HANDBOOK OF THEORIES FOR PURCHASING, SUPPLY CHAIN AND MANAGEMENT RESEARCH

Handbook of Theories for Purchasing, Supply Chain and Management Research

Edited by

Wendy L. Tate

William J. Taylor Professor of Business and Ray and Joan Myatt Faculty Research Fellow, Department of Supply Chain Management, Haslam College of Business, University of Tennessee, USA

Lisa M. Ellram

University Distinguished Professor and Rees Distinguished Professor of Supply Chain Management, Farmer School of Business, Miami University, USA

Lydia Bals

Professor of Supply Chain and Operations Management, Mainz University of Applied Sciences, External Post-Doctoral Research Fellow, EBS Universität, Germany and Visiting Scholar, Copenhagen Business School, Denmark

EE **Edward Elgar**
PUBLISHING

Cheltenham, UK • Northampton, MA, USA

Cover image: Susan Q Yin on Unsplash

Published by
Edward Elgar Publishing Limited
The Lypiatts
15 Lansdown Road
Cheltenham
Glos GL50 2JA
UK

Edward Elgar Publishing, Inc.
William Pratt House
9 Dewey Court
Northampton
Massachusetts 01060
USA

Paperback edition 2023

A catalogue record for this book
is available from the British Library

Library of Congress Control Number: 2022932711

This book is available electronically in the **Elgar**online
Business subject collection
http://dx.doi.org/10.4337/9781839104503

ISBN 978 1 83910 449 7 (cased)
ISBN 978 1 83910 450 3 (eBook)
ISBN 978 1 0353 1891 9 (paperback)

Printed and bound by CPI Group (UK) Ltd, Croydon, CR0 4YY

Contents

Contributors

Lojain Alkhuzaim is a PhD Candidate in Operations Management within the Business School at Worcester Polytechnic Institute, USA. Her research focuses on the applications of emergy analysis and system dynamics within the context of sustainable supply chain management.

Björn Axelsson, at the time of writing, was Professor Emeritus of the Stockholm School of Economics (SSE), Sweden. His research centered around B2B operations, foremost procurement, and marketing and sales. He earned his PhD degree from Uppsala University, Sweden, in 1981. During a period of almost 15 years he served as director and teacher in the Uppsala Executive MBA Program. He was appointed his first chair as professor at the Jönköping International Business School and moved to SSE in 2002. He published in journals such as *Industrial Marketing Management*, the *Journal of Business and Industrial Marketing* and the *Journal of Purchasing and Supply Management*. Björn has also published several books, the latest published in 2018 (edited together with Andersson and Rosenqvist). Early on, Björn Axelsson was part of the Industrial Marketing and Purchasing (IMP) Group. Björn passed away on 19 April 2021, shortly after he and his co-authors finished their chapter in this book.

Arash Azadegan is an Associate Professor at Rutgers Business School, USA, and the Director of Supply Chain Disruption Research Laboratory (SCDrl). His research focuses on supply chain disruptions, and the effect of interorganizational response and recovery effort to mitigate them. Specific to humanitarian supply chains, Dr Azadegan has several ongoing projects on response and recovery from humanitarian disasters in the United States (for example, hurricanes) and how collaboration among non-governmental organizations (NGOs) and governmental entities can be strengthened. Dr Azadegan's work is published in several top operation/supply chain management journals including the *Journal of Operations Management*, *Journal of Supply Chain Management*, *Production and Operations Management*, and the *Decision Sciences Journal* among others. Dr Azadegan has acted as an officer (treasurer) of the OM Division at the Academy of Management, and is an active member of the Decision Sciences Institute. Dr Azadegan is a board member of Safe-America Foundation, an NGO focused on safety and preparedness in the United States.

Jenny Bäckstrand is Associate Professor in Supply Chain and Operations Management at the School of Engineering at Jönköping University, Sweden. She has published articles on various topics related to purchasing and customized products in a triadic setting as well as engaged research methods. Her current research interests include university–industry interaction and information sharing, specifically in small and medium-sized enterprises and engineering-to-order (ETO) contexts.

Lydia Bals has been Full Professor of Supply Chain and Operations Management at the University of Applied Sciences Mainz, Germany since 2014, and an external Post-Doc Research Fellow at EBS Universität, Germany since 2019. She has been affiliated with Copenhagen Business School, Denmark for research since 2008. She also works as an independent consultant, moderator and speaker (https://source4future.de/). Until the end of 2013 she was Head of the Department Global Procurement Solutions (for example, procurement strategy, sustainability, controlling, Source2Contract and Purchase2Pay processes, methods, tools and systems; benchmarking and excellence) at Bayer CropScience (BCS) AG. Prior to this she worked as a Project Manager at Bayer Business Consulting, Germany, the in-house consulting unit of Bayer. She teaches purchasing and supply management, operations, logistics and supply chain management courses. She has published in the *Journal of Operations Management, Journal of Supply Chain Management, Journal of Purchasing and Supply Management, Journal of International Management*, and other academic outlets.

John E. Bell is the Ratledge Endowed Associate Professor of Supply Chain Management and Bartley Family Faculty Research Fellow at the University of Tennessee, USA. He holds a PhD from Auburn University, USA, an MS from the Air Force Institute of Technology, and a BS from the US Air Force Academy. He is an Associate Editor of four leading supply chain journals and has published over 30 peer-reviewed articles. Dr Bell is currently the Director of the Supply Chain PhD and Aerospace and Defense MBA Programs at the University of Tennessee (UT). Before coming to UT, Dr Bell served 20 years on active duty as a US Air Force officer. His current research interests are in last mile delivery, strategic facility location and sustainability. His publications have appeared in the *Journal of Business Logistics, European Journal of Operational Research, Transportation Journal, Advanced Engineering Informatics, Computers and Operations Research*, and other top journals.

Philip Beske-Janssen is an Assistant Professor in the Department for Operations Management at the Copenhagen Business School, Denmark. His research interests are primarily sustainability in supply chains, circular economy and sustainability accounting.

Amanda Bille is a PhD Fellow at the Department of Operations Management, Copenhagen Business School, Denmark. Bille's research is centred around providing political and ethical perspectives on SCM that make it possible to embrace the complexity of the twenty-first century. She particularly interested in corporate responsibility as well as power structures. She is a part of the research project 'The Supply Chain of the 21st Century – Towards Ethical, Social and Circular Business Models', a joint research effort between NORDAKADEMIE University of Applied Sciences and Copenhagen Business School. Bille holds an MSc in International Business and Politics as well as a BSc in Business, Language and Culture, both from Copenhagen Business School.

Sebastian Brockhaus is an Associate Professor of Supply Chain Management at the Boler College of Business at John Carroll University, USA. He received his Doctoral degree from the Hamburg University of Technology. He has published in the *Journal of Business Logistics, International Journal of Operations and Production Management*, and *International Journal of Logistics Management*, among others. He is interested in supply chain sustainability, collaboration, and product development.

Federico Caniato is Full Professor of Supply Chain and Purchasing Management at the School of Management of Politecnico di Milano, Italy, and is Rector's Delegate for Life Long Learning. He is the director of the International Master in Digital Supply Chain Management of MIP Politecnico di Milano Graduate School of Business. He has authored several international publications on various operations and supply chain management journals, and he is Associate Editor of the *Journal of Purchasing and Supply Management* and the *International*

Journal of Operations and Production Management. The research interests of Federico Caniato are in the field of supply chain and purchasing management; in recent years he has focused on supply chain finance, supply chain sustainability and supply chain resilience. He has focused in particular on the food and fashion industries.

David E. Cantor (PhD, University of Maryland, USA) is Professor of Supply Chain Management and holds the Mark and Terri Walker Professorship in Logistics and Supply Chain Management at the Debbie and Jerry Ivy College of Business at Iowa State University, USA. His supply chain research interests include motor carrier safety, environmental management and behavioral operations management. Dr Cantor's research has been awarded best paper awards from the *Journal of Operations Management* and *Transportation Journal.* His research has been published in many journals including the *Journal of Business Logistics, Journal of Operations Management, Production and Operations Management Journal* and *Journal of Supply Chain Management.*

Steven Carnovale, PhD holds the rank of Assistant Professor of Supply Chain Management, and Graduate Programs Director (Management Department) at the Saunders College of Business, Rochester Institute of Technology, USA. In addition, he serves as Associate Editor of both the *Journal of Supply Chain Management* and the *Journal of Purchasing and Supply Management.* Steven specializes in supply chain strategy focused on interfirm networks, risk management and global sourcing networks. His research has appeared in the *Journal of Supply Chain Management, Journal of Business Logistics, Journal of Purchasing and Supply Management, International Journal of Production Economics, European Journal of Operational Research* and *Annals of Operations Research,* among others. Steven earned his BS and PhD degrees at Rutgers University, USA (Supply Chain Management and Marketing Sciences). Steven frequently speaks on topics related to supply chain analytics/strategy, focused on how firms can use these concepts to increase visibility and performance within their supply chains.

Thomas Y. Choi is a Professor of Supply Chain Management at the W.P. Carey School of Business at Arizona State University, USA. He leads the study of the upstream side of supply chains, where a buying company interfaces with many suppliers organized in various forms of networks. He has published articles in numerous leading journals. From 2014 to 2019, he served as Harold E. Fearon Chair of Purchasing Management and Executive Director of CAPS Research. From 2011 to 2014, he served as Co-Editor-in-Chief of the *Journal of Operations Management.* Since 2018, he has been listed as a Highly Cited Researcher by Clarivate Web of Science.

Donna F. Davis is a Professor of Marketing and Supply Chain Management and serves as Academic Director of the Monica Wooden Center for Supply Chain Management and Sustainability in the Muma College of Business at the University of South Florida, USA. She holds PhD and MBA degrees from the University of Tennessee, USA. Dr Davis has presented her research at numerous domestic and international academic and professional conferences. Her current research focuses on logistics-led economic development and digital supply chain transformation.

Christian von Deimling holds the Endowed Junior Professorship for General Business Administration, in particular for Industrial Procurement, at the Department of Economics and Management at the Bundeswehr University Munich, Germany. In his research and teaching, Christian von Deimling focuses on issues in industrial supply management and public procurement. He is interested in changes and future developments in supply management (understood as a function in companies and organizations with a significant influence on their market position). Therefore, he is intensively concerned with the development and successful introduction of supply and procurement strategies, with the influence of innovation on and through procurement and on the market position of companies and organizations, with the role and use of life cycle costs for different decision gates in investment projects as well as with the design and the success of cooperative purchasing. His applied understanding of research is grounded on data-based observations (both qualitative and quantitative) and corresponding data triangulation.

Kevin J. Dooley is a Distinguished Professor of Supply Chain Management in the W.P. Carey School of Business at Arizona State University, USA, Chief Scientist of The Sustainability Consortium, and a Senior Sustainability Scientist in the Julie Ann Wrigley Global Institute of Sustainability. At The Sustainability Consortium, Dooley leads a global research team that works with over 100 of the world's largest retailers and manufacturers to develop tools that measure and track progress on critical product sustainability issues. He has published more than 100 research articles and has provided training or consultation for over 200 companies in the areas of sustainability, supply chain management, quality, and technology and innovation. He obtained his PhD in Mechanical Engineering at the University of Illinois, USA.

Lisa M. Ellram, PhD (Ohio State University, USA) is University Distinguished Professor and the Rees Distinguished Professor of Supply Chain Management at the Farmer School of Business, Miami University, Oxford, OH, USA. Her primary areas of research interest include sustainability; buyer–supplier relationships; services purchasing and supply chain management; offshoring and outsourcing; and supply chain cost management. She has published in numerous top journals spanning a variety of disciplines, and has presented her work on six continents and in more than 30 countries. She has been Co-Editor-in-Chief Emeritus of the *Journal of Supply Chain Management* (2007–2016), and is Senior Associate Editor for *Journal of Purchasing and Supply Management*. She is the 2019 winner of the Distinguished Scholar Award from the Supply Chain and Operations Management Division of the Academy of Management.

Reham Eltantawy is the Coggin Endowed Strategic Professor, Professor of Marketing, and Chair of the Department of Marketing and Logistics at the Univesity of North Florida, USA. Areas of focus are purchasing and supply chain management, strategic sourcing, and purchasing and supply management.

Michael Eßig holds the Chair for Purchasing and Supply Management at the Bundeswehr University Munich, Germany. His research focuses on the areas of strategic supply (chain) management, public procurement and defence supply management. He has published extensively in major journals including the *Journal of Purchasing and Supply Chain Management*, *Supply Chain Management: An International Journal* and *Industrial Marketing Management*, and works with major industrial and public (buying) institutions such as Audi, Federal Ministry of the Interior, Federal Office for Defence Acquisition (amongst others). He serves as Associate Editor of the *Journal of Purchasing and Supply Management* as well as the *Journal of Public Procurement*; additionally in several academic and professional organizations such as the Management Board and the Scientific Board of the German Purchasing Association (BME) and the Scientific Advisory Board of the Austrian Minister of Defence. He teaches in Munich and also at the University of St Gallen, Switzerland and the Vienna University of Economics and Business, Austria.

Amydee M. Fawcett is the Chief Executive Officer of Engage2E and a Professor of Supply Chain Management. She earned her PhD at the University of Arkansas, USA. Her interests are in relational dynamics (that is, teaming, trust, change management, leadership through people and negotiation) and creating an engaged learning environment. Since entering the academic world, Dee has received three best paper awards (h-index: 19, i10-index: 23).

Stanley E. Fawcett (PhD, Arizona State University, USA) is a member of the Logistikum team at the University of Applied Sciences, Upper Austria. His interests are in supply chain collaboration and global supply chain design. An award-winning teacher, Stan has taught around the world in English, German and Spanish. Stan has developed and led action-learning, experiential-education workshops that demonstrate how a deliberate practice pedagogy can elevate learning. The winner of over a dozen best paper awards, Stan has published 200+ articles and 12 books (h-index: 61; i10-index: 122; RG Score: 35.39). He also served as Co-Editor-in-Chief of one of the supply chain profession's top journals, the *Journal of Business Logistics*, and is behind the innovative MyEducator online supply chain curriculum.

Sajad Fayezi, PhD (Deakin University, Australia) is an Associate Professor of Supply Chain Management in the Faculty of Business Administration at Memorial University in St John's, Canada. Dr Fayezi has published in both academic and practitioner journals in the field of supply chain management. His main research areas involve social issues in the supply chain, including business human rights, modern slavery and responsible sourcing, sustainable supply chain management, and resilient supply chains. He has published research in top-tier international journals, including the *International Journal of Operations and Production Management*, *International Journal of Management Reviews*, *Industrial Marketing Management*, *Supply Chain Management* and *International Journal of Physical Distribution and Logistics Management*.

Javad Feizabadi is an Associate Professor at Asia School of Business, Malaysia (in Collaboration with MIT Sloan School of Management). Dr Feizabadi's primary research interest focuses on designing and managing supply chains as complex adaptive systems in a highly volatile business landscape. He has published in several international referred journals such as *Strategic Management Journal, International Journal of Production Economics, International Journal of Physical Distributions and Logistics Management, Supply Chain Management: An International Journal* and *Journal of Business Logistics*.

Barbara B. Flynn is the Richard M. and Myra Louise Buskirk Professor of Manufacturing Management at the Kelley School of Business, Indiana University, USA. She is a Co-Editor-in-Chief of the *Journal of Supply Chain Management* and past Editor of *Decision Sciences Journal of Innovative Education* and *Quality Management Journal*. Her research on operations strategy topics has appeared in top journals including *Journal of Supply Chain Management, Journal of Operations Management, Management Science, Decision Sciences*, and *Academy of Management Journal*. Her research has been funded by the National Science Foundation and the US Department of Education. She is Past President of the Decision

Sciences Institute and winner of the Distinguished Scholar Award from the operations management division of the Academy of Management.

Brian Fugate is the Chair of the Department of Supply Chain Management, Professor, and Oren Harris Endowed Chair in Transportation at the University of Arkansas Sam M. Walton College of Business, USA. He was formerly an MIT Fulbright Senior Research Scholar and Co-Editor-in-Chief of the *Journal of Supply Chain Management*. His recent publications focus on advancing the consumer-oriented integration of demand across the supply network through collaboration and enabling technologies. Dr Fugate has published articles in premiere journals such as the *Journal of Supply Chain Management, Academy of Management Journal, Journal of Operations Management, Journal of Business Logistics* and *Decision Sciences Journal*.

Lars-Erik Gadde is an Emeritus Professor of Industrial Marketing at Chalmers University of Technology in Gothenburg, Sweden. His research interest is devoted to two aspects of what is now identified as supply chain management, but previously labelled channels of distribution and purchasing and supply. When the Industrial Marketing and Purchasing (IMP) Group project was launched, he adopted these concepts and models, and since that time his studies have relied on the network framing. Research outlets include *Journal of Supply Chain Management, International Journal of Physical Distribution and Logistics Management, Journal of Management Studies, Industrial Marketing Management* and *International Journal of Research in Marketing*. He is also a co-author of several IMP books.

Myles D. Garvey, PhD is an Assistant Teaching Professor of Analytics and Marketing at the D'Amore-Mckim School of Business at Northeastern University, USA. Prior to receiving his PhD from Rutgers Business School, USA, Dr Garvey was a software consultant for RedHat. His research interests are currently within the areas of social media analytics, natural language generation, supply chain risk propagation, social network analytics, and general marketing analytics. He also is currently the Co-Director of the DATA Initiative at Northeastern University, whose main purpose is to help organizations turn data into insight by way of student engagement and the application of business analytics methodologies.

John Gattorna is Executive Chairman of Gattorna Alignment, a Sydney, Australia-based firm specialising in supply chain 'thought leadership'. He has held a number of professorships, with the most recent being Adjunct Professor at the University of Technology, Sydney, the SP Jain School of Global Management, Australia, and Foundation Professor to CIPS Australia.

Cees J. Gelderman is Associate Professor of Purchasing and Marketing Management at the Open University of the Netherlands. He has developed several courses, all based on the principles of distance education. As leading author, he published the Dutch-language book *Professioneel Inkopen* (*Professional Purchasing*) and the textbook *Business Marketing*. In 2003 he completed his PhD research project on purchasing portfolio approaches. His research is primarily focused on managing buyer–supplier relationships, with a special interest in purchasing portfolio management, public procurement, contracting and governance, power and dependence, opportunism, and sustainability. He has published in numerous journals and has presented many competitive papers at IPSERA conferences. He is a member of the Editorial Review Board of the *Journal of Public Procurement*.

Larry Giunipero, CPSM, CPSD, CPM is a Professor of Supply Chain Management at Florida State University, USA. His primary research, teaching and consulting interests are in the area of supply management. Current interests lie in strategic and global sourcing, talent development and supply chain technologies.

Andreas H. Glas is Assistant Professor for Procurement and Supply Management at Bundeswehr University Munich, Germany. His research investigates the buyer–supplier cooperation and is in particular related to performance-based contracts and service innovation. He co-edited the books *Performance-based Logistics* and *Einkauf 4.0* and is currently working on several research topics linked to projects in the automotive, manufacturing and aerospace industries. His research findings have appeared in a number of academic journals in the field including *Journal of Purchasing and Supply Management, Industrial Marketing Management, Journal of Supply Chain Management: An International Journal, International Journal of Physical Distribution and Logistics Management, International Journal of Production Economics, Journal of Business and Industrial Marketing, International Journal of Operations and Production Management*. He is a member of several review and editorial boards, highlighting the editorial role for the *Journal of Defense Analytics and Logistics Management*.

Tim Gruchmann is a Professor of Logistics and Supply Chain Management at Westcoast University of Applied Sciences, Germany and a member of the Westcoast Institute of Human Resources (WinHR). His research interests lie within employee and customer-centred logistics and sustainable supply chain management. His research contributions have been published in international, peer-reviewed journals such as *International Journal of Logistics Management, Supply Chain Management: An International Journal, Journal of Business Economics, International Journal of Production Economics* and *Journal of Industrial Ecology*.

Árni Halldórsson is Professor in Supply Chain Management at Chalmers University of Technology, Sweden. His research interests concern supply chain management, sustainable development, and advancing service supply chains in various sectors. Key focus areas include logistics services (energy efficiency, development, service blueprinting); supply chain design; buyer-supplier relationships; logistics services for enhanced circularity; end-users in the supply chain; supply chain resilience; research methodology and theory development.

Robert Handfield is the Bank of America University Distinguished Professor of Supply Chain Management at North Carolina State University, USA, and Director of the Supply Chain Resource Cooperative (http://scm.ncsu.edu/). Handfield is considered a thought leader in the field of supply chain management, and is an industry expert in the field of strategic sourcing, supply market intelligence, and supplier development. He has spoken on these subjects across the globe, including in China, Azerbaijan, Turkey, Latin America, India, Europe, Korea, Japan and Canada, in multiple presentations and webinars. Handfield has published more than 120 peer-reviewed journal articles and is regularly quoted in global news media such as the *Wall Street Journal, Bloomberg, NPR, CNBC*, the *Financial Times*, the *San Francisco Chronicle* and *CNN*. He has recently published articles on the shortage of personal protective equipment (PPE) in the *Harvard Business Review* and the *Milbank Quarterly Journal*.

Christine M. Harland is the Gianluca Spina Chair of Supply Strategy at the Politecnico di Milano, Italy. Her research interests are in policy and practice in procurement in complex confederal public sector supply networks, notably healthcare. As co-founder of the International Research Study of Public Procurement (IRSPP), Christine has researched public procurement's role in responding to global crises, stimulating innovation, delivery of community benefits, and small and medium-sized enterprise development. Christine is a former Editor and current Associate Editor of the *Journal of Purchasing and Supply Management*. Widely published in books and journals, she is lead editor of the *SAGE Handbook of Strategic Supply Management* (2013), co-author of the world's leading text and case book in operations management, and co-editor of a text on public procurement. In 2019 Christine was awarded the Lifetime Achievement Award by the International Purchasing and Supply Education and Research Association (IPSERA).

Feigao (Kelly) Huang is a Doctoral student in the Department of Supply Chain Management at the University of Tennessee, Knoxville, USA. Prior to joining the PhD Program in 2018, Kelly worked in Walmart Stores (China) for several years. Kelly holds a Master of Arts degree in English Language and Literature from Beijing Foreign Studies University, China, and a Bachelor of Arts degree in English from Xi'an University of Architecture and Technology, China. Kelly's research interests include sustainable supply chain management, base of the pyramid (BoP) supply chains, and socially useful supply chains.

Yao 'Henry' Jin, PhD is an Associate Professor of Supply Chain Management at Richard T. Farmer School of Business at Miami University, USA. He received his Doctoral degree from the Sam M. Walton College of Business, University of Arkansas, USA. Drawing on his retail industry experience, his main research interest focuses on retail supply chain and operations concerning issues related to collaboration and demand planning. He has published his research in journals such as the *Journal of Operations Management, Journal of Retailing* and *Journal of Business Logistics*, among others. Currently, he is working on projects regarding counterfeit products, and service failures in omni-channel retailing.

Thomas E. Johnsen (MSc, Phd, HDR) is Professor of Purchasing and Supply Management at Audencia Business School in France and Visiting Professor at Copenhagen Business School, Denmark. Prior to this he was Gianluca Spina Professor of Supply Chain Management at Politecnico di Milano in Italy, and he has also held full-time or part-time positions at Rennes Business School (France), University of Bath (UK), Jönköping International Business School (Sweden) and the University of Southern Denmark. He is Associate Editor of the *Journal of Purchasing and Supply Management*. His book (with M. Howard and J. Miemczyk) *Purchasing and Supply Chain Management: A Sustainability Perspective*, published by Routledge, is now in its second edition.

Katri Kauppi (née Karjalainen) is an Associate Professor of Logistics (tenured) at Aalto University School of Business in Finland. Prof. Kauppi got her PhD from Helsinki School of Economics, Finland in 2009 and has since then also worked at Manchester Business School and at Nottingham University Business School in the UK. Her main research interests are in purchasing organizational behaviour, public procurement, buyer–supplier relationships and social sustainability in supply chains. In particular much of her research work deals with organizational theory applications in a purchasing or supply chain context, most notably using either institutional theory or agency theory. She has published in several leading journals in the supply chain management, operations management and public administration areas. She teaches purchasing and supply chain management related topics at Aalto University School of Business.

Mahtab Kouhizadeh is an Assistant Professor of Supply Chain Management at the University of Rhode Island, USA. Her research focuses on the applications of blockchain technology in supply chain management and sustainability. She has co-authored a book chapter on 'Global Perspectives on Green Business Administration and Sustainable Supply Chain Management', published by IGI Global. She is a member of the Academy of Management, the Institute for Operations Research and the Management Sciences, Production and Operations Management Society, and Decision Sciences Institute.

Gyöngyi Kovács is the Erkko Professor in Humanitarian Logistics, and the Subject Head of Supply Chain Management and Social Responsibility at the Hanken School of Economics, Helsinki, Finland. She is a founding Editor-in-Chief of the *Journal of Humanitarian Logistics and Supply Chain Management* (*JHLSCM*) and is on the editorial board of several other journals. She was the first Director of the Humanitarian Logistics and Supply Chain Research Institute (HUMLOG Institute) and has published extensively in the areas of humanitarian logistics and sustainable supply chain management. She was awarded Humanitarian Logistics Researcher of the Year 2020 by the American Logistics Aid Network ALAN. Currently, she is leading a Horizon 2020 (European Union) COVID-19 project called 'HERoS' (Health Emergency Response in Interconnected Systems).

Anna Land is an Assistant Professor of Supply Chain Management at Boise State University, USA. She teaches various operations and supply chain management courses at the undergraduate and MBA levels. Her research addresses sustainability topics in operations, supply chain and logistics management, such as supplier relationship management in developing countries and data analytics in rail transportation to improve financial and environmental performance. She has published conceptual, empirical and pedagogical articles in the *International Journal of Production Economics*, *Supply Chain Management: An International Journal*, *International Journal of Operations and Production Management*, *Journal of Cleaner Production*, *IEEE Engineering Management Review* and *Operations Management Education Review*.

Teresa M. McCarthy-Byrne is an Associate Professor of Marketing and Global Supply Chain Management (GSCM) at Bryant University, USA. She has over 30 years of supply chain-related experience in both industry and academia. Her current research topics include supply chain risk management and omnichannel fulfillment. Dr McCarthy-Byrne has published in *International Journal of Physical Distribution and Logistics Management*, *Journal of Forecasting*, *Transportation Journal*, *Journal of Business Forecasting*, *Foresight: The Journal of Future Studies*, *Strategic Thinking and Policy*, *Industrial Marketing Management*, *Decision Sciences Journal of Innovative Education*, and *Journal of Marketing Education*. Dr McCarthy-Byrne received her PhD from the University of Tennessee, USA; her MS from the University of Rhode Island, USA; and her BS from the University of Massachusetts at Amherst, USA.

Mark Pagell holds a Chair in Global Leadership and is a Professor of Sustainable Supply Chain Management at University College Dublin, Ireland. He is also the Co-Editor-in-Chief of the *Journal of Supply Chain Management* and an Adjunct Scientist at the Institute for Work and Health in Toronto, Canada. Dr Pagell's research on topics such as sustainable supply chain management and human resource issues, including employee safety in operational environments, has appeared in a number of premier outlets including the *Journal of Supply Chain Management, Management Science, Journal of Operations Management, Production and Operations Management, Sloan Management Review* and *Journal of Management Studies.* Dr Pagell's research has won a number of awards including two Emerald Citation of Excellence Awards (2013 and 2016), best papers published in the *Journal of Supply Chain Management* (2009) and *Journal of Operations Management* (2002 and 2019).

William Pasmore is a Professor of Practice at Teachers College, Columbia University, USA. He is the author or editor of 30 books and numerous articles dealing with the topics of organization design and change leadership. He also heads his own consulting firm, Advanced Change.

Peter M. Ralston is an Assistant Professor of Supply Chain Management at Iowa State University, USA. His research centres around two general areas. One is supply chain relationships, with supply chain collaboration and supply chain integration being prime interests. The other research area focuses on factor market rivalry and how firms compete for needed supply-side resources. He spent nearly six years in the cosmetics and office products industries as a customer specialist and distribution centre manager before pursuing and earning his PhD.

Jens K. Roehrich is a Professor of Supply Chain Innovation at the University of Bath, School of Management, UK. Prior to this, Jens was a researcher at Imperial College London, UK. Significant strands of his research agenda explore the long-term interplay of contractual and relational governance mechanisms in complex projects, and the management of public–private relationships. More recently, he has started to explore the dark side of relationships by investigating coordination failures, conflicts and trust breaches. His research is multidisciplinary, drawing theoretical inspiration and methodological support from operations management, economics, strategy, innovation management, healthcare and policy management. His research has been published in journals such as *Journal of Management Studies, International Journal of Operations and Production Management, British Journal of Management, Social Science and Medicine, Journal of Purchasing and Supply Management,* and *Industrial Marketing Management.*

Eugenia Rosca is an Assistant Professor of Supply Chain Management at the Tilburg School of Economics and Management, Tilburg University, the Netherlands. Her main research interests revolve around sustainability and social issues in value chains in the context of subsistence markets. In particular, she is interested in value chain inclusion of low-income producers and consumers in developing economies, and the mechanisms employed by social enterprises and multinational companies to enable social impact. She has published articles in several peer-reviewed academic journals such as the *International Journal of Physical Distribution and Logistics Management, Journal of Cleaner Production, International Business Review* and *Technological Forecasting and Social Change.*

Joseph Sarkis is a Professor of Management within the Business School at Worcester Polytechnic Institute, USA. He earned his PhD from the University of Buffalo, USA. His research and teaching interests include sustainability, technology, operations and supply chain management. He has authored over 500 publications. He is an AT&T Industrial Ecology

Fellow and has served as a research scholar at universities throughout the world. He is a coordinator of the Future Earth Circular Economy Working Group; and also an international programme coordinator for the Greening of Industry Network. He is currently Editor-in-Chief of *IEEE Engineering Management Review* and Associate Editor for the journal *Resources Conservation and Recycling* on the topic of sustainable supply chains. He holds editorial positions for a number of other leading journals. He has edited and published books on green supply chain management and greener manufacturing and design.

habil Holger Schiele has held the chair of Technology Management – Innovation of Purchasing, Production and Logistics at the University of Twente in Enschede (Netherlands) since 2009. Prior to this he was at Leibniz Universität Hannover, Germany, and Jacobs University in Bremen, Germany, after working for ten years in industry and in consulting (PricewaterhouseCoopers, and with the purchasing consultancy h&z). He gained his PhD from Leibniz Universität Hannover with a work on cluster theory and strategic management. His current research focuses on innovation from and with suppliers, supplier satisfaction and preferred customership, and Industry 4.0 (I4.0) in purchasing. He regularly scores among the most published scholars in the field, with papers appearing in purchasing journals (*Journal of Purchasing and Supply Management, Journal of Supply Chain Management, Industrial Marketing Management*, among others) and in innovation management journals (*Research Policy, R&D Management*, among others).

Tobias Schoenherr is the Hoagland-Metzler Endowed Professor of Purchasing and Supply Management in the Eli Broad College of Business at Michigan State University, USA. He holds a PhD in Operations Management and Decision Sciences from Indiana University, Bloomington, USA. His research focuses on buyer–supplier relationships, especially at the intersection of the themes of innovation, technology, sustainability and globalization. He has published more than 75 journal articles in outlets such as *Management Science, Journal of Operations Management, Production and Operations Management, Decision Sciences, Journal of Marketing Research* and *Journal of Supply Chain Management*. He is Co-Editor-in-Chief of the *International Journal of Operations and Production Management* and an Associate Editor for the *Journal of Operations Management, Decision Sciences* and the *Journal of Purchasing and Supply Management*.

Matthew A. Schwieterman is an Assistant Professor of Supply Chain Management at Miami University, USA. He completed his PhD in Business Administration at Ohio State University, USA. Prior to Joining Miami University, he was an Assistant Professor of Supply Chain Management at Michigan State University, USA. His primary research interests include customer and supplier portfolio structure, and firm growth and diversification. Prior to his academic career, he held various positions within logistics and operations management.

Erik Siems is a Research Assistant at the Chair of Supply Chain Management at the University of Kassel, Germany. His interests and research areas focus specifically on business strategy, operations research and sustainable supply chain management.

Wendy L. Tate, PhD (Arizona State University, USA, 2006) is the Taylor Professor of Business and the Ray and Joan Myatt Faculty Research Fellow at the University of Tennessee, Haslam College of Business, Department of Supply Chain Management, USA. She teaches strategic sourcing to undergraduate, MBA, Executive and PhD students. Her research interests revolve around strategic sourcing and include the financial impacts of decisions on the supply chain, sustainable supply chain design, and the supplier location decision. She is co-Editor-in-Chief of the *Journal of Purchasing and Supply Management*. She has published in the *Journal of Operations Management*, *Journal of Supply Chain Management*, *Journal of Purchasing and Supply Management*, *Journal of Business Logistics*, and other academic outlets.

Anurag Tewari is a Lecturer of Logistics, Procurement and Supply Chain Management at Cranfield University, UK. He earned his MSc in supply chain, Master of Research in management and a PhD in complex system's research from Cranfield University. Prior to joining Cranfield, he earned a Bachelor of Technology in Chemical Engineering from Sir Harcourt Butler Technological Institute, Kanpur, India, and has extensive industrial experience. His current research interest lies in the study and modelling of supply chain information flows and machine learning-driven supply chain analytics. His expertise is in modelling, visualizing, and interpreting large complex systems and networks.

Virpi Turkulainen works at Haaga-Helia University of Applied Sciences in Finland. In the past she has worked at the University College Dublin, School of Business in Ireland, and Aalto University, School of Science in Finland, among others. Her research interests are in areas of organization design, organizational integration, management and organization of project-based operations, and operations strategy. Dr Turkulainen has published in *Journal of Operations Management*, *Journal of Supply Chain Management*, *International Journal of Operations and Production Management*, *Journal of Purchasing and Supply Management* and *Project Management Journal*, among others.

Diego Vega is an Assistant Professor of Supply Chain Management, Social Responsibility and Humanitarian Logistics at Hanken School of Economics, Finland; and Director of the Humanitarian Logistics and Supply Chain Research (HUMLOG) Institute, Finland. In 2013, Diego completed his Doctoral studies at Aix-Marseille University, France, in collaboration with Médecins Sans Frontières (MSF) France; he has over ten years of experience in conducting research in the humanitarian context. His current research interests include logistics services in humanitarian supply chains, shelter and temporary settlements, strategic management and qualitative methods.

Carl Marcus Wallenburg is a Professor of Supply Chain Management and holds the Chair of Logistics and Service Management of WHU – Otto Beisheim School of Management, Germany. He is the European Editor of the *Journal of Business Logistics* and Co-Chair of the Council of Supply Chain Management Professionals (CSCMP) European Research Seminar on Logistics and SCM. His research focuses on online and omnichannel retailing, logistics services and third-party logistics (3PL), different supply chain matters (for example, risk management and logistics innovation), and how they are influenced by vertical and horizontal relationships. His work has appeared in various journals, including *European Journal of Marketing*, *International Journal of Operations and Production Management*, *International Journal of Physical Distribution and Logistics Management*, *Journal of Business Logistics*, *Journal of Purchasing and Supply Management*, *Journal of Supply Chain Management*, *Journal of Service Management* and *Transportation Journal*.

Andreas Wieland is an Associate Professor of Supply Chain Management at Copenhagen Business School, Denmark. His current research reinterprets global supply chains as social-ecological systems. His articles have appeared in journals such as the *International Journal of Logistics Management*, *International Journal of Physical Distribution and Logistics Management*, *Journal of Business Logistics*, *Journal of International Management*, *Journal of Supply Chain Management* and *Supply Chain Management: An International Journal*. He is the European Co-Editor of the *Journal of Business Logistics* and Co-Chair of the Council of Supply Chain Management Professionals (CSCMP) European Research Seminar. He is also the editor of the blog scmresearch.org.

Professor Richard Wilding is Full Professor and Chair in Supply Chain Strategy at the Centre for Logistics, Procurement and Supply Chain Management, Cranfield School of Management UK. Richard works with European and international companies on logistics and supply chain projects in all sectors including pharmaceutical, retail, automotive, high technology, food, drink and professional services to name a few. He was appointed a National Teaching Fellow in 2019 and is recognized by the BBC and DHL as one of 'the world's foremost supply chain experts'. He is a champion for encouraging evidence-based decision making within the logistics industry, and is an advocate for ensuring knowledge can create action and impact within the organizations he works with. His Doctoral research in the 1990s pioneered the application of chaos theory to supply chain management.

Zhaohui Wu, PhD (Arizona State University, USA) is a Professor of Supply Chain Management at Oregon State University, USA; and an Honorary Professor at the University of Exeter, UK. He has received multiple research grants from the National Science Foundation (US), Agriculture of the Middle (US) and the Leverhulme Trust Visiting Professorship (UK). He is currently teaching and conducting research on supply networks, alternative food systems, agricultural co-operatives, and the informal economy concerning migrant workers and refugees.

Finn Wynstra is a Professor of Purchasing and Supply Management at Rotterdam School of Management, Erasmus University (Netherlands). He conducted his PhD training at Eindhoven University of Technology (Netherlands) and Uppsala University (Sweden), where he had been an exchange student earlier (to study the industrial network approach, INA). His research focuses on purchasing and supply management, in particular the interplay of supply and innovation processes and buyer–supplier relations in business service contexts. His work has appeared in journals spanning different disciplines, including *Journal of Operations Management*, *International Journal of Research in Marketing*, *Journal of Product Innovation Management* and *Accounting, Organizations and Society*.

George A. Zsidisin, PhD (Arizona State University, USA), CPSM, CPM., is the John W. Barriger III Professor and Director of the Supply Chain Risk and Resilience Research (SCR3) Institute at the University of Missouri – St Louis, USA. Professor Zsidisin's research focuses on how firms assess and manage risk associated with supply disruptions and price volatility in their supply chains. His research has been funded by and/or received awards from organizations including the AT&T Foundation, IBM, Institute for Supply Management, Deutsche Post, the Council of Supply Chain Management Professionals and the Decision Sciences Institute. Further, he is one of the founding members of the International Supply Chain Risk Management (ISCRiM) network; teaches and leads discussions with various executive education programmes and numerous companies in the USA and Europe; is Co-Editor Emeritus of the *Journal of Purchasing and Supply Management* and serves on the editorial review boards of several academic supply chain journals.

1. Introduction to the *Handbook of Theories for Purchasing, Supply Chain and Management Research*

Wendy L. Tate, Lisa M. Ellram and Lydia Bals

INTRODUCTION

There has been a strong call for theory application and theory development in the purchasing and supply management (PSM) and supply chain management (SCM) literature (Carter, 2011; van Weele and van Raij, 2014). However, it is not always clear to researchers which theories are appropriate to apply, and how to best apply such theories, or when it is advisable to build theory (Smith and Hitt, 2007). The goal of this edited book is to present some background on the development and application of theory in PSM and SCM to date, and provide a mapping of major types of theories to give guidance on which theory might be appropriate to apply, and when new theory development is needed. Most of these theories that are incorporated in this *Handbook* are also relevant to management research, and some developed primarily out of the strategic management area.

The aspiration of the edited book was to compile a valuable overview of theories that can serve as the foundation for management research. This collection of chapters provides high-quality, state-of-the-art overviews of theories relevant to PSM, SCM and other management fields, and creates a standard reference for researchers and students in this and related fields. Senior scholars in PSM and SCM were contacted to contribute chapters on key theories and theory development in the field. Experts on theories within and outside the field of SCM/PSM were also contacted and asked to contribute and review chapters.

The chapters consistently provide understanding of the assumptions of a given theory or family of theories (for example, the resource-based view as a family of theories), including appropriate levels of analysis, unit of analysis, variables and relationships as well as key findings. Each chapter includes references to selected seminal literature applying that theory, and applications of the theory in the PSM, SCM and related fields such as management and marketing literature.

The idea to create a book on theories arose out of a series of meetings that began with conversations among scholars globally regarding why the range of topics seemingly unrelated to PSM were being presented, applying an increasing array of theories. The term 'identity crisis' was used in numerous conversations as some began to question the identity of our field. To explore this further, a group of PSM scholars met in the autumn of 2017 to discuss and debate the evolution of PSM's identity in research and practice. This included a range of PSM academics primarily from Western Europe and the United States; some more practice-based and applied, others pushing for PSM to become a distinct academic discipline. The diversity of views presented during the meeting sparked enough interest by the participants that a meeting involving more PSM scholars was held the following autumn (Ellram et al., 2020).

It was interesting that among this relatively small group of established PSM scholars, including numerous past and current journal editors, there were so many differing views on PSM as an applied field of study versus an academic discipline, as well as differences in what the nature of research and identity building should be in the future. Almost an entire day was spent debating and discussing the role of theory in PSM, whether PSM needed its own theory, and what would constitute good PSM theory. This issue was not settled, but participants gained insight from the variety of positions discussed.

One thing that was agreed upon was the importance of grounding PSM research in theory; either in existing theory, or building discipline-specific theory. Theory is important to present a common framework and body of knowledge for a discipline. It creates an understanding of the phenomenon being studied, and a common language and understanding of a discipline. It can help to strengthen a discipline from both an academic and a practical perspective. It facilitates the systematic generation, accumulation, extension and dissemination of knowledge. It creates a common language for a discipline.

Those who were present at the meetings of PSM scholars agreed that theory is often improperly applied and misunderstood, and that it is sometimes difficult to determine whether a theory is appropriate in a given situation. If researchers had a starting point in understanding the assumptions, levels and units of analysis and key variables considered in a theory, they could better decide which theories are most appropriate and investigate those theories further. Out of this discussion, the idea for this book was born. We saw the issue of theory building and application as relevant to all areas of supply chain management: purchasing, logistics, operations, and the supply chain processes and interfaces. We believe that this book is also relevant to other disciplines such as management and marketing, which often study similar issues from different perspectives. The early chapters (Chapters 2 to 6) focus on the fundamentals of theory building and theory application. The following chapters provide an overview of specific theories (Chapters 7 to 33), while the final chapter looks at potential theories for the sustainability research area. After a three-year journey from the first call for contributions, we are confident that with the help of a great advisory board and a fantastic group of chapter authors, we are delivering a high-quality guidebook that will be used by PSM and SCM scholars, as well as in other disciplines.

THEORIES COVERED

The original scope of which theories to include in this collection relied on systematic literature reviews that had been conducted, for example, Glock and Hochrein (2011), Spina et al. (2013), Spina et al. (2016), Johnsen et al. (2017) and Giunipero et al. (2019). Theories intersecting between those reviews, such as the resource-based view, were included in the initial scope. In addition, well-recognized theories only covered in one of the literature reviews, such as the Industrial Marketing and Purchasing (IMP) Group perspective, were initially included on the long list. During the process of contacting potential authors, and from the advisory board, there were additional theory suggestions such as socio-technical theory and panarchy theory. Creating a broad scope was seen as particularly fruitful for this endeavour of creating a *Handbook*, as the intuition was both to encourage better understanding and further application of established theories, as well as to bring additional theories into the field of vision.

Moreover, some overarching topics of interest emerged, such as theory development in general, which led to the creation of five more general chapters.

Beginning with Chapter 7, each chapter covers a specific theory. To fulfill the goal of the edited book to provide a standard resource for researchers, each chapter related to theories covers the following basic elements:

- a brief history of how the theory developed;
- (meta) unit of analysis,[1] as well as examples of applied units of analysis; for example, the resources and processes engaged in producing goods and services, or the social exchanges in a dyadic relationship;
- level(s) of analysis appropriate for that theory: individual level, functional level, organization level, dyadic level, supply chain level, supply network level, supply systems level.

Following Wacker (1998, 2008) four elements of theory were also incorporated: (1) definitions of terms or constructs; (2) identification of the domain(s) where the theory applies; (3) description of key set(s) of relationships of constructs; and (4) specific predictions (factual claims).

Each theory chapter also covers how the theory has been applied in the following disciplines, if applicable: purchasing and supply management; another aspect of supply chain management, including logistics, operations or other aspects of supply chain management; management if relevant; marketing if relevant. Finally, each of the chapters lists seminal or important papers and books. The book closes with a chapter focused on sustainability, discussing a number of theories to spur future research in this area; see Table 1.1 for an overview. Some chapters evolved in unexpected ways. For example, Chapter 26 was originally about chaos theory. As the authors wrote that chapter, and during the evolution of that work, it ultimately converged towards complex adaptive systems, which are also covered in Chapter 22.

APPLICATIONS OF THIS HANDBOOK

This *Handbook* is not meant to be the primary reference for each of the theories, since it is always good practice to go back to the original sources. However, this is an excellent reference for future research ideas in the individual theory chapters, and for the content of the more general articles (for example, on mid-range theory) in the *Handbook*. This should be a 'go-to' resource, for those writing theses (bachelor, master, doctoral), and for the postdoctoral level to broaden scope beyond 'favourite' theories, and to understand appropriate theories for their research. The *Handbook* can help to expand knowledge of the field to better comprehend other people's research, and understand how various theories and the application of those theories is evolving, including mid-range theory building. It can provide insight into when theory building is appropriate, and an introduction to some methods of theory building.

From an educational standpoint, this is an excellent addition to a graduate seminar where it can be used to discuss theories with respect to student projects, published research or current research projects. The *Handbook* can help to identify key work in the field that uses a particular theory, and to discuss different applications. It provides different lenses that might be used to view new and interesting problems. For editors, associate editors and reviewers who may not be well versed in a particular theory, the *Handbook* can be used to validate the level and unit of analysis and the appropriate tenets of the theories.

Table 1.1   *Future research by chapter*

Chapter #	Chapter title	Suggestions for future research
Chapter 2	Foundations of theory	• Create new theoretical propositions that make interesting and important contributions to the extant theory.
Chapter 3	Developing purchasing and supply management theory	• Meld discipline with imagination to enhance and build purchasing and supply management theory. • Utilize new sources of data and analytical approaches for theory development including dark data, data mining, data visualization, ethnography, data virtualization, 'live' big data, meta-analysis, predictive analytics, operating and sensing data, and thick data.
Chapter 4	Theories relevant to purchasing and supply management research: status quo and future suggestions	• Use attribution theory to understand how managers interpret PSM outcomes. • Use of reverse auctions in the sourcing cycle offer multiple opportunities for researchers to apply auction theory. • Increase usage of information processing theory (IPT) along with the growth of artificial intelligence, machine learning and robotics in PSM. • Utilize institutional theory to inform PSM research exploring bounded rationality and time constraints leading to solutions where no efficiency gains have been realized. • Take a multi-level theoretical perspective to explore how a PSM participant, such as a buyer or supplier, decisions and behaviour foster organizational learning. • Integrate the concept of power within complex dynamics to increase the utility of studies of power in PSM to be theoretically meaningful and useful in practice. • Study relational governance in the PSM context. • Use resource orchestration theory to highlight the importance of supply management actions for the organization to realize the full value of its resources. • Apply social network theory in PSM to investigate how buyer–supplier firms interact with each other, describe the many informal connections that tie their executives together, as well as associations and connections between individual employees at partner firms.
Chapter 5	Systems levels in purchasing and supply chain management (PSCM) research: exploring established and novel theories to address PSCM problems and challenges	• Consider novel (at least to PSCM) theoretical approaches to exploring and understanding key business and societal challenges. • Elaborate, test and develop theory.
Chapter 6	Enhancing theorizing in purchasing and supply management through middle-range theories	• Perform a comprehensive literature review to populate a greater list of MRT in PSM to complement the examples presented. • Conceptualize the relationship between engaged scholarship and MRT is encouraged.

Chapter #	Chapter title	Suggestions for future research
Chapter 7	Transaction cost economics	• Combine the frequency of transactions with increasing uncertainty and measurement problems and determine how it influences the make versus buy decision, or even the location decision. • Understand the role of opportunism in market versus hierarchy decisions. • Determine the influence of big data and blockchain on transaction costs with increased information availability and transparency.
Chapter 8	Resource-based view	• Explore the strategic capabilities needed to enable firms to succeed in new contexts such as base of the pyramid (BoP) markets which are characterized by institutional voids. • Identify natural resource-based view (NRBV) contingencies which affect the environmental–financial performance relationship. • Extend the scope in the social resource-based view (SRBV) far beyond 'typical' business stakeholders to include non-governmental organizations (NGOs), but also local communities and the natural environment. • Explore the necessary and sufficient conditions for achieving triple bottom line (TBL) value, in particular the role of social capabilities and whether capabilities from all views are needed to create integrated TBL value. • Understand the interrelations between the economic, environmental and social performance outcomes especially in the context of a broad stakeholder network.
Chapter 9	The knowledge-based view	• Build, recombine and integrate knowledge in complex settings (compared to the static supply chain).
Chapter 10	Resource-advantage theory	• Financial performance needs to be further explored and tested. • Examine when and how organizational learning spurs incremental innovation in adopting best practices of competitors versus major innovation that disrupts the status quo and sets a new benchmark for the industry. • Understand the external factors that moderate or mediate the relationships among the key variables of resource-advantage (R-A) theory. • Examine non-resources and contra-resources to provide insight into the dynamic nature of competition. • Determine whether R-A theory provides a framework for understanding superior performance in the competition for suppliers.
Chapter 11	Resource and natural resource dependence theories in supply chains	• Integrate resource dependence theory (RDT) and other theoretical lenses to investigate organizational interdependencies. • Explore updated mechanisms to manage dependencies and organizational power that would be more tailored to deal with recent challenges of an extremely uncertain environment. • Investigate the role of integrated and interorganizational technologies such as those from Industry 4.0 and other digitalization technologies. • Understand how organizations manage their ecosystem services and environmental rents.
Chapter 12	Resource orchestration: managers' role in developing and deploying resources to create distinctive advantage	• Explore the why, when and how questions related to managers' influence on the development of true core competencies. • Provide more nuanced insight into how specific managerial skills and organization routines affect structuring, bundling and leveraging resources.

Chapter #	Chapter title	Suggestions for future research
Chapter 13	Agency theory in purchasing and supply management	• Apply agency theory to continue extending beyond the dyads of buyer and supplier firms.
Chapter 14	Playing to win: applying game theory to purchasing and supply management	• Study the intersection of artificial intelligence, and purchasing behaviour in the presence of 'smart' machines. • Research the competitive dynamics between different (levels of) actors in the supply chain (i.e., people competing with machines). • Consider the structure of competitive dynamics between smart machines.
Chapter 15	Paradox theory	• Study the implications of a paradoxical response to the contradictory and competing demands of social, environmental and economic stakeholders in various tiers of the supply chain. • Explore how power regimes interplay with paradoxical thinking when creating system-wide changes. • Integrate and leverage research from behavioural operations management with psychological, sociological and organizational paradox to study the micro-foundations of the paradoxical mindset/cognition in the supply chain.
Chapter 16	Contingency theory and the information processing view	• Engage in theory-based empirical research to develop elaborated and more detailed understanding of a variety of managerial practices in PSM or other topic areas. • Engage in an in-depth conversation of conceptualizing and empirically assessing effectiveness in that specific PSM setting. • Consider different forms of fit.
Chapter 17	Social exchange theory	• Research internal dynamics that require purchasing to mediate the internal relationships with stakeholders and external relationships with sellers. • Mapping and understand the relative forms of value among multiple engaged parties. • View global buyer–seller relationships, espousing a view that interpersonal links between firm boundary spanners and the concomitant links between firms are mutually affected.
Chapter 18	The relational view	• Study the RV in newly emerging research contexts such as alliances and partnerships in the context of organizations undergoing digital transformations. • Explore how digital technologies and new software solutions reshape alliances, collaborations and the resulting relational rents. • Apply the RV to new contexts, namely, different types of partners (e.g., NGOs, community associations) and different types of relational rents (e.g., social impact, environmental value). • Incorporate sustainability considerations with novel definition and conceptualization of 'relational rents' beyond traditional economic measures and might unravel new variables. • Explore the interrelationships between the four sources of relational rents.
Chapter 19	Supply networks: dyads, triads and networks	• Develop network perspectives and suggest that social network concepts such as ego-network structure, structural holes, node centrality, network cohesion and structural equivalence might be applied to supply chain management. • Understand network structure and structuring, collaboration and network governance gains urgency as we tackle new challenges.

Chapter #	Chapter title	Suggestions for future research
Chapter 20	Stakeholder theory	• Combine stakeholder theory with other theories. • Use stakeholder theory beyond stakeholder classification in supply chain management to embrace its full potential when analysing global supply chains. • Look at the relationships between stakeholders to understand how they influence one another, and how that influence contributes to the dynamics of their salience.
Chapter 21	Institutional theory	• Include uncertainty as a variable in empirical studies on institutional theory. • Examine the three pressures and their linkages. • Understand the role of operations and supply chain management (OSCM) academics as a source of institutional pressure.
Chapter 22	Complex adaptive systems	• Partner with researchers from other disciplines who have skills related to complexity science. • Develop process theories of supply network evolution and adaptation.
Chapter 23	Factor market rivalry: a general theory of supply chain management	• Build upon the temporal nature of resource scarcity. • Examine the role factor market rivalry (FMR) plays in the development of exclusivity agreements between trading partners. • Research mergers and acquisitions (M&A) activities, and vertical and horizontal integration in the supply chain to better understand how competition for resources is executed using M&A in the supply chain. • Use FMR as a guiding theory could extend into the academic area of legal scholarship where antitrust laws and the litigated competition over resources is documented in lawsuits. • Defend firms from FMR, by making them less reliant on scarce resources. • Examine the role that preferred resources play in the development of rivalry and resource competition. • Consider which factors can breakdown FMR and lessen the negative impact of FMR activities. • Develop the strategic competition aspect of FMR.
Chapter 24	The industrial network approach and purchasing and supply management research	• Apply the industrial network perspective in purchasing and supply management (PSM) research related to the strategic role of procurement, supplier relations, supplier base configurations, organizing procurement, offshoring and international sourcing, service procurement, logistics and distribution channels, collaborative innovation, public sector procurement and research methods.
Chapter 25	Dynamic capabilities theory	• Shift from conceptual work to empirical studies investigating the validity of the dynamic capabilities theory, for example, through longitudinal research.
Chapter 26	Supply chains as complex adaptive systems	• Investigate network level cascading processes or discussed supply chain phenomena linked to agent adaptation. • Assess how local interactions, driven by a simple set of rules, could alter network properties. • Establish indirect causalities linked to supply chain performance. • Expand the understanding of 'entropy' in a supply network context.

Chapter #	Chapter title	Suggestions for future research
Chapter 27	Cluster theory and purchasing science: geographical proximity as a strategic decision factor in sourcing	• Test the generalizability of cluster relevance. • Research the intersection of purchasing and strategic management using a cluster theory lens. • Explore how governments foster the formation of regional clusters.
Chapter 28	Organizational learning theory and its application to purchasing management and supply chain management research	• Investigate theoretically and empirically the implications of artificial intelligence and machine learning adoption by firms and supply chains for organizational learning and developing intelligent organizations.
Chapter 29	Signalling theory	• Question whether and how signals are passed and treated in a supply chain. • Involve additional stakeholders (others than already involved in the supply chain) and their potential influence on signalling. • Expand the level of analysis from dyadic to network-like arrangements (supply chains), including signalling in buyer–buyer relationships or in supplier–supplier relationships. • Understand decisions related to make-or-buy, global versus localized sourcing, supplier relationship management, supplier involvement (also in new product development), supplier development or strategic cost management, through a signalling theory lens. • Assess topics that occur *ex ante* to a contractual relationship. • Look at enablers for successful purchasing and supply management activities. • Question how to ensure the realization of these priorities by also using supplier-induced signals. • Investigate each of the constructs in more detail in the context of purchasing and supply management in a business-to-business (B2B) environment.
Chapter 30	Portfolio theory	• Assess the selection and measurement of purchasing portfolio variables. • Understand the impact of the context which companies work in. • Understand the effectiveness of purchasing portfolio models. • Perform longitudinal studies to provide information about the long-term impact and usefulness of the portfolio approach.
Chapter 31	Supply chains as dynamic socio-technical systems	• Learn how to minimize design features that produce less-than-optimal supply chain operations. • Investigate design features that allow more ready adaptation to turbulent business conditions. • Research the design of supply chains that operate under conditions of extreme volatility to add to our understanding of the factors that are most important to consider as we witness the ever-increasing turbulence and connectedness of global business conditions.
Chapter 32	Panarchy theory	• Investigate the possibilities of using panarchy theory as a means to address sustainability issues. • Research how to determine the number of scales and levels necessary when using panarchy theory in SCM. • Apply different methodological approaches and their use of panarchy theory in SCM.

Chapter #	Chapter title	Suggestions for future research
Chapter 33	Preferred customer theory: benefiting from preferential treatment from suppliers through measures on buyer attractiveness and supplier satisfaction	• Map the cycle stages as one dimension in preferred customer research. • Identify opportunities for future research at these levels of analysis: micro (individual), meso (buyer–supplier) and macro (country).
Chapter 34	On theories for researching sustainability	• Extend the scope of analysis to the multiple tiers of the supply chain and the relationships with relevant stakeholders, thus broadening the perspective of stakeholder and institutional theories by combining them with the IMP approach. • Identify and compare reactive and proactive strategies to respond and manage the multiple pressures by actors and stakeholders to achieve sustainable competitive advantage at network level. • Extend the NRBV approach to include social and ethical perspectives, to understand how they can become sources of competitive advantage, while broadening the scope from focal firms to the supply chain or network. The SRBV is a first and very promising attempt in this direction.

CONCLUSIONS AND OUTLOOK

We applaud the collective effort that made this *Handbook* possible; from the initial discussion to the commitment of a very diverse and international set of 65 authors from 11 countries (35 authors from outside the United States; and almost a third female authors). We would also like to recognize the active advisory board that helped us to manage the challenges inherent in a significant endeavour such as this *Handbook*: Christine M. Harland, Finn Wynstra, Erik van Raaij, Craig Carter, Michael Eßig, Frank Rozemeijer and Stefan Seuring.

A theoretical contribution is expected in empirical research today. This book provides a resource for supporting theory application and development. Fortunately, this *Handbook* is intended to be (mostly) timeless. While the future applications sections are a mirror of the current issues at the time this is written in, such as the ongoing Covid-19 pandemic, we hope to have many future editions.

There are some theories that are not yet well integrated into purchasing and supply chain research to date and need further development. One example is panarchy theory. Its focus is to help explain complex changes that occur in the processes and structures of ecosystems, exploring the 'continual adaptive cycles of growth, accumulation, restructuring, and renewal' that are part of dynamic environments we face in the real world every day. This fits well with many purchasing and supply chain challenges: from how we can effectively deal with adapting to changes due to the spread of Covid-19, to how to implement sustainability goals and action to move towards science-based targets in order to slow and even stop global climate disruption.

Other theories, such as transaction cost economics, have been applied in purchasing and supply chain research for several decades. However, these grand theories are still relevant to studying and understanding emerging areas of supply chain research. These include areas such as blockchain, crypto currencies, supply chain finance and the implications of greater digitalization on supply chain governance.

There are many suggestions for future research related to the various theories in the chapters and in Table 1.1. These ideas are meant to inspire you, not to limit you. We hope that you can use this table as a jumping-off point for exploring new theories and supporting future research. We wish each of you the best in the journey of research and discovery that lies ahead.

Editing this book has been a great experience. We would like to thank the authors both for their chapters and for their feedback in the peer review process; the advisory board for their input; and Ellen Pearce and Sarah Brown from Edward Elgar Publishing for their thoroughness and thoughtfulness throughout this process.

NOTE

1. Unit of analysis information and level of analysis information can often be found in seminal works in the field.

REFERENCES

Carter, Craig R. (2011). A call for theory: the maturation of the supply chain management discipline. *Journal of Supply Chain Management*, 47 (2), 1523–2409.

Ellram, L.M., Harland, C.M., van Weele, A., Essig, M., Johnsen, T., et al. (2020). Purchasing and supply management's identity: Crisis? What crisis? *Journal of Purchasing and Supply Management*, 25th Anniversary Issue, 26 (1), 1–8.

Giunipero, L. C., Bittner, S., Shanks, I., & Cho, M. H. (2019). Analyzing the sourcing literature: over two decades of research. *Journal of Purchasing and Supply Management*, 25 (5), 100521.

Glock, C.H., & Hochrein, S. (2011). Purchasing organization and design: A literature review. *Business Research*, 4 (2), 149–191.

Johnsen, T. E., Miemczyk, J., & Howard, M. (2017). A systematic literature review of sustainable purchasing and supply research: Theoretical perspectives and opportunities for IMP-based research. *Industrial Marketing Management*, 61, 130–143.

Smith, Ken G., & Hitt, Michael A. (eds) (2007). *Great Minds in Management: The Process of Theory Development*. Oxford: Oxford University Press.

Spina, G., Caniato, F., Luzzini, D., & Ronchi, S. (2013). Past, present and future trends of purchasing and supply management: An extensive literature review. *Industrial Marketing Management*, 42 (8), 1202–1212.

Spina, G., Caniato, F., Luzzini, D., & Ronchi, S. (2016). Assessing the use of external grand theories in purchasing and supply management research. *Journal of Purchasing and Supply Management*, 22 (1), 18–30.

van Weele, Arjan J., & van Raaij, Erik M. (2014). The future of purchasing and supply management research: About relevance and rigor. *Journal of Supply Chain Management*, 50 (1), 1523–2409.

Wacker, J.G. (1998). A definition of theory: research guidelines for different theory-building research methods in operations management. *Journal of Operations Management*, 16 (4), 361–385.

Wacker, J.G. (2008). A conceptual understanding of requirements for theory-building research: Guidelines for scientific theory building. *Journal of Supply Chain Management*, 44 (3), 5–15.

2. Foundations of theory

Barbara B. Flynn, Mark Pagell, Brian Fugate and David E. Cantor

INTRODUCTION

Theory is an important part of research in all disciplines. Although sometimes viewed only as a submission requirement to be satisfied (Hambrick 2007; Sutton and Staw 1995), theory is an essential part of developing high-quality research. In fact, 'nothing is as practical as good theory' (Van de Ven 1989), because it guides researchers toward important research questions that can be used to scientifically advance related knowledge (Wacker 1998).

An important goal of any research endeavour is the systematic accumulation of knowledge to better understand a phenomenon and make predictions about it. Theory-driven research allows systematically addressing a research problem, to help researchers develop new knowledge related to it, reinforce existing knowledge, and uncover opportunities for new theoretical directions. In a way, theory is like a roadmap for investigating an interesting research question. It tells what the relevant constructs are, describes expected relationships between them, articulates the domain in which they are applicable, and predicts how the constructs will operate (Hambrick 2007). Without this roadmap, researchers would run the risk of accumulating statistically significant relationships without understanding the big picture or why relationships were significant (Wacker 2008). This can lead to 'false theories' (Huff 2009) that cause researchers to draw conclusions without adequate knowledge, synthesis or analysis. False theories are not unusual, particularly in light of the speed with which they can be disseminated by social and traditional media. Consider the development and spread of the many false theories about Covid-19's origins, treatments, prevention and potential causes. Using theory as a research roadmap is a way of combating false theory and making sense of empirical findings, to generate coherent explanations that contribute to the knowledge about a phenomenon.

Alternatively, theory can emerge from empirical observation of qualitative or quantitative evidence. For example, much of the seminal operations strategy theory, such as the product–process matrix (Hayes and Wheelwright 1979), stages of manufacturing effectiveness (Wheelwright and Hayes 1985), focus (Skinner 1974) and order winners/order qualifiers (Hill 2000), was based on the authors' observations in their consulting experience. Thinking about their observations theoretically helped them to move from simply developing practices to thinking about why the practices worked, and avoiding seemingly plausible constructs and relationships that were actually extraneous. Thus, thinking theoretically is critical in developing a coherent explanation for findings resulting from empirical evidence (Hambrick 2007; Weick 1989, 1995; Whetton 1989).

To summarize, theory provides researchers with a way to generate coherent explanations for empirical findings, in order to contribute to the systematic accumulation of knowledge, whether the goal of a research project is to test theory or to develop theory. Employed effectively, theory provides a roadmap for designing a high-quality empirical research project and a framework for positioning the findings in the extant knowledge.

WHAT IS THEORY?

Theory 'is about the connections among phenomena, a story about why actions, events, structure, and thoughts occur' (Sutton and Staw 1995, p. 378). According to Weick (1995), a good theory predicts, explains and delights. Theory operates through development and accumulation of a system of coherent, disciplined and rigorous knowledge and explanation (Huff 2009). It is coherent in that terminology is clearly defined and does not overlap with existing terminology. Theory seeks to systematically accumulate knowledge and explanation to provide a foundation for the work of other researchers. Whether that knowledge is generated by quantitative or qualitative empirical data or analytical mathematical modelling, the methods used to gather it are disciplined and rigorous, providing assurance that other researchers approaching the phenomenon in the same way would arrive at similar conclusions. Theory is informed by practice, and it informs focused, disciplined, empirical research inquiry. Although purchasing and supply management is closely linked with practice (Ellram et al. 2020), theory provides a way of elevating research to a level that predicts and explains phenomena that cut across specific applications.

In developing a better understanding of what theory is, we contrast it with what theory is not (Suddaby 2006; Sutton and Staw 1995; Weick 1995). While a literature review positions a research study in the extant literature and is a necessary part of a good research paper, a literature review does not provide a roadmap for addressing the research problem, specify key constructs and relationships between them, or describe how the research advances scientific knowledge (Sutton and Staw 1995). Further, pointing out the limitations to a theory's range of application, although important, is not the same as making a theoretical contribution (Hambrick 2007; Whetton 1989). Although a model is important in guiding deductive research, and theories almost always incorporate models, a model is a smaller element of a theory that graphically portrays proposed relationships between variables and outcomes (Huff 2009); models 'should be considered as stage props, rather than as the performance, itself' (Sutton and Staw 1995, p. 376). Finally, while good theory always tells an interesting story, telling an interesting story is not the same thing as inductively developing good theory. Qualitative data that describes which patterns of behaviour, but not why they were observed or are to be expected, is not theory (Sutton and Staw 1995). The key is to be able to hear the story that the empirical evidence is telling, and frame it in a way that is generalizable and robust.

Developing theory is something that some purchasing and supply chain researchers may be reluctant to tackle, because they are more comfortable with approaches that apply the scientific method to develop laws for predicting outcomes. Yet, there is a wealth of exciting new sources of empirical evidence for developing theory, providing researchers with the opportunity to develop relevant theory specific to the purchasing and supply management context (Flynn et al. 2020; Melnyk et al. 2018).

Table 2.1   Overview of philosophical orientations

	Positivism	Interpretivism	Critical theory
Foundation	● Scientific method	● Real-world problems	● Obstacles presented by ideology
Approach	● Hypothesis testing	● Search for patterns of meaning and symbolic acts	● Overturn theory that is false, dogmatic, or cannot be proven
			● Replace it with scientific insights that better inform theory
View of reality	● Objective	● Socially constructed	● Disguised by ideologies and exploitation
Goal	● Establish universal laws to predict outcomes	● Develop a deep understanding of key constructs and how they related to each other	● Change the world
Research methods	● Experiments	● Ethnography	● Field research
	● Surveys	● Engaged research	● Dialectical analysis
	● Secondary analysis of archival data	● Interviews	● Historical analysis
		● Content analysis	● Deconstruction
		● Textual analysis	● Textual analysis
		● Case studies	
		● Grounded theory development	
Evaluation	● Ability to predict	● Trustworthiness	● Theoretical consistency
	● Rigour	● Authenticity	● Implications for action, mobilization and change
	● Internal validity		● Historical insights
	● External validity		● Transcendent interpretations
	● Reliability		

TYPES OF THEORY

Theories can be described by their philosophical orientation and their level of abstraction. There is no 'right' type of theory; each of these is a valid perspective for purchasing and supply theory. The type of theory employed or developed in a particular research project should be a logical outcome of the research question.

Philosophical Orientation

Theory development is not limited to a particular philosophical orientation. Different philosophical orientations (Table 2.1) are useful in guiding different phases of the theory development process, as well as in applying and developing theory in different contexts (Huff 2009).

Positivism
A positivist orientation is based on the scientific method (Huff 2009); it is reflected in the hypothesis testing approach of much of the purchasing and supply management research. Positivism views reality as objective, and the task of the researcher is establishing universal laws to predict outcomes, in the way that the natural sciences do. However, since purchasing and supply management research focuses on people, relationships and organizations, truly universal laws, akin to the boiling or freezing point of water, are not possible. Rather, researchers focus on predicting relationships between constructs and outcomes within a specific domain.

Research based on a positivist orientation uses theory to generate hypotheses, operationalizes key constructs, and collects data for testing hypotheses. For example, Blount and Li (2021) surveyed 277 buyers in large United States (US) and United Kingdom purchasing organizations about their willingness to purchase from minority businesses. Skilton et al.'s (2020) study of absorptive capacity's support for different product development strategies used archival data from the US pharmaceutical industry. Lu et al. (2020) used a scenario-based experiment to study the impact of informal interactions by boundary-spanning supply managers on later formal sourcing collaborations.

Because positivism seeks to uncover quantitative relationships among constructs, a positivist theory's validity is evaluated in terms of its ability to predict, its rigour, internal and external validity, and reliability. Research methods associated with a positivist orientation include experiments, surveys and secondary analysis of archival data (Huff 2009).

Interpretivism

Interpretive research philosophies view human behaviour as too complex to be described by the universal laws and relationships sought by positivistic research (Huff 2009). Interpretivism capitalizes on the messy, cross-disciplinary nature of real-world problems, rather than attempting to reduce them to manageable constructs and relationships. It uses nuanced interpretation of rich data sources to develop a deep understanding of key constructs and how they relate to each other. Thus, rather than viewing reality as objective and quantifiable, an interpretivist orientation views reality as a social construction.

Interpretivist researchers search for patterns of meaning to understand how people's perceptions of a situation influence their reality. Rather than variables, interpretivism focuses on symbolic acts and meaning. Research is comprised of developing abstract descriptions of meanings and situations as they occur in their natural setting. Interpretivist theory is assessed by its trustworthiness and authenticity, using research methods such as ethnography; engaged research; interviews; content and textual analysis of descriptions, documents and conversations; case studies; and grounded theory development (Huff 2009).

For example, the engaged research approach actively involves researchers in the research context, rather than adhering to positivism's unbiased, disengaged orientation (Touboulic et al. 2020). Researchers draw upon their participation in decision making and action to engage in disciplined reflection, to search for insights that lay the foundation for theory building. Examples include Touboulic and Walker's (2016) study of supply chain sustainability, Coughlan et al.'s (2003) examination of collaborative relationships during periods of discontinuity, Harland and Knight's (2001) longitudinal engaged research on supply network strategy, and Eltantaway et al.'s (2015) examination of information flows in a multi-tier supply chain. Interpretivism's primary challenge for researchers is making the transition from reporting observations to developing them into a system of coherent, disciplined and rigorous knowledge.

Critical theory

Moving from a goal of understanding and explaining the world, a critical theory orientation focuses on changing the world (Huff 2009). It views ideology as a major obstacle to changing society. Thus, a critical theory orientation seeks to overturn theory that is false, dogmatic, or cannot be proven, challenging processes and policies that reinforce the status quo, removing tacit ideological biases, and exposing processes and policies that prevent people from realizing their full potential. Although much critical theory research is based on advancing a political agenda, its fundamental questioning of all assumptions by breaking traditional thought paradigms is important to building theory in any discipline.

A critical theory orientation focuses on searching for disguised contradictions (Poole and Van de Ven 1989) hidden by ideologies and incidents that reveal exploitation. By exposing them, it seeks to replace ideology with scientific insights and enable better-informed thinking. Because of critical theory's focus on contradictions in structural or historical thinking, key assessment criteria include theoretical consistency, implications for action, mobilization and change, historical insights and transcendent interpretations. Research methods associated with critical thinking include field research, dialectical analysis, historical analysis, deconstruction and textual analysis (Huff 2009).

Examples of applying a critical theory orientation to topics relevant to purchasing and supply management are Springett's (2013) analysis of stakeholder power and hegemony in sustainable development, Reed's (1999) critical theory analysis of stakeholder theory, and Hilt's (1995) application of critical theory to vulnerable populations. There is substantial opportunity for more direct application of critical theory and related approaches to purchasing and supply management.

Although the positivist, interpretivist and critical thinking orientations are very different from each other, they can potentially inform each other in developing and testing theory. For example, research with a critical theory orientation might expose the way that traditional thinking leads to exploitation of vulnerable local communities that gather nuts and berries in the Amazon region to supply the production of lotions and creams. Interpretivist researchers might build on this in conducting in-depth examination of local communities that supply lotions and creams manufacturers versus cosmetics manufacturers in several regions, comparing and contrasting them on important dimensions to refine key constructs. Building on these findings, positivist researchers might then collect data from a large number of firms that source raw materials from local communities, to isolate key antecedents to exploitation. By being open to research with different philosophical orientations, researchers can generate more coherent explanations to make a meaningful contribution to the systematic accumulation of knowledge.

Levels of Abstraction

Theory that focuses at different levels of abstraction also contributes to the systematic accumulation of knowledge. A camera metaphor is useful in understanding different levels of theoretical abstraction (Huff 2009): each generates coherent explanations that contribute to the systematic accumulation of knowledge, but in a different way (Table 2.2).

Grand theory
Grand theory is like a photograph taken using a wide-angle lens. It provides a broad, comprehensive view of the big picture, while the details are fuzzy. Grand theory is at the highest level of abstraction, with a goal of establishing universally applicable predictions and principles. It is frequently employed in purchasing and supply management research with a positivist orientation, and it is often borrowed from other disciplines due to its broad applicability. Many examples of grand theory are covered in other chapters of this book, including the resource-based view (Barney et al. 2001), transaction cost economics theory

Table 2.2   *Levels of theory*

	Grand theory	Middle-range theory	Local theory
Level of abstraction	Highest	Middle	Lowest
Big picture	Broad, comprehensive, generalizable	Less emphasized	Blurred or missing
Details	Fuzzy	Clearer	Very clear
Goal	Establish universally applicable predictions and principles	• Systematic accumulation of knowledge • Prediction of outcomes for a limited set of phenomena • Prediction of outcomes within a limited domain	• Understand unexpected or counterintuitive findings • Generate insights about unique phenomenon or event
Source	Often borrowed from other disciplines	Developed or modified by researcher	Developed by researcher
Examples	• Resource-based view • Transaction cost economics • Social network theory • Behavioural economics • Agency theory	Domains with unique characteristics: • Healthcare • Logistics and transportation • Regulated industries	Unique phenomena or events: • Post-Covid buyer–supplier relationships in specific industry • Emergency supply chains following 2011 earthquake, tsunami and nuclear power plant meltdown in Japan

(Williamson (1975, 1985), institutional theory (DiMaggio and Powell 1983), social network theory (Granovetter 1973), complex adaptive systems theory (Pathak et al. 2007), behavioural economics (Tversky and Kahneman 1974) and agency theory (Jensen and Meckling 1976). These and other grand theories have guided purchasing and supply management research that has led to important insights, despite being originally developed for other domains, including economics, strategic management, marketing, computer science and psychology.

Care should be taken in adapting grand theories to purchasing and supply management due to unit of analysis issues, since many potentially relevant grand theories predict and explain the behaviour of individuals, rather than interorganizational relationships (Flynn et al. 2020; Melnyk et al. 2018). Grand theories are sometimes applied by purchasing and supply management researchers using a 'one size fits all' approach, dropping in a favourite theory as an explanation for almost any phenomenon. This type of research is characterized by a paragraph or two describing a theory, then failing to use it to guide development of the key constructs, relationships, domain and predictions (Boer et al. 2015). These 'bolted on' (Boer et al. 2015) theory and 'ceremonial citations' (Weick 1995) approaches fail to accomplish the goals of advancing the systematic accumulation of knowledge, articulating key constructs, or providing a compelling argument for expected relationships between them.

Middle-range theory

Middle-range theory is analogous to a photograph taken with an intermediate-range lens. It reveals rich details, with less emphasis on the big picture and, thus, less generalizability to other domains. Middle-range theory systematically accumulates knowledge and predicts outcomes for a limited set of phenomena (Wacker 1998) or phenomena within a limited domain, functioning at the middle level of abstraction.

In purchasing and supply management research, middle-range theory is common within domains with unique characteristics. For example, healthcare purchasing and supply management research sometimes develops middle-range theory to incorporate the unique challenges associated with third-party payers (government, employers), fiscal intermediaries (insurance companies, health maintenance organizations), the US Affordable Care Act, physician preference items and group purchasing organizations (GPOs). Another domain where middle-range theory is sometimes developed is logistics and transportation. This industry's unique challenges include equipment that is constantly in motion and operational personnel (truck drivers) making important decisions with limited supervision. An example of middle-range purchasing and supply management theory is provided by Davis et al.'s (2019) survey of owners and managers of over 5000 wineries in the US. They sought to develop a deep understanding of buyer–supplier relationships in an industry where regulations vary by state, often limiting choice of supply partners. In doing so, they developed middle-range theory about the nuances and complexities of purchasing and supply management in the unique context of this industry and its regulatory institutions.

Local theory
A local theory is analogous to a close-up or cutaway photograph. While the details are very clear, the 'scene' is blurred or missing. Thus, local theories are the least abstract, identifying relationships that lead to empirical generalization of very limited scope (Wacker 1998). Often, local theory is developed as researchers attempt to understand an unexpected or counterintuitive finding, or generate insights about a unique phenomenon or event (Huff 2009).

For example, Marques et al. (2020) used a single case study approach to develop local theory to extend prevailing theory on knowledge diffusion that is based on long-term, trust-based, collaborative relationships. They pointed out that in a globally dispersed supply network, relationships are often at arm's length, characterized by competitive tensions and weak ties. Thus, Marques et al. (2020) extended extant theory to a context more realistic for a global supply network. They examined knowledge diffusion in a closed-network platform used by members of the single focal firm's globally dispersed supply network, examining written discussion forum posts over two years, supplemented with semi-structured interviews, demographic data about network members, validation workshops and observation of supply network webinars. Marques et al.'s (2020) focus is clearly local theory development, yet its positioning in the context of global supply networks makes it easy to see its potential for future research to demonstrate its generalizability.

BUILDING BLOCKS OF THEORY

There are four building blocks of theory: constructs, relationship, domain and predictions (Wacker 1998). We describe them in the following sections, adopting Whetton's (2009) terminology.

Basic Building Blocks

We begin with the basic building blocks of constructs and relationships, which can be linked to form theoretical propositions. Developing meaningful theoretical propositions gives a researcher the ability to enter the theoretical discourse on a phenomenon (Huff 2009). As theoretical propositions are refined, they become the foundation for a full-blown theory (Weick 1995).

Constructs

A construct is the 'who' or 'what' of a theory (Whetton 1989), portrayed in a graphic model by a box. If a theory were a play, constructs would be the central characters (Whetton 2009).

It is important that constructs are named to reflect the concepts underlying them (Osigweh 1989). Constructs should be named as broadly as possible, while avoiding stretching them so broadly that they are meaningless in theoretical propositions (Osigweh 1989); for example, broad names such as 'supply chain relationships', 'sustainability' or 'environmental conditions' are not very useful in a theoretical proposition. Rather, constructs should be named following the same conventions as variables, connoting a range from low to high, such as 'supply chain relationship quality', 'sustainability standards' or 'environmental competitiveness'. Further, constructs should be capable of acting or being acted upon; they should describe a cause or an effect. Construct names should be theoretical (not completely defined by empirical measures), in order to allow extension to other domains (Osigweh 1989); a construct should retain its meaning when it is used at various levels of abstraction. Construct names should be the same as in the extant literature, to avoid confusion. If a construct is unique, it should be carefully differentiated from related constructs (Wacker 1998).

Whetton (2009) describes two types of constructs. The focal construct is the central interest of a research project, like the central character in a play. For example, a researcher may be interested in developing middle-range theory related to group purchasing organizations (GPOs) that aggregate demand from multiple hospitals. On the other hand, complementary constructs are constructs that seem related to the focal construct in some way, based on the literature review or preliminary empirical evidence from interviews; they are like the supporting characters in a play. Whetton (2009) recommends considering up to seven complementary constructs in developing theoretical propositions about a focal construct. For example, in developing theory about GPOs (the focal construct), complementary constructs might include cost of purchased items, physician preference items, purchasing group power, clinical outcomes, patient satisfaction, hospital size, physician preference items and government financial support. Combinations of complementary and focal constructs are the basis of forming theoretical propositions.

Clarification of the role of focal and complementary constructs is important in framing a theory. For a researcher interested in contributing to the theoretical discourse about GPOs, a basic X-focused theoretical proposition is that GPO use (X) is inversely related to the cost of purchased items (Y); it is X-focused because the focal construct explains the (lower) cost of purchased items. On the other hand, a basic Y-focused theoretical proposition is that hospital size (X) is related to GPO use (Y); it is Y-focused because the focal construct is the outcome.

Relationships

Relationships are explanations between two or more constructs, portrayed in a graphic model as arrows. Each arrow signifies a testable proposition; thus, relationships are the 'hows' and 'whys' of a theory (Whetton 1989). In a play, relationships would be the storyline that connects the central characters (Whetton 2009).

Every construct should be connected by one or more arrows that propose relationships between them. Each arrow signifies an explanation, rather than simply a descriptive prediction or a statistical relationship. A direct relationship links one construct to another without any intermediate links (X → Y), while an intermediate relationship between two constructs is mediated by another construct Z, such that X → Z → Y. A useful tip for ensuring that every arrow serves a theoretical purpose is to write a brief explanation on each arrow in a graphic model, such as 'X → Y because ...'). For example, for the relationship between external collaboration and lower supply expense in a hospital setting, the brief explanation might be: 'As a form of lateral relations, information processing theory predicts that external collaboration will increase a hospital's information processing capacity. This reduces supply expense because information processing occurs closer to the source, avoiding moving between hierarchical levels for processing.'

Using basic building blocks to create theoretical propositions
Relationships between constructs are described by theoretical propositions (Bacharach 1989). A theoretical proposition is comprised of at least two constructs and one relationship. Developing theoretical propositions allows a researcher to make a unique contribution to an ongoing theoretical discourse (Huff 2009). Repeating a basic theoretical proposition that is already well established does not contribute to theory, thus an important first step is to become familiar with existing research on the focal construct and to note established theoretical propositions. The basic X-focused and Y-focused theoretical propositions described above are already well known and would not make a meaningful contribution to theoretical discourse on GPOs. However, there are several ways in which a basic theoretical proposition can be enhanced to create new theoretical propositions that make interesting and important contributions to the extant theory; these are summarized in Table 2.3.

Change an antecedent or outcome
One way to contribute to the theoretical discourse on GPOs is by proposing a different antecedent or outcome to a basic X-focused or Y-focused theoretical proposition, in order to improve its accuracy (Whetton 2009). A researcher could propose new dimensions of an existing construct (for example, public versus private hospitals, or large versus small hospitals), broaden or narrow the scope of an existing construct (for example, teaching hospitals only), or substitute a different construct for the original antecedent or outcome in the basic theoretical proposition (for example, clinical outcomes or patient satisfaction). For example, a researcher could contribute to the middle-range theory on GPOs by proposing that the size of a GPO (X_a) explains the cost of hospitals' purchased items (Y), because GPOs that aggregate demand across more hospitals or purchase greater volumes have greater purchasing power, substituting X_a for X in basic theoretical proposition [1]. Another change to basic theoretical proposition [1] would be to examine the effect of a hospital's use of single versus multiple GPOs (X_a) on the cost of purchased supplies (Y), because hospitals might select the mix of GPOs offering the greatest benefits for certain product groups, for example generic supplies such as gauze and cotton versus specialized items such as implantable devices or surgical instruments. By changing the focal construct in an X-focused theoretical proposition, a researcher can contribute to the theoretical discourse on GPOs by refining the GPO construct and examining its use in different ways.

A second way to make a theoretical contribution through modifying a basic theoretical proposition is through developing a different Y-focused proposition, where the focal con-

Table 2.3   *Basic and advanced theoretical propositions*

Type	Notation	Purchasing and supply chain examples
Basic theoretical proposition		
X-focused	$X^* \rightarrow Y$	A hospital's GPO use explains its cost of purchased items [1].
Y-focused	$X \rightarrow Y$	The Affordable Care Act explains hospitals' use of GPOs [2].
Change antecedent or outcome construct		
Change antecedent construct	$X_a \rightarrow Y$	The size of a hospital explains its use of GPOs [3].
Change outcome construct	$X \rightarrow Y_a$	A hospital's GPO use explains its clinical outcomes [4].
Add moderator or mediator construct		
Add moderator construct	$X \rightarrow Y$ $\uparrow$ Z	The extent to which a hospital's GPO use explains its cost of purchased items depends on whether it is a comprehensive or specialized hospital [5].
Add mediator construct	$X \rightarrow Z \rightarrow Y$	The size of a hospital explains its use of GPOs through the intermediate impact of the power of its purchasing group [6].
Add antecedent or outcome construct		
Add antecedent construct	$X_1 \searrow$ Y $X_2 \nearrow$	Both the size of a hospital and its extent of specialization explain its use of GPOs [7].
Add outcome construct	Y_1 $X \nearrow$ $\searrow$ Y_2	A hospital's GPO use explains both its cost of purchased items and its clinical outcomes [8].

Note: * In each model, the focal construct is shown in **bold** type.

struct explains a different outcome. By changing the outcome, the researcher is asking a new research question. While the relationship between GPO use (X) and a hospital's cost of purchased items (Y) in basic theoretical proposition [1] is already known, how is GPO use related to patient clinical outcomes (Y_a)? Does the use of GPO-provided items have an impact on the speed with which a patient recovers? This may be related to the more limited product selection and availability offered by GPOs, but it may also reflect more subtle conditions. For example, Ngaya et al. (2015) estimate that hospital clinical personnel spend up to 50 per cent of their time locating and ordering items needed to provide care; if using GPOs frees up some of this time, clinical outcomes might improve (Tucker and Edmondson 2003). Thus, by examining different outcomes potentially associated with the focal construct (GPOs), a researcher contributes to the theoretical discourse on GPOs. The important takeaway is that making a theoretical contribution need not be intimidating; it can be as simple as changing the antecedent or outcome construct in a basic theoretical relationship.

Add a moderator or mediator
A basic theoretical proposition can be enhanced through the addition of a third construct that functions as a moderator or mediator. A moderator describes a condition that alters the relationship between the antecedent and outcome proposed in a basic theoretical proposition, improving its accuracy (Whetton 2009). A moderator is appropriate in situations where the basic theoretical proposition is true in some conditions, but not in others, such as contingency theories that specify when, where and with whom a theory applies (Whetton 2009). Thus, the addition of a moderator enhances a basic theoretical proposition by addressing 'when'

and 'where' questions, in addition to the 'what' and 'why' questions addressed by the basic theoretical proposition. Because a moderator describes the context in which a theoretical relationship holds, context moves from the theory's domain to its core theoretical propositions.

A good way to think about the effect of adding a moderator is like an 'on–off' switch (Whetton 2009). When the moderator is 'on', the proposed relationship is expected to hold, but not when it is 'off'. Thus, a moderator is often measured as a nominal variable, which classifies observations into nominal groups (male versus female) or an ordinal variable, which classifies observations into groups that can be placed in order (high versus low). For example, a researcher might enhance middle-range theory related to GPOs by proposing hospital scope (comprehensive versus specialized) as a moderator. In other words, the researcher expects that the basic inverse theoretical relationship between GPO use and the cost of purchased items will be stronger for a comprehensive hospital such as the Mayo Clinic or Cleveland Clinic in the US (McDermott and Stock 2011) than it will be for a specialized hospital such as MD Anderson Cancer Center or Shouldice Hospital (Plsek 2003). Another example would be using regional versus national hospital systems (Burns and DeGraaff 2002) as a moderator.

In contrast, a mediator improves understanding of how a basic $X \rightarrow Y$ relationship occurs, through functioning as an intermediary. Thus, a basic $X \rightarrow Y$ relationship is changed from a direct to an indirect relationship conveyed through Z, which functions as both an outcome of X and an antecedent to Y (Whetton 2009). Adding a mediator improves the theoretical specificity of a theoretical proposition, addressing 'how', in addition to the 'what' and 'why' questions addressed by the basic theoretical proposition. Adding a mediator transforms a basic $X \rightarrow Y$ theoretical proposition into a compound proposition comprised of two direct relationships, $X \rightarrow Z$ and $Z \rightarrow Y$ (Whetton 2009). Considering the addition of a mediator is useful when it is not obvious how X explains Y, typically in an X-focused proposition (Whetton 2009). Thus, adding a mediator is a way of justifying an unproven X (Whetton 2009). For example, purchasing group power could be added as a mediator to the $X \rightarrow Y$ theoretical proposition [1] to explain how this relationship operates. Because most hospitals are structured as a professional services organization superimposed on a bureaucratic organization (Abdulsalam et al. 2018), the goals of physicians (in the professional services organization) and the purchasing group (in the bureaucratic organization) may be misaligned. Physicians in this environment sometimes function as 'surrogate buyers' (Abdulsalam et al. 2018), who make independent purchasing decisions. A more powerful purchasing group may be able to overrule these decisions and shift more orders away from 'surrogate buyers' to GPOs. Further, a larger hospital is more likely to have a more powerful purchasing group to coordinate purchasing for its large number of professionals and departments. Thus, proposing purchasing group power as a mediator between hospital size and GPO use makes an interesting contribution to the theoretical discourse about GPOs.

Add an antecedent or outcome
Adding a direct antecedent or outcome to a basic theoretical proposition expands the scope of the proposition, in order to learn more about the focal construct by expanding its theoretical domain (Whetton 2009). A single X can be changed into a vector of Xs, or a single Y can be changed into a vector of Ys, to improve their ability to explain, or be explained by, the focal construct. In order to avoid 'downgrading' the focal construct, expansion should occur on the side of the theoretical proposition that contains the complementary construct, by adding a construct that provides an alternative explanation, shifting the focus from individual to cat-

egories of antecedent constructs, populating categories of antecedents with specific instances, or nesting antecedents within categories (Whetton 2009).

For example, adding the extent of a hospital's specialization to basic theoretical proposition [3] would result in the theoretical proposition that both the size of a hospital and its extent of specialization explain its GPO use. Because a more specialized hospital concentrates a high amount of its patient volume in a small number of clinical services (Sampson et al. 2015), it may have high enough volumes of related purchases that it would not benefit substantially from using GPOs. Comprehensive hospitals, on the other hand, must accommodate a much broader set of patient needs, requiring numerous medical specialties and protocols (Sampson et al. 2015); thus, they may benefit more from aggregating their demand with that of other hospitals through a GPO.

The explanatory power of the focal construct can also be improved by adding an outcome. For example, a researcher might propose that a hospital's GPO use explains both its cost of purchased items and its clinical outcomes. Although the way that GPO use explains cost is known, clinical outcomes could be improved by the consistent quality of items provided by GPOs, as well as freeing up the time that nurses use to locate materials, so that they can focus more on clinical care (Tucker and Edmondson 2003).

Create a chain of theoretical propositions
Although purchasing and supply management researchers seem to be fond of complex graphical models, a well-crafted theoretical proposition can function as a theory in and of itself (Melnyk et al. 2018); there is often no need to develop a theory based on a complex collection of boxes and arrows. However, a theory can also be created by grafting well-thought-out propositions together (Wacker 2008). This will result in an antecedent or outcome being reformulated as a mediator linking two theoretical propositions into an emergent compound proposition. As with adding an antecedent or outcome, the existing theoretical proposition should be expanded on the side opposite the location of the focal construct (Whetton 2009). For example, combining theoretical propositions [6] and [7], we could propose that both the size of a hospital (mediated by the power of its purchasing group) and its extent of specialization explain its use of GPOs. It could be further expanded by adding antecedents to purchasing group power, while the focal construct (GPO use) remains as a bookend at the right side of the model. Similarly, theoretical proposition [8] could be expanded by adding moderators or mediators to its two basic propositions, keeping the focal construct as the left bookend.

Advanced Building Blocks

Although the 'what' and 'how' of the basic building blocks are important in developing theoretical propositions, stronger theoretical contributions are often made through domain and predictions, which focus on when, where and who. Important enhancements to a theory result from its application in different domains and from reflection on surprising results related to its predictions (Whetton 1989).

Domain
A theory's domain is the set of assumptions it is based upon, indicating when and where it can be applied (Boer et al. 2015) and where it does not apply (Huff 2009). The domain places limitations on a theory (Whetton 1989) by addressing questions about when, where and to whom

a theory applies (Wacker 1998). It is like the owner's manual for a complex piece of machinery, listing the terms and conditions that govern its safe use (Whetton 2009). Explicitly listing these assumptions is part of the thought process that pushes a researcher to think critically about the theoretical arguments being posed. Both contextual and conceptual assumptions are included in the domain of a theory.

Contextual assumptions are boundary conditions that can modify or nullify a theory's predictions (Whetton 2009). Contextual assumptions are important, because they identify the conditions under which a theory is expected to hold (Melnyk et al. 2018); readers develop an understanding of what is going on through their appreciation of where and when it happened (Whetton 1989). Thus, contextual assumptions are important for theories in context. Contextual assumptions include political, cultural and economic features of the environment. Level of analysis is another important contextual factor that purchasing and supply management researchers need to be cognizant of when borrowing grand theory originally developed in other disciplines. For theories in context, contextual assumptions are incorporated into hypothesis testing as control variables. Contextual assumptions are also important in theorizing about context; these are theories of context. Theories of context are common in comparative research, such as purchasing and supply management research that takes a cross-cultural or cross-industry perspective. Contextual features of a theory are used to explain cross-context similarities and differences in practices, values and beliefs (Whetton 2009). In theories of context, context is incorporated into theoretical propositions as predictors or moderators.

On the other hand, conceptual assumptions are the boundary conditions of a theory that are based on the researcher's perspective, including the researcher's philosophical orientation, values and choice of paradigm; positivist, interpretivist and critical theory orientations are based on different conceptual assumptions. Thus, conceptual assumptions reflect a particular researcher's mindset. They should be shared with readers, in order to help the theoretical propositions make sense. Conceptual assumptions are often described by purchasing and supply management researchers in the limitations part of a manuscript's 'Discussion' section. Limitations do not necessarily indicate weaknesses; rather, they provide information about when and where a theory is relevant. Testing a theory in different domains can lead to both verification and refinement through the feedback loop provided (Van Weele and Van Raaij 2014; Whetton 1989).

Predictions

Because the goal of any theory is to make predictions, assessing how 'good' a theory is should be based on the extent to which it is able to make accurate predictions (Huff 2009). The extent to which a theory is able to make predictions is its generalizability; the more phenomena that a theory can be applied to, the better the theory is (Wacker 1998, 2008). A related criterion is a theory's fecundity, which is a theory's ability to generate new hypotheses that expand future research into new conceptual areas (Wacker 1998, 2008). Generalizability and fecundity are typically addressed in the 'Discussion' section of a purchasing and supply management manuscript.

The generalizability and fecundity of a theory can be improved by several strategies described by Whetton (2009). First, outcomes should be broad enough that their measures will exhibit sufficient variance to demonstrate the effects suggested by the theory. Second, a theory that is associated with reasonable data collection requirements is more likely to be applied in future research projects. For example, cross-sectional purchasing and supply management data is easier for researchers to collect than longitudinal data. Similarly, monadic (from the perspective of a single respondent) relationships have easier data collection requirements than dyadic or polyadic relationships (Flynn et al. 2018). Third, theories that include some standard constructs for which reliable and valid measures already exist are more likely to be applied in future research projects. Finally, the difficulty of operationalizing new constructs is related to a theory's use by other researchers. In describing new constructs, using examples that hint at their potential operationalization is helpful. These suggestions are not meant to imply that theory development should be limited to constructs that are easy to measure, or relationships that are obvious, but rather to provide guidelines for researchers seeking to improve the generalizability and fecundity of their theories.

Another important factor to consider is the extent to which a theory causes theoretical tensions that result in awareness of contradictions between different theories that explain the same phenomenon (Poole and Van de Ven 1989). Although researchers are trained to value internal consistency (logical compatibility of the constructs and relationships with each other) and parsimony (all other things being equal, the fewer the assumptions, the better) (Wacker 1998, 2008), obsession with developing a perfect theory may cause 'less and less correspondence to the multifaceted reality it seeks to portray' (Poole and Van de Ven 1989, p. 563). Alternatively, less-perfect theory may stimulate development of more encompassing theories, as other researchers seek ways to enhance or integrate them. Thus, intentional pursuit of theoretical inconsistencies can stimulate development of additional theory. Focusing on this paradox provides a way to increase the theoretical discourse on a phenomenon by shifting its perspective (Melnyk et al. 2018).

Assessing the accuracy of theoretical productions is difficult to address in the short term. Accuracy is ultimately proven over time; each application of a theory is like an experiment that demonstrates or refutes a theory's accuracy and indicates areas for refinement in future applications. More applicable theories advance knowledge within a discipline, guide research and enlighten practice (Van de Ven 1989). Researchers can help to improve the predictive accuracy of their theories by explicitly describing domain issues. There should be sufficient information about contextual and conceptual assumptions that other researchers will be able to design appropriate tests to precisely reflect the accuracy of the theory's predictions. Further, accuracy of theoretical predictions can be enhanced by developing theories that are empirically risky, allowing a clear path to refutation (Wacker 1998, 2008). Obvious theories are not interesting and not likely to undergo further empirical testing, while non-obvious relationships are more interesting and potentially more important. Thus, the more counterintuitive a theoretical proposition is, the better the theory is. Finally, the substantive significance of a theory is important in the accuracy of its predictions (Wacker 2008). Relying only on statistical significance can allow inclusion of variables that are only significant due to chance. Thus, the conceptual importance of the constructs and relationships is a criterion for substantive significance.

CONCLUDING THOUGHTS

Purchasing and supply management theory exists at multiple levels of abstraction and can be borrowed from other disciplines or developed specifically for the purchasing and supply management context. The common thread that cuts across this diversity of theory is that it is comprised of constructs, relationships, domain and predictions. Understanding these building blocks is essential to effectively developing or testing purchasing and supply management theory.

REFERENCES

Abdulsalam, Y., Gopalakrishnan, M., Maltz, A., and Schneller, E. (2018), 'The impact of physician–hospital integration on hospital supply management', *Journal of Operations Management*, 57, 11–22.

Bacharach, S.B. (1989), 'Organizational theories: some criteria for evaluation', *Academy of Management Review*, 14(4), 496–515.

Barney, J., Wright, M., Ketchen, D.J. Jr. (2001), 'The resource-based view of the firm: ten years after 1991', *Journal of Management*, 27(6), 625–641.

Blount, I., and Li, M. (2021), 'How buyers' attitudes toward supplier diversity affect their expenditures with ethnic minority businesses', *Journal of Supply Chain Management*, 56(4), 3–24.

Boer, H., Holweg, M., Kilduff, M., Pagell, M., Schmenner, R., and Voss, C. (2015), 'Making a meaningful contribution to theory', *International Journal of Operations and Production Management*, 35(9), 1231–1352.

Burns, L.R., and DeGraaff, R.A. (2002), 'Importance of the health care value chain', in Burns, L.R. and Wharton School Colleagues (eds), *The Health Care Value Chain: Producers, Purchasers, and Providers*. Hoboken, NJ: Jossey Bass, pp. 27–40.

Coughlan, P. Coglan, D., and Lombard, F. (2003). 'Managing collaborative relationships in a period of discontinuity', *International Journal of Operations and Production Management*, 35(6), 1246–1259.

Davis, D.F., Davis-Sramek, B., Golicic, S.L., and McCarthy-Byrne, T.M. (2019), 'Constrained choice in supply chain relationships: the effect of regulatory institutions', *International Journal of Logistics Management*, 30(4), 1101–1123.

DiMaggio, J., and Powell, W.W. (1983), '"The iron cage revisited:" institutional isomorphism and collective rationality in organizational fields', *American Sociological Review*, 48, 147–160.

Ellram, L.M., Harland, C.M., van Weele, A., Essig, M., Johnsen, T., et al. (2020), 'Purchasing and supply management's identity: Crisis? What crisis?', *Journal of Purchasing and Supply Management*, 26, 1–8.

Eltantawy, R., Paulraj, A., Guinipero, L., Naaslune, D., and Thute, A.A. (2015), 'Toward supply chain coordination and productivity in a three-echelon supply chain', *International Journal of Operations and Production Management*, 35(6), 895–924.

Flynn, B.B., Pagell, M., and Fugate, B. (2018), 'Survey research design in supply chain management: the need for evolution in our expectations', *Journal of Supply Chain Management*, 54(1), 1–15.

Flynn, B.B., Pagell, M., and Fugate, B. (2020), 'Introduction to the emerging discourse incubator on the topic of emerging approaches for developing supply chain management theory', *Journal of Supply Chain Management*, 56(2), 3–6.

Granovetter, M.S. (1973), 'The strength of weak ties', *American Journal of Sociology*, 78(6), 1360–1380.

Hambrick, D.C. (2007), 'The field of management's devotion to theory: too much of a good thing?', *Academy of Management Journal*, 50(5), 1346–1352.

Harland, C.M., and Knight, L.A. (2001), 'Supply network strategy: role and competence requirements', *International Journal of Operations and Production Management*, 21(4), 476–489.

Hayes, R.H., and Wheelwright, S.C. (1979), 'Link manufacturing process and product life cycles', *Harvard Business Review*, January–February, 133–140.

Hill, T. (2000), *Manufacturing Strategy: Text and Cases*, 3rd edn. Boston, MA: Irwin McGraw-Hill.

Hilt, R.P. (1995), 'Researching sensitive topics in marketing: the special case of vulnerable populations', *Journal of Public Policy and Marketing*, 14(1), 143–155.

Huff, A.S. (2009), *Designing Research for Publication*. Los Angeles, CA: SAGE.

Jensen, M.C., and Meckling, W.H. (1976), 'Theory of the firm: managerial behavior, agency costs, and ownership structure', *Journal of Financial Economics*, 3(4), 305–360.

Lu, J., Kaufmann, L., and Carter, C.R. (2020), 'How informal exchanges impact formal sourcing collaboration (and what supply managers can do about it)', *Journal of Supply Chain Management*, 56(4), 26–62.

Marques, L., Yan, T., and Matthews, L. (2020), 'Knowledge diffusion in a global supply network: a network of practice view', *Journal of Supply Chain Management*, 56(1), 33–53.

McDermott, C.M., and Stock, G.N. (2011), 'Focus as emphasis: conceptual and performance implications for hospitals', *Journal of Operations Management*, 29(6), 616–626.

Melnyk, S.A., Flynn, B.B., and Awaysheh, A. (2018), 'The best of times and the worst of times: empirical operations and supply chain research', *International Journal of Operations and Production Management*, 56(1–2), 164–192.

Nyaga, G.N., Young, G.J., and Zepeda, E.D. (2015), 'An analysis of the effects of intra- and interorganizational arrangements on hospital supply chain efficiency', *Journal of Business Logistics*, 36(4), 340–354.

Osigweh, C.A.B. (1989), 'Concept fallibility in organizational science', *Academy of Management Review*, 14(4), 579–594.

Pathak. D.D., Day, J.M., Nair, A., and Sawaya, W.J. (2007), 'Complexity and adaptivity in supply chains: building supply network theory using a complex adaptive systems perspective', *Decision Sciences*, 38(4), 547–580.

Plsek, P. (2003), 'Complexity and the adoption of innovation in health care', *Accelerating Quality Improvement in Health Care: Strategies to Accelerate the Diffusion of Evidence-Based Innovations*. Washington, DC: National Institute for Healthcare Management Foundation and National Committee for Quality in Health Care.

Poole, M.S., and Van de Ven, A.H. (1989), 'Using paradox to build management and organizational theories', *Academy of Management Journal*, 14(4), 562–578.

Reed, D. (1999), 'Stakeholder management theory: a critical theory perspective', *Business Ethics Quarterly*, 9(3), 453–483.

Sampson, S.E., Schmidt, G., Gardner, J.W., and Van Order, J. (2015), 'Process coordination within a health care service supply network', *Journal of Business Logistics*, 36(4), 355–373.

Skilton, P.F., Bernandes, E., Li, M., and Creek, S.A. (2020), 'The structure of absorptive capacity in three product development strategies', *Journal of Supply Chain Management*, 56(3), 47–65.

Skinner, W. (1974), 'The focused factory', *Harvard Business Review*, 52(3), 113–121.

Springett, D. (2013), 'Critical perspectives on sustainable development', *Sustainable Development*, 21(2), 73–82.

Suddaby, R. (2006), 'What grounded theory is not', *Academy of Management Journal*, 49(4), 633–542.

Sutton, R.K., and Staw, B.M. (1995), 'What theory is not', *Administrative Science Quarterly*, 40(3), 371–384.

Touboulic, A., McCarthy, L., and Matthews, L. (2020), 'Re-imagining supply chain challenges through critical engaged research', *Journal of Supply Chain Management*, 56(2), 36–51.

Touboulic, A., and Walker, H. (2016), 'A relational, transformative and engaged approach to sustainable supply chain management: the potential of action research', *Human Relations*, 69(2), 301–343.

Tucker, A.L., and Edmondson, A.C. (2003), 'Why hospitals don't learn from failure: organizational and psychological dynamics that inhibit system change', *California Management Review*, 45(2), 54–72.

Tversky, A. and Kahneman, D. (1974), 'Judgment under uncertainty: heuristics and biases', *Science*, 185, 1124–1130.

Van de Ven, A.H. (1989), 'Nothing is quite so practical as good theory', *Academy of Management Review*, 14(4), 486–489.

Van Weele, A.J., and Van Raaij, E.M. (2014), 'The future of purchasing and supply management research: about rigor and relevance', *Journal of Supply Chain Management*, 50(1), 56–72.

Wacker, J.G. (1998), 'A definition of theory: research guidelines for different theory-building research methods in operations management', *Journal of Operations Management*, 16, 361–385.

Wacker, J.G. (2008), 'A conceptual understanding of requirements for theory-building research: guidelines for scientific theory building', *Journal of Supply Chain Management*, 44(3), 5–15.

Weick, K.E. (1989), 'Theory construction as disciplined imagination', *Academy of Management Review*, 14(4), 516–531.

Weick, K.E. (1995), 'What theory is not, theorizing is', *Administrative Science Quarterly*, 40(3), 385–390.
Wheelwright, S.C., and Hayes, R.H. (1985), 'Competing through manufacturing', *Harvard Business Review*, 63(1), 99–110.
Whetton, D.A. (1989), 'What constitutes a theoretical contribution?', *Academy of Management Review*, 14(4), 490–495.
Whetton, D.A. (2009), 'Modeling theoretical propositions', in Huff, A.S. (ed.), *Designing Research for Publication*. Los Angeles, CA: SAGE, pp. 217–247.
Williamson, O.E. (1975), *Markets and Hierarchies*. New York: Free Press.
Williamson, O.E. (1985), *The Economic Institutions of Capitalism*. New York: Free Press.

SUGGESTED FURTHER READING

Development of Interesting Research Questions

Barley, S.R. (2000), 'When I write my masterpiece: thoughts on what makes a paper interesting', *Academy of Management Journal*, 49(1), 16–20.
Bartunek, J.M., Ryner, S.L., and Ireland, R.D. (2006), 'What makes research interesting and why does it matter?', *Academy of Management Journal*, 49(1), 9–16.
Davis, M.S. (1971), 'That's interesting! Towards a phenomenology of sociology and a sociology of phenomenology', *Philosophy of the Social Sciences*, 1(4), 309–344.
Weick, K.E. (1999), 'That's moving!', *Journal of Management Inquiry*, 8, 134–142.

Middle-Range Theory

Calantone, R., Whipple, J.M., Wang, J.F., Sardashti, H., and Miller, J.W. (2017), 'A primer on moderated mediation analysis: exploring logistics involvement in new product development', *Journal of Business Logistics*, 38(3), 161–169.
Craighead, C.W., Ketchen, D.J. Jr., and Cheng, L. (2016), '"Goldilocks" theorizing in supply chain research: balancing scientific and practical utility via middle-range theory', *Transportation Journal*, 30(1), 241–257.

Theory Development

Suddaby, R. (2006), 'What grounded theory is not', *Academy of Management Journal*, 49(4), 633–542.
Whetton, D.A. (2002), 'Modeling-as-theorizing: a systematic methodology for theory development', in Portingtor, J.D. (ed.), *Essential Skills for Management Research*. London: SAGE Publications, pp. 45–71.

3. Developing purchasing and supply management theory

Mark Pagell, Barbara B. Flynn, Brian Fugate and David E. Cantor

INTRODUCTION

Why Theory?

Imagine a world without theory. At one extreme, research would consist of digging through empirical data in search of statistically significant relationships. While the outcome could be a plethora of significant results (or perhaps a set of observations with no coherence), researchers would not develop an understanding of why they occurred, the dynamics underlying relationships between key constructs or why those relationships are important. At the other extreme, researchers would compile practices without guidance as to why they work; while effective in a local context, this is not generalizable to other contexts. Theory that develops a coherent explanation for findings resulting from empirical evidence is what makes purchasing and supply management research a science, rather than a set of practices.

The Need for Theory Unique to Purchasing and Supply Management

Grand theory, such as resource-based theory, transaction cost economics theory, institutional theory or agency theory, has been important in guiding purchasing and supply management research. It is widely understood, and its constructs and relationships are clearly articulated and supported by prior empirical testing. However, most grand theories were developed for domains other than purchasing and supply management, including economics, strategic management, marketing, computer science, psychology, and other disciplines. There are opportunities to develop new insights through developing theories that are unique to the purchasing and supply management domain, which differs from the domains where grand theories have their roots, in several important ways.

First, as Carter et al. (2017) describe, although many researchers are conducting purchasing and supply management research, we have failed to agree on what a supply chain is. Supply chains do not exist physically; thus, they are a socially constructed, sometimes ill-defined construct. This leads to a wide variety of definitions and lack of the agreement on key constructs and problems that characterizes other fields. There is a steady stream of new research questions (Durach et al., 2017), causing a wide range of potential theoretical boundaries and perspectives to be relevant.

Second, the unit of analysis in purchasing and supply management varies widely, from individual purchasing managers to supply chain dyads, networks, and extended networks that include all actors that contribute to the flow of products, services, money and information (Durach et al., 2017). However, the focus of much grand theory is on individuals and interpersonal relationships. Although organizations are comprised of individuals working as agents representing them, a single individual's thoughts or a collection of individuals' thoughts may not be indicative of organizational decisions. Although purchasing managers are individuals, they operate within decision parameters set by their organizations, which means that purchasing and supply management researchers are able to apply only a subset of the assumptions of various grand theories (Durach et al., 2017).

Third, by their very nature, buyers and suppliers have conflicting goals; they are simultaneously independent and interdependent. For instance, suppliers seek the highest price they are able to charge to cover their expenses and generate some profit, while buyers seek the lowest prices for acceptable quality levels to be profitable. This independence inevitably leads to buyer–supplier conflict. However, buyers and suppliers are also necessarily interdependent, with individual profitability depending, in part, on the success of all members of their supply chain. This becomes even more complicated when supply relationships include non-governmental organizations (NGOs) (Johnson et al., 2018), social enterprises (Longoni et al., 2019; Pullman et al., 2019) or governments (Quarshie and Leuschner, 2020), each with their own goals.

Fourth, many purchasing and supply management researchers focus on a simplified representation of a supply chain as a dyadic buyer–supplier relationship. Although purchasing relationships are between a buyer and supplier, supply chains extend well beyond a relationship between two entities, with important implications for buying companies. Complex supply chains may lack transparency beyond a tier or two, yet consumers are increasingly holding companies responsible for behaviour in their extended supply chains (Lund-Thomsen and Lindgren, 2014). Thus, there is increasing recognition that 'the expected line of responsibility needs to extend along the full extent of a firm's supply chains into its products, processes, and relationships' (Ashby et al., 2012, p. 497), and that supply chains are more appropriately conceptualized as networks rather than as dyadic relationships. Social network theory (Borgatti and Foster, 2003) and complex adaptive systems theory (Holland, 2001) are expressly designed for networks and may better incorporate some of these challenges.

Finally, as global supply networks become increasingly dynamic, and contain many heterogeneous actors, not all of whom have a profit motive (for example, Pagell et al., 2018), their behaviour is driven by complex interactions and the need for information to coordinate operations between independent, yet interdependent, supply chain (SC) members increases. Although these characteristics may also apply to marketing, an additional characteristic that differentiates purchasing and supply management is that it operates with a finite, diminishing set of resources. In contrast, marketing has the ability to create and stimulate demand. Understanding and dealing with supply markets and resource constraints is central to purchasing and supply management.

These unique characteristics drive the need for theory specific to the purchasing and supply management domain. Applying grand theory designed for a different context and level of analysis may seem like pounding a square peg into a round hole, leading to references to theory that are dropped in to meet publication requirements, rather than effectively guiding research to reveal important insights. Further, purchasing and supply management has the potential for developing theory that can inform other disciplines.

Theory Development as Disciplined Imagination

Weick (1989) famously described theory development as 'disciplined imagination'. It is disciplined through consistent application of criteria and analysis to qualitative and quantitative data, and it is imaginative because it is based on diverse thought processes and intentional broadening of perspectives to discern the story that the data tells. It combines deep observation, creativity and emotion with discipline, rigour and technique (Caniato et al., 2020). In the following sections, we provide an overview of several approaches that meld discipline with imagination to develop purchasing and supply management specific theory (see Figure 3.1). We describe both theory enhancement and theory building approaches, moving roughly from those where the discipline–imagination mix is on the imagination side to those that are more disciplined, within each section. Theory enhancement begins with established theory, then modifies it (for example, by refining constructs or relationships) or elaborates upon it (for example, by applying it in a different domain). On the other hand, theory building inductively extracts meaning from empirical observations, moving from local observation to developing generalizable constructs, relationships and propositions.

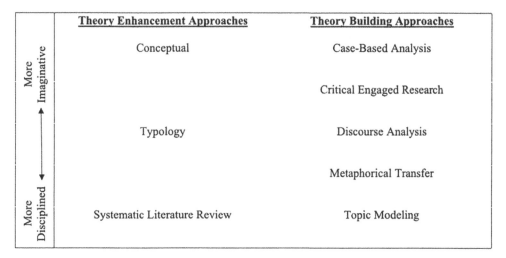

Figure 3.1   *Examples of theory enhancement and theory building approaches as disciplined imagination*

THEORY ENHANCEMENT APPROACHES

Theory enhancement starts with an established theory, notes empirical findings that do not fit, then uses imagination to resolve the apparent paradox (Alvesson and Kärreman, 2007). The oppositions and contradictions within a paradox (Poole and Van de Ven, 1989) allow researchers to play different perspectives off against each other, highlighting opportunities to develop theory that is a better fit (Alvesson and Kärreman, 2007). One approach to resolving a paradox is to apply spatial, temporal and domain separation. Poole and Van de Ven (1989) recommend using spatial separation to resolve a theoretical paradox by clarifying levels of analysis. For example, Reimann et al. (2017) extended the domain of extant theory on supplier-induced disruptions from single-level to multiple-level analysis, where individual cognitive decision making is nested in organizational decision making. They applied fuzzy set analysis to analyse response processes from dyadic interviews of decision makers in Western buying firms and their Chinese suppliers to develop five theoretical types. Similarly, temporal separation can be effective in resolving a paradox by understanding that one 'horn' (Poole and Van de Ven, 1989) of the paradox holds at one point in time, while the other holds at a different point in time. For example, Ni et al. (2015) studied shippers' voluntary adoption of the Customs–Trade Partnership Against Terrorism (C-TPAT) standard, which gives them access to the fast lane at international borders and ports, in exchange for submitting to Customs and Border Protection inspection of their facilities and developing SC security plans. Using prospect theory, they found that early C-TPAT adopters were motivated by avoiding the potential reputational damage of a SC breach (loss aversion), while later adopters were motivated by the economic benefits of accessing the fast lane at international border crossings. Thus, Ni et al. (2015) enhanced prospect theory by applying it to the domain of SC shipping and temporally separating the early adopters of a voluntary standard from later adopters.

Conceptual Theory Enhancement

A third approach to resolving a theoretical paradox is through domain separation, where one horn of the paradox holds in one domain, while the other holds in a different domain. This approach has significant potential for the development of purchasing and supply management theory, due to the unique characteristics of this domain. Carter et al. (2017) used this approach to enhance existing theory on the practice-based view (PBV) (Bromiley and Rau, 2014), a variant of resource-based theory (RBT) (Barney, 2012), in order to make it relevant to a SC. The PBV focuses on the domain of practices that are imitable and transferable, and whose use results in a range of performance outcomes, unlike RBT's focus on the domain of resources that are valuable, rare, inimitable and non-substitutable (VRIN). Thus, the dependent variable in the PBV is performance, rather than RBT's sustained competitive advantage (limited to the top performer in an industry). Independent variables in the PBV are imitable, transferable practices, rather than RBT's VRIN resources. Thus, the basic relationship in the PBV is that differences in firm performance are explained by the practices they employ, moving from RBT's resource domain to the PBV's practice domain. Carter et al. (2017) pose relational performance as the focal construct. It is defined as performance benefits generated by two or more firms beyond those they could generate individually. Rather than firm performance, the SC practice view (SCPV) focuses on relational performance, which is at the interorganizational level. Like the PBV, however, the SCPV uses performance as the dependent variable, rather than sustained competitive advantage. Also like the PBV, the SCPV explains performance across its entire range, rather than only for SC leaders.

Thus, the SCPV's focal construct (relational performance) includes both the intra-organizational performance of each firm in a SC relationship and its appropriated relational performance at the intersection between the firms. A buyer's performance is thus a function of its intra-organizational practices plus the interorganizational SC management practices that the buyer appropriates from its relationship with a supplier. As the buyer bundles its own intra-organizational practices, which are complementary interorganizational practices that span organizational boundaries, performance gains are made. The same arguments can be made for a supplier, members of a triad, or members of an extended supply network. Thus, the value of relational performance comes from the use of interorganizational practices beyond what an individual buyer or supplier could use. Thus, by starting with the existing PBV and enhancing it by considering it in an interorganizational domain, Carter et al. (2017) provide an example of purchasing and supply management theory enhancement.

Typologies

Moving from the creative approach of conceptual theory enhancement, building a typology provides a somewhat more disciplined approach to theory enhancement. A typology is a set of conceptually developed ideal types that constitute a theory (Doty and Glick, 1994). Rather than precise, measurable operationalizations, typologies use rich descriptions to give a 'feel' for each ideal type (Doty and Glick, 1994).[1] Typologies, like all theories, can be described in terms of constructs, relationships, domain and predictions. There are two types of constructs in a typology. An ideal type is a complex, abstract construct described using multiple attributes. Ideal types can be independent multidimensional profiles such as Porter's (1980, 1985) low cost, differentiation and focus strategies; endpoints on a continuum such as Cameron and Quinn's (2005) competing values typology of organizational culture; or a continuum of ideal types such as the product–process matrix (Hayes and Wheelwright, 1979). While an ideal type describes a phenomenon that might exist, empirical examples of organizations that embody all the dimensions of an ideal type are rare or non-existent; thus, an ideal type is an abstract construct.

The second type of construct in a typology is the individual unidimensional constructs that comprise each ideal type. They are first-order constructs, while the ideal types are second-order constructs. Typology relationships primarily focus on internal consistency among the first-order constructs that comprise an ideal type. Combined, they explain why an ideal type explains the dependent variable; 'greater similarity to an ideal type is posited to result in greater effectiveness' (Doty and Glick, 1994, p. 234). The domain of a typology exists at two levels, corresponding to the type of theory associated with it. Grand theory exists at the level of the ideal types, generalizable to all organizations. For example, any assembly line is expected to be efficient, compared with any job shop (Hayes and Wheelwright, 1979). Mid-range theory exists at the level of the individual dimensions that comprise the ideal types; an assembly line in a cafeteria has very different characteristics compared to an assembly line in an automotive plant. A typology's predictions are related to its domain. Typologies are Y-focused theories, explaining the dependent variable (Y); thus, the product–process matrix is a theory of efficiency and customization, rather than a theory of assembly lines and job shops. Predictions are made about the dependent variable of a typology, based on how similar organizations are to the ideal types (Doty and Glick, 1994).

Kim and Choi (2015) provide an illustration of developing purchasing and supply management theory using a typology. They started with the widely used relative posture (cooperative versus adversarial) typology of buyer–supplier relationships, which they described as incomplete, because it ignores relational intensity (amount and strength of transactions). SC members whose operations are tightly linked do not necessarily engage in mutually accommodating practices, and arm's length buyer–supplier relationships are not always adversarial. Positioning relational posture and relational intensity as the axes, Kim and Choi (2015) developed a 2x2 matrix that describes four ideal types of buyer–supplier relationships. A 'sticky' buyer–supplier relationship is closely tied, but adversarial. Although their operations are synchronized, buyers and suppliers consider their relationship as a 'necessary evil' (Kim and Choi, 2015). They engage in power games, where the more powerful party tries to shape the relationship to its advantage, and the weaker party engages in covert actions to 'get even'. In contrast, a 'deep' buyer–supplier relationship is closely tied and cooperative. The buyer and supplier respond to each other's needs, jointly developing efficient communications mechanisms for coordinating production activities and willingly becoming operationally and strategically interdependent. A 'transient' buyer–supplier relationship is adversarial and short-term. Most transactions are discrete, established through competitive tendering and aggressive price negotiations. The buyer and supplier are willing to enforce or adhere to the terms of their contract to avoid the open market, but their relationship is, at best, indifferent and more likely confrontational. Finally, a 'gracious' buyer–supplier relationship is at arm's length, but cooperative. Although the buyer and supplier hold each other in high regard, their collaborative activities are sporadic, perhaps because of only occasional need for a certain part or material. While the buyer and supplier retain autonomy in their relationship and neither is highly dependent on the other, they are positive toward each other and maintain goodwill.

In this example, the key constructs are the first-order multidimensional sticky, deep, transient and gracious ideal types, as well as the potential outcomes. There are also unidimensional second-order constructs, including the length of a buyer–supplier relationship, the intensity of exchange, the type of contract governing the relationship, trust, collaboration, cooperation, and so on. The key theoretical relationships are between the second-order constructs comprising the ideal types; the stronger they are, the more closely an organization resembles an ideal type. The domain of this theoretical typology is a buyer–supplier relationship. Predictions are related to specific outcomes; for example, a gracious buyer–supplier relationship is associated with faster deliveries, product innovation or SC integration. Thus, typology development offers substantial potential for enhancing purchasing and supply management research.

Systematic Literature Review

A third approach to theory enhancement is through use of a systematic literature review (SLR). While literature reviews often apply creative ways to synthesize the extant literature, search for paradoxes or unexplored questions, and extract opportunities for theory enhancement, systematic literature reviews provide a more disciplined approach to structuring this process. Originally developed in medicine as a means of knowledge development, Durach et al. (2017) argue that systematic literature reviews are also a powerful approach for enhancing purchasing and supply management theory. A theoretical SLR is based on analysis, integration and synthesis of the extant literature; it is 'more than a description (stock taking) of existing literature; instead, it is aimed at refining or revising predetermined theoretical frameworks' (Durach et al. 2017, p. 78). Durach et al. (2017) refined the SLR process used in fields such as medicine and management to reflect the unique context of purchasing and supply management theory; Table 3.1 describes the steps in this process.

Zimmermann and Foerstl (2014) provide an example of using a SLR within the domain of purchasing and supply management. They built on resource-based theory, which assumes that firms have limited access to strategic resources that are associated with performance. Barney (2012) describes the potential of supply chain management to serve as a strategic resource that contributes to the performance of a buying firm, through helping buyers and suppliers work together to develop distinct attributes that are difficult to imitate and would be time-consuming

Table 3.1   *Steps in conducting a systematic literature review*

Step	Description
Define purpose	Develop an initial theoretical framework specifying unit of analysis, context, and construct definitions. Limit the literature reviewed to one or two perspectives.
Articulate characteristics of primary studies	Define criteria for inclusion and exclusion of primary studies, based on the research question, purpose and initial theoretical framework.
Select baseline sample of literature	Use keywords to search for potentially relevant published and unpublished primary studies, ensuring they cover all aspects of the initial theoretical framework, research purpose and inclusion/exclusion criteria. They should also address potential limitations of the initial theoretical framework and the breadth of construct definitions and terminology used in the literature.
Develop synthesis sample	Apply the inclusion and exclusion criteria to select primary studies with strong potential to inform the initial theoretical framework. It is not necessary to generate a large volume of primary studies; a smaller sample that makes a stronger contribution is ideal. This step is prone to both inclusion criteria bias and selector bias. Durach et al. (2017) recommend applying exclusion criteria to titles and inclusion criteria to abstracts and highlighting factors explaining differences in primary study findings.
Code data in synthesis sample	Develop codes reflecting the extraction template based on the initial theoretical framework, as well as themes that emerge during the coding process. Summarize the evidence using contingency statements ('if … then', 'when' and 'for whom'). Constructs may be split to reflect more refined definitions and ultimately transition to an improved theoretical framework.
Develop narrative propositions	Develop narrative propositions reflecting mechanisms, context and outcomes. They should combine insights from different methodological approaches and research settings. Identification of contradictory empirical results, outliers and real-world paradoxes reflected in the literature plays a central role in this step.
Compile results into manuscript	Write a manuscript describing how the primary studies were identified and analysed, as well as highlighting the thematic theoretical knowledge resulting from the analysis. It should describe the initial framework and contrast it with the resulting refined framework, to develop theoretical propositions based on conceptual, contextual and temporal contingencies.

Source: Adapted from Durach et al. (2017).

for the buying firm to develop by itself. Zimmermann and Foerstl's (2014) research sought to enhance resource-based theory by extending Barney's (2012) domain from supply chain management to purchasing and supply management.

Their research question was whether purchasing and supply management (PSM) practices influence buyer performance, in other words, whether PSM serves a strategic purpose. Their initial theoretical framework grouped PSM practices into two groups. Supplier-facing (external) PSM practices include relational PSM practices (deployment of resources by both the buyer and the supplier) and non-relational PSM practices (deployment of resources by just the buyer; for example, supplier selection or supply base reduction). Internal PSM practices include vertically aligned PSM practices (aligned with corporate strategy), cross-functional integration practices (joint practices with other internal functions, such as manufacturing, research and development, or marketing), within-PSM practices (negotiation preparation, order processing, and so on), and enabling PSM practices (information technology, skill development, employee evaluation, and so on). The two groups of PSM practices were hypothesized to be related to buying firm performance, including operational, market and financial performance.

In the second step, Zimmermann and Foerstl (2014) articulated the characteristics of the primary studies to be reviewed, to inform the aspects of their initial theoretical framework. Their inclusion and exclusion criteria were based on methodological approach, scope of their topic, and availability of the type of data they sought to analyse. Methodologically, they sought to include empirical research studies, excluding case studies, conceptual papers, conceptual literature reviews, mathematical modelling and simulation research studies. The scope of the findings they sought was defined as including specific performance results associated with the use of PSM practices, rather than more general studies. Because their intent was to use a meta-analysis approach to analyse the data, a third inclusion criterion was that the studies were required to include correlations between various PSM practices and types for performance.

In the third step of their SLR, Zimmermann and Foerstl (2014) selected their baseline sample of potentially relevant literature. They developed a comprehensive list of keywords including 'suppl*', 'purchasing', 'sourcing*', 'vendor manag*', 'procur*', 'vertical alliance*' and 'performance'. They applied them to search 17 leading peer-reviewed journals that were known to have published PSM research, using the EBSCO Business Source Complete, Science Direct and Emerald Management Xtra databases. They also obtained articles recommended by knowledgeable PSM researchers and searched the reference lists of the most frequently cited PSM studies to obtain additional studies that had not been found in the database search. This process resulted in a baseline sample of 659 potentially usable primary studies.

Zimmermann and Foerstl (2014) then applied the inclusion and exclusion criteria to develop the synthesis sample. Starting with the baseline sample of 659 studies, 244 were eliminated because of their method, and another 269 were eliminated because their definition of PSM practices was not consistent with Zimmermann and Foerstl's (2014) initial theoretical framework. An additional 41 studies did not include the correlation data that was required; the authors were contacted, and some were able to provide the needed data. The final synthesis sample contained 108 articles about 99 independent studies of a total of 22 971 buying firms.

In the fifth step, the data in the synthesis sample was coded by the two authors, using codes based on the initial theoretical framework. To ensure consistency between them, they coded the first ten studies together, then compared codes after every 20 studies had been coded. They achieved an inter-rater reliability score of 94 per cent, resolving any inconsistencies through further discussion. The authors also evaluated whether the measures they evaluated were consistent with the definitions associated with the initial theoretical framework, exceeding the threshold value of 75 per cent content validity. Zimmermann and Foerstl (2014) used meta-analysis techniques with artifact distribution to correct for sampling or measurement error.

Finally, Zimmermann and Foerstl (2014) used the result of the meta-analysis to develop narrative propositions. They found that PSM practices were related to buying firm performance, and that this effect was greater than the effect on performance of other practice groups, such as human resource practices or research and development (R&D) practices. More specifically, they found that both relational and VRIN PSM practices had the strongest impact on buying firm performance. Thus, they were able to enhance resource-based theory to include the context of purchasing and supply management.

As SLRs bring discipline to the literature review process, it is important to consider several potential sources of bias (Durach, 2017). Sampling bias, which refers to failing to capture all studies relevant to the initial theoretical framework, can be addressed by consulting data structure experts, such as librarians, in developing the list of search keywords. Selection bias is related to proper design of inclusion and exclusion criteria, as well as ensuring that the researchers apply the inclusion and exclusion criteria consistently. Within-study bias is variability in coding between researchers, which can be addressed through development of well-defined codes, calibration training of the coders, and including coders with a variety of backgrounds, ideally without preconceptions about the theoretical framework. Thus, although there is the potential for bias in an SLR, it can be addressed through effective study design.

THEORY BUILDING APPROACHES

Developing theory from rich, unstructured data uses an inductive approach, building on an interpretivist perspective (Huff, 2009), where meaning is linked to observations in specific domains. Although this process may appear to be primarily creative and imaginative, disciplined approaches can be used to reveal themes and aggregate dimensions, providing the basis for developing new constructs, proposing new ways in which constructs are related, and using them to develop theory.

Case-Based Analysis

Case-based research has been used in building theory across many disciplines. One of the challenges in case-based research is retaining and capitalizing on the richness of the qualitative data, while avoiding storytelling and accusations of selecting case data to support researchers' preconceptions (Gehman et al., 2018). Eisenhardt's well-known approach to case research design provides an effective guide to strategic selection of research cases, developing an interview protocol, conducting interviews, and applying discipline to compiling the results into transcripts and developing detailed case narratives that synthesize multiple sources of case data. Within- and between-case analysis (Eisenhardt, 1989) articulates emerging themes that form the foundation for propositions. The summary documents for each case are individually coded by each research team member, using both a priori codes, based on the protocol and tentative theoretical background, and emergent codes developed during the within-case analysis. Between-case analysis uses disciplined methods for comparing insights about the cases in a variety of ways, to allow insights to emerge. Eisenhardt (1989) recommends grouping the cases in various ways, then comparing them on various criteria to reveal insights. For example, cases could be grouped by large versus small focal firms, domestic versus global SCs, or by the ideal types they represent. A good way to think about this is as a spreadsheet, where the columns are cases, the rows are comparison criteria, and the cells are simple descriptions such as large, old, multinational, high or sticky. The order of the columns is repeatedly changed to group the cases differently, and the entries in the cells for each group are compared and contrasted, revealing insights for the research team to consider. The result is a set of tentative propositions. The case study database is then searched for specific evidence to support or refute each tentative proposition. In this way, tentative propositions are refined into a final set of theoretical propositions, enriched by a diverse chain of case evidence.

For example, Krause and Pullman (2020) applied case-based research to develop middle-range theory on the management of supply chains in the emerging legal cannabis industry. Although black market cannabis supply chains have existed for many years, cannabis products are just beginning to be legal, with 24 countries and 33 United States (US) states allowing cannabis sales for medical use, and five countries and 11 US states allowing sales for recreational use. This industry is unique because of its stringent regulations for ingestible products, unpredictable turbulence, and rapidly changing regulations. Krause and Pullman (2020) studied value-added producers (VAPs) that process cannabis into various types of products. They strategically selected nine VAP companies in Oregon to include ingestible, inhalable and topical products and a range of company sizes. The cases were studied longitudinally from 2016 to 2019, using semi-structured interviews of primary SC decision makers (typically company owners) that were repeated annually. The qualitative interview data were supplemented with information from company websites, online information, industry publications, field notes and company reports, resulting in over 1000 pages of qualitative data. These were synthesized in the within-case analysis, which provided a summary of each case that integrated data from all sources. Coding of the within-case analysis was done by both researchers, explicitly developing codes for a priori concepts and identifying major emergent themes. The researchers applied the codes using NVivo software and axial coding to connect common themes. In the between-case analysis, multiple tables were developed to identify and explore patterns between the cases to develop emerging themes. Iterative triangulation of case evidence was then used to flesh out, support or refute emergent themes and refine them into theoretical propositions supported by rich qualitative data. Krause and Pullman (2020) then developed a theoretical typology of maladaptive, adaptive and transformative cannabis VAPs, elaborating on the characteristics differentiating between them. Other approaches to building theory through case-based analysis use longitudinal or process-oriented approaches.

The Gioia methodology (Gioia et al., 2012; Gehman et al., 2018) for analysing rich qualitative case data brings further discipline to the imaginative process of building theory from case research. It uses three stages of coding that increase in their abstraction, culminating in development of a data structure that clearly articulates the chain of evidence. A key feature of the Gioia methodology is that it explicitly builds on the voice of the informants, as well as the voice of the researchers. The first stage codes interview transcripts and case notes using the informant's terminology and perspectives, in order to reflect their lived experience. As the analysis unfolds, similarities and differences between first-order categories are noted, leading to their combination in a smaller number of categories that begin to reveal a deeper structure, similar to Strauss and Corbin's (1998) axial coding. The second-order analysis reflects the perspectives of the researchers and extant theory. The research team examines the first-order categories to determine whether they reflect existing or emergent theoretical constructs, iterating between first-order categories and the theoretical literature until 'theoretical saturation' (Glaser and Strauss, 1967) is reached. The third stage of analysis focuses on distillation of emergent second-order themes into aggregate dimensions. A data structure is then developed, providing a visual aid reflecting the progression from the raw data (informants' words) to theoretical terms and themes (constructs). The data structure provides the foundation for building a grounded theory model, through the addition of relationships between constructs, and propositions.

Quarshie and Leuschner's (2020) study of interorganizational interactions between members of humanitarian SCs following Hurricane Sandy, and Villena and Gioia's (2018) study of lower-tier SC members, provide examples of analysing case data using the Gioia methodology. Quarshie and Leuschner (2020) interviewed informants from state government agencies, NGOs, faith-based organizations, long-term recovery groups, utility firms and retailers, resulting in 475 pages of interview transcripts and detailed notes. Villena and Gioia (2018) conducted 165 interviews with informants from three multinational corporations, nine tier-one suppliers, and 22 lower-tier suppliers in Mexico, the US and China. Both articles provide nice examples of developing first-order category labels based on the informant's language, then distilling the emergent themes into theoretical dimension during the second-order analysis. Their data structures clearly illustrate the chain of evidence leading to their propositions. Villena and Gioia (2018) also employ Eisenhardt's (1989) multiple between-case comparisons approach at different levels, comparing two employees in the same firm, cases across international boundaries, data from different sources (interviews, job shadowing and meeting memos) and data between firms, encouraging nuanced themes to emerge. Thus, Eisenhardt's (1989) approach and the Gioia methodology (Gioia et al., 2012) can be used hand-in-hand to improve the credibility of theory building from case research.

Critical Engaged Research

Critical engaged research is based on deep engagement of a researcher with research participants, in order to avoid being constrained by the assumptions that underlie traditional theories. Critical engaged research is a synthesis of two approaches: traditional engaged research and a critical orientation. In traditional engaged research approaches, researchers are embedded in the process of generating deep situational knowledge to inform theory development, based on the understanding that it is never possible for researchers to completely detach themselves from the phenomena they are observing. The knowledge produced through engaged research has a problem solving, contextual knowledge focus. The goal is changing practices, rather than conducting unbiased observation; although some aspects of theory that is developed through engaged research may be generalizable, this is not its overarching goal (Cunliffe and Scaratti, 2017). Extended embedding of the researcher in the context develops mutual trust with participants, leading to deep knowledge of key constructs and relationships. Traditional engaged research is based on dialogical sensemaking, which is defined as giving researchers a useful purpose in their embedded role, surfacing, questioning and exploring themes, multiple meanings, and developing new directions (Cunliffe and Scaratti, 2017). There is constant interplay between context, people, relationships, interactions and actions (movement) and cognizance of the 'veil' that obstructs vision (opacity). Thus, the researcher is an active participant in the process, bringing unique value through academic training and perspective. For example, Akkermans et al. (2019) worked within a digital services provider to examine project ramp up and ramp down, and offer advice to management on how to improve these processes.

The other essential element of critical engaged research is its critical orientation, with a goal of pushing a socially useful agenda (Cunliffe and Scaratti, 2017). A critical orientation is normative and emphasizes the political and ethical aspects of a social organization, such as an SC or a purchasing group, focusing on power, exploitation and emancipation (Touboulic et al., 2020). Building on a critical orientation causes researchers to question dominant ideologies and their assumptions. For example, Touboulic et al. (2020) describe the dominant discourse in global SC research as shaped by history, especially colonialism, which is embodied in asymmetric relationships, where buying firms tend to be large corporations in developed countries, while suppliers are smaller firms in developing countries. Suppliers are often marginalized stakeholders whose voices have been silenced in the dominant discourse of free trade and global supply management, which is shaped by the perspective of Western firms based on their agenda. Critical research engages the perspectives of diverse participants, such as indigenous people, defenders of the environment, consumers from all backgrounds, the natural environment, lower-tier suppliers, and workers at all levels, in the discourse that informs theory development. Imaginative reflection is important in analysing this data in conjunction with research participants. A researcher might offer tentative insights to research participants after being embedded with them, engage in deep conversation with them about the insights, then return to reflect further and refine the insights. This iterative reflection–discussion–reflection process continues as insights are refined into theory.

Actively involving participants, including those marginalized by traditional theory, lays the foundation for creative reframing of problems (Touboulic et al., 2020). Further, the theory is more complete because of incorporating diverse voices and integrating cognition, emotion and behaviour. Understanding an SC phenomenon from multiple perspectives, ranging from the buying corporation to marginalized workers for lower-tier suppliers, supports development of multi-level theory and greater relevance to practice.

Discourse Analysis

Discourse analysis is the disciplined study of texts; a discourse is a collection of textual materials related to a phenomenon. Like critical engaged research seeks to move researchers' thinking beyond traditional assumptions, discourse analysis looks at the effects of language on the way a phenomenon is conceptualized and how this shapes meanings and practices (Hardy et al., 2020). In a dominant discourse, the texts build upon and inform each other, resulting in convergence of explanations for a phenomenon that creates a unified, taken-for-granted view of reality that reveals what is considered normal in a domain. By 'ruling in' some ways of thinking, the dominant discourse can also 'rule out' alternative ways of thinking; thus, the language used to describe a phenomenon shapes how it is experienced as reality (Hardy et al., 2020).

Like critical engaged research, discourse analysis incorporates a critical orientation, viewing textual materials within their social context. Analysis of author position or location within the social space from which texts are produced can reveal insights about the 'rights' of various author positions to produce texts (Phillips et al., 2008). Texts can also be examined in the 'expressive sphere of culture' (Phillips et al., 2008), which is the constructs that emerge from the realm of ideas that exist in the texts through which people understand the world. Finally, while constructs only exist in the expressive sphere, objects exist when constructs are used to make sense of physical objects or social relationships. Thus, discourse analysis focuses on relationships between constructs, objects and authors.

For example, Hardy et al. (2020) describe how the dominant discourse of lean is a 'shorthand' for cost cutting, and new forms of dominating employees and rendering them invisible. In contrast, Hardy et al. (2020) use discourse analysis to analyse why, although sustainability is a mature research area, it is not dominant in purchasing and supply management due to absence of a well-known, authoritative text that supports sustainability in purchasing and supply management – unlike *The Machine That Changed the World* (Womack et al., 2007) for lean – leading to a plethora of sometimes conflicting definitions. Further, sustainability texts conflict over meaning: is sustainability subordinate to economic profitability, or on an equal or higher footing? Hardy et al. (2020) describe the discourse on modern slavery in SCs as emerging from the United Nations Sustainable Development Goals and recent legislation on SC transparency that requires buying firms to clearly identify all upstream tiers and report their strategies for mitigating risks to vulnerable populations. Thus, the SC discourse is evolving to include formerly invisible marginalized employees, through the discourse on modern slavery that recognizes organizational risks related to modern slavery in power relationships among companies. Another interesting application of discourse analysis is presented by Meehan et al. (2017), which applies this approach to healthcare procurement.

Discourse analysis opens the door to new sources of qualitative data for developing theory. However, it is less clear about moving from reflection and insight to theory. Fairhurst and Putnam (2019) suggest that discourse analysis and the disciplined analytical approaches associated with case-based research can go hand-in-hand in developing theory based on tensions, paradoxes and contradictions. Line-by-line coding of a narrative document can be used to code terminology, actions and arguments in texts to identify patterns and allow themes to emerge. Coding can identify language that reflects tension or emotion, leading researchers to analyse push–pull opposition in texts and remind researchers how discourses can exert power.

Metaphorical Transfer

The metaphorical transfer approach applies discipline to the creative and imaginative approach of building theory from observation. Metaphorical transfer is a way of moving from a casually invoked metaphor (such as rocks in a river, a funnel or a bullwhip) to a theory-constitutive metaphor (Chen et al., 2013). Terminology that was originally developed for a source phenomenon in a different domain is applied to a target phenomenon by elaborating the extent to which source characteristics are aligned with characteristics of the target phenomenon at various levels of abstraction. For example, Garud and Kotha (1994) used the human brain to develop a theory constitutive metaphor for flexible production systems. Three stages of metaphorical transfer establish correspondence between the building blocks of theory in two different domains.

The ontology stage establishes a logical correspondence between the 'whats' (constructs) of the target and source phenomena. For example, Chen et al. (2013) established the ontologic equivalence between marital infidelity and the use of alternative suppliers, between spousal alimony and breach-of-contract payments, and between child support and parts warranty support, in their study of SC relationship dissolution. Lu and Koufteros (2017) established equivalence between elements of the human immune system and SC security systems by highlighting that both are designed to ensure well-being (of a human or SC), are complex and multilayered, need to be tolerant (to the immune system itself, or to efficiency needs), learn (from previously encountered pathogens or previous SC breaches), and must act quickly to eliminate pathogens or resolve SC security breaches.

The analogy level establishes correspondence between relationships among elements of the target and source. Thus, analogic equivalence focuses on the 'hows' and 'whys' of the relationship between constructs by subsuming ontology-level abstractions into higher-level abstractions, constructing a graphic model of interrelationships. Chen et al. (2013) used material aspects, psyche aspects and social network aspects of divorce and SC relationship dissolution to establish equivalence at the analogy level. Lu and Koufteros (2017) focused on systems to prevent, detect, react to and restore diseases and supply chain security breaches to establish analogic equivalence.

The identity level establishes propositions, based on ontologic and analogic equivalence between the source and target phenomena. The goal is to describe, explain and predict relationships for both the source and target phenomenon, often based on literature in the source's domain. For example, Chen et al. (2013) adapted sociological principles that underlie divorce into principles for dissolution of SC relationships (Chen et al., 2013). Lu and Koufteros (2017) used propositions related to the human immune system to develop propositions to explain and predict relationships in SC security systems. The disciplined approach described by metaphorical transfer (Chen et al., 2013) provides structure to the imaginative process of developing theory.

Topic Modelling

Topic modelling combines disciplined machine learning analysis of co-occurring words in textual materials with imaginative formulation of the themes they embody, to identify theoretical constructs from which researchers can derive relationships and formulate propositions. Topic modelling is a text mining technique for extracting useful information from textual big data (Schmiedel et al., 2019). It uses an algorithm for unsupervised machine learning, where researchers lack a priori knowledge about constructs and relationships (Bansal et al., 2020; Schmiedel et al., 2019). Topic modelling is different from content analysis in several important ways. First, content analysis focuses on individual words; for example, Tate et al.'s (2010) content analysis examined influential words in corporate social responsibility (CSR) reports, constructing a network reflecting their influence on the triple bottom line. Topic modelling, on the other hand, is based on the distributional hypothesis of linguistics: 'words that occur in the same contexts tend to have similar meanings' (Turney and Pantel, 2010, p. 142). Meanings result from relationships between words, rather than from the words themselves. Second, the scope of content analysis and of topic modelling research is different. While Tate et al.'s (2010) content analysis examined 100 socially and environmentally responsible global companies, the average topic modelling study uses 38 000 documents (Schmiedel et al., 2019), known as a corpus. Thus, topic modelling establishes patterns of words that occur in the same context.

In topic modelling, relevant textual data is scraped from the web and stored as documents, whose length can range from a sentence to a chapter (Bansal et al., 2020). Preparation of the scraped documents for analysis is critical: trimming documents to remove unnecessary words and reducing words to their stems. A topic modelling algorithm is applied to the prepared corpus to extract co-occurring words, forming topics (Bansal et al., 2020). Like cluster analysis in statistics, the power of topic modelling relies on researchers' ability to discern the relationship between the stems comprising a topic and give it an appropriate name. For example, Schmiedel et al. (2019) cite the co-occurrence of the stems 'employe', 'manag', 'door', 'polic', 'open', 'concern' and 'listen' as comprising a topic which they named 'Is management really listening?'. Researchers then consider the relationship among topics and formulate propositions. Bansal et al. (2020) recommend working iteratively, first using individual researchers, then groups, to resolve inconsistencies by discussing each other's perspectives to identify the building blocks of emergent theory.

Topic modelling is useful for dealing with very large volumes of textual material to help identify topics that researchers might not normally see, and overcome some of the systematic biases associated with coding. Through the research team's discussion and interpretation of the meaning of co-occurring words, new insights are revealed (Bansal et al., 2020). Bansal et al. (2020) illustrate developing theory using topic modelling by proposing a purchasing and supply management example of conceptualizing SCs as complex adaptive systems, in order to examine co-evolutionary mechanisms between SC members widely separated in space and context, although connected through the transfer of goods. They conclude with a list of potential research traps embodied in topic modelling, as well as an appendix containing useful sources of qualitative big data that could inform developing purchasing and supply management theory.

CONCLUDING THOUGHTS

This chapter introduces existing and emerging approaches to developing purchasing and supply management theory by synthesizing discipline with imagination. Caniato et al. (2020) describe this synthesis using the metaphor of a researcher as being like Leonardo da Vinci. Leonardo is described as a polymath; like other Renaissance scholars, he excelled in several fields, including engineering, science, technology and mathematics, as well as the arts. Because he was both a painter and a designer, Leonardo had to combine and integrate both creativity and technique in his work, building on both emotion and rigour. Thus, although he was primarily known as an artist, his notebooks include unique insights related to astronomy, botany, cartography, anatomy, and even paleontology. Theory development poses similar challenges for researchers. For example, a properly executed systematic literature review can result in simply a counting exercise that adds up the number of articles in different categories or, through the application of creativity and imagination, it can lead to unique insights and novel enhancements to an existing theory that lay the foundation for exciting new research opportunities. Thus, the challenge to researchers is to meld discipline with imagination, to enhance and build purchasing and supply management theory.

More detail about specific approaches is provided in the cited references, as well as in the suggestions for further reading. Perhaps some of the most exciting opportunities for theory enhancement and development lie in new sources of data and analytical approaches for theory development include dark data, data mining, data visualization, ethnography, data virtualization, 'live' big data, meta-analysis, predictive analytics, operating and sensing data, and thick data. Some of these approaches and data sources have their origins in other disciplines, while others are completely new as a means of developing theory. These and many other approaches have the potential to guide researchers in developing theory that is unique to purchasing and supply management, overcoming the limitations associated with grand theory.

NOTE

1.   A typology should not be confused with a taxonomy, which is a scheme for classifying organizations or phenomena using decision rules that result in mutually exclusive and exhaustive classifications. While taxonomies can be useful in understanding a phenomenon and developing mid-range theory, taxonomies are not theory themselves, but rather empirically developed.

REFERENCES

Akkermans, H., Voss C., and van Oers, R. (2019), 'Ramp up and ramp down dynamics in digital services', *Journal of Supply Chain Management*, 55 (3), 3–23.

Alvesson, M., and Kärreman, D. (2007), 'Constructing mystery: empirical matters in theory development', *Academy of Management Review*, 32 (4), 1265–1281.

Ashby, A., Leat, M., and Hudson-Smith, M. (2012), 'Making connections: a review of supply chain management and sustainability literature', *Supply Chain Management: An International Journal*, 17 (5), 497–516.

Bansal, P., Gualandris, J., and Nahyun, K. (2020), 'Theorizing supply chains with qualitative big data and topic modeling', *Journal of Supply Chain Management*, 56 (2), 7–18.

Barney, J. (2012), 'Purchasing, supply chain management and sustained competitive advantage: the relevance of resource-based theory', *Journal of Supply Chain Management*, 48, 3–6.

Borgatti, S.P., and Foster, P.C. (2003), 'The network paradigm in organizational research: a review and typology', *Journal of Management*, 29, 991–1013.

Bromiley, P., and Rau, D. (2014), 'Towards a practice-based view', *Strategic Management Journal*, 35, 1249–1256.

Cameron, K.S., and Quinn, R.D. (2005), *Diagnosing and Changing Organizational Culture: Based on the Competing Values Framework*. New York: John Wiley & Sons.

Caniato, F., Harland, C., Johnsen, T., Moretto, A., and Ronchi, S. (2020), 'The art and science of procurement: revisiting Leonardo da Vinci: Editorial of the 2019 IPSERA Conference Special Issue', *Journal of Purchasing and Supply Management*, 26 (4), 1–7.

Carter, C.R., Kosmol, T., and Kaufman, L. (2017), 'Toward a supply chain practice view', *Journal of Supply Chain Management*, 53 (1), 114–122.

Chen, Y.S., Rungtusanatham, M., Goldstein, S.M., and Koerner, A.F. (2013), 'Theorizing through metaphorical transfer in OM/SCM research: divorce as a metaphor for strategic buyer–supplier relationship dissolution', *Journal of Operations Management*, 31 (7–8), 579–586.

Cunliffe, A.L., and Scaratti, G. (2017), 'Embedding impact in engaged research: developing socially useful knowledge through dialogical sensemaking', *British Journal of Management*, 28, 29–44.

Doty, D.H., and Glick, W.H. (1994), 'Typologies as a unique form of theory building: toward improved understanding and modeling', *Academy of Management Review*, 19 (2), 230–250.

Durach, C.F., Kembro, J., and Wieland, A. (2017), 'A new paradigm for systematic literature reviews in supply chain management', *Journal of Supply Chain Management*, 53 (4), 67–85.

Eisenhardt, K.M. (1989), 'Building theories from case study research', *Academy of Management Review*, 14 (4), 532–550.

Fairhurst, G.T., and Putnam, L.L. (2019), 'An integrative methodology for organizational oppositions: aligning grounded theory and discourse analysis', *Organizational Research Methods*, 22 (4), 917–940.

Garud, R., and Kotha, S. (1994), 'Using the brain as a metaphor to model flexible production systems', *Academy of Management Review*, 19 (4), 671–698.

Gehman, J., Glaser, V.L., Eisenhardt, K.N., Gioia, D., Langley, A., and Corley, K.D. (2018), 'Finding the theory-method fit: a comparison of three qualitative approaches to theory building', *Journal of Management Inquiry*, 27, 284–300.

Gioia, D.A., Corley, K.G., and Hamilton, A.L. (2012), 'Seeking qualitative rigor in inductive research: notes on the Gioia methodology', *Organizational Research Methods*, 16, 15–31.

Glaser, B.G., and Strauss, A.L. (1967). *The Discovery of Grounded Theory: Strategies for Qualitative Research*. Hawthorne, NY: Aldine de Gruyter.

Hardy, C., Bhakoo, V., and Maguire, S. (2020), 'A new methodology for supply chain management: discourse analysis and its potential for theoretical advancement', *Journal of Supply Chain Management*, 56 (2), 19–35.

Hayes, R., and Wheelwright, S.C. (1979), 'Link manufacturing process and product life cycles', *Harvard Business Review*, January–February, 133–140.

Holland, J.H. (2001), 'Studying complex adaptive systems', *Journal of Systems Science and Complexity*, 19 (1), 1–8.

Huff, A.S. (2009), *Designing Research for Publication*. Los Angeles, CA: SAGE.

Johnson, J.L., Dooley, K.L., Hyatt, D.G., and Hutson, A.M. (2018), 'Cross-sector relations in global supply chains: a social capital perspective', *Journal of Supply Chain Management*, 54 (2), 21–33.

Kim, Y., and Choi, T.Y. (2015), 'Deep, sticky, transient, and gracious: an expanded buyer–supplier relationship typology', *Journal of Supply Chain Management*, 51 (3), 63–86.

Krause, D., and Pullman, M. (2020), 'Fighting to survive: how supply chain managers navigate the emerging legal cannabis industry', *Journal of Supply Chain Management*, 56 (4).

Longoni, A., Luzzini, E., Pullman, M., and Habiague, M. (2019), 'Business for society is society's business: tension management in a migrant integration supply chain', *Journal of Supply Chain Management*, 55 (4), 3–33.

Lu, G., and Koufteros, X. (2017), 'Toward a taxonomy of food supply chain security practices', *Journal of Marketing Channels*, 24 (3), 190–203.

Lund-Thomsen, P., and Lindgren, A. (2014), 'Corporate social responsibility in global value chains: where are we now and where are we going?', *Journal of Business Logistics*, 123 (1), 11–22.

Meehan, J., Menzies, L., and Michaelides, R. (2017), 'The long shadow of public policy: barriers to a value-based approach in healthcare procurement', *Journal of Purchasing and Supply Management*, 23 (4), 229–241.

Ni, J.Z., Melnyk, S.A., Ritchie, W.J., and Flynn, B.B. (2015), 'Why be first if it doesn't pay? The case of early adopters of C-TPAT supply chain security certification', *International Journal of Operations and Production Management*, 36 (10), 1161–1181.

Pagell, M., Fugate, B., and Flynn, B.B. (2018), 'From the editors: introduction to the emerging discourse incubator on the topic of research where the focal actor in the network is not a for-profit firm', *Journal of Supply Chain Management*, 54 (2), 1–2.

Phillips, N., Sewall, G., and Jaynes, S. (2008), 'Applying critical discourse analysis in strategic management research', *Organizational Research Methods*, 11 (4), 770–789.

Poole, M.S., and Van de Ven, A.H. (1989), 'Using paradox to build management theories', *Academy of Management Review*, 14 (4), 562–578.

Porter, M.E. (1980), *Competitive Strategy: Techniques for Analyzing Industries and Competitors*. New York: Free Press.

Porter, M.E. (1985), *Competitive Advantages: Creating and Sustaining Superior Performance*. New York: Free Press.

Pullman, M., Longini, A., and Luzzini, D. (2019), 'The roles in institutional complexity and hybridity in social impact supply chain management', *Journal of Supply Chain Management*, 54 (2), 3–20.

Quarshie, A.M., and Leuschner, R. (2020), 'Interorganizational interaction in disaster response networks: a government perspective', *Journal of Supply Chain Management*, 56 (3), 3–25.

Reimann, F., Kosmol, T., and Kaufmann, L. (2017), 'Response to supplier-induced disruptions: a fuzzy set analysis', *Journal of Supply Chain Management*, 53 (4), 37–66.

Schmiedel, F., Müller, O., and vom Brocke, J. (2019), 'Topic modeling as a strategy of inquiry in organizational research: a tutorial with an example of organizational culture', *Organizational Research Methods*, 22 (4), 941–968.

Strauss, A., and Corbin, J. (1998), *Basics of Qualitative Research: Techniques and Procedures for Developing Grounded Theory* (2nd edn). Thousand Oaks, CA: SAGE.

Tate, W.L., Ellram., L.M., and Kirchoff, J.F. (2010), 'Corporate social responsibility reports: a thematic analysis related to supply chain management', *Journal of Supply Chain Management*, 46 (1), 19–44.

Touboulic, A., McCarthy, L., and Matthews, L. (2020), 'Re-imagining supply chain challenges through critical engaged research', *Journal of Supply Chain Management*, 56 (2), 36–51.

Turney, P.D., and Pantel, P. (2010), 'From frequency to meaning: vector space modeling semantics', *Journal of Artificial Intelligence Research*, 37, 141–188.

Villena, V.H., and Gioia, D.A. (2018), 'On the riskiness of lower-tier suppliers: managing sustainability in supply networks', *Journal of Operations Management*, 64, 65–87.

Weick, K.E. (1989), 'Theory construction as disciplined imagination', *Academy of Management Review*, 14 (4), 516–531.

Womack, J.P., Jones, D.T., and Roos, D. (2007), *The Machine That Changed the World*. New York: Free Press.

Zimmerman, F., and Foerstl, K. (2014), 'A meta-analysis of the purchasing and supply management practice–performance link', *Journal of Supply Chain Management*, 50, 37–54.

SUGGESTED FURTHER READING

Theory Development

Carter, C.R., Meschnig, G., and Kaufmann, L. (2015), 'Moving to the next level: why our discipline needs more multilevel theorization', *Journal of Supply Chain Management*, 51, 94–102.

Ketokivi, M., and Mantere, S. (2010), 'Two strategies for inductive reasoning in organizational research', *Academy of Management Review*, 35, 315–333.

Pinder, C.C., and Moore, L.F. (1979), 'The resurrection of taxonomy to aid the development of middle-range theories of organization behavior', *Administrative Science Quarterly*, 24, 99–118.

Rich, P. (1992), 'The organizational taxonomy: definition and decision', *Academy of Management Review*, 17, 758–781.

Weick, K.G. (1974), 'Middle-range theories of social systems', *Behavioral Science*, 21, 1–19.

Case-Based Theory Development

Barratt, M., Choi, T.Y., and Li, M. (2011), 'Qualitative case studies in operations management: trends, research outcomes, and future research implications', *Journal of Operations Management*, 29, 329–342.

Bitektine, A. (2008), 'Prospective case study design: qualitative method for deductive theory testing', *Organizational Research Methods*, 11, 160–171.

Corbin, J., and Strauss, A. (1990), 'Grounded theory research: procedures, canons and evaluative criteria', *Qualitative Sociology*, 13, 3–21.

Eisenhardt, K.M. (1991), 'Better stories and better constructs: the case for rigor and comparative logic', *Academy of Management Review*, 16, 620–627.

Eisenhardt, K.M., and Graebner, M.E. (2007), 'Theory building from cases: opportunities and challenges', *Academy of Management Journal*, 50 (1), 25–32.

Ketokivi, M., and Choi, T.Y. (2014), 'Renaissance of case research as a scientific method', *Journal of Operations Management*, 32 (5), 232–240.

Langley, A. (1999), 'Strategies for theorizing from process data', *Academy of Management Review*, 24, 691–710.

Leonard-Barton, D. (1990), 'A dual methodology for case studies: synergistic use of a longitudinal single site with replicated multiple sites', *Organization Science*, 1, 1–19.

Pratt, M.G. (2008), 'Tensions in evaluating and publishing qualitative researching top-tier North American journals', *Organizational Research Methods*, 11, 481–509.

Stake, R.E. (1995), *The Art of Case Study Research*. London: SAGE Publications.

Metaphorical Transfer

Cornelissen, J.P. (2006), 'Making sense of theory construction: metaphor and disciplined imagination', *Organizational Studies*, 27 (11), 1579–1597.

Foropon, C., and McLachlin, R. (2012), 'Metaphors in operations management theory building', *International Journal of Operations and Production Management*, 33 (2), 181–196.

Hunt, S.D., and Menon, A. (1995), 'Metaphors and competitive advantage: evaluating the use of metaphors in theories of competitive strategy', *Journal of Business Research*, 33 (2), 81–90.

Morgan, G. (1980), 'Paradigms, metaphors, and puzzle solving in organization theory', *Administrative Science Quarterly*, 25 (4), 605–622.

O'Malley, L., Patterson, M., and Kelly-Holmes, H. (2008), 'Death of a metaphor: reviewing the "marketing as relationships" frame', *Marketing Theory*, 8 (2), 167–187.

Tsoukas, H. (1991), 'The missing link: a transformation view of metaphors in organizational science', *Academy of Management Review*, 6 (3), 566–585.

Engaged Research

Van de Ven, A.H. (2007), *Engaged Scholarship: A Guide for Organizational and Social Research*. Oxford: Oxford University Press.

4. Theories relevant to purchasing and supply management research: status quo and future suggestions

Larry Giunipero and Reham Eltantawy

INTRODUCTION

Recognition of the increased complexity of purchasing and supply management (PSM) phenomena calls for increasingly diverse theoretical frameworks. Scholars have argued for the need for interdisciplinary and multidisciplinary research in PSM (e.g., Knight et al., 2016). Despite the multiple calls for the use of theory in PSM, little formal research has been produced examining and describing the actual theories being used, and the extent of their usage in the field. The purpose of this research is to address this gap in the PSM body of knowledge. The aim of this chapter is to promote and support learning and innovation about novel and underutilized theoretical perspectives that can help to promote new insights into the PSM disciple. Thus, this chapter explores the prevalent theories found in contemporary PSM research and discusses promising, but sporadically adopted, theories that can further future PSM research.

To understand the extent to which these theories were used, we relied on a study by Giunipero et al. (2019). They reviewed 520 PSM sourcing articles, published in 20 supply chain, operations and marketing journals from 1995 to 2018. The analysis presented on the following pages summarizes the results of this review and extends the discussion to include currently underutilized theories that can be further applied to advance a future research agenda in PSM. The remainder of the chapter is organized as follows. First, we present the findings describing the trends and the use of various theories during the sampled period and link their use to PSM topics. Next, we elaborate on the theories being frequently used and their applications. Finally, we take a step back from the analysis and present our thoughts on theory use going forward.

HISTORICAL OVERVIEW: PSM THEORETICAL DEVELOPMENT

Theory is a systematized structure capable of explaining and predicting phenomena to distinguish theoretically based works from atheoretical ones (Hunt, 1991). Theory is important for PSM researchers and practitioners as it provides a framework for analysis, an efficient method for field development, and clear explanations for the pragmatic world (Wacker, 1998). Therefore, a total of 20 journals were selected by Giunipero et al. (2019), and 520 articles addressing relevant topics were identified from 1995 to 2018.

PSM researchers are increasingly applying a theoretical lens to underpin their studies. Most articles from 2010 forward used theory to underpin their research propositions. Approximately

Table 4.1   *Theories by time period*

Theories	1995–1999	2000–2004	2005–2009	2010–Present	Total	% of total theories used	% of theory/ total articles
Transaction cost	6	15	11	18	50	14	10
Resource-based view	0	3	7	19	29	8	6
Game	0	2	7	14	23	6	4
Agency	1	3	3	10	17	5	3
Social exchange	0	1	3	8	12	3	2
Resource dependency	1	2	3	5	11	3	2
Stakeholder	0	0	1	10	11	3	2
Knowledge-based theory	1	2	4	3	10	3	2
Contingency	2	1	1	6	10	3	2
Auction theory	0	1	2	4	7	2	1
Institutional	0	2	1	4	7	2	1
Power	1	0	0	3	4	1	1
Total quality	0	4	0	0	4	1	1
Classical economic	1	1	0	2	4	1	1
Prospect	1	1	1	1	4	1	1
Other	9	35	31	77	152	43	29
Total	23	73	75	184	355		
%	6	21	21	52			

Source: Giunipero et al. (2019).

52 per cent of all sampled articles published between 1995 and 1999 used theories, which then increased to 71 per cent between 2000 and 2004, before decreasing to 58 per cent between 2005 and 2009. This since increased to approximately 75 per cent of articles between 2010 and 2018. Clearly, a theory-based approach to sourcing research will be the norm for journal publications moving forward.

More specifically, as indicated in Table 4.1, trends seen in theories used include an increase in the overall number of theory-based articles and, conversely, a decrease in the use of transaction cost economics (TCE). TCE was used in 14 per cent of all articles in the time periods of 1995–1999 and 2000–2004. However, this declined to 9 per cent and then 7 per cent in the time periods of 2005–2009 and 2010–2018, respectively. Meanwhile the resource-based view (RBV) has seen a steady increase since 1995. In the time period of 1995–1999, the RBV was not used. However, its usage increased to 3 per cent, then 5 per cent, and finally 8 per cent in the three following time periods. One possible explanation is that sourcing has evolved to be viewed as strategic activity, versus being more tactical in the past. Other theories that have seen a steady upward trend include game theory, agency theory and social exchange theory.

The following section provides an overview of the three top widely used theories (TCE, RBV and agency theory) through the lens of PSM scholarship.

WIDELY USED THEORIES AND THEIR PSM APPLICATION

Based on the work of Giunipero et al. (2019), the following discussion highlights the top three most frequently used theories and their PSM applications. The three are: transaction cost economics, the resource-based view and agency theory.

Transaction Cost Economics

Williamson's (1975) transaction cost economics (TCE) was adapted from Coase's (1937) work and essentially states that firms use the most economical choice of markets or hierarchies to govern transactions. In selecting to use markets, the organization will incur governance costs to guard against suppliers taking advantage of buyers (opportunism). The organizational hierarchy will govern internal transactions. The methods to control opportunism have been a subject of research in PSM. TCE considers supplier relationships as discrete transactions, which is the unit of analysis adopted, that need to be managed with the goals of minimizing costs involved and curbing partners' opportunism (Williamson, 1985). Williamson (1975) proposed a classification of transaction costs that are comprised of market costs and hierarchy costs. On the one hand, market costs include: costs of the selection of the supplier offering the best quality at the most competitive price; costs of finding target customers for the products of the firm; costs for contract drafting and approval; costs for contract enforcing. On the other hand, hierarchy costs, which correspond to costs of the entrepreneurial organization, include: costs for human resources selection and management; costs of control on contracts regarding human resources; costs of contract enforcement; costs of coordination and information transmission within the firm (Costantino et al., 2012).

TCE, therefore, can be used as a lens to understand decisions throughout the PSM process. For example, TCE explains influencing decisions and behaviour of suppliers through fiat and use of delivery and quality control, annual audits, on-site visits, and direct control over second-tier suppliers (Bello et al., 2004). TCE has also been crucial in understanding the resources devoted to lower-tier suppliers in terms of identifying (*ex ante*) and monitoring (*ex post*) critical lower-tier suppliers (Meinlschmidt et al., 2018). The salient relevance of these tenets of the TCE explains its historical prominence in the PSM literature. Therefore, there continues to be room to utilize and extend TCE to explain PSM phenomenon.

Resource-Based View

The resource-based view (RBV) focuses attention on a firm's assets as a unit of analysis. The most important assets are 'strategic' resources that are rare, valuable, and difficult to purchase or imitate (Barney, 1991). These resources provide competitive advantages over rivals lacking such resources. Patents, strong reputations and positive organizational cultures, for example, may serve as strategic resources for some organizations. In contrast, non-strategic assets (for example cash) are possessed by many organizations and thus do not distinguish an organization's ability to be competitive. Specifically, Barney (1991) identified four essential requirements for a resource to be a source of competitive advantage. First, the resource must be valuable, in that it improves firm efficiency and/or effectiveness. Second, the resource must be rare, so that by exercising control over it, the firm can exploit it to the disadvantage of its competitors. Third, the resource must be imperfectly mobile, to discourage the *ex post* competition for the resource that would offset the advantages of maintaining control of the resource. Fourth, the resource must not be substitutable; otherwise, competitors would be able to identify equivalent resources to be used for the same purpose.

While TCE helps to explain why firms exist, the RBV focuses on why firms differ in performance; both very relevant in making PSM decision (Halldorsson et al., 2015). The RBV suggests that a mature PSM function will often exhibit attributes that contribute to being a source of sustained competitive advantage to the firm (Barney, 2012). Competitive advantage is the value that a firm creates for its customers through cost leadership and/or meaningful differentiation (Porter, 1985). For example, relationships with key suppliers, if well managed, can be valuable, rare and difficult to imitate. RBV identifies conditions under which PSM can be a source of competitive advantage.

Agency Theory

Agency theory has been deployed by PSM researchers to explain the behaviour of agents for the organization. An agency relationship exists in any joint effort in which one party (that is, the principal) delegates authority to a second (that is, the agent). Because the parties often possess divergent goals, agents often elevate their own aims above those of principals. In response, the principal must either monitor agent behaviour or offer strong incentives to ensure that agents act in the principal's best interest (Eisenhardt, 1989). The deviation from the principal's interest by the agent is called agency cost (Jensen and Meckling, 1976). The focus of the theory is on determining the most efficient contract to govern a particular relationship, given the characteristics of the parties involved and the fact that environmental uncertainty and the costs of obtaining information make it impossible for the principal to monitor the agent completely (Bergen et al., 1992). Principals and agents, therefore, must choose between a course of action that benefits their firm versus one that benefits both parties. Leveraging tools such as reward structures and cultural competitiveness to ensure alignment among participants' interests removes the temptation to take advantage of other parties in the relationship (Ketchen and Hult, 2007).

Given that most PSM functions consist of multiple employees at various firm levels (buyer, category manager, procurement manager, and so on), developing and implementing PSM strategies and programmes necessarily involves managing agency relationships (Tate et al., 2010). Ideally, if the buyer–supplier relationship is strong, all members prosper. However, individual relationship imbalances can make certain participants vulnerable to opportunism. The buyer or seller may take advantage of their partner to maximize their own gain. Similarly, the buyer (agent) has authority to enter into contracts and commit the organization's (principal's) funds. In essence, the agent is given the authority to act on behalf of the principal and enter into contracts with suppliers (Monczka et al., 2016). Agency theory offers a natural fit with PSM research with applications including ethical conduct, buyer–supplier relationships, and relationships with internal stakeholders.

UNDERUTILIZED THEORIES AND A FUTURE RESEARCH AGENDA

A more prescient question might be: are we overlooking important research opportunities by focusing so much attention on only a few theories in most of the PSM research? This can limit the scope of investigation in the discipline and create blind spots in our knowledge base. For this reason, we selected the ten most promising theories based on the literature review and analysis by Giunipero et al. (2019). These theories were reported by Giunipero et al. (2019) to have been used three or fewer times in the contemporary PSM literature, despite their potential to inform PSM future research and provide additional insight into the PSM phenomenon. This is not to say that the rest of the theories listed in the literature review by Giunipero et al. (2019) as underutilized theories cannot be successfully used by scholars to shed light on PSM phenomena. Rather, we were constrained by space limitations to offer only a more detailed description for a few selected promising theories. Our goal is to help inform future PSM research via novel theoretical lenses, and promote learning and innovation about underutilized theoretical perspectives in the discipline. Below we highlight these ten promising, but sporadically adopted theories, and within the PSM context.

Attribution Theory

Attribution theory attempts to describe and explain the mental and communicative processes involved in everyday explanations, most typically of individual and social events (Kelley, 1973). Attribution theory rests on three causal dimensions (Bettman and Weitz, 1983): (1) internal (for example, ability, effort) or external (for example, task difficulty, luck, environmental constraints); (2) causal stability, which refers to the temporal nature of the causes that is, causes can be permanent and unchanging (for example, ability) or temporary and unstable (for example, luck); and (3) controllability of the cause or the extent to which a firm has power to change or alter the cause.

PSM scholars can use attribution theory to understand how managers interpret PSM outcomes. This has important implications: different interpretations can lead to different strategic responses (for example, ending a relationship with a supplier or continuing to work with the supplier) with different performance outcomes (Wowak et al., 2016). Broadly speaking, attribution theory can be used to examine who or what gets credit or blame for value creation or destruction within PSM. For example, purchasing managers must ensure that their suppliers are compliant with sustainability standards if they face higher pressures from their stakeholders to meet social/environmental sustainability criteria (Goebel et al., 2018). This may induce higher purchasing costs and, as a consequence, force a trade-off between (short term) economic criteria (that is, purchasing cost reduction) and social/environmental sustainability criteria.

Auction Theory

An auction is a form of market with specific rules that determine resource allocation and prices on the basis of bids coming from market participants (McAfee and McMillan, 1987). Auction theory is a branch of game theory, where auctions are a type of game characterized by incomplete information and information asymmetry (Costantino et al., 2012). Auction theory assumes that bidders are risk-neutral; bidders are symmetric; and payments are a function of the bids alone (McAfee and McMillan, 1987).

A reverse auction (RA) is defined as an electronic bidding process where multiple sellers are vying for the business of a single buyer, resulting in intense price competition among sellers (Monczka et al., 2016, p. 725). Consequently, auction theory offers a valid framework to study the bidding process in PSM. It fits nicely with the growing popularity of reverse auctions as a sourcing tool. This theory can explain and predict buyer–supplier bidding behaviour under various conditions. For example, Li and Zheng (2009) show that the equilibrium bidding behaviour can become less aggressive because of entry costs, so that bidders become discouraged from entering the competition as the expected number of bidders increases. Pearcy et al. (2007) found that partitioning the RA process into offer and execution phase will lessen the negative impact on the buyer–supplier relationship. Overall, auction theory essentially deals with buyer and supplier behaviour in auction markets, and the properties and rules used to judge behaviour when auctions are used to establish a price in markets. PSM's use of reverse auctions in the sourcing cycle offers multiple opportunities for researchers to apply this theory.

Information Processing Theory

For buying firms, one of the most pressing challenges is that they frequently do not possess sufficient information on what is occurring in their complex supply chains (Busse et al., 2017). Information processing theory (IPT) posits that the uncertainty arising from a firm's business environment creates information processing needs which must be managed appropriately by the firm (Tushman and Nadler, 1978). IPT evolved in the 1970s with an intra-organizational focus, in response to organizational design problems of large firms (Galbraith, 1973). It was later extended to a dyadic, interorganizational level to assess buyer–supplier relationships (Bensaou and Venkatraman, 1995). Information processing encompasses the gathering, interpreting and synthesizing of information (Tushman and Nadler, 1978).

IPT is concerned with the link between environmental uncertainty and PSM-related information processing needs, as well as with the question of how buyers and suppliers can cope with these needs (Trautmann et al., 2009). Uncertainty as the root cause of information processing needs is 'the difference between the amount of information required to perform the task and the amount of information already possessed by the organization' (Galbraith, 1973). The effect of the fit between information processing needs and capabilities on PSM performance (Premkumar et al., 2005) calls for applications of the IPT to examine the complexities of related phenomena. Understanding PSM information processing needs thoughtful analysis of the features of different sources of uncertainty that augment it (Duncan, 1972), such as complexity (that is, the plurality of relevant factors) and dynamism (that is, a measure of temporal change) (Bensaou and Venkatraman, 1995; Premkumar et al., 2005). The use of IPT should increase along with the growth of artificial intelligence, machine learning and robotics in PSM.

Innovation Theory

The theory of the adoption and diffusion of innovations (innovation theory, for short) developed by Rogers (1962) is one of the most widely accepted academic works on innovation adoption that has been applied to a variety of contexts over an extended period of time (e.g.,

Moore and Benbasat, 1991; Premkumar and Roberts, 1999). Innovation diffusion is the process by which an innovation is communicated through certain channels over time among the members of a social system (Debnath et al., 2016).

Historically, the strategic focus on innovation and competence-based thinking has changed and elevated the role of PSM (Van Weele and Van Raaij, 2014). The PSM function has been deemed to be a driver of key strategic processes and supplier relationships. However, contributions on how to leverage purchasing and supply knowledge and expertise within and across organizations in the mainstream literature remain limited (Van Weele and Van Raaij, 2014). Innovation theory can inform the adoption of PSM innovations and technology within the firm and across partner organizations. It can also provide an assessment of the key characteristics that drive innovation diffusion success (Rogers, 1962). These characteristics include: perceived relative advantage of an innovation, the perceived compatibility of an innovation, the perceived complexity of an innovation, perceived trialability, and the perceived observability of an innovation. Since innovation diffusion requires communication through the supply chain channels over time (Debnath et al., 2016), the measurement of divergence and convergence in these perceptions among buyer–supplier partner firms can inform the innovation diffusion phenomenon in PSM.

Institutional Theory

Institutional theory is traditionally concerned with how various groups and organizations better secure their positions and legitimacy by conforming to the rules and norms of the institutional environment (Debnath et al., 2016; Scott and Davis, 2007). According to institutional theory, organizations are subject to three types of forces: normative, placed on organizations by market forces, such as customers, to adopt certain practices; mimetic, placed by the competitive environment and the need to be aware of the activities of their competitors; and coercive pressure to conform or adopt certain practices based on the demands from regulatory authorities or other pressure groups (DiMaggio and Powell, 1983).

These external pressures consequently make buyer–supplier organizations adopt or abandon purchasing practices, regardless of their efficiency and effectiveness, as they grow increasingly similar; due to their need to adopt very similar industry practices and structures out of a concern for legitimacy even in the absence of viable performance gains (Ahmed et al., 2013; Tate et al., 2009). For example, buyers create pressures to adopt programmes such as ISO 9000 that many suppliers would not otherwise implement; and professional organizations such as the Institute for Supply Management (ISM) create normative pressures through their publications and managerial certifications, leading purchasing professionals to embrace standard practices as a critical part of their jobs. Institutional theory can inform PSM research in exploring bounded rationality and time constraints leading to solutions where no efficiency gains have been realized.

Organizational Learning Theory

March (1991) introduced the theory of the learning organization and presented the challenges of managing the trade-off between different types of learning-related capabilities. Organizational learning represents a process of creation, transfer and/or modification of knowledge initiated by an organizational member and/or groups of members for the purpose of improving organizational performance and outcomes (Real et al., 2014). This theory highlights that the learning capacity of an organization depends on factors such as: top-level leaders' behaviours; organizational structure, culture and flexibility; and uncertainties in the environment in which the organization functions. According to this theory, organizational learning is composed of the process of learning and the structure of the learning organization (Slater and Narver, 1995). The structure of a learning organization is based on how it is 'skilled at creating, acquiring, and transferring knowledge and at modifying its behavior to reflect new knowledge and insights' (Garwin, 1993). According to Peter Senge (1990, 2006), five disciplines create organizational learning: (1) a shared vision; (2) mental models; (3) team learning; (4) personal mastery; and (5) system thinking.

Organizational learning has long been recognized as an important determinant of PSM performance and sustainability (e.g., Dawes et al., 2007; Hult et al., 2000). This said, existing PSM research has commonly focused on the perspectives of a single group and viewed organizational learning as a single-level, top-down and organized organizational event initiated by the leader. This particular perspective may fall short of explaining the effects of PSM multi-level participants and spontaneous behaviours on organizational learning. PSM learning activities take place among, and are influenced by the power of, stakeholders such as management, buyers, suppliers, customers, local community and public (Chou and Ramser, 2019). Therefore, we suggest developing a multi-level theoretical perspective in exploring how the decisions and behaviour of a PSM participant, such as a buyer or supplier, foster organizational learning. It is evident that organizational learning has many applications for organizations in technology and even in dealing with the current Covid-19 pandemic (Dawes et al., 2007).

Power Dependence Theory

Emerson (1962) defined power as the ability of an actor to influence another to act in a manner that they would not have otherwise. In his seminal work, he suggests that power: exists in a dyadic relationship when each actor seeks to acquire resources controlled by the other party; is directly proportional to one party's motivational investment in goals mediated by the other party; and is inversely proportional to the availability of those goals to the party outside of the relation. Pfeffer and Salancik (1978) applied Emerson's philosophy to the context of buyer–supplier relationships, with the fundamental premise that power in an exchange relationship is a relative concept determined by which firm is more dependent on the other firm for needed resources. Buchanan (1992), characterized power–dependence imbalances in buyer–supplier relationships as the difference in value that buyers and sellers attach to the relationship. In balanced relationships neither party dominates, as opposed to asymmetric relationships where the most independent party dominates.

Although the concept of power has a wide scope of applications in PSM, empirical PSM studies that investigate the impact of buyer–supplier relationship power are sparse, and many debates on the bases and impacts of power within the supply network remain unresolved (Meehan and Wright, 2012). Explanations could be that power dependence theory requires precise context-specific definitions for research (Pfeffer and Salancik, 1978), and the differing schools of thought with respect to the relevant unit of analysis adopted. Most of the literature views power in interorganizational relationships as an attribute of an organization (Chicksand, 2015; Pulles et al., 2014). Yet, one organization's dependence on another is not only contingent on the criticality of the resources sought, but also proportional to the availability of alternative sources (Huff, 2016). The lack of integration of these levels of analysis creates attenuated conceptual positions on the origins of power, and a narrowness in the view of power. Integration to locate the concept of power within complex dynamics is needed to increase the utility of studies of power in PSM to be theoretically meaningful and useful in practice.

Relational Exchange Theory

Relational exchange theory (RET) is an offshoot of and is largely based on Blau's (1964) social exchange theory (SET). Macneil's (1980) relational exchange theory describes exchanges along a continuum from discrete, characterized by a short-term orientation, limited communications, competitive behaviours, and pursuit of individual goals limited to buying and selling issues and interactions; to relational, characterized by extensive communications, commitment and a long-term orientation. Morgan and Hunt's (1994) treatise on commitment and trust has also evolved from SET (Blau, 1964) and has been regarded as one of the main pillars of studies on RET (Lee et al., 2010). In one of the foundational works on exchange relationships, Dwyer et al. (1987) differentiated between various types of relationships, market-governed transactions and discrete exchanges, and proposed that relational exchanges gain benefits from reducing uncertainty, managing dependence, increasing efficiency and providing social satisfactions. RET espouses that the historical and social contexts should be taken into account in managing buyer–supplier relationships (Heide, 1994). Accordingly, scholars forwarded informal mechanisms that are based on moral and social norms (Liu et al., 2009) and that thrive on relationship elements such as open communication, trust, solidarity and joint cooperation (Heide, 1994) to make PSM decisions.

The area of relational governance in general is ripe with applications and unanswered questions in the PSM context. For example, on the one hand, unilateral governance in exchange relationships emerges as a substitute for market governance when it is more efficient due to external or internal uncertainty or transaction-specific investments (Heide, 1994). On the other hand, bilateral governance focuses on reducing uncertainty as well, but also on managing dependence by promoting cooperation, collaboration, commitment, dependency, power, trust, risk and uncertainty (Gummesson, 1999; Hunt and Morgan, 1995). Despite potential gains, bilateral governance is costly. As buyers and suppliers manage their respective dependence in a relationship, it is simultaneously increased through specific investments which make the dissolution of the relationship very costly (Aistrich, 2002). For example, the supplier's dependence on a buyer cannot be removed, but the buyer can become tied to the supplier as well by virtue of the relationship and making specific investments in it. Therefore, understanding and measuring the buyer–supplier bonds, the related activity links and the resource ties involved (Gummesson, 1999) is important for the PSM function, because relationships are recognized to constrain and/or enhance the ability to act. However, a conceptual and methodological gap in PSM relationship management scholarship remains as it pertains to how to measure such relationship aspects and to gauge the impact of multiple and interconnected buyer–supplier relationships on organizations.

Resource Orchestration Theory

Resource orchestration theory (ROT) is an extension of the RBV which suggests that it is the combination of resources, capabilities and managerial acumen that ultimately results in superior firm performance (Helfat, 2007). In his work, Helfat defined resource orchestration as the capacity of managers to purposefully create, extend or modify the resource base of an organization by assembling and orchestrating configurations of its co-specialized resources. Therefore, ROT can provide the lens to understand and predict the PSM firm-level decisions as they relate to the three dimensions suggested by Sirmon et al. (2007): (1) structuring – resources must be acquired, accumulated and divested; (2) bundling – resources must be bundled and tailored to meet the firm's unique needs once acquired; and (3) leveraging – resources must be mobilized, coordinated and deployed to exploit market opportunities and to create value for customers after they have been successfully structured and bundled.

As suggested by strategic management scholars (Chadwick et al., 2015; Sirmon et al., 2011), PSM scholarship can use ROT to highlight the importance of supply management actions for the organization to realize the full value of its resources when the breadth (resource orchestration across the scope of the firm), life cycle (resource orchestration at various stages of firm maturity) and depth (resource orchestration across levels of the firm) of these resources are managed effectively. This, in turn, provides an opportunity for PSM scholarship to inform buyers' and suppliers' decisions to orchestrate relevant resources as they structure their resources, bundle them into capabilities, and leverage from those capabilities to help both achieve their goals.

Social Network Theory

Social network theory (SNT) examines social structures as systems or networks of relations (Scott, 1991) and views social relationships in terms of nodes and ties. More specifically, a social network is a set of entities (for example, individuals, departments, firms or countries) connected to one another by a series of relationships that can be represented graphically by a set of nodes connected by lines (Lincoln, 1982). Nodes are the individual actors within the frameworks; ties are the relationships between the actors (Lincoln, 1982). Within this framework, a basic assumption is that structure is important (Chabowski et al., 2011); that is, the focus of this theory is relationships and ties with other entities within the network, rather than the attributes of such entities. As such, the focus of this perspective is on relationship patterns as well as their causes and consequences (Tichy and Fombrun, 1979).

SNT explicates the properties of today's PSM networks, including the nature of the links between joined entities (Tichy et al., 1979) and the transactional content, defined as the consistent flows or exchange of knowledge, influence and ideas from one entity to another. It helps in understanding how interactions and interconnectedness across the nodes and links in a supply chain impact the overall performance of PSM. That is, it parallels the shift in focus from each individual firm in the supply chain, to how those firms interact with one another to create value (Gligor et al., 2019). The increased use of social media tools for sourcing make this a very useful theory for the future. Social networks are primarily associated with personal interactions, but also can have a business purpose. We also know that often social and business interactions can be complementary. Certainly, the popularity of LinkedIn as a professional business site and Facebook, while more social, can serve business purposes. This theory has

Table 4.2   *Suggested theories and examples of PSM applications*

Theory	Applicability examples
Attribution theory	Examine who or what gets credit or blame for value creation or destruction within PSM. Understand how different interpretations can lead to different strategic responses (for example, ending a relationship with a supplier or continuing to work with the supplier). This will be important in the next decade in PSM practice, as new technologies such as artificial intelligence and machine learning impact upon supplier selection, retention and relationships.
Auction theory	This can be helpful in explaining and predicting buyer–supplier bidding behaviour through electronic reverse auctions and expressive bidding software platforms. Examining entry costs and their impact on bidder decisions in both the offer and the execution phase will help to explain the resultant buyer–supplier relationship.
Information processing theory (IPT)	Understanding the link between environmental uncertainty and PSM-related information processing needs and how buyers and suppliers cope with these needs. The applications of IPT should increase along with the growth of technology such as artificial intelligence, machine learning and robotics in PSM.
Innovation theory	Inform the adoption of PSM innovations and technology within the firm and across partner organizations. Investigate how the diffusion of new technologies and innovations themselves are influenced by specific groups. Supply base innovation is necessary to support internal innovation. Thus, this theory can provide an assessment of buyers' and suppliers' divergence and convergence in perceptions of key innovation characteristics. These include the perceived: relative advantage, compatibility and complexity of an innovation, and its impact on successfully driving innovation practices among buyer–supplier partner firms.
Institutional theory	Inform the bounded rationality in PSM decisions leading to solutions where no efficiency gains have been realized. The normative pressures and time constraints that buyers face lead to adopting programmes that many suppliers would not otherwise implement. This theory can examine the external pressures that make buyer and supplier organizations adopt or abandon purchasing practices regardless of their efficiency and effectiveness.
Organizational learning theory	Examine how multi-level learning takes place in PSM contexts and how stakeholder feedback serves as a source of PSM's practices and strategies. Also, link individuals, groups and the organization to develop a multi-level organizational learning model explaining the PSM learning phenomenon.
Power dependence theory	Understand buyer–supplier negotiations. Integrate organizational, individual and relationship levels of analysis to understand perceptions of power within PSM complex dynamics. Inform our understanding of how in dyadic relationships the dominant party can impact upon the behaviour of the other party. This, in turn, can help to provide additional insights into the factors that lead to successful PSM relationships.
Relational exchange theory	Understand how buyers and suppliers can be better motivated in the relationship to perform the tasks required of them. This is informed by examining and measuring the characteristics of buyer–supplier bonds, the related activity links, and the resource ties involved. This theory also can inform the impact of multiple and interconnected buyer–supplier relationships on organizations.
Resource orchestration theory	Inform buyers' and suppliers' decisions to orchestrate relevant resources as they structure their resources, bundle them into capabilities, and leverage from those capabilities to help both achieve their goals. Also, explain how resource versatility is linked to higher levels of performance with respect to the allocation of resources across different members of the supply chain
Social network theory	Understand how members of the supply chain interact and relate to one another and how these interactions, in turn, impact upon the PSM performance of buyers and suppliers. The increased use of social media tools for sourcing make this a very useful theory for the future. Also, it can help to investigate the many informal connections that tie employees and their executives together, as well as associations and connections between individual employees at partner firms.

been used to investigate how executives across firms interact with each other (Chabowski et al., 2011). Therefore, there is a wide spectrum of applications of the social network theory in PSM to investigate how buyer–supplier firms interact with each other, describe the many informal connections that tie their executives together, as well as associations and connections between individual employees at partner firms.

CONCLUSIONS AND IMPLICATIONS

Theory is critical to the development of any field of research. The first objective of this chapter was to elaborate on the extent of theory use in PSM research and describe the most frequently used theories in PSM research published in the past two decades. As stated earlier in this chapter, theory is becoming a necessary requirement to publish PSM scholarly work. TCE and the RBV have been the dominant theoretical lenses used to explain PSM phenomena. Other theories that we discussed were much less used, but have experienced some upward movement, and include game theory, agency theory and social exchange theory.

Going forward, we discussed ten promising, but sporadically adopted theories that can be applied to future PSM research. The broad variety of theory use that exists in recent PSM research may confirm that earlier calls for greater use of theory have been answered to some extent. The discussion, summarized in Table 4.2, shows that these ten theories can be utilized in suggested applications by PSM researchers, editors and reviewers to expand the scope of investigation and promote new insights in the discipline.

REFERENCES

Ahmed, D., Das, A. and Pagell, M. (2013), 'The influence of product life cycle on the efficacy of purchasing practices', *International Journal of Operations and Production Management*, 33 (4), 470–498.

Aistrich, Matti M. (2002), 'Trust us, trust me, trust in the future: determinants of the supplier's success in managing a global account relationship', Unpublished DBA, Harvard University.

Barney, Jay (1991), 'Firm resources and sustained competitive advantage', *Journal of Management*, 17 (1), 99–120.

Barney, Jay B. (2012), 'Purchasing, supply chain management and sustained competitive advantage: the relevance of resource-based theory', *Journal of Supply Chain Management*, 48 (2), 3–6.

Bello, D.C., Lohtia, R. and Sangtani, V. (2004), 'An institutional analysis of supply chain innovations in global marketing channels', *Industrial Marketing Management*, 33 (1), 57–64.

Bensaou, M. and Venkatraman, N. (1995), 'Configurations of interorganizational relationships: a comparison between U.S. and Japanese automakers', *Management Science*, 41 (9), 1471–1492.

Bergen, M., Dutta, S. and Walker Jr, O.C. (1992), 'Agency relationships in marketing: a review of the implications and applications of agency and related theories', *Journal of Marketing*, 56 (3), 1–24.

Bettman, J.R. and Weitz, B.A. (1983), 'Attributions in the board room: causal reasoning in corporate annual reports', *Administrative Science Quarterly*, 28 (2), 165–183.

Blau, Peter (1964), *Exchange and Power in Social Life*. New York: Wiley.

Buchanan, Lauranne (1992), 'Vertical trade relationships: the role of dependence and symmetry in attaining organizational goals', *Journal of Marketing Research*, 29 (1), 65–75.

Busse, C., Meinlschmidt, J. and Foerstl, K. (2017), 'Managing information processing needs in global supply chains: a prerequisite to sustainable supply chain management', *Journal of Supply Chain Management*, 53 (1), 87–113.

Chabowski, B.R., Mena, J.A. and Gonzalez-Padron, T.L. (2011), 'The structure of sustainability research in marketing, 1958–2008: a basis for future research opportunities', *Journal of the Academy of Marketing Science*, 39 (1), 55–70.

Chadwick, C., Super, J.F. and Kwon, K. (2015), 'Resource orchestration in practice: CEO emphasis on SHRM, commitment-based HR systems, and firm performance', *Strategic Management Journal*, 36 (3), 360–376.

Chicksand, Daniel (2015), 'Partnerships: the role that power plays in shaping collaborative buyer–supplier exchanges', *Industrial Marketing Management*, 48, 121–139.

Chou, S.Y. and Ramser, C. (2019), 'A multilevel model of organizational learning: incorporating employee spontaneous workplace behaviors, leadership capital and knowledge management', *Learning Organization*, 26, 132–145.

Coase, R.H. (1937), 'The nature of the firm', *Economica*, 4 (16), 386–405.

Costantino, N., Dotoli, M., Falagario, M. and Sciancalepore, F. (2012), 'Balancing the additional costs of purchasing and the vendor set dimension to reduce public procurement costs', *Journal of Purchasing and Supply Management*, 18 (3), 189–198.

Dawes, P.L., Lee, D.Y. and Midgley, D. (2007), 'Organizational learning in high-technology purchase situations: the antecedents and consequences of the participation of external IT consultants', *Industrial Marketing Management*, 36 (3), 285–299.

Debnath, R., Datta, B. and Mukhopadhyay, S. (2016), 'Customer relationship management theory and research in the new millennium: directions for future research', *Journal of Relationship Marketing*, 15 (4), 299–325.

DiMaggio, P.J. and Powell, W.W. (1983), 'The iron cage revisited: institutional isomorphism and collective rationality in organizational fields', *American Sociological Review*, 48 (2), 147–160.

Duncan, Robert B. (1972), 'Characteristics of organizational environments and perceived environmental uncertainty', *Administrative Science Quarterly*, 17 (3), 313–327.

Dwyer, F.R., Schurr, P.H. and Oh, S. (1987), 'Developing buyer–seller relationships', *Journal of Marketing*, 51 (2), 11–27.

Eisenhardt, Kathleen M. (1989), 'Agency theory: an assessment and review', *Academy of Management Review*, 14 (1), 57–74.

Emerson, Richard M. (1962), 'Power–dependence relations', *American Sociological Review*, 27 (1), 31–41.

Galbraith, Jay (1973), *Designing Complex Organizations*. Boston, MA: Addison-Wesley Publishing Co.

Garwin, David A. (1993), 'Building a learning organization', *Harvard Business Review*, 71 (4), 73–91.

Giunipero, L.C., Bittner, S., Shanks, I. and Cho, M.H. (2019), 'Analyzing the sourcing literature: over two decades of research', *Journal of Purchasing and Supply Management*, 25 (5), 100521.

Gligor, D., Bozkurt, S., Russo, I. and Omar, A. (2019), 'A look into the past and future: theories within supply chain management, marketing and management', *Supply Chain Management: An International Journal*, 24 (1), 170–186.

Goebel, P., Reuter, C., Pibernik, R., Sichtmann, C. and Bals, L. (2018), 'Purchasing managers' willingness to pay for attributes that constitute sustainability', *Journal of Operations Management*, 62 (1), 44–58.

Gummesson, Evert (1999), *Total Relationship Marketing*. Oxford: Butterworth-Heinemann.

Halldorsson, A., Mikkola, J.H. and Kotzab, H. (2015), 'Complementary theories to supply chain management revisited – from borrowing theories to theorizing', *Supply Chain Management*, 20 (6), 574–586.

Heide, Jan B. (1994), 'Interorganizational governance in marketing channels', *Journal of Marketing*, 58 (1), 71–86.

Helfat, Constance E. (2007), *Dynamic Capabilities: Understanding Strategic Change in Organizations*. New York: Wiley Blackwell.

Huff, Jerry (2016), 'Friends of my enemies: a longitudinal investigation into supply base management', Unpublished PhD, Arizona State University.

Hult, G.T.M., Hurley, R.F., Giunipero, L.C. and Nichols Jr, E.L. (2000), 'Organizational learning in global purchasing: a model and test of internal users and corporate buyers', *Decision Sciences*, 31 (2), 293–325.

Hunt, Shelby D. (1991), *Modern Marketing Theory: Critical Issues in the Philosophy of Marketing Science*. Cincinnati: OH: South Western Publishing.

Hunt, S.D. and Morgan, R.M. (1995), 'The comparative advantage theory of competition', *Journal of Marketing*, 59 (2), 1–15.

Jensen, M. and Meckling, W. (1976), 'Theory of the firm: managerial behavior, agency costs and capital structure', *Journal of Financial Economics*, 3 (October), 305–360.

Kelley, Harold H. (1973), 'The process of causal attribution', *American Psychologist*, 28, 103–128.

Ketchen, D.J. and Hult, G.T.M. (2007), 'Bridging organization theory and supply chain management: the case of best value supply chains', *Journal of Operations Management*, 25 (2), 573–580.

Knight, L., Tate, W.L., Matopoulos, A., Meehan, J. and Salmi, A. (2016), 'Breaking the mold: research process innovations in purchasing and supply management', *Journal of Purchasing and Supply Management*, 22 (4), 239–243.

Lee, J.W.C., Mohamad, O. and Ramayah, T. (2010), 'Outsourcing: is the social exchange theory still relevant in developing countries?', *Journal of Research in Interactive Marketing*, 4 (4) , 316–345.

Li, T. and Zheng, X. (2009), 'Entry and competition effects in first-price auctions: theory and evidence from procurement auctions', *Review of Economic Studies*, 76 (4), 1397–1429.

Lincoln, James R. (1982), 'Intra- (and inter-) organizational networks', in S.B. Bacharach (ed.), *Research in the Sociology of Organizations*. Greenwich: JAI Press, pp. 1–38.

Liu, Y., Luo, Y. and Liu, T. (2009), 'Governing buyer–supplier relationships through transactional and relational mechanisms: evidence from China', *Journal of Operations Management*, 27 (4), 294–309.

Macneil, Ian R. (1980), *The New Social Contract: An Inquiry Into Modern Contractual Relations*. New Haven, CT: Yale University Press.

March, James G. (1991), 'Exploration and exploitation in organizational learning', *Organization Science*, 2 (1), 71–87.

McAfee, R. P. and McMillan, J. (1987), 'Auctions and bidding', *Journal of Economic Literature*, 25 (2), 699–738.

Meehan, J. and Wright, G. (2012), 'The origins of power in buyer–seller relationships', *Industrial Marketing Management*, 41 (4), 669–679.

Meinlschmidt, J., Schleper, M. and Foerstl, K. (2018), 'Tackling the sustainability iceberg: a trans-action cost economics approach to lower tier sustainability management', *International Journal of Operations and Production Management*, 38, 1888–1914.

Monczka, R.M., Handfield, R.B., Giunipero, L.C. and Patterson, J.L. (2016), *Purchasing and Supply Chain Management* (6th edn). Boston, MA: Cengage Learning.

Moore, G.C. and Benbasat, I. (1991), 'Development of an instrument to measure the perceptions of adopting an information technology innovation', *Information Systems Research*, 2 (3), 192–222.

Morgan, R.M. and Hunt, S.D. (1994), 'The commitment–trust theory of relationship marketing', *Journal of Marketing*, 58 (3), 20–38.

Pearcy, D., Giunipero, L. and Wilson, A. (2007), 'A model of relational governance in reverse auctions', *Journal of Supply Chain Management*, 43 (1), 4–15.

Pfeffer, J. and Salancik, G.R. (1978), *The External Control of Organizations: A Resource Dependence Perspective*. New York: Harper & Row.

Porter, Michael E. (1985), *The Competitive Advantage: Creating and Sustaining Superior Performance*. New York: Free Press.

Premkumar, G., Ramamurthy, K. and Saunders, C.S. (2005), 'Information processing view of organiza-tions: an exploratory examination of fit in the context of interorganizational relationships', *Journal of Management Information Systems*, 22 (1), 257–294.

Premkumar, G. and Roberts, M. (1999), 'Adoption of new information technologies in rural small busi-nesses', *Omega*, 27 (4), 467–484.

Pulles, N.J., Veldman, J., Schiele, H. and Sierksma, H. (2014), 'Pressure or pamper? The effects of power and trust dimensions on supplier resource allocation', *Journal of Supply Chain Management*, 50 (3), 16–36.

Real, J.C., Roldán, J.L. and Leal, A. (2014), 'From entrepreneurial orientation and learning orientation to business performance: analysing the mediating role of organizational learning and the moderating effects of organizational size', *British Journal of Management*, 25 (2), 186–208.

Rogers, Everett M. (1962), *Diffusion of Innovation*. New York: Free Press.

Scott, John (1991), *Social Network Analysis: A Handbook*, Newbury Park: SAGE Publications.

Scott, W.R. and Davis, G.F. (2007), *Organizations and Organizing: Rational, Natural, and Open System Perspectives*. Hoboken, NJ: Pearson Prentice Hall.

Senge, Peter M. (1990), *The Art and Practice of the Learning Organization*. New York: Doubleday.

Senge, Peter M. (2006), *The Fifth Discipline: The Art and Practice of the Learning Organization*. New York: Broadway Business.

Sirmon, D.G., Hitt, M.A. and Ireland, R.D. (2007), 'Managing firm resources in dynamic environments to create value: looking inside the blackbox', *Academy of Management Review*, 32 (1), 273–292.

Sirmon, D.G., Hitt, M.A., Ireland, R.D. and Gilbert, B.A. (2011), 'Resource orchestration to create competitive advantage: breadth, depth, and life cycle effects', *Journal of Management*, 37 (5), 1390–1412.

Slater, S.F. and Narver, J.C. (1995), 'Market orientation and the learning organization', *Journal of Marketing*, 59 (3), 63–74.

Tate, W., Ellram, L., Bals, L. and Hartmann, E. (2009), 'Offshore outsourcing of services: an evolutionary perspective', *International Journal of Production Economics*, 120, 512–524.

Tate, W., Ellram, L., Bals, L., Hartmann, E. and van der Valk, W. (2010), 'An agency theory perspective on the purchase of marketing services', *Industrial Marketing Management*, 39, 806–819.

Tichy, N. and Fombrun, C. (1979), 'Network analysis in organizational settings', *Human Relations*, 32 (11), 923–965.

Tichy, N.M., Tushman, M.L. and Fombrun, C. (1979), 'Social network analysis for organizations', *Academy of Management Review*, 4 (4), 507–519.

Trautmann, G., Turkulainen, V., Hartmann, E. and Bals, L. (2009), 'Integration in the global sourcing organization – an information processing perspective', *Journal of Supply Chain Management*, 45, 57–74.

Tushman, M.L. and Nadler, D.A. (1978), 'Information processing as an integrating concept in organizational design', *Academy of Management Review*, 3 (3), 613–624.

Van Weele, A.J. and Van Raaij, E.M. (2014), 'The future of purchasing and supply management research: about relevance and rigor', *Journal of Supply Chain Management*, 50 (1), 56–72.

Wacker, John G. (1998), 'A definition of theory: research guidelines for different theory-building research methods in operations management', *Journal of Operations Management*, 16 (4), 361–385.

Williamson, Oliver E. (1975), *Markets and Hierarchies: Analysis and Antitrust Implications: A Study in the Economics of Internal Organization*. New York: Free Press.

Williamson, Oliver. E. (1985), *The Economics Institutions of Capitalism: Firms, Markets, Relational Contracting*. New York: Free Press.

Wowak, K.D., Craighead, C.W., Ketchen, D.J.J.R. and Hult, G.T.M. (2016), 'Toward a "theoretical toolbox" for the supplier-enabled fuzzy front end of the new product development process', *Journal of Supply Chain Management*, 52 (1), 66–81.

5. Systems levels in purchasing and supply chain management (PSCM) research: exploring established and novel theories to address PSCM problems and challenges

Christine M. Harland and Jens K. Roehrich

INTRODUCTION

Purchasing and supply management (PSM) scholars have traditionally focused on purchasing's role in an organisation and the organisation's relationships with its suppliers (Webster and Wind, 1972; Leenders et al., 1980). Operations management (OM), in contrast, originally focused on operations internal to firms, with its origins dating back to the time of the industrial revolution. Meredith and Amoako-Gyumpah (1990) traced the genealogy of OM from 'factory management' through 'production management' to 'production/operations management'. The term 'supply chain management' (SCM) was first used in 1982 to denote the internal value chain within a manufacturing organisation from in- to outbound ends of the business (Oliver and Webber, 1992), that is traditional production/operations management. It was not until the late 1980s that OM as a field widened its perspective beyond the boundary of the firm to include consideration of sourcing and supplier relationships (Hayes et al., 1988; Hill, 1989). In *The Machine that Changed the World*, Womack et al. (1990) incorporated examination of supplier relationships, coining the phrase 'lean' supply. SCM has since been conceptualised as a field encompassing traditional internal OM and connected relationships with suppliers, suppliers' suppliers, customers and customers' customers, operating at multiple systems levels of internal supply chains, dyadic relationships, external supply chains and wider supply networks (Harland, 1996). These multiple systems levels were conceived from the perspective of the 'focal firm' (Harland, 2021). Purchasing and supply chain management (PSCM) is one of a myriad of terms used to define boundaries, and argue territory rights, of the field of research and practice that includes these multiple systems levels and examines contractual, relational, physical and transformational perspectives (Ellram et al., 2020).

During the COVID-19 crisis, several calls have been made for more holistic approaches to management in general, and PSCM in particular, to deal with complex problems associated with interconnected, global phenomena (Chesbrough, 2020; Craighead et al., 2020; Harland, 2021). Additionally, a call has also been made to increase the relational and 'softer' rather than 'hard' science approaches to PSCM (Caniato et al., 2020). These calls have led us to bring systems theory, systems thinking and systems levels to the foreground for this chapter, to examine established and novel theories to address PSCM problems and challenges in a more open, interconnected and holistic way, beyond traditional firm-based perspectives.

In this chapter, we start by providing a brief review of systems thinking, and how it emerged from organismic biology and cybernetics. We particularly discuss systems thinking by identifying, conceptualising and problematising different systems levels; our assertion is that this is crucial to clarify key levels and their importance in PSCM research and practice (and their strong connections). This is followed by a discussion of established theories used at these systems levels within prior PSCM work, positioning (novel) theories popular in related and adjacent fields at different levels, and reflecting on particular chapters in this book on individual theories which may advance research in PSCM.

SYSTEMS THINKING: HIERARCHIES AND LEVELS

Biologists pioneered systems thinking, desiring to study the complexity of the whole biology of an organism, rather than only its physical and chemical components (Pantin, 1968). So-called 'organismic biologists' were frustrated with reductionist, hard science approaches that promoted the scientific method of the so-called restricted sciences of physics and chemistry, seeking instead to understand the organisation of the complexity of the whole organism. Checkland (1981) illustrated this holism simply, explaining that the shape of an apple is not meaningfully described in terms of the cells and molecules that make up the apple; the complexity of the whole apple gives rise to its overall shape. Ludwig von Bertalanffy (1951) developed the foundations of systems theory from organismic biology, to a more generalised view of all systems including management systems (von Bertalanffy, 1968), becoming what is now recognised as 'general systems theory'. In Kevin Dooley's Chapter 22 in this book, he explores understanding of complexity and how complex adaptive systems theory deals with complex interactions and feedback loops within complex systems. In this chapter, we complement this by focusing on holism, and how hierarchies and levels within hierarchies comprise the whole, and give sense, organisation and meaning to the whole.

Systems thinking has at its centre the notion of organised complexity (Checkland, 1981), where complex systems comprise a hierarchy of systems levels, each level more complex than the level below it in the hierarchy. Each hierarchical level contains emergent properties that are not present in the lower levels. Hierarchy theory explains the structure, the relative position of different levels within a system, and how the levels relate to each other. Used particularly in ecology (for a comprehensive introduction, see Odum and Barrett, 1971), hierarchy theory focuses on differences between one level of complexity and another. What emerges at each level is constrained by the fact that it operates within the context, or environment, of the next higher level. To understand the whole system requires understanding of the linkages between levels and what is communicated up and down these levels.

Checkland (1981) proposed that systems thinking is based on two pairs of principles: 'emergence and hierarchy' and 'communications and control'. In organised complexity, there exists a hierarchy of levels of organisation. Emergence and hierarchy are paired because each hierarchical level is characterised by emergent features that do not exist at the lower level; hierarchy theory is concerned with the differences between each level of complexity in the hierarchy (Simon, 1957). Communications and control are paired, influenced by von Bertalanffy (1951) who proposed that systems open to environmental influence – open systems – require communication between different levels of the hierarchy to enable control of the system, in line with control systems thinking from cybernetics (Wiener, 1948). In management, two of the most notable uses of hierarchy theory are Maslow's hierarchy of needs from psychology (Maslow, 1943), and Williamson's (1975) examination of markets and hierarchies. There have been calls for greater use of hierarchy theory in management (Wahba and Bridwell, 1973), although with the exception of these two examples, neither hierarchy theory nor, indeed, systems thinking seem to have gained much traction in the last few decades in management research.

It is argued by systems thinkers that a more holistic perspective of complex, real-world problems – a 'big picture' – is achieved through combining organismic systems thinking from biology (giving rise to emergence and hierarchy), with cybernetics thinking (giving rise to communications and control), supplemented and complemented with scientific reductionist approaches (Checkland, 1981; Jackson, 2003). But how does this more holistic perspective enhance understanding in management and, more specifically, in PSCM?

The classical approach to management theory, based on the behavioural theory of the firm, focuses management researchers on firm-based decision making (Cyert and March, 1963). Systems thinking views the organisation both as a whole and as part of a larger environment (Jackson, 2003). The systems approach sees the organisation as an interdependent, unified system composed of interrelated subsystems or parts, rather than separate entities. More specifically, systems thinking requires a shift in mindset, away from linear to circular. In contrast to a more linear, structured 'mechanical worldview', the holism of systems thinking offers a dynamic, chaotic, interconnected array of relationships and feedback loops, giving rise to organised complexity of the whole management system. Another key concept in systems thinking is synthesis, as opposed to analysis; analysis dissects complexity (in a scientific, reductionist way, wielding Ockham's razor) into manageable components, whereas synthesis looks at the whole. Analysis fits into the mechanical and reductionist worldview, where the world is broken down into parts. But all management systems are dynamic and often complex; therefore, we need a more holistic approach to understanding phenomena, and thus synthesis offers an understanding of the whole and the parts at the same time, along with the relationships and the connections that make up the dynamics of the whole. Similarly, systems thinking also considers the concept of emergence (the natural outcome of parts of the management system coming together). Emergence is about non-linearity and self-organisation, and we often use the term 'emergence' to describe the outcome of things interacting together. Since everything is interconnected, there are also constant feedback loops and flows between elements of a system. We can observe, understand and intervene in feedback loops once we understand their type and dynamics. Understanding feedback loops is about gaining perspective of causality: how one thing results in another thing in a dynamic and constantly evolving system (all systems are dynamic and constantly changing in some way).

In the next section we relate systems thinking, particularly levels and hierarchy, to PSCM research and practice.

SYSTEMS LEVELS IN PSCM RESEARCH AND PRACTICE

Purchasing and supply chain management concerns complex, multilevel systems. Consider, for example, the supply of vaccines for COVID-19, with local health authorities managing implementation of vaccine plans to supply the local population; national government health departments forming the strategy for vaccination and allocation of vaccines to supply localities; international trading blocs forming framework agreements for vaccine supply to member nations; and global organisations, such as the World Health Organisation, liaising with governments for the supply of vaccines to poorer countries globally. As another example, a global food products manufacturing organisation may permit local plant sourcing for highly perishable ingredients; regional sourcing for bulky foods that are costly to transport; but insist on global, centralised sourcing for high-value, critical supplies for all plants. Each organisation within these supply systems deals every day with emergence and hierarchy, communications and control, within these complex, multilevel systems.

In addition to dealing with multilevel system complexity, PSCM has three distinct features: its roots in practice, its research methodologies and its theoretical underpinnings. PSCM work in practice is often deeply embedded in individual behaviours, organisational, supply chain or network practices and challenges, using a range of methods, including in-depth case work, ethnographic or action research studies and field experiments. This chapter (and book) is particularly concerned with the theoretical underpinnings in prior and future PSCM work and its impact on practice. This section, therefore, first explores the importance and relationship between theory across levels and practice, before exploring some exemplary theories used in prior PSCM research.

The Importance of, and Relationship Between, Theory Across Levels and Practice

It is a widely held view in PSCM that theoretical contributions are important for publication in leading (PSCM) journals (Carter, 2011; Colquitt and Zapata-Phelan, 2007; Hambrick, 2007). Theories are statements of relations among concepts within sets of boundary assumptions (Bacharach, 1989), and are vital to interpret empirical work. Following Dubin (1978), all theories are constrained by their specific critical bounding assumptions, setting limitations in theory application. Two key boundaries – spatial and temporal – have been emphasised (Bacharach, 1989). Whilst spatial boundaries are conditions restricting the use of the theory to specific units of analysis or levels, temporal contingencies constrain the historical applicability of a theory. Both boundaries together restrict the empirical generalisability of the theory. In this book, more details regarding theory can be found in Chapter 2 by Flynn et al. about the foundations of theory, and Chapter 3 by Pagell et al. about developing PSM theory. In this chapter, we are mainly concerned with different systems levels and their challenges for PSCM research and practice.

The development path of theory testing and building, and, more recently, theory elaboration (see, for example, Ketokivi and Choi, 2014), has sparked debates amongst academics. While some researchers advocate consensus and unity akin to a 'well-tended garden' (Pfeffer, 1993, 1995), others favour less structured plurality of inquiries for theory building, encouraging multiple theories to compete, as in a 'weed-patch' (Van de Ven, 1989; Van Maanen, 1995). Theory building, testing and elaborating are closely interrelated in the process of knowledge creation and refinement within a discipline (Colquitt and Zapata-Phelan, 2007). Academic fields and disciplines (and PSCM is no exception here), need to consider a careful balance between theory building and elaboration to allow original ideas to be introduced, and theory testing, a process which ascertains whether the empirical evidence supports or does not support a given theory.

PSCM has been criticised for lacking sufficient theoretical development and underpinning to be considered an academic discipline (Harland et al., 2006; Chicksand et al., 2012; Spina et al., 2016). This has led to simplified conceptualisations of key concepts and their contexts, and lack of generalisability, highlighting the importance of using theories to understand complex environments across levels in which individuals, teams and organisations are operating (Chicksand et al., 2012). For instance, a literature review by Croom et al. (2000) showed a relative lack of theoretical work compared to empirical-based studies. Whilst there are more promising recent developments over the last two decades to build on and elaborate theories, PSCM research would benefit greatly from theorising work at different levels (hence this chapter and the whole book are crucial to support these future research efforts).

Management theory (including when applied to PSCM challenges) focuses on facts and sound principles, which often prescribe what to do to meet desired outcomes in and outside organisations, thereby informing and advancing PSCM research and practice. The relationship between theory and practice is closely intertwined for management, and in particular for PSCM scholars, as follows:

> management theory provides the basis for management practice, and the practice in turn helps to reinforce the development of management theory. Management practice therefore involves the translation of existing management knowledge and theories into action that will result in the achievement of the dual goals of organizational efficiency and effectiveness. Management practitioners and professionals are in the vanguard of management practice, and their practice provides the opportunity for reviewing existing management theories and even developing new ones. Management theorists and practitioners reinforce one another and are in a continuous process of interaction. The knowledge of both is required to improve our understanding of management in society. (Inyang, 2008, pp. 124–125)

Along the same lines, prior work (Alvesson and Kärreman, 2007; Van Maanen et al., 2007) has also emphasised the relationship between the validity and power of a theory and its relation to empirical reality. It is widely recognised, and prior PSCM work is a good example, that the empirical nourishes the conceptual as data are used as evidence to support, refine and further develop a theory (Van Maanen et al., 2007). Thus, as practised by PSCM scholars, the engagement with practical problems opens up avenues for a theory to emerge, to be elaborated and to be tested. We argue that an understanding of different theories across levels is vital for PSCM researchers, as a theoretical base is a key underpinning for the field to develop into a legitimate management discipline and inform and shape practice.

Table 5.1 applies a systems thinking lens to examine theory relevant to PSCM. Specifically, it is structured into systems levels within a hierarchy, allowing examination of emergence, communication and control, and key challenges associated with research at each level. It offers a brief overview of key theories (most of which are discussed in much more detail across chapters in this book).

Theories at Different PSCM Systems Levels

This section builds on the various systems levels discussed in the previous section by identifying key theories used in prior PSCM work (mainly based on the chapters in this book). We then propose exemplary theories across these levels which have so far received limited attention in prior PSCM studies, but which we believe offer ample opportunities to augment and develop our thinking and practical insights. By bringing together different theoretical perspectives from PSCM as well as related research fields and adjacent disciplines, we hope to support future theoretically informed efforts to advance PSCM research and practice.

Despite some prior studies arguing that PSCM lacks theoretical underpinnings when compared to other management fields and adjacent disciplines, prior PSCM studies have used a myriad of theories across different levels. Prior studies have used theories from a number of disciplines including, but not limited to, economics, sociology, engineering and psychology to

Table 5.1   *System levels: their scope, definition, exemplary challenges and theories*

Systems level in a hierarchy/chapter	Definition and scope	Emergence, communication and control	Exemplary challenges	Exemplary theories and references
Individuals, and the PSCM internal supply chain team (organisation) Chapter 8 Chapter 10 Chapter 25	This is about the job (job role) of PSCM including, but not limited to, individual buyers, supply chain planners and boundary-spanners. Purchasing teams, project teams, supply chain teams, management teams. Members of a PSCM department managing inbound to outbound physical and information flows.	Individual identity; communication and control within PSCM team dynamics and performance; communication and control across internal supply chain functional boundaries; PSCM strategy and alignment with corporate strategy; relationships with stakeholders; communication and control with supply base.	Identity coherence and legitimacy, training and education requirements, professionalism, career progression. Category management; supply market research, supplier development, supply portfolio management, risk management, sustainable and ethical procurement.	Attribution theory – Kelley, 1973 Dynamic capabilities – Teece et al., 1997 Event system theory – Morgeson et al., 2015 Expectancy disconfirmation theory – Oliver, 1977 Game theory – von Neumann and Morgenstern, 1944; Parkhe, 1993 Information processing theory (IPT) – Tushman and Nadler, 1978; Deci et al., 1994 Knowledge-based view (KBV) – Kogut and Zander, 1992 Natural resource-based-view (NRBV) – Hart (1995) Organisational learning theory – March, 1991 Population ecology – Hannan and Freeman, 1977 Prospect theory – Kahneman and Tversky 1979 Real options – Hult et al., 2010 Resource-based view (RBV) – Barney, 1991 Self-determination theory (SDT) – Deci et al., 2017 Strategic choice – Child, 1972 Structural inertia theory – Hannan and Freeman, 1984 Transaction costs economics/analysis (TCE/TCA) – Williamson, 1975; Rindfleisch and Heide, 1997
Dyadic and triadic relationships Chapter 7 Chapter 19 Chapter 29	This is concerned with the interorganisational relationships with suppliers. Buyer–supplier, supplier–supplier, public–private organisation. Buyer and two first-tier suppliers, buyer and one first-tier and one second-tier supplier.	Power, trust and dependence in supplier dyadic and triadic relationships; dyadic and triadic social capital; dyadic and triadic learning; communication and control with external supply chain.	Contractual and relational governance; psychological and relational issues vs. operational and informational issues; vendor rating; investment in relationship specific assets; cooperation, competition and coopetition, new product development and innovation, horizontal cooperation; make or buy/outsourcing.	Agency theory – Eisenhardt; 1989; Tate et al., 2010 Regulatory focus theory (RFT) – Weber and Mayer, 2011 Signalling theory – Spence, 1973 Social exchange theory (SET) – Blau, 1964 Power dependency theory – Emerson, 1962

Systems level in a hierarchy/chapter	Definition and scope	Emergence, communication and control	Exemplary challenges	Exemplary theories and references
External supply chain Chapter 32	This is about flows and integration of materials and information across tiers in a supply chain. Supplier, buyer, customer (plus possibly sub-suppliers and customers' customers).	Supply chain dynamics emerge. Communication and control with the broader supply network.	Vertical integration/ disintegration; CPFR; integrated enterprise resource planning (ERP).	Institutional theory – DiMaggio and Powell, 1991; Scott, 1995 Panarchy theory – Allen et al., 2014 Resource orchestration theory – Sirmon et al., 2007; Barney et al., 2010 Stakeholder theory – Freeman, 1984
Supply network Chapter 32	This is concerned with a more shared, collaborative effort. Focal organisation supply network nested within interorganisational networks (containing overlapping innovation, learning and social networks). Supply network boundary is around entities and processes whose core purpose is to supply a product, service or solution.	Supply network collaboration and network social capital emerge. Communication and control with the broader supply system occurring in confederal supply systems, or with industry groups in a sector.	Extended ERP (ERPII); keiretsu; network cooperation vs. network competition; strategic position in the network; network innovation.	Social network theory/analysis (SNT/SNA) – Scott, 1988 Weak ties theory – Granovetter, 1973
Supply system Chapter 22 Chapter 27 Chapter 32	Networks of supply within sectors or industries; industry groups.	Cultures emerge within confederal supply systems (for example United Nations culture). Communication and control to develop and manage supply markets.	Supply system governance; supply exchanges and platforms; sustainable and ethical supply.	Complexity theory – Byrne, 1998; Dooley, 2020 Complex adaptive systems (CAS) – Holland, 1995; Choi et al., 2001 Cluster theory – Manzini and Di Serio, 2017 Institutional theory – DiMaggio and Powell, 1991; Scott, 1995 Systems theory – von Bertalanffy, 1951; Forrester, 1994
Supply market	All available suppliers in a particular sector or industry.	Impact of supply market concentration and competition emerges. Communication and control with wider economy and society.	Innovation exploration; supply market development; supply market concentration; scarce resource strategies; factor market rivalry.	Factor market rivalry – Ellram et al., 2013 Supply market concentration – DeWitt et al., 2006

Note: This is not an exhaustive list of challenges and theories, and merely an illustration of them across levels; some theories are used across different system levels.

understand phenomena and address challenges in practice (Sarkis et al., 2011; Touboulic and Walker, 2015). The evolution of the uptake of these theories is also informed by changing historical conditions such as across markets and industries over the last decades. In this section, we provide an illustrative (rather than exhaustive) overview of popular (that is, in terms of frequency of use in prior PSCM work) theories. Further details for most of these theories can be found in individual chapters in this book (please see Table 5.1). While pluralism in terms of using different theories is a strength of PSCM, researchers need to be aware of the benefits and limitations of individual theories. Thus, we offer a discussion of different theories and their usage across levels, as each perspective and level provide a unique set of theoretical insights.

The process of looking across levels (as offered in this chapter) and across complementary theoretical perspectives (as offered in this book) is vital and timely. This is coupled with the increasing visibility and popularity of behavioural perspectives in OM and PSCM more specifically, as well as emerging challenges (for example, digital technologies, the COVID-19 pandemic; Kache and Seuring, 2017; Craighead et al., 2020). Each management theory provides valuable insight into different aspects (such as resources, transactions, relations and capabilities) at different levels (from individuals to markets, and sometimes across levels). Selecting a theory for a particular research study depends on a number of factors including, but not limited to, the research question(s) and hypotheses the study seeks to answer, the key aspects under study (for example, resources, capabilities and behaviours), the boundaries and limitations of a particular theory, as well as the level of analysis. Thus, mapping and bridging multiple perspectives and levels in the field and across fields and disciplines is vital.

Within prior PSCM work, there is a preference of using theories that take a more organisational and strategic perspective rather than an individual and behavioural one. These theories (such as transaction cost economics, stakeholder theory and institutional theory) utilised in PSCM have favoured the prevalence of large (often private) buyer organisations' perspective as the unit of analysis. There has also been a stream of research, albeit smaller, that focuses on public organisations and small and medium-sized enterprises (SMEs) (Amann et al., 2014) and the relationships between public and private organisations (Zheng et al., 2008; Caldwell et al., 2009). Public–private relationship may offer further opportunities to explore a range of key PSCM areas ranging from relationship management to complex contracting for products, services and more integrated solutions (Barlow et al., 2013; Roehrich and Lewis, 2014; Roehrich and Kivleniece, 2021). For example, when institutional theory is applied to a supply chain context, it enables consideration of whether supply chain practices should mimic industry best practices or reflect the participants' unique characteristics. The study by Preuss (2009) shows that the adoption of ethical sourcing codes is strongly influenced by isomorphic and public pressures. Institutional theory has also been used as a lens that offers insights into the pressure that firms put on one another in the movement towards adopting more sustainable supply chain practices (for example, mimetic isomorphism; Hoejmose et al., 2014). Similarly, Tate et al. (2010) use institutional theory to analyse the content of CSR reports and highlight that although institutional pressure is clear across various industries, the way in which it is interpreted and translated within reports varies according to the size of the company and its geographic location.

Another popular theory used in prior PSCM work is transaction cost economics (TCE) (Williamson, 1975; Grover and Malhotra, 2003). TCE is powerful with regard to the interorganisational aspects and issues such as defining firm boundaries (Coase, 1937; Williamson, 1981; Grimm, 2008). An initial step for purchasing and supply chain managers is to decide which components they will produce in-house and which they will source from external suppliers. TCE has been used to explain make-or-buy and outsourcing or offshoring decisions in different industries (Ellram et al., 2008). The theory posits that firms will prefer internal hierarchy, or making components internally, as opposed to purchasing them from external suppliers via the market, when transaction costs (costs of using the market) are high. Transaction costs are driven by the degree of asset specificity, frequency and uncertainty. Once a firm determines which components will be produced outside the firm, the firm must then establish and manage relationships with various suppliers. One key decision is the degree to which firms employ a short- or long-term relationship (and its nature: transactional versus relational) with a particular supplier. These relationships are often governed by a detailed contract (Essig et al., 2016; Roehrich et al., 2021). Again, TCE suggests that where transaction costs are high, due to elevated asset specificity, frequency and/or uncertainty, the firm would be more likely to establish long-term relationships (Grimm, 2008). Furthermore, the nature of the contract will also be driven by the extent of transaction costs. Where costs are high, firms will tend to develop longer-term contracts, and contracts with more complex features, and with detailed control and coordination clauses (Roehrich et al., 2020) in order to frame the relationship (for example, its impact on justice; Bouazzaoui et al., 2020) and tackle emerging issues in relationships such as coordination failures and curb opportunism (Howard et al., 2019; Kalra et al., 2021). Emerging research on contractual and relational governance mechanisms has also started to explore their individual roles and interplay to realise a range of performance outcomes (Hartmann et al., 2014; Roehrich and Lewis, 2014; Kreye et al., 2015; Caldwell et al., 2017).

In summary, as we have briefly shown and is evident across chapters in this book, PSCM researchers have utilised theory pluralism to explain and make sense of PSCM phenomena to inform theory and practice alike. We now turn to theories which are yet underutilised in prior PSCM studies, but which we believe could offer further powerful theoretical insights to inform the advancement of the field and improvement of practice.

THEORIES USED OUTSIDE PSCM

This section pays particular attention to theories which are used more frequently in other management fields, and also takes a closer look at theories used in adjacent disciplines such as psychology. An understanding of these and other theories is important for PSCM scholars, as our thinking can be advanced by learning about (as well as testing and elaborating) theories from other fields and disciplines. Please note that this is an exemplary, rather than an exhaustive, list of theories which might prove powerful to uncover, understand and explain processes, activities, behaviours and relationships in future research to address PSCM problems and challenges. We urge PSCM scholars also to look outside PSCM (and even management), to detect, explore and then utilise theories which would help to advance our thinking and practices.

At an individual level, self-determination theory (SDT) focuses on human motivation concerned with how individuals interact with the social environment and engage in a behaviour (Ryan and Deci, 2000; Deci et al., 2017). A central tenet of SDT is that individuals possess innate tendencies and mechanisms to optimise their well-being, development and motivation (Ryan and Deci, 2000). The theory positions two types of motivation: autonomous and controlled (Deci et al., 1994; Gagné and Deci, 2005). Autonomous motivation shows that the behaviour an individual engages in is congruent with the individual's own interests and values (that is value internalisation) (Reinholt et al., 2011), and hence, it leads to effort and persistence in engagement of that behaviour (Robson et al., 2012). In contrast, controlled motivation reflects engagement in behaviour due to an external source of pressure; that is, lack of autonomy and self-determination (Ryan and Deci, 2000). For instance, individuals may engage in an activity to meet an external expectation, comply with regulations, or maintain their reputation in the social environment.

SDT argues that the social context can facilitate value internalisation through satisfaction of three innate needs: autonomy, competence and relatedness (Deci et al., 1994; Weibel, 2007). The need for autonomy focuses on the experience of freedom, which is the sentiment of being the perceived source or origin of an individual's own behaviour. In other words, autonomy is the feeling of freedom based an individual choice. Individuals who experience autonomy have a sense of ownership of behaviour (Gagné and Deci, 2005) that is central to the ability to transform actively external factors (for example, regulations and initiatives) into an individual's inner principles. The need for competence refers to when individuals feel effective in their ongoing interactions with the environment, and try to maintain and increase their capacity and skills through actions (Ryan and Deci, 2000). Lastly, the need for relatedness refers to the feelings of being connected to other people, that is important to an individual within society or business environments (Van den Broeck et al., 2016).

SDT was originally developed in social psychology and more recently has been adopted in management studies (Van den Broeck et al., 2016). Researchers have used SDT to investigate a range of topics such as creativity (Liu et al., 2011), knowledge sharing (Reinholt et al., 2011), citizenship behaviour (Chiniara and Bentein, 2015) and employees' performance (Aryee et al., 2015) within organisations. However, SDT and its key dimensions are underutilised in prior PSCM studies, apart from a very few exceptions. One of the first studies in PSCM to explicitly use SDT is the work by Roehrich et al. (2017), who explore how realising improved performance in green supply chain management is contingent upon SDT mechanisms of autonomy, competence and relatedness in the aerospace industry.

Other theories on an individual level include attribution theory, which seeks to explain the mental and communicative processes involved in everyday explanations, most typically of individual and social events (Kelley, 1973; Chapter 4 in this book by Giunipero and Eltantawy). Similarly, PSCM researchers may want to explore other theories that are useful on an individual level including, but not limited to, real options (Hult et al., 2010), strategic choice (Child, 1972) and prospect theory (Kahneman and Tversky, 1979).

At an organisational (and market level), PSCM researchers may want to consider population ecology (Craighead et al., 2020), which provides insights on which organisations survive or die based on the natural selection process, which is beyond organisations' control (Hannan and Freeman, 1977). This perspective provides a contrasting view to resource and capability perspectives (for example, the resource-based view, dynamic capabilities) as they are centred on wilful adaptation by the organisation. The theory points towards structural inertia in providing an explanation of why some organisations cannot adapt to changing (for example market/ sector) conditions (Hannan and Freeman, 1984). For example, Kodak once held a dominant position in photographic film, but struggled to adjust to digital photography, which has since adversely affected its market position.

Craighead et al. (2020) have also recently argued that within PSCM research, structural inertia theory has been sparely used. A rare example in PSCM is the study by Rungtusanatham and Salvador (2008) which seeks to explain the reasons why organisations find it difficult to realise major shifts (for example, from mass production to customisation). Structural inertia, Craighead et al. (2020) posit, may be a promising lens to investigate why certain organisations do better than others during a crisis or pandemic. Whilst under 'normal conditions' smaller firms fail more often than larger ones due to limited resources (Hannan and Freeman, 1984), but during a pandemic this issue might be amplified as smaller firms may lack required resources for survival, as evidenced during the COVID-19 pandemic (Craighead et al., 2020). However, during lockdowns, larger firms were not immune to resource challenges. Assessing the impact of structural inertia before, during and after a pandemic (or crisis situation) would offer fruitful future research opportunities (Craighead et al., 2020).

Future PSCM studies at the level of the organisation may also benefit from exploring the use of organisational learning theory (March, 1991). This theory highlights that the learning capacity of an organisation depends on a myriad of factors, such as top-level leaders' behaviours, organisational structure and culture (Chapter 4 in this book by Giunipero and Eltantawy). Similarly, event system theory can be applied on multiple levels, but especially at an organisational level (Morgeson et al., 2015). The theory outlines how important events are, how they become more meaningful and eventually impact upon organisations across space and time.

At a dyadic relationship level, regulatory focus theory (RFT), an as yet underexplored theory in PSCM research, has been used to address the role of contract framing and expectations on contractual relationships (Weber and Mayer, 2011; Selviaridis and van der Valk, 2019). RFT differentiates between a prevention frame and a promotion frame, each of which leads to distinct interpretations of goals in the relationship, emotional and behavioural reactions as well as views and expectations of the relationship. A prevention framing of a negotiation between two organisations results in minimal goal-inducing, high-intensity negative emotions if the goal is not attained, and low-intensity, positive emotions when the goal is accomplished. In contrast, when a negotiation between two parties has a promotion framing, parties view the same goal as something that would be ideal if reached. When a promotion framing is used and the goal is not attained, low-intensity negative emotions result, whereas participants experience high-intensity, positive emotions when the goal is accomplished.

Future PSCM research may also consider power dependency theory (Emerson, 1962), which defines power as the ability of an actor to influence another to act in a manner that they would not have otherwise. Pfeffer and Salancik (1978) applied Emerson's philosophy to the context of relationships with the fundamental premise that power in an exchange relationship is a relative concept determined by which firm is more dependent on the other for needed resources (Chapter 4 in this book by Giunipero and Eltantawy).

At an organisational, supply chain, network and system level, resource orchestration theory might prove to be a useful lens (Chapter 4 in this book by Giunipero and Eltantawy). Sirmon et al. (2007) (building on Barney, 1991) argue that strategic resources, including assets such as a sophisticated supply network, are valuable, rare and difficult to substitute or imitate, and these can lead to sustainable competitive advantage. Resource orchestration theory suggests that strategic resources are accompanied by three types of actions: (1) structuring (management of a firm's resource portfolio); (2) bundling (actions that bring together and integrate resources by stabilising, enriching and pioneering processes that tweak, extend or develop capabilities); and (3) leveraging (actions taken to generate value from a firm's resources, including mobilising and deploying) (Sirmon et al., 2011). Similarly, Helfat (2007) defines resource orchestration as the capacity of managers to create, extend or modify purposefully the resource base of an organisation by assembling and orchestrating configurations of its co-specialised resources. Sirmon et al. (2007, 2011) uncovered the processes by which these effects unfold. Prior work investigating performance management (Koufteros et al., 2014) and product recalls (Ketchen et al., 2014) has adopted a resource orchestration perspective, but Craighead et al. (2020) point out that the theory is yet to be properly utilised within PSCM research. Considering the various orchestration challenges firms face (which are especially pronounced during pandemics or crisis situations), Craighead et al. (2020) position that this would be an ideal place to build momentum for resource orchestration theory within PSCM research.

CONCLUSIONS

In this chapter, we have suggested that PSCM scholars might want to consider novel (at least to PSCM) theoretical approaches to exploring and understanding key business and societal challenges. Building on other calls, we argued that the field of PSCM is uniquely positioned to attempt multilevel theoretical perspectives to gain a comprehensive understanding of key practical challenges (Astley and Van de Ven, 1983; Klein et al., 1999; Craighead et al., 2020). The richness of PSCM settings and phenomena for empirical studies (including supply chains and networks, and global crises such as COVID-19) should be exploited towards elaborating, testing and even developing theory. These efforts should capitalise on the strong connections with practice as evidenced in prior PSCM work. Public and private organisations (small and large) are faced with the reality of addressing a range of PSCM challenges. Theories may constitute useful frames and lenses through which PSCM may make sense of these challenges in an effort to advance practice, policy and science. It is important for PSCM scholars to remember that a good theory (and there are plenty of them to choose from in this book) is practical because it advances our knowledge in a scientific discipline, guides research toward crucial research questions and enlightens the profession of management (Van de Ven, 1989). We hope that discussions provided in this chapter (and the book) will help to bring together prior PSCM work building on management theories and pave the way for as yet underutilised theoretical perspectives from other fields and disciplines to inform future PSCM research efforts and guide practice.

REFERENCES

Allen, C.R., Angeler, D.G., Garmestani, A.S., Gunderson, L.H. and Holling, C.S. (2014). Panarchy: Theory and application. *Ecosystems*, 17(4), 578–589.
Alvesson, M. and Kärreman, D.A.N. (2007). Constructing mystery: Empirical matters in theory development. *Academy of Management Review*, 32(4), 1265–1281.
Amann, M., Roehrich, J.K., Essig, M. and Harland, C. (2014). Driving sustainable supply chain management in the public sector: The importance of public procurement in the EU. *Supply Chain Management: An International Journal*, 19(3), 351–366.
Aryee, S., Walumbwa, F.O., Mondejar, R. and Chu, C.W.L. (2015). Accounting for the influence of overall justice on job performance: Integrating self-determination and social exchange theories. *Journal of Management Studies*, 52, 231–252.
Astley, W.G. and Van de Ven, A.H. (1983). Central perspectives and debates in organization theory. *Administrative Science Quarterly*, 28, 245–273.

Bacharach, S.B. (1989). Organizational theories: Some criteria for evaluation. *Academy of Management Review*, 14(4), 496–515.

Barlow, J., Roehrich, J.K. and Wright, S. (2013). Europe sees mixed results from public-private partnerships for building and managing health care facilities and services. *Health Affairs*, 32(1), 146–154.

Barney, J.B. (1991). Firm resources and sustained competitive advantage. *Journal of Management*, 17(1), 99–120.

Barney, J.B., Ketchen Jr, D.J., Wright, M., Sirmon, D.G., Hitt, M.A., et al. (2010). Resource orchestration to create competitive advantage: Breadth, depth, and life cycle effects. *Journal of Management*, 37 (5), 1390–1412.

Blau, P. (1964). *Exchange and Power in Social Life*. New York: Wiley.

Bouazzaoui, M., Wu, H.-J., Roehrich, J.K., Squire, B. and Roath, T. (2020). Justice in inter-organizational relationships: A literature review and future research agenda. *Industrial Marketing Management*, 87, 128–137.

Byrne, D. (1998). *Complexity Theory and the Social Sciences*. London: Routledge.

Caldwell, N.D., Roehrich, J.K. and Davies, A.C. (2009). Procuring complex performance in construction: London Heathrow Terminal 5 and a Private Finance Initiative Hospital. *Journal of Purchasing and Supply Management*, 15(3), 178–186.

Caldwell, N., Roehrich, J.K. and George, G. (2017). Social value creation and relational coordination in public-private collaborations. *Journal of Management Studies*, 54(6), 906–928.

Caniato, F., Harland, C., Johnsen, T., Moretto, A. and Ronchi, S. (2020). The art and science of procurement: Revisiting Leonardo da Vinci: Editorial of the 2019 IPSERA Conference Special Issue. *Journal of Purchasing and Supply Management*, 26(4), 100650.

Carter, C.R. (2011). A call for theory: The maturation of the supply chain management discipline. *Journal of Supply Chain Management*, 47(2), 3–7.

Checkland, P. (1981). *Systems Thinking, Systems Practice*. Chichester: Wiley.

Chesbrough, H. (2020). To recover faster from Covid-19, open up: Managerial implications from an open innovation perspective. *Industrial Marketing Management*, 88, 410–413.

Chicksand, D., Watson, G., Walker, H., Radnor, Z. and Johnston, R. (2012). Theoretical perspectives in purchasing and supply chain management: An analysis of the literature. *Supply Chain Management: An International Journal*, 17(4), 454–472.

Child, J. (1972). Organizational structure, environment, and performance – The role of strategic choice. *Sociology*, 6, 1–22.

Chiniara, M. and Bentein, K. (2015). Linking servant leadership to individual performance: Differentiating the mediating role of autonomy, competence and relatedness need satisfaction. *Leadership Quarterly*, 27(1), 124–141.

Choi, T., Dooley, K. and Rungtusanatham, M. (2001). Supply networks and complex adaptive systems: Control versus emergence. *Journal of Operations Management*, 19, 351–366.

Coase, R.H. (1937). The nature of the firm. *Economica*, 4(16), 386–405.

Colquitt, J.A. and Zapata-Phelan, C.P. (2007). Trends in theory building and theory testing: A five decade study of the Academy of Management Journal. *Academy of Management Journal*, 50(6), 1281–1303.

Craighead, C.W., Ketchen Jr, D.J. and Darby, J.L. (2020). Pandemics and supply chain management research: Toward a theoretical toolbox. *Decision Sciences*, 51(4), 838–866.

Croom, S.R., Romano, P. and Giannakis, M. (2000). Supply chain management: An analytical framework for critical literature review. *European Journal of Purchasing and Supply Management*, 6, 67–83.

Cyert, R.M. and March, J.G. (1963). *A Behavioral Theory of the Firm*. Englewood Cliffs, NJ: Prentice Hall.

Dahlmann, F. and Roehrich, J.K. (2019). Sustainable supply chain management and partner engagement to manage climate change information. *Business Strategy and the Environment*, 28, 1632–1647.

Deci, E.L., Eghrarl, H., Patrick, B.C. and Leone, D.R. (1994). Facilitating internalization: The self determination theory perspective. *Journal of Personality*, 62, 119–142.

Deci, E.L., Olafsen, A.H. and Ryan, R.M. (2017). Self-determination theory in work organizations: The state of a science. *Annual Review of Organizational Psychology and Organizational Behavior*, 4, 19–43.

DeWitt, T., Giunipero, L.C. and Melton, H.L. (2006). Clusters and supply chain management: the Amish experience. *International Journal of Physical Distribution & Logistics Management*, 36(4), 289–308.

DiMaggio, P.J. and Powell, W.W. (1983). The iron cage revisited: Institutional isomorphism and collective rationality in organizational fields. *American Sociological Review*, 147–160.

Dooley, K. (2020). Complexity science and the organization sciences: 1999–2018. In D. Kiel (ed.), *Chaos Theory in the Social Sciences*. Ann Arbor, MI: University of Michigan Press.

Dubin, R. (1978). *Theory Development*. New York: Free Press.

Eisenhardt, K.M. (1989). Agency theory: An assessment and review. *Academy of Management Review*, 14(1), 57–74.

Ellram, L.M., Harland, C.M., van Weele, A., Essig, M., Johnsen, T., et al. (2020). Purchasing and supply management's identity: Crisis? What crisis? *Journal of Purchasing and Supply Management*, 26(1), 100583.

Ellram, L.M., Tate, W.L. and Billington, C. (2008). Offshore outsourcing of professional services: A transaction cost economics perspective. *Journal of Operations Management*, 26(2), 148–163.

Ellram, L.M., Tate, W.L. and Feitzinger, E.G. (2013). Factor-market rivalry and competition for supply chain resources. *Journal of Supply Chain Management*, 49(1), 29–46.

Emerson, R.M. (1962). Power-dependence relations. *American Sociological Review*, 27(1), 31–41.

Essig, M., Glas, A., Selviaridis, K. and Roehrich, J.K. (2016). Performance-based contracting in business markets. *Industrial Marketing Management*, 59, 5–11.

Forrester, J.W. (1994). System dynamics, systems thinking, and soft OR. *System Dynamics Review*, 10(2–3), 245–256.

Freeman, R.E. (1984). *Strategic Management: A Stakeholder Approach*. Boston, MA: Pitman.

Gagné, M. and Deci, E.L. (2005). Self-determination theory and work motivation. *Journal of Organizational Behavior*, 26(4), 331–362.

Granovetter, M.S. (1973). The strength of weak ties. *American Journal of Sociology*, 78(6), 1360–1380.

Grimm, C.M (2008). The application of industrial organization economics to supply chain management research. *Journal of Supply Chain Management*, 44(2), 16–21.

Grover, V. and Malhotra, M.K. (2003). Transaction cost framework in operations and supply chain management research: theory and measurement. *Journal of Operations Management*, 21(4), 457–473.

Hambrick, D.C. (2007). The field of management's devotion to theory: too much of a good thing? *Academy of Management Journal*, 50(6), 1346–1352.

Hannan, M.T. and Freeman, J. (1977). The population ecology of organizations. *American Journal of Sociology*, 82(5), 929–964.

Hannan, M.T. and Freeman, J. (1984). Structural inertia and organizational change. *American Sociological Review*, 49(2), 149–164.

Harland, C.M. (1996). Supply chain management: Relationships, chains and networks. *British Journal of Management*, 7, S63–S81.

Harland C.M. (2021). Discontinuous wefts: weaving a more interconnected supply chain management tapestry. *Journal of Supply Chain Management*, 57(1), 27–40.

Harland, C.M., Lamming, R.C., Walker, H., Phillips, W.E., Caldwell, N.D., et al. (2006). Supply management: Is it a discipline? *International Journal of Operations and Production Management*, 26(7), 730–753.

Hart, S.L. (1995). A natural-resource-based view of the firm. *Academy of Management Review*, 20(4), 986–1014.

Hartmann, A., Roehrich, J.K., Frederiksen, L. and Davies, A. (2014). Procuring complex performance: The transition process in public infrastructure. *International Journal of Operations and Production Management*, 32(2), 174–194.

Hayes, R.H., Wheelwright, S.C. and Clark, K.B. (1988). *Dynamic Manufacturing: Creating the Learning Organization*. New York: Simon & Schuster.

Helfat, C.E. (2007). *Dynamic Capabilities: Understanding Strategic Change in Organizations*. New York: Wiley Blackwell.

Hill, T. (1989). *Manufacturing Strategy: Text and Cases*. Homewood, IL: Richard D. Irwin.

Hoejmose, S.U., Roehrich, J.K. and Grosvold, J. (2014). Is doing more, doing better? The relationship between responsible supply chain management and corporate reputation. *Industrial Marketing Management*, 43(1), 77–90.

Holland, J. (1995). *Hidden Order: How Adaptation Builds Complexity*. New York: Basic Books.

Howard, M.B., Roehrich, J.K., Lewis, M.A. and Squire, B. (2019). Converging and diverging govern-ance mechanisms: The role of (dys)function in long-term inter-organizational relationships. *British Journal of Management*, 30(3), 624–644.

Hult, G.T.M., Craighead C.W. and Ketchen Jr, D.J. (2010). Risk uncertainty and supply chain decisions: A real options perspective. *Decision Sciences*, 41, 435–458.

Inyang, B.J. (2008). The challenges of evolving and developing management indigenous theories and practices in Africa. *International Journal of Business Management*, 3(12), 122–132.

Jackson, M.C. (2003). *Systems Thinking: Creative Holism for Managers*. Chichester: Wiley.

Kache, F. and Seuring, S. (2017). Challenges and opportunities of digital information at the intersec-tion of big data analytics and supply chain management. *International Journal of Operations and Production Management*, 37(1), 10–36.

Kahneman, D. and Tversky, A. (1979). Prospect theory: An analysis of decision under risk. *Econometrica*, 47(2), 263–291.

Kalra, J., Lewis, M.A. and Roehrich, J.K. (2021). Manifestation of coordination failures in service triads. *Supply Chain Management: An International Journal*, 26(3), 341–358.

Kelley, H.H. (1973). The process of causal attribution. *American Psychologist*, 28, 103–128.

Ketchen Jr, D.J., Crook, T.R. and Craighead, C.W. (2014). From supply chains to supply ecosystems: Implications for strategic sourcing research and practice. *Journal of Business Logistics*, 35(3), 165–171.

Ketokivi, M. and Choi, T. (2014). Renaissance of case research as a scientific method. *Journal of Operations Management*, 32(5), 232–240.

Klein, K.J., Tosi, H. and Canella, A.A. (1999). Multilevel theory building: benefits, barriers, and new developments. *Academy of Management Review*, 24(2), 243–248.

Kogut, B. and Zander, U. (1992). Knowledge of the firm, combinative capabilities, and the replication of technology. *Organization Science*, 3(3), 383–397.

Koufteros, X., Verghese, A.J. and Lucianetti, L. (2014). The effect of performance measurement systems on firm performance: A cross-sectional and a longitudinal study. *Journal of Operations Management*, 32(6), 313–336.

Kreye, M., Roehrich, J.K. and Lewis, M.A. (2015). Servitizing manufacturers: The importance of service complexity and contractual and relational capabilities. *Production Planning and Control*, 26(14–15), 1233–1246.

Leenders, M.R., Fearon, H.E. and England, W.B. (1980). *Purchasing and Materials Management*. Burr Ridge, IL: Irwin Professional Publishing.

Liu, Y., Zhang, J. and Huang, G. (2011). The working mechanism of organizational justice's effects on counterproductive work behavior: A self-determination-theory approach. *Science of Science and Management of S. & T*, 32(8), 162–172.

Manzini, R.B. and Di Serio, L.C. (2017). Current thinking on cluster theory and its translation in economic geography and strategic and operations management: Is a reconciliation possible? *Competitiveness Review*, 27(4), 366–389.

March, J.G. (1991). Exploration and exploitation in organizational learning. *Organization Science*, 2(1), 71–87.

Maslow, A.H. (1943). Theory of human motivation, *Psychological Review*, 50(4), 370–396.

Meredith, J.R. and Amoako-Gyampah, K. (1990). The genealogy of operations management. *Journal of Operations Management*, 9(2), 146–167.

Morgeson, F.P., Mitchell, T.R. and Liu, D. (2015). Event system theory: An event-oriented approach to the organizational sciences. *Academy of Management Review*, 40, 515–537.

Odum, E.P. and Barrett, G.W. (1971). *Fundamentals of Ecology*. Philadelphia, PA: Saunders.

Oliver, R.L. (1977). Effect of expectation and disconfirmation on postexposure product evaluations – An alternative interpretation. *Journal of Applied Psychology*, 62(4), 480–486.

Oliver, R.K. and M.D. Webber (1992). Supply chain management: Logistics catches up with strategy. In M. Christopher (ed.), *Logistics: The Strategic Issues*. London: Chapman & Hall.

Pantin, C.P.A. (1968). *The Relations Between the Sciences*. Cambridge: Cambridge University Press.

Parkhe, A. (1993). Strategic alliance structuring: A game theoretic and transaction cost examination of interfirm cooperation. *Academy of Management Journal*, 36(4), 794–829.

Pfeffer, J. (1993). Barriers to the advance of organisational science: Paradigm development as a dependent variable. *Academy of Management Review*, 18, 599–620.

Pfeffer, J. (1995). Mortality, reproducibility, and the persistence of styles of theory. *Organization Science*, 6(6), 681–686.

Pfeffer, J. and Salancik, G.R. (1978). *The External Control of Organizations: A Resource Dependence Perspective*. New York: Harper & Row.

Preuss, L. (2009). Ethical sourcing codes of large UK-based corporations: Prevalence, content, limitations. *Journal of Business Ethics*, 88(4), 735–747.

Reinholt, M., Pedersen, T. and Foss, N.J. (2011). Why a central network position isn't enough: The role of motivation and ability for knowledge sharing in employee networks. *Academy of Management Journal*, 54(6), 1277–1297.

Rindfleisch, A. and Heide, J.B. (1997). Transaction cost analysis: Past, present, and future applications. *Journal of Marketing*, 61(4), 30–54.

Robson, M.J., Schlegelmilch, B.B. and Bojkowszky, B. (2012). Resource deployment stability and performance in international research and development alliances: A self-determination theory explanation. *Journal of International Marketing*, 20(1), 1–18.

Roehrich, J.K., Hoejmose, S. and Overland, V. (2017). Driving green supply chain management performance through supplier selection and value internalisation: A self-determination theory perspective. *International Journal of Operations and Production Management*, 37(4), 489–509.

Roehrich, J.K. and Kivleniece, I. (2021). Creating and distributing sustainable value through public-private collaborative projects. In G. George, M.R. Hass, H. Joshi, A. McGahan and P. Tracey (eds), *Handbook on the Business of Sustainability: The Organization, Implementation, and Practice of Sustainable Growth*. Cheltenham, UK and Northampton, MA, USA: Edward Elgar Publishing.

Roehrich, J.K. and Lewis, M.A. (2014). Procuring complex performance: Implications for exchange governance complexity. *International Journal of Operations and Production Management*, 32(2), 221–241.

Roehrich, J.K., Selviaridis, K., Kalra, J., van der Valk, W. and Fang, F. (2020). Inter-organisational governance: A review, conceptualisation and extension. *Production Planning and Control*, 31(6), 453–469.

Roehrich, J.K., Tyler, B.B, Kalra, J. and Squire, B. (2021). The decision process of contracting in supply chain management. In T. Choi, J. Li, D. Rogers, J. Rungtusanatham, T. Schoenherr, T. and S. Wagner (eds), *Handbook of Supply Chain Management*. Oxford: Oxford University Press.

Rungtusanatham, M.J. and Salvador, F. (2008). From mass production to mass customization: Hindrance factors, structural inertia, and transition hazard. *Production and Operations Management*, 17(3), 385–396.

Ryan, R.M. and Deci, E.L. (2000). Self-determination theory and the facilitation of intrinsic motivation, social development, and well-being. *American Psychologist*, 55(1), 68–78.

Sarkis, J., Zhu, Q. and Lai, K.-h. (2011). An organizational theoretic review of green supply chain management literature. *International Journal of Production Economics*, 130(1), 1–15.

Scott, J. (1988). Social network analysis. *Sociology*, 22(1), 109–127.

Scott, W.R. (2005). Institutional theory: Contributing to a theoretical research program. *Great Minds in Management: The Process of Theory Development*, 37(2), 460–484.

Selviaridis, K. and van der Valk, W. (2019). Framing contractual performance incentives: Effects on supplier behaviour. *International Journal of Operations and Production Management*, 39(2), 190–213.

Simon, H. A. (1957). *Models of Man: Social and Rational*. Oxford: Wiley.

Sirmon, D.G., Hitt, M.A. and Ireland, R.D. (2007). Managing firm resources in dynamic environments to create value: Looking inside the black box. *Academy of Management Review*, 32, 273–292.

Sirmon, D.G., Hitt, M.A., Ireland, R.D. and Gilbert, B.A. (2011). Resource orchestration to create competitive advantage breadth, depth, and life cycle effects. *Journal of Management*, 37, 1390–1412.

Spence, M. (1973). Job market signaling. *Quarterly Journal of Economics*, 87(3), 355–374.

Spina, G., Caniato, F., Luzzini, D. and Ronchi, S. (2016). Assessing the use of external grand theories in purchasing and supply management research. *Journal of Purchasing and Supply Management*, 22(1), 18–30.

Tate, W.L., Ellram, L.M., Bals, L., Hartmann, E. and Van der Valk, W. (2010). An agency theory perspective on the purchase of marketing services. *Industrial Marketing Management*, 39(5), 806–819.

Tate, W.L., Ellram, L.M. and Kirchoff, J.F. (2010). Corporate social responsibility reports: A thematic analysis related to supply chain management. *Journal of Supply Chain Management*, 46(1), 19–44.

Teece, D.J., Pisano, G. and Shuen, A. (1997). Dynamic capabilities and strategic management. *Strategic Management Journal*, 18(7), 509–533.

Touboulic, A. and Walker, H.L. (2015). Theories in sustainable supply chain management: a structured literature review. *International Journal of Physical Distribution and Logistics Management*, 45(1–2), 16–42.

Tushman, M.L. and Nadler, D.A. (1978). Information processing as an integrating concept in organizational design. *Academy of Management Review*, 3(3), 613–624.

Van den Broeck, A., Ferris, D.L., Chang, C.H. and Rosen, C.C. (2016). A review of self-determination theory's basic psychological needs at work. *Journal of Management*, 42(5), 1195–1229.

Van de Ven, A.H. (1989). Nothing is quite so practical as a good theory. *Academy of Management Review*, 14(4), 486–489.

Van Maanen, J. (1995). Style as theory. *Organization Science*, 6(1), 133–143.

Van Maanen, J., Sorensen, J.B. and Mitchell, T.R. (2007). The interplay between theory and method. *Academy of Management Review*, 32(4), 1145–1154.

von Bertalanffy, L. (1951). General system theory – A new approach to unity of science. *Human Biology*, 23, 303–361.

von Bertalanffy, L. (1968). *General Systems Theory*. New York: Braziller.

Von Neumann, J. and Morgenstern, O. (1944). *Theory of Games and Economic Behavior*. Princeton, NJ: Princeton University Press.

Wahba, M.A. and Bridwell, L.G. (1973). Maslow reconsidered: A review of research on the need hierarchy theory. *Academy of Management Proceedings*, 1, 514–520.

Weber, L. and Mayer, K.J. (2011). Designing effective contracts: Exploring the influence of framing and expectations. *Academy of Management Review*, 36(1), 53–75.

Webster, F.E. and Wind, Y. (1972). *Organizational Buying Behavior*. Upper Saddle River, NJ: Prentice Hall.

Weibel, A. (2007). Formal control and trustworthiness: Shall the twain never meet? *Group and Organization Management*, 32(4), 500–517.

Wiener, N. (1948). *Cybernetics or Control and Communication in the Animal and the Machine*. Cambridge, MA: Technology Press.

Williamson, O.E. (1975). *Markets and Hierarchies*. New York: Free Press.

Williamson, O.E. (1981). The economics of organization: The transaction cost approach. *American Journal of Sociology*, 87(3), 548–577.

Womack, J., Jones, D. and Roos, D. (1990). *The Machine that Changed the World*. New York: Macmillan Publishing.

Zheng, J., Roehrich, J.K. and Lewis, M.A. (2008). The dynamics of contractual and relational governance: Evidence from long-term public–private procurement arrangements. *Journal of Purchasing and Supply Management*, 14(1), 43–54.

6. Enhancing theorizing in purchasing and supply management through middle-range theories

Jenny Bäckstrand and Árni Halldórsson

INTRODUCTION

With this chapter we present middle-range theory (MRT) as a promising way of both specifying what theory is in the context of purchasing and supply management (PSM), and how these theories come about, that is, theorizing. MRT derives from specific practical problems and pertains to a local setting but can, due to its modifiable feature, be transferred to other industrial sectors than the one being investigated.

Research in purchasing and supply management (PSM) aims to develop and test theory that advances knowledge relevant to practitioners, but has yet to establish a firm status as an academic discipline as 'it lacks its own theories and common themes of research' (Ellram et al., 2019). Whilst one key aim of advancing knowledge of PSM is theory development, the approaches towards this vary. Current knowledge creation approaches take different forms. One approach is borrowing theories and concepts from external grand theories (EGTs), for example transaction cost analysis to analyse PSM problems such as outsourcing and supplier relationship management. Another emerging approach to theorizing is situated in PSM practice, in which MRT offers a relevant venue. Followed by a definition of MRT and the call for these in PSM, the chapter argues that the broad scope of PSM, ranging from professional to theoretical knowledge, can benefit from MRT. The intellectual foundation of MRT as it could apply to PSM is established, and based on this, examples of MRT in PSM are presented. Whilst the chapter first sets out the concepts and basics of MRT in PSM, it then seeks to advance this by identifying guiding principles for theorizing PSM through MRT.

WHAT IS MRT?

In contrast to well-established EGTs which are commonly used in PSM, such as transaction cost analysis, that build upon a well-established range of concepts and assumptions, MRT can be defined in terms of 'solutions to problems that contain a limited number of assumptions and considerable accuracy and detail in the problem specification' (Weick, 1989). More specially, MRT pertain to 'Context-specific conceptualization providing theoretically grounded insight readily applicable to an empirical context' (Craighead et al., 2016).

At first glance, MRT can be regarded as a way of categorizing frameworks and models and enhance their legitimacy in a larger hierarchy of theories. To further understand MRT, it is important to not only take such a static perspective, but also view these from the perspective of 'how do MRTs come about?'. This is where the concept of theorizing becomes a helpful distinction in our overall theory development endeavour. Swedberg (2012) states the following:

The expression "to theorize" roughly means what you do to produce a theory. While *theorizing* is primarily a process, *theory* is the end-product. The two obviously belong together and complement each other. But to focus mainly on theory, which is what is done today, means that the ways in which a theory is actually produced are being neglected.

Following this logic, MRT does not refer to a specific theory but is rather a theory level and an approach to theorizing that aims to integrate theoretical and empirical research. For PSM, MRT can be seen as an acting bridge between 'grand', established theories such as EGTs, and concepts and frameworks that capture a particular managerial situation or a challenge. MRTs in PSM stem from knowledge that the researcher has, for example, gained through empirical case studies and conceptualized analytically or vice versa (Wacker, 1998). Theorizing a middle-range theory is hence inherently abductive in its approach (Kovács and Spens, 2005).

WHY IS MRT NEEDED IN PSM?

Adopting the logic of MRT in PSM can be motivated in various ways. First of all, the debate on whether PSM can be regarded as a mature academic field is still quite lively (see, e.g., Ellram et al., 2019). Instead of relying upon the use of EGTs, PSM scholars may want to revisit their view on what theory is and how it comes about, to avoid misconceptions with respect to status of the field. Perhaps more importantly, we need to be more confident that our concepts and frameworks are indeed significant as theoretical contributions on their own. We do not always need EGTs to gain legitimacy when pursuing academic publications. Second, MRT considers the local and the situational when displaying research synthesis into a conceptual framework and seeks to enhance application and successful intervention in a particular setting rather than presenting a more overall and abstract view. In this respect, MRT aligns well with recent calls for engaged scholarship (e.g., Bäckstrand and Halldórsson, 2019) and engaged theorization (Touboulic et al., 2020). By introducing MRT, we suggest that it is less relevant to aim for the state of having one single theory in or of PSM; rather, we should advance our ability to theorize and develop applicable knowledge.

BASIC CONCEPTUALIZATION AND EXAMPLES

PSM as Profession and Theory: A Quest for a Broad Approach to Theorizing

PSM entails a broad range in its contribution to knowledge advancement. On one hand, PSM is associated with increased professionalization of managerial practices in purchasing and supply management in public and private organizations. Within these, PSM ranges from operational processes to strategic issues at the highest management level. Externally, PSM has a significant contribution to the strategic success of the organization by managing relationships with one key stakeholder, namely the supplier base. On the other hand, PSM can be seen as an applied field of research closely related to, and growing out of, areas such as operations management, industrial marketing, supply chain management and logistics, which are all seeking to achieve status as an academic discipline using and contributing to theories.

Our point of departure is that this range – professionalization of managerial practices and the strive for theoretical maturity – should shape our way of theorizing PSM. To underpin this view, we introduce Boyer's (1990) view of scholarship and research as a principle that sets the foundation for our view on research in PSM, and that becomes the fundamental principle for viewing MRT as a means to enhance theorizing in and of PSM. This perspective advocates a broader view on research than only discovery (what is to be known? what is yet to be found?), two features of which can serve as the intellectual underpinning of the abovementioned range of PSM: scholarship of integration, and scholarship of application, respectively.

First, scholarship of integration suggests that knowledge is created at intersections: 'at the boundaries where fields converge'. Advancement of knowledge is rooted in established theory. However, in applied fields such as PSM where few, if any, comprehensive theories or even a set of internal theories exist, and where the roles and competences of professionals are constantly developing (Bals et al., 2019), a common way to speed up development, boost maturity and increase the ability to deal with complex problems is to 'borrow' concepts and frameworks from EGTs (Halldórsson et al., 2015; Spina et al., 2016). Albeit not necessarily all-encompassing, EGTs present a rather high level of abstraction and are rooted in more mature fields of social sciences (management, business, economics, sociology). Examples of EGTs and their application in PSM are:

1. Transaction cost analysis: make-or-buy/outsourcing decision; information sharing between buyers and suppliers; supply chain governance; adversarial relationships.
2. Resource-based view: competitive advantage in and through unique buyer–supplier relationships; criticality of suppliers.
3. Agency theory: incentives and risk in contracts; cost monitoring of suppliers; supplier risk.
4. Network theory: relationship management; supplier selection; interdependence in supply networks.

These theories differ in terms of, for example, unit of analysis, problem orientation and behavioural assumptions. An EGT concerns an overall problem or a core question. For example, transaction cost analysis seeks to explain the most efficient boundaries of the firm, that is, 'why do firms exist?' (Williamson, 1979), and the resource-based view concerns competitive advantage by asking 'how do firms differ?' (Teece et al., 1994). Although the application of these theories gives legitimacy to the individual researcher and PSM as such, the key reason for their use must always be the conceptual proximity between the core concepts of EGTs and the PSM problem at hand. For example, agency theory departs from the problem of information asymmetry between two actors; in PSM, this resonates very well with buyer–supplier relationships, and corresponding problems and concepts that have emerged from within PSM, such as collaborative arrangements, contract management, and supply risk are intended to overcome some of these problems (Halldórsson et al., 2015). Since there are few if any specific and well-established theories at the core of PSM, this borrowing has had a great influence on theorizing and the status of PSM today. Whilst EGTs give us the necessary theoretical embeddedness, PSM gives us the view of the professionals and the vocabulary that catches their perspective.

Second, scholarship of application states that knowledge creation goes in both directions between practice and theory. It requires research design that is sensitive to the context, that is, able to establish closeness to people, processes and practices within which the phenomenon under study takes place. It also requires a process orientation: an interaction between the researcher and practitioner over time. Whilst this dimension of scholarship is less developed than that of integration, recent calls for increased focus on relevance in PSM (Knight et al., 2016) have been followed up by more specific observations on what this may entail. In particular, PSM has been encouraged to follow the logic of engaged scholarship as set out by Van de Ven and Johnson (2006, p. 803): 'a collaborative form of inquiry in which academics and practitioners leverage their different perspectives and competencies to co-produce knowledge about a complex problem or phenomenon that exists under conditions of uncertainty found in the world'. In PSM, this underpins research designs that are very much in line with 'proximity to practice' as the core feature of MRT; professionals and researchers interact closely in a co-creative manner in order to enhance the relevance of the problem, but also to promote transfer of knowledge and create opportunity for interventions and to study efforts and impact of transformative actions (Bäckstrand and Halldórsson, 2019; Touboulic et al., 2020). Ultimately, these research designs, which are based on the idea of engaged scholarship, aim to present an actionable knowledge, which resonates well with the view of Craighead et al. (2016) on MRT as being 'readily applicable'. By this, MRT contributes to the learning of individuals and organizations that enhances their capabilities in future actions.

PSM cannot be regarded as an EGT itself and the field does not have one overall EGT to refer to. However, the theoretical status of PSM and the way in which it develops resonates well with MRT. Based on the two underpinnings of scholarship outlined above, Figure 6.1 provides a summary of two key components of theorizing aiming for actionable knowledge, suggesting that theorizing in PSM rests on scholarship of integration and application.

Figure 6.1   Two key components of theorizing in PSM that lead to actionable knowledge

Whilst scholarship of both integration and application serve as an intellectual prelude to MRT, we observe that MRT itself entails attributes and has been given an aim that to some extent combines these two types of scholarship. MRT departs from a practical problem and may be presented with the use of sensitizing concepts, that is, concepts that emerge from the empirical field and that may be specific to PSM; for example 'portfolio analysis' and 'early supplier involvement'. These emerge from concrete, practical problems and contain *in vivo* codes – that is, language used by the practitioners – but can be further embedded in EGTs such as contingency theory and knowledge-based theories of the firm, respectively. MRT offers thus a complementary approach to theorizing in PSM where the theory-development potential of research should start with but also lead to practical relevance.

EXAMPLES OF MRT IN PSM

In PSM, key features of MRT are multiple levels of analysis and proximity to practice, hence making them more actionable than grand theories. Based on a literature review and input from the International Purchasing and Supply Education and Research Association (IPSERA) community, this section provides analysis of current frameworks in PSM that can be regarded as MRT.

One example of a middle-range theory in PSM is the Kraljic matrix (Kraljic, 1983) that was conceptualized based on empirical experience (Beer, 2006), adapted to align with local applications in PSM literature, and is used in various versions by a large number of PSM professionals. The upper part of Figure 6.2 depicts the original version of the Krajlic matrix as described in the paper, though never depicted in the original publication in a figurative form. The horizontal and vertical dimensions serve as determinants for the categorization into one of the four areas in the middle. The vocabulary in the framework consists largely of sensitizing concepts, which emerged out of the empirical field, but are specific to PSM. With its multiple dimensions, the matrix resonates with various EGTs. Overall, the use of dimensions to determine a particular category in the matrix resonates with contingency theory; the course of action is dependent upon situations particular to the individual organization. More specificly, amongst the preferred courses of actions, the labels of 'leverage' and 'bottleneck' refer to a power imbalance between the buyer and the supplier, which has its theoretical roots in political science (Cox, 2004).

Over time, the original Krajlic matrix has been subject to discussion amongst scholars in PSM, and accordingly developed to capture a variety of different situations, especially through the determinant dimensions of the framework. The lower levels of Figure 6.2 depict four adaptions of the original matrix, the layouts are based on the works of the original authors but illustrated here in a uniform way. Starting from the left, a new focus becomes the 'type of purchase' (Olsen and Ellram, 1997), followed by 'supply strategies' and a more outspoken power-perspective (Gelderman and van Weele, 2002). Somewhat contrary to this is 'management strategies' (Dubois and Pedersen, 2002), which is more relationship-oriented than the power approach. Finally, furthest to the right is an example of a quantified model for 'decision support' (Montgomery et al., 2018). Another indicator of MRT in PSM is the visualization of the purchasing process model in Figure 6.3; all illustrations are based on the original authors' work, but the layouts are modified for uniformity across the different models.

There are many different ways of illustrating the purchasing process models available (Bäckstrand et al., 2019) but the illustration by van Weele (2002) was found to be the most widespread process model, both in its original form and in adopted forms. As with the Kraljic matrix, the process model has been subject to adaptions to capture different situations. Some adaptions propose a model with fewer steps (Lysons and Farrington, 2006) and some with

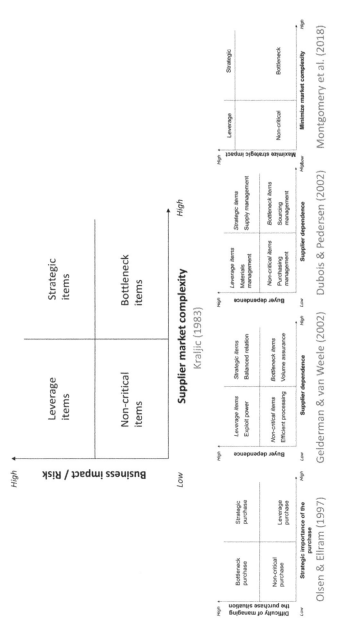

Figure 6.2   *The purchasing matrix portfolio analysis (top) and four adaptions (below)*

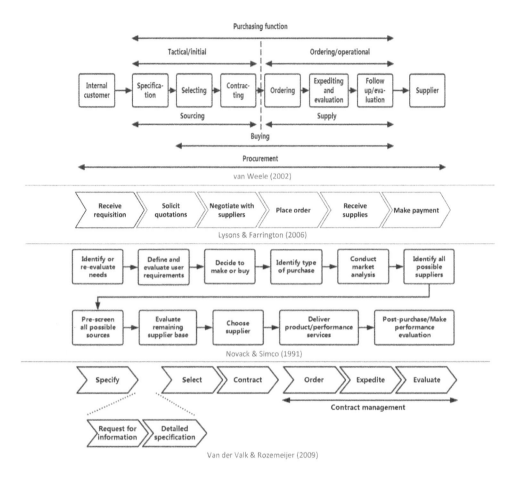

Figure 6.3   The purchasing process model by van Weele (top) and three adaptions (below)

more steps (Novack and Simco, 1991), whereas others have adapted the model to serve a specific purpose, such as buying business services (Van der Valk and Rozemeijer, 2009).

THEORIZING PSM WITH MRT: A COCKTAIL WITH A TWIST

It is evident from the above that MRT suggests a pluralist approach to PMS. However, this is not a matter of having many concepts or frameworks. Rather, MRT pertains to a modifiable feature of theory and theorizing that makes it attractive to use. To explain this further we draw upon an analogy to the skills in mixology. Every serious bartender seeks to make the customers the best drink they ever tasted. To do so, they not only need to identify the right cocktail for the customer, but also need to master the skills of art and theatre when building, twisting and delivering the drink. Now, what has this to do with MRT and PSM?

The cocktail metaphor helps us to understand MRT as a type of theory in PSM, but more importantly it helps in illustrating its creation, that is, theorizing. A cocktail is a creation of various ingredients using specific dimensions such as taste, appearance, temperature, nose-flavour and texture-mouthfeel (Kaplan et al., 2014). The bartender uses a mix of these to create a local experience to the customer, often departing from a specific situation or occasion. Whilst the deep, smoky-sweet flavor of rum in Dark 'N' Stormy may suit well to a melancholic November evening in Scandinavia, the refreshing, sparkling and citrusy French 75, which uses gin to give an extra punch, is well suited to celebrations on a sunny day. A good cocktail delivers experience, just as MRT seeks to bring principles into practice; it is situational, departing from the manager's own context, aiming to create a positive experience to the solution of a practical problem.

MRT is not pure or grand, like transaction cost analysis and the resource-based view. An EGT is to MRT what spirits – gin, vodka, rum or tequila – are to many cocktails. They are the base; they set the baseline for the taste, for the solution. They give us a core concept at a higher level of abstraction. Like an EGT, these spirits are well known and widely used; but seldom on their own. They hardly deliver a unique consuming experience, apart from booziness, if consumed without any modification or guidelines. Just as MRT often either implicitly relates to EGTs or even explicitly makes use of concepts and logics from an EGT, cocktails are in most cases built on a base. Think of MRT as a tasteful, classic cocktail such as the Margarita. Classic in the sense that it is not only old but has turned out to be useful to the manager over a longer period and in a variety of situations. A Margarita is embedded in tequila as the base, just as the power concept in the Krajlic matrix refers to political science as the base.

To prelude a unique experience by the consumer, the base must relate to something specific: a context or a situation. To give the cocktail a character, or make a theoretical framework situational, we need modifying agents. This is the role of lime and the liqueur Cointreau in a Margarita. In MRT, we decide which dimensions or items to use, and how to operationalize them. In the Krajlic matrix, for example, we would define supplier base complexity not from a long list of items from a textbook, but rather by selecting a few dimensions from such a list that the manager finds useful. Over time, the view on supply risk, as part of that concept, has developed as businesses have faced new and often formerly unknown major disruptions. Similarly, a Margarita has developed over time; it can be twisted into a frozen creation, made on ice or even frozen pineapple.

A third element in the cocktail are the special flavouring and colouring agents; or in our case, a dash of syrup to further enhance the local – visual and aromatic – character of the experience. Temperature and appearance contribute to the final touch, just like the shape and the way by which MRT is displayed. In PSM, two-by-two matrixes seem to be quite popular. Finally, as for cocktails, MRT does not deliver experience on its own, through the mix outlined in the recipe; it relies upon the bartenders' – or the researchers' – theatric and artistic skills in mixing and communicating with the receiver.

ADVANCED GUIDING PRINCIPLES FOR MRT IN PSM

Whilst the previous sections gave us the underpinnings of MRT and illustrated this by examples from PSM, the following opens for increased use of MRT and its logic when developing and presenting theoretical perspectives in MRT. Two perspectives on MRT in PSM are presented. First, based upon the definition of MRT and our analysis of PSM above, by positioning MRT as a particular level of theory in a wider hierarchy of theories. Second, MRT is given a complementary role of theorizing PSM to the current borrowing theories from other disciplines and engaged scholarship by presenting four modes of theorization.

Theories as Levels: Positioning PSM Research as MRT

Departing from the examples of MRT in PSM above are the Krajlic matrix and the purchasing process models, which contain concepts that originate in an EGT, but the shape of the framework helps to operationalize these and bring them closer to practical use. Figure 6.4 presents a view of theories as a hierarchy (or levels of abstraction), ranging from theories about theories – that is, philosophy of science – through EGTs and MRT towards conceptual frameworks that lie closer to practice.

Figure 6.4   Levels of theory and the bridging role of MRT

A great deal of theorizing in PSM has built upon borrowing theories from other disciplines, or the EGT level. The figure positions MRT in PSM as an 'in-between' kind of theory, bridging the two knowledge creation cycles that, according to the amount of literature, often appear as separate entities. In the ideal world, however, the relationships between the levels are two-sided. Next to this bridging role of MRT, three additional distinct features of MRT in PSM can be derived from this: extension of criteria for rigour and relevance; bottom-up; and cumulative.

First, whereas relevance and rigour are considered as difficult to comprehend simultaneously, the levels in Figure 6.4 suggest that the criteria for rigour and relevance must be understood with respect to the level of abstraction at which the researcher operates. Traditionally, much research in PSM refers to external validity as a core quality criterion without considering what level of theory is being proposed. Our notion is that this criterion is valid as regards the higher levels of theory, and when comparing particular results with current theory as we do when establishing an analytical generalizability (Yin, 2018). However, as we move towards lower levels of abstraction such as MRT, and given the nature and role of these in PSM as exemplified above, using this notion of generalizability runs the risk of losing the connection with the applied nature of PSM and the professionals in the field. Therefore, scholars should perhaps rather consider the transferability (Halldórsson and Aastrup, 2003) or even adaptability of their theories as quality criteria to create an impact (Elg et al., 2020). To enhance transferability of the results, research quality criteria must assert both local actionability of the results as well as adaptability of these to other local settings. Second, moving from the bottom and upwards: being an applied discipline, theorizing in PSM has its roots at the bottom of the figure, in the practices and profession of PSM, and moves upwards. Although this is motivated by notions such as phenomenon-driven research (Schwarz and Stensaker, 2014), responding to business challenges, or 'nothing as theoretical as good practice' (Ployhart and Bartunek, 2019), however, too often theorization ends with the presentation of a framework in an academic article. Such output could be given clearer theoretical merits if conceptualized as MRT. Finally, following Bourgeois (1979) who sees MRT as cumulative, ranging from a descriptive, substantive theory towards a formal theory. In this respect, the Krajlic matrix originated as a conceptual framework and substantive theory but has developed into a more formal theory as it gained popularity among professionals and was further advanced by scholars in PSM. Speeding up the process of this upwards transition requires an extension of the quality criterion (see the right-hand side of Figure 6.4) used for assessing the quality of engaged research, as well as use of engaged scholarship-based research design.

MRT as Mode of Theorization

Although PSM might not yet have reached the status of having internal theories (Spina et al., 2016), the field is rich in frameworks and concepts that are specific to the field and/or have emerged during empirical studies of PSM professionals. Given this richness of PSM, and the intellectual background of MRT and its combinatory ability of being context-specific and situational but also theoretically grounded, we suggest that PSM frameworks could benefit from being considered as MRT. To illustrate this, and to understand the position of MRT with respect to the status of PSM, Figure 6.5 presents three different modes of theorizing.

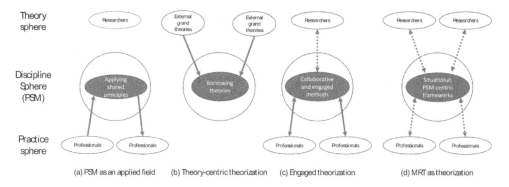

Figure 6.5   *Modes of theorization: MRT as complementary to borrowing theories and engaged theorization*

Beginning from the left, PSM has grown from an applied field (a), with few if any established theories or frameworks, but consisting of concepts and principles that have emerged from practice. This can be seen as precursor to the more advanced modes of theorizing. The second mode of theorizing outlined above is 'theory-centric theorizing' (b), borrowing concepts and frameworks from EGTs to investigate PSM practices (Halldórsson et al., 2015; Spina et al., 2016). The third mode, 'engaged theorizing' (c), is phenomenon-driven research that puts great requirements on the research design and methods to create proximity (Knight et al., 2016) to the practitioners through collaborative research design (Walker et al., 2008), engaged scholarship (Bäckstrand and Halldórsson, 2019) or engaged theorization (Touboulic et al., 2020). Finally, 'MRT as theorization' (d) is depicted as theories that relate to both theory and practice spheres, yet not at the same depth as borrowing theories does with EGTs, or engaged theorization does with the practice. To this end, MRT entails a combinatory approach of theorizing PSM, moving vertically across the three spheres in Figure 6.5 (d). Features of this mode of theorizing include (but are not limited to):

1. Orientation. Situated in a practical problem in the practice sphere (bottom up) that seeks to generate theory that falls between more abstract EGTs at a researcher level and a theory about a specific topic area in PSM.
2. Accumulative. Make use of existing concepts and framework but seek to bring these towards a higher level of abstraction to contribute to (rather than borrow from) current EGTs. For example, PSM provides a firm interorganizational dimension to the resource-based view, that is resources and capabilities that reside in the buyer–supplier relationship.
3. Methodological inseparability. The selection of a research design with features that entail use of the research results (for example, in the form of a prototype) not only enhances the situational feature of MRT but also helps the researcher to understand the adaptability and actionability of the framework proposed.
4. Contributions. By using Whetten's (1989) criterion for contribution, MRT encourages sensitivity to the context, which in turn should result in frameworks that contain factors meaningful to the manager's context and that can be acted upon, that is, be actionable. Moreover, the situational feature of MRTs will encourage contributions with respect to what factors are relevant, and even how they are related. Aiming for Whetten's fourth type of contribution, the 'why' that leads to questioning fundamental assumptions is more likely to occur using higher level of abstraction of EGTs rather than MRT.
5. Research quality. First, in line with Miles et al. (2020), MRT should be of pragmatic value for the participants involved; that is, be actionable, have a certain action orientation. Second, qualitative research that is sensitive to the context: the traditional criterion of external validity as a measure for generalizability is replaced by transferability (Halldórsson and Aastrup, 2003). This is where MRT shows its true strength: factors and their relationships that are explicitly related to the specific context help in creating similarities between the sender and the receiver of the framework. Establishing such similarities and the fact that MRT contains dimensions that are modifiable will enhance applicability of knowledge outside the context in which it is originally generated.

Modes (c) and (d) of theorizing in Figure 6.5 entail active participation of both researchers and practitioners, and aim to generate transformative opportunities or relevant and actionable knowledge. In this way, theorizing becomes to a certain extent inseparable from the research design.

These modes are intended to encourage PSM scholars to conceptualize their research contribution with respect to MRT. We do not necessarily agree with the notion that PSM has no internal theories. Rather, by broadening our understanding of research and scholarship into both integration and application, this allows us to consider the richness of PSM with respect to concepts and frameworks, that have developed over time and that have turned out to be applicable in various sectors.

CONCLUDING REMARKS

As an applied field, purchasing and supply management (PSM) has developed towards an academic discipline through the borrowing of theories and concepts from other more established disciplines, and more recently by emphasizing research design that promotes close interaction between researchers and PSM professionals. Some misconception exists in the field about what theory is, and too often it is primarily defined with respect to grand theories, leaving PSM-specific theories to be labelled as models, frameworks or concepts. When compared with external grand theories (EGTs), a common notion is that PSM lacks an internal theory or a theory of its own. Notably, however, PSM is very rich in frameworks and perspectives that have turned out to be useful across a variety of industrial and public sectors, other than those which were initially being investigated.

MRT can add to not only clarification but also legitimacy of scholarship in PSM with respect to theoretical maturity of the field. This chapter conceptualizes MRT with respect to theorizing in an applied field, such as PSM. Examples of MRT and PSM are presented, and guiding principles for further theorizing in PSM are outlined. Based on this, we want to encourage PSM scholars to make use of MRT as a point of reference in their research, and to be brave in claiming theory and theoretical contributions.

Our conception of MRT suggests that PSM scholars can present good and solid theories without opting to borrow theories and frameworks from external grand theories. MRT is introduced as a way of theorizing, complementing theory-centric approaches such as borrowing concepts and framework from grand theories, as well as methods that emphasize proximity (Knight et al., 2016) to the practitioners through engaged scholarship (Bäckstrand and Halldórsson, 2019) and collaborative research design (Walker et al., 2008). The theoretical frameworks in Figures 6.4 and 6.5 encourage PSM scholars to conceptualize their theoretical contribution with respect to MRT. To enhance transferability of the results, research quality criteria must assert both local applicability of the results as well as adaptability of these to other local settings.

Considering the potential and limitations of the perspective presented above, at least two venues of future research should be considered. First, a comprehensive literature review is needed to populate a greater list of MRTs in PSM to complement the examples presented above. Second, following the lead suggested by Bäckstrand and Halldórsson (2019) and Touboulic et al. (2020), a firmer conceptualization of the relationship between engaged scholarship and MRT is encouraged.

Finally, metaphorically speaking, like a cocktail, MRT is intersectional and situational; it is the result of a creation of ingredients and experience. Cocktails deliver experiences in a certain time and space. The philosophy of cocktails resonates well with PSM as MRT; the ultimate experience of the cocktail, and accordingly the problem-solving capacity of the specific MRT, is not defined by a recipe that is generalizable. Rather, it is based on the adaptability of the recipe, which ultimately becomes actionable, resulting in a true customer experience.

REFERENCES

Bäckstrand, J., and Halldórsson, Á. (2019), 'Engaged scholar(ship) in purchasing and supply management (PSM): creative tension or squeezed in the middle?', *Journal of Purchasing and Supply Management*, 25 (4), 100557. https://doi.org/https://doi.org/10.1016/j.pursup.2019.100557.

Bäckstrand, J., Suurmond, R., van Raaij, E.M., and Chen, C. (2019), 'Purchasing process models: inspiration for teaching purchasing and supply management', *Journal of Purchasing and Supply Management*, 25 (5), 100577. https://doi.org/https://doi.org/10.1016/j.pursup.2019.100577.

Bals, L., Schulze, H., Kelly, S., and Stek, K. (2019), 'Purchasing and supply management (PSM) competencies: current and future requirements', *Journal of Purchasing and Supply Management*, 25 (5), 100572.

Beer, J. (2006), 'To make or to buy – that is (still) the question', *Efficient Purchasing*, 1 (2), 26–35.

Bourgeois, L.I. (1979), 'Toward a method of middle-range theorizing', *Academy of Management Review*, 4 (3), 443–447. https://www.jstor.org/stable/257201bu.

Boyer, E.L. (1990), *Scholarship Reconsidered: Priorities of the Professoriate*. Princeton University Press.

Cox, A. (2004), 'The art of the possible: relationship management in power regimes and supply chains', *Supply Chain Management: An International Journal*, 9 (5), 346–356.

Craighead, C.W., Ketchen Jr, D.J., and Cheng, L. (2016), '"Goldilocks" theorizing in supply chain research: balancing scientific and practical utility via middle-range theory', *Transportation Journal*, 55 (3), 241–257.

Dubois, A., and Pedersen, A.-C. (2002), 'Why relationships do not fit into purchasing portfolio models – a comparison between the portfolio and industrial network approaches', *European Journal of Purchasing and Supply Management*, 8 (1), 35–42. https://doi.org/https://doi.org/10.1016/S0969-7012(01)00014-4.

Elg, M., Gremyr, I., Halldorsson, A., and Wallo, A. (2020), 'Service action research: review and guidelines', *Journal of Services Marketing*, 34 (1), 87–99.

Ellram, L.M., Harland, C.M., van Weele, A., Essig, M., Johnsen, T., et al. (2019), 'Purchasing and supply management's identity: Crisis? What crisis?', *Journal of Purchasing and Supply Management*, 100583. https://doi.org/https://doi.org/10.1016/j.pursup.2019.100583.

Gelderman, C.J., and van Weele, A.J. (2002), 'Strategic direction through purchasing portfolio management: a case study', *Journal of Supply Chain Management: A Global Review of Purchasing and Supply*, 38 (2), 30–37.

Halldórsson, Á., and Aastrup, J. (2003), 'Quality criteria for qualitative inquiries in logistics', *European Journal of Operational Research*, 144 (2), 321–332.

Halldórsson, Á., Hsuan, J., and Kotzab, H. (2015), 'Complementary theories to supply chain management revisited – from borrowing theories to theorizing', *Supply Chain Management: An International Journal*, 20 (6), 574–586.

Kaplan, D., Fauchald, N., and Day, A. (2014), *Death & Co: Modern Classic Cocktails, with More Than 500 Recipes*. Ten Speed Press.

Knight, L., Tate, W.L., Matopoulos, A., Meehan, J., and Salmi, A. (2016), 'Breaking the mold: research process innovations in purchasing and supply management', *Journal of Purchasing and Supply Management*, 22 (4), 239–243. https://doi.org/https://doi.org/10.1016/j.pursup.2016.09.003.

Kovács, G., and Spens, K.M. (2005), 'Abductive reasoning in logistics research', *International Journal of Physical Distribution and Logistics Management*, 35 (2), 132–144.

Kraljic, P. (1983), 'Purchasing must become supply management', *Harvard Business Review*, 61 (5), 109–117.

Lysons, K., and Farrington, B. (2006), *Purchasing and Supply Chain Management* (7th edn). Pearson Education.

Miles, M.B., Huberman, A.M., and Saldaña, J. (2020), *Qualitative Data Analysis: A Methods Sourcebook* (4th edn). SAGE Publications.

Montgomery, R.T., Ogden, J.A., and Boehmke, B.C. (2018), 'A quantified Kraljic Portfolio Matrix: using decision analysis for strategic purchasing', *Journal of Purchasing and Supply Management*, 24 (3), 192–203. https://doi.org/https://doi.org/10.1016/j.pursup.2017.10.002.

Novack, R.A., and Simco, S.W. (1991), 'The industrial procurement process: a supply chain perspective', *Journal of Business Logistics*, 12 (1), 145–167.

Olsen, R.F., and Ellram, L.M. (1997), 'A portfolio approach to supplier relationships', *Industrial Marketing Management*, 26 (2), 101–113. https://doi.org/https://doi.org/10.1016/S0019-8501(96)00089-2.

Ployhart, R.E., and Bartunek, J.M. (2019), 'Editors' comments: there is nothing so theoretical as good practice – a call for phenomenal theory', *Academy of Management Review*, 44 (3), 493–497. https://doi.org/10.5465/amr.2019.0087

Schwarz, G., and Stensaker, I. (2014), 'Time to take off the theoretical straightjacket and (re-)introduce phenomenon-driven research', *Journal of Applied Behavioral Science*, 50 (4), 478–501.

Spina, G., Caniato, F., Luzzini, D., and Ronchi, S. (2016), 'Assessing the use of external grand theories in purchasing and supply management research', *Journal of Purchasing and Supply Management*, 22 (1), 18–30. https://doi.org/https://doi.org/10.1016/j.pursup.2015.07.001

Swedberg, R. (2012), 'Theorizing in sociology and social science: turning to the context of discovery', *Theory and Society*, 41 (1), 1–40.

Teece, D.J., Rumelt, R.P., and Schendel, D.E. (1994), *Fundamental Issues in Strategy: A Research Agenda*. Harvard Business Press.

Touboulic, A., McCarthy, L., and Matthews, L. (2020), 'Re-imagining supply chain challenges through critical engaged research', *Journal of Supply Chain Management*, 56 (2), 36–51. https://doi.org/10.1111/jscm.12226.

Van de Ven, A.H., and Johnson, P.E. (2006), 'Knowledge for theory and practice', *Academy of Management Review*, 31 (4), 802–821.

Van der Valk, W., and Rozemeijer, F. (2009), 'Buying business services: towards a structured service purchasing process', *Journal of Services Marketing*, 23 (1), 3–10.

Van Weele, A.J. (2002), *Purchasing and Supply Chain Management: Analysis, Planning and Practice* (3rd edn). Thomson Learning.

Wacker, J.G. (1998), 'A definition of theory: research guidelines for different theory-building research methods in operations management', *Journal of Operations Management*, 16 (4), 361–385.

Walker, H., Harland, C., Knight, L., Uden, C., and Forrest, S. (2008), 'Reflections on longitudinal action research with the English National Health Service', *Journal of Purchasing and Supply Management*, 14 (2), 136–145. https://doi.org/https://doi.org/10.1016/j.pursup.2008.02.003.

Weick, K.E. (1989), 'Theory construction as disciplined imagination', *Academy of Management Review*, 14 (4), 516–531.

Whetten, D.A. (1989), 'What constitutes a theoretical contribution?', *Academy of Management Review*, 14 (4), 490–495. http://www.jstor.org/stable/258554.

Williamson, O.E. (1979), 'Transaction-cost economics: the governance of contractual relations', *Journal of Law and Economics*, 22 (2), 233.

Yin, R.K. (2018), *Case Study Research and Applications: Design and Methods* (6th edn). SAGE.

7. Transaction cost economics

Wendy L. Tate and Lisa M. Ellram

INTRODUCTION

The basic premise of transaction cost analysis is that firms are profit maximizing, and as part of achieving that goal of profit maximization the firm must determine its most efficient boundaries between buying in the market and creating goods and services internally (Williamson 1981), referred to as market versus hierarchy. This is often referred to as the 'make versus buy' decision, or the decision of whether to outsource (if something is currently being done internally). The correct governance structure (market, hierarchy, or a hybrid form) depends on the characteristics of the transaction. The right type of governance structure should be based on what is most economical, considering both the purchase (production) costs and the transaction costs (Williamson 1979). The right type of structure, considering market, hierarchy, or some hybrid approach between the two, should be continually reviewed, with the organization adapting as conditions change (Williamson 2008).

KEY VARIABLES AND DEFINITIONS

Transaction cost economics considers that in addition to the price paid for the item in the marketplace, there are many potential transaction costs and risks associated with using the market. If not for these additional costs, a frictionless marketplace would always be better than hierarchy, because market specialists should be more efficient than hierarchy. However, one must consider the frequency of the transaction, the specificity of assets needed to fulfil the transaction, the uncertainty and complexity in the transaction that may give rise to potential opportunism (Tadelis and Williamson 2012), and the associated specific types of transaction costs. Human behaviour comes into play regarding fully understanding the contract and monitoring contractual behaviour.

Two dimensions of human behaviour play a critical role: bounded rationality and opportunism (Rindfleisch and Heide 1997). These characteristics determine the most appropriate form of contractual governance. Each of these areas is expanded below. Basic definitions of the transaction cost economics variables are provided in Table 7.1.

Frequency of the Transaction

When considering market versus hierarchy (vertical integration), the frequency of the transaction is important, because with greater frequency it is more worthwhile to invest in specialized governance in order to mitigate risk (Williamson 1985). While it may seem that high-volume activities are favourable to vertical integration, this is not necessarily the case. This is noted as the least important and least studied of the three dimensions of transaction frequency, asset specificity and uncertainty (Williamson 1985; Rindfleisch and Heide 1997). In addition, the

Table 7.1   *Definitions of TCE variables*

Element	Explanation	References supporting
Unit of analysis	The transaction, often characterized through the lens of the contract	Williamson 1979, 1981, 1985; Macher and Richman 2008
Level of analysis	Firm level, analysing the transaction or the contract	Williamson 1979, 1981; Tadelis and Williamson 2012
Key variables/definitions		
Frequency of transaction	Ongoing, regular transaction versus an occasional transaction	Williamson 1985, 2008
Asset specificity	Requirements for very specialized, specific assets required to meet the contractual needs	Walker and Weber 1984; Williamson 2008
Uncertainty and complexity	The more complex the task/purchased item, and the more difficult it is to determine whether it has been performed properly, the greater the risk of opportunism in the marketplace	Rindfleisch and Heide 1997; Williamson 1979
Major transaction costs to consider	Cost of search and information gathering, bargaining costs, policing and enforcement costs	North 1990; Rindfleisch and Heide 1997; Tate et al. 2011
Assumptions about human nature		
Bounded rationality	Limited ability to process all data and behave fully rationally even though we may want to	Rindfleisch and Heide 1997
Opportunism	Taking advantage of the situation due to some weakness in the other party's position, made possible by incomplete contracts and bounded rationality	Ellram et al. 2020; Williamson 2008

current level of automation and digitization of transactions shifts the importance of this issue, as high frequency is not necessarily associated with high transaction cost or set-up (Ellram et al. 2008; Schmidt and Wagner 2019).

Asset Specificity

Asset specificity is a critical dimension. It deals with the issue of whether the seller has to make investments in specific human or physical assets in order to support the firm's business. Asset specificity is characterized as 'durable investments that are undertaken in support of particular transactions' (Williamson 1985, p. 55). These investments may be in physical facilities, such as specialized capital equipment for production, a specialized building, or a building in a specific area of interest to others, and can even be specialized human capabilities, such as a dedicated account representative who is intimate with all aspects of a buyer's business.

Transactions or contracts based on highly specialized assets are idiosyncratic and are often a good candidate for vertical integration to avoid dependence on a supplier. Due to the specialized nature of the assets, it is in the interest of the buyer to limit the number of suppliers in order to gain economies of scale, and avoid paying multiple set-up costs to pay for those assets at a number of different suppliers. At the same time, the seller interested in utilizing these assets fully will cooperate with the buyer, as it has no other use for these specialized assets (Williamson 1979). A cooperative working relationship and a good contract with clauses specifying how to deal with changes in pricing and demand are essential, as the dependence created by asset specificity can pose risks to both sides of the contracting equation (Williamson 1979;

Buvik and Reve 2001). In addition, there are other risks posed by uncertainty surrounding the transaction, and human tendencies towards bounded rationality and opportunism.

Uncertainty and Complexity

Uncertainty makes transactions more complex and laden with problems. Uncertainty relates to the timespan of transactions, which in turn influences the breadth of future contingencies for which contractual adaptations are required (Akbar and Tracongna 2018). Uncertainty includes unexpected contingencies that could not be anticipated in advance. Another type of uncertainty is ambiguity regarding whether both parties have really fulfilled their side of the contract. There could be judgement regarding the level of quality of the transacted item, the completeness, and even the execution in cases of something intangible. Uncertainty is the most critical among the transaction attributes of frequency of transactions, asset specificity and uncertainty (Williamson 1979, 1985). The greater the uncertainty, the more safeguards are needed in the contract to protect both parties to the contract. But not every situation can be anticipated.

Transaction Costs to Consider

Many of the costs typically associated with transactions are caused by the uncertainty and complexity risks associated with opportunism (Tate et al. 2011). Given these three elements that affect transaction costs, the three types of transaction costs that organizations often concern themselves with are costs of search and information gathering; bargaining costs; policing and enforcement costs (Rindfleisch and Heide 1997; Tate et al. 2011).

Information costs or search costs refer to the potential time and monetary outlays associated with data gathering to determine the supplier's best course of action (Heide and Stump 1995). Gathering information is pre-emptive, to balance uncertainty and avoid moral hazard. It is also proactive, to create understanding of the true scope of commitment that each party is making to the contract. The cost of information deals with determining the characteristics of what you would like to purchase, gaining information about what is available in the market place that meets those characteristics, then identifying the suppliers of those items.

Bargaining costs have been defined as the direct costs of negotiating, documenting and enforcing an agreement (Knez and Simester 2000). These costs accrue primarily due to the time and effort involved in bargaining and developing an agreement. The amount of effort that a supplier will invest in bargaining is a function of the perceived value of the expected gains versus the expected bargaining costs (Cramton 1991; Tate et al. 2011). Bargaining costs tend to increase as certainty increases, because more contingencies have to be built into the contracts.

Enforcement costs are also called monitoring costs and are a policing function. These costs relate to reducing opportunism risks from others. Performance monitoring and measurement are essential in preventing opportunistic behaviour and hidden actions (Narayanan and Raman 2004). When performance is not monitored, or behaviour is difficult to define, or the monitoring is not cost-beneficial, then opportunism is likely to occur (Williamson 1985). The costs of non-compliance must also be exacted, with the associated costs considered.

North (1987), Coase (1937), and other economists argue that transaction costs associated with conducting business can be substantial, and should be considered as part of the cost of conducting business. These transaction costs can apply to both buyers and suppliers. As the transaction costs become high, the contractual relationship will become less attractive to whichever side incurs the costs (Tate et al. 2011). If the transaction costs become too high, a supplier may refuse the business, and a buyer may decide to vertically integrate.

ASSUMPTIONS REGARDING HUMAN NATURE

Human actors are determined to be rational but behave only limitedly so (Williamson 2008). There are bounds on their rationality, which means that all contracts will be incomplete. There will be gaps, errors, omissions, and so on. However, if the boundedly rational parties have the capacity to look ahead, or obtain knowledge, then contracts can be adapted to deal with unanticipated disturbances to the contracting process (or additional costs) and realize mutual gains (Simon 1955). Self-interest or opportunism also creates problems in contracting. In general, most people will do what they say they will do, and some will do more most of the time (Williamson 2008). However, without proper controls, as circumstances change, so can self-interest, meaning that opportunism is introduced.

Bounded Rationality

Williamson relies on Herbert Simon, who coined the term, with the following definition: bounded rationality has reference to behaviour that is '*intendedly* rational, but only *limited* so' (Simon 1972). This term means that although people may intend to make a rational decision, their capacity to evaluate accurately all possible decision alternatives is physically limited. It is because of these constraints of cognitive capabilities that comprehensive contracting covering all contingent situations or future changes is not feasible (Williamson 1985). Also, pairing exists between bounded rationality and uncertainty/complexity. Bounded rationality poses a problem only in situations of uncertainty/complexity where people cannot make a fully rational decision due to the cognitive limits. In particular, an adaptation problem is created when a firm with decision makers that are limited by bounded rationality has difficulty modifying contractual agreements to changes in the external environment.

Opportunism

Opportunism has been defined by Williamson (1979) as self-interest seeking with guile. In other words, it recognizes that businesses and individuals will sometimes seek to exploit a situation to their own advantage. According to Williamson (1993), opportunism is the cause for the failure of markets and the existence of organizations. And the risk of opportunism is greater when there exists a small number of alternatives. Opportunism poses a problem in cases of asset specificity. Specifically, a safeguarding problem arises when a firm deploys specific assets and fears that its partner may opportunistically exploit these investments. Ghoshal and Moran (1996) criticized this strong assumption, saying that it can have wrong and dangerous implications for corporate managers. This was clarified by Williamson (1987), indicating that transactions should be organized in a way that economizes on bounded rationality while simultaneously safeguarding them against the hazards of opportunism. However, there are behaviours that cannot be verified, introducing uncertainty into the transaction.

The 'Element 1 – Variables' is summarized in Figure 7.1. All further elements are discussed in the following sections.

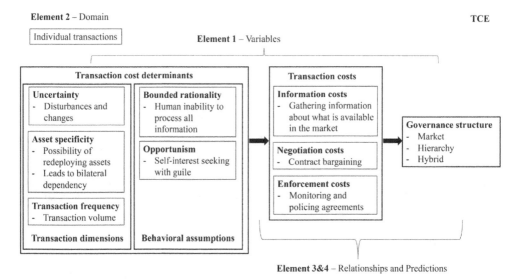

Figure 7.1   Overview of transaction cost economics theory elements

DOMAIN WHERE THE THEORY APPLIES

The domain of the research represents the areas to which the theory applies. Transaction cost economics (TCE) has some broad applications but in its most narrow sense, the domain of TCE applies to a transaction between two entities. However, as you start to think about what that means, the domain of TCE expands significantly. Transaction cost economics fundamentally guides when an entity (organization, individual) should perform an activity itself (hierarchy), and when it should go the market to purchase the item. This affects how the firm organizes to complete the tasks it needs to perform in order to be successful in the market. Thus, decisions guided by TCE affect the entities' governance and structure. It has an impact on relationships and contracts with third parties.

TCE applies in all types of transactions between entities. These can be single transactions, though we often consider contracts of varying lengths in TCE (Williamson 2008). The primary domain of TCE includes the buyer–supplier contracts and transactions of all types. It provides guidance regarding the make–buy decision, including outsourcing, offshoring, nearshoring and reshoring.

RELATIONSHIPS BETWEEN THE VARIABLES

Most contracts are not straightforward arrangements that go just as they were planned when originally executed. TCE brings in numerous variables to help explain some of the things that can happen in contractual relationships, as well as some ways to safeguard against potential problems. Because of the human conditions of bounded rationality, it is impossible to build all possible scenarios and contingencies into a contract. At the same time, there may be a tendency for humans to behave opportunistically in the face of incomplete contracts, so TCE explains when problems are most likely to occur, and possible ways to safeguard the contract/ transactions from opportunistic behaviours.

Whether an organization should choose markets or hierarchies is dependent upon the transaction dimensions of uncertainty, asset specificity and frequency of transactions (Williamson 1975, 1981). Greater uncertainty over whether the other party to the contract is behaving as promised creates more risk through the potential for opportunistic behaviour. Greater asset specificity also creates risk as it generates dependence, and essentially invalidates the potential advantage of using markets (Williamson 1985). The transition dimensions coupled with human behaviour assumptions determine the possible level of risk. In summary, if the risk is too high, the transaction costs increase, as it is more expensive to scan the market to determine the least-risk situation, and negotiations and monitoring become more complex and expensive. The cost and risk associated with a particular transaction (contract) determine the relative attractiveness of market, hybrid or hierarchy.

THEORETICAL PREDICTIONS (FACTUAL CLAIMS)

As stated above, in theory, if information was perfect and the market frictionless, the market would always be preferred as the most economical for transactions. At another extreme is vertical integration or performing an operation internally. In the middle of these extremes there are various types of hybrid, bilateral relationships that attempt to induce shared rewards and risks to reduce the potential opportunism and increase positive outcomes of the relationship (Carter and Hodgson 2006).

Among the key transaction dimensions, uncertainty is generally believed to be the most influential on governance structure, followed in importance by the degree of required asset-specific investments, then transaction frequency (Williamson 1979). The relationship of these dimensions is illustrated in Figure 7.1. Williamson (1979) often associates asset specificity with uncertainty. When asset specificity is high or mixed, that creates high uncertainty due to dependence upon whoever owns the assets. Nonetheless, if the transaction frequency is relatively low, it would not be worthwhile to vertically integrate.

Assuming that these specialized investments are relatively important, Williamson (1979) suggests using 'trilateral' contracting rather than establishing a relationship. He suggests that a trilateral contract is most efficient because it relies on an outside arbitrator for settlement in the case of a disagreement, rather than requiring a court settlement. This would be faster and more efficient. Since dependence and uncertainty create greater risk of opportunism, this type of contracting provides a buffer from that risk. He applies the same logic to mixed use assets, though the risk is probably less because there is less dependence, and greater potential application of the assets (Williamson 1979).

TCE posits that non-specific use assets face the least uncertainty regardless of transaction frequency, as the assets can be put to another use. Uncertainty in investment increases as the assets become more specific. However, when reviewing many empirical studies conducted on the application of TCE, Carter and Hodgson (2006) found inconclusive results. In particular, they found that prior studies provided mixed results on when vertical integration was best, and

Table 7.2   *Impact of transaction frequency and investments on governance structure*

		Investment characteristics		
		Non-specific use	Mixed use	Idiosyncratic or dedicated
		(least uncertainty)	(some uncertainty)	(most uncertainty)
Transaction frequency	Low	Market governance (classical contracting)	Trilateral governance (neoclassical contracting)	
	Recurring	Market governance (classical contracting)	Bilateral governance (relational contracting)	Unified governance vertical integration (relational contracting)

little support for hybrid relationships such as trilateral relationships and relational contracting. They call for further empirical testing and alternative explanations. Williamson's later work acknowledges that in some cases vertical integration might be appropriate for obligational contracts as well, as such contracts attempt to buffer against some uncertainty and provide protection from some types of dependence-induced opportunism. For example, Williamson (1979, p. 250):

> Highly idiosyncratic transactions are ones where the human and physical assets required for production are extensively specialized, so there are no obvious scale economies to be realized through inter-firm trading that the buyer (or seller) is unable to realize himself (through vertical integration). In the case, however, of mixed transactions, the degree of asset specialization is less complete. Accordingly, outside procurement for these components may be favored by scale-economy considerations.

See Table 7.2.

Williamson predicts that specificity and uncertainty heavily influence market versus hierarchy:

1. High asset specificity increases the risk of the market due to dependence; low asset specificity creates opportunity for competition and lower switching costs.
2. Uncertainty over whether the supplier is really behaving as contracted drives toward hierarchy and increases the transaction costs associated with information gathering, negotiations (which become more complex) and enforcement (monitoring behaviours).

HOW HAS THIS THEORY BEEN USED?

Purchasing and Supply Management and Supply Chain Management

In the purchasing and supply chain management literature, transaction cost economics has been used to look at the outsourcing and location decisions such as offshoring and reshoring. Other research has focused on environmental supply chain decision making. More recently the influence of blockchain on supply chain relationships used a transaction cost lens. Below are some examples from this stream of literature:

1. Ellram, L.M., Tate, W.L. and Billington, C. (2008), 'Offshore outsourcing of professional services: A transaction cost economics perspective', *Journal of Operations Management*, 26(2), 148–163.

2. Grover, V. and Malhotra, M.K. (2003), 'Transaction cost framework in operations and supply chain management research: theory and measurement', *Journal of Operations Management*, 21(4), 457–473.

3. Hobbs, J.E. (1996), 'A transaction cost approach to supply chain management', *Supply Chain Management: An International Journal*, 1(2), 15–27.

4. McIvor, R. (2009), 'How the transaction cost and resource-based theories of the firm inform outsourcing evaluation', *Journal of Operations Management*, 27(1), 45–63.

5. Schmidt, C.S. and Wagner, S.M. (2019), ,Blockchain and supply chain relations: A transaction cost theory perspective', *Journal of Purchasing and Supply Management*, 25(4), 100552.

6. Tate, W.L., Dooley, K.J. and Ellram, L.M. (2011), 'Transaction cost and institutional drivers of supplier adoption of environmental practices', *Journal of Business Logistics*, 32(1), 6–16.

7. Tate, W.L., Ellram, L.M. and Dooley, K.J. (2014), 'The impact of transaction costs and institutional pressure on supplier environmental practices', *International Journal of Physical Distribution, and Logistics Management*, 44(5), 353–372.

8. Wacker, J.G., Yang, C. and Sheu, C. (2016), 'A transaction cost economics model for estimating performance effectiveness of relational and contractual governance', *International Journal of Operations & Production Management*, 36(11), 1551–1575.

9. Wever, M., Wognum, P.M., Trienekens, J.H. and Omta, S.W.F. (2012), 'Supply chain-wide consequences of transaction risks and their contractual solutions: Towards an extended transaction cost economics framework', *Journal of Supply Chain Management*, 48(1), 73–91.

10. Williamson, O.E. (2008), 'Outsourcing: Transaction cost economics and supply chain management', *Journal of Supply Chain Management*, 44(2), 5–16.

11. Ketokivi, M. and Mahoney, J. T. (2020), 'Transaction cost economics as a theory of supply chain efficiency', *Production and Operations Management*, 29(4), 1011–1031.

12. Piboonrungroj, P. and Disney, S. M. (2015), 'Supply chain collaboration in tourism: a transaction cost economics analysis', *International Journal of Supply Chain Management*, 4(3), 25–31.

13. Wacker, J.G., Yang, C. and Sheu, C. (2016), 'A transaction cost economics model for estimating performance effectiveness of relational and contractual governance', *International Journal of Operations & Production Management*, 36(11), 1551–1575.

14. Lumineau, F. and Oliveira, N. (2020), 'Reinvigorating the study of opportunism in supply chain management', *Journal of Supply Chain Management*, 56(1), 73–87.

15. Liu, J., Feng, Y., Zhu, Q. and Sarkis, J. (2018), 'Green supply chain management and the circular economy', *International Journal of Physical Distribution & Logistics Management*, 48(8), 794–817.

Management

The management literature employing transaction cost economics focuses on market entry decisions and relationships. Much of the research here looks at contractual safeguarding, cooperation and opportunism. Some examples are below:

1. Brouthers, K.D., Brouthers, L.E. and Werner, S. (2003), 'Transaction cost-enhanced entry mode choices and firm performance', *Strategic Management Journal*, 24(12), 1239–1248.
2. Buvik, A. and Reve, T. (2001), 'Asymmetrical deployment of specific assets and contractual safeguarding in industrial purchasing relationships', *Journal of Business Research*, 51(2), 101–113.
3. Chiles, T. H. and McMackin, J. F. (1996), 'Integrating variable risk preferences, trust, and transaction cost economics', *Academy of Management Review*, 21(1), 73–99.
4. David, R. J. and Han, S. K. (2004), 'A systematic assessment of the empirical support for transaction cost economics', *Strategic Management Journal*, 25(1), 39–58.
5. Geyskens, I., Steenkamp, J. B. E. and Kumar, N. (2006), 'Make, buy, or ally: A transaction cost theory meta-analysis', *Academy of Management Journal*, 49(3), 519–543.
6. Hill, C. W. (1990), 'Cooperation, opportunism, and the invisible hand: Implications for transaction cost theory', *Academy of Management Review*, 15(3), 500–513.
7. Jones, G. R. and Hill, C. W. (1988), 'Transaction cost analysis of strategy-structure choice', *Strategic Management Journal*, 9(2), 159–172.
8. Mayer, K. J. and Salomon, R. M. (2006), 'Capabilities, contractual hazards, and governance: Integrating resource-based and transaction cost perspectives', *Academy of Management Journal*, 49(5), 942–959.
9. Robertson, T.S. and Gatignon, H. (1998), 'Technology development mode: a transaction cost conceptualization', *Strategic Management Journal*, 19(6), 515–531.
10. Zhao, H., Luo, Y. and Suh, T. (2004), 'Transaction cost determinants and ownership-based entry mode choice: A meta-analytical review', *Journal of International Business Studies*, 35(6), 524–544.

Marketing

The marketing literature uses transaction cost economics to explore relationships between the seller and the buyer. It also looks at contractual governance and the role of marketing in both internal and supplier relationships. Examples of articles from marketing journals are below:

1. Cannon, J.P., Achrol, R.S. and Gundlach, G.T., (2000), 'Contracts, norms, and plural form governance', *Journal of the Academy of Marketing Science*, 28(2), 180–194.
2. Heide, J. B. and John, G. (1992), 'Do norms matter in marketing relationships?, *Journal of Marketing*, 56(2), 32–44.
3. Heide, J.B. and Stump, R.L. (1995), 'Performance implications of buyer-supplier relationships in industrial markets: a transaction cost explanation', *Journal of Business Research*, 32(1), 57–66.
4. Klein, S., Frazier, G.L. and Roth, V.J. (1990), 'A transaction cost analysis model of channel integration in international markets', *Journal of Marketing Research*, 27(2), 196–208.

5. Mudambi, R. and Mudambi, S.M. (1995), 'From transaction cost economics to relationship marketing: a model of buyer-supplier relations', *International Business Review*, 4(4), 419–433.
6. Noordewier, T.G., John, G. and Nevin, J.R. (1990), 'Performance outcomes of purchasing arrangements in industrial buyer-vendor relationships', *Journal of Marketing*, 54(4), 80–93.
7. Pemer, F., Werr, A. and Bianchi, M. (2014), 'Purchasing professional services: A transaction cost view of the antecedents and consequences of purchasing formalization', *Industrial Marketing Management*, 43(5), 840–849.
8. Pitt, L.F. and Foreman, S.K. (1999), 'Internal marketing role in organizations: a transaction cost perspective', *Journal of Business Research*, 44(1), 25–36.
9. Rindfleisch. A. and Heide, J.B. (1997), 'Transaction Cost Analysis: Past, Present, and Future Applications', *Journal of Marketing*, 61(4), 30–54.
10. Williamson, O. and Ghani, T. (2012), 'Transaction cost economics and its uses in marketing', *Journal of the Academy of Marketing Science*, 40(1), 74–85.

OUTLOOK ON FUTURE RESEARCH OPPORTUNITIES

Because of the constantly changing environment, there are many opportunities for future research looking through the lens of transaction cost economics. In general, transaction frequency is increasing significantly because of new technologies and more data availability. The theory says that when uncertainty and measurement problems are combined with high frequency, internal procurement is expected to dominate; in these circumstances the firm has an incentive to incur the set-up costs of organizing the transaction (Aubert et al. 1996). If the levels of uncertainty and measurement problems are lower, relational contracting can emerge; this is the realm of outsourcing and strategic alliances (Williamson 1985, 1987). The question is: how does the frequency of transactions combined with increasing uncertainty and measurement problems influence our make versus buy decision; or even the location decision? Does it make sense to 'reshore' from low cost countries to the home country to decrease uncertainty and improve the ability to measure? What happens if there is a big movement from low cost countries to higher cost countries: will this change the frequency of transacting?

More research is also needed to understand the role of opportunism in market versus hierarchy decisions. In research by Ellram et al. (2020) related to cost savings, the idea that people behave in a 'passively' opportunistic way was revealed. Research that broadens the definition of opportunism is necessary to better understand the impact of passive opportunism on the market versus hierarchy decision.

With increased information availability and transparency, what is the influence of big data and blockchain on transaction costs? Significantly improved analytics and data accuracy is emerging to monitor relationship performance. That change in monitoring capabilities will influence uncertainty which will change our decision making. More research is also needed to understand the impact of big data on purchasing decision making. More research is needed to look at the influence of blockchain through a transaction cost economics lens. Some research has started to address the influence of information availability and transparency on sustainability, which is another context for fruitful research. There appears to be much hidden information and possibly opportunism in lower tiers of organizations' supply chains, particularly in relation to human rights and environmental degradation. TCE's framing of risk and uncertainty, and assumptions regarding human behaviour, could shed light on this phenomenon. Related to this, the COVID-19 pandemic has brought to light some additional problems with offshoring, risk and resiliency; can we view changes in decision-making through a TCE lens? Will it make sense in the future to continue to offshore spending to low cost countries? Will it make sense to reshore?

These are just a few ideas for future research. Transaction cost economics is a valuable lens to view decision making in a market versus a hierarchy. Understanding the tenets of TCE is crucial as research is completed that helps to inform decision making.

REFERENCES

Akbar, Y.H. and Tracogna, A. (2018), 'The sharing economy and the future of the hotel industry: Transaction cost theory and platform economics', *International Journal of Hospitality Management*, 71, 91–101.

Aubert, B.A., Rivard, S. and Patry, M. (1996), 'A transaction cost approach to outsourcing behavior: Some empirical evidence', *Information and Management*, 30 (2), 51–64.

Buvik, A. and Reve, T. (2001), 'Asymmetrical deployment of specific assets and contractual safeguarding in industrial purchasing relationships', *Journal of Business Research*, 51 (2), 101–113.

Carter, R. and Hodgson, G.M. (2006), 'The impact of empirical tests of transaction cost economics on the debate on the nature of the firm', *Strategic Management Journal*, 27 (5), 461–476.

Coase, R.H. (1937), 'The nature of the firm', *Economica*, 4 (16), 386–405.

Cramton, P.C. (1991), 'Dynamic bargaining with transaction costs', *Management Science*, 37 (10), 1221–1233.

Ellram, L.M., Tate, W.L. and Billington, C. (2008), 'Offshore outsourcing of professional services: A transaction cost economics perspective', *Journal of Operations Management*, 26 (2), 148–163.

Ellram, L.M., Tate, W.L. and Choi, T.Y. (2020), 'The conflicted role of purchasing in new product development costing', *Journal of Supply Chain Management*, 56 (1), 3–32.

Ghoshal, S. and Moran, P. (1996), 'Bad for practice: A critique of the transaction cost theory', *Academy of Management Review*, 20 (1), 13–47.

Heide, J. B. and Stump, R. L. (1995), 'Performance implications of buyer-supplier relationships in industrial markets: a transaction cost explanation', *Journal of Business Research*, 32 (1), 57–66.

Knez, M. and Simester, D. (2000), 'Direct and indirect bargaining costs and the scope of the firm', Social Science Research Network Working Paper, accessed 15 January 2020 at www.ssrn.com/.

Macher, J. and Richman, B. (2008), 'Transaction Cost Economics: An Assessment of Empirical Research in the Social Sciences', *Business and Politics*, 10 (1), 1–63.

Narayanan, V.G. and Raman, A. (2004), 'Aligning incentives in supply chains', *Harvard Business Review*, 82 (11), 94–103.

North, D.C. (1987), 'Institutions, transaction costs and economic growth', *Economic Inquiry*, 25 (3), 419.

North, Douglass C. (1990), 'Institutions and a transaction-cost theory of exchange', in James Alt and Kenneth A. Shepsle (eds), *Perspectives on Positive Political Economy*, Cambridge, MA: Cambridge University Press, pp. 182–194.

Rindfleisch, A. and Heide, J.B. (1997), 'Transaction cost analysis: Past, present, and future applications', *Journal of Marketing*, 61 (4), 30–54.

Schmidt, C.G. and Wagner, S.M. (2019), 'Blockchain and supply chain relations: A transaction cost theory perspective', *Journal of Purchasing and Supply Management*, 25 (4), 100552.

Simon, H.A. (1955), 'A behavioral model of rational choice', *Quarterly Journal of Economics*, 69 (1), 99–118.

Simon, H.A. (1972), 'Theories of bounded rationality', *Decision and Organization*, 1 (1), 161–176.

Tadelis, S. and Williamson, O.E. (2012), 'Transaction cost economics', in Robert S. Gibbons and John Roberts (eds), *The Handbook of Organizational Economics*, Princeton, NJ: Princeton University Press, pp. 150–191.

Tate, W.L., Dooley, K.J. and Ellram, L.M. (2011), 'Transaction cost and institutional drivers of supplier adoption of environmental practices', *Journal of Business Logistics*, 32 (1), 6–16.

Walker, G. and Weber, D. (1984), 'A transaction cost approach to make-or-buy decisions', *Administrative Science Quarterly*, 29 (3), 373–391.

Williamson, Oliver E. (1975), *Markets and Hierarchies: Analysis and Antitrust Implications*, New York: Free Press.

Williamson, O.E. (1979), 'Transaction-cost economics: The governance of contractual relations', *Journal of Law Economics*, 22 (2), 233–262.

Williamson, O.E. (1981), 'The economics of organization: The transaction cost approach', *American Journal of Sociology*, 87 (3), 548–577.

Williamson, Oliver E. (1985), *The Economic Institutions of Capitalism: Firms, Markets, Relational Contracting*, New York: Free Press.

Williamson, O.E. (1987), 'Transaction cost economics: The comparative contracting perspective', *Journal of Economic Behavior and Organization*, 8 (4), 617–625.

Williamson, O.E. (1993), 'Opportunism and its critics', *Managerial and Decision Economics*, 14 (2), 97–107.

Williamson, O.E. (2008), 'Outsourcing: Transaction cost economics and supply chain management', *Journal of Supply Chain Management*, 44 (2), 5–16.

SUGGESTED FURTHER READING

For more information on industrial economics and its roots:

Chandler, A. (1992), 'Organizational capabilities and the economic history of the industrial enterprise', *Journal of Economic Perspectives,* 6 (3), 79–100. Accessed 15 January 2020 at http://www.jstor.org/stable/2138304.

For an excellent review of the historical development of TCE, see:

Tadelis, S. and Williamson, O.E. (2012), 'Transaction cost economics', in R.S. Gibbons and J. Roberts (eds), *The Handbook of Organizational Economics*, Princeton , NJ: Princeton University Press, pp. 150–191.

For an opposing perspective:

Ghoshal, S. and Moran, P. (1996), 'Bad for practice: A critique of the transaction cost theory', *Academy of Management Review*, 20 (1), 13–47.

Good literature reviews on the application of TCE:

David, R.J. and Han, S.K. (2004), 'A systematic assessment of the empirical support for transaction cost economics', *Strategic Management Journal*, 25, 39–58.

Geyskens, I., Steenkamp, J.B.E. and Kumar, N. (2006), 'Make, buy, or ally: A transaction cost theory meta-analysis', *Academy of Management Journal*, 49 (3), 519–543.

Macher, J. and Richman, B. (2008), 'Transaction cost economics: An assessment of empirical research in the social sciences', *Business and Politics*, 10 (1), 1–63.

8.   Resource-based view

Lydia Bals and Eugenia Rosca

INTRODUCTION TO THE RESOURCE-BASED VIEW

The resource-based view (RBV) is another of the most commonly applied theories in supply chain management (SCM) and purchasing and supply management (PSM) research today. The RBV is rooted in insights from economics stemming from Penrose (1995) and Richardson (1972) and it is widely applied across many business disciplines, including economics (Lockett and Thompson, 2001). A fundamental issue of interest in management studies focuses on understanding how firms can leverage the internal resources and capabilities to achieve sustained competitive advantage (Barney, 1991; Teece et al., 1997). While significant efforts have been undertaken to explore capabilities for superior financial performance, there is much less understanding of the capabilities and resource bundles needed to create social and environmental value (Hart and Milstein, 2003; Norman and MacDonald, 2004). The influential RBV has paved the way for significant theory development and extension leading to numerous theories such as the relational view, knowledge-based view, resource advantage and dynamic capabilities. In the light of ever increasing concerns for the environment and global inequality, two notable RBV extensions have been proposed. The natural resource-based view (NRBV), which incorporates environment as a key constraint, explicates the links between environmental strategies, capabilities and outcomes (Hart, 1995; Hart and Dowell, 2011); while the social resource-based view (SRBV) highlights capabilities and resources needed to create social, environmental and economic value (Sodhi, 2015; Tate and Bals, 2018). Figure 8.1 summarizes the key theory elements (Wacker, 1998, 2008). The elements are discussed in the following sections.

Figure 8.1 highlights the variables, domain, relationships and outcome predictions, following (Wacker, 1998), for the three theoretical perspectives: the RBV, NRBV and SRBV. Following the basic requirements and characteristics of firm resources, capabilities are outlined following the original RBV logic with a focus on economic performance of the focal firm and its shareholders. This traditional view is extended to incorporate environmental capabilities of the NRBV and social capabilities of the SRBV. The outcome predictions are conceptualized drawing on the shared triple bottom line (TBL) value – economic, environmental and social – to account for competitive advantage, environmental and social performance. These capabilities are needed to create TBL value in a context with a broad range of traditional (economic) and non-traditional (social and environmental) stakeholders.

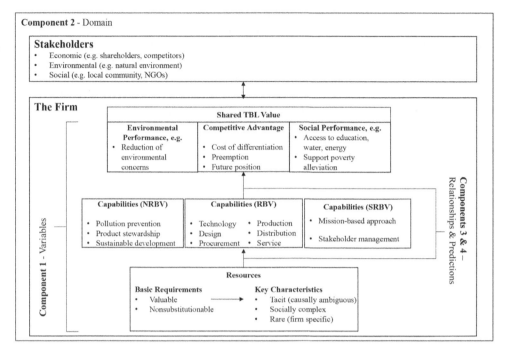

Source: Adapted from Tate and Bals (2018, p. 819).

Figure 8.1   *Overview of RBV, NRBV and SRBV theory elements*

KEY VARIABLES AND DEFINITIONS

RBV

The RBV has emerged as an alternative theory to the existing environmental models of competitive advantage which seek to explain environment-based conditions which favour high levels of firm performance (Barney, 1991). The fundamental argument behind the RBV is that firms can achieve sustained competitive advantage based on internal factors. Rooted in the seminal works of Penrose (1995), Learned et al. (1969), Selznick (1984), the RBV has paved the way for significant theory development and extension, with many other theories emerging to explain how acquisition and deployment of resources enables firms to achieve superior rents, for instance, resource advantage (Hunt and Morgan, 1995) and dynamic capabilities (Eisenhardt and Martin, 2000; Teece, 2007; Teece et al., 1997). The initial RBV contribution has been positioned relative to the structure–conduct–performance (SCP) models of competitive advantage from economics (Barney, 2001). Positioning the RBV in evolutionary economics would have helped to explain how capabilities and resources change over time, while the neoclassical microeconomics would have helped to explain whether the RBV is tautological and equilibrium analysis could be used in the context of the RBV (Barney et al., 2001). Despite the original SCP positioning, further developments of the RBV followed both the neoclassical microeconomics view (Peteraf, 1993) and the evolutionary view (Teece et al., 1997). While the neoclassical view of the RBV has given rise to 'resource-picking' theories, the evolutionary versions of the RBV have been known as 'capability building' theories (Makadok, 1999).

As a starting point, Wernerfelt (1984) distinguishes between tangible and intangible firm resources, and argues that there is a relationship between firm profitability and resource position barriers. This initial approach was extended by Barney (1991), who introduced the conditions under which firm resources can lead to sustained competitive advantage: firm resources need to be valuable, rare, imperfectly imitable and non-substitutable. By leveraging such resources, firms can develop distinct capabilities. In the context of the RBV, resources are 'basic units of analysis and include physical and financial assets as well as employees' skills and organizational (social) processes' (Hart, 1995). In contrast to resources, capabilities result from bundles of resources and can be used by firms to perform certain value-adding tasks (Winter, 2003). Examples of valuable resources include human capital in the form of managerial roles and experiences (Ireland and Hitt, 1999), tacit and explicit knowledge (Ireland and Hitt, 1999; Kogut and Zander, 1993); while examples of capabilities include research and development (R&D) and technological capabilites (Peteraf, 1993; Prahalad and Hamel, 1990; Wernerfelt, 1984).

There is sufficient evidence to suggest that the RBV has reached its maturity stage, achieving a high level of precision and sophistication, giving birth to numerous spin-offs, proving sufficient empirical work to enable integration with other perspectives and publications of collective assessments for the body of RBV research (Barney et al., 2011).

NRBV

The NRBV proposed by Hart (1995) and extended by Hart and Dowell (2011) expanded the domain to include the natural environment as a constraint. They changed the traditional context of economic activities to incorporate the needs of the future society at large and the natural environment as a primary constituent (Montabon et al., 2016). The incorporation of the natural environment as a primary constituent in the firm's context is valuable given recent challenges related to climate change, population and economic growth, expansion of global industrial activities and fossil fuel consumption, all leading to significant environmental damage (Tate et al., 2010). The NRBV focuses on strategic capabilities needed for firms to achieve both financial success and positive environmental outcomes. The strategic capabilities under the NRBV include pollution prevention, product stewardship, clean technology and base of the pyramid (BoP) business models and they are based on key firm resources such as continuous improvement, stakeholder integration and embedded innovation (Hart and Dowell, 2011).

SRBV

Building on the RBV and the NRBV, the SRBV has been proposed to explain how businesses with a strong mission to conduct business sustainably can create TBL value. In terms of variables proposed, the SRBV focuses on capabilities needed for firms to fulfil their missions in the context of a wide stakeholder network. Social businesses entail traditional RBV capabilities such as production, distribution, the NRBV such as pollution prevention and product stewardship, and essential social capabilities which are further outlined by the SRBV. Two social capabilities are put forward by the SRBV: the mission-driven approach and stakeholder management. The mission-driven approach is important since most social businesses are developed around a specific issue in the local context and their primary goal is to employ the business to improve the situation. Stakeholder management capability relates to managing a broad network of actors which are needed for their different inputs for the social business. The various inputs relate to provision of financial resources, products delivered by suppliers, knowledge for business model development or context shaping. Context shaping has been regarded as a key capability for firms creating TBL outcomes since the current business context requires further adaptations and special support services are needed for social businesses to succeed (Glavas and Mish, 2015). The SRBV proposes social capabilities in the previously suggested areas of commitments, connections and consistency (Meehan et al., 2006). The commitment is reflected in the strong mission underlying social businesses at inception, while pursuing this throughout later stages of enterprise development relates to consistency (mission-driven approach). The connections aspect is reflected in the stakeholder management capability since it refers to managing a wide range of links with economic, social and environmental stakeholders with different motivations and governance structures (Bals and Tate, 2018; Tate and Bals, 2018).

DOMAIN WHERE THE THEORY APPLIES

RBV

The domain assumed by the RBV includes a focus on superior rents, a competitive market situation and integration of traditional business stakeholders such as investors, customers, shareholders and competitors. In the context of the RBV, value creation is defined as profits for the focal firm and sustained competitive advantage (Peteraf, 1993). The nature of the competitive market is defined by competition between firms on commercial terms (Chatain, 2011). An important assumption underlying the RBV is that firms are heterogeneous within an industry due to differences in their resource base (Hitt et al., 2016).

NRBV

As a theoretical extension of the RBV, the NRBV entails a wider application domain and has integrated the natural environment as a key constraint to traditional economic activities (Gladwin et al., 1995). The NRBV has been instrumental in linking research on organizations to the environment by providing specific theoretical mechanisms to establish the link between environmental strategy and profits (Hart and Dowell, 2011). While the proposed mechanisms are different in nature (for example, pollution prevention or product stewardship), the measure of performance remains the same, with a focus on lower costs, legitimacy, long-term growth and reputation. Subsequently, the NRBV can be regarded as a continuation of the traditional instrumental logic which aims to identify win–win situations for firms to establish both financial profits and environmental success. More recently, current practice and literature show that this traditional logic does not necessarily lead to more sustainable firms and supply chains, and therefore the ecologically dominant logic has been proposed as an 'outside-in' approach to decision making where environmental viability is assessed first, then social and economic viability (Montabon et al., 2016).

SRBV

The creation of economic, social and environmental value demands the extension of traditional firm-oriented boundaries to consider the focal firm within a given context, a local community, societal needs and the environment (Glavas and Mish, 2015). Along the same lines, the SRBV domain broadly considers a wide network of stakeholders and has an explicit focus on understanding the needs of the local communities and advocating for the natural environment. This goes beyond the traditional firm-centric approach and shareholder focus of the RBV. The SRBV integrates various economic stakeholders (for example investors, financial institutions), social stakeholders (for example, low-income families, local communities, not-for-profit organizations) and environmental stakeholders (for example, local ecosystems) in the value creation (Bals and Tate, 2018). A related extension of the RBV is the stakeholder resource-based view which aims to inform decision making of managers so that they maximize the utility of various stakeholders beyond the shareholders (Sodhi, 2015). Drawing on the RBV, utility and stakeholder theory, this extension aims to conceptualize social responsibility in operations management and includes two foci of interest: the operations as the basic unit of observation, and the firm stakeholders, all treated equally. In this context, all stakeholders entail important resources, routines, dynamic capabilities and utility considerations (Sodhi, 2015).

RELATIONSHIPS BETWEEN THE VARIABLES AND THEORETICAL PREDICTIONS (FACTUAL CLAIMS)

RBV

The basic relationship proposed by the RBV is that firms can generate sustained competitive advantage by leveraging internal firm resources which are valuable, rare, imperfectly imitable and non-subsitutable. Yet, an important condition for achieving competitive advantage relates to the firm's ability to accumulate, recombine and reconfigure its resource base and apply it to new market opportunities (Dierckx and Cool, 1989). This RBV extension is important to explain why firms with similar resource bundles or making similar investments may not have the same resulting performance outcomes (Hitt et al., 2016).

NRBV

The NRBV examines the relationship between environmental strategies and various performance measures for competitive advantage (Hart, 1995). Originally, Hart (1995) proposed three interconnected strategic capabilities for the NRBV: pollution prevention, product stewardship and sustainable development (Hart, 1995). The proposed strategic capabilities are different in nature: they are driven by different environmental forces, leverage different key resources, and present different sources for competitive advantage. For instance, pollution prevention capabilities can enable firms to achieve significant cost reductions through reduced waste and emissions, while product stewardship capabilities can enable firms to include external stakeholders in the product development and planning processes, which in turn can lead to gains in reputation and external legitimacy (Hart, 1995).

The original NRBV predictions have been further refined by distinguishing between 'greening' strategies (pollution prevention and product stewardship) with a focus on incremental improvements, and 'beyond greening' strategies (clean technology and BoP) which focus on building new capabilities for the future (Hart and Dowell, 2010). Again, each capability can lead to different sources of competitive advantage: while clean technology can enable firms to strengthen their future market position, BOP strategies can enable firms to tap the market potential of populations living in poverty conditions and thereby achieve long-term market growth. The BOP capability within the NRBV goes beyond environmental considerations and resembles a very first move towards integrating the social aspects of sustainable development.

SRBV

The major contribution of the SRBV in terms of outcomes prediction relates to 'shared TBL value' as a unit measure for performance. This goes beyond the traditional instrumental logic employed by both the RBV and the NRBV where the ultimate measures of competitive advantage are economic indicators such as market share and rents (Barney, 1991; Mahoney and Pandian, 1992; Peteraf, 1993).

Shared TBL value suggests that economic, social and environmental dimensions need to be managed to deliver value for the broad range of stakeholders involved, including the local communities and the environment (Bowen, 1953; Carroll, 1979, 1999). Drawing on the initial definition of 'shared value' provided by Porter and Kramer (2006, 2011), the SRBV argues that shared TBL value goes beyond philanthropy or social responsibility, and actively redefines economic success with societal and environmental needs at the core of the value creation processes.

Regarding outcome preditions, the SRBV proposes that social capabilities are needed to create shared TBL value. Social businesses tend to employ capabilities from the RBV and NRBV, and social capabilities from the SRBV, to reach their objectives: they tend to show a strong desire to create TBL value for all stakeholders involved in their operations. While economic viability is a key concern for them too, the underying goal remains the creation of TBL value.

The SRBV proposes that a mission-driven approach positively influences TBL value creation. This capability can serve as a constant reference for decision making processes inside the firm, ensures that the social mission does not allow an overemphasis on economic outcomes, and maintains shared value creation across the extended supply chain (Bals and Tate, 2018). The conceptualization of the mission-driven approach can differ depending on the timing of empirical measurement: while in the early stages of venture development this refers to 'commitment', towards later stages this can be seen as 'consistency' (Bals and Tate, 2018).

The SRBV proposes that stakeholder management capabilities positively impact upon shared TBL value creation. Social businesses operate in a context with a broad range of stakeholders, and therefore they need important capabilities to configure, design and maintain relationships with both economic and non-economic actors. These capabilities can enable focal firms to better understand the local context and develop local embeddedness. Managing stakeholders with complementary capabilities and integrating them in the focal firm's supply chains is essential to create additional value and prevent destruction of value. While testing this relationship empirically, the timing again serves as a moderating factor. While in early stages, the capability 'value chain partner network design' is more relevant; later on, this relates more to '(supply/value chain) collaboration in terms of suppliers and/or financial partners' and '(supply chain) monitoring'. For more on sustainable supply chain designs, Bals and Tate (2018) offered a framework in line with the theory of the supply chain (Carter et al., 2015).

HOW HAS THIS THEORY BEEN USED?

RBV empirical testing has faced numerous methodological challenges over the years, for example measuring intangible resources, the need for longitudinal analysis to account for the notion of sustained competitive advantage, and the use of new, multidisciplinary methodologies (Barney et al., 2001). Despite this, the RBV has made significant contributions in various fields such as human resource management, economics and finance, entrepreneurship, marketing, international business, and more. Early on, the focus was on empirical mapping of resources and then testing of relationships between the presence of resources and development of sustainained competitive advantages (Barney et al., 2011). More recently, the focus of RBV work has been more on exploring the origins of resources. For instance, Sirmon et al. (2011) show how managers actively structure, bundle and leverage resources by coining the terms 'resource orchestration' and resource orchestration theory (ROT), respectively.

The RBV has been extensively used in the context of supply chains and operations with significant contributions in four areas: (1) analysis of supply chain activities individually and collectively; (2) operations strategies and effective use of process capabilities; (3) achieving effectiveness and efficiency; and (4) product and service innovations (Hitt et al., 2016). The application of the RBV to the operations and supply chain context has also resulted in new insights for RBV; for example, Allred et al. (2011) proposed a new capability – that is, superior coordination among diverse supply chain members – with important implications for firm performance.

Empirical studies employing the NRBV have focused on testing the strategic capabilities put forward. Many studies have been dedicated to exploring the impact of pollution prevention on firm performance (for example, King and Lenox, 2002), but more recently empirical work has focused on identifying moderating factors which can affect the firm's abilities to gain financial benefits from pollution prevention capabilities (Hart and Dowell, 2011). An exemplary study drawing on the NRBV is by Sharma and Vredenburg (1998), who found that proactive environmental strategies require stakeholder integration, higher-order learning and continuous integration.

Since the SRBV has been proposed only recently, further empirical work is needed to expand and test the proposed capabilities. The SRBV has been developed based on exploratory qualitative research in the context of social businesses. Recently, Lashitew et al. (2020) have provided new evidence for capabilities needed to sustain social businesses.

The integration of the RBV, NRBV and SRBV has been used in recent work to distinguish the broad range of economic, environmental and social capabilities that firms can take advantage of to drive corporate financial performance (Ratajczak, 2021).

Examples in Purchasing and Supply Management and Supply Chain Management

RBV

Peng, D.X., Schroeder, R.G., and Shah, R. (2008). Linking routines to operations capabilities: a new perspective. *Journal of Operations Management, 26*(6), 730–748.

Hitt, M.A., Xu, K., and Carnes, C.M. (2016). Resource based theory in operations management research. *Journal of Operations Management, 41*, 77–94.

Bromiley, P., and Rau, D. (2016). Operations management and the resource based view: another view. *Journal of Operations Management, 41*, 95–106.

Lai, F., Li, D., Wang, Q., and Zhao, X. (2008). The information technology capability of third-party logistics providers: a resource-based view and empirical evidence from China. *Journal of Supply Chain Management, 44*(3), 22–38.

NRBV

Miemczyk, J., Howard, M., and Johnsen, T.E. (2016). Dynamic development and execution of closed-loop supply chains: a natural resource-based view. *Supply Chain Management: An International Journal, 21*(4), 453–469.

SRBV

Tate, W.L., and Bals, L. (2018). Achieving shared triple bottom line (TBL) value creation: toward a social resource-based view (SRBV) of the firm. *Journal of Business Ethics, 152*(3), 803–826.

Sodhi, M. S. (2015). Conceptualizing social responsibility in operations via stakeholder resource-based view. *Production and Operations Management, 24*(9), 1375–1389.

Examples in Management

RBV

Newbert, S.L. (2008). Value, rareness, competitive advantage, and performance: a conceptual-level empirical investigation of the resource-based view of the firm. *Strategic Management Journal, 29*(7), 745–768.

Ray, G., Barney, J.B., and Muhanna, W.A. (2004). Capabilities, business processes, and competitive advantage: choosing the dependent variable in empirical tests of the resource-based view. *Strategic Management Journal, 25*(1), 23–37.

NRBV

Sharma, S., and Vredenburg, H. (1998). Proactive corporate environmental strategy and the development of competitively valuable organizational capabilities. *Strategic Management Journal, 19*(8), 729–753.

Pujari, D., Wright, G., and Peattie, K. (2003). Green and competitive: influences on environmental new product development performance. *Journal of Business Research, 56*, 657–671.

Christmann, P. (2000). Effects of 'best practices' of environmental management on cost advantage: the role of complementary assets. *Academy of Management Journal, 43*, 663–680.

SRBV

Lashitew, A.A., Bals, L., and van Tulder, R. (2020). Inclusive business at the base of the pyramid: the role of embeddedness for enabling social innovations. *Journal of Business Ethics, 162*(2), 421–448.

Examples in Marketing

RBV
Srivastava, R.K., Fahey, L., and Christensen, H.K. (2001). The resource-based view and marketing: the role of market-based assets in gaining competitive advantage. *Journal of Management, 27*(6), 777–802.
Capron, L., and Hulland, J. (1999). Redeployment of brands, sales forces, and general marketing management expertise following horizontal acquisitions: a resource-based view. *Journal of Marketing, 63*(2), 41–54.
Kozlenkova, I.V., Samaha, S.A., and Palmatier, R.W. (2014). Resource-based theory in marketing. *Journal of Academy of Marketing Science, 42*(1), 1–21.

NRBV
Fraj, E., Martínez, E., and Matute, J. (2013). Green marketing in B2B organisations: an empirical analysis from the natural-resource-based view of the firm. *Journal of Business and Industrial Marketing, 28*(5), 396–410.

OUTLOOK ON FUTURE RESEARCH OPPORTUNITIES

As outlined earlier, the original RBV and the extensions such as ROT have reached significant maturity. Regarding the spin-off theories, the NRBV and SRBV, the NRBV needs further empirical and conceptual development. In terms of key variables, the strategic capabilities behind BoP strategies require further empirical investigation. Moreover, the domain can be expanded and the role of the external environment in shaping firm's responses to environmental concerns should be further understood (Hart and Dowell, 2011). Still, further research is needed to explore the strategic capabilities needed to enable firms to succeed in new contexts such as BoP markets which are characterized by institutional voids (Hart and Dowell, 2011). Regarding factual claims, future research directions for NRBV include the identification of contingencies which affect the environmental–financial performance relationship (Van der Byl and Slawinski, 2015). Moreover, investigating the applicability of the ecologically dominant logic (Montabon et al., 2016) and the capabilities needed to reconsider the priorities between ecological, social and economic aspects, is important.

In terms of the SRBV, the extended domain offers ample future research opportunities, extending the scope far beyond 'typical' business stakeholders to also include non-governmental organizations (NGOs), but also local communities and the natural environment. In terms of variables, future research should explore the necessary and sufficient conditions for achieving TBL value, in particular the role of social capabilities, and whether capabilities from all views are needed to create integrated TBL value. In terms of factual claims, an important aspect for further research relates to the interrelations between the economic, environmental and social performance outcomes, especially in the context of a broad stakeholder network. The specific order of priorities between the three areas can be explored from the ecologically dominant view (Montabon et al., 2016) as well as the anthropocentric versus ecocentric perspective (Borland et al., 2016). Exploring these questions in different research contexts is also very important, since there are major differences between traditional firms, social businesses, B-Corps and non-profits. In terms of research streams, SRBV provides a link between social entrepreneurship (Torugsa et al., 2012), sustainable supply chain management (SSCM) research (Klassen and Vachon, 2003; Klassen and Vereecke, 2012), as well as performance measurement and supplier relationship management in SSCM (Ahi and Searcy, 2013; Gold et al., 2010; Hassini et al., 2012; Klassen and Vachon, 2003; Klassen and Vereecke, 2012). Bridging between those streams in future research to ensure common progress across disciplines also represents a research opportunity.

REFERENCES

Ahi, P., and Searcy, C. (2013). A comparative literature analysis of definitions for green and sustainable supply chain management. *Journal of Cleaner Production*, *52*, 329–341.

Allred, C.R., Fawcett, S.E., Wallin, C., and Magnan, G.M. (2011). A dynamic collaboration capability as a source of competitive advantage. *Decision Sciences*, *42*(1), 129–161.

Bals, L., and Tate, W.L. (2018). Sustainable supply chain design in social businesses: advancing the theory of supply chain. *Journal of Business Logistics*, *39*(1), 57–79.

Barney, J.B. (1991). Firm resources and sustained competitive advantage. *Journal of Management*, *17*, 49–61.

Barney, J. B. (2001). Resource-based theories of competitive advantage: a ten-year retrospective on the resource-based view. *Journal of Management*, *27*(6), 643–650.

Barney, J.B., Ketchen Jr, D.J., and Wright, M. (2011). The future of resource-based theory: revitalization or decline? *Journal of Management*, *37*(5), 1299–1315.

Barney, J.B., Wright, M., and Ketchen Jr, D.J. (2001). The resource-based view of the firm: ten years after 1991. *Journal of Management*, *27*(6), 625–641.

Borland, H., Ambrosini, V., Lindgreen, A., and Vanhamme, J. (2016). Building theory at the intersection of ecological sustainability and strategic management. *Journal of Business Ethics*, *135*, 293–307.

Bowen, H.R. (1953). *Social Responsibility of the Businessman*. New York: Harper & Row.

Carroll, A.B. (1979). A three-dimensional conceptual model of corporate performance. *Academy of Management Review*, *4*(4), 497–505.

Carroll, A.B. (1999). Corporate social responsibility evolution of a definitional construct. *Business and Society*, *38*(3), 268–295.

Carter, C.R., Rogers, D.S., and Choi, T.Y. (2015). Toward the theory of the supply chain. *Journal of Supply Chain Management*, *51*(2), 89–97.

Chatain, O. (2011). Value creation, competition, and performance in buyer–supplier relationships. *Strategic Management Journal*, *32*(1), 76–102.

Dierckx, I., and Cool, K. (1989). Asset stock accumulation and sustainability of competitive advantage. *Management Science*, *35*(12), 1504–1511.

Eisenhardt, K.M., and Martin, J. (2000). Dynamic capabilities: What are they? *Strategic Management Journal*, *21*(10–11), 1105–1121.

Gladwin, T.N., Kennelly, J.J., and Krause, T.S. (1995). Shifting paradigms for sustainable development: implications for management theory and research. *Academy of Management Review*, *20*(4), 874–907.

Glavas, A., and Mish, J. (2015). Resources and capabilities of triple bottom line firms: going over old or breaking new ground? *Journal of Business Ethics*, *127*(3), 623–642.

Gold, S., Seuring, S., and Beske, P. (2010). Sustainable supply chain management and inter-organizational resources: a literature review. *Corporate Social Responsibility and Environmental Management*, *17*(4), 230–245.

Hart, S.L. (1995). A natural-resource-based view of the firm. *Academy of Management Review*, *20*(4), 986–1014.

Hart, S.L., and Dowell, G. (2010). A natural-resource-based view of the firm: fifteen years after. *Journal of Management*, *37*(5), 1464–1479.

Hart, S.L., and Dowell, G. (2011). Invited editorial: a natural-resource-based view of the firm: fifteen years after. *Journal of Management*, *37*(5), 1464–1479.

Hart, S.L., and Milstein, M.B. (2003). Creating sustainable value. *Academy of Management Executive*, *17*(2), 56–69.

Hassini, E., Surti, C., and Searcy, C. (2012). A literature review and a case study of sustainable supply chains with a focus on metrics. *International Journal of Production Economics*, *104*(1), 69–82.

Hitt, M.A., Xu, K., and Carnes, C.M. (2016). Resource based theory in operations management research. *Journal of Operations Management, 41*, 77–94.

Hunt, S.D., and Morgan, R.M. (1995). The comparative advantage theory of competition. *Journal of Marketing, 59*(2), 1–15.

Ireland, R.D., and Hitt, M.A. (1999). Achieving and maintaining strategic competitiveness in the 21st century: the role of strategic leadership. *Academy of Management Executive, 13*(1), 43–57.

King, A., and Lenox, M. (2002). Exploring the locus of profitable pollution reduction. *Management Science, 48*(2), 289–299.

Klassen, R.D., and Vachon, S. (2003). Collaboration and evaluation in the supply chain: the impact on plant-level environmental investment. *Production and Operations Management, 12*(3), 336–352.

Klassen, R.D., and Vereecke, A. (2012). Social issues in supply chains: capabilities link responsibility, risk (opportunity), and performance. *International Journal of Production Economics, 140*(1), 103–115.

Kogut, B., and Zander, U. (1993). Knowledge of the firm and the evolutionary theory of the multinational corporation. *Journal of International Business Studies, 24*(4), 625–645.

Lashitew, A.A., Bals, L., and van Tulder, R. (2020). Inclusive business at the base of the pyramid: the role of embeddedness for enabling social innovations. *Journal of Business Ethics, 162*(2), 421–448.

Learned, E., Christensen, C., Andrews, K. and Guth, W. (1969). *Business Policy: Text and Cases.* Homewood, IL: Irwin.

Lockett, A., and Thompson, S. (2001). The resource-based view and economics. *Journal of Management, 27*(6), 723–754.

Mahoney, J.T., and Pandian, J.R. (1992). The resource-based view within the conversation of strategic management. *Strategic Management Journal, 13*(5), 363–380.

Makadok, R. (1999). Interfirm differences in scale economies and the evolution of market shares. *Strategic Management Journal, 20*(10), 935–952.

Meehan, J., Meehan, K., and Richards, A. (2006). Corporate social responsibility: the 3C-SR model. *Journal of Social Economics, 33*(5/6), 386–398.

Montabon, F., Pagell, M., and Wu, Z. (2016). Making sustainability sustainable. *Journal of Supply Chain Management, 52*(2), 11–27.

Norman, W., and MacDonald, C. (2004). Getting to the bottom of 'triple bottom line'. *Business Ethics Quarterly, 14*(2), 243–262.

Penrose, E. (1995). *The Theory of the Growth of the Firm,* 1959. Oxford: Basil Blackwell and Mott.

Peteraf, M.A. (1993). The cornerstones of competitive advantage: a resource-based view. *Strategic Management Journal, 14*(3), 179–191.

Porter, M.E., and Kramer, M.R. (2006). Strategy and society: the link between competitive advantage and corporate social responsibility. *Harvard Business Review, 84*(12), 78–92.

Porter, M.E., and Kramer, M.R. (2011). Creating shared value: redefining capitalism and the role of the corporation in society. *Harvard Business Review, 89*(1/2), 62–77.

Prahalad, C.K., and Hamel, G. (1990). Core competency concept. *Harvard Business Review, 64*(3), 70–92.

Ratajczak, P. (2021). The mediating role of natural and social resources in the corporate social responsibility–corporate financial performance relationship. *Managerial and Decision Economics, 42*(1), 100–119.

Richardson, G.B. (1972). The organization of industry. *Economic Journal, 82*(327), 883–896.

Selznick, P. (1984). *Leadership in Administration: A Sociological Interpretation.* Berkeley, CA: University of California Press.

Sharma, S., and Vredenburg, H. (1998). Proactive corporate environmental strategy and the development of competitively valuable organizational capabilities. *Strategic Management Journal, 19*(8), 729–753.

Sirmon, D.G., Hitt, M.A., Ireland, R.D., and Gilbert, B.A. (2011). Resource orchestration to create competitive advantage breadth, depth, and life cycle effects. *Journal of Management, 37*(5), 1390–1412.

Sodhi, M.S. (2015). Conceptualizing social responsibility in operations via stakeholder resource-based view. *Production and Operations Management, 24*(9), 1375–1389.

Tate, W.L., and Bals, L. (2018). Achieving shared triple bottom line (TBL) value creation: toward a social resource-based view (SRBV) of the firm. *Journal of Business Ethics, 152*(3), 803–826.

Tate, W.L., Ellram, L.M., and Kirchoff, J. (2010). Corporate social responsibility reports: a thematic analysis related to supply chain management. *Journal of Supply Chain Management, 46*(1), 19–44.

Teece, D.J. (2007). Explicating dynamic capabilities: the nature and microfoundations of (sustainable) enterprise performance. *Strategic Management Journal, 28*(13), 1319–1350.

Teece, D.J., Pisano, A., and Shuen, A. (1997). Dynamic capabilities and strategic management. *Strategic Management Journal, 18*(7), 509–533.

Torugsa, N.A., O'Donohue, W., and Hecker, R. (2012). Capabilities, proactive CSR and financial performance in SMEs: empirical evidence from an Australian manufacturing industry sector. *Journal of Business Ethics, 109*(4), 483–500.

Van der Byl, C.A., and Slawinski, N. (2015). Embracing tensions in corporate sustainability: a review of research from win–wins and trade-offs to paradoxes and beyond. *Organization and Environment, 28*(1), 54–79.

Wacker, J.G. (1998). A definition of theory: research guidelines for different theory-building research methods in operations management. *Journal of Operations Management, 16*(4), 361–385.

Wacker, J.G. (2008). A conceptual understanding of requirements for theory-building research: guidelines for scientific theory building. *Journal of Supply Chain Management, 44*(3), 5–15.

Wernerfelt, B. (1984). A resource-based view of the firm. *Strategic Management Journal, 5*(2), 171–180.

Winter, S.G. (2003). Understanding dynamic capabilities. *Strategic Management Journal, 24*(10), 991–995.

SUGGESTED FURTHER READING

For More Information on the RBV and Its Roots

For a critical discussion of its origins and implications, please see:
Barney, J.B., and Arikan, A.M. (2001). The resource-based view: origins and implications. In: Hitt, M.A., Freeman, R.E. and Harrison, J.S. (eds), *The Blackwell Handbook of Strategic Management.* Hoboken, NJ: Wiley-Blackwell, pp. 124–188.

For an excellent review of main challenges faced by the RBV, see:
Priem, R.L., and Butler, J.E. (2001). Is the resource-based 'view' a useful perspective for strategic management research? *Academy of Management Review, 26*(1), 22–40.

For an opposing perspective and criticism of the RBV, see:
Kraaijenbrink, J., Spender, J.C., and Groen, A.J. (2010). The resource-based view: a review and assessment of its critiques. *Journal of Management, 36*(1), 349–372.

Good Literature Reviews on the Application of the RBV

Armstrong, C.E., and Shimizu, K. (2007). A review of approaches to empirical research on the resource-based view of the firm. *Journal of Management, 33*(6), 959–986.

Ferreira, M.P., Serra, F.R., Costa, B.K., and Almeida, M. (2016). A bibliometric study of the resource-based view (RBV) in international business research using Barney (1991) as a key marker. *Innovar, 26*(61), 131–144.

Hitt, M.A., Xu, K., and Carnes, C.M. (2016). Resource based theory in operations management research. *Journal of Operations Management, 41*, 77–94.

Lopes, J., Ferreira, J.J.M., and Farinha, L. (2021). Entrepreneurship and the resource-based view: what is the linkage? A bibliometric approach. *International Journal of Entrepreneurial Venturing, 13*(2), 137–164.

Newbert, S.L. (2007). Empirical research on the resource-based view of the firm: an assessment and suggestions for future research. *Strategic Management Journal, 28*(2), 121–146.

Wade, M., and Hulland, J. (2004). The resource-based view and information systems research: review, extension, and suggestions for future research. *MIS Quarterly, 28*(1), 107–142.

9. The knowledge-based view

Tobias Schoenherr

INTRODUCTION

The knowledge-based view (KBV) has been experiencing increased interest and application across disciplines in general, and more specifically also within the domains of both supply chain management (SCM) and purchasing and supply management (PSM). The basic premise of the KBV is that knowledge constitutes the primary and 'most strategically-significant resource of the firm' (Grant, 1996a, p. 375; see also Quinn, 1992). With this framing, the KBV provides a framework and associated approaches for integrating this knowledge within firms (Grant, 1996b). This integration of knowledge for the building of organizational capabilities is the fundamental tenet of the KBV. As such, obtaining, disseminating and utilizing knowledge is positioned as a unique source for a company's competitive differentiation and long-lasting success (Kogut and Zander, 2008). Of critical importance for sustainable competitive advantage is that knowledge is idiosyncratic, and not easily transferable or replicable (Grant, 1991). The KBV has thus at its core the investigation of mechanisms for how organizations process and integrate knowledge, as well as how knowledge is created (Nonaka, 1994).

Western epistemologists view knowledge as justified true belief and have been studying its nature, as well as what elevates a belief to become knowledge. Management scholars, however, generally deviate from this strict, traditionalist understanding of epistemological knowledge, which focuses on the 'absolute, static, and nonhuman nature of knowledge, traditionally expressed in propositional forms in formal logic' (Nonaka, 1994, p. 15). This traditional view focuses on the truthfulness aspect of knowledge, rather than a subjective belief for which justification is sought. The latter has been the focus of management scholars, studying human processes responsible for the justification of personal beliefs and aspiring for truth in them, rather than viewing truth as an absolutely necessary condition for beliefs to constitute knowledge. In this chapter, I consider knowledge from the perspective of management scholars. With this framing, the chapter provides background on the development and application of the KBV, with a particular focus on SCM and PSM research.

The chapter commences with an outline of the foundations that contributed to the development of the KBV, going back to the seminal work of Adam Smith, but then fast-forwarding to the last century and discussing the contributions of Machlup, Drucker, and others who aided in the formation of the theory. This serves as the background for the more rapid evolution of the knowledge-based view over the last decade of the prior century. These more recent developments were influential in shaping the KBV as we know it today.

I then describe the key tenets, variables and definitions of the KBV. This discourse starts with an exposition of the theory of the firm, which aids in our understanding of companies' actions by an abstraction of complexities inherent in real life. The theory helps in the application of the theoretical perspectives to actual companies. This is followed by the key themes and definitions that make up the KBV, including the distinction between knowledge and information, and between explicit and tacit knowledge, with the latter pair referring to the degree of transferability of knowledge between individuals. Other aspects discussed include an individual's commitment to create knowledge, as well as aggregation, which determines how effectively knowledge can be transferred. I also discuss appropriability, which refers to how easily knowledge can be imitated, and the concept of common knowledge, which is critical as it serves as infrastructure for how more advanced knowledge can be integrated and applied. I further outline knowledge conversion and integration mechanisms, capturing the evolutionary pathways of explicit and tacit knowledge, and describe how knowledge can help in building organizational capability. This section concludes with a brief overview of organizational learning, which serves as a foundation for the KBV. The major variables discussed are summarized in Table 9.1, with their relationships captured in Figure 9.1.

I then review some of the most prominent application domains of the KBV within the SCM and PSM literature. This review, which is structured into three subsections (knowledge management and organizational capabilities; strategic sourcing; and supplier and customer

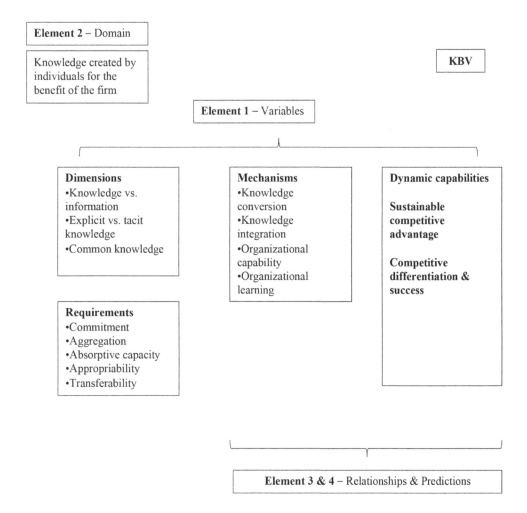

Figure 9.1   Overview of KBV theory elements

Table 9.1   Definitions of KBV variables

Elements	Explanation	Supporting references
Unit of analysis	Knowledge created by individuals for the benefit of the firm, often conceptualized as collective knowledge resident in the firm	Grant, 1996b; Nonaka, 1994
Level of analysis	Project, firm or relationship level, analysing the effects of knowledge	Grant, 1996a, 1996b
Dimensions		
Information	A flow of messages, which is different to knowledge	Dretske, 1981; Machlup, 1983; Nonaka, 1994
Knowledge	A belief for which justification is sought, aspiring for the truth in it; knowledge is the outcome of information flows anchored in the commitment and beliefs of its holder	Dretske, 1981; Machlup, 1983; Nonaka, 1994
Explicit knowledge	Knowledge that can be easily codified, communicated and transferred; often captured in books or policies	Grant, 1996a, 1996b; Nonaka, 1994
Tacit knowledge	Knowledge that is implied and subjective, and part of an individual's experience, beliefs, mental models and perspectives; it is reflected in actions and behaviours; it can be difficult to transfer this knowledge, which is often 'learned by doing'	Grant, 1996a, 1996b; Kogut and Zander, 1992; Polanyi, 1966
Common knowledge	Knowledge that is known and accepted by all members of the firm, offering a foundation and common understanding that facilitates the integration of non-common knowledge	Grant, 1996b; Nonaka and Takeuchi, 1995
Requirements		
Commitment	An important element in the creation of knowledge, emphasizing that individuals need to be committed to be able to create knowledge; commitment can be fostered through an individual's intention (how an individual views the world, their value judgement), autonomy (offering freedom and motivation to consider new knowledge) and fluctuation (making knowledge more robust)	Nonaka, 1994
Aggregation	A determinant for how efficiently knowledge can be transferred and applied; absorptive capacity can aid this endeavour	Cohen and Levinthal, 1990; Grant, 1996b
Absorptive capacity	The foundation of prior knowledge upon which the new knowledge can be built	Cohen and Levinthal, 1990
Appropriability	Factors 'that govern an innovator's ability to capture the profits generated by an innovation' (Teece, 1986)	Grant, 1996b; Teece, 1986
Transferability	The ease with which knowledge can be shared and applied by someone else; based on the degree of transferability, explicit and tacit knowledge	Grant, 1996b
Mechanisms		
Knowledge conversion	The interaction between explicit and tacit knowledge dimensions, which can take the form of socialization, combination, externalization and internalization	Nonaka, 1994
Socialization	The conversion of tacit knowledge into tacit knowledge	Nonaka, 1994
Combination	The conversion of explicit knowledge into explicit knowledge	Nonaka, 1994
Externalization	The conversion of tacit knowledge into explicit knowledge	Nonaka, 1994

Elements	Explanation	Supporting references
Internalization	The conversion of explicit knowledge into tacit knowledge	Nonaka, 1994
Knowledge integration	The ways and ease with which knowledge can be transferred and integrated; integrating knowledge forms the essence for building organizational capability	Grant, 1996a
Organizational learning	Deals with the mechanisms for new information and knowledge to be absorbed and applied by individuals	Levitt and March, 1988; Penrose, 1959
Organizational capability	A firm's ability to repeatedly carry out a task that creates value; central to this capability is the integration of specialized knowledge	Grant, 1996a
Dynamic capabilities		
Sustainable competitive advantage	Long-lasting and persistent superior performance of the firm, enabling it to set itself apart from competing firms	Dyer, 1996; Dyer and Nobeoka, 2000; Grant, 1991
Competitive differentiation and success	A company's ability to create a unique value proposition, effectively setting it apart from rival firms	Kogut and Zander, 2008

integration), is meant to be illustrative, rather than exhaustive, with a focus on publications that appeared over the last five years.

The final section offers some concluding thoughts, including whether the KBV can be considered as a theory, and where the future of the KBV may lie.

TOWARD A KNOWLEDGE-BASED VIEW

Foundations

The importance of knowledge and our transitioning to a knowledge society has been a topic of constant debate, exchange and development. As such, it has been fundamental to economic analysis, which has been relying on knowledge as a factor in decision making; for instance, in terms of investments and the desire to achieve the best possible outcomes with the least amount of resources. This is reflected in Adam Smith's (1776) *The Wealth of Nations*, in which he compares production workers 'educated at the expense of much labour and time' to 'expensive machines', substantiating the different wages between skilled and common labour. Along similar lines, he positioned knowledge as a critical ingredient for the success of a merchant.

These early thoughts were developed further in the last century by Machlup's (1962) discourse on the production and distribution of knowledge in the United States. In this book, he traces the early beginnings of a knowledge society and predicts that future development will shift the demand from physical labour to 'brain workers' (p. 9). In addition to noting that countries are becoming increasingly concerned with the production of knowledge, he advances the hypothesis suggesting that more innovation-minded firms employ white collar workers to a greater degree, which goes hand in hand with technological advances. While this relationship is well accepted today, Machlup (1962) was one of the first to call attention to these dynamics, and hence to propose the notion of knowledge industries; that is, industries whose success is intricately linked to knowledge.

These arguments were further extended by Drucker (1969), highlighting changes happening in our society and the emergence of the knowledge society. Drucker argues that with knowledge being the 'central cost of the American economy', it has become 'the key to productivity, competitive strength, and economic achievement', as well as a critical ingredient to a country's international economic strength (p. 264). A compelling analogy which Drucker provides is that with steel being the economic measurement in 1910, if all knowledge workers had been taken away back then, the economy would have paid very little notice, since steel production relied on skill rather than on knowledge. However, Drucker also cautions that knowledge will not take the place of skill, but rather that knowledge is the foundation for advanced and sophisticated skills to develop and improve productivity. In this vein, Grant (1996b) stresses knowledge as a critical input to production, with machines and equipment simply being 'embodiments of knowledge' (p. 112).

Drucker (1969) further emphasizes several milestones over the last centuries that contributed to this development and the fostering of a knowledge economy. As such, recognizing that knowledge can be systematically applied was the foundation for the success of toolmakers in England during the 1800s, most notably Joseph Whitworth, who built their knowledge into the tools and thus codified the best ways to carry out a particular task; the 'go/no go' gauges were just some of the innovations that came out of this development. A further milestone during the late 1800s highlighted by Drucker was Frederick Taylor's scientific management, which introduced the notion that more work can be accomplished not only by working harder, but also by working smarter (and more effectively so). Promoting knowledge to push skills to the next level was also the objective of the Morrill Act of 1962 in the United States, which established land-grant colleges to develop farming into a discipline for the advancement of knowledge and skills.

Another influential writer foreshadowing the changing times was Bell (1973), who envisions the structural changes in a post-industrial society moving towards the information age. He correctly predicts the shift from an 'economy of goods' to an 'economy of information'. The importance of knowledge for society was also dealt with in a highly influential discourse by Hayek (1945), who emphasizes the need for knowledge sharing and combination, due to the dispersed nature of knowledge. The concept and importance of knowledge also increasingly became a theme at conferences, such as the one held at the Technische Hochschule Darmstadt in Germany in fall 1984, whose major contributions were captured in Böhme and Stehr (1986).

At the beginning of the 1990s, Kogut and Zander (1992) forwarded the notion that firms are effective vehicles for knowledge sharing and transfer among individuals and groups. The basic premise of the article is that information and know-how can yield combinative capabilities, enabled by internal and external learning, which in turn can generate opportunities and growth. Their framework considers information as knowledge that 'can be transmitted without loss of integrity' (p. 386), while know-how refers to accumulated skill of expertise that has to be acquired.

Recent Developments

Building on these seminal works, authors in the second part of the 1990s started to take these foundations further to develop a 'knowledge-based theory of the firm'. While there are numerous scholars that contributed to the development and refinement of what we now know as the KBV, I would like to highlight especially the works by Robert Grant, Ikujiro Nonaka and Hirotaka Takeuchi.

One of the earliest proponents of the knowledge-based view was Robert Grant (1996a), who positions organizational capabilities as a key ingredient for firms' long-term strategy and competitiveness. Taking this concept further, he notes that with knowledge being inherent to individuals, the objective of organizational capabilities should then be the integration of this specialized knowledge. As such, Grant (1996a) develops a knowledge-based theory of organizational capabilities, and in doing so leverages tenets from the resource-based view (RBV), organizational learning and capabilities, and competitive dynamics. Already in this seminal work, an emphasis is placed on the mechanisms through which knowledge is integrated and then applied, rather than just focusing on its possession.

That same year, Grant (1996b) followed up this discourse by conceptualizing the firm as an 'institution for integrating knowledge' (p. 109) and highlighting the need for coordination mechanisms in this endeavour. Grant (1996b) differentiates his perspective in that knowledge resides in the individual, with firms then applying this knowledge, rather than creating it; this was also an important distinction made later on by Felin and Hesterly (2007). Within this context, Grant (1996b) positions knowledge as the most strategically important resource a firm possesses, and in this vein, the KBV can be considered as an extension of the RBV.

Overall, Grant's 1996 article in the *Strategic Management Journal* (Grant, 1996b) continues to be one of the most influential pieces in the development of the KBV and is his most highly cited article.

Grant's immersion into the RBV can also be seen in some of his earlier work (Grant, 1991). The RBV was initially proposed by Penrose (1959) in his theory of the growth of the firm, and later expanded and refined by Wernerfelt (1984), Barney (1991) and Conner (1991). The basic tenet of the RBV is that firms can achieve sustainable competitive advantage through the development and protection of resources. This is the case when a resource can be characterized as being valuable, rare, inimitable and non-substitutable: the so-called VRIN characteristics (the RBV is discussed more in-depth in Chapter 8 in this book). Within the KBV, these properties are related to the concept of knowledge, with knowledge being able to represent such a VRIN resource.

Dynamic capabilities represent another closely related theoretical concept. With dynamic capabilities referring to 'difficult-to-replicate enterprise capabilities required to adapt to changing customer and technological opportunities' (Teece, 2007, pp. 1319–1320), the connection to the KBV is obvious. As such, the ability to 'integrate, build, and reconfigure internal and external competences to address rapidly changing environments' (Teece et al., 1997, p. 516) can be readily related to a company's knowledge management capability. This capability has been conceptualized as knowledge management competencies related to the acquisition, conversion, application and protection of knowledge (Schoenherr et al., 2014).

Equally as influential as Grant in the development of the KBV was Ikujiro Nonaka, most notably with his book *The Knowledge-Creating Company: How Japanese Companies Create Dynamics of Innovation*, which he co-authored with Hirotaka Takeuchi (Nonaka and Takeuchi, 1995). The scholars start out the book by noting that the success of Japanese companies continues to be an enigma to Western companies, and then shed light on this observation by emphasizing the Japanese companies' capability of 'organizational knowledge creation' (p. 3). Nonaka and Takeuchi (1995) explain what may have contributed to this capability to develop among Japanese firms first (history, industrial development, overall status of international competitiveness), and position knowledge as a competitive resource. Key to the success of Japanese companies was the recognition that knowledge cannot always be written down, and that especially tacit knowledge has great potential to yield competitive differentiation.

Nonaka and Takeuchi (1995) outline three characteristics responsible for effective knowledge creation. The first is a heavy emphasis on metaphor and analogy, which is an attempt to 'express the inexpressible' (p. 12). As such, figurative language can go a long way, especially in new product development, since it enables individuals to relate to what they know to a new situation without any constraints. With this approach, creativity is encouraged, and fundamental breakthroughs are possible. The second characteristic is that individual knowledge must be shared with others. As such, the creation of organizational knowledge is not possible without individuals sharing knowledge with each other, or the refining and elevating of it to a new level through discussion and debate. The third is that knowledge is created amidst ambiguity, which again triggers creativity and outside-of-the-box thinking. Ambiguity, however, is coupled with redundancy, which ensures a common understanding of basic principles, and which enables individuals to help each other manage the ambiguous environment. In the extreme case, this can even lead to the institution of competing product development teams pursuing different approaches for the new product (Nonaka, 1990), with the ensuing debate then being invaluable to produce the best product possible.

A highly influential piece, preceding the publication of the book, was Nonaka's (1994) dynamic theory of organizational knowledge creation, which outlines the mechanisms with which organizational knowledge can be developed. The essence of this development is the ongoing dialogue between tacit and explicit knowledge dimensions, captured in four different patterns, and reflecting the ways in which current knowledge can be converted into new knowledge. Nonaka (1994) further points out that while knowledge resides in individuals, it is the interaction among them that can elevate and amplify knowledge. Nonaka (1994) refers to these dynamics as 'communities of interaction' and as the 'ontological' dimension of knowledge creation (p. 15). Similarly to Grant (1996b), Nonaka (1994) stresses that while knowledge is created by and resides within individuals, organizations play a major part in knowledge articulation and amplification.

KEY TENETS, VARIABLES AND DEFINITIONS

Theory of the Firm

The 'theory of the firm' concept helps in our understanding of companies' actions, and relies on an abstraction of complexities inherent in real-life companies. In order to do so, the concept is founded on singling out specific behaviours and leveraging insight into these to explain the influence of actions or characteristics on firm strategy and subsequent success (Machlup, 1967). Along these lines, Grant (1996b) positions the role of firms as offering mechanisms through which individuals can integrate and combine their specialized knowledge to create something that is greater than the sum of the individual knowledge assets. In fact, Grant (1996a, p. 385) went so far as to suggest that the 'fundamental role of the firm is the integration of individuals' specialist knowledge', and that 'organizational capabilities are the manifestation of this knowledge integration'.

In contrast to Spender (1989), who focuses on the generation and application of organizational knowledge, Grant (1996b) considers the creation of knowledge as an individual activity, with firms then providing the context within which this knowledge can be applied to the provision of products and services; appropriate incentives for individuals to do so can be provided by firms. As such, the firm is viewed as providing structures for coordinating and integrating individuals' contributions, which are needed since an individual cannot feasibly learn all needed specialized knowledge resident in others (Grant, 1996a). This view parallels Simon's (1991), and also explains the extended label of the KBV often used: that is, the 'knowledge-based view of the firm'.

Within this framing, the assumptions underlying Grant's (1996a, p. 385) development of the knowledge-based theory of organizational capability are that: (1) knowledge is a firm's principal productive resource; (2) tacit knowledge (in contrast to explicit knowledge) is of particular importance, due to its limited transferability; (3) tacit knowledge is stored in a highly specialized form; and (4) a wide array of knowledge is needed for production. These assumptions serve as the foundation for the ensuing discussion in which they will be expanded upon.

Knowledge versus Information

While the terms 'knowledge' and 'information' are frequently used interchangeably, it is critical to note their differences. While Machlup (1962) calls attention to the differential uses of 'information' versus 'knowledge', in that information is understood as disconnected facts, and knowledge as an ordered or systematic view about information, he advocates that 'all information is knowledge' (p. 8), expressing a preference for just using 'knowledge'. Nonaka (1994), also capturing prior work by Machlup (1983) and Dretske (1981), however delineates the differences by describing information as 'a flow of messages', while knowledge is created by this 'very flow of information, anchored on the commitment and beliefs of its holder' (p. 15). As such, information is needed to generate knowledge. Of particular relevance here is semantic information, that is, its content, rather than the form in which it is shared; this content has the ability to bring new meaning to contexts.

Explicit versus Tacit Knowledge

Central to the RBV is a resource's transferability so that its strengths can be leveraged in different contexts (Barney, 1986). This characteristic is extended to the KBV, where the transfer of knowledge both within and across firms can be instrumental in sustaining a firm's or a supply chain's competitive success. While there are various distinctions based on the degree of knowledge transferability, the most common ones utilized by SCM and PSM scholars include explicit and tacit knowledge. This dichotomy is also highlighted by Nonaka (1994), who refers to this distinction as the 'epistemological dimension to organization knowledge creation' (p. 15), and notes that the interplay of explicit and tacit knowledge can yield new discoveries.

Explicit knowledge is characterized by its ability to be codified, and to be easily communicated and transferred (Nonaka, 1994). As such, explicit knowledge can be captured in books and articles, but also in policies and procedures. Grant (1996b, p. 111) describes it as 'knowing about facts and theories', rather than 'knowing how', which he associates with tacit knowledge. Explicit knowledge can thus generally be integrated with great ease (Grant 1996a), due to the ability to capture it readily in unambiguous written form. Advances in information technology in the late 1980s and 1990s, primarily in the form of enterprise resource planning (ERP) systems, have further elevated this knowledge integration, dissemination and retrieval to entirely new heights (Rockart and Short, 1989; Bendoly and Schoenherr, 2005).

In contrast, tacit knowledge is difficult to conceptualize, since it is often implicit and subjective, and part of an individual's experience, beliefs, mental models and perspectives, rather than knowledge captured in written form. As such, tacit knowledge is reflected in actions and behaviours, and is characterized by its frequently ambiguous nature (Venkitachalam and Busch, 2012); it cannot be written down (Grant, 1996a). Tacit knowledge also often cannot be acquired immediately but develops over time and is encapsulated in someone's skill. The philosopher Polanyi (1966) fittingly describes it as knowing more than one can tell; that is, knowledge that cannot be readily expressed, but which becomes evident via its application. Along these lines, Grant (1996b) describes it as 'knowing how to do something'. The tacit nature of this type of knowledge can make it difficult or even impossible to transfer, since it can also be context-dependent (Kogut and Zander, 1992). While this may pose challenges for an internal knowledge transfer, it may also offer an opportunity for the firm to leverage this knowledge as a competitive differentiator, since it is difficult to copy or imitate by other firms. As such, Nonaka (1991) attributed tacit knowledge to the success of Japanese companies. These properties make tacit knowledge the more intriguing form of knowledge to study.

Common Knowledge

While the power of the KBV relies on the integration of specialized knowledge resident in individuals, a key prerequisite of this integration is the existence of common knowledge. As the label implies, this knowledge is known and accepted by all members of the firm, offering a foundation and common understanding that facilitates the integration of non-common knowledge. Grant (1996b, p. 115) describes common knowledge as 'the intersection of ... individual knowledge sets' and draws parallels to Nonaka and Takeuchi's (1995) redundancy concept that captures knowledge known across functions. Grant (1996b) differentiates between five types of common knowledge: (1) a common language, which enables seamless verbal communication between stakeholders; (2) other forms of symbolic communication, which include literacy and familiarity with, for instance, computer programs, software and statistical principles; (3) common specialized knowledge, which considers a deeper overlap of more specific knowledge between individuals; (4) shared meaning, which captures a common understanding of knowledge aspects that are tacit; and (5) individual knowledge domains, which reflect an individual's awareness of the knowledge repertoire of others. In this vein, organizational culture can also be considered as a form of common knowledge (Grant, 1996a).

Other Knowledge Classifications

In addition to the dichotomy between explicit and tacit knowledge described above, other classification schemes were suggested. For instance, Machlup (1962) differentiates between five classes of knowledge: (1) practical knowledge applicable for someone's work activities; (2) intellectual knowledge to respond to someone's intellectual curiosity; (3) small-talk and pastime knowledge, which includes aspects such as gossip, stories or jokes; (4) spiritual knowledge, referring to religious knowledge; and (5) unwanted knowledge, which is obtained by accident. In a later work, Machlup (1980) further introduced 13 elements of knowledge, which relate to: '(1) being acquainted, (2) being familiar, (3) being aware, (4) remembering, (5), recollecting, (6) recognizing, (7) distinguishing, (8) understanding, (9) interpreting, (10) being able to explain, (11) being able to demonstrate, (12) being able to talk about, and (13) being able to perform' (p. 47).

While Spender (1996) differentiates between explicit and implicit knowledge, he also distinguishes between individual and social knowledge. Individual knowledge can be transferred with the individual, with social knowledge being publicly available or collective and embedded within the structure of firms.

Alavi and Leidner (2001), within the context of information systems, suggest several perspectives with which knowledge can be viewed. As such, knowledge is described as a state of mind, where information contributes to a better understanding and learning. Knowledge can also be viewed as an object that can be stored and manipulated; or a process, where knowledge is applied and shared. Knowledge can also pertain to an organized access to information; or a capability, where knowledge is associated with the potential to influence action.

Commitment

Since it is an individual that creates knowledge, a crucial element in this vein is their commitment to this endeavour. Nonaka (1994) defines three factors contributing to this commitment. The first is the individual's intention, which refers to how they view the world and aim to make sense of it. Inherent to this view is a value judgement, based on which the information received is evaluated and its value appropriated. The second is an individual's autonomy, which enables them to have the freedom and flexibility to acquire and interpret information and use their judgement to elevate it to knowledge. Autonomy can also serve as a motivation to generate knowledge in the first place. The third factor is fluctuation, which fosters a refinement of knowledge based on the continuous interaction with the environment, making the knowledge more robust and elevating it to greater applicability. An individual's identification with their organization can also be a valuable element in promoting knowledge throughout the organization. This was confirmed, for instance, by Van den Hooff and de Ridder (2004), who established a positive relationship between affective commitment and an individual's desire to share their knowledge with others in the organization.

Commitment, however, can also be viewed from an organizational level, an aspect that can subsume individual commitment. For instance, Garrido-Moreno et al. (2014) capture organizational commitment as comprising the commitment from both top management and employees, in addition to the investment in appropriate training and reward systems, as well as executive leadership and support. In the authors' study on the influence of customer relationship management technology (CRM) infrastructure on CRM success, organizational commitment had a significant influence on knowledge management, with both of these dimensions fully mediating the relationship between CRM technology infrastructure and CRM success. A similar angle was taken by Mao et al. (2016), who investigate the role of resource commitment, which reflects an organization's efforts for improving infrastructure and capabilities. While resource commitment directly influences knowledge management capability, it also was able to play an enabling role for enhancing the impact of human and relationship resources on knowledge management capability. Yet another way to look at commitment is from the interorganizational level, a view which was taken by Zheng et al. (2011). In their study, commitment was part of relational embeddedness, able to influence knowledge-based dynamic capabilities.

Aggregation

Grant (1996b) describes aggregation as a determinant for how effectively knowledge can be transferred. This is a critical aspect, since not only does relevant knowledge need to be shared, but this knowledge now also needs to be received and absorbed, that is, put to good use. This receptiveness factor has been studied with the concept of absorptive capacity, a term which was coined by Cohen and Levinthal (1990). Absorptive capacity refers to the foundation of prior knowledge upon which the new knowledge can be built, and which can be a key determinant for the innovation capabilities of a firm. This prior knowledge helps individuals make sense of the newly acquired knowledge, and hence supports individuals 'to recognize the value of new, external information, assimilate it, and apply it to commercial ends' (Cohen and Levinthal, 1990, p. 128). Grant (1996b) refers to this as the 'additivity between different elements of knowledge' (p. 111).

Appropriability

The concept of appropriability within the context of business strategy was introduced by Teece (1986), who describes it as the environmental factors 'that govern an innovator's ability to capture the profits generated by an innovation' (p. 287). Within the KBV context, appropriability essentially then refers to how easily knowledge can be imitated. In the case of explicit knowledge, legal instruments such as patents, copyrights and trade secrets can ensure appropriability to some degree. However, if such protection is not available – that is, under conditions of weak appropriability – explicit knowledge needs to be tightly guarded. While this is also the case for tacit knowledge, the potential for imitation is reduced due to the knowledge's implicit nature. As such, tacit knowledge cannot be directly transferred, but must be appropriated through its application (Grant, 1996b).

Even if knowledge is easily transferable, whether this is done depends on an individual's willingness. As such, Nickerson and Zenger (2004) caution that opportunism associated with knowledge exchange discourages the sharing of knowledge, and label knowledge appropriation as a knowledge formation hazard. A solution to this would be the embedding of knowledge into salable products, so that the individual sharing the knowledge can extract value from it. A related hazard is that of strategic knowledge accumulation, in which an individual may shape the knowledge search heuristic to showcase their expertise and thus make their knowledge appear more valuable.

Knowledge Conversion Mechanisms

The concept of knowledge conversion can be traced back to Anderson (1983), who classified knowledge into declarative knowledge (analogous to explicit knowledge) and procedural knowledge (analogous to tacit knowledge), with the former needing to be converted to the latter to generate cognitive skills. Nonaka (1994), however, extended this unidirectional notion to a continuous and reciprocal dialogue between explicit and tacit knowledge.

The conversion of tacit knowledge – that is, the sharing of one's own tacit knowledge so that it becomes the tacit knowledge of others – is referred to as socialization. This conversion of tacit knowledge to tacit knowledge can be accomplished by on-the-job training, apprenticeships or internships. In this manner, experiences can be shared within the context, which is essential for the transfer of tacit knowledge.

The conversion of explicit knowledge – that is, the sharing of one's own explicit knowledge and combining it with the explicit knowledge of others – is referred to as combination. This sharing can help in the reconfiguration and recontextualization of one's own knowledge. Information technology has been a great enabler in this regard, for instance in the form of enterprise resource planning systems enabling cross-functional integration, or the use of supplier portals enabling the sharing of knowledge across companies.

The conversion of tacit into explicit knowledge is referred to as externalization. This can be accomplished by 'successive rounds of meaningful "dialogue"' (Nonaka, 1994, p. 20) and is facilitated by the use of metaphors. As such, aspects are articulated and cultivated until they become more concrete, often by a 'trial and error' approach.

The conversion of explicit into tacit knowledge is referred to as internalization. Internalization takes place when knowledge created by individuals is aimed to be crystalized within the context of a different application. Crystallization involves testing the 'reality and applicability' of a concept (Nonaka, 1994, p. 25), enabled by experimentation. The outcome is referred to as tacit since the process needed for it relies on the social and synergetic interaction of team members.

Knowledge Integration Mechanisms

The KBV considers knowledge integration as the essence for building organizational capability (Grant, 1996a), which hinges on the firm's ability to access and integrate knowledge effectively. Determining elements in this vein constitute the effectiveness of mechanisms with which knowledge can be integrated within the firm, as well as the firm's level and sophistication of common knowledge. Favourable conditions on these elements may help this organizational capability to lead to competitive advantage. The sustainability of this advantage then depends on the degree of the capability's inimitability.

Since explicit knowledge can be written down and easily communicated, it faces less, if any, challenges for integration. As such, explicit knowledge can be encoded and captured in procedures, norms, processes and rules (March, 1991). Similar approaches are aimed to be employed for the integration of tacit knowledge, although this is more challenging. Specifically, Grant (1996a) suggests the use of direction and routines. On the one hand, directions can be provided in the form of an operating manual addressing almost every aspect of an operation, embodying the collective knowledge of specialists. On the other hand, organizational routines provide for coordination mechanisms without the need for communication. Routines are dependent on informal processes and an understanding of everyone's role in them. This can be achieved through training, observation or repetition (Grant, 1996a).

Grant (1996a) identifies three characteristics of knowledge integration that foster the development of competitive advantage. The first pertains to the efficiency of integration, which captures the ease with which individual, specialized knowledge can be accessed and applied. Efficiency can be enhanced by greater levels of common knowledge, a greater frequency with which tasks are performed and a lower degree of task variability, and an organizational structure that minimizes the need for communication required in knowledge integration (modularity can be a great enabler in this regard). The second characteristic is the breadth of the knowledge that is being integrated, with a greater breadth being reflected in terms of both different types and a broader scope of knowledge. These properties make it more challenging for competitors to imitate the knowledge for similar gains. The third characteristic is the flexibility of integration, which captures the degree to which knowledge can be reconfigured via new forms of integration to yield new capabilities.

Organizational Learning

Fundamental to the KBV is organizational learning, which provides a deeper understanding of the mechanisms responsible for new information and knowledge being absorbed and applied by individuals within their firms. Through organizational learning, inferences can be encoded into routines that guide behaviour (Levitt and March, 1988), and thus form the foundation for the growth of the firm (Penrose, 1959). Of note here is the organizational context in which learning takes place, which can be fertile ground and provide a structure for learning. Brown and Duguid (1991) aptly refer to this context as 'communities of practice', and Senge (1990) coins the term 'the learning organization'.

Beneficial to the acquisition of knowledge can be specialization, for which the larger organizational setting also provides opportunities. Due to an individual's bounded rationality (Simon, 1991), individuals possess a limited capacity to absorb, process and apply new knowledge, which is why Grant (1996b) suggests that individuals specialize in specific knowledge areas. With this approach, new specific knowledge can be quickly put to use and applied.

APPLICATION DOMAINS

While the KBV has been applied in a variety of domains, our emphasis in this illustrative review is on the application of the theory to the domains of SCM and PSM. This review is not meant to be exhaustive, but rather illustrative of how the KBV has been applied in SCM and PSM, with an emphasis on the last five years. The illustrative snapshot of SCM and PSM research applying the KBV is structured around the following three themes: knowledge management and organizational capabilities, strategic sourcing, and supplier and customer integration.

Knowledge Management and Organizational Capabilities

Knowledge management pertains to the recognition, creation, transformation and distribution of knowledge (Gold et al., 2001), captures the flows of knowledge (Alavi and Leidner, 2001), and has as its objective the development of mechanisms for the best management of these flows. This can lead to the development of organizational capabilities. The management of knowledge, especially within a supply chain setting, has received significant attention, as illustrated by two recent literature reviews on the topic (Cerchione and Esposito, 2016; del Rosario Pérez-Salazar et al., 2017). While knowledge management across firms is certainly more challenging than it is within firms, it also carries with it greater promises through the integration of diverse knowledge assets from supply partners.

In this vein, Gold et al. (2001) outline both infrastructural capabilities (technology, structure and culture) and process capabilities (acquisition, conversion, application and protection processes) to enhance the organizational effectiveness in managing knowledge. Schoenherr et al. (2014) translate these process capabilities to the supply chain context, devising the concept of supply chain knowledge management capability (SCKMC). Specifically, *knowledge acquisition* captures approaches with which knowledge can be accumulated (Lyles and Salk, 1996); *knowledge conversion* refers to the translation of the obtained knowledge into formats that can be applied; *knowledge application* includes methods to utilize this knowledge to solve problems; and *knowledge protection* pertains to approaches aimed at shielding the knowledge from outside dissemination (Norman, 2004). Schoenherr et al. (2014) then position SCKMC as a dynamic capability able to generate both explicit and tacit knowledge, eventually enhancing supply chain performance.

The KBV has been leveraged quite a bit to investigate and explain the enhancement of operational capabilities in a manufacturing operations context. Since the development of capabilities may hinge on the combination of specialized knowledge sources within the firm, the role of human resources management can therefore not be neglected (Malik et al., 2020). An illustrative study is provided by Roscoe et al. (2019), who rely on the KBV to understand how structures and processes aid stakeholders to interact and share knowledge, leading to the emergence of operating routines and operational capabilities. The authors differentiate between discrete and system technologies, which are ideally matched with authority-based and consensus-based hierarchies, respectively. A further illustration is provided by Lam et al. (2016), who explore the impact of a firm's internal social media initiatives (enabling knowledge exchange) on operational efficiency and innovativeness.

Onofrei et al. (2019) position operational intellectual capital as a knowledge-based resource, able to enhance the effect of the investment in lean practices on operational performance. A similar context of lean production systems is chosen by Secchi and Camuffo (2016), who characterize lean implementation processes founded in a principles-based knowledge replication strategy as more effective and efficient. Capabilities for the management of technology are the focus of Argote and Hora (2017), who consider knowledge to be embedded in members, tasks and tools of the organization. Within the context of operational capabilities, knowledge is also associated with absorptive capacity. For instance, Ambulkar et al. (2016) consider absorptive capacity as a second-order construct consisting of knowledge usage, dissemination and acquisition, which is developed by an individual's risk mitigation orientation and which is able to lead to risk mitigation competency.

Strategic Sourcing

The KBV has been relied upon extensively in the realm of strategic sourcing, as indicated for instance in the review by Wynstra et al. (2019) on PSM being a multidisciplinary research field. As such, the authors identify the KBV to be especially popular among strategy and organization journals. Similarly, Spina et al. (2016), in their review of external grand theories in PSM, suggest the KBV to be particularly suitable when taking a buyer's perspective, and the theory has had a continued presence in papers presented at the International Purchasing and Supply Education and Research Association (IPSERA) conferences (for example, Kamann and Johnsen, 2019).

An illustrative study, having applied the KBV within the context of strategic sourcing, is by Schütz et al. (2020), who leverage KBV tenets to argue for the positive effect of purchasing knowledge on both cost savings and strategic performance at the same time, also considering the moderating role of purchasing integration. In addition, Kilpi et al. (2018) consider knowledge acquired from the supply market and the supply base as leading to both an exploitative and an explorative PSM orientation, ultimately enhancing supply performance. Knowledge is also identified as a key ingredient for developing competences to drive sustainable PSM by Schulze and Bals (2020). The KBV is further relied upon in a study on SCM experience in top management teams and its impact on proactive environmental strategy by Kumar and Paraskevas (2018). However, it also depends on *how* knowledge is integrated. Revilla and Knoppen (2015) illustrate this in their study on buyer–supplier relationships, in which knowledge integration mechanisms (specifically, joint sense making and joint decision making) play a critical role in fostering innovation and operational efficiency. Knowledge integration mechanisms, in turn, can be elevated by strategic supply management and trust in buyer–supplier relationships.

Outsourcing literature has applied the KBV to explain firms' motivations for outsourcing (Mihalache and Mihalache, 2016), which may stem from the ability to identify, explore and transfer knowledge from suppliers to the firm (Shook et al., 2009). In this view, sourcing is a boundary spanning mechanism contributing to the competitive differentiation of the firm

(Combs and Crook, 2007). In addition to the internalization of the knowledge, this can also involve the hiring of knowledge workers from other firms, the development of joint ventures or alliances, or even the acquisition of other firms themselves (Shook et al., 2009). Within this context, the KBV has also helped to facilitate the make-or-buy decision (Tsay et al., 2018). While the KBV has mostly been applied in empirical studies, it also received application in Chen et al.'s (forthcoming) game-theoretic model looking at the impact of outsourcing knowledge on a buying firm's decision to use a supply chain intermediary or agent.

A further illustrative study in this domain is Verwaal (2017), who associates greater cognitive and normative barriers in knowledge exchange when outsourcing, leading to explorative innovation to negatively mediate the link between global outsourcing and firm financial performance. What may alleviate this situation, however, is the development of relational capital built with the foreign supplier.

Supplier and Customer Integration

A large body of research within the SCM and PSM domains focuses on the benefits associated with supplier and customer integration, and sometimes even the integration of competitor knowledge (for example, Schoenherr and Swink, 2012). While numerous advantages can be derived from such better integration, including better coordination and information sharing abilities, as well as the opportunity for enhanced collaboration, a central benefit from a KBV perspective is the integration and leveraging of knowledge from both suppliers and customers for the benefit of the firm. This knowledge obtained from external partners has the ability to offer new insights and information, enabling better decision making based on a more comprehensive understanding of the context and complexities.

What makes this type of knowledge integration, which leverages the insight of many different stakeholders, so powerful is that knowledge can be elevated to an entirely new level, as the result of this integration can often be much more than the simple sum of the knowledge assets; an expectation that goes back to Senge's (1992) concept of the learning organization. Access to such external knowledge can serve as a primary driver for companies to foster closer supplier relationships (Lanier et al., 2010). The significant potential of knowledge integration across company boundaries was also highlighted by Grant (1996a), who emphasizes the importance of relational contracts as an efficient and effective means to access, transfer and integrate knowledge. Kogut (2000) also makes the case for knowledge generated within firm networks and posits this knowledge as the source of value. How the complexity of such supply networks can impact a firm's financial performance is the topic in Lu and Shang (2017), who rely on the KBV to explain the positive effect of supplier knowledge on a firm's innovation and financial performance. Overall, the predictions formulated by Grant (1996a) have held true, as indicated in the review of supply chain integration by Danese et al. (2020), who identify the KBV as a theory that has been used to explain the effects of such integration. As such, knowledge management and knowledge management processes can serve as important mediators and moderators to provide finer-grained insight into the impact of integration on performance.

The integration of specialized knowledge is also at the foundation of innovation and the development of new products (Nonaka, 1990). Innovation can be accomplished not only by the application of new knowledge, but also by the reconfiguration of existing knowledge (Grant, 1996a). These tenets were relied upon extensively in SCM and PSM research. For example, Schoenherr (2018) investigates the moderating role of structural, human and social capital on the relationship between supplier leveraging and product innovation performance. In this model, supplier leveraging refers to the application of knowledge obtained from suppliers for the benefit of the firm. While the influence of this construct on innovation was supported, Schoenherr (2018) also confirmed this relationship to be stronger under higher levels of both structural and human capital. In contrast, higher levels of social capital diminish the influence of supplier leveraging on innovation, due to social capital being associated with greater autonomy and confidence (Marcus, 1988), which in turn may not provide a fertile ground for outside (supplier) knowledge to be welcomed (Kim et al., 2015).

While most research has taken the buyer's perspective, similar benefits can, however, also be derived by the supplier. This was confirmed by Preston et al. (2017), who were able to find support for their expectations of buyer–supplier social capital leading to buyer-enabled enrichment of supplier knowledge, eventually resulting in greater cost efficiency and innovation on behalf of the supplier. Similarly, the effect of knowledge transfer activities driven by the buying firm on the supplier's operational performance improvement was investigated by Kim et al. (2015), highlighting key supplier characteristics that can enhance this effect (the supplier's perceived overlapping knowledge, their cognitive congruence and their trust) or detract from it (the supplier's innovativeness).

CONCLUDING THOUGHTS

It is undeniable that the KBV has had a fundamental impact on the SCM and PSM disciplines. Its appeal is eminent, since it offers a fitting framework and associated approaches for integrating and leveraging knowledge for the benefit of the firm. This ability to obtain, disseminate and utilize knowledge can serve as a unique source for a company's competitive differentiation and long-lasting success.

The setting of the supply chain offers particularly intriguing and powerful opportunities for the leveraging of knowledge from the various stakeholders involved. This can be attributed to the reality of supply chains competing against supply chains (as opposed to companies competing against companies), necessitating the help and support of supply chain partners, particularly regarding their knowledge resources, in order to remain competitive – for instance quickly bringing innovative products to market (Schoenherr, 2018). One of the earliest works adapting this framing was Dyer (1996), who considered specialized supplier networks as a source of competitive advantage. The power of such 'knowledge-sharing networks' was later also illustrated by Dyer and Nobeoka (2000) with the case of Toyota. These findings further parallel arguments by Cohen and Levinthal (1990), who view outside knowledge (that is, knowledge from supply chain partners) as a critical element for driving innovation.

Ever since these early studies, the KBV has been establishing itself as a foundational perspective to be applied within a supply chain setting. This was evidenced, for instance, in the review by Defee et al. (2010), who provide an inventory of theories used in logistics and SCM research; but also by Shook et al. (2009) in their 'theoretical toolbox' for strategic sourcing, which includes the KBV as one of the ten theories reviewed.

Given the prevalence of the KBV, can it thus be considered a theory? The debate on how this question should be answered is still ongoing. When Grant (1996a) first formulated the KBV, he was explicit in noting that it is not yet a theory of the firm, since there is 'insufficient consensus as to its precepts or purpose, let alone its analysis and predictions' (p. 110). The review of Eisenhardt and Santos (2002) also concludes that the KBV is not yet a theory of strategy that significantly extends the RBV or the dynamic capabilities perspective.

These views stand in contrast to those of Kogut and Zander (1992), who consider organizations as 'social communities in which individual and social expertise is transformed into economically useful products and services by the application of a set of higher-order organizing principles' (p. 384). These early inroads in labelling the KBV as a theory were faced by harsh criticism, for instance by Foss (1996a, 1996b). While Foss (1996a) acknowledges the value of the KBV perspective, he does not agree that it is a theory, since it is not able to provide reasons for the existence of firms in the absence of incentives, property rights and opportunism/moral hazard. He continues these arguments in Foss (1996b), arguing that the KBV cannot sufficiently characterize the firm. This view was then again countered by Kogut and Zander (1996), arguing that knowledge 'has an economic value over market transactions when identity leads to social knowledge that supports coordination and communication' (p. 502)

In recent years, an increasing consensus seems to be appearing that suggests the KBV constitutes a theory. This is evidenced, for instance, in Spina et al.'s (2016) review of external grand theories applied in the PSM domain, which highlights the KBV as one of the most frequently applied theories, behind transaction cost economics and the RBV. The KBV was also included as a grand theory in Wynstra et al.'s (2019) review. To delineate the KBV as a theory, some articles have deliberately moved away from the 'view' label and replaced it with 'theory', that is, referring to it as the 'knowledge-based theory' (KBT) (for example, Spina et al., 2016). The 'KBV' term, however, is still the more prevalent label used to date.

Where do we go from here? In my view, the KBV is a perspective that is now probably more important than it has ever been. In our hyper-competitive and risk-prone environment, knowledge is essential for companies to continuously transform and reinvent themselves, to be able to remain relevant and competitive. Substantiation for this view can be drawn from the notion that data is the world's most valuable resource, rather than oil, as headlined in a 2017 article in *The Economist* (Parkins, 2017). This data can be equated to information; which, however, in and of itself does not necessarily lead to value generation. What needs to happen is a transformation of this information into valuable knowledge that can be applied for the benefit of the firm. When this is done, knowledge can lead to the development of dynamic capabilities, sustainable competitive advantage, and competitive differentiation and success.

The KBV carries great potential in serving as the theoretical foundation for a multitude of applications. While I expect the theory to continue to be applied to the themes reviewed in this chapter, I believe it will be especially powerful when aiming to push companies to their next frontiers. While companies may be able to do so themselves, a more effective and efficient approach may lie in the leveraging of external stakeholders and partners, since with this approach, unique and different knowledge resources can be recombined for the benefit of the network. This view is becoming increasingly prevalent, as indicated by the emergence of the term 'business ecosystems', which refers to dynamic, collaborative, semi-permanent, multi-company systems (Fuller et al., 2019). As such, these systems are a 'middle ground' between traditional (static) supply chains and the open market, and are widely considered the 'hotbeds of industry knowledge' (Zahra and Nambisam, 2012, p. 220). How to effectively build, recombine and integrate knowledge in these more complex settings (compared to the static supply chain) carries great promise for investigation.

REFERENCES

Alavi, M. and D.E. Leidner (2001), 'Review: Knowledge management and knowledge management systems', *MIS Quarterly*, 25 (1), 107–136.

Ambulkar, S., J.V. Blackhurst and D.E. Cantor (2016), 'Supply chain risk mitigation competency: An individual-level knowledge-based perspective', *International Journal of Production Research*, 54 (5), 1398–1411.

Anderson, J.R. (1983), *The Architecture of Cognition*, Cambridge, MA: Harvard University Press.

Argote, L. and M. Hora (2017), 'Organizational learning and management of technology', *Production and Operations Management*, 26 (4), 579–590.

Barney, J.B. (1986), 'Organizational culture: Can it be a source of sustained competitive advantage?', *Academy of Management Review*, 11 (3), 656–665.

Barney, J.B. (1991), 'Firm resources and sustained competitive advantage', *Journal of Management*, 17 (1), 99–120.

Bell, D. (1973), *The Coming of Post-Industrial Society: A Venture in Social Forecasting*, New York: Basic Books.

Bendoly, E. and T. Schoenherr (2005), 'ERP system and implementation-process benefits: Implications for B2B e-procurement', *International Journal of Operations and Production Management*, 25 (4), 304–319.

Böhme, G. and N. Stehr (eds) (1986), *The Knowledge Society: The Growing Impact of Scientific Knowledge on Social Relations*, Dordrecht: D. Reidel Publishing Company.

Brown, J.S. and P. Duguid (1991), 'Organizational learning and communities of practice: Toward a unified view of working, learning and innovation', *Organization Science*, 2 (1), 40–57.

Cerchione, R. and E. Esposito (2016), 'A systematic review of supply chain knowledge management research: State of the art and research opportunities', *International Journal of Production Economics*, 182, 276–292.

Chen, Q., G. Özkan-Seely, S. Wang and A. Roth (forthcoming), 'Knowledge-based view of the use of an intermediary in new product manufacturing outsourcing', *Decision Sciences*. https://doi.org/10.1111/deci.12496.

Cohen, W.M. and D.A. Levinthal (1990), 'Absorptive capacity: A new perspective on learning and innovation', *Administrative Science Quarterly*, 35 (1), 128–152.

Combs, J. and T. Crook (2007), 'Sources and consequences of bargaining power in supply chains', *Journal of Operations Management*, 25 (2), 546–555.

Conner, K.R. (1991), 'A historical comparison of the resource-based theory and five schools of thought within industrial organization economics: Do we have a new theory of the firm?', *Journal of Management*, 17 (1), 121–154.

Danese, P., M. Molinaro and P. Romano (2020), 'Investigating fit in supply chain integration: A systematic literature review on context, practices, performance links', *Journal of Purchasing and Supply Management*, 26 (5), 100634.

Defee, C.C., B. Williams, W.S. Randall and R. Thomas (2010), 'An inventory of theory in logistics and SCM research', *International Journal of Logistics Management*, 21 (3), 404–489.

del Rosario Pérez-Salazar, M., A.A. Aguilar Lasserre, M.G. Cedillo-Campos and J.C. Hernández González (2017), 'The role of knowledge management in supply chain management: A literature review', *Journal of industrial Engineering and Management*, 10 (4), 711–788.

Dretske, F. (1981), *Knowledge and the Flow of Information*, Cambridge, MA: MIT Press.

Drucker, P. (1969), *The Age of Discontinuity: Guidelines to Our Changing Society*, New York: Harper & Row.

Dyer, J.H. (1996), 'Specialized supplier networks as a source of competitive advantage: Evidence from the auto industry', *Strategic Management Journal*, 17 (4), 271–291.

Dyer, J.H. and K. Nobeoka (2000), 'Creating and managing a high-performance knowledge-sharing network: The Toyota case', *Strategic Management Journal*, 21 (3), 345–367.

Eisenhardt, K.M. and F.M. Santos (2002), Knowledge-based view: A new theory of strategy. In A. Pettigrew, H. Thomas, and R. Whittington (eds), *Handbook of Strategy and Management*, Thousand Oaks, CA: SAGE Publications, pp. 139–164.

Felin, T. and W.S. Hesterly (2007), 'The knowledge-based view, nested heterogeneity, and new value creation: Philosophical considerations on the locus of knowledge', *Academy of Management Review*, 32 (1), 195–218.

Foss, N.J. (1996a), 'Knowledge-based approaches to the theory of the firm: Some critical comments', *Organization Science*, 7 (5), 470–476.

Foss, N.J. (1996b), 'More critical comments on knowledge-based theories of the firm', *Organization Science*, 7 (5), 519–523.

Fuller, J., M.G. Jacobides and M. Reeves (2019), 'The myths and realities of business ecosystems', *MIT Sloan Management Review*, 60 (3), 1–9.

Garrido-Moreno, A., N. Lockett and V. García-Morales (2014), 'Paving the way for CRM success: The mediating role of knowledge management and organizational commitment', *Information and Management*, 51 (8), 1031–1042.

Gold, A.H., A. Malhotra and A.H. Segars (2001), 'Knowledge management: An organizational capabilities perspective', *Journal of Management Information Systems*, 18 (1), 688–698.

Grant, R.M. (1991), 'The resource-based theory of competitive advantage: Implications for strategy formulation', *California Management Review*, 33 (3), 114–135.

Grant, R. (1996a), 'Prospering in dynamically competitive environments: Organizational capability as knowledge integration', *Organization Science*, 7 (4), 375–387.

Grant, R. (1996b), 'Towards a knowledge-based view of the firm', *Strategic Management Journal*, 17, 109–122.

Hayek, F.A. (1945), 'The use of knowledge in society', *American Economic Review*, 35 (4), 519–530.

Kamann, D.-J. F. and T.E. Johnsen (2019), 'Coping with the future: Picking your battles', *Journal of Purchasing and Supply Management*, 25 (1), 1–4.

Kilpi, V., H. Lorentz, T. Solakivi and J. Malmsten (2018), 'The effect of external supply knowledge acquisition, development activities and organizational status on the supply performance of SMEs', *Journal of Purchasing and Supply Management*, 24 (3), 247–259.

Kim, H., D. Hur and T. Schoenherr (2015), 'When buyer-driven knowledge transfer activities really work: A motivation–opportunity–ability perspective', *Journal of Supply Chain Management*, 51 (3), 33–60.

Kogut, B. (2000), 'The network as knowledge: Generative rules and the emergence of structure', *Strategic Management Journal*, 21 (3), 405–425.

Kogut, B. and U. Zander (1992), 'Knowledge of the firm, combinative capabilities, and the replication of technology', *Organization Science*, 3 (3), 383–397.

Kogut, B. and U. Zander (1996), 'What firms do? Coordination, identity, and learning', *Organization Science*, 7 (5), 502–518.

Kogut, B. and U. Zander (2008), *What Firms Do: Coordination, Identity, and Learning, Knowledge, Options, and Institutions*, Oxford: Oxford University Press.

Kumar, A. and J.P. Paraskevas (2018), 'A proactive environmental strategy: Analyzing the effect of SCM experience, age, and female representation in TMTs', *Journal of Supply Chain Management*, 54 (4), 20–41.

Lam, H.K., A.C. Yeung and T.E. Cheng (2016), 'The impact of firms' social media initiatives on operational efficiency and innovativeness', *Journal of Operations Management*, 47, 28–43.

Lanier, D., Jr., W.F. Wempe and Z.G. Zacharia (2010), 'Concentrated supply chain membership and financial performance: Chain- and firm-level perspectives', *Journal of Operations Management*, 28 (1), 1–16.

Levitt, B. and J.G. March (1988), 'Organizational learning', *Annual Review of Sociology*, 14 (1), 319–338.

Lu, G. and G. Shang (2017), 'Impact of supply base structural complexity on financial performance: Roles of visible and not-so-visible characteristics', *Journal of Operations Management*, 53, 23–44.

Lyles, M.A. and J.E. Salk (1996), 'Knowledge acquisition from foreign parents in international joint ventures: An empirical examination in the Hungarian context', *Journal of International Business Studies*, 27 (5), 877–903.

Machlup, F. (1962), *The Production and Distribution of Knowledge in the United States*, Princeton, NJ: Princeton University Press.

Machlup, F. (1967), 'Theories of the firm: Marginalist, behavioral, managerial', *American Economic Review*, 57, 201–220.

Machlup, F. (1980), *Knowledge: Its Creation, Distribution, and Economic Significance*, Princeton, NJ: Princeton University Press.

Machlup, F. (1983), 'Semantic quirks in studies of information', in F. Machlup and U. Mansfield (eds), *The Study of Information*, New York: John Wiley, pp. 641–671.

Malik, A., F.J. Froese and P. Sharma (2020), 'Role of HRM in knowledge integration: Towards a conceptual framework', *Journal of Business Research*, 109, 524–535.

Mao, H., S. Liu, J. Zhang and Z. Deng (2016), 'Information technology resource, knowledge management capability, and competitive advantage: The moderating role of resource commitment', *International Journal of Information Management*, 36 (6), 1062–1074.

March, J.G. (1991), 'Exploration and exploitation in organizational learning', *Organization Science*, 2 (1), 71–87.

Marcus, A.A. (1988), 'Responses to externally induced innovation: Their effects on organizational performance', *Strategic Management Journal*, 9 (4), 387–402.

Mihalache, M. and O.R. Mihalache (2016), 'A decisional framework of offshoring: Integrating insights from 25 years of research to provide direction for future', *Decision Sciences*, 47 (6), 1103–1149.

Nickerson, J. and T. Zenger (2004), 'A knowledge-based theory of the firm: The problem-solving perspective', *Organization Science*, 15 (6), 617–632.

Nonaka, I. (1990), 'Redundant, overlapping organization: A Japanese approach to managing the innovation process', *California Management Review*, 32 (3), 27–38.

Nonaka, I. (1991), 'The knowledge-creating company', *Harvard Business Review*, 69 (6), 96–104.

Nonaka, I. (1994), 'A dynamic theory of organizational knowledge creation', *Organization Science*, 5 (1), 14–37.

Nonaka, I. and H. Takeuchi (1995), *The Knowledge-Creating Company: How Japanese Companies Create Dynamics of Innovation*, New York: Oxford University Press.

Norman, P.M. (2004), 'Knowledge acquisition, knowledge loss, and satisfaction in high technology alliances', *Journal of Business Research*, 57 (6), 610–619.

Onofrei, G., J. Prester, B. Fynes, P. Humphreys and F. Wiengarten (2019), 'The relationship between investments in lean practices and operational performance', *International Journal of Operations and Production Management*, 39 (3), 406–428.

Parkins, D. (2017), 'The world's most valuable resource is no longer oil, but data', *The Economist*, 7 May. https://www.economist.com/leaders/2017/05/06/the-worlds-most-valuable-resource-is-no-longer-oil-but-data.

Penrose, E. (1959), *The Theory of the Growth of the Firm*, Oxford: Basil Blackwell.

Polanyi, M. (1966), *The Tacit Dimension*, Garden City, NY: Doubleday.

Preston, D.S., D.Q. Chen, M. Swink and L. Meade (2017), 'Generating supplier benefits through buyer-enabled knowledge enrichment: A social capital perspective', *Decision Sciences*, 48 (2), 248–287.

Quinn, J.B. (1992), *Intelligent Enterprise*, New York: Free Press.

Revilla, E. and D. Knoppen (2015), 'Building knowledge integration in buyer–supplier relationships', *International Journal of Operations and Production Management*, 35 (10), 1408–1436.

Rockart, J.F. and J.E. Short (1989), 'IT in the 1990s: Managing organizational interdependence', *Sloan Management Review*, 30 (2), 17–33.

Roscoe, S., P.D. Cousins and R. Handfield (2019), 'The microfoundations of an operational capability in digital manufacturing', *Journal of Operations Management*, 65 (8), 774–793.

Schoenherr, T. (2018), 'Leveraging suppliers for product innovation performance: The moderating role of intellectual capital', *Transportation Journal*, 57 (4), 365–398.

Schoenherr, T., D.A. Griffith and A. Chandra (2014), 'Knowledge management in supply chains: The role of explicit and tacit knowledge', *Journal of Business Logistics*, 35 (2), 121–135.

Schoenherr, T. and M. Swink (2012), 'Revisiting the arcs of integration: Cross-validations and extensions', *Journal of Operations Management*, 30 (1–2), 99–115.

Schulze, H. and L. Bals (2020), 'Implementing sustainable purchasing and supply management (SPSM): A Delphi study on competences needed by purchasing and supply management (PSM) professionals', *Journal of Purchasing and Supply Management*, 26 (4), 100625.

Schütz, K., M. Kässer, C. Blome and K. Foerstl (2020), 'How to achieve cost savings and strategic performance in purchasing simultaneously: A knowledge-based view', *Journal of Purchasing and Supply Management*, 26 (2), 100534.

Secchi, R. and A. Camuffo (2016), 'Rolling out lean production systems: A knowledge-based perspective', *International Journal of Operations and Production Management*, 36 (1), 61–85.

Senge, P.M. (1990), *The Fifth Discipline: The Art and Practice of the Learning Organization*, New York: Doubleday Currency.

Senge, P.M. (1992), 'Mental models', *Planning Review*, 20(2), 4–44.

Shook, C.L., G.L. Adams, D.J. Ketchen and C.W. Craighead (2009), 'Towards a "theoretical toolbox" for strategic sourcing', *Supply Chain Management: An International Journal*, 14 (1), 3–10.

Simon, H.A. (1991), 'Bounded rationality and organizational learning', *Organization Science*, 2 (1), 125–134.

Smith, A. (1776), *An Inquiry into the Nature and Causes of the Wealth of Nations*, London: Strahan & Cadell.

Spender, J.-C. (1996), 'Making knowledge the basis of a dynamic theory of the firm', *Strategic Management Journal*, 17 (S2), 45–62.

Spender, J.-C. (1989), *Industry Recipes: The Nature and Sources of Managerial Judgment*, Oxford: Blackwell.

Spina, G., F. Caniato, D. Luzzini and S. Ronchi (2016), 'Assessing the use of external grand theories in purchasing and supply management research', *Journal of Purchasing and Supply Management*, 22 (1), 18–30.

Teece, D.J. (1986), 'Profiting from technological innovation: Implications for integration, collaboration, licensing and public policy', *Research Policy*, 15 (6), 285–306

Teece, D.J. (2007), 'Explicating dynamic capabilities: The nature and microfoundations of (sustainable) enterprise performance', *Strategic Management Journal*, 28 (13), 1319–1350.

Teece, D.J., G.P. Pisano and A. Shuen (1997), 'Dynamic capabilities and strategic management', *Strategic Management Journal*, 18 (7), 509–533.

Tsay, A.A., J.V. Gray, I.J. Noh and J.T. Mahoney (2018), 'A review of production and operations management research on outsourcing in supply chains: Implications for the theory of the firm', *Production and Operations Management*, 27 (7), 1177–1220.

Van Den Hooff, B. and J.A. De Ridder (2004), 'Knowledge sharing in context: The influence of organizational commitment, communication climate and CMC use on knowledge sharing', *Journal of Knowledge Management*, 8 (6), 117–130.

Venkitachalam, K. and P. Busch (2012), 'Tacit knowledge: Review and possible research directions', *Journal of Knowledge Management*, 16 (2), 356–371.

Verwaal, E. (2017), 'Global outsourcing, explorative innovation and firm financial performance: A knowledge-exchange based perspective', *Journal of World Business*, 52 (1), 17–27.

Wernerfelt, B. (1984), 'A resource-based view of the firm', *Strategic Management Journal*, 5 (2), 171–180.

Wynstra, F., R. Suurmond and F. Nullmeier (2019), 'Purchasing and supply management as a multidisciplinary research field: Unity in diversity?', *Journal of Purchasing and Supply Management*, 25 (5), 100578.

Zahra, S.A. and S. Nambisan (2012), 'Entrepreneurship and strategic thinking in business ecosystems', *Business Horizons*, 55 (3), 219–229.

Zheng, S., W. Zhang and J. Du (2011), 'Knowledge-based dynamic capabilities and innovation in networked environments', *Journal of Knowledge Management*, 15 (6), 1035–1051.

10. Resource-advantage theory

Donna F. Davis and Teresa M. McCarthy-Byrne

INTRODUCTION

Resource-advantage (R-A) theory is a general theory of competition that combines a resource-based view of the firm with heterogeneous demand theory to describe an evolutionary process of competition. R-A theory was introduced in the 1990s in a series of articles published in marketing journals co-authored by Shelby Hunt and Robert Morgan (1995, 1997), culminating in a monograph that sets forth the historic foundation and basic tenets of the theory (Hunt, 2000). Subsequent articles develop R-A theory across multiple disciplines including purchasing, supply chain management, management, economics, ethics, law and public policy.

Resource-advantage theory posits that firms pursue comparative advantages in resources to achieve marketplace positions of competitive advantage that, in turn, generate superior financial performance (Hunt, 2000). Here, 'superior' implies that a firm surpasses competitors in terms of relative efficiency through reduced costs and/or relative effectiveness by delivering higher value. Feedback loops spur organizational learning and innovation by systematically cycling back marketplace signals of relative performance as inputs to inform future actions. That is, superior financial performance signals a marketplace position of competitive advantage which, in turn, signals a higher level of comparative advantage in resources (see Figure 10.1). Hence, R-A theory views competition as an inherently dynamic process that provokes disequilibrium in the marketplace as firms strive for comparative advantages in resources to secure marketplace positions of competitive advantage.

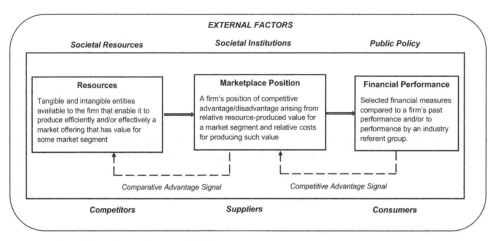

Source: Adapted from Hunt and Morgan (1997).

Figure 10.1   Resource-advantage theory conceptual framework

Both R-A theory and the resource-based view (RBV) posit that firms possess bundles of resources that are unique to the firm and heterogenous across firms, and those resource bundles are imperfectly mobile. However, RBV theorists suggest competition is equilibrating whereas R-A theory views competition as disequilibrating as firms continually attempt to gain positions of comparative advantage (Hunt and Davis, 2008). Further, the RBV considers market demand as an external environmental factor. In contrast, R-A theory extends the RBV by assuming heterogeneous demand. That is, R-A theory proposes that industry demand is a collection of market segments with significantly different demand curves that reflect consumer's preferences. Thus, heterogenous demand theory assumes different bundles of resources are required to meet expectations of multiple market segments within an industry. The combination of heterogenous, imperfectly mobile resources, and heterogenous demand across market segments, generates a competitive landscape characterized by significant diversity among firms in the same industry as well as across industries.

The following sections outline the foundational premises, define key variables of R-A theory, and explain relationships among the variables. The domain where the theory applies is then described, along with the use of R-A theory across disciplines. The chapter concludes with opportunities for future research.

KEY VARIABLES AND DEFINITIONS

As shown in Figure 10.1, the R-A theory of competition emphasizes the importance of: (1) organizational resources; (2) marketplace positions of competitive advantage; and (3) financial performance. As set forth by Hunt and Morgan (1995, 1997) and further developed by Hunt (2000, p. 106), nine foundational premises undergird R-A theory:

- P1. Demand is heterogeneous across industries, heterogeneous within industries, and dynamic.
- P2. Consumer information is imperfect and costly.
- P3. Human motivation is constrained self-interest seeking.
- P4. The organization's objective is superior financial performance.
- P5. The organization's information is imperfect and costly.
- P6. The organization's resources are financial, physical, legal, human, organizational, informational and relational.
- P7. Resource characteristics are heterogeneous and imperfectly mobile.
- P8. The role of management is to recognize, understand, create, select, implement and modify strategies.
- P9. Competitive dynamics are disequilibrium-provoking, with innovation endogenous.

The nine foundational premises underpin the theoretical framework displayed in Figure 10.1. The following sections define the key variables of R-A theory.

Organizational Resources

Following the resource-based view of the firm, organizational resources are defined as 'the tangible and intangible entities available to the firm that enable it to produce efficiently and/ or effectively a market offering that has value for some market segment' (Hunt, 2000, p. 128).

This definition conveys three important aspects of organizational resources. First, resources comprise not only tangible resources but also intangible entities. Second, the firm is not required to own the resources; rather, resources must only be available to the firm for the purpose of creating value. Third, entities are classified as resources only when they contribute to producing value for a specific market segment.

As noted in R-A theory's foundational premises, resources are heterogeneous and imperfectly mobile. As firms accumulate portfolios of resources, the characteristics of these assortments are distinctive – and some are unique – to the firm. Imperfect mobility implies that these bundles of resources are, to varying degrees, not easily bought or sold in the marketplace. Because these resources are imperfectly mobile, the heterogenous nature of resources can persist over time (Deirickx and Cool, 1989).

As specified in the foundational premises, R-A theory assumes heterogeneity of demand. That is, consumers' tastes and preferences are homogeneous within market segments, vary across market segments within an industry, and are constantly changing. Further, consumers have imperfect information about which market offers best meet their needs and wants. These characteristics of consumer behaviour generate a dynamic competitive environment as consumers discover new ways to satisfy their changing needs and firms jockey for positions of comparative advantage in resources to meet or exceed consumer expectations.

R-A theory groups resources into seven categories. Examples of each include:

1. Financial: cash reserves, access to financial markets.
2. Physical: plants, inventory, equipment.
3. Legal: trademarks, licences.
4. Human: skills and knowledge of individual employees.
5. Organizational: controls, routines, culture, competencies.
6. Informational: knowledge about market segments, competitors, technology.
7. Relational: relationships with suppliers, customers, competitors.

An asset is a resource only when it contributes to creating value for the firm's market offering. This premise implies that an entity can be a 'non-resource' when it does not contribute to creating value. For example, retailers continue to close brick-and-mortar locations as consumers increasingly shop online. Given the change in consumer behaviour, a retailer's physical resources may now be a non-resource, failing to contribute to comparative advantage. More concerning, an entity can be a 'contra-resource' if it diminishes the value of a firm's market offering. Consider the case of a strong relationship with a supplier that earns a negative reputation and thereby damages the firm's value proposition (Nichols et al., 2019). This previously valuable relational resource is now a contra-resource.

Marketplace Position

In R-A theory, a marketplace position of competitive advantage refers to one of nine possible locations on a 3x3 matrix of competitive advantage, based on a firm's relative resource-produced value for a specific market segment and relative cost for producing that value (Figure 10.2). 'Value' here refers to the total of all benefits that consumers in the market segment perceive as part of the firm's market offering. As shown in Figure 10.2, an organization may have several such matrices, one for each market segment served.

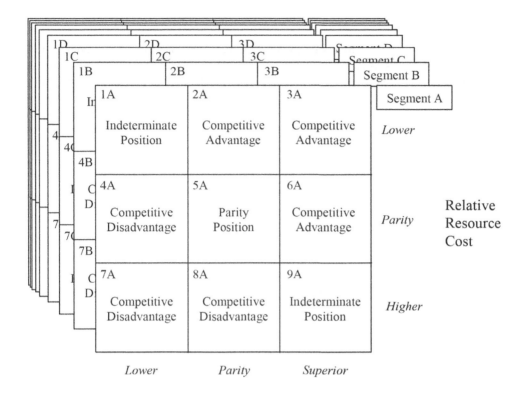

Figure 10.2   Marketplace position competitive matrix

Firms that occupy marketplace positions reflected in Cells 2, 3 and 6 realize a competitive advantage by delivering higher relative value at lower relative costs. Firms that produce lower relative value at equal (Cell 4) or higher (Cell 7) relative cost are at a competitive disadvantage. Similarly, firms that produce relative value on par with competitors but at relatively higher cost (Cell 8) are at a competitive disadvantage.

In Cell 1, lower resource costs are associated with lower relative value, and the competitive position is indeterminate. That is, firms in this competitive position could be in positions of parity, competitive advantage or competitive disadvantage, depending on the extent to which a market segment is willing to accept lower prices along with reduced value. Cell 9 is the opposite case, where firms create higher levels of value by assembling resources at greater costs. Again, the firm may hold a position of parity, competitive advantage or competitive disadvantage, depending on some market segment's willingness to pay a higher price for greater value.

Firms in Cell 5, the parity position, have no comparative advantage in either relative cost or value. The parity position is unlikely to persist over time, as firms seek to move toward competitive advantage by lowering relative resource costs or improving relative value.

Financial Performance

Recall that competition is a process of ongoing rivalry among firms to achieve comparative advantages in resources to attain marketplace positions of competitive advantage which, in turn, yield superior financial performance. P4 of the foundational premises states the firm's objective is to achieve superior financial performance. 'Superior' implies comparison to a baseline, which could be the firm's own performance in a previous period, performance of competitors, or industry averages (Hunt and Morgan, 1997). A wide variety of measures of financial performance could be used, such as profits, return on investment, return on assets, return on equity or stock market prices. The financial measures and referents will change over time as external factors change the basis of competition.

External Factors

A firm's comparative advantage can be enhanced, neutralized or eliminated by external factors such as changes in societal resources, societal institutions and public policy, as well as changing behaviour of suppliers, competitors and consumers.

Societal institutions provide structure for commerce in the form of regulations or industry norms that influence the relationship between resources and comparative advantage. For example, regulatory pressure can constrain a firm's ability to leverage relational resources for comparative advantage by limiting or prescribing potential supply chain partners (Davis et al., 2019). Trade agreements can boost or eliminate the contribution of a firm's resources to comparative advantage.

As mentioned previously, changes in consumer shopping behaviour can shift brick-and-mortar stores from a resource to a non-resource. A global pandemic can neutralize the value of an airlines' vast network of airport franchises. Competitors can neutralize the contribution of a firm's comparative resource advantage to its marketplace position of competitive advantage by acquiring the same resource, identifying a strategically equivalent resource or developing a superior resource (Barney, 1991).

To summarize, the key variables of R-A theory are: (1) organizational resources; (2) marketplace positions of competitive advantage; and (3) financial performance. These key variables are set in a context of external factors. The following section explains how key variables and contextual factors interact in a dynamic process wherein firms continuously vie for comparative advantages in resources to achieve competitive advantage.

RELATIONSHIPS AMONG THE VARIABLES

Figure 10.1 illustrates the relationships among the key variables in R-A theory. Organizations assemble bundles of resources that contribute to various levels of comparative advantage in resources that, in turn, predict marketplace positions of competitive advantage.

In addition to the direct and indirect effects of organizational resources on performance, feedback loops among key variables are the mechanisms that generate competitive dynamics proposed by R-A theory. That is, superior financial performance signals a marketplace position of competitive advantage supported by higher value associated with equal or lower costs (that is, Figure 10.2, cells 2, 3 or 6). Inferior financial performance signals a marketplace position of competitive disadvantage where lower value is produced with higher or equal costs (that is, Figure 10.2, cells 4, 7 or 8).

Marketplace positions signal the location of firms in the competitive landscape in terms of more efficiently creating value, or efficiently creating greater value. Based on the firm's competitive position, management is stimulated to better manage existing resources to enhance efficiency and/or effectiveness, triggering organizational learning (Hunt and Morgan, 1997). As predicted in the resource-based view (Barney, 1991), firms may seek to neutralize competitors' advantages by acquisition, imitation, substitution or innovation. Firms can quickly neutralize a competitor's advantage through acquisition when resources are relatively mobile and available in the marketplace. Imitation or substitution of a strategically equivalent resource requires innovation. Major innovation seeks to surpass the competition by creating a new, superior resource that is difficult to imitate, thereby securing a robust position of competitive advantage.

Recall that management's goal is to secure superior financial performance. Management enhances financial performance by refining existing strategies and/or creating and implementing new strategies to stabilize or improve marketplace positions of competitive advantage. Strategies aimed toward securing a position of competitive advantage rely on assembling the resources needed to increase value and/or lower costs. Firms will seek to neutralize competitors' comparative advantages by acquiring or imitating value-producing resources. Importantly, firms will also innovate to secure new resources that can result in a marketplace position of competitive advantage.

As illustrated in Figure 10.1 and described above, resource-advantage theory is a theory of competition. Key variables are linked in a dynamic, evolutionary process. The following section describes the domain and levels of analysis where R-A theory applies.

DOMAIN WHERE THEORY APPLIES AND LEVELS OF ANALYSIS

The domain of a theory refers to when and where the theory applies (Wacker, 2008) and which stakeholders are in the theoretical scope (Bals and Tate, 2018). As an evolutionary, disequilibrium-provoking, process theory of competition, R-A theory can be applied very broadly to understand competition in any environment within market-based economies (Hunt, 2000). Whereas command economies lack provisions for stimulating and rewarding innovation and financial performance, rewards in market-based economies are realized by firms and individuals engaged in ongoing, disequilibrating innovation resulting in new resources producing comparative advantages that yield marketplace positions of competitive advantage and thus superior financial performance (Hunt, 2000).

A theory's domain reflects its generalizability and the population to which the theory can be applied, and the choice of sample selected for empirical research (Wacker, 2008). As a general theory of competition, the stakeholders and contexts to which R-A theory applies are vast. In market-based economies, heterogeneity is evident within and across firms, industries and countries (Hunt, 2000). Thus, the levels of analysis in which competition manifests include competition between firms, buyers and suppliers, dyads, supply chains, nations and trading regions. The discussion below provides examples of the various domains and levels of analysis to which the theory can be applied.

At the firm level of analysis, consider that Firm A may be competing with direct competitor Firm B for market share within the same industry. Sales, marketing and new product development are among the business unit stakeholders Firm A may leverage to develop imperfectly mobile and inimitable resources to capture and grow market share. Alternatively, if the two firms are competing for constrained capacity at an offshore low-cost manufacturer, Firm A may turn to its purchasing department to secure the volume by developing superior negotiation and contracting advantages that create unique sources of value for both Firm A and the supplier.

Consider another example of firm-versus-firm level of analysis, in which Firm A is lobbying for and promoting policies with lawmakers that differ from the policy interests of competitor Firm C. A comparative advantage for Firm A will derive from access to experienced lobbyists with established political connections to multiple stakeholders in state and federal agencies. Such an advantage over Firm C can be further enhanced with competence leveraging (Sanchez et al., 1996) as firms and supply chains apply other existing resources to the lobbying effort.

For example, in the context of e-waste recycling, after more than a decade of making substantial investments in e-waste recycling processes and infrastructure, in 2001 Hewlett-Packard (HP) executives began drafting and lobbying to accelerate the adoption of aggressive e-waste legislation placing the burden of responsibility on manufacturers rather than consumers (Fremeth and Richter, 2011). Consequently, the state of California was the first of many to enact an e-waste law in 2003, thereby establishing a source of competitive advantage for HP which had already invested in the processes and infrastructure, and a competitive disadvantage for rivals such as Dell whose non-compliant e-waste recycling programme required substantial investment (Davis and Smith, 2003).

However, such legislative actions could provoke disequilibrium, by stimulating the disadvantaged competitors to partner with and leverage the resources of an established recycling company or to collaborate with suppliers on developing more easily recyclable materials. In addition to the supply chain partners, lobbyists and policy makers, other stakeholders include the environmentalist groups and the environmentally conscious end consumer.

Another level of analysis that can lead to a marketplace position of competitive advantage is the buyer–supplier dyad. Perhaps Firm A has rationalized its supply base and developed long-term relationships with a small group of preferred suppliers with distinctive capabilities that support Firm A's strategic goals. These dyadic relationships are often socially and technologically complex and can result in scale economies through increased purchasing and production volumes (Hunt and Davis, 2008) as well as unique value co-creation (Fawcett et al., 2012). Thus, the ability of other firms or dyads to neutralize the relational competitive advantage is diminished.

If competitive advantage derives from disequilibrating innovation among firms, dyads and supply chains in market-based economies, why are some market-based nations and trade regions wealthier than others? R-A theory suggests that vigorous competition among firms is fostered by a favourable institutional environment, hence variance across nations in per capita economic growth can be explained by established societal institutions that favour competition (Hunt, 2000). Therefore, competition among nations and trade regions falls within the domain of R-A theory.

Nations can facilitate competition and thus economic growth by establishing institutions that protect physical and intellectual property rights of individuals and firms (North, 1990), such as patent systems and trademark protection, and by investing in infrastructure to facilitate trade logistics and supply chain performance. For example, the World Bank's Logistics Performance Index (LPI) is used by organizations to inform global decisions regarding where to establish new facilities, outsource processes and target new customer segments. The LPI is a comparative assessment of the country-level logistics performance based on six dimensions of trade logistics: customs, infrastructure, international shipments, logistics quality and competence, tracking and tracing, and timeliness (Arvis et al., 2018). Indeed, a 1 per cent improvement in a country's LPI score increases trade by 16 per cent (Arvis et al., 2018). For a nation to develop a comparative advantage in trade logistics performance requires substantial investment in and coordination of all seven R-A categories of resources (that is, financial, physical, legal, human, organizational, informational and relational). The complexity involved in the disequilibrium-provoking decision to compete on trade logistics performance requires an evolution in the institutional environment involving substantial policy implications for governments, non-governmental organizations, private enterprises and other stakeholders. Institutional environments in which firms and individuals can directly benefit from infrastructure investment and innovation are conducive to a nation's productivity, economic growth and global competitive position.

As described above, R-A theory has relevance at multiple levels of analysis including firm, dyad, supply chain, nation and trading region, and is thus widely generalizable across many populations. Accordingly, R-A theory has been empirically researched across diverse disciplines, as presented in the following section.

INTERDISIPLINARY USES OF RESOURCE-ADVANTAGE THEORY

As a general theory of competition, R-A theory has been applied in a wide variety of disciplines. In his monograph, Hunt (2000) cites dozens of conceptual articles in which the theory has been developed across disciplines such as marketing, management, economics, general business and ethics. R-A theory has also been broadly tested empirically. The following sections provide selective (not exhaustive) examples of studies that apply the theory in the disciplines of management, marketing, purchasing and supply management, and supply chain management.

Management

Doherty (2011) employs a theory-building multiple case study approach to identify the competitive resources of firms founded on a social mission, specifically fair trade (FT) social enterprises. The author attempts to identify how two FT social enterprises can compete in the highly concentrated United Kingdom chocolate confectionary and coffee sectors. Following key assumptions of R-A theory (Hunt and Morgan, 1995), heterogeneous demand implies that different demand curves exist in each of these industry sectors, reflecting a variety of consumer preferences, including consumer preferences for social and ethical objectives that align with the firm's mission and objectives. Firms possessing a bundle of heterogenous, imperfectly mobile resources to meet those preferences will have a competitive advantage within that segment (Hunt and Morgan, 1995).

Doherty (2011) argues that the study contributes to explaining the success of FT social enterprises founded on a social mission, despite Hunt and Morgan's (1995) assertion that superior financial performance must be a primary objective before social objectives can be entertained. Findings from the case studies reveal the strategic importance for FT enterprises of social resources as a source of comparative advantage, resulting in strong performance across a variety of distribution channels. Social resources are comprised of three elements: ethical and social commitments, connections with partners (upstream and downstream), and consistency of behaviour (engendering trust, and absence of opportunism). As such, the author suggests that the foundational premise P6 in R-A theory should include the addition of social resources.

Marketing

Building on R-A theory, Cacciolatti and Lee (2016) analyse moderators of the marketing capability–firm performance relationship, including market orientation, strategic orientation and organizational power. The study focuses on intangible marketing capabilities that, according to R-A theory tenets, can enable more efficient and/or effective value creation for some heterogeneous market segments (Hunt and Morgan, 1995). Specifically, the study measures the direct and moderated effects of accountability of the marketing department, customer connection, perceived creativity of the marketing department, level of interdepartmental collaboration, and level of perceived innovation within the marketing department.

The authors suggest that extant marketing research reveals a tension between a shift to a service-dominant logic and a concurrent diminishing importance of the marketing department within firms. Application of R-A theory guided novel operationalizations of intangible marketing capabilities and identification of important moderators, demonstrating various approaches to marketing competitive advantage leading to improved firm performance, thus ameliorating concerns of diminished importance of marketing within the firm.

Golicic et al. (2012) propose that logistics service providers can increase brand equity by leveraging an informational resource advantage. Through the lens of R-A theory, the study reveals that two intangible resources – information quantity and information quality – comprise informational advantage. The marketplace advantage derives from access to information resources that are superior to those of competitors, including accurate, complete, timely and credible information, allowing the carrier to match information characteristics with user needs and thus more efficiently and effectively identify and serve its customers' needs. Because informational resources are heterogeneous and imperfectly mobile, they can provide an enduring, inimitable comparative resource advantage.

Purchasing and Supply Management

Unal and Donthu (2014) adopt R-A theory to explore how the task-specific and social resources of a buyer–supplier dyad in an existing outsourcing relationship contribute to competitive advantage and improved performance. The study takes a consumer packaged goods (CPG) manufacturer's perspective of outsourcing the sales and marketing process to a sales and marketing agency (SMA). Results reveal that higher levels of complementarity of task-specific resources, and of absorptive capabilities associated with learning from a shared understanding of goals and processes, result in improved partnership performance.

Reimann et al. (2017) measure the use of power by a buyer (supplier) to negotiate lower-cost resources from their supplier (buyer) in a multimarket environment in which multiple business units of the focal firm have business relationships with the trading partner. Using a vignette experimental design, the cost reduction sought by wielding power involves adoption by the trading partner of a streamlined delivery process resulting in cost savings to the buyer (supplier) and cost increase for the supplier (buyer). The dependent variable in this study is the type of power that would likely be used in the situation (that is, reward, coercion or legal legitimate), given various scenario manipulations. Results suggest that different forms of power can be leveraged as a resource by buyers and suppliers to obtain cost savings from trading partners, given the level of multimarket contact and centralization of the focal firm's buying or selling processes.

Supply Chain Management

Grounded in R-A theory, Adams et al. (2014) explore the impact of supply chain collaboration and integration on performance, mediated by technology. The study distinguishes collaboration and integration as operant resources and technology as a more tangible operand resource. Operant resources are characterized as intangible human resources that act on other resources. Operand resources are characterized as tangible, physical resources upon which an operation is performed, such as technology, capital equipment or raw materials (Constantin and Lusch, 1994). Examples of operant resources include: skill- and/or knowledge-based resources possessed by individual employees; organizational-level routines, cultures and competences; informational resources, such those emerging from superior customer, competitor and macroenvironmental analysis; and relational resources with supply chain partners (Madhavaran and Hunt, 2008), including collaboration and integration (Adams et al., 2014). In this study, the operant resources were operationalized as the respondents' perceptions of their firm's level of integration and collaboration externally across supply chain relationships (Adams et al., 2014). Following the foundational premises of R-A theory (Hunt and Morgan, 1995, 1997), the authors suggest that these operant resources, compared to operand resources, are more inimitable and more imperfectly mobile and, thus, a greater source of competitive advantage. They also recognize the hierarchical nature of operant resources, with those that are more complex and interconnected than others as possessing the potential for greater competitive advantage. Specifically, the collective impact of the higher-order resources of collaboration and integration – through the operand vehicle of interfirm technology – positively influences logistics service competency and firm performance. The study demonstrates the R-A premise that a comparative advantage stemming from a properly bundled heterogeneous portfolio of operant and operand resources constitutes a marketplace position of enduring competitive advantage generating superior firm performance.

OUTLOOK ON FUTURE RESEARCH OPPORTUNITIES

A review of the literature reveals that the preponderance of studies in management, purchasing and supply chain management that reference resource-advantage theory are conceptual rather than empirical. R-A theory supplies a robust, detailed framework for examination of competition at multiple levels of analysis and across several disciplines. The lack of empirical studies opens up several areas of inquiry that would be useful to understand the phenomenon of competition in these domains.

The dependent variable in R-A theory – financial performance – needs to be further explored and tested. Purchasing and supply chain management are replete with financial indicators of performance. Which financial performance measures provide the strongest signals of competitive position? Studies suggest that financial performance alone may not be a sufficient indicator of an organization's position of competitive advantage. As suggested by Doherty (2011), enterprises founded on social missions also measure their ability to deliver social goods (for example, meals served, vaccinations provided, carbon footprint reduced), in addition to financial performance. Are there additional performance measures that reflect an organization's competitive position?

The feedback loops in R-A theory are critical mechanisms of the dynamic nature of competition. These relationships provide a theoretical basis for examining the roles of organizational learning and innovation in driving competition. Adams et al. (2014) provide insight into the characteristics of resource advantages that are more or less likely to contribute to a sustainable position of competitive advantage. Rapid technological advances across multiple business disciplines offer a laboratory for examining when and how organizational learning spurs incremental innovation in adopting best practices of competitors, versus major innovation that disrupts the status quo and sets a new benchmark for the industry.

Understanding external factors that moderate or mediate the relationships among the key variables of R-A theory are increasingly important in today's global marketplace. Social resources, societal institutions and public policy vary widely across regions of the world, affecting the contribution levels of portfolios of resources on competitive advantage. For example, when does public policy effectively leverage the resources of a region and when does it constrain the effective use of resources? Are there institutions that accelerate or block innovation?

An examination of non-resources and contra-resources could provide considerable insight into the dynamic nature of competition. For example, what conditions are most likely to eliminate the contribution of a resource to value creation? Which external factors more likely to trigger the change? How does management detect the shift? What are the challenges associated with removing non-resources and contra-resources from a firm's resource portfolio?

R-A theory is premised on an examination of competition for market segments. However, competition exists not only for downstream customers but also for upstream suppliers. Different bundles of resources are likely to be antecedents to comparative advantage in the competition for suppliers. For example, human and organizational resources could be more important than other resources in attracting and retaining critical suppliers of scarce resources. Does R-A theory provide a framework for understanding superior performance in the competition for suppliers?

As a general theory of competition, R-A theory is well suited to the examination of not only the micro-phenomenon of firm-to-firm competition but also the macro-phenomena of competition among supply chains, countries and trading regions. These higher-level analyses are needed to understand phenomena relevant to management, purchasing and supply chain management such as sustainability, risk management and cybersecurity. For example, can R-A theory explain the dynamics of competitive positions of trading regions in the competition for advanced manufacturing? Can R-A theory account for competition among trading regions in innovations such as autonomous vehicles, blockchain platforms or robotics?

CONCLUSION

In this chapter, we provide an introduction and overview of the basic tenets and uses of resource-advantage theory. Importantly, we highlight R-A theory as a general theory of competition that opens the door to a rich range of research in management, purchasing and supply chain management at multiple levels of analysis. Studies that reference R-A theory are largely conceptual, leaving a great deal of opportunity to apply and further develop the theory in empirical studies. As an evolutionary process theory, R-A theory seems to be particularly well suited for research questions that seek to understand and explain business phenomena situated in the increasing pace of change of today's global business environment.

Researchers who would like to consider R-A theory as a theoretical lens for their studies should read the monograph by Shelby Hunt (2000). As Hunt notes in the introduction, we routinely 'assume competition' as a condition of business and life. R-A theory offers a framework for thinking about competition and organizing our studies in a way that supports a programme of research that can inform multiple disciplines.

REFERENCES

Adams, F.G., Richey, R.G., Autry, C.W., Morgan, T.R., and Gabler, C.B. (2014). Supply chain collaboration, integration, and relational technology: How complex operant resources increase performance outcomes. *Journal of Business Logistics*, 35(4), 299–317.

Arvis, J.F., Ojala, L., Wiederer, C., Shepherd, B., Raj, A., Dairabayeve, K., and Kiiski, T. (2018). *Connecting to Compete: Trade Logistics in the Global Economy*. Washington, DC: World Bank. Retrieved from https://lpi.worldbank.org/report.

Bals, L., and Tate, W.L. (2018). Sustainable supply chain design in social businesses: Advancing the theory of supply chain. *Journal of Business Logistics*, 39(1), 57–79.

Barney, J.B. (1991). Firm resources and sustained competitive advantage. *Journal of Management*, 17(1), 99–120.

Cacciolatti, L., and Lee, S. H. (2016). Revisiting the relationship between marketing capabilities and firm performance: The moderating role of market orientation, marketing strategy and organisational power. *Journal of Business Research*, 69(12), 5597–5610.

Constantin, J.A., and Lusch, R.F. (1994). *Understanding Resource Management: How to Deploy Your People, Products, and Processes for Maximum Productivity*. Oxford: Planning Forum.

Davis, D.F., Davis-Sramek, B., Golicic, S.L., and McCarthy-Byrne, T.M. (2019). Constrained choice in supply chain relationships: the effects of regulatory institutions. *International Journal of Logistics Management*, 30(4), 1101–1023.

Davis, S. and Smith, T. (2003). Cororate strategies for electronics recycling: A tale of two systems. *Silicon Valley Toxics Coalition*. Accessed on 29 March 2021 at http://svtc.org/wp-content/uploads/prisno_final.pdf.

Dierickx, I., and Cool, K. (1989). Asset stock accumulation and sustainability of competitive advantage. *Management Science*, 35 (December), 1504–1511.

Doherty, B. (2011). Resource advantage theory and fair trade social enterprises. *Journal of Strategic Marketing*, 19(4), 357–380.

Fawcett, S.E., Fawcett, A.M., Watson, B.J., and Magnan, G.M. (2012). Peeking inside the black box: Toward an understanding of supply chain collaboration dynamics. *Journal of Supply Chain Management*, 48(1), 44–72.

Fremeth, A.R., and Richter, B.K. (2011). Profiting from environmental regulatory uncertainty: Integrated strategies for competitive advantage. *California Management Review*, 54(1), 145–165.

Golicic, S.L., Fugate, B.S., and Davis, D.F. (2012). Examining market information and brand equity through resource-advantage theory: A carrier perspective. *Journal of Business Logistics*, 33(1), 20–33.

Hunt, S.D. (2000). *A General Theory of Competition: Resources, Competences, Productivity, Economic Growth.* Thousand Oaks, CA: SAGE Publications.

Hunt, S.D., and Davis, D.F. (2008). Grounding supply chain management in resource-advantage theory. *Journal of Supply Chain Management*, 44(1), 10–21.

Hunt, S.D., and Morgan, R.M. (1995). The comparative advantage theory of competition. *Journal of Marketing*, 59(2), 1–15.

Hunt, S.D., and Morgan, R.M. (1997). Resource-Advantage theory: A snake swallowing its tail or a general theory of competition? *Journal of Marketing*, 61(3), 74–82.

Madhavaram, S., and Hunt, S.D. (2008). The service-dominant logic and a hierarchy of operant resources: Developing masterful operant resources and implications for marketing strategy. *Journal of the Academy of Marketing Science*, 36(1), 67–82.

Nichols, B.S., Stolze, H., and Kirchoff, J.F. (2019). Spillover effects of supply chain news on consumer perceptions of product quality: An examination within the triple bottom line. *Journal of Operations Management*, 65(6), 536–559.

North, D.C. (1990). *Institutions, Institutional Change, and Economic Performance.* Cambridge: Cambridge University Press.

Reimann, F., Shen, P., and Kaufmann, L. (2017). Multimarket contact and the use of power in buyer–supplier relationships. *Journal of Business Logistics*, 38(1), 18–34.

Sanchez, R., Heene, A., and Thomas, H. (1996). *Dynamics of Competence-Based Competition.* New York: Elsevier Science.

Unal, B., and Donthu, N. (2014). Role of absorptive capabilities in outsourcing the headquarters selling task in the United States. *Industrial Marketing Management*, 43(6), 1079–1084.

Wacker, J.G. (2008). A Conceptual understanding of requirements for theory-building research. *Journal of Supply Chain Management*, 44(3), 5–15.

11. Resource and natural resource dependence theories in supply chains

Lojain Alkhuzaim, Mahtab Kouhizadeh and Joseph Sarkis

INTRODUCTION

The concept of resource dependence is very broad and has roots in other fields; for example, economics and ecology. Resource dependence theory (RDT) is an organizational theory that explains and informs the extent of relationships between organizations and their external environment (Pfeffer and Salancik, 1978). The theory of resource dependence essentially states that entities may be dependent on other organizations for resources, especially when critical resources are scarce (Pfeffer and Salancik, 1978). It is especially pertinent in supply chain management (SCM) because the management of supplies means the management of resources; typically, between two independent entities. Also, RDT provides a conceptualization of organizational interrelationships dealing with issues of dependence, uncertainty, power and scarcity with regard to resource supply (Nienhüser, 2008).

From an RDT perspective, resources characterized by criticality and scarcity can shape and control organizational relationships (Johnson, 1995). The theory elaborates upon possible organizational actions taken to deal with interorganizational dependencies to manage uncertainty (Pfeffer and Salancik, 1978). Additionally, RDT explains supply chain instability from the perspective of all involved entities; for example, suppliers and the focal company (Bode et al., 2011).

Expanding on the basic view of RDT, the network of organizational relationships is not only part of a socio-economic environment but also interacts directly and indirectly with the natural or ecological environment (Tashman, 2011). This broader view extends RDT to natural resource dependence theory (NRDT).

Tashman (2011) introduced NRDT as an extension of RDT, highlighting the importance of the dynamic mutual relationship between organizations and the natural environment. Similar to RDT, the natural view of resource dependence addresses uncertainty, dependence and scarcity. Socio-ecological systems (SESs) may be linked to NRDT as a broader-level perspective. SESs consider organizations and the natural environment as two interacting entities (Bergmann et al., 2016; Tashman, 2020). NRDT focuses on three important relationships: organizational dependence on natural environment, ecological impact on organizations, and organizational impact on natural environment (Tashman, 2011).

From an SCM perspective, dependence on the natural environment and scarcity of natural resources may greatly affect the stability of supply chains (Kalaitzi et al., 2018). In other words, with the increasing consumption of natural resources, resource depletion becomes a concern especially if organizational survival is associated with the availability of scarce resources. Thus, sustainability practices within supply chains can help to manage complex relationships from the NRDT viewpoint; efforts to manage resources in a way that conserves them, or finding substitutes, would be examples of avenues and relationships that can be studied.

For this chapter, the two theoretical lenses, RDT and NRDT, are reviewed from a broader SCM perspective, taking into consideration the external factors affecting organizations' relationships and performance. Also, multiple levels of analysis are discussed in relation to these two theories. Lastly, future research opportunities are presented from the SCM viewpoint.

KEY VARIABLES AND DEFINITIONS

Building on the premises of open systems theory (Katz and Kahn, 1971), RDT includes emphasis on the effect of external resources dependence on interorganizational relationships, and the degree of uncertainty associated with such dependence. According to Pfeffer and Salancik (1978), key variables of RDT include: (1) criticality of the resource needed to survive in the current environment; (2) power; and (3) availability of alternatives. As the role of the natural environment became increasingly significant with regard to organizational relationships, an emergent view of the RDT was developed to include the natural resource dimension. NRDT is an extension of RDT highlighting the importance of direct and indirect dependence of organizations on the natural environment (Tashman, 2011). Thus, the main variables of NRDT are: (1) organizational ecosystem dependence; (2) ecological impacts on organizations; and (3) organizational impacts on the ecosystem, rather than organizational interdependence.

With regard to the level of analysis, RDT is more suitable to be applied within an organizational or dyadic level of analysis. However, some scholars have extended the theory to a broader level which will be explained in more detail in a later section. As for NRDT, the macro level analysis – including environmental as well as multiple organizational relationships – fits the theory's construct and elements. Table 11.1 summarizes the main aspects of RDT and NRDT, including their elements, key variables and definitions.

Criticality of Resources

From the RDT perspective, the ability to survive in the competitive environment is determined by the organizational capability to obtain critical resources found outside the boundary of the organization. To consider a resource as critical it has to be essential to the survival of the organization in a given market (Pfeffer and Salancik, 2003).

Power

The role of power varies according to the degree of control and ownership of critical resources. Figure 11.1 illustrates an interdependent relationship where organization A is dependent on organization B which consequently has power over the former. Dependence on an external organization grows as the latter organization exercises ownership of the critical resource needed by a dependent organization for its own survival (Emerson, 1962). Strategies to manage such dependencies are discussed later in the chapter. The other direction is also a concern, where the supplying organization may be dependent on the buying organization. The power structure and imbalance may occur in either direction.

Table 11.1 *Definitions of variables of resource dependence theory and natural resource dependence theory*

Theory	Element	Explanation	Supporting references
RDT	Unit of analysis	Organizations, organizational resources and organizational relationships	Johnson (1995)
	Level of analysis	Organizational level, focusing on interorganizational relationships between organizations and external environment	Pfeffer and Salancik (1978)
	Key variables/definitions		
	Criticality of resources	Resources essential to the survival of the organization in market	Pfeffer and Salancik (2003)
	Power	Degree of control and ownership of critical resources	Hillman et al. (2009); Weiner (1984)
	Availability of alternatives	Scarce critical resources increase the level of dependence on the external environment	Johnson (1995)
NRDT	Unit of analysis	Socio-ecological system	Bergmann et al. (2016); Tashman (2020)
	Level of analysis	Macro level: regional, global, due to resources across geographies	Tashman (2011)
	Key variables/definitions		
	Organizational ecosystem dependence	Degree of criticality of natural resources	Tashman (2011)
	Ecological impacts on organizations	Impact of natural forces on increasing uncertainty and the ability of organizations to obtain critical natural resources	
	Organizational impacts on ecosystem	Impact of organizational activities on the ecosystem	

Availability of Alternative Resources

Scarcity of critical resources plays a role in the level of dependence experienced between organizations (Pfeffer and Salancik, 1978). Moreover, this variable intersects with the other two variables in determining the degree of dependence. For example, if an organization is in possession of a scarce critical resource that has no substitutable alternatives, its power and control over dependent parties increases significantly.

Organizational Ecosystem Dependence

NRDT assumes that organizational dependence on the natural environment is affected by how critical the natural resources are to the organization (Tashman, 2011). The theory states that organizations are directly dependent on natural resources and services. Thus, if a critical natural resource is required to sustain a business, dependence on the ecosystem increases proportionally.

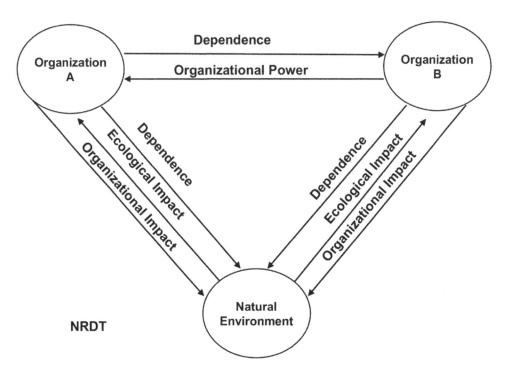

Note: This figure integrates the RDT framework provided by Pfeffer and Salancik (2003) and the NRDT framework presented by Tashman (2011). The figure illustrates a broad presentation of the two theoretical frameworks.

Figure 11.1   *Resource dependence theory and natural resource dependence theory integrative framework*

Ecological Impacts on Organizations

This relationship is reflected by forces of nature that can cause uncertainty, and eventually affects the ability of organizations to obtain critical natural resources (Tashman, 2011). In other words, according to NRDT, organizations with high dependency on natural resources are highly susceptible to natural forces which are nearly impossible to manage (Winn et al., 2011).

Organizational Impacts on the Ecosystem

This variable focuses on the impact of organizational activities on the ecosystem (Tashman, 2011). Organizational practices and activities can greatly affect the quality of the surrounding natural environment, which eventually impacts upon the availability of natural resources. For instance, overconsumption of renewable and non-renewable resources causes disruption to the ability of the ecosystem to regenerate.

The following sections provide a more detailed foundational review of the constructs, definitions and historical overviews of RDT and NRDT. They also present the theoretical applications of the two theories in different research areas and disciplines.

RESOURCE DEPENDENCE THEORY

Theoretical Constructs and Historical Overview

Studies have viewed organizations as a network of social, economic and professional relationships that interact dynamically with their surrounding environments. These relationships are scientifically explained on the premises of open systems theory (Katz and Kahn, 1971). The idea of resource dependence was introduced in the 1970s to explain economics-related issues – such as mergers and board interrelations – as an attempt to provide an alternative theoretical grounding for economic theories of organizational relationships (Pfeffer and Salancik, 2003).

The foundation of the RDT was built around the idea of critical resource acquisition from external sources, instead of focusing on internal resource use and capability building that has been highlighted by many other theories (Pfeffer and Salancik, 2003), especially the resource-based view (Barney, 1991). Introduced into the organizational theoretic literature by Pfeffer and Salancik (1978), RDT focuses on the interorganizational relationships to manage the degree of dependency on the external environment. According to RDT, instead of adopting a self-sufficient approach in providing strategic resources, organizations operate within an open system that allows for continuous exchange of materials, information, skills and experts.

The highly interactive environment in which organizations function contributes to dependence playing a fundamental role in shaping organizational decisions in addition to contributing to uncertainty and risk. This situation helps to explain how RDT may explain aspects of organizational behaviour and structure by emphasizing the effect of external power relations (Nienhüser, 2008). The direction of influence between organizations is affected by dependence and power imbalances, and is related to the distribution of critical resources (Casciaro and Piskorski, 2005).

Nienhüser (2008) supports the theoretical basis of RDT which considers uncertainty and criticality and their relation to the distribution of critical resources. According to Pfeffer and Salancik (1978), organizational interdependencies are determined by three factors: (1) criticality of the resource needed to survive in the current environment; (2) power, degree of control and ownership of the critical resource; and (3) availability of alternatives.

Scholars have suggested two different ways to address resource dependencies: bridging and buffering. As regards bridging, organizations adapt to being dependent on external parties for resources supplies and manage this dependence with a number of actions or activities. Pfeffer and Salancik (1978) identified five different bridging activities to reduce interdependency and uncertainty: (1) mergers and acquisitions; (2) joint ventures; (3) boards of directors; (4) political action; and (5) executive succession. From the RDT perspective, these strategies are adopted by organizations with high dependency on external resources in an attempt to reduce interdependencies and thus absorb competition (Hillman et al., 2009; Pfeffer, 1972a). Additionally, to reduce uncertainty, these strategies are useful in acquiring power and securing a consistent resource supply, especially with the increasing complexity of interorganizational relationships (Pfeffer, 1987).

With regard to the board of directors, studies suggest that RDT provides a logical explanation of the relationship between board size and external resources. In other words, the board of directors can facilitate the procurement of critical external resources that are essential to sustain anticipated organizational performance (Kroll et al., 2007; Pfeffer, 1972b). As for the political actions, Hillman et al. (2009) highlighted the linkages between regulatory actions and interdependencies as an attempt by organizations to manage their control over external resources. An example of using buffering and bridging for managing a political crisis are the environmental issues faced by the Shell Oil corporation in its environmental crisis around the Brent Spar drilling platform from the early 1990s (Van den Bosch and Van Riel, 1998). This relationship focuses on stakeholder management in addition to building buffering capabilities for these types of crises; in this case, a corporate social responsibility and environmentally oriented crisis.

Finally, Pfeffer and Salancik (1978) used RDT to explain the connection between interdependencies and the transitioning phase prior to executive replacement. Studies show that intra-organizational distribution of control and power is affected by degree of dependency on the external environment (Hillman et al., 2009; Weiner, 1984).

Buffering differs from bridging in that organizations try to mitigate external uncertainties by focusing on internal activities (Thompson, 1967); for instance, securing sufficient inventory to avoid supply uncertainty. The buffering aspects may relate to building internal capabilities and resources such that external dependence imbalances are lessened. Buffering may also provide greater power to organizations who may have been more dependent on external resources. For example, certifying backup suppliers, and access to multiple modes of transportation, help to build buffers by providing the ability to multi-source or to use alternative forms of transportation (Manhart et al., 2020). Buffering and bridging have a significant influence on the growing number of research investigations around supply chain risk management.

Theoretical Applications

Within the SCM literature, RDT is broadly used to deal with environmental interdependency and uncertainty issues, and has been integrated with other theories to give a holistic theoretical perspective of a specific research area (Ozturk, 2021). RDT highlights the role of dependency, uncertainty and power/control affecting the supply chain's stability where maintaining a certain flow of inputs and outputs is crucial (Pfeffer and Salancik, 1978).

Supply chains consist of a number of organizations that are highly connected and involved in operational activities forming complex relationships that require elucidation of some sort (Hajmohammad and Vachon, 2016). In this regard, an important role of RDT lies in the fact that interdependencies act as a catalyst for collaborative sustainable relationships between related parties (Paulraj and Chen, 2007).

Accordingly, RDT has been used within the SCM context to explain series of relationships linking focal firms with their suppliers and customers (Crook and Combs, 2007). The study by Crook and Combs (2007) discusses the effect of resources quality on bargaining power in supply chains, and the overall implications of such power on different supply chain members. RDT is considered one of the first organizational theories that analyses interorganizational relationships from a socio-economic perspective; however, it does not explain the type of power – for example, coercive or non-coercive – and can be integrated with other organizational theories such as institutional theory (Ireland and Webb, 2007).

The significance of supply chain instability and risk management has been viewed from the perspective of RDT in which responses of such disruptions have also been addressed to reduce related uncertainties (Bode et al., 2011). In line with managing supply chain disruption, Hajmohammad and Vachon (2016) addressed risk management from two theoretical lenses – RDT and agency theory – suggesting four different strategies to mitigate related risks: risk avoidance, monitoring-based risk mitigation, collaboration-based risk mitigation, and risk acceptance.

It is evident that supply chain risk management has been widely addressed from the perspective of RDT, proposing multiple mitigating strategies, along with other theories such as organizational information processing theory (Manhart et al., 2020). For instance, buyer–supplier contract design is presented as an important strategy for supply chain parties to manage associated risks (Eckerd and Girth, 2017). Moreover, in an empirical study informed by RDT principles, Elking et al. (2017) tested three different hypotheses: supply chain dependence, lean inventory, and financial performance. Similarly, Carr et al. (2008) empirically investigated the effect of suppliers' dependence on supplier training and participation in product development, incorporating RDT as a theoretical lens in their study.

Other studies have integrated RDT at a broader level. Darby et al. (2020) used RDT to explain supply chain operations strategies at both the macro and the industry level. At the macro level, studies investigate the effect of uncertainty caused by government policy on a firm's ability to access critical resources. Moreover, this line of study suggests that uncertainty at the industry level makes organizations more inclined to adopt buffering strategies. There are implications here for multiple levels of analysis research, including industry, supply chain and organizational-level joint analyses.

A recent research study used a case study of a Norwegian coopetition alliance to explain the effect of resource dependencies on the strategic organizational relations from the perspective of RDT (Jakobsen, 2020). The idea of coopetition seeks to join resources horizontally with competitors, to build efficiencies (Trapp et al., 2020). Another study focused on the effect of top management support on the adoption of Sustainable Development Goals (SDGs) in developing economies such as Pakistan by incorporating RDT (Ilyas et al., 2020).

Also drawing on RDT, Lai et al. (2013) tested the feasibility of logistics integration and interorganizational relationships on enhancing financial performance by helping organizations deal with third party logistics challenges and dependencies. Lastly, RDT has been integrated to address the potential benefits of implementing the Internet of Things (IoT) into the service transformation of manufacturers to strengthen the buyer–supplier relationship (Boehmer et al., 2020). These latest directions are broadly juxtaposed to exemplary major developments of RDT in the supply chain literature; for example, resource-dependent topics such as sustainability, and risk management technology development (Kim and Fortado, 2021).

NATURAL RESOURCE DEPENDENCE THEORY

Theoretical Constructs and History Overview

Because of the vital significance of natural resources and their effect on organizational performance, Tashman (2011) introduced an expanded perspective of RDT by adding an ecological perspective to it. The main focus of NRDT is on the dependency between organizations and their natural environment as resources are exchanged from one party with more power and control to a dependent party. Hence, the difference between Pfeffer and Salancik's (1978) RDT proposition and Tashman's (2011) proposition is that the latter expanded the level of analysis from an interorganizational level to an SES level. SESs inclusively account for interconnected elements of social, biological and physical systems (Chapin et al., 2009). SESs are comprised of complex ecosystems, where larger ecosystems with greater complexity generate greater uncertainties (Young et al., 2006). An SES and NRDT perspective allows theoreticians and scholars to consider conflicting institutional logics and their impact on how organizations view natural resources and ecosystems management (Tashman, 2020).

Tashman (2011) introduced NRDT to extend the traditional perspective of RDT. The case example to introduce the concept was to measure the corporate climate change vulnerability of the skiing industry in the United States.

NRDT states that organizations are directly and indirectly dependent on natural resources, such as sun, water, energy, land and air. Ecological economists have also used the terminology of environmental rents and internalizing externalities – to name a couple of examples – to help explain this relationship. NRDT is constructed around the idea that organizations are a subsystem of the social and ecological system where organizations and natural resources are the two main elements of its construct (Bergmann et al., 2016).

Tashman (2011, p. 62) describes natural resource dependence as: 'a function of *organizational ecosystem dependence, ecological impacts on organizations*, and *organizational impacts on ecosystem rather than organizational interdependence*'. Therefore, organizational behaviour and performance are affected by both social systems and ecosystems. Additionally, NRDT constructs seek to evaluate the mutual effect between organizations and their natural environment in a way that has been ignored in some ecological theories. Thus, based on NRDT, organizations and the natural environment interact directly with each other.

The organizational dependence on the natural environment is affected by how critical the natural resources are to the organizational survivor (Tashman, 2011). With regard to the ecological impact on organizations, this relationship is reflected by forces of nature that can cause uncertainty and eventually affect the ability of organizations to obtain critical natural resources (Tashman, 2011). Thus, the ecological impact on organizations is influenced by the degree of dependency that organizations have on natural resources. With regard to the reciprocal relationship between organizations and the natural environment, organizational activities place numerous pressures on the ecosystem. Overconsumption of natural resources, and organizational waste, exemplify the impact that organizations have on the ecological system. On the other hand, some organizations are becoming more environmentally conscious by developing sustainable practices initiatives to conserve natural resources.

Theoretical Applications

The effect and relationship of the natural environment on organizations have been studied through a variety of theoretical perspectives and lenses, including the resource-based view, the trade-off phenomenon, and managerial opportunism (Bergmann et al., 2016). However, studies that address how dependency on the natural environment affects organizational performance remain limited. For instance, one of the few studies has been by Bergmann et al. (2016), who used NRDT to explain the effect of extreme weather conditions on organizational financial performance.

The issue of natural resource scarcity – the shortage of natural resources that companies depend upon – has rarely been addressed in the supply chain literature. Some aspects of material scarcity are part of earlier research streams in manufacturing supply chains that addressed the issues related to the availability of raw materials and rare earth elements (REEs), including metals, water and energy (Alonso, 2010). Natural resource depletion and limited access to natural resources are supply chain risk factors that can jeopardize both companies and societies, especially as anthropocentric activities have caused stresses on many planetary boundaries (Mekonnen and Hoekstra, 2016). Supply chains need to manage their dependencies on the natural environment to deal with uncertainty and mitigate the associated risk of potential disruption (Bode et al., 2011). In fact, early arguments for 'greening' of supply chains were based on business continuity afforded by environmentally sound practices (Sarkis and Dou, 2017).

Natural resource dependence and scarcity has not been extensively addressed in the SCM literature. Major supply chain studies that investigated natural resources were primarily conceptual. For example, Autry et al. (2013) highlighted the importance of supply chain managers understanding resource scarcity dynamics to achieve a competitive advantage. Bell et al. (2012) proposed a natural resource scarcity typology based on the resource consumption and degradation state. The proposed model can help supply chain companies to choose the best mitigation strategies while improving supply chain performance. Bell et al. (2013) developed a conceptual framework based on the resource advantage theory for addressing natural resource scarcity in closed loop supply chains.

Among the few empirical studies in this context, a study by Kalaitzi et al. (2018) explored supply chain strategies at diverse natural resource dependence levels, and found that organizations use buffering strategies when critical resources are scarce, and use buffering and bridging strategies when supplier substitutability of the scarce natural resource exists. The lack of empirical validation is a gap in the studies that address natural resource dependence in a supply chain context. Despite the growing literature on the green initiatives and sustainability in supply chains that mainly aim to secure sustainable resources (Gold et al., 2010; Lee et al., 2012; Sarkis et al., 2011), there is a lack of research and empirically tested studies on the impact of the natural resource dependence on supply chain relationships, structures and performance. Supply chain companies should comprehend the risks of natural resource dependency and mitigate those risks by appropriate strategies and responses.

Figure 11.1 integrates and summarizes the constructs and elements of RDT and NRDT (Pfeffer and Salancik, 2003; Tashman, 2011). The top section within Figure 11.1 illustrates RDT where interorganizational relationships between two organizations are highlighted. Organization A is dependent on organization B, which consequently has power over organization A. This power continues as long as organization B is in possession of a critical resource needed by organization A to survive. But organization B may also be dependent on organization A for financial resources.

The lower part of Figure 11.1 focuses on the role of the natural environment and its relation to individual organizations. Organizations are dependent on the natural environment by using resources naturally generated by the ecological system; for example, water, sunlight, soil and minerals. Furthermore, the natural environment places some constraints on organizational performance; for example, natural forces and crises from both short-term and long-term perspectives. Alternatively, organizational activities impact upon the natural environment either positively – for example, green initiatives – or negatively, such as pollutant emissions.

OUTLOOK ON FUTURE RESEARCH OPPORTUNITIES

RDT is a growing area of importance in SCM but limited literature exists supporting the integration of natural resources within the construct of RDT from an SCM perspective. Although RDT is widely used to address environmental uncertainty issues (López-Gamero et al., 2011) underrepresented opportunities still exist. One potential area for future research is the integration between RDT and other theoretical lenses to investigate organizational interdependencies (Wry et al., 2013); specifically, highlighting the dynamic relationship between organizations and their environment by adopting an integrative approach with regard to the theoretical lenses used to explain a particular organizational behaviour. Moreover, current applications of RDT are significantly directed to strategic management issues; thus, there is a need to expand the theory to multiple organizational areas (Ozturk, 2021). In other words, future research can give more insights about the role of operational decisions (for example, sourcing) in managing interdependencies.

Another potential area to investigate is exploring updated mechanisms to manage dependencies and organizational power that would be more tailored to deal with recent challenges of an extremely uncertain environment. Also, as supply chains expand regionally and globally, different types of uncertainties may emerge, opening new venues of unexplored aspects of RDT. Additional work is needed to investigate the role of government policies and regulations on uncertainties related to resource acquisition at an organizational level (Darby et al., 2020). Lastly, more empirical studies are needed in the context of RDT to test the network of relationships suggested by the theory (Roundy and Bayer, 2019).

One potential area of investigation is the role of integrated and interorganizational technologies such as those from Industry 4.0 and other digitalization technologies (Sarkis et al., 2020). A specific example that may provide increased re-evaluation is the issue of how blockchain technology may influence power structures and dependence on resources that may be more easily available or monitored due to blockchain transparency and traceability characteristics (Kouhizadeh et al., 2019).

As for the NRDT, there are many possible relationships that exist between the natural environment and sustainable supply chain management (SSCM) at various levels. Based on that, applying NRDT into SCM is an emergent area that needs to be developed and tailored to address SCM issues and practices. We can begin by considering industry characteristics. For example, some industries are heavily dependent on natural resources, and faced with environmental rents. Extractive industries that include mining and petroleum are heavily dependent on land resources; irreversible affects will often occur due to their resources usage. How irreversibility – a type of power structure – affects the relationships between supply chains and the natural environment is an important aspect from the theoretical development of NRDT.

Agriculture, although many might consider this a renewable type of natural resource usage, is still is influenced by natural resources dependence. In this case the temporal effects may play a larger role in how NRDT relationships exist. That is, climate change can cause agricultural geography to change immensely, therefore how policy and practices from agriculture change based on this dependency, and at least awareness, of natural resource use and depletion, can potentially be studied.

Related to the NRDT relationships, scarcity may become a concern for the continuity of some supply chains. Natural resource depletion provides greater power relationships; corporations practicing sustainable practices in the seafood industry, for example, can help to maintain a balance in NRDT. In this case, extending to the type of practices to help manage resources such that the balance remains can be explained, to help organizations and their supply chain build resilience. This can help to build a relationship with nature where dependence may lessen, through such activities as sustainable fishing; or even, in some other industries, circular economy practices and alternative sources of natural resources. How these various activities can help organizations to manage their ecosystem services and environmental rents can be investigated from an NRDT perspective (Tashman, 2020).

Outside of NRDT there is a belief that nature should be treated as an entity, or as a stakeholder (Driscoll and Starik, 2004). However, this can be very difficult for organizations and supply chains to accept; and it is debated amongst scholars (Laine, 2011; Starik, 1995). Although nature cannot speak for itself, there are human proxies that speak for nature – albeit imperfectly – and can play a role in this power struggle over resource dependence. Nature requires more of a balance as well with its dependency on anthropocentric activities; trusting supply chains not to damage biodiversity, resources or the general climate are all part of this dependency on the activities of supply chains. What level of dependency and cooperation between nature – and its proxies – can result in a more sustainable supply chain environment is a basic issue and concern. As an example, are sustainability certification policies, whether required or not, and managed by non-governmental organizations, part of a resource dependency arrangement with nature (Soundarajan and Brown, 2016)?

NRDT from two institutional logic perspectives – economizing versus ecologizing – may also cause organizations and their supply chains to behave very differently (Tashman, 2020). An economizing logic focuses on 'win–win' opportunities such as those in eco-efficiency, and may have very different resource dependence perspective from an ecologizing logic, which focuses on planetary boundaries and limitations of resources. These competing logics may alter the viewpoint of organizations and their supply chains on their dependency perspective and associated environmental actions. Finally, for both theories, RDT and NRDT, empirical testing and investigations of their elements using quantitative methodologies can significantly contribute to the current literature.

CONCLUSION

Studies have viewed organizations as a network of social, economic and professional relationships that interact dynamically with their surrounding environments. These relationships are scientifically explained by the premises of open system theory (Katz and Kahn, 1971). RDT focuses on the interorganizational relationships to manage the degree of dependency on the external environment by using a set of strategies to mitigate power and dependence (Pfeffer and Salancik, 1978).

Expanding the traditional view of RDT, emergent perspectives have been developed to give a broader understanding by considering the interactive relationship between organizations and the natural environment. NRDT was introduced to fill a significant gap in the literature by grounding this relationship to RDT (Tashman, 2011).

This chapter provides a review of the extension of RDT into NRDT, explaining their constructs, historical development and current applications from an SSCM perspective. We provide a slightly more detailed evolutionary overview of NRDT, as it is still an emergent area. Furthermore, this chapter presents some of the latest research that is investigating this topic, in a short review of the literature. Finally, some future opportunities are highlighted for expanding the research in this area, especially for SCM and SSCM.

REFERENCES

Alonso, E. (2010). Material scarcity from the perspective of manufacturing firms: case studies of platinum and cobalt. Thesis, Massachusetts Institute of Technology.

Autry, C.W., Goldsby, T.J., and Bell, J.E. (2013). *Global Macrotrends and Their Impact on Supply Chain Management: Strategies for Gaining Competitive Advantage*. Upper Saddle River, NJ: Pearson Education.

Barney, J. (1991). Firm resources and sustained competitive advantage. *Journal of Management, 17*(1), 99–120.

Bell, J.E., Autry, C.W., Mollenkopf, D.A., and Thornton, L.M. (2012). A natural resource scarcity typology: theoretical foundations and strategic implications for supply chain management. *Journal of Business Logistics, 33*(2), 158–166.

Bell, J.E., Mollenkopf, D.A., and Stolze, H.J. (2013). Natural resource scarcity and the closed-loop supply chain: a resource-advantage view. *International Journal of Physical Distribution and Logistics Management, 43*(5–6), 351–379.

Bergmann, A., Stechemesser, K., and Guenther, E. (2016). Natural resource dependence theory: impacts of extreme weather events on organizations. *Journal of Business Research, 69*(4), 1361–1366.

Bode, C., Wagner, S.M., Petersen, K.J., and Ellram, L.M. (2011). Understanding responses to supply chain disruptions: insights from information processing and resource dependence perspectives. *Academy of Management Journal, 54*(4), 833–856.

Boehmer, J.H., Shukla, M., Kapletia, D., and Tiwari, M.K. (2020). The impact of the Internet of Things (IoT) on servitization: an exploration of changing supply relationships. *Production Planning and Control, 31*(2–3), 203–219.

Carr, A.S., Kaynak, H., Hartley, J.L., and Ross, A. (2008). Supplier dependence: impact on supplier's participation and performance. *International Journal of Operations and Production Management, 28*(9), 899–916.

Casciaro, T., and Piskorski, M.J. (2005). Power imbalance, mutual dependence, and constraint absorption: a closer look at resource dependence theory. *Administrative Science Quarterly, 50*(2), 167–199.

Chapin III, F. S., Kofinas, G.P., Folke, C., and Chapin, M.C. (2009). *Principles of Ecosystem Stewardship: Resilience-Based Natural Resource Management in a Changing World*. New York: Springer Science and Business Media.

Crook, T.R., and Combs, J.G. (2007). Sources and consequences of bargaining power in supply chains. *Journal of Operations Management, 25*(2), 546–555.

Darby, J.L., Ketchen Jr, D.J., Williams, B.D., and Tokar, T. (2020). The implications of firm-specific policy risk, policy uncertainty, and industry factors for inventory: a resource dependence perspective. *Journal of Supply Chain Management, 56*(4), 3–24.

Driscoll, C., and Starik, M. (2004). The primordial stakeholder: advancing the conceptual consideration of stakeholder status for the natural environment. *Journal of Business Ethics, 49*(1), 55–73.

Eckerd, A., and Girth, A.M. (2017). Designing the buyer–supplier contract for risk management: assessing complexity and mission criticality. *Journal of Supply Chain Management, 53*(3), 60–75.

Elking, I., Paraskevas, J.P., Grimm, C., Corsi, T., and Steven, A. (2017). Financial dependence, lean inventory strategy, and firm performance. *Journal of Supply Chain Management, 53*(2), 22–38.

Emerson, R.M. (1962). Power–dependence relations. *American Sociological Review, 27*(1), 31–41.

Gold, S., Seuring, S., and Beske, P. (2010). Sustainable supply chain management and inter-organizational resources: a literature review. *Corporate Social Responsibility and Environmental Management, 17*(4), 230–245.

Hajmohammad, S., and Vachon, S. (2016). Mitigation, avoidance, or acceptance? Managing supplier sustainability risk. *Journal of Supply Chain Management, 52*(2), 48–65.

Hillman, A.J., Withers, M.C., and Collins, B.J. (2009). Resource dependence theory: a review. *Journal of Management, 35*(6), 1404–1427.

Ilyas, S., Hu, Z., and Wiwattanakornwong, K. (2020). Unleashing the role of top management and government support in green supply chain management and sustainable development goals. *Environmental Science and Pollution Research*, 27(8), 8210–8223.

Ireland, R.D., and Webb, J.W. (2007). A multi-theoretic perspective on trust and power in strategic supply chains. *Journal of Operations Management*, 25(2), 482–497.

Jakobsen, S. (2020). Managing tension in coopetition through mutual dependence and asymmetries: a longitudinal study of a Norwegian R&D alliance. *Industrial Marketing Management*, 84, 251–260.

Johnson Jr, B.L. (1995). Resource dependence theory: a political economy model of organizations. University of Utah, Department of Educational Administration College of Education.

Kalaitzi, D., Matopoulos, A., Bourlakis, M., and Tate, W. (2018). Supply chain strategies in an era of natural resource scarcity. *International Journal of Operations and Production Management*, 38(3), 784–809.

Katz, D., and Kahn, R. (1971). Open-systems theory. In Maurer, J.G. (ed.), *Readings in Organization Theory: Open-System Approaches* (pp. 13–32). New York: Random House.

Kim, D.-Y., and Fortado, B. (2021). Outcomes of supply chain dependence asymmetry: a systematic review of the statistical evidence. *International Journal of Production Research*, 59(19), 5844–5866.

Kouhizadeh, M., Sarkis, J., and Zhu, Q. (2019). At the nexus of blockchain technology, the circular economy, and product deletion. *Applied Sciences*, 9(8), 1712.

Kroll, M., Walters, B.A., and Le, S.A. (2007). The impact of board composition and top management team ownership structure on post-IPO performance in young entrepreneurial firms. *Academy of Management Journal*, 50(5), 1198–1216.

Lai, F., Chu, Z., Wang, Q., and Fan, C. (2013). Managing dependence in logistics outsourcing relationships: evidence from China. *International Journal of Production Research*, 51(10), 3037–3054.

Laine, M. (2011). The nature of nature as a stakeholder. *Journal of Business Ethics*, 96(1), 73–78.

Lee, S.M., Kim, S.T., and Choi, D. (2012). Green supply chain management and organizational performance. *Industrial Management and Data Systems*, 112(8), 1148–1180.

López-Gamero, M.D., Molina-Azorín, J.F., and Claver-Cortés, E. (2011). Environmental uncertainty and environmental management perception: a multiple case study. *Journal of Business Research*, 64(4), 427–435.

Manhart, P., Summers, J.K., and Blackhurst, J. (2020). A meta-analytic review of supply chain risk management: assessing buffering and bridging strategies and firm performance. *Journal of Supply Chain Management*, 56(3), 66–87.

Mekonnen, M.M., and Hoekstra, A.Y. (2016). Four billion people facing severe water scarcity. *Science Advances*, 2(2), e1500323.

Nienhüser, W. (2008). Resource dependence theory – how well does it explain behavior of organizations? *Management Revue*, 19(1–2), 9–32.

Ozturk, O. (2021). Bibliometric review of resource dependence theory literature: an overview. *Management Review Quarterly*, 71(3), 525–552.

Paulraj, A., and Chen, I.J. (2007). Environmental uncertainty and strategic supply management: a resource dependence perspective and performance implications. *Journal of Supply Chain Management*, 43(3), 29–42.

Pfeffer, J. (1972a). Merger as a response to organizational interdependence. *Administrative Science Quarterly*, 17(3), 382–394.

Pfeffer, J. (1972b). Size and composition of corporate boards of directors: the organization and its environment. *Administrative Science Quarterly*, 17(2), 218–228.

Pfeffer, J. (1987). A resource dependence perspective on intercorporate relations. *Intercorporate Relations: The Structural Analysis of Business*, 1(1), 25–55.

Pfeffer, J., and Salancik, G.R. (1978). *Social Control of Organizations: The External Control of Organizations*. New York: Harper & Row.

Pfeffer, J., and Salancik, G.R. (2003). *The External Control of Organizations: A Resource Dependence Perspective*. Stanford, CA: Stanford University Press.

Roundy, P.T., and Bayer, M.A. (2019). To bridge or buffer? A resource dependence theory of nascent entrepreneurial ecosystems. *Journal of Entrepreneurship in Emerging Economies*, 11(4), 550–575.

Sarkis, J., and Dou, Y. (2017). *Green Supply Chain Management: A Concise Introduction*. New York: Routledge.

Sarkis, J., Kouhizadeh, M., and Zhu, Q.S. (2020). Digitalization and the greening of supply chains. *Industrial Management and Data Systems, 121*(1), 65–85.

Sarkis, J., Zhu, Q., and Lai, K.-H. (2011). An organizational theoretic review of green supply chain management literature. *International Journal of Production Economics, 130*(1), 1–15.

Soundararajan, V., and Brown, J.A. (2016). Voluntary governance mechanisms in global supply chains: beyond CSR to a stakeholder utility perspective. *Journal of Business Ethics, 134*(1), 83–102.

Starik, M. (1995). Should trees have managerial standing? Toward stakeholder status for non-human nature. *Journal of Business Ethics, 14*(3), 207–217.

Tashman, P. (2011). Corporate climate change adaptation, vulnerability and environmental performance in the United States ski resort industry. Thesis, George Washington University.

Tashman, P. (2020). A natural resource dependence perspective of the firm: how and why firms manage natural resource scarcity. *Business and Society,* 0007650319898811.

Thompson, J.D. (1967). *Organizations in Action: Social Science Bases of Administrative Theory.* New York: McGraw-Hill.

Trapp, A.C., Harris, I., Rodrigues, V.S., and Sarkis, J. (2020). Maritime container shipping: does coopetition improve cost and environmental efficiencies? *Transportation Research Part D: Transport and Environment, 87,* 102507.

Van den Bosch, F.A., and Van Riel, C.B. (1998). Buffering and bridging as environmental strategies of firms. *Business Strategy and the Environment, 7*(1), 24–31.

Weiner, N. (1984). Executive succession. An examination of the resource dependence model. *Canadian Journal of Administrative Sciences/Revue Canadienne des Sciences de l'Administration, 1*(2), 321–337.

Winn, M., Kirchgeorg, M., Griffiths, A., Linnenluecke, M.K., and Günther, E. (2011). Impacts from climate change on organizations: a conceptual foundation. *Business Strategy and the Environment, 20*(3), 157–173.

Wry, T., Cobb, J.A., and Aldrich, H.E. (2013). More than a metaphor: assessing the historical legacy of resource dependence and its contemporary promise as a theory of environmental complexity. *Academy of Management Annals, 7*(1), 441–488.

Young, O.R., Berkhout, F., Gallopin, G.C., Janssen, M.A., Ostrom, E., and Van der Leeuw, S. (2006). The globalization of socio-ecological systems: an agenda for scientific research. *Global Environmental Change, 16*(3), 304–316.

SUGGESTED FURTHER READING

For More Information on the RDT and NRDT

For a more detailed review of the resource dependence theory:
Hillman, A.J., Withers, M.C., and Collins, B.J. (2009). Resource dependence theory: a review. *Journal of Management, 35*(6), 1404–1427.
Pfeffer, J., and Salancik, G.R. (1978). *Social Control of Organizations: The External Control of Organizations.* New York: Harper & Row.
For a more detailed review of natural resource dependence theory:
Bergmann, A., Stechemesser, K., and Guenther, E. (2016). Natural resource dependence theory: impacts of extreme weather events on organizations. *Journal of Business Research, 69*(4), 1361–1366.
Tashman, P. (2011). Corporate climate change adaptation, vulnerability and environmental performance in the United States ski resort industry. Thesis, George Washington University.
Tashman, P. (2020). A natural resource dependence perspective of the firm: how and why firms manage natural resource scarcity. *Business and Society,* 0007650319898811.

Good Literature Reviews on the RDT

Ozturk, O. (2021). Bibliometric review of resource dependence theory literature: an overview. *Management Review Quarterly*, *71*(3), 525–552.

12. Resource orchestration: managers' role in developing and deploying resources to create distinctive advantage

Stanley E. Fawcett, Yao 'Henry' Jin, Sebastian Brockhaus, Diego Vega and Amydee M. Fawcett

INTRODUCTION

Strategy's enduring question is, 'Why do some companies succeed and others do not?' One of the primary theory streams designed to answer this question focuses on the resources that a company possesses (see Figure 12.1). Resource orchestration theory is firmly grounded in this resource-based perspective. Resource orchestration extends the understanding of resource-based theories by explicitly considering how managers influence resource acquisition and development to cultivate distinctive competitive advantage.

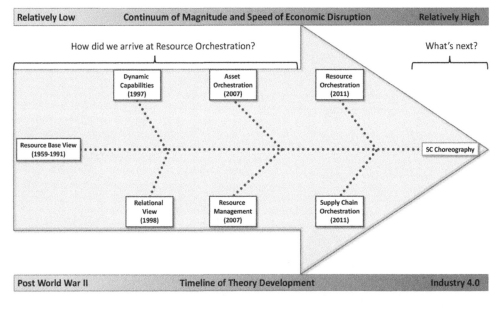

Figure 12.1   The historical development of resource orchestration theory

The basic premise of resource-based theories is that a firm is a heterogeneous 'collection of productive resources' that are imperfectly mobile (Penrose, 1959; Wernerfelt, 1984). Jay Barney popularized the resource-based view (RBV), noting that the more valuable, rare, inimitable and non-substitutable (VRIN) the resources, the greater the competitive advantage a firm could attain (Barney, 1991). The RBV led managers to seek to acquire a unique resource base.

Over time, theorists transitioned from what resources a firm possesses to how a firm configures those resources within a dynamic marketplace. This dynamic capabilities approach emphasizes a firm's ability to 'integrate, build, and reconfigure internal and external competences' (Teece et al., 1997, p. 516). Terms such as 'combine', 'coordinate' and 'integrate' describe the process of organizing resources into a valued capability (Barreto, 2010; Eisenhardt and Martin, 2000; Ettlie and Pavlou, 2006). Strategists also recognized that critical resources often reside beyond the firm's boundaries, 'embedded in inter-firm resources and routines' (Dyer and Singh, 1998, p. 650). Effective governance and knowledge sharing emerged as critical organizing capabilities.

The process of organizing became the focus of two follow-on theories:

1. Resource management is 'the comprehensive process of structuring the firm's resource portfolio, bundling the resources to build capabilities, and leveraging those capabilities with the purpose of creating and maintaining value' (Sirmon et al., 2007, p. 273).
2. Asset orchestration posits that distinctive value emerges as managers search for, select, configure and deploy resources (Helfat et al., 2007).

Resource orchestration integrates these theories. Essentially, resource orchestration theory argues that proactive managerial action is required to find complementary resources and fit them together into distinctive capabilities that deliver superior firm performance (Chadwick et al., 2015).

KEY VARIABLES AND DEFINITIONS

Under resource orchestration (RO) the most fundamental building blocks of a firm are its assets, which are configured into resources. RO considers that resources, as classically defined in prior resource-based literature, can be comingled or integrated in a way that brings distinctive value to the firm. Central to this value creation process is the role of the managers, who act as orchestrators responsible for synchronizing firm assets based on strategy and market position to create valuable capabilities in pursuit of competitive advantage. Moreover, RO recognizes that any competitive advantage generated through resource orchestration can and will erode over time. Managerial activities involved in orchestrating firm assets to create valuable and unique resources and capabilities must therefore be ongoing, particularly as the pace of change continues to increase in the market. In other words, resource orchestration as an effective organizational and managerial process needs to be routinized in firms to achieve continuous synchrony and sustainable advantage.

RO recognizes two general categories of managerial activities: resource management and asset orchestration (see Figure 12.2). Resource management comprises structuring, bundling and leveraging. Asset orchestration involves search and selection as well as configuration and deployment. These activities are intertwined. As a firm defines its strategic vision and desired competitive position in the market, it must assess whether it has the necessary assets to support its strategy. Once required assets are acquired, managers bundle/configure and deploy/leverage the derived resources to gain competitive advantage. As the competitive environment and firm strategies change over time, resources may not retain their value, in which case the firm can either reconfigure underlying assets into newer, more valuable resources, or divest them altogether.

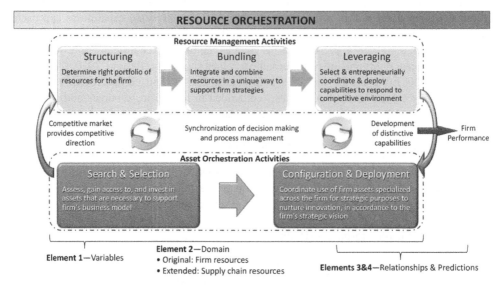

Source: Adapted from Sirmon et al. (2011).

Figure 12.2   Overview of RO theory elements

The nature and type of activities that comprise resource orchestration depend on two organizational issues: location of resources across the firm, and governance mechanisms across levels of the firm. Sirmon et al. (2007) call these breadth and depth, respectively. Because resource richness varies across different stages of the firm life cycle, resource orchestration will look and behave differently over time. Basic resource orchestration variables and their definitions are provided in Table 12.1.

Resource Management Activities

According to resource management, managerial actions focus on three primary activities: structuring, bundling, and leveraging (Sirmon et al., 2007). Structuring through the lens of RO theory considers how a firm determines what resources to acquire, build and dispose of. Structuring recognizes that firm resources are not simply 'endowed', and that their heterogeneity should change as the competitive environment changes. Over time, firms may acquire new resources corresponding to new needs. As the value of firm resources diminish, managers may consider divesting them. For instance, Rojo Gallego Burin et al. (2020) found that firms can acquire information technology competence to unlock supply chain ambidexterity and flexibility. By contrast, Nixon et al. (2004) argue that resources no longer serving a competitive purpose may be divested. In doing so, the underlying assets can be freed to be reconfigured into other valuable resources that yield new competitive capabilities (Morrow et al., 2007).

Table 12.1   *Resource orchestration variables and their definitions*

Element	Explanation	References supporting
Unit of analysis	Managerial decisions, such as resource acquisition and deployment	(Davis-Sramek et al., 2015; Ketchen et al., 2014)
Level of analysis	Firm level, analysing managerial decision or firm strategies with an emphasis on resources and capabilities	(Chadwick et al., 2015; Chirico et al., 2011)
Key variables/definitions		
Resource management activities		
Structuring	Acquire and dispose of resources to achieve the right asset portfolio for the firm	(Chadwick et al., 2015; Rojo Gallego Burin et al., 2020)
Bundling	Integrate and combine resources in a unique way to support firm competitive strategies	(Sirmon et al., 2007, 2011)
Leveraging	Selectively and entrepreneurially coordinate, mobilize and deploy resources in response to the competitive environment	(Sirmon et al., 2007, 2011)
Asset orchestration activities		
Search and selection	Assess, gain access to and invest in assets that are necessary to support a business model	(Helfat et al., 2007; Sirmon et al., 2011)
Configuration and Deployment	Coordinate use of specialized assets across the firm to fulfil strategic needs and nurture innovation in accordance to the firm's strategic vision	(Helfat et al., 2007; Sirmon et al., 2011)
Strategic determinants of resource orchestration		
Breadth	Breadth refers to resource orchestration across the scope of the firm and is determined by the firm's strategy as well as the competitive environment.	(Sirmon et al., 2011)
Depth	Depth refers to orchestration across the levels of the firm; complex organizational structures have greater communications requirements for successful resource orchestration, which is further influenced by information flow (i.e., top-down versus bottom-up)	(Davis-Sramek et al., 2015; Sirmon et al., 2011)
Firm life cycle	Newer firms (e.g., start-up) have different goals and assets than mature firms; proper resource management can help both newer and mature firms to configure assets into the resources needed to sustain growth	(Sirmon et al., 2007, 2011)

Bundling focuses on properly configuring resources to derive unique capabilities and maximize their collective value. Properly comingling these resources enables managers to unleash the full potential of the whole of these resources to be greater than the sum of their parts. One way for managers to configure the firm's resource portfolio is to integrate them to achieve new capabilities (Cui and Pan, 2015). Integration should be continuous and iterative, as the uniqueness of capabilities tends to erode due to competitive imitation or substitution. By identifying resources for augmentation, managers can extend or prolong the distinctive value of capabilities (Carnes et al., 2017). Visionary managers, in particular, can exploit market opportunities by configuring resources in novel bundles that yield pioneering capabilities (Baert et al., 2016; Carnes et al., 2017). Altogether, bundling under RO describes how managers configure and comingle resources to create distinctive value.

Leveraging recognizes that bundling diverse resources to create value is not enough to achieve competitive advantage. Managers need to deploy them to meet market needs. This is the key to harnessing the value creation potential of the firm's resource portfolio. That is, deploying a single capability can offer temporary competitive advantage that could quickly erode as managers from rival firms achieve similar capabilities. Managers need to have a vision for how different firm capabilities are interconnected and can potentially form synergistic capabilities that create a defensive moat around its performance edge (Efrat et al., 2018). Indeed, market opportunities emerge and evolve, requiring managers to proactively reconfigure resources to continuously create timely and relevant capabilities (Badrinarayanan et al., 2019).

Asset Orchestration Activities

Looking through the lens of asset orchestration, managerial actions focus on two activities: search and selection, as well as configuration and deployment (Helfat et al., 2007). Asset orchestration activities may be considered as precursors to resource development, in which managers must first determine if the firm possesses the necessary assets to be strategically configured into valuable resources.

Search and selection engages managers in understanding and acquiring the assets needed to achieve market success. Specifically, managers must assess the assets which the firm currently possesses that are of potential use, as well as those assets needed to achieve desired competitive outcomes. Often, these assets are either already possessed by the firm or under control of other firms. Once a useful asset is identified, managers need to determine whether, and how, to acquire that asset. If the asset is not under the firm's direct control, managers need to consider how to engage the firm controlling the asset in order to gain access. Ultimately, asset control relies on organizational and supply chain governance structures (Dyer and Singh, 1998; Grossman and Hart, 1980).

Configuration and deployment recognizes that assets are rarely single-purposed. They are also not omni-purpose. Importantly, some assets are localized within the firm, whereas other assets are under simultaneous control and accessible by multiple functional groups. Asset ownership may enable or inhibit managers' ability to access, configure and deploy the asset as part of a distinctive capability.

An overarching firm strategy, often communicated through vision and mission statements, can help managers to understand how best to achieve competitive goals through resource configuration and provide a direction for resource innovation. A vision also helps managers to understand their roles, and facilitates the cross-functional collaboration needed to minimize conflict over co-specialized assets. Managers must evolve configuration and deployment initiatives to correspond to new competitive manoeuvres and to respond to market opportunities.

Search and selection, and configuration and deployment, perform essentially the same role as structuring, bundling and leveraging: that is, managers perform these activities to turn assets into distinctive capabilities to achieve competitive advantage. Simply put, resource orchestration is the process of capability development.

STRATEGIC DETERMINANTS OF RESOURCE ORCHESTRATION

RO builds off the notion that a firm is a heterogeneous 'collection of productive resources' that are imperfectly mobile (Penrose, 1959; Wernerfelt, 1984). Some firms are resource rich; some are resource poor. The RBV would argue that resource-rich companies would possess significant competitive advantage in a free-market economy. Yet, many resource-disadvantaged firms do not just succeed, they grow into industry leaders; think about the start-ups now known as Amazon, Microsoft, Nucor Steel and Walmart. RO explains this incongruity by positing that managers can proactively manage assets to create unique capabilities. The fundamental research question is, 'How?'. Three strategic determinants influence how, and how effectively, managers can orchestrate resources to create distinctive capabilities: breath, depth and stage in the firm's life cycle.

Breadth

Firm assets are allocated across functions and geography. Organizational boundaries – both structural and psychological – define who 'owns' these assets. These boundaries also hinder managers' efforts to identify, access and uniquely configure these assets to create unique value. Breadth refers to orchestration that takes place across these boundaries within the firm. The breadth of a manager's resource orchestration efforts is primarily determined by three different moderating factors.

The first is the extent of market diversification. The range of resources needed to synchronize efforts increases as product assortment and physical presence widen. For instance, managers must tap into different supplier and customer bases. Effective resource orchestration enables managers to co-create value with both suppliers and customers. In effect, newly available resources can be used to create new competitive capabilities.

The second moderating factor is business strategy. Strategic choices regarding cost leadership versus differentiation (e.g. Snow and Miles, 1983; Thornhill and White, 2007) influence managers' RO efforts. Differentiation requires managers to invest in and synchronize processes that create and sustain innovative capabilities beyond those of competitors. Cost leadership, by contrast, requires managers to coordinate resources among upstream entities internally (for example, procurement) and externally (for example, suppliers) to effectively drive down cost.

The third moderating factor is the competitive environment. Intense competition not only results in heated rivalry for customers and resources but also influences the overall need and pace of innovation (Sirmon et al., 2011). In highly competitive and disruptive industries, managers must recognize necessary shifts in firm strategy and tactics. Asset portfolios must be adjusted and quickly reconfigured to bring new capabilities to market. In less competitive environments, orchestration must enable incremental innovations through extracting more value from existing resource portfolios while maintaining some efforts to develop novel capabilities.

Sirmon et al. (2011) emphasize that bridging boundaries involves integrating assets and coordinating efforts across the firm. They note that governance, measurement and incentives, and information sharing are critical to these orchestration initiatives.

Depth

Depth refers to orchestration across levels or hierarchy of the firm. Extant research focuses on upper-level managers who supposedly possess the influence to direct resource orchestration; a reality that is seldom true. A better understanding of managerial behaviour across levels of the firm is needed because the ideas that underlie distinctive capabilities can emerge anywhere within an organization. Indeed, truly distinctive capabilities emerge as managers up and down a firm's hierarchy work together in unique ways. Bower's (1970) work on strategy development highlights the importance and challenge of direction, either top-down or bottom up.

- Top-down managerial action. When ideas for distinctive capabilities emerge at the top, capability development follows a direct–implement–conform sequence as ideas move from top-level to mid-level to operational managers.
- Bottom-up managerial action. When ideas for distinctive capabilities are generated by operational managers, the capability development process follows an experiment–champion–ratify sequence.

Many companies pursue a hybrid bi-directional capability development process, inviting both top managers and operational managers to generate ideas for distinctive capabilities.

Sirmon et al. (2011, p. 1404) posit that 'the structuring, bundling, and leveraging subprocesses of resource orchestration likely differ by managerial level'. Thus, RO likely looks and behaves differently depending on where an initiative emerges. For instance, how information is communicated can impact upon performance outcomes of resource orchestration. Davis-Sramek et al. (2015) showed that a centralized decision making structure weakens the link between research and development investment and firm performance. This result echoes the RO tenet that increased depth risks information distortion (Sirmon et al., 2011). Similarly, hierarchy complexity influences RO. Complex hierarchical structures require more clearly defined managerial roles and responsibilities, which must be aligned with a unified strategy. By contrast, relatively flat organizational hierarchies are likely easier to orchestrate.

Firm Life Cycle

Orchestrating resources to achieve supernormal returns is also likely to differ based on the life cycle stage of the firm.

1. Start-up stage. Managers at entrepreneurial start-ups prize acquiring and stabilizing assets critical to assure the firm's viability. Further, experimental resource configuration patterns provide the necessary agility to pursue distinctive processes and products.
2. Growth stage. Managers guiding firms through the growth stage focus on developing capabilities to profitably expand their operating scale. For instance, managers must develop the skills to access and build relationships with supply chain partners, including investors, to support continued growth and rapidly turn ideas into new revenue streams.
3. Maturity stage. Managerial efforts in maturity shift toward acquiring and bundling resources to enhance process efficiency. Managers seek ambidexterity to simultaneously innovate new products and services in order to enter new markets to rekindle firm growth.

4. Decline stage. Managers navigating decline focus on rationalizing resource portfolios. Specifically, resources that no longer serve a firm's new strategic purpose should be judiciously divested to free up resources to invest in a new, more relevant asset portfolio.

Regardless of life cycle stage, the question is, 'What are the managerial skills and organizational routines that enable the coordination and collaboration needed to transform firm assets into highly valued capabilities in each stage of the firm life cycle?'

RELATIONSHIPS BETWEEN THE VARIABLES

Resource orchestration is both a contingency and a dynamic process theory. Sirmon et al.'s (2011) explicit discussion of strategic determinants highlights the importance of context and strategic response. This is the contingent environment–strategy–performance relationship. RO's fundamental question – that is, 'What is the role of managers' actions to effectively structure, bundle and leverage firm resources to develop distinctive capabilities?' – focuses on the dynamic process of how a firm uses its resources to achieve competitive success. The nature of RO theory calls out several key relationships among variables:

1. Contextual variables – that is, competitive environment and competitive strategy – define the nature of the capabilities that managers need to invest in and develop.
2. Contextual variables and desired capabilities define the asset portfolio that managers need to assemble.
3. Desired capabilities create a need to gain a nuanced understanding of how to uniquely structure, bundle and leverage assets to build and manage distinctive capabilities.
4. The nature of structuring, bundling and leveraging determine the managerial skills and organizational routines that firms must inculcate to consistently and effectively orchestrate resources to build distinctive capabilities.
5. Managers' ability to effectively orchestrate resources to cultivate distinctive capabilities contributes to a firm's ability to craft and execute a successful competitive strategy.

Importantly, a cyclical interplay exists between strategy and capability development. Managers' ability to consistently incubate and cultivate distinctive capabilities enables a firm to adopt more disruptive strategies, which may drive supernormal returns. These returns can be invested in assets and orchestration capabilities, which promote a virtuous cycle of new capabilities and competitive advantage.

DOMAIN WHERE THE THEORY APPLIES

Asset management and resource orchestration theories have inspired numerous studies on how firm resources contribute to unique competencies and superior performance. Since resource orchestration emerged as an integrated theory, scholars have continued this general focus on translating firm assets into competitive advantage. RO has been applied to specific fields such as information and communication technologies, e-commerce, entrepreneurship, manufacturing, innovation and sales management at both individual (manager) and organizational (firm) levels.

Table 12.2   RO streams in organizational research

Stream	Topic	Author
E-commerce	Manufacturer's e-commerce adoption using the RBV and RO	Cui and Pan (2015)
	E-commerce enabled social innovation by social entrepreneurs using RO	Cui et al. (2017)
Entrepreneurship	RO processes to enable exploration and exploitation of new opportunities in venture portfolios	Baert et al. (2016)
	RO as enhancer of entrepreneurial orientation and firm performance	Wales et al. (2013)
	RO processes as enablers to achieve sustainable growth of university spin-offs	Wright et al. (2012)
Innovation	RO processes at different stages of the firm's life cycle to sustain innovation	Carnes et al. (2017)
Manufacturing	RO as central to competitive advantage when defining manufacturing strategy and resource configuration	Efrat et al. (2018)
Sales management	Sales managers as resource orchestrators in achieving strategic sales force and selling organization outcomes	Badrinarayanan et al. (2019)

Within supply chain management (SCM), RO's firm-level focus has been extended to evaluate the coordination of resources across firm boundaries. This extension of RO to an interorganizational perspective is analogous to the relational view's extension of classic RBV theory. That is, considering how to orchestrate assets that reside beyond the firm's boundaries was not explicitly part of the original RO lens. In SCM, RO has so far only been employed on the organizational level and does not directly address the individual or managerial competence level.

HOW HAS RESEARCH ORCHESTRATION THEORY BEEN USED?

Application of RO in Organizational Research

The organizational RO research primarily evaluates the underlying fundamentals of RO; that is, the role of structuring, bundling and leveraging in cultivating unique capabilities that lead to enhanced performance. Resource orchestration theory has been used by different scholars to explain the performance effect of technology adoption, social entrepreneurship and innovation. Studies that are representative of the extant research are presented in Table 12.2. The extant research is quite limited.

Application of RO within SCM

Resource orchestration theory has been adopted and adapted by supply chain researchers. Specifically, the traditionally internally focused perspective of RO is extended to include assets that reside beyond the firm's organizational boundaries. Although Hitt (2011) and Hitt et al. (2016) specifically suggest that RO be employed as a theoretical lens for SCM research based on this interorganizational view, RO-based SCM research remains limited.

We identified two streams of SCM literature around the notion of resource orchestration. The first (e.g. Gong et al., 2018; Liu et al., 2016) employs RO as an extension of the RBV that broadens the view of RO to include intercompany resources and relationships. The second

Table 12.3   *RO streams in SCM*

Stream	Topic	Author
RO as extension of RBV	Resource orchestration and integration to successfully promote sustainability learning in the firm's supply chain	Gong et al. (2018)
	Resource orchestration as a solution for resource underutilization in product recalls	Ketchen et al. (2014)
	Resource orchestration as enabler of better supply chain integration of information technology systems	Lui et al. (2016)
3PL as supply chain orchestrator	3PLs as particularly well-positioned neutral arbitrators that coordinate interactions between firms with full visibility of the whole supply chain while being one step removed from internal politics	Zacharia et al. (2011)

stream (Zacharia et al., 2011) conceptualizes third-party logistics providers (3PLs) as supply chain orchestrators. However, they merely introduce the 'orchestrator' terminology for the established concept of a proactive supply chain manager. Thus, we find that RO in SCM research has been underutilized. Potential exists to establish and better understand orchestration as a supply chain capability. Topics under both streams are highlighted in Table 12.3.

Summary of the Use of RO

RO has been employed as an extension and elaboration of the RBV. Specifically, the emphasis has been on how resources are used, over simply possessing unique resources. The reviewed studies employ both the breadth versus depth, as well as the structuring, bundling and leveraging perspective of RO. However, the extant literature lacks a more detailed analysis of the actual tenets of RO. Especially in the SCM realm, the reviewed manuscripts tend to employ the language of RO, without actually applying the theory in a systematic way by fleshing out the details of how resources are structured, bundled and leveraged. Further, although company resources and capabilities are discussed from an orchestration perspective, current research does not address how specific managerial skills and organizational routines enable or impede structuring, bundling and leveraging. This gap provides an opportunity for a more nuanced and impactful application of RO.

THEORETICAL PREDICTIONS (FACTUAL CLAIMS)

The theoretical predictions of RO can be grouped into two main categories: direct predictions and moderating predictions. Direct predictions inform how resource orchestration enables or supports company strategy and, by extension, firm performance. Alternatively, direct predications may inform the relationship between how managerial skills and organization routines enable unique structuring, bundling and leveraging processes. Moderating predictions explore how RO changes and evolves as breadth and depth of the management processes increase and mature over time. We detail some of RO's predictions as they relate to general organizational research as well as their application in SCM.

Direct Organizational Predictions of RO

Improved asset and resource orchestration can improve firm performance if those orchestration efforts are aligned with and embedded in company strategy. As such, RO predicts that a company's managerial capabilities can enhance a firm's competitive position in the following ways (Sirmon et al., 2007, 2011):

1. Coordination and collaboration capabilities differentiate managerial attempts at synchronizing asset orchestration and resource management capabilities.
2. Greater understanding of the firm's competitive strategy and market position will lead managers to make more effective asset search and selection decisions as well as resource structuring and deployment decisions.
3. Visionary leadership will allow managers to more effectively coordinate assets and resources into innovative capabilities.
4. Providing timely and accurate information related to competitive outcomes will lead to superior asset orchestration activities.

Direct SCM Predictions of RO

According to RO, the managerial capabilities of a firm extend beyond its boundaries into the supply chain, both upstream and downstream. Importantly, appropriate internal alignment of resources and strategy must precede attempts to coordinate resources successfully across company borders (Gong et al., 2018; Liu et al., 2016). Specifically, RO predicts the following:

1. Successful internal resource orchestration (depth) is an antecedent to successful interorganizational resource orchestration (breadth).
2. Successful proactive management of a firm's supply chain requires effective structuring, bundling and leveraging of resources, both within and across company boundaries.
3. Leveraging resources across company boundaries requires an alignment of the individual with the organizational levels of resource orchestration.
4. The ability of a firm to act as the supply chain 'orchestrator' depends on its capability to successfully influence the RO processes of other firms in the supply chain. This influence can either be derived channel power or the ability to act as a neutral arbitrator.

Moderating General Predictions of RO

The impact and influence of RO activities will change over time. As firms elaborate and refine their strategy and orchestration processes over the course of their life cycle, resource orchestration offers additional benefits as well as posing new challenges (Carnes et al., 2017). We posit the following:

1. The breadth of orchestration activities will increase as firm competitive strategy entails more products and/or a presence in more markets.
2. The complexity and difficulty of RO will increase as breadth of orchestration activities increases.
3. The depth of orchestration activities will increase as firm adopts an increasingly complex organizational hierarchy.

4. The complexity of RO will increase as information feedback becomes bidirectional.
5. Demands of RO differ among firms in different life cycle stages:
   a.   start-ups will focus on RO activities that most directly influence short-term viability;
   b.   growing firms will focus on RO activities that allow them to effectively scale up operations;
   c.   mature firms will focus on RO activities that allow them to strike a balance between improving cost performance and identifying new innovations;
   d.   declining firms will have to focus on RO activities that would allow them to transform their business;
   e.   need for innovation will be the greatest for start-up and declining firms;
   f.   need for stability will be the greatest for growing and mature firms.

Moderating SCM Predictions of RO

The benefits and challenges of resource orchestration increase and evolve along with maturity in the life cycle of the firm but also with its level of supply chain integration. This interaction between resource orchestration processes and supply chain integration leads to increased detail and dynamic complexity (Gong et al., 2018; Liu et al., 2016). Specifically, RO predicts the following:

1. The breadth of RO will increase as proactive supply chain management extends beyond the first tier of suppliers and customers.
2. The complexity of RO will increase disproportionately as the breadth of RO extends across more than one tier of companies in a supply chain.
3. Both breadth and depth of RO will have to evolve and change as companies in a supply chain transition between different stages in their life cycle.
4. Interorganizational hierarchies and dynamics affect breadth and depth of RO, determining which company can fulfil the different roles of supply chain 'orchestrator'.

OUTLOOK ON FUTURE RESEARCH OPPORTUNITIES

In many respects, RO research has followed the trajectory of preceding resources-based theories; think RBV, dynamic capabilities and the relational view. As a general theory, it is easy to cite as a frame or lens for a wide variety of research that focuses on the question, 'Why do some companies succeed and others do not?' However, much of the research remains rather superficial. Further, many research issues identified by Sirmon et al. (2011) have yet to be explored (see Figure 12.3).

A more nuanced approach is needed that helps decision makers to better understand the dynamic processes involved in orchestrating assets into distinctive capabilities. More specifically, research needs to dig much more deeply into the underlying tenet of RO; that is, what is the role of managers in building distinctive capabilities that improve firm performance? Three high-level questions merit further investigation.

First, why pursue resource orchestration? Managers orchestrate resources to create distinctive capabilities. More research is needed to understand appropriate motivations. RO can be used to take costs out of processes; to develop unique processes, products and services; and

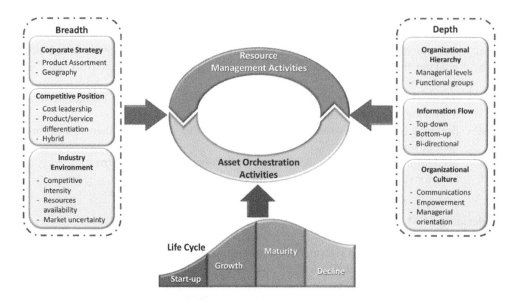

Figure 12.3   Research issues identified by Sirmon et al. (2011)

to create unique customer experiences. Each motivation may require distinctive mixing and meshing of assets. How does motivation influence RO processes?

Second, when to pursue resource orchestration? RO is neither free nor easy. Some circumstances call for efforts to create distinctive capabilities; others push back. To know when to pursue RO, we must examine diverse boundary conditions. External context (for example, competitive intensity, market dynamism, technology emergence) matters. Readiness at the focal firm as well as among supply chain partners also likely influences RO.

Third, how to pursue resource orchestration? 'How' builds on 'why' and 'when'; a reality that has not been critically explored in the extant research. We need research that delineates and explicates the capability development process, especially as it relates to managers' role in mixing and meshing organizational and supply chain resources.

Specifically, what are the managerial skills and organizational routines that are needed to proactively structure, bundle and leverage assets/resources under different motivations and boundary conditions? See Table 12.4 for examples (this is not a comprehensive list). Similarly, how do managers use these skills/routines to define system boundaries, evaluate asset fit, enhance asset value, understand environmental shifts and enable change, and explore new possibilities? Ultimately, what are the dynamics of resource orchestration, and how do they vary across different motivations and boundary conditions?

HOW WILL THIS THEORY EVOLVE?

RO posits that managers can proactively assemble and configure assets to create distinctive value. It explicitly asks, 'What is the role of managers?' Then it identifies a variety of roles that managers must perform, including structuring, bundling and leveraging. As conceptualized and operationalized, RO is primarily focused on how assets fit together; that is, how they can

Table 12.4   *Opportunities for future research*

	Structuring	Bundling	Leveraging
Managerial skills			
Change management	How can managers use resource acquisition and new partner selection to motivate and sustain change needed to develop new capabilities?	How can managers motivate functional managers (internal) and supply chain partners (external) to reconfigure resources to support new supply chain strategies?	How can managers convince functional managers (internal) and supply chain partners (external) to synchronously deploy resources to support new supply chain strategies?
Empowerment	How can managers empower team members to more effectively acquire and develop a unique resource portfolio?	How can managers determine the appropriate degree of functional (internal) and supply chain partner's (external) autonomous control over certain resources to support new capabilities and new supply chain strategies?	How do different levels and types of empowerment enable managers to orchestrate deployment of resources residing within the firm across different functions, and outside the firm among supply chain partners, to execute new supply chain strategies in response to the competitive environment?
Influence	How can managers determine and exert the necessary degree of influence in order to acquire informal access to and control of desirable resources located outside the firm?	What influence levers most effectively promote cross-functional comingling and configuration of resources? How does the role of influence levers change based on context?	How can managers convince supply chain partners to synchronously deploy resources and capabilities to execute supply chain strategies?
Storytelling	How can managers craft a narrative to successfully translate novel supply chain strategies into necessary resource portfolios?	How can managers use storytelling to promote the collaboration needed to configure resources to build unique new competencies?	Which narratives best promote agile deployment of newly developed capabilities? Who should create and share these stories?
Team building	What differences exist between resource portfolios and human resource portfolios in terms of cost and ease to acquire, divest and reconfigure assets?	How can managers engage and encourage supply chain partners with complementary resources and capabilities to work together to comingle them to create unique value?	How can customer and supplier advisory boards improve the speed and agility of unique capability deployment?
Trust construction: signalling and swift trust development	How does trust signalling influence a company's ability to gain access to scarce resources?	How can managers build trust internally among functions and externally among supply chain partners to increase sharing of co-specialized resources?	What is the role of interorganizational trust in synchronized execution of supply chain strategies?
Organizational routines			
Recruitment and hiring	How can managers assess and develop the talent needed to collaborate with supply chain partners to acquire a distinctive resource portfolio?	How can managers assess new hires' ability to effectively work across boundaries to reconfigure resources into unique capabilities?	How can managers promote the improvization needed to rapidly deploy new capabilities in a dynamic and disruptive market?

	Structuring	Bundling	Leveraging
Leadership development	Does cross-functional training of managers enhance the value of resource portfolios?	To what extent does hiring from supply chain partners improve capability development?	What leadership style most effectively motivates functions and supply chain partners to behave synchronously? Does it differ by context?
Measurement and reward design	How do measures influence a firm's ability to acquire a unique resource base?	What is the role of incentives in configuring co-specialized resources among functions and supply chain partners?	How can managers design incentive systems to encourage functions and supply chain partners to synchronously deploy strategic resources and capabilities?
Information sharing	What is the longevity of shared information's value as a resource and how does it influence portfolio structuring?	What type of data, and how timely should they be shared, to enhance the speed and process of configuration to create new capabilities?	How can information sharing among supply chain partners facilitate synchronous tactical execution under a unified supply chain strategy?

be configured and reconfigured. Although Sirmon et al. (2011) refer to enriching and pioneering, RO does not emphasize the notion or need to elevate assets, especially the human asset.

Fawcett et al. (2020) argue that in today's dynamic and disruptive marketplace, developing unique capabilities and distinctive core competencies requires more focus on unleashing the ideation of every member of an organization and supply chain. Building on the notion of orchestration, they propose that supply chain choreography is the next step in the evolution of resource-based theory and capability development. They define choreography as follows:

Choreography = Orchestration + Elevated Empowerment + Improvisation

Specifically, choreography posits that fit is a necessary but not sufficient condition for the creation of distinctive and enduring competencies. Elevated empowerment leverages the 'living, collective learning' of everyone who touches a value-added process, inviting open ideation and ensuring that the best ideas rise to the top. Elevated empowerment acknowledges that value creation ultimately belongs to the people who do the work and interact with partners – both suppliers and customers – to deliver an experience that builds deep customer satisfaction and loyalty.

Improvisation recognizes that glitches happen. When they do, improvisation is the process of effectively adapting 'on the fly'. It can only exist as a spontaneous capability in a culture of elevated empowerment. Together, elevated empowerment and improvisation invite experimentation, the ability and willingness to ask, 'If an idea, element, or system doesn't work, what will?'. These capabilities are vitally important in a disruptive marketplace where response time matters more and more. They enable decision makers to 'design out problems, build in contingencies and build bubbles around pain points' (Fawcett et al., 2020, p. 44).

As with resource management and asset orchestration, there are similarities and differences between orchestration and choreography. The differences are, importantly, complementary. Specifically, choreography puts forth two central propositions:

1. Choreography is the alpha competence that precedes the development and perpetuation of valued and valuable core competencies.

2. Choreography is a shared or collaborative design/development process that encourages more ideas to be shared, assures that the best ideas are adopted, and enables improvisation to meet the needs of a demanding and disruptive marketplace.

Figure 12.4 depicts five managerial roles that comprise choreography. These five roles are co-requisite to the choreographic process, which actively involves every actor – within and across firms – in the development of distinctive capabilities. As a process, choreography goes beyond focusing on managers' role in competence development, to include individual workers. These are the individuals who analyse the data, operate the machines and interact with customers. Their empowerment, improvisation and experimentation enable the high levels of efficiency and agility required to earn supranormal returns in a disruptive market. Choreography is the next stage for exploring how resources can be developed and deployed to achieve distinctive advantage.

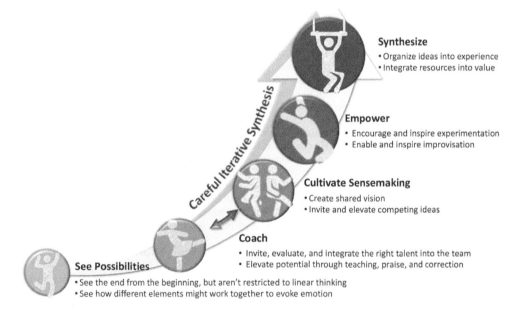

Figure 12.4   The nature of supply chain choreography

To summarize, RO extends the RBV by more deeply exploring the 'how' behind distinctive value creation. RO focuses on managers' role in bringing together, configuring and deploying resources in a way that helps a company to better meet market demands and customer needs. RO research remains underdeveloped. The time has come to more thoroughly explore the 'why', 'when' and 'how' questions related to managers' influence on the development of true core competencies. Research that provides more nuanced insight into how specific managerial skills and organization routines affect structuring, bundling and leveraging resources is needed to help companies succeed in tomorrow's chaotic marketplace.

REFERENCES

Badrinarayanan, V., Ramachandran, I. and Madhavaram, S. (2019), 'Resource Orchestration and Dynamic Managerial Capabilities: Focusing on Sales Managers as Effective Resource Orchestrators', *Journal of Personal Selling and Sales Management*, 39 (1), 23–41.

Baert, C., Meuleman, M., Debruyne, M. and Wright, M. (2016), 'Portfolio Entrepreneurship and Resource Orchestration', *Strategic Entrepreneurship Journal*, 10 (4), 346–370.

Barney, J. (1991), 'Firm Resources and Sustained Competitive Advantage', *Journal of Management*, 17 (1), 99–120.

Barreto, I. (2010), 'Dynamic Capabilities: A Review of Past Research and an Agenda for the Future', *Journal of Management*, 36 (1), 256–280.

Bower, J.L. (1970), *Managing the Resource Allocation Process*, Division of Research, Harvard Business School, Boston, MA.

Carnes, C.M., Chirico, F., Hitt, M.A., Huh, D.W. and Pisano, V. (2017), 'Resource Orchestration for Innovation: Structuring and Bundling Resources in Growth- and Maturity-Stage Firms', *Long Range Planning*, 50 (4), 472–486.

Chadwick, C., Super, J.F. and Kwon, K. (2015), 'Resource Orchestration in Practice: CEO Emphasis on SHRM, Commitment-Based HR Systems, and Firm Performance', *Strategic Management Journal*, 36 (3), 360–376.

Chirico, F., Sirmon, D.G., Sciascia, S. and Mazzola, P. (2011), 'Resource Orchestration in Family Firms: Investigating How Entrepreneurial Orientation, Generational Involvement, and Participative Strategy Affect Performance', *Strategic Entrepreneurship Journal*, 5 (4), 307–326.

Cui, M. and Pan, S.L. (2015), 'Developing Focal Capabilities for E-Commerce Adoption: A Resource Orchestration Perspective', *Information and Management*, 52 (2), 200–209.

Cui, M., Pan, S.L., Newell, S. and Cui, L. (2017), 'Strategy, Resource Orchestration and E-Commerce Enabled Social Innovation in Rural China', *Journal of Strategic Information Systems*, 26 (1), 3–21.

Davis-Sramek, B., Germain, R. and Krotov, K. (2015), 'Examining the Process R&D Investment–Performance Chain in Supply Chain Operations: The Effect of Centralization', *International Journal of Production Economics*, 167, 246–256.

Dyer, J.H. and Singh, H. (1998), 'The Relational View: Cooperative Strategy and Sources of Interorganizational Competitive Advantage', *Academy of Management Review*, 23 (4), 660–679.

Efrat, K., Hughes, P., Nemkova, E., Souchon, A.L. and Sy-Changco, J. (2018), 'Leveraging of Dynamic Export Capabilities for Competitive Advantage and Performance Consequences: Evidence from China', *Journal of Business Research*, 84, 114–124.

Eisenhardt, K.M. and Martin, J.A. (2000), 'Dynamic Capabilities: What Are They?', *Strategic Management Journal*, 21 (10–11), 1105–1121.

Ettlie, J.E. and Pavlou, P.A. (2006), 'Technology-Based New Product Development Partnerships', *Decision Sciences*, 37 (2), 117–147.

Fawcett, S.E., Fawcett, A.M., Knemeyer, A.M. and Brockhaus, S. (2020), 'Thriving on the Supply Chain High Wire', *Supply Chain Management Review*, 16 January.

Gong, Y., Jia, F., Brown, S. and Koh, L. (2018), 'Supply Chain Learning of Sustainability in Multi-Tier Supply Chains: A Resource Orchestration Perspective', *International Journal of Operations and Production Management*, 38 (4), 1061–1090.

Grossman, S.J. and Hart, O.D. (1980), 'Disclosure Laws and Takeover Bids', *Journal of Finance*, 35 (2), 323–334.

Helfat, C., Finkelstein, S., Mitchell, W., Peteraf, M., Singh, H., et al. (2007), *Dynamic Capabilities: Understanding Strategic Change in Organizations*, Blackwell, Malden, MA.

Hitt, M.A. (2011), 'Relevance of Strategic Management Theory and Research for Supply Chain Management', *Journal of Supply Chain Management*, 47 (1), 9–13.

Hitt, M.A., Xu, K. and Carnes, C.M. (2016), 'Resource Based Theory in Operations Management Research', *Journal of Operations Management*, 41, 77–94.

Ketchen, D.J., Wowak, K.D. and Craighead, C.W. (2014), 'Resource Gaps and Resource Orchestration Shortfalls in Supply Chain Management: The Case of Product Recalls', *Journal of Supply Chain Management*, 50 (3), 6–15.

Liu, H., Wei, S., Ke, W., Wei, K.K. and Hua, Z. (2016), 'The Configuration Between Supply Chain Integration and Information Technology Competency: A Resource Orchestration Perspective', *Journal of Operations Management*, 44, 13–29.

Morrow, J.L., Sirmon, D.G., Hitt, M.A. and Holcomb, T.R. (2007), 'Creating Value in the Face of Declining Performance: Firm Strategies and Organizational Recovery', *Strategic Management Journal*, 28 (3), 271–283.

Nixon, R.D., Hitt, M.A., Lee, H.-U. and Jeong, E. (2004), 'Market Reactions to Announcements of Corporate Downsizing Actions and Implementation Strategies', *Strategic Management Journal*, 25 (11), 1121–1129.

Penrose, E.G. (1959), *The Theory of the Growth of the Firm*, Wiley, New York.

Rojo Gallego Burin, A., Perez-Arostegui, M.N. and Llorens-Montes, J. (2020), 'Ambidexterity and IT Competence Can Improve Supply Chain Flexibility? A Resource Orchestration Approach', *Journal of Purchasing and Supply Management*, 26 (2), 100610.

Sirmon, D.G., Hitt, M.A. and Ireland, R.D. (2007), 'Managing Firm Resources in Dynamic Environments to Create Value: Looking Inside the Black Box', *Academy of Management Review*, 32 (1), 273–292.

Sirmon, D.G., Hitt, M.A., Ireland, R.D. and Gilbert, B.A. (2011), 'Resource Orchestration to Create Competitive Advantage: Breadth, Depth, and Life Cycle Effects', *Journal of Management*, 37 (5), 1390–1412.

Snow, C.C. and Miles, R.E. (1983), 'The Role of Strategy in the Development of a General Theory of Organizations', *Advances in Strategic Management*, 2 (1), 213–259.

Teece, D.J., Pisano, G. and Shuen, A. (1997), 'Dynamic Capabilities and Strategic Management', *Strategic Management Journal*, 18 (7), 509–533.

Thornhill, S. and White, R.E. (2007), 'Strategic Purity: A Multi-Industry Evaluation of Pure vs. Hybrid Business Strategies', *Strategic Management Journal*, 28 (5), 553–561.

Wales, W.J., Parida, V. and Patel, P.C. (2013), 'Too Much of a Good Thing? Absorptive Capacity, Firm Performance, and the Moderating Role of Entrepreneurial Orientation', *Strategic Management Journal*, 34 (5), 622–633.

Wernerfelt, B. (1984), 'A Resource-Based View of the Firm', *Strategic Management Journal*, 5 (2), 171–180.

Wright, M., Clarysse, B. and Mosey, S. (2012), 'Strategic Entrepreneurship, Resource Orchestration and Growing Spin-Offs from Universities', *Technology Analysis and Strategic Management*, 24 (9), 911–927.

Zacharia, Z.G., Sanders, N.R. and Nix, N.W. (2011), 'The Emerging Role of the Third-Party Logistics Provider (3PL) as an Orchestrator', *Journal of Business Logistics*, 32 (1), 40–54.

13. Agency theory in purchasing and supply management

George A. Zsidisin

INTRODUCTION

Agency theory, in its essence, concerns settings in which one party (the principal), whether an individual or organization, delegates work to another party (the agent) to perform. Agency theory has been applied in various organizational contexts for decades, such as executive compensation (Jensen and Murphy, 1990), auditing (Adams, 1994; Morris, 1987), incentivizing salesforce personnel (Anderson and Oliver, 1987) and franchising (Carney and Gedajlovic, 1991; Lafontaine, 1992). In the domain of supply chain management, scholars have grounded their research applying agency theory in studying topics such as outsourcing and channel relationships (Celly and Frazier, 1996; Lassar and Kerr, 1996; Logan, 2000), service supply chains (Kudla and Klass-Wissing, 2012; Selviaridis and Norrman, 2014; Tate et al., 2010), security (Belzer and Swan, 2011), vendor-owned inventory management (Rungtusanatham et al., 2007), quality (Whipple and Roh, 2010; Zu and Kaynak, 2012), risk (Zsidisin and Ellram, 2003; Zsidisin et al., 2004; Zsidisin and Smith, 2005) and sustainability (Kudla and Klass-Wissing, 2012; Shafiq et al., 2017; Wilhelm et al., 2016). Several of these articles, including Zsidisin and Ellram (2003), Zsidisin and Smith (2005) and Tate et al. (2010), focus on purchasing and supply management (PSM) and its management of suppliers.

Although these and other supply chain scholars have used agency theory as a theoretical framework in their research, these studies represent only a small portion of published supply chain academic research. Fayezi et al. (2012), in their structured literature review of agency theory in supply chain management, discovered only 19 published journal articles to include in their analysis. Further, Defee et al. (2010) found that agency theory only represents 1.9 per cent of theoretical incidents in their analysis of 364 logistics (supply chain management) publications using at least one theory. Despite agency theory still not quite garnering the same level of adoption compared with rival theories such as transaction cost economics and the resource-based view of the firm, the foundations of agency theory align well for studying facets of the PSM phenomenon.

The unit of analysis in agency theory is the analogy of a 'contract between principal and agent' (Eisenhardt, 1989, p. 59), where the principal delegates work to the agent (Lassar and Kerr, 1996). Agency theory assumes that there is partial goal conflict and different risk preferences between the principal and agent. The form of the 'contract' is dichotomized into behaviour-oriented and outcome-oriented contracts. Behaviour-oriented contracts, traditionally conceptualized in terms such as salaries and hierarchical structures, serve to reduce the risk exposure of the agent when working for the principal. Outcome-oriented contracts, on the other hand, place the burden of risk on the agent in fulfilling its duties to the principal. Examples of outcome-oriented contracts include commissions, stock options, transfer of property rights and market governance (Eisenhardt, 1989). In some ways, agency theory parallels transaction cost economics with regard to determining whether it is more efficient for the principal to structure contracts and incentives based on hierarchies and vertical integration (behaviours) or markets (outcomes) as the dependent variable.

Eisenhardt (1989) provides a seminal analysis of agency theory and its respective applications in business, including mention of its utilization in buyer–supplier exchanges. In the context of PSM, agency theory has usually been applied in the context of a buying organization being the principal, which delegates work to a supplier organization serving as the agent (Camuffo et al., 2007; Norrman, 2008; Zsidisin and Ellram, 2003). However, as will be discussed in this chapter, there are other settings and units of analysis which may be appropriate for utilizing agency theory in PSM scholarship. For example, agency theory may be applicable in settings where the PSM function serves as an agent for internal customers, such as the production and marketing functions of a corporation, as well as other units of analysis, such as individual buyers and commodity managers working as agents for superiors in the same function or external function personnel.

This chapter coninues with a discussion of agency theory variables through the lens of PSM scholarship and practice. The chapter concludes with suggestions as to how agency theory can be utilized in the future for guiding and informing PSM practice and scholarship, and specifically with regard to different units of analysis and applications of PSM phenomena and practice.

AGENCY THEORY IN PURCHASING AND SUPPLY MANAGEMENT

The following section begins with a description of the dependent variable, which is the metaphor of contracts, followed by its independent variables. The essence of agency theory offers insight as to how and why variables such as information systems, outcome uncertainty, risk aversion, programmability, relationship length and goal conflict influence the most efficient contract to implement. It is critical to note that the term 'contract' is used as a metaphor in the great majority of supply chain research adopting agency theory as its theoretical underpinning. In research, 'contracts' have often been associated with a specific overt management technique buying firms would adopt to most efficiently align a supplier to perform as needed to meet the buyer's requirements in a given setting (Eisenhardt, 1989). As previously highlighted, these settings have included activities such as outsourcing, sustainability, inventory management, quality management and risk management.

DEPENDENT VARIABLE: THE METAPHOR OF BEHAVIOUR- AND OUTCOME-BASED CONTRACTS

The dependent variable in agency theory is the form of the contract, which is most frequently applied as a binomial of either behaviour- or outcome-based contracts. A behaviour-based contract addresses agent (supplier) processes rather than simply outcomes (Anderson and Oliver, 1987; Choi and Liker, 1995). Agents are evaluated on their behaviours, which would then have an effect on outcomes.

Behaviour-based contracts have been applied and described in a variety of ways, depending on the context of the research. Celly and Frazier (1996), in their study of supplier–distributor relationships, utilize the construct 'behaviour-based coordination efforts', consisting of selling techniques used by distributor sales representatives, extent of distributor promotional efforts, and distributor's customer education and support activities. In a different investigation of incentivizing distributors, Lassar and Kerr (1996) use the term 'behavior orientation', describing how manufacturers attempt to approximate a behaviour-based contract with distributors. The three items comprising the scale focus on the level of effort by the manufacturer in monitoring distributors' conformance to specific behavioural standards.

Zu and Kayank (2012) frame behaviour-based approaches associated with quality management in terms of tasks and activities associated with suppliers' processes, subsequently leading to positive outcomes. Examples of behaviour-based approaches in their study include supplier quality certification, supplier quality audits, supplier process management and supplier quality development. Research investigating supply risk management processes classify supplier certification, quality management programmes, target costing, supplier development (Zsidisin and Ellram, 2003) and earlier supplier involvement (Zsidisin and Smith, 2005) as behaviour-based management approaches. Prosman et al. (2016) utilize the term 'behavior-based governance management' in their study of suppliers defaulting on their contracts and the viability of improving their performance.

The challenge associated with behaviour-based contracts is that the agent's behaviour has to be monitored. As summarized by Whipple and Roh (2010), this may require the principal to invest in information monitoring capabilities to reduce information asymmetry (Fama, 1980; Fama and Jensen, 1983; Lassar and Kerr, 1996). Information monitoring capabilities are investments that provide the principal with information which reveals the agent's behaviour (Eisenhardt, 1989) and can include investments such as external audit/inspection services or information/instrumentation technology. In more modern applications, these may include the use of Industry 4.0 approaches to monitor supplier processes (Arcidiacono et al., 2019). These activities are not so necessary when circumstances warrant the use of outcome-based contracts where risk is minimal and subsequently no longer require the buyer to actively monitor supplier behaviours.

Outcome-based contracts or management emphasize results regardless of how the agents achieve them (Choi and Liker, 1995). In supplier–distributor (principal–agent) relationships, Celly and Frazier (1996) examine outcome-based coordination efforts in terms of total sales volume, market share performance and sales growth. Zu and Kaynak (2012), from a quality management perspective, view outcome-based quality management in terms of penalties for quality failure inspections, from no inspection, sampling inspection, to 100 per cent inspection. However, some studies do not elaborate on outcome-based contracts or management, such as Prosman et al. (2016), Zsidisin and Ellram (2003) and Zsidisin and Smith (2005).

In a buyer–supplier relationship, outcome-based contracts would typically involve some type of price premium (Klein and Leffler, 1981) in order to make cheating unprofitable (Mishra et al., 1998). Thus, outcome-based contracts in a literal 'contracting' application can range from cost-plus incentives and/or risk/gain sharing, which place some of the risk burden on suppliers, to firm fixed price contracts, which place most to all of the risk on suppliers to fulfil their obligations to the customer. With this mechanism both principals and agents can observe outcomes, and the principals reward agents based on measured performance outcomes (Ekanayake, 2004).

Outcome-based contracts are often conceptualized and examined in terms of performance-based contracting (Randall et al., 2010; Selviaridis and Wynstra, 2015). As summarized by Randall et al. (2010), performance-based contracting (PBC) promotes customer value by specifying contractual outcomes (Datta and Roy, 2011) for improving goal alignment and incentives in the supply chain (Randall et al., 2011), increasing risk and rewards for the supplier by aligning financial bonuses and/or penalties on performance and enabling co-creation of specified outcomes (Guo and Ng, 2011).

Selviaridis and Norrman (2014) summarize PBC in terms of specifying service performance and linking that to payment, thereby transferring some or all of the risk to the provider/agent (Doerr et al., 2005; Selviaridis and Wynstra, 2015). However, one challenge is that these systems often require elaborate processes for measuring and reporting performance (Datta and Roy, 2011). Selviaridis and Norrman (2014) provide examples of 'fixed price plus incentive fee' structures in the transportation industry, where the incentive fee (bonus) is linked to product availability and supply chain cost reduction targets specified by the customer (principal). In the context of performance-based logistics (PBL) and post-production support, Randall et al. (2011) argue that PBL involves contracting for performance, or an outcome, rather than repeatedly contracting for discrete products and services. However, it is also suggested that performance-based contracting should move towards a more systemic approach for understanding behavioural as well as contractual approaches for incentivizing suppliers (Selviaridis and Norrman, 2014). The challenge is that incentive alignment is not well established in practice. Instead, simple mechanisms that are performance- or outcome-based are more commonly used, as compared with behaviour-based contracts that are considered more sophisticated to employ (Norrman and Naslund, 2019) and often require extensive monitoring (Whipple and Roh, 2010).

INDEPENDENT VARIABLES: FACTORS INFLUENCING CONTRACT SELECTION

There are several factors in agency theory influencing whether behaviour- or outcome-based 'contracts' are appropriate. Some of the more prevalent factors are discussed below, which are information systems, outcome uncertainty, risk aversion, programmability, relationship length and goal conflict. Table 13.1 provides definitions of agency theory independent variables (factors) and examples in PSM, while Table 13.2 summarizes the appropriate 'contract' given the independent variable, where 'x' signifies a positive relationship between the variable and contract form.

Information Systems

Information systems, within the context of agency theory, consist of approaches for accumulating, processing and disseminating information (Eisenhardt, 1989). From the perspective of the principal, information systems can be used to monitor the behaviour of the agent, thereby more closely aligning their work with the requirements of the principal, as well as reducing risk associated with adverse selection (misrepresentation of ability) and moral hazard (lack of agent effort) (Logan, 2000). Information asymmetry and its monitoring challenges is one of the two essential agency problems (with goal congruency) that arise when a principal del-

Table 13.1   Agency theory independent variable definitions and PSM examples

Independent variable	Definition	PSM example
Information systems	Approaches for accumulating, processing and disseminating information	Industry 4.0 tools; supplier designed representative; vendor managed inventory
Outcome uncertainty	Degree of uncertainty about obtaining desired results	Commodity price volatility; new product development; demand volume heterogeneity
Risk aversion	The extent to which a party (principal or agent) desires to avoid risk	Capital investments; developing technologies
Programmability	The degree to which appropriate agent behaviours can be specified in advance	Specifications or statement of work
Relationship length	The length of time that the relationship is anticipated to endure	Experience with supplier
Goal conflict	The extent to which alignment exists between the goals of the principal and those of the agent	Supplier providing product to competitors; supplier as competitor; profitability; future strategic direction

Sources: Definitions adapted from Eisenhardt (1989) and Zsidisin and Smith (2005).

Table 13.2   Agency theory variables and contract type

Behaviour-based		Outcome-based
X	Information systems	
X	Outcome uncertainty	
	Risk aversion (principal)	X
X	Risk aversion (agent)	
X	Programmability	
X	Relationship length	
	Goal conflict	X

Source: Adapted from Eisenhardt (1989).

egates tasks to an agent (Norrman, 2008; Whipple and Roh, 2010). As shown in Table 13.2, the use of information systems is positively associated with the use of behaviour-oriented contracts due to the ability to monitor and assess the agent's behaviour.

In the context of PSM scholarship, there are several examples where information systems are conceptualized and measured for monitoring supplier behaviours and performance. Maestrini et al. (2018) examine information systems in terms of monitoring supplier quality, delivery and order accuracy. Zu and Kaynak (2012) describe how buyers can reduce information asymmetries associated with quality management by collecting data associated with suppliers' process quality performance and capabilities, their quality control procedures, their quality improvement programmes and the results of these programmes. Lassar and Kerr (1996) examine distributor (supplier) monitoring in terms of monitoring ability, task observability and clarity of outcome measures. Zsidisin and Smith (2005) describe information systems in their application with early supplier involvement for assessing supplier capabilities, monitoring supplier processes and providing information to suppliers during new product development in order to reduce risk exposure.

Information systems are arguably necessary for both behaviour- and outcome-based contracts in a PSM context; they are just applied in different ways. As traditionally concep-tualized, information systems can be used for monitoring supplier behaviours by reducing the buying organization's risk associated with supplier adverse selection and moral hazard (Eisenhardt, 1989; Zsidisin and Smith, 2005). However, from a performance-based contract-ing (outcome-based contracts) perspective, information systems can be viewed in terms of assessing supplier performance and rewarding/penalizing suppliers based on those results (Randall et al., 2011; Datta and Roy, 2011). Therefore, depending on the context, information systems and supplier monitoring may be necessary when incentivizing suppliers with either behaviour- or outcome-based contracts or management approaches; it is the application and intentions of these monitoring systems that may differ, putting a different twist on the way we perceive and contextualize the use of information systems.

Outcome Uncertainty

Outcome uncertainty is associated with the extent to which the agent can effectively control its performance outcomes when meeting the requirements of the principal (Eisenhardt, 1989; Whipple and Roh, 2010). Uncertainty in business and supply chain is prevalent in many ways. These include, but are not limited to, government policies (Eisenhardt, 1989), economic climate (Celly and Frazier, 1996), competitor actions, technological change, demand vola-tility, product churning (Claycomb et al., 2002), commodity price volatility (Gaudenzi et al., 2018) and foreign exchange valuation shifts (Gaudenzi et al., 2021; Zsidisin et al., 2020).

Whipple and Roh (2010) examine outcome uncertainty with regard to quality 'fade' from shippers. Zsidisin et al. (2004) argue that the purchasing organizations in their study are able to reduce the level of uncertainty associated with inbound supply through the use of formal risk assessment tools and proactive supply management techniques. Zu and Kaynak (2012) propose when buying firms perceive a high degree of supplier uncertainty in attaining quality levels, behaviour-based approaches are more appropriate. Likewise, Selviaridis and Norrman (2014) argue that outcome-based contracts are appropriate under conditions of low outcome uncertainty performance, because the cost of transferring risk is low. Overall, the central argument is that under conditions of significant outcome uncertainty it is very difficult for the buyer to efficiently transfer the associated risk to suppliers without having to pay a risk premium, and instead it is better to incentivize suppliers based on their behaviours and efforts to attain performance requirements.

Risk Aversion

Zu and Kaynak (2012) state that, in essence, risk aversion is about settling for a lower profit to avoid the risk of an uncertain return; or in other words, being willing to pay more to avoid risks. When the level of agents' risk aversion decreases or principals become more risk averse, it is easier to transfer risk to agents and outcome-based control is preferred (MacCrimmon and Wehrung, 1986). For suppliers who are more risk averse, it becomes increasingly expensive to pass risk to these suppliers, and then behaviour-based approaches become more appealing (Eisenhardt, 1989).

From a quality management perspective, risk averse suppliers are more likely to apply strict quality control procedures and invest in quality management practices to improve their process and product quality, so that they can reduce the proportion of defective goods going into each delivered lot and deliver better-quality products to buyers (Starbird, 1994). Under these conditions, behaviour-based approaches to managing supplier quality, especially supplier process management and supplier quality development practices, are more effective in managing supplier quality than outcome-based approaches, because risk averse suppliers are more willing to cooperate with buyers to improve their capabilities, thereby reducing their risk of quality problems and failures (Zu and Kaynak, 2012). In the case of new product development, suppliers are often exposed to risk associated with design failures in meeting their customer requirements. Strategic supply chain processes such as early supplier involvement help to reduce risk exposure and improve goal congruence between the buyer and strategic suppliers (Zsidisin and Smith, 2005). However, in other circumstances where there is minimal uncertainty, and hence risk in the transaction, it is usually more efficient to transfer what little risk there is to the supplier, and instead focus on performance outcomes.

Programmability

Programmability refers to the standardization and clarity of processes and procedures in tasks, job responsibility and results (Goodale et al., 2008; Stroh et al., 1996). In the context of PSM, task programmability occurs when buyers can specify appropriate supplier behaviours (Eisenhardt, 1989; Zu and Kaynak, 2012). It becomes easier to observe the supplier's work when tasks are more programmable (Rungtusanatham et al., 2007; Stroh et al., 1996). Therefore, when information about a supplier's behaviour can be easily obtained, behaviour-based approaches are preferable (Eisenhardt, 1989). A standard product implies high task programmability because the required production process can be precisely defined; whereas a unique product implies low task programmability (Keebler, 2001). When purchasing standard products from suppliers, it is easier for buyers to know what the production process should be and to evaluate whether suppliers are managing quality as they should. It is thus easier to apply behaviour-based approaches with suppliers, such as monitoring suppliers' processes, performing quality audits, or offering technical assistance and guidance. These approaches can help buyers to stipulate suppliers' behaviour toward their desired performance level (Eisenhardt, 1989).

Relationship Length

Relationship length from an agency theory perspective simply refers to the duration of buyer–supplier relationships in a supply chain setting (Eisenhardt, 1989), and is usually tested using the number of years doing business with a supplier (Buvik and Haugland, 2005; Kotabe et al., 2003). Zu and Kaynak (2012), basing their arguments on the work of Flynn and Flynn (2005), Fynes et al. (2005) and Kaynak and Hartley (2008), state that successful long-term relationships encourage suppliers to become involved in product or service design process improvement efforts, thereby leading to improvements in product and service quality. Long-term relationships provide a platform where the purchasing organization will learn about the supplier and establish organizational routines (Li et al., 2015; Zsidisin et al., 2004).

Early supplier involvement (ESI) in new product development, which requires a long-term relationship and orientation with suppliers (Zsidisin and Smith, 2005), has been found to serve as a behaviour-based management approach for managing supply risk (Zsidisin and Ellram,

2003). Zsidisin and Ellram's (2003) study discovered that relationship length has a positive moderating effect on the influence of sharing information about risk and firm performance. ESI tends to extend relationships, increasing the likelihood of goal alignment between the supplier and the buyer (Zsidisin and Smith, 2005).

Goal Conflict

Goal conflict is the second of the two essential agency problems that arise when a principal delegates tasks to an agent (Norrman, 2008; Whipple and Roh, 2010). Goal conflict (congruence) concerns the extent to which alignment exists between the goals and strategies of the principal and agent (Eisenhardt, 1989; Rungtusanatham et al., 2007; Zsidisin and Ellram, 2003; Zsidisin and Smith, 2005), where conflict implies different or opposing directions, and congruence refers to alignment.

Goal conflict (congruence), from an agency perspective, has been studied in several different contexts in the supply chain literature. Zu and Kaynak (2012) examine goal conflict in terms of the degree to which buying firms perceive that suppliers disagree on goals and strategies for ensuring quality. Maestrini et al. (2018) found empirical support for goal congruence positively moderating the influence of supplier monitoring and incentives on supplier operational performance. Zsidisin and Smith (2005) argue that goal congruence between buyers and suppliers is positively associated with ESI, a behaviour-based risk management approach, in attaining final customers' product/service requirements.

SUMMARY AND FUTURE DIRECTIONS

As discussed in this chapter, the core of agency theory concerns aligning and incentivizing an entity (individual or organization) via the metaphor of a contract. Agency theory is currently one of the lesser-utilized theoretical frameworks in supply chain scholarship, but has the potential to provide scholars with insight and grounding when investigating PSM phenomena.

Stock (1997) posits that agency theory may assist managers in understanding supply chain issues such as the development of inter- and intra-organizational relationships; the maintenance of complex relationships between suppliers, customers and third parties; the dynamics of risk sharing, capital outlay, power and conflict between channel intermediaries; and identifying the costs and benefits of supply chain integration. These topics, and other settings and phenomena where a buyer, whether in terms of the organization, PSM function or individual, delegates or is delegated work to or from another organization, function or individual, can potentially glean insight from the theoretical underpinnings of agency theory. However, the great majority of agency theory-informed purchasing and supply chain management scholarship focuses on buyer–supplier dyads (Fayezi et al., 2012; Selviaridis and Norrman, 2014).

One opportunity that has not yet been fully seized in PSM research is adopting agency theory from different units of analysis. Future research applying agency theory in PSM should continue extending beyond the dyads of buyer and supplier firms. Agency problems can exist within the firm, involving the PSM function. For example, it can be argued that in some capacities the PSM function has an agency relationship with production, where PSM is the agent performing the task of arranging and providing the inputs for manufacturing, whereas manufacturing serves as the principal. Although each function works for the same company, there may be instances where there is goal conflict, such as engineers or plant managers wanting to use a specific supplier due to reputation or perceived quality, and PSM seeking to use a supplier providing the best business value to the company.

Another example can concern the individual level, such as a commodity manager as the agent tasked by a director of supply management for managing a respective spend category. Although the commodity manager may have done due diligence in selecting a supplier, there may also be outcome uncertainty, such as changing market conditions and prices, detrimentally affecting cost or product availability; as well as programmability or information system factors influencing how the commodity manager should be evaluated and incentivized in their performance evaluation or compensation structure.

However, agency theory may have limitations extending beyond the investigation of dyadic relationships. Supply chain research during the last decade and a half has extended towards investigating the dynamics of supply chain and service triads (Wynstra, 2010) and networks (Choi and Dooley, 2009). Several scholars have attempted to make initial associations of agency theory applied to supply chain triads and networks, but only with high-level generalizations. Cheng and Kam (2008) provide and discuss a conceptual framework using the setting of multiple principal–agent relationships in a supply network, but none of the assumptions or variables of agency theory are examined or introduced. Zhang et al. (2015) adopt an agency perspective of triad relationships in franchiser–franchisee–customer relationships, but the key dependent variable of 'contracts' is never mentioned, nor any empirical examination of its independent variables. Wynstra et al. (2015) briefly state that 'agency theory has immediate relevance for the study of contracting in triads, due to its focus on structuring arrangements between entities' (p. 10), but do not provide any specific guidance on how this can be done.

Tate et al. (2010) provide a rare exception by investigating agency 'triads' in the purchases of marketing services, with marketing and supply management from the same organization serving as the principals and the supplier as the agent. Studies such as this illustrate the complexity of interorganizational and intra-organizational goals and behaviours, where in their study marketing management prefers behaviour-based contracts focusing on the relationship and building loyalty so that the supplier will do a 'good job'. In contrast, supply management prefers outcome-based contracts that track fulfillment of requirements along the purchasing process (monitoring) and initiate consequences when necessary if failures arise. This study provides a rare glimpse into intra-organizational relationships, but with two different business functions (marketing and PSM) serving as principals, and the complex dynamics of incentivizing supplier performance. They discovered conflicting guidance and incentives between purchasing and marketing in incentivizing supplier performance. Further, the work of Tate et al. (2010) is one of the only supply chain studies directly adopting the core tenets of agency theory assumptions, its dependent variable, and select independent variables (information systems/monitoring, goal conflict, and programmability) in their analysis of a triadic relationship. However, one key difference, in relation to other supply chain triadic or network studies, is that it is still focused on two distinct companies: the principal is dichotomized by the two business functions of PSM and marketing, and the supplier serves as an agent in the relationship.

Agency theory can provide initial insight into some of the conflicting dynamics with multiple relationships, but translating those initial insights into creating an effective system of contracts among those entities is arguably beyond our current understanding and utilization of agency theory in PSM and supply chain research. As discussed in this chapter, there are numerous variables influencing whether behaviour- or outcome-based contracts are most appropriate. Triads and networks exponentially compound this analysis by simultaneously considering multiple relationships among three or more entities at arguably two or more units of analysis. In some ways this was identified by Fayezi et al. (2012), who noted that extended networks of firms, which characterize most supply chains today, are not well addressed within agency theory research due to those complexities.

This may also be a reason why agency theory is not as frequently used as compared with other theories in supply chain scholarship. Most scholars today would argue that supply chains need to consist of a minimum of three entities; usually the bare minimum being a supplier, producer and customer. The realities of supply chain management today is that they are more of a collection or network of firms.

Agency theory is one of many theoretical frameworks that PSM scholars can consider adopting in their research agendas. This chapter provides a high-level view of agency theory in scholarship, with a focus on PSM and supply chain management research examining factors influencing the efficient use of behaviour- or outcome-based 'contracts'. Although most supply chain research has focused on the use of buyer–supplier dyads, agency theory is ripe for examining PSM phenomena in a variety of settings and dyadic units of analysis, but also has its limitations when extending into networks. I hope this chapter encourages you to consider agency theory in your toolbox of theoretical frameworks.

REFERENCES

Adams, Michael (1994), 'Agency theory and the internal audit', *Managerial Auditing Journal*, 9 (8), 8–12.

Anderson, E. and R.L. Oliver (1987), 'Perspectives on behavior-based versus outcome-based salesforce control systems', *Journal of Marketing*, 51 (4), 76–88.

Arcidiacono, F., A. Ancarani, C. Di Mauro and F. Schupp (2019), 'Where the rubber meets the road. Industry 4.0 among SMEs in the automotive sector', *IEEE Engineering Management Review*, 47 (4), 86–93.

Belzer, M.H. and P.F. Swan (2011), 'Supply chain security: agency theory and port drayage drivers', *Economic and Labour Relations Review: ELRR*, 22 (1), 41–63.

Buvik, A. and S.A. Haugland (2005), 'The allocation of specific assets, relationship duration, and contractual coordination in buyer–seller relationships', *Scandinavian Journal of Management*, 21 (1), 41–60.

Camuffo, A., A. Furlan and E. Rettore (2007), 'Risk sharing in supplier relations: an agency model for the Italian air-conditioning industry', *Strategic Management Journal*, 28 (12), 1257–1266.

Carney, M. and E. Gedajlovic (1991), 'Vertical integration in franchise systems: agency theory and resource explanations', *Strategic Management Journal*, 12 (8), 607–629.

Celly, K.S. and G.L. Frazier (1996), 'Outcome-based and behavior-based coordination efforts in channel relationships', *Journal of Marketing Research*, 33 (2), 200–210.

Cheng, S.K. and B.H. Kam (2008), 'A conceptual framework for analysing risk in supply networks', *Journal of Enterprise Information Management*, 22 (4), 345–360.

Choi, T.Y. and K.J. Dooley (2009), 'Supply networks: theories and models', *Journal of Supply Chain Management*, 45 (3), 25–27.

Choi, T.Y. and J.K. Liker (1995), 'Bringing Japanese continuous improvement approaches to US manufacturing: the roles of process orientation and communications', *Decision Sciences*, 26 (5), 589–620.

Claycomb, C., C. Dröge and R. Germain (2002), 'Applied product quality knowledge and performance', *International Journal of Quality and Reliability Management*, 19 (6), 649–671.

Datta, P.P. and R. Roy (2011), 'Operations strategy for the effective delivery of integrated industrial product-service offerings: two exploratory defense industry case studies', *International Journal of Operations and Production Management*, 31 (5), 579–603.

Defee, C., B. Williams, W.S. Randall and R. Thomas (2010), 'An inventory of theory in logistics and SCM research', *International Journal of Logistics Management*, 21 (3), 404–489.

Doerr, K., I. Lewis and D.R. Eaton (2005), 'Measurement issues in performance-based logistics', *Journal of Public Procurement*, 5 (2), 164–186.

Eisenhardt, Kathleen M. (1989), 'Agency theory: an assessment and review', *Academy of Management Review*, 14 (1), 57–74.

Ekanayake, Samson (2004), 'Agency theory, national culture and management control systems', *Journal of American Academy of Business*, 4 (1), 49–54.

Fama, E.F. (1980), 'Agency problems and the theory of the firm', *Journal of Political Economy*, 88 (2), 288–307.

Fama, E.F. and M.C. Jensen (1983), 'Agency problems and residual claims', *Journal of Law and Economics*, 26 (2), 327–349.

Fayezi, S., A. O'Loughlin and A. Zutshi (2012), 'Agency theory and supply chain management: a structured literature review', *Supply Chain Management*, 17 (5), 556–570.

Flynn, B.B. and E.J. Flynn (2005), 'Synergies between supply chain management and quality management: emerging implications', *International Journal of Production Research*, 43 (16), 3421–3436.

Fynes, B., C. Voss and S. de Búrca (2005), 'The impact of supply chain relationship quality on quality performance', *International Journal of Production Economics*, 96 (3), 339–354.

Gaudenzi, B., G.A. Zsidisin, J.L. Hartley and L. Kaufmann (2018), 'An exploration of factors influencing the choice of commodity price risk mitigation strategies', *Journal of Purchasing and Supply Management*, 24 (3), 218–237.

Gaudenzi, B., G.A. Zsidisin and R. Pellegrino (2021), 'Measuring the financial effects of mitigating commodity price volatility in supply chains', *Supply Chain Management: An International Journal*, 26 (1), 17–31.

Goodale, J.C., D.F. Kuratko and J.S. Hornsby (2008), 'Influence factors for operational control and compensation in professional service firms', *Journal of Operations Management*, 26 (5), 669–688.

Guo, L. and I. Ng (2011), 'The co-production of equipment-based services: An interpersonal approach', *European Management Journal*, 29 (1), 43–50.

Jensen, M.C. and K.J. Murphy (1990), 'Performance pay and top-management incentives', *Journal of Political Economy*, 98 (2), 225–264.

Kaynak, H. and J.L. Hartley (2008), 'A replication and extension of quality management into the supply chain', *Journal of Operations Management*, 26 (4), 468–489.

Keebler, James S. (2001), 'Measuring performance in the supply chain', in J.T. Mentzer (ed.), *Supply Chain Management* (pp. 411–435), Thousand Oaks, CA: SAGE Publications.

Klein, B. and K.B. Leffler (1981), 'The role of market forces in assuring contractual performance', *Journal of Political Economy*, 89 (4), 615–641.

Kotabe, M., X. Martin and H. Domoto (2003), 'Gaining from vertical partnerships: knowledge transfer, relationship duration, and supplier performance improvement in the US and Japanese automotive industries', *Strategic Management Journal*, 24 (4), 293–316.

Kudla, N.L. and T. Klaas-Wissing (2012), 'Sustainability in shipper-logistics service provider relationships: A tentative taxonomy based on agency theory and stimulus–response analysis', *Journal of Purchasing and Supply Management*, 18 (4), 218–231.

Lafontaine, Francine (1992), 'Agency theory and franchising: some empirical results', *RAND Journal of Economics*, 23 (2), 263–283.

Lassar, W.M. and J.L. Kerr (1996), 'Strategy and control in supplier–distributor relationships: an agency perspective', *Strategic Management Journal*, 17 (8), 613–632.

Li, G., H. Fan, P.K. Lee and T.C.E. Cheng (2015), 'Joint supply chain risk management: an agency and collaboration perspective', *International Journal of Production Economics*, 164, 83–94.

Logan, M.S. (2000), 'Using agency theory to design successful outsourcing relationships', *International Journal of Logistics Management*, 11 (2), 21–32.

MacCrimmon, K. and D. Wehrung (1986), *Taking Risks: The Management of Uncertainty*, New York: Free Press.

Maestrini, V., D. Luzzini, F. Caniato and S. Ronchi (2018), 'Effects of monitoring and incentives on supplier performance: an agency theory perspective', *International Journal of Production Economics*, 203, 322–332.

Mishra, D.P., J.B. Heide and S.G. Cort (1998), 'Information asymmetry and levels of agency relationships', *Journal of Marketing Research*, 35 (3), 277–295.

Morris, R.D. (1987), 'Signalling, agency theory and accounting policy choice', *Accounting and Business Research*, 18 (69), 47–56.

Norrman, A. (2008), 'Supply chain risk-sharing contracts from a buyers' perspective: content and experiences', *International Journal of Procurement Management*, 1 (4), 371–393.

Norrman, A. and D. Naslund (2019), 'Supply chain incentive alignment: The gap between perceived importance and actual practice', *Operations and Supply Chain Management*, 12 (3), 129–142.

Prosman, E.J., K. Scholten and D. Power (2016), 'Dealing with defaulting suppliers using behavioral based governance methods: an agency theory perspective', *Supply Chain Management: An International Journal*, 21 (4), 499–511.

Randall, W.S., D.R. Nowicki and T.G. Hawkins (2011), 'Explaining the effectiveness of performance-based logistics: a quantitative examination', *International Journal of Logistics Management*, 22 (3), 324–348.

Randall, W.S., T.L. Pohlen and J.B. Hanna (2010), 'Evolving a theory of performance-based logistics using insights from service dominant logic', *Journal of Business Logistics*, 31 (2), 35–61.

Rungtusanatham, M., E. Rabinovich, B. Ashenbaum and C. Wallin (2007), 'Vendor-owned inventory management arrangements in retail: an agency theory perspective', *Journal of Business Logistics*, 28 (1), 111–135.

Selviaridis, K. and A. Norrman (2014), 'Performance-based contracting in service supply chains: A service provider risk perspective', *Supply Chain Management*, 19 (2), 153–172.

Selviaridis, K. and F. Wynstra (2015), 'Performance-based contracting: a literature review and future research directions', *International Journal of Production Research*, 53 (12), 3505–3540.

Shafiq, A., P.F. Johnson, R.D. Klassen and A. Awaysheh (2017), 'Exploring the implications of supply risk on sustainability performance', *International Journal of Operations and Production Management*, 37 (10), 1386–1407.

Starbird, S.A. (1994), 'The effect of acceptance sampling and risk aversion on the quality delivered by suppliers', *Journal of the Operational Research Society*, 45 (3), 309–320.

Stock, J. (1997), 'Applying theories from other disciplines to logistics', *International Journal of Physical Distribution and Logistics Management*, 27 (9), 515–539.

Stroh, L.K., J.M. Brett, J.P. Baumann and A.H. Reilly (1996), 'Agency theory and variable pay compensation strategies', *Academy of Management Journal*, 39 (3), 751–767.

Tate, W.L., L.M. Ellram, L. Bals, E. Hartmann and W. Van der Valk (2010), 'An agency theory perspective on the purchase of marketing services', *Industrial Marketing Management*, 39 (5), 806–819.

Whipple, J.M. and J. Roh (2010), 'Agency theory and quality fade in buyer–supplier relationships', *International Journal of Logistics Management*, 21 (3), 338–352.

Wilhelm, M.M., C. Blome, V. Bhakoo and A. Paulraj (2016), 'Sustainability in multi-tier supply chains: understanding the double agency role of the first-tier supplier', *Journal of Operations Management*, 41, 42–60.

Wynstra, Finn (2010), 'What did we do, who did it and did it matter? A review of fifteen volumes of the (European) Journal of Purchasing and Supply Management', *Journal of Purchasing and Supply Management*, 16 (4), 279–292.

Wynstra, F., M. Spring and T. Schoenherr (2015), 'Service triads: a research agenda for buyer–supplier–customer triads in business services', *Journal of Operations Management*, 35, 1–20.

Zhang, J.J., B. Lawrence and C.K. Anderson (2015), 'An agency perspective on service triads: linking operational and financial performance', *Journal of Operations Management*, 35, 56–66.

Zsidisin, G.A. and L.M. Ellram (2003), 'An agency theory investigation of supply risk management', *Journal of Supply Management*, 39 (2), 15–27.

Zsidisin, G.A., L.M. Ellram, J.R. Carter and J.L. Cavinato (2004), 'An analysis of supply risk assessment techniques', *International Journal of Physical Distribution and Logistics Management*, 34 (5), 397–413.

Zsidisin, G.A., B. Gaudenzi and R. Pellegrino (2020), 'Five principles for creating a supply chain foreign exchange risk mitigation strategy', *CSCMP Quarterly*, (3), 20–23.

Zsidisin, G.A. and M.E. Smith (2005), 'Managing supply risk with early supplier involvement: a case study and research propositions', *Journal of Supply Chain Management*, 41 (4), 44–57.

Zu, X. and H. Kaynak (2012), 'An agency theory perspective on supply chain quality management', *International Journal of Operations and Production Management*, 32 (4), 423–446.

14. Playing to win: applying game theory to purchasing and supply management

Steven Carnovale and Myles D. Garvey

INTRODUCTION

Since the dawn of time, existence has been defined by competition. With the increasing length and complexity of modern supply chains, coupled with heightened geopolitical interconnectedness, businesses are forced into competition on a global scale. Such complexity requires a methodological way in which to study and analyse these competitive dynamics. One such approach is game theory. Game theory, at its core, is the analytical process by which the dynamics of competition are modelled and analysed. Though, perhaps, implicit in the psychology of human beings forever, game theory was codified as a formal mathematical approach to understanding strategy by Morgenstern and Von Neuman (1953) in the book *Theory of Games and Economic Behavior*, and widely popularized by John Nash (1951), when the so-called Nash equilibrium was formalized. As inputs, game theory takes into account all possible courses of action for each player in the game, the resources that each player has, and the value that those players put on those resources. The ultimate goal of using game theory is to determine the optimal course of action to maximize the gain for the player(s). Formally, game theory studies the intersection of three things: (1) rational economic agents; (2) what those agents value (that is their utilities); and (3) the pay-offs/consequences of various strategies/ actions. In the decades since Morgenstern and Von Neuman's book, game theory has firmly entered into the toolboxes of researchers in disciplines such as computer science, economics, political science, business, biology, and many more. Indeed, the proliferation and expansiveness of game theory over the past eight decades suggests just how useful it is in answering important basic research questions, such as:

1. What is the nature of competition within my industry?
2. How/why does one, or should one, cooperate in the presence of competition?
3. What is the best strategy to take, given how my competitor might react?
4. Is it better to be the first mover into a market/product, or the second?
5. How should I react to my competition, in the presence (or absence) of complete information?

And many more.

Indeed, even a cursory review of the literature in game theory would render the reader overwhelmed and wondering where to begin. So, how might scholars get started in understanding what game theory is, what it includes, and which problems it helps purchasing and supply researchers to solve? Further, where might game theory be used in purchasing and supply research in the coming decades? These are the questions that this chapter seeks to answer. In what follows we first describe the lens that we use to think about supply chain management's many intricacies and layers. Then, leveraging the framework established in Wacker (2008) we advance an ontology of game theory through four key elements: (1) the 'who' and 'what' of game theory (that is, definitions); (2) the 'when' and 'where' of game theory (that is, its domain); (3) the 'how' and 'why' of game theory (that is, its relationships); and finally (4) the 'should', 'could' and 'would' of game theory (that is, its predictions). We then transition into a brief, yet pointed, literature review focusing on some key applications of game theory that are relevant to purchasing and supply management. Finally, we tie it all together with a heuristic of sorts for the aspiring game theory researcher, providing examples of when and why game theory might be applicable.

As a brief, and necessary aside, we should remark on what purpose this chapter will serve and, perhaps more importantly, what purpose it will not serve. In what follows we will explore game theory from a grounding lens. That is, we will focus on breaking it down to the atomic level, and then building up its foundation so that the reader can understand whether game theory is an appropriate way to study the research problem at hand. Certainly, the reader may hold the view that game theory is more mathematical and formulaic, rather than grounding. While it is true that applications of game theory utilize a fair bit of mathematics, the logic of why/when/where to use game theory does not. What this chapter is not: this is not a comprehensive review of the history and theoretical development of game theory. For that purpose, we direct the readers to Weintraub (1992) and Walker (1995). In addition, if after reading this chapter the reader is curious about the analytical approaches to derive closed form mathematical solutions, we refer the reader to Morgenstern and Von Neumann (1953), Nash (1950, 1951), Hamilton (1992) and Mazalov (2014). Further, within the world of game theory, there are several nuances that a brief review of the literature will yield. Things such as: cooperative versus competitive games; symmetric versus asymmetric competition; simultaneous versus sequential games; perfect versus imperfect information; and so on. This chapter does not cover those dynamics, instead we would direct the reader to Bonanno (2018a, 2018b) for a comprehensive overview in non-cooperative game theory, and Peleg and Sudholter (2007) for a comprehensive overview of cooperative games.

FOUR ELEMENTS OF GAME THEORY

What is Game Theory?

Depending on the lens through which one views game theory, it is possible to date the historic rudiments back to the Babylonian Talmud as the source of strategy in the face of cooperative decision making. Serving as the bedrock of the Jewish religious traditions, the Talmud details a 'marriage contract problem' where, in the case of one man with three wives, he bequeaths a sum to each one in differing quantities. Specifically, the problem is stated as: 'a man has three wives whose marriage contracts specify that in the case of his death they receive 100, 200 and 300 respectively' (Walker, 1995, p. 1). The allocation, it turns out, is in contradiction with what the prescriptions of the Talmud advise, which are contingent on the size of the estate. Leveraging game theory, specifically a specific branch of game theory known as 'cooperative game theory', Aumann and Maschler (1985) resolve the contradiction, and establish the fact that the parts of the Talmud are reminiscent of cooperative game theory whereby some of the wives could/should group together to garner a higher portion of the estate (Walker, 1995).

Transitioning out of antiquity, and into the eighteenth century, the bedrock of modern game theory was born. In 1713, James Waldegrave articulated the idea of a minimax approach/ strategy to a two-player game called 'le Her' in his correspondence with Nicolas Bernoulli and Pierre-Remond de Montmort (Walker, 1995). 'Le Her' is 'a game of strategy and chance played with a standard deck of fifty-two playing cards' (Bellhouse and Fillion, 2015, p. 27), and a perfect backdrop against which to understand an 'optimal' strategy. The simplest case of this problem focuses on a two-player scenario where player A deals a card to player B, and one to themselves. Player B has the option to switch for player A's card, and player A is only allowed to switch if player A is holding a King. After player B chooses their course of action, player A now can either hold the card dealt, or switch with one from the deck. If, however, player A draws a King from the deck, player A must retain the original card dealt. The player with the highest card wins the sum of money in the pot. Thus, this game requires information pertaining to: (1) the probabilities associated with the drawing of each of the 52 cards, and the likelihood of subsequent cards being drawn, contingent on what the card dealt is; and (2) information on the opponent, such that their relative risk tolerance can be estimated. Ultimately, it represents an outstanding early example of strategy and interdependence. The correspondence between these gentlemen yielded the idea that solving the game (that is, determining the best course of action) would be the strategy that ensures the best minimal gain, later deemed the minimax approach.

Since these two early examples of strategy, other profound advances have been made. For example: (1) in Augustin Cournot's analysis of political economy, he discussed a solution for optimality in duopolistic[1] competition; (2) Ernst Zermelo advanced the notion of rationality and pay-off in games that are strictly determined;[2] and (3) Emile Borel advanced the idea of a mixed (as opposed to a pure[3]) strategy for determining the minimax solution, under certain circumstances (that is, games with a small number of strategies), among several other developments. Arguably, though, the most important work in the modern canon of game theory is by Oskar Morgenstern and John Von Neuman (1953) in the book *Theory of Games and Economic Behavior*. This work was so groundbreaking because it provided an axiomatic take on the theory of utility, which provided for a concrete way in which to gauge how players will act/react based on their values. Ultimately, this provided scholars working in the field with the mathematical grounding to analytically, and comprehensively, understand competitive dynamics and reaction.

From there, it was 'off to the races' with game theory. The common and frequently referenced (including in this chapter) game called 'The Prisoner's Dilemma' was created through work at the RAND Corporation in 1950. This famous two-person game examines how two alleged criminals, recently apprehended in connection with the commission of a crime, should react in the presence of two interdependent choices: cooperate, or defect from law enforcement. Then, in the years that followed the creation of this game, John Nash established the modern notion of equilibrium (more on this below), named the 'Nash equilibrium', which is a solution concept[4] whereby a player in a game has no incentive to deviate from their initial strategy, assuming that the competitor in the game also chooses their initial strategy. This contribution was profound, as it established an optimal outcome based on the interaction of the strategies of decision makers. Since this work, game theory has made its way into the fields of economics, computer science, international relations and business, among several others. In fact, on 24 August 2020 we conducted an initial search of the literature using the phrase 'game theory'. The preliminary search yielded 24,649 results in the discipline of economics, 19,881 in engineering, 13,688 in business, 12,840 in mathematics, and 12,436 in computer science. From the humble beginnings of analysing a simple game of chance, to the modelling of nuclear war, game theory has forged its way as a fundamental theory of analysing behaviour. For readers interested in a more comprehensive history of game theory, we suggest reading Weintraub (1992) and Walker (1995).

Wacker's Four Elements

As established above, game theory is an elegant lens through which to study the dynamics of competition. Fundamentally, we can analyse the best course of action to take, contingent on our understanding of our opponent's utility, potential pay-offs and strategy. Further, the levels of supply chain analysis provided above allow for a delineated framework for understanding who is competing against whom, and at what level of the supply chain the game is being played. Yet, in order to provide a useful guide for researchers, we must boil down game theory to its most fundamental components. To do so, we use Wacker's (2008) framework, where theory is defined as 'an explained set of conceptual relationships', and where all of these share four common elements:

1. Definitions (the 'who' and 'what').
2. Domain (the 'when' and 'where').
3. Relationships (the 'how' and 'why').
4. Predictions (the 'should', 'could', 'would').

A brief comment regarding the nuances and complexities of game theory, as the reader may be anecdotally familiar with them, is required. As noted above, there are overarchingly two branches of game theory: competitive and cooperative. The greatest distinction between the two is that one (cooperative) allows for potential opponents banding together (that is, a cartel) against another group. This does not detract from the framework we establish below (that is, competition is still at the heart of this branch). Our approach is general and applies to both branches. In addition, there are other nuances associated with simultaneity, information asymmetry, sequencing, and so on. These nuances, too, are taken into account in our framework, and can be induced using it.

Game Theory Element 1: Who and What (Definitions)

In science, definitions are critical. Precisely crafted definitions allow for the communication of what phenomena are under scrutiny. We offer a pertinent summary of the definitions for game theory in Table 14.1, with more detail to follow.

Who
The 'who' essentially refers to the objects being studied in game theory. Broadly, there are two constituencies to which we refer:

1. Actors, typically made up of individuals, organizations (either individuals grouped together in a firm, or some other group of individuals). In the purchasing and supply management space, this can be a purchasing agent or a buying centre, for example.
2. The environment in which the actors exist and participate in the game.

Table 14.1   Game Theory Element 1 Summary

Who	
Actors	Typically made up of individuals, organizations (either individuals grouped together in a firm, or some other group of individuals, that is, a purchasing agent/department).
Environment	The external setting in which the actors exist and participate in the game.
What	
Properties of actors	
Information	In game theory, information is power. Game theory requires information in order to map out the possible strategy for an actor to take. This information is not, however, unidimensional.
Payout	The reward as a result of an action that can occur in a game. In effect, this is the incentive for the player to compete, and also represents what the potential outcome is for the player's competitor.
Resource	The resource refers to something that the actor values and desires; hence the competition.
Behaviours of actors	
Strategy	A player's strategy represents a roadmap for choosing a move, contingent on the possible actions of a player's competitor. In effect, a strategy can be thought of as an algorithm of sorts, guiding the player on the best course of action as the player's competitor makes their moves. Optimal strategy is determined by enumerating all of the possible outcomes in a given game, for both the player and their competitor.
Reaction function	Sometimes referred to as a 'best response', the player's reaction function is the course of action that yields the best results for the player. Recall that a core assumption underpinning game theory is that the actors operating within the game are doing so rationally.
Properties of environment	
Information	Much like the information enumerated above, the players are able to ascertain information about the environment in which they are competing. This ultimately feeds into their decision making.
Resource and allocation	The source of the scarcity that drives competitive behaviour is scarcity associated with finite resources in the environment. The degree to which these resources are allocated, as well as their upper bounds, are critical pieces of information for players to have in determining their strategies.
Actors	The participants in the games being played in a particular environment.
Behaviours of the environment	
Time	The increments that govern the duration of the game, and the horizon over which it is to be played.
Events	The decision points which impact upon the players of a game. That is, for every action of a player's competitor, that player will also have a reaction.
Outcomes of the environment	
Competition	The principal outcome of the environment, specifically in the context of game theory, is striving to beat one's opponent and gain more resources.

If either firm is looking at the outcomes of each course of action they might map out the elements as shown in Figure 14.1.

What

In defining the 'what' of game theory, we rely on three concepts: properties, behaviours and outcomes. Properties describe the unique, game-theoretic elements of the 'who' described above. Behaviours describe the unique, game-theoretic actions that the 'who' of game theory take in response to the properties they have. Outcomes describe the unique, game-theoretic consequences at the intersection of the properties and behaviors of the 'who' participating in the game. Specifically:

1. Properties of actors:

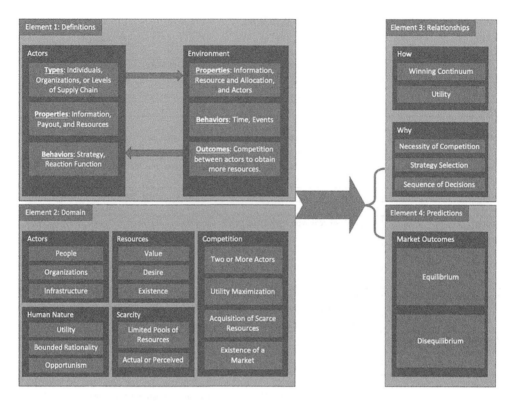

Figure 14.1   Four elements of game theory

    a.   Information. In game theory, as in many things, information is power. Game theory requires information in order to map out the possible strategy for an actor to take. This information is not, however, unidimensional. As a property of an actor, information can come in the form of:

       i.   Information about the actors (themselves and other actors in the game).

      ii.   Information about the environment.

     iii.   Information about the payout.

     iv.   Information about the strategy.

      v.   Information about resources.

     vi.   Information about reaction functions.

    b.   Payout. The reward as a result of an action that can occur in a game. In effect, this is the incentive for the player to compete, and also represents what the potential outcome is for the player's competitor.

    c.   Resource. The resource refers to something that the actor values and desires, hence the competition.

2.   Behaviours of actors:

    a.   Strategy. A player's strategy represents a roadmap for choosing a move, contingent on the possible actions of a player's competitor. In effect, a strategy can be thought of as an algorithm of sorts, guiding the player on the best course of action as the player's competitor makes their moves. Optimal strategy is determined by enumerating all of the possible outcomes in a given game, both for the player and their competitor. Once each of these outcomes are enumerated, methods such as backwards induction or other analytical techniques used to determine the optimal strategy for the player to take in order to maximize their own utility. The specific analytical techniques and details of these methods are outside the scope of this chapter, but for reference we guide the reader to Mazalov (2014).

    b.   Reaction function. Sometimes referred to as a 'best response', the player's reaction function is the course of action that yields the best results for the player. Recall that a core assumption underpinning game theory is that the actors operating within the game are doing so rationally. Thus, they each have an implicit utility function that governs what alternatives they value. In addition, and assuming full information, the players either know, or can estimate, their competitor's utility functions.

3. Properties of the environment:

    a.   Information. Much like the information enumerated above, the players are able to ascertain information about the environment in which they are competing. This ultimately feeds into their decision making.

    b.   Resource and allocation. The source of the scarcity that drives competitive behaviour is that scarcity associated with finite resources in the environment. The degree to which these resources are allocated, as well as their upper bounds, are critical pieces of information for players to have in determining their strategies.

    c.   Actors. The participants in the games being played in a particular environment.

4. Behaviours of the environment:

    a.   Time. The increments that govern the duration of the game, and the horizon over which it is to be played.

    b.   Events. The decision points which impact upon the players of a game. That is, for every action of a player's competitor, that player will also have a reaction.

5. Outcomes of the environment:

    a.   Competition. The principal outcome of the environment, specifically in the context of game theory, is striving to beat one's opponent and gain more resources. Leveraging the framework noted above, this competition can occur in the following manner:

        i.   Internal: actors within a specific firm, competing in the supply chain.

        ii.   External: firms competing with other firms in the supply chain.

        iii.   Mixed level: this is a rare form of competition, when a firm and an actor (within a supply chain) are competing against each other. Take, for example, a firm competing in a procurement auction against one individual operating independently. A rare, but still possible example of competition.

        iv.   Bi-level/hierarchical competition that occurs at different levels, within a specific firm.

Game Theory Element 2: When and Where (Domain)

Equally as important as appropriately, and concisely, defining the elements that exist in game theory is to establish the boundaries around which game theory is applicable. Game theory is applicable when there exists competition over resources, between or among actors. That is, when scarcity exists (either perceived or actual) the drive to acquire more resources than your competitor naturally follows. While this generalized scenario is clear, it is necessary, however, to understand the assumptions that govern the applicability of game theory's use. Specifically, these assumptions are:

1. Actors. As noted above, actors represent the oft-referenced players of a game. Typically, we assume that 'actors' refers to participants, that is organizations, people, or infrastructure with the ability to make decisions (for example, artificial intelligence-driven machines), competing for resources.
2. Human nature. In order for game theory to be appropriate as an approach to answer a research question, there must be a notion of utility. Broadly, all actors place a utility on the resource over which they are competing, and this utility is specific to the individual actors competing. As such, we further assume the following governing principles about human nature:
   a.   Utility: each actor competing must have a notion of what they value. All actors have some unique utility function.
   b.   Bounded rationality is assumed in all actors participating in the game. In this context, bounded rationality refers to the notion that actors will make decisions based on the information they have about other actors, and the environment, such that those decisions will maximize their individual utility.
   c.   Opportunism, we also assume, will exist in the context of human nature. In this case, opportunism refers to 'self seeking with guile' (Williamson, 1985, p. 30), and relates to the idea that when possible an actor will maximize their utility to the intentional detriment of another actor.
3. Resources. As noted previously, resources are something the actors in competition value and desire. It is necessary to assume that there exist resources over which the competition is being played, otherwise the notion of competition becomes meaningless.
4. Scarcity. Game theory requires the idea that there are limited pools of resources over which actors will compete. This scarcity, either actual or perceived, is the antecedent of competition, and is thus a necessary assumption.
5. Competition. The essence of game theory, competition assumes that or more parties strive for the same resource to maximize their utility, under conditions of scarcity. Competition exists when there is little or no centralized allocation of resources, and actors are permitted to make decisions that they believe could lead to the acquisition of resources.
6. Market structure. In order for the dynamics of game theory to work, there needs to exist a collection of actors (as defined above) where at least two are competing. This organization of a market allows for competition to exist, and renders game theory an effective means through which to study it.

Game Theory Element 3: How and Why (Relationships)

Wacker (2008) suggests that a good 'theory is interpreted to mean a "new" theory may explain the current phenomena but also offer new areas to research' (p. 10). Indeed, while game theory is not new, at the time of its conception and formulation it certainly met this standard. Noteworthy is that much of Wacker's (2008) requirement for 'relationships' is certainly framed by an empirical (that is, statistical) testing approach. While game theory in certain circumstances can leverage such an approach, more often than not the analysis of mathematical models (that is, setting up a system and deriving a closed form solution) is used to understand the logical actions and reactions of actors participating in the game at hand. The most desirable outcome is to derive a closed form solution with equations from which the researcher can derive meaningful insight. Thus, while Wacker discusses notions of statistical parsimony and related concepts, this section will largely focus on the determinants of an actor's strategy, from a game-theoretic perspective. The 'how' and 'why' of game theory are as follows:

1. How? In order to understand how an actor can/should formulate their strategy, the critical element is to understand the purpose of the competition (that is, why the actors are competing). Typically, the purpose is for the actor to win, thereby increasing/maximizing their utility. As noted above, such competition is driven by scarcity, and winning (in the most general sense) is for the actor to acquire more resource(s) than it previously had. Note that this does not imply that the other actor(s) in the game necessarily have to acquire no resources, just that the focal actor has to acquire enough such that its utility is maximized. Hence we note the following:

   a. Winning is a continuum, on which there are two absolutes: 0 per cent and 100 per cent. On this continuum, the result of the competition can yield the following:

      i. I win it all and you lose everything; or of the total pot of resource we allocate it in some manner in-between (so-called zero-sum games). In the setting of purchasing and supply management, consider a contract negotiation where one side completely dominates the other.

      ii. Yet, in order for the concept of a win to make any sense, the utility has to be taken into account and defined. As noted above, utility is that thing which the actors playing the game value. Hence, the definition of the utility is such that it is individualized to the focal actor. This utility informs strategy, and governs how the actor will play the game, in response to the competitors of the game.

2. Why? Perhaps the best way to tackle the question of 'why game theory' is to frame it as a discussion of sorts. That is:

   a. Why is competition necessary? Well, this has been rather straightforwardly answered above: scarcity. For competition to make sense as a construct, there must exist a degree of scarcity. Indeed, the outcome of the competition will be governed by each player's strategy, utilities, initial resource allocations, and the time allotment; but simply put, competition and scarcity have a symbiotic relationship with each other.

   b. Why do actors choose the strategies that they do? They do so in response to the rules of the game, their strategy and the strategies of the other players in the game, their reaction functions and their utility.

   c. Why do the sequences/events of games unfold as they do? This makes direct reference to each player's strategy. The oft-referenced Prisoner's Dilemma is a great example of this. As described by Steven Kuhn (2019):

   Tanya and Cinque have been arrested for robbing the Hibernia Savings Bank and placed in separate isolation cells. Both care much more about their personal freedom than about the welfare of their accomplice. A clever prosecutor makes the following offer to each: 'You may choose to confess or remain silent. If you confess and your accomplice remains silent I will drop all charges against you and use your testimony to ensure that your accomplice does serious time. Likewise, if your accomplice confesses while you remain silent, they will go free while you do the time. If you both confess I get two convictions, but I'll see to it that you both get early parole. If you both remain silent, I'll have to settle for token sentences on firearms possession charges. If you wish to confess, you must leave a note with the jailer before my return tomorrow morning.'

The 'dilemma' faced by the prisoners here is that, whatever the other does, each is better off confessing than remaining silent. But the outcome obtained when both confess is worse for each than the outcome they would have obtained had both remained silent.

The Prisoner's Dilemma elegantly provides an answer to the question of why the events unfold as they do: there is a delicate balance between my actions and your reaction, and my utility and your utility. This version of the game involves two participants, but extensions have been made for larger numbers of actors. Of course, the decision making becomes more complex (hence the use of various mathematical modelling techniques). Ultimately, by understanding the properties, behaviours and outcomes of the game, each actor can establish a sound strategy with a clear course of action. It is this very precise and calculated enumeration of (interdependent) outcomes that makes game theory so appealing in many situations.

    d.   What are the relationships that game theory seeks to understand? We can answer this question by asking the following questions:

        i.   How do/will all actors compete to achieve their objectives? There is a dynamic interplay between the actor and the environment in which the actor competes. First, the actor has an a priori strategy which is induced based on the environment (that is, who else is competing, resource scarcity, and so on). Then, after interacting and observing with the environment, the actor is left with a subset of possible strategies (that is, based on the observations/responses).

        ii.   Why are actors competing in the first place (that is, where does the scarcity exist)? In short: to maximize their utility.

Game Theory Element 4: Should, Could and Would (Predictions)

So, why game theory? What can it do for us as purchasing and supply management scholars? What will it predict? In the simplest terms possible, game theory suggests that actors playing the game will gravitate towards their equilibrium, or the best possible outcome given the constraints and rules of the game. What, exactly, does that mean? Generally, when people refer to this concept they are referring to the so called 'Nash equilibrium',[5] which as noted above refers to a solution concept whereby a player in a two-plus player game has no incentive to deviate from their initial strategy, assuming that the competitor in the game also chooses their initial strategy. In other words, this is the choice that (conditionally) maximizes the player's utility. Key behind this notion are the assumptions that we have enumerated above.

For the purposes of exposition, let us use an example. In classical economics, an oligopoly exists when there is a state of limited competition such that buyers in the market have few choices among large, typically powerful sellers. These large and powerful sellers typically control a majority of the market, or at least a dominant one. From a practical setting, take the example of soft drinks. Let us assume that there are two large sellers (that is, a duopoly) of cola: Big Cola 1 and Big Cola 2, and they produce two colas: cola 1 and cola 2. Let us further assume that each of these products are substitutes[6] (in the economic sense) for one another, and that the goal of each firm is to maximize their own market share, respectively. In such an industry, dominated by few large companies and where the products are substitutes for one

Table 14.2   *Example two-player game pay-off matrix (% market share)*

		Big Cola 2		
	Price decisions	Decrease to $1.00	Decrease to $1.50	Keep at $2.00
Big Cola 1	Decrease to $1.00	(50%/50%), reduced profits	Big Cola 1: 75% Big Cola 2: 25% reduced profits	Big Cola 1: 100% Big Cola 2: 0% reduced profits
	Decrease to $1.50	Big Cola 1: 25% Big Cola 2: 75% reduced profits	(50%/50%), reduced profits	Big Cola 1: 75% Big Cola 2: 25% reduced profits
	Keep at $2.00	Big Cola 1: 0% Big Cola 2: 100% reduced profits	Big Cola 1: 25% Big Cola 2: 75% reduced profits	(50%/50%), maintain profits

another, price and quantity end up being the two factors that impact upon a firm's market share. Of course, the notion of brand preference comes into play, but for the purposes of this example we have assumed that the products are substitutes for one another, and thus without loss of generality it will not pose an issue.

Now, let us frame the game-theoretic problem. This is a classic case where competition is spawned by a finite resource – the size (in dollars) of the market – and the competition between Big Cola 1 and Big Cola 2 is to capture as much as possible. This also works well for our framework because the assumptions of human nature (namely, rationality) will govern the firms' decisions and formulate their strategies. In this scenario, we also assume that price is the competitive dimension on which the firms are competing. In other cases, quality or advertising may also be used. There are several examples of this in the literature, but for the purposes of parsimony we assume that only price is being manipulated in this example. Let us assume that the size of the market is $1 million, and that they currently each have 50 per cent share of the market. Let us further assume that the cost of each cola is $2.00 per unit. Now, there are three possible situations for each firm: keeping the price the same, raising the price of the cola, or lowering the price. If both companies keep the price the same, then nothing changes and the 50 per cent market shares are maintained. Let us also assume the following dynamics surrounding the elasticity of the products: If cola 1's price is decreased to $1.50, and cola 2's price is kept constant, then the market share of cola 1 increases to 75 per cent and the market share for cola 2 decreases to 25 percent (the opposite is also true); if cola 1 further decreases the price to $1.00, cola 1 will own all of the market and cola 2 will own none of the market (with, of course, the opposite also being true). There is a trade-off that must be taken into account, and that is the net profit that each firm gains or loses as it increases or decreases its price. While either firm can certainly reduce its price down to $1.00, and capture the entire market, what if the cost of that is 90 per cent, or 95 per cent, or even nearly 100 per cent of its profits? Clearly, because we assume that these firms are rational in their decision making, and that their goal is market share while keeping profit in mind, they will not choose the option that sacrifices profit at the expense of market share.

So, how might this simple game be analysed? Well, if either firm is looking at the outcomes of each course of action they might map out the matrix shown in Table 14.2.

These dynamics perfectly illustrate the idea of equilibrium: each firm knows that by reducing its price, the competitor will respond in kind so as to maintain market share, thereby negatively affecting each one's profit. So, when the transition is examined from $2.00 each to a reduction (by either competitor), the rational choice is to reduce pricing by the exact amount that the competitor did, thus minimizing the maximum loss, maintaining market share, and keeping the oligopolistic dynamics the same as the previous state (with the consumer surplus now being higher, of course). So, a rational firm (in this case, both firms) will gravitate towards the outcome of maintaining prices at $2.00, thereby adhering to the fundamental prediction of game theory: actors will choose the option that maximizes their utility.

Of course, it must be said that this option is simplistic and reductive. There are myriad considerations that would go into the decision making process to reduce prices, and we have only captured one decision making criterion: market share. Consider, for example, if production quantities and economies of scale are taken into account. This would shift the unit cost to the producer, and likely change the decision making process where one of the actors in the game may be able to reduce prices, gain market share, and still maintain profits at an acceptable level. So, while this simplistic example, we hope, is illustrative of how game theory tends to govern and predict behaviour in such situations, it certainly does not encapsulate all of the possibilities. Hopefully, the research that the reader will conduct, can fill these gaps.

LEVELS OF SUPPLY CHAIN ANALYSIS

In order to understand the structure of competition, utility and strategy, it is necessary to understand the ethos within which all of these concepts exist; presently, this ethos is supply chain management. As such, to reconcile language and messaging, we offer this section as an organizing mechanism, and a tool with which to look at where game theory and purchasing/ supply chain management can intersect favourably.

First, in order to study any concepts within the body of knowledge known as supply chain management, one must have an understanding of what specifically is being managed; that is, the supply chain (Carter et al., 2015). So, what is a supply chain? Many academics differ in their definition, but generally agree that it can be thought of as the collection of entities, beginning at the raw materials source and ending at the individual consumer, all of which engage in activities to plan, source, make, deliver and return a product, usually through the help of value-adding and non-value-adding processes throughout the various entities involved in these five major activities. Supply chains are usually conceptualized as networks (Carnovale and Yeniyurt, 2014, 2015; Carnovale et al., 2017, 2016; Carnovale et al., 2019), and the various approaches to their study, be they conceptual, empirical or analytical, tend to use this mathematical conceptualization to better understand the strategies undertaken across the entities in the supply chain.

Common practice, when analysing a firm, is to restrict the scope of inquiry to the level of the organization. The scholar of any subdiscipline within business is usually aware that their studies are primarily relevant to micro or macro levels of the business. The usual conceptualization of these levels is itself in a hierarchical structure, and entails the strategic layer, the tactical layer and the operational layer, from top to bottom, respectively, and in that order. However, scholars of supply chain management over the prior two decades have rarely transcended this conceptualization to when multiple firms are involved. Just as academics within any area of study of business must be cognizant as to which level of the organization they intend to better understand, supply chain scholars must also have a similar conceptualization of the supply chain.

Indeed, there are vast constituencies of people, processes and organizations that impact upon, and are impacted upon by, the supply chain's very existence. So why do many scholars have different definitions of what constitutes an 'entity' and what constitutes a 'link' within a supply chain? It is simply due to their background and area of expertise. More appropriately, we argue, it is due to a lack of existence of a hierarchy of levels of the supply chain. Scholars can certainly agree that they are studying different facets of an organization, be they strategic or operational. Yet they still agree on the definition of 'the organization'. The supply chain, not so much. We argue that in order to ground any theory, including our grounding of game theory, within the context of supply chain management, one must first agree that a supply chain is a supply chain, and that the disagreement among scholars over the prior 20 years has not actually been about the definition of 'what is', but rather, a disagreement about 'at which level'.

So, in order to properly ground how game theory may be a useful tool for supply chain management research, we advance a concept which we refer to as the hierarchical levels of the supply chain. Establishing this hierarchy allows for the usefulness of game theory in purchasing and supply management to become clear, and allows for scholars applying game theory in purchasing and supply management to know at what level of analysis their game is being played. Effectively, we argue that this hierarchy comprises five foundational levels: people, infrastructure, agents, processes and organizations. The use of the word 'hierarchy' is deliberate. There is a necessary ordering of each of these levels, and they build on each other in order to develop the overall framing of supply chain management. The primary motivation of this hierarchy comes from the observation of the traditional view of the firm being composed of three levels. We expand beyond the three levels, since connections among entities in a supply chain are more complex and all-encompassing than those within a traditional organization. We can think of each level being its own network of entities (with each respective entity described below) and connections. At the next level up in the hierarchy, a single entity could be a collection of entities and connections within a network on a lower level of hierarchy.

We consider people and infrastructure to be in different non-overlapping networks, somewhat parallel to each other. Together, people and/or infrastructure constitute a single agent. Collections of people, agents and infrastructure constitute a single process. Lastly, collections of people, infrastructure, agents and processes constitute a single organization. We conceptualize a supply chain to essentially be composed of these five levels, where each level is its own network. Each entity in each respective network is either an indivisible unit, or is a composition of entities and connections from 'lower' levels. For example, when we speak of Apple's supply chain, we will have five different networks to define 'Apple's Supply Chain'.

The collection of people across firms and their associations and personal or professional communications and other associations constitutes the people network level. The infrastructure may be composed of facilities that serve as the location for manufacturing of Apple's products, as well as computer systems to enable Apple's product development. The links between these may represent transportation routes of supplies, or physical computer network wires or wireless connections. The agent network may constitute a collection of infrastructure (that is, computers) or people that act as representative agents for Apple and the various firms in the network. The process network may constitute a collection of processes and their connections, specific to a single product of Apple, where a single process entails a collection of people and infrastructure, with resources flowing through this network of processes. And lastly, the organizational network may constitute the firms themselves, where a single firm has as its constituent parts sub-networks of the people, infrastructure, agents and processes within each of their respective network levels. Each network in this hierarchy comes together to form the supply chain. Having this conceptualization allows us to ground game theory, so that we know precisely who, or what, is competing over what, and how, as well as why they compete within the supply chain. In summary, each level's entity and connections between entities are defined thus:

1. People. The indivisible units in/on the supply chain. A supply chain cannot exist without people. People interact with infrastructure, processes and organizations. Even in the most extreme cases of all computerized and mechanized supply chains, they still exist to serve end consumers, who are people.
2. Infrastructure. Another indivisible unit, necessary for supply chains to exist. Infrastructure constitutes the non-human assets of the supply chain, as is defined in accounting: property, plant, land and equipment. Within the definition of infrastructure, we recognize that there are physical and non-physical infrastructure components (for example, plant versus information).
3. Agent. Defined as the authorized representation by a person or an infrastructure component with the ability to make decisions on behalf of an organization with other agents of other organizations.
4. Process. Defined as a collection of people, infrastructure, relationships among people and among infrastructure, respectively, and between people and infrastructure. The purpose of the process is to convert inputs into outputs.
5. Organization. At the organizational level of analysis, collections of people, processes and infrastructure are combined for the purpose of fulfilling a mission. Organizations have connections by way of transactions or relationships.

GAME THEORY AND PURCHASING, SOURCING AND SUPPLY CHAIN MANAGEMENT: WHAT HAS BEEN DONE, AND HOW CAN WE USE IT?

What has been done at the intersection of Game Theory and Purchasing?

As we have illustrated thus far, game theory lends itself to natural applications that happen to involve actors competing over scarce resources with the goal of maximizing their own utilities, while accounting for the potential strategies of other actors, and externalities in the environment within which they compete. While the obvious application of game theory is implicit in the name (games, such as the 'le Her' game noted above) there are clearly other applications. Previously, as we noted in describing the historical development of the field, game theory was seen to easily apply to economic applications involving competition amongst various firms, in a market competing over consumers by way of the design, pricing and delivery of their respective products. However, the applications of game theory extend beyond the general area of economics and often trickle down to the more specialized areas of purchasing, sourcing and supply chain management.

As it relates to the context of purchasing, various authors have used game theory in trying to explain the behaviour of actors when they are leveraging bidding and auction-based systems so as to exercise their purchasing responsibilities. For example, Rob (1985) leveraged a Stackleberg[7] model to study competitive bidding in the presence of asymmetrical information. Similarly, game theory has been applied to study reverse auctions (Engelbrecht-Wiggans et al., 2007; Fugger et al., 2019), bidding with multi-stage qualification contexts (Chen et al., 2018), as well as the impact of the lack of information of exogenous factors such as bidder quality on an actor's revenue (Haruvy and Katok, 2013).

Game-theoretic elements have also been leveraged to better understand the decisions made in the branding of products. This branch of the literature has focused attention on the application of game theory to study the positioning of brands (Sayman et al., 2002) as well as the dynamics of brand competition (Amaldoss and Jain, 2015; Ansari et al., 1994). Game theory applications are not only restricted to the study of competition of brands and the dynamics of auction systems, but have also reached the literature streams of pricing (Aviv and Pazgal, 2008; Cachon and Feldman, 2015; Rao and Shakun, 1972), negotiation (Miller, 1972; Rapoport et al., 1995; Samuelson, 1980), and of sequential (August et al., 2015), service (Li et al., 2016) and internet (Hsiao and Chen, 2014) channel distribution, as well as the behaviour of consumer shopping (Amaldos and Jain, 2005; Iyer and Kuksov, 2012; Kuksov and Kangwang, 2014; Pazgal et al., 2013).

Another branch of literature that has introduced game-theoretic concepts is that of supply chain management, broadly defined. Various applications within this body of knowledge have leveraged game theory to better understand decision making in capacity management (Cachon and Lariviere, 1999a), inventory management (Özen et al. 2008), buyer–supplier relationships (Narasimhan et al., 2009), risk and disruption management (Lee et al., 2004), as well as various problems within production and operations management in the supply chain context (Fang and Wang, 2010). In the area of capacity management, equilibriums and dominant strategies[8] have been derived and used to characterize capacity allocation decisions (Cachon and Lariviere, 1999b). Similar methods have been used to study the conditions that must hold for an equilibrium to exist in the cases of quick-response inventory competition (Caro and Martínez-de-Albéniz, 2010), supply chain design in the presence of positive and negative externalities (Netessine and Zhang, 2005), as well as in profit allocations under the strategy of inventory centralization (Kemahlioğlu-Ziya and Bartholdi, 2011).

Most of the relevant applications of game theory within the intersection of supply chain management and purchasing have been demonstrated in the areas of buyer–supplier management as well as contracting. The same concepts of game design and the study of equilibriums and the various types of dominant strategies have been leveraged in the study of long-term contracts when suppliers are at risk of default (Swinney and Netessine, 2009), outsourcing decisions with contract manufacturers (Gray et al., 2009), contracting decisions between firms with opposing profit seeking and survival seeking objectives (Wei et al., 2013), the construction of project management contracts in the scope of delayed payments (Kwon et al., 2010), as well as the study of fostering buyer–supplier relationships in the salience of organizational trade-offs (Chatain and Zemsky, 2007). Likewise, these concepts have been applied to issues within supply chain security (Cho et al., 2015), disruption and risk management (Bakshi and Kleindorfer, 2009; Gupta et al., 2016; Toyasaki et al., 2017), product quality (Chao et al., 2009; Guan and Chen, 2017; Sheu, 2016), and cost allocation across members in the supply chain (Elomri et al., 2012).

The common thread that weaves this diverse body of literature within the fields of purchasing, sourcing and supply chain management is the theory of games. As we previously illustrated, so long as the situation at hand involves actors competing over scarce resources within an environment, each with their own utility maximizing goals under the information that is available to each of them, respectively, game theory offers an interesting approach to predict and explain the behaviours of the various actors in these diverse ecosystems. We can clearly see that these applications have been applied to various types of actors, such as buyers, suppliers and consumers, as well as across various levels of the supply chain, ranging from individual people (that is, consumers) to entire organizations (that is, buyers/suppliers). The extant literature contends that game theory is indeed not only a useful methodology for explaining and predicting the behaviours of these actors, but also a useful grounding theory for theorizing the behaviours in the context of competition in environments with scarce resources with congruent and incongruent goals of respective actors.

How can we use Game Theory?

Often, it is better to show the path rather than to prescribe the solution. In this chapter that is the approach we have chosen to take. In Table 14.3 we highlight a few papers that demonstrate the use-cases of game theory in areas related to purchasing and supply management. This, we hope, will serve as a heuristic of sorts for the aspiring game theorist working in the space of purchasing and supply management.

MACHINES AS COMPETITIVE ACTORS

Traditional and neoclassical economic thought has, up to this point, considered the notion of an actor to be defined as a person, company, university, government, or any other general organization that engages within some form of economic transaction. However, due to recent advances in technology, one could pose the argument that the definition of 'actor' should no longer be constrained to this small laundry list of entities, and should be revised to include newer entities: machines. While it is true that machines have technically engaged in economic transactions over the prior century, such as through automated teller machines and automated order placement, these transactions have traditionally been rule-based, where the rules have been well defined by another actor.

Put simply, when machines make 'decisions', those decisions are technically preordained by other economic actors and purely delegated to the machine to make, as though the actor were making them. However, we argue that with the recent advancement and replacement of these traditional rule-based machines, each one reflective of the specific decisions made by a traditional non-machine economic actor, with newer learning, and soon to be 'self-aware' machines, that these machines are themselves their own actors. While they may indeed be learning and acting in the best interest and on the behalf of other economic actors, one could argue that since these machines operate on rules no longer strictly derived from other actors, but rather from themselves by way of their observations and the analysis of these observations by way of machine learning, these machines have their own collection of utility, resources and strategies to undertake to play within the game.

We also argue, by way of experience and transitivity from other actors, that these machines will also act with bounded rationality, since they are only privileged to certain information that is fed to them; and with opportunism, since they make decisions with a utility, that is, objective

Table 14.3   *Areas of game theory applied to purchasing and supply management*

Purchasing and supply management focus area	Research question	Game theory approach	Insights
Negotiation (Bard, 1987)	Broadly, the research examines whether cooperative or competitive dynamics are better in buyer–supplier negotiations.	The author sets up two distinct approaches: one cooperative and one competitive. The competitive scenario reaches a Nash equilibrium, and provides for normative prescriptions for a more conservative strategy.	Several dynamics are explored around individual bargaining power, cost minimization, and so on. Ultimately, based on several equilibria derived via analytical examination, performance of various strategies can be examined and compared.
Competitive purchasing under demand uncertainty (Nti, 1987)	The research addresses the optimal method of stockpiling such that competition is attended to and that price is considered as uncertain.	The author sets up two broad scenarios: a non-cooperative, and a cooperative approach. In the non-cooperative approach a Nash equilibrium is proposed where stockpiling is contingent on other parties who are also engaging in such procurement behaviour. The cooperative approach includes coordination.	The authors use the case of petroleum stockpiling with price uncertainly, and find that with the cooperative approach, where parties are coordinating and jointly purchasing, better outcomes are gained.
Category management and coordination (Cachon and Kök, 2007)	This research studies the problem of planning a purchasing assortment where consumers buy from multiple categories. The goal is to determine the optimal assortment.	The authors present a duopoly model where retailers choose pricing and breadth within a category. The consumers are allowed to choose to buy (or not), to maximize their own utilities.	The authors find that category management, conducted in this way, often results in less than optimal pricing and assortment decisions, because category management is decentralized (that is, category managers are competing with one another).

Purchasing and supply management focus area	Research question	Game theory approach	Insights
Procurement of technology (Chu and Wang, 2015)	The goal is to analyse bundled procurement, a phenomenon whereby the outcome of the purchasing scenario is to achieve a dual mandate: accomplish the project, and acquire the underlying technology. This is particularly game theory-driven, because the scarce resource here is quite proprietary.	The authors set up a dynamic game with n players, and use backward induction to analyse how different bidding scenarios will lead to increased likelihood of success. The authors also leverage this set-up to understand extensions such as technology adoption failure, bargaining power and technology advancements.	The authors are able to understand how and under what conditions the procurement of a technology bundled project are likely to be successful, and what the limiting factors will be. This allows for a specific strategy to maximize the purchaser's likelihood of success.
Supplier selection and quality evaluation (Hwang et al., 2006)	What is better in supplier selection: appraisal of quality or certification of quality?	Two separate instances are set up: (1) the appraisal regime where suppliers are penalized when quality issues arise; and (2) the certification regime where the supplier attains external certification and the buyer pays the unit price (given the certification of quality).	Optimal strategy for supplier selection can be ascertained if situations are studied rigorously and comprehensively. In this case the agency costs between certification and appraisal are examined. The strategic dimension that the firm intends to compete on becomes pre-eminent, and game theory can dictate how to best choose a supplier under these competing objectives.

function, defined by other actors. When the time of machine 'self-awareness' arrives, this utility, we argue, could very well change from being derived by other actors to that of its own, based on its own experiences and learnings. Even without self-awareness, it is plausible to assume that machines currently have the ability to learn their own utility based on their own observations. Hence, we posit that machines are actors, and as is currently the case in practice, they do engage in economic transactions with other actors, such as humans, companies, more general organizations, and even other machines.

CONCLUDING REMARKS

If the reader takes but one thing away from this chapter it should be this: game theory is the formal study of competition in the presence of scarcity. That, of course, reduces years of elegant and rigorous work down to one phrase, but it solves the core objective we set out to achieve. Stated differently, the goals of this chapter are twofold: (1) to present game theory as a grounding theory, complete with a comprehensive examination of its definitions, its domain, its relationships and its predictions; and (2) to provide scholars in the area of purchasing and supply management with a rough idea of how to start using game theory to solve challenging research problems and questions. We first provided a unique conceptualization of the hierarchical levels of supply chain analysis, so that the scholar knows at what level and with whom the competition is occurring. Then, to advance game theory as a formal grounding theory, we leveraged Wacker's (2008) framework. Next, we transitioned into how game theory has been used in purchasing and supply management, either directly or tangentially. We then provided a few specific and exemplary works in the field to provide a heuristic of sorts, to allow the researcher to start their journey in this elegant and rigorous realm of knowledge. Just remember: scarcity breeds competition, and competition engenders understanding it through game theory.

NOTES

1. A duopoly is an oligopoly with two participants, and it is often used to model competition because of natural ease in exposition.
2. 'Strictly determined' refers to a two-person, zero-sum game.
3. A pure strategy implies certainty with respect to how the player will play the game, whereas a mixed strategy uses a probability to describe the likelihood that the player will take a course of action.
4. A 'solution concept' refers to the rule or rules for how a game will be played.
5. Also of note is that the Nash equilibrium is only relevant in the context of competitive games, as opposed to cooperative games. As briefly alluded to above, competitive games are those where it is actor against actor, rather than groups of actors competing against one another. For example, in the case of cartels, where groups of countries are joining together to compete, this would be considered cooperative game theory. In the cooperative case, the analogous solution concept is referred to as the Shapley value (Shapley, 1951). The logic, however, is quite similar.
6. Such that consumers have little to no issue switching between them.
7. A so-called Stackleberg game involves a leader and a follower, typically utilizing the concept of leadership and first mover advantage.
8. So-called dominant strategies are those that result in the highest payoff for actors, regardless of the other actors' actions.

REFERENCES

Amaldoss, W. and Jain, S. (2005), 'Conspicuous consumption and sophisticated thinking', *Management Science*, 51(10), 1449–1466.

Amaldoss, W. and Jain, S. (2015), 'Branding conspicuous goods: An analysis of the effects of social influence and competition', *Management Science*, 61(9), 2064–2079.

Ansari, A., Economides, N. and Ghosh, A. (1994), 'Competitive positioning in markets with nonuniform preferences', *Marketing Science*, 13(3), 248–273.

August, T., Duy, D. and Hyoduk, S. (2015), 'Optimal timing of sequential distribution: The impact of congestion externalities and day-and-date strategies', *Marketing Science*, 34(5), 755–774.

Aumann, R.J. and Maschler, M. (1985), 'Game theoretic analysis of a bankruptcy problem from the Talmud', *Journal of Economic Theory*, 36(2), 195–213.

Aviv, Y. and Pazgal, A. (2008), 'Optimal pricing of seasonal products in the presence of forward-looking consumers', *Manufacturing and Service Operations Management*, 10(3), 339–359.

Bakshi, N. and Kleindorfer, P. (2009), 'Co-opetition and investment for supply-chain resilience', *Production and Operations Management*, 18(6), 583–603.

Bard, J.F. (1987), 'Developing competitive strategies for buyer–supplier negotiations', *Management Science*, 33(9), 1181–1191.

Bellhouse, D.R. and Fillion, N. (2015), 'Le Her and other problems in probability discussed by Bernoulli, Montmort and Waldegrave', *Statistical Science*, 30(1), 26–39.

Bonanno, G. (2018a), *Game Theory: Volume 1: Basic Concepts*, CreateSpace Independent Publishing Platform, 2nd edn, 1983604631

Bonanno, G. (2018b) *Game Theory: Volume 2*, CreateSpace Independent Publishing Platform, 2nd edn, 1985862514

Cachon, G.P. and Feldman, P. (2015), 'Price commitments with strategic consumers: Why it can be optimal to discount more frequently ... Than optimal', *Manufacturing and Service Operations Management*, 17(3), 399–410.

Cachon, G.P. and Kök, A.G. (2007), 'Category management and coordination in retail assortment planning in the presence of basket shopping consumers', *Management Science,* 53(6), 934–951.

Cachon, G.P. and Lariviere, M.A. (1999a), 'Capacity allocation using past sales: When to turn-and-earn', *Management Science*, 45(5), 685–703.

Cachon, G.P. and Lariviere, M.A. (1999b), 'Capacity choice and allocation: Strategic behavior and supply chain performance', *Management Science*, 45(8), 1091–1108.

Carnovale, S., Rogers, D.S. and Yeniyurt, S. (2016), 'Bridging structural holes in global manufacturing equity based partnerships: A network analysis of domestic vs. International joint venture formations', *Journal of Purchasing and Supply Management*, 22(1), 7–17.

Carnovale, S., Rogers, D. and Yeniyurt, S. (2019), 'Broadening the perspective of supply chain finance: The performance impacts of network power and cohesion', *Journal of Purchasing and Supply Management*, 25(2), 134–145.

Carnovale, S. and Yeniyurt, S. (2014), 'The role of ego networks in manufacturing joint venture formations', *Journal of Supply Chain Management*, 50(2), 1–17.

Carnovale, S. and Yeniyurt, S. (2015), 'The role of ego network structure in facilitating ego network innovations', *Journal of Supply Chain Management*, 51(2), 22–46.

Carnovale, S., Yeniyurt, S. and Rogers, D.S. (2017), 'Network connectedness in vertical and horizontal manufacturing joint venture formations: A power perspective', *Journal of Purchasing and Supply Management*, 23(2), 67–81.

Caro, F. and Martínez-De-Albéniz, V. (2010), 'The impact of quick response in inventory-based competition', *Manufacturing and Service Operations Management*, 12(3), 409–429.

Carter, Craig R., Rogers, Dale S. and Choi, Thomas Y. (2015), 'Toward the theory of the supply chain', *Journal of Supply Chain Management*, 51(2), 89–97.

Chao, G.H., Iravani, S.M.R. and Savaskan, R.C. (2009), 'Quality improvement incentives and product recall cost sharing contracts', *Management Science*, 55(7), 1122–1138.

Chatain, O. and Zemsky, P. (2007), 'The horizontal scope of the firm: Organizational tradeoffs vs. buyer–supplier relationships', *Management Science*, 53(4), 550–565.

Chen, W., Dawande, M. and Janakiraman, G. (2018), 'Optimal procurement auctions under multistage supplier qualification', *Manufacturing and Service Operations Management*, 20(3), 566–582.

Cho, Soo-Haeng, Fang, X. and Tayur, S. (2015), 'Combating strategic counterfeiters in licit and illicit supply chains', *Manufacturing and Service Operations Management*, 17(3), 273–289.

Chu, L.Y., and Wang, Y. (2015), 'Bundled procurement for technology acquisition and future competition', *Manufacturing and Service Operations Management*, 17(2), 249–261.

Elomri, A., Ghaffari, A., Jemai, Z. and Dallery, Y. (2012), 'Coalition formation and cost allocation for joint replenishment systems', *Production and Operations Management*, 21(6), 1015–1027.

Engelbrecht-Wiggans, R., Haruvy, E. and Katok, E. (2007), 'A comparison of buyer-determined and price-based multiattribute mechanisms', *Marketing Science*, 26(5), 629–641.

Fang, X. and Wang, Y. (2010), 'A model for partial product complementarity and strategic production decisions under demand uncertainty', *Production and Operations Management*, 19(3), 322–342.

Fugger, N., Katok, E. and Wambach, A. (2019), 'Trust in procurement interactions', *Management Science*, 65(11), 5110–5127.

Gray, J.V., Tomlin, B. and Roth, A.V. (2009), 'Outsourcing to a powerful contract manufacturer: The effect of learning-by-doing', *Production and Operations Management*, 18(5), 487–505.

Guan, X. and Chen, Y.J. (2017), 'The interplay between information acquisition and quality disclosure', *Production and Operations Management*, 26(3), 389–408.

Gupta, S., Starr, M.K., Farahani, R.Z. and Matinrad, N. (2016), 'Disaster management from a pom perspective: Mapping a new domain', *Production and Operations Management*, 25(10), 1611–1637.

Hamilton, J. (1992), 'Game theory: Analysis of conflict, by Myerson, R.B., Cambridge: Harvard University Press', *Managerial and Decision Economics*, 13, 369–369. doi:10.1002/mde.4090130412.

Haruvy, E. and Katok, E. (2013), 'Increasing revenue by decreasing information in procurement auctions', *Production and Operations Management*, 22(1), 19–35.

Hsiao, L. and Chen, Y.J. (2014), 'Strategic motive for introducing internet channels in a supply chain', *Production and Operations Management*, 23(1), 36–47.

Hwang, I., Radhakrishnan, S. and Su, L. (2006), 'Vendor certification and appraisal: Implications for supplier quality', *Management Science*, 52(10), 1472–1482.

Iyer, G. and Kuksov, D. (2012), 'Competition in consumer shopping experience', *Marketing Science*, 31(6), 913–933.

Kemahlioğlu-Ziya, E. and Bartholdi Iii, J.J. (2011), 'Centralizing inventory in supply chains by using Shapley value to allocate the profits', *Manufacturing and Service Operations Management*, 13(2), 146–162.

Kuhn, Steven (2019), 'Prisoner's Dilemma', in Edward N. Zalta (ed.), *The Stanford Encyclopedia of Philosophy* (Winter 2019 edn), https://plato.stanford.edu/archives/win2019/entries/prisoner-dilemma/.

Kuksov, D. and Kangwang, W. (2014), 'The bright side of loss aversion in dynamic and competitive markets', *Marketing Science*, 33(5), 693–711.

Kwon, H.D., Lippman, S.A., Mccardle, K.F. and Tang, C.S. (2010), 'Project management contracts with delayed payments', *Manufacturing and Service Operations Management*, 12(4), 692–707.

Lee, H.L., Padmanabhan, V. and Seungjin, W. (2004), 'Comments on "information distortion in a supply chain: The bullwhip effect"', *Management Science*, 50, 1887–1893.

Li, X., Li, Y., Cai, X.Q. and Shan, J. (2016), 'Service channel choice for supply chain: Who is better off by undertaking the service?', *Production and Operations Management*, 25(3), 516–534.

Mazalov, V. (2014), *Mathematical Game Theory and Applications*. Chichester: John Wiley & Sons.

Miller, R.B. (1972), 'Insurance contracts as two-person games', *Management Science*, 18(7), 444–447.

Morgenstern, Oskar and Von Neumann, John (1953), *Theory of Games and Economic Behavior*. Princeton, NJ: Princeton University Press.

Nash, John (1950), 'Equilibrium points in n-person games', *Proceedings of the National Academy of Sciences*, 36(1), 48–49.

Nash, John (1951), 'Non-cooperative games', *Annals of Mathematics*, 54(2), 286–295.

Narasimhan, R., Nair, A., Griffith, D.A., Arlbjørn, J.S. and Bendoly, E. (2009), 'Lock-in situations in supply chains: A social exchange theoretic study of sourcing arrangements in buyer–supplier relationships', *Journal of Operations Management*, 27(5), 374–389.

Netessine, S. and Zhang, F. (2005), 'Positive vs. negative externalities in inventory management: Implications for supply chain design', *Manufacturing and Service Operations Management*, 7(1), 58–73.

Nti, Kofi O. (1987), 'Competitive procurement under demand uncertainty', *Management Science*, 33(11), 1489–1500.

Özen, U., Fransoo, J., Norde, H. and Slikker, M. (2008), 'Cooperation between multiple newsvendors with warehouses', *Manufacturing and Service Operations Management*, 10(2), 311–324.

Pazgal, A., Soberman, D. and Thomadsen, R. (2013), 'Profit-increasing consumer exit', *Marketing Science*, 32(6), 998–1008.

Peleg, B. and Sudholter, P. (2007), *Introduction to the Theory of Cooperative Games (Theory and Decision Library C(34))*, 2nd edition. Heidelberg and New York: Springer.

Rao, A.G., and Shakun, M.F. (1972), 'A quasi-game theory approach to pricing', *Management Science*, 18(5 Part 2), 110–228.

Rapoport, A., Erev, I., and Zwick, R. (1995), 'An experimental study of buyer–seller negotiation with one-sided incomplete information and time discounting', *Management Science*, 41(3), 377–394.

Rob, R. (1985), 'A note on competitive bidding with asymmetric information', *Management Science*, 31(11), 1431–1439.

Samuelson, W. (1980), 'First-offer bargains', *Management Science*, 26(2), 155–164.

Sayman, Serdar, Hoch, Stephen J. and Raju, Jagmohan S. (2002), 'Positioning of store brands', *Marketing Science*, 21(4), 378–397.

Shapley, Lloyd S. (1951, 21 August), 'Notes on the n-Person Game – II: The value of an n-person game' (PDF), Santa Monica, CA: RAND Corporation.

Sheu, J.B. (2016), 'Buyer behavior in quality-dominated multi-sourcing recyclable-material procurement of green supply chains', *Production and Operations Management*, 25(3), 477–497.

Swinney, R. and Netessine, S. (2009), 'Long-term contracts under the threat of supplier default', *Manufacturing and Service Operations Management*, 11(1), 109–127.

Toyasaki, F., Arikan, E., Silbermayr, L. and Falagara Sigala, I. (2017), 'Disaster relief inventory management: Horizontal cooperation between humanitarian organizations', *Production and Operations Management*, 26(6), 1221–1237.

Wacker, J.G. (2008), 'A conceptual understanding of requirements for theory-building research: Guidelines for scientific theory building', *Journal of Supply Chain Management*, 44(3), 5–15.

Walker, P. (1995), 'An outline of the history of game theory', Discussion Paper 9504, University of Canterbury, Department of Economics.

Wei, M.M., Yao, T., Jiang, B. and Young, S.T. (2013), 'Profit seeking vs. survival seeking: An analytical study of supplier's behavior and buyer's subsidy strategy', *Production and Operations Management*, 22(2), 269–282.

Weintraub, E.R. (ed.) (1992), *Toward a History of Game Theory* (Vol. 24), Durham, NC: Duke University Press.

Williamson, O.E. (1985). *The Economic Institutions of Capitalism: Firms, Markets, Relational Contracting*. New York: Free Press.

15. Paradox theory

Sajad Fayezi

INTRODUCTION

In a broad sense, paradox theory is a paradigm of organization and management with its roots in philosophy, psychology, and literature. Philosophers (Plato), psychologists (Jung) and poets (Shakespeare) have long made use of paradoxes to convey wide-ranging meanings, including inseparability, coexistence and coevolution of contradictions (for example, life and death, being and becoming, unity and plurality) to broaden our view of the intricacies of human experience and existence (Schad et al., 2016). Paradoxical thinking allows us to shift our mindset from 'either/or' to 'both/and' (Smith et al., 2016), which is particularly relevant to a modern environment characterized by uncertainty and ambiguity. Paradoxical thinking often reveals vulnerabilities in our traditional approaches to organization and management and shows that growth and sustainability require space for unconventional, counterintuitive approaches. We explain the paradox theory and its applications (outlined in Table 15.1), and invite purchasing and supply chain management (PSCM) scholars to explore its utility for advancing theory and practice.

KEY VARIABLES AND DEFINITIONS

Tensions: Mechanisms

Organization and management scholars have been engaging with paradox debates since the 1980s, exploring its role in organization theory (Poole and van de Ven, 1989), developing theoretical frameworks (Lewis, 2000), and applying paradox to investigate tensions embroiled in management decisions (Eisenhardt, 2000; Smith and Tushman, 2005; Tushman and O'Reilly, 1996). This has contributed to the advancement of paradox theory through, for example, dissecting the notion of paradoxical tensions and exploring their antecedents and manifestations, while shedding light on interrelationships between contradictory elements, including their simultaneity and persistence (Ford and Backoff, 1988; Lewis, 2000). Scholarly conversations have allowed us to understand organizational elements of paradoxical tensions in a variety of forms, such as mindsets, emotions, demands, interests, identities and practices (Lewis, 2000).

Tensions associated with contradictory, yet interrelated elements of paradox can be an inherent feature of organizational systems in the form of action (or ontological realities of tensions) (Schad and Bansal, 2018). These tensions may be socially constructed by actor cognition. Organizations, and actors within them, often put themselves under exorbitant pressure as a result of polarized socially constructed, diametrically opposed interaction logics of paradoxes (for example, social versus financial goals). This is described as a process for simplifying contradictions by adopting a frame of reference that encourages abstraction and bipolarization of complex realities (Kelly, 1955), which fails to capture the notion of inter-

Table 15.1   Definitions

Element	Explanation	References
Level of analysis	Individual, team, functional, business unit, organizational, interorganizational, multi-level	See Appendix
Unit of analysis	Project, performance, relationship, sensemaking, corporate sustainability, process, scandal, teams, supply network, function, discourse, strategy	See Appendix
Variables and definitions		
Tensions	Competing objectives or values that appear to be in conflict and opposition but in fact support each other	Quinn (2015)
Types of tensions	Paradox: 'Contradictory yet interrelated elements that exist simultaneously and persist over time.' These resemble the symbol of *yin–yang*, where the paradoxical choices 'reflect polarities that are interrelated aspects of a greater whole.' Dilemma: 'Competing choices, each with advantages and disadvantages' Dialectic: 'Contradictory elements (thesis and antithesis) resolved through integration (synthesis), which, over time, will confront new opposition'	Smith and Lewis (2011, p. 387)
Categories of tensions	Learning (knowledge): Surfaces during organizational changes and innovations involving tensions between old and new Belonging (identity): Involves conflicts surrounding individual and group interactions embodying self versus other Organizing (processes): Results when organizations adopt competing design and production processes reflecting demands for both control and flexibility Performing (goals): Arises from differing and conflicting needs of internal and external stakeholders	Smith and Lewis (2011, p. 383)
Vicious cycle	Stems from consistency schemes (individual), defensive mechanisms (individual), inertia forces (organizational)	Smith and Lewis (2011)
Virtuous cycle	Stems from cognitive and behavioural complexity (individual), emotional composure (individual), dynamic capabilities (organizational)	Smith and Lewis (2011)

relatedness. However, paradox theory rests on the premise that organizations may follow paradoxical demands to safeguard both short- and long-term goals and enhance performance (Smith and Lewis, 2011). It is therefore important to understand how the paralyzing defensiveness of actors against competing demands can be tackled and, correspondingly, how the power of paradoxical thinking can be harnessed. Such questions have contributed to the advancement of theory and practice of paradoxical management, and this is a continuing journey (De Keyser et al., 2019; Schad et al., 2016).

Tensions: Types

Three types of organizational tensions are identified and discussed in the paradox literature: paradox, dilemma and dialectic. Paradox refers to tensions associated with contradictory yet interrelated demands that exist simultaneously and persist over time (Lewis, 2000; Smith and

Lewis, 2011). In relation to dilemma (or trade-off), tensions are centred on competing choices, each with advantages and disadvantages that must be weighed up (Smith and Lewis, 2011). With dialectic (or compromise), tensions relate to contradictory demands whose similarities can be integrated to develop a (short-lived) synergy (Lewis et al., 2014). This typology of tensions reflects varied decision making approaches to competing demands, and as such serves two primary purposes: (1) it fosters understanding of the features of paradox by juxtaposing similar types of tensions; and (2) it encourages reflection on how we characterize dualities based on their state of contradiction, interrelationship, simultaneity and persistence. For example, studies of exploration–exploitation tensions describe their sequential recharacterization from dilemma (Burgelman, 2002) and dialectic (Farjoun, 2010) to paradox (Andriopoulos and Lewis, 2009).

Tensions: Categories

Building on Lewis (2000) and Lüscher and Lewis (2008), Smith and Lewis (2011) develop a comprehensive categorization of paradoxes that represents core activities of any organization: learning, belonging, organizing and performing. Learning paradoxes surface during organizational changes and innovations involving tensions between old and new. Belonging (identity) paradoxes involve conflicts surrounding individual and group interactions embodying self versus other. Organizing paradoxes can result when organizations adopt competing design and production processes reflecting demands for both control and flexibility. Finally, performing paradoxes arise from differing and conflicting needs of internal and external stakeholders (Jarzabkowski et al., 2013). As noted earlier, not only are tensions inherent in organizational systems, but also they can be cognitively and socially constructed (Smith and Lewis, 2011). It is these characteristics that shed light on forces that render latent tensions salient.

Tensions: Assumptions

Paradox theory holds important assumptions in its conception and articulation of organizational tensions associated with contradictory elements. According to paradox theory, organizations are viewed as replete with inherent tensions embedded across complex systems and subsystems (for example, industries, firms, teams and individuals) that constantly interact (Lewis and Smith, 2014). Tensions are seen as emerging due to differing goals, expectations and functions of these subsystems (Lewis and Smith, 2014). Importantly, lack of understanding of the interactions between subsystems and their outcomes, as well as bounded rationality of decision makers, can significantly aggravate organizational tensions (Merton and Barber, 1976). Paradox theory also assumes that paradoxes are cognitively and/or socially constructed polarities, resulting from actor responses to tensions. These responses are proposed to be centred on defensiveness aiming to reduce actor discomfort and anxiety (Ford and Backoff, 1988; Lewis, 2000). Actors are assumed to have a tendency to ignore or mask interdependence of contradictory choices through polarization, which fosters either/or thinking whereby actors simply choose one of two opposing elements (Sharma and Bansal, 2017). Finally, paradox theory emphasizes the persistence of tension as a phenomenon that can never be resolved (Smith and Lewis, 2011), but can be leveraged through paradoxical thinking that accepts this persistence, moves beyond contradictions and identifies synergies (Sharma and Bansal, 2017).

ENVIRONMENTAL FOCI AND ACTOR COGNITION

Building on the assumptions of paradox theory, researchers distinguish between latent and salient tensions (Smith and Lewis, 2011). This distinction acknowledges that tensions, while embedded in organizational systems and persistent due to their complexity and adaptability, are experienced phenomena (Schad and Bansal, 2018). As such, their paradoxical nature can be recognized, intensified and aggravated subject to environmental foci (that is, plurality, change, scarcity) and/or actor cognition and sensemaking (Miron-Spektor et al., 2018; Smith and Lewis, 2011). These factors accentuate the juxtaposition of contradictory elements, spurring ambiguity and stress that escalate susceptibility to polarization (either/or thinking).

Plurality denotes the multiplicity of views, claims and demands associated with an organization's internal and external stakeholders (Meixell and Luoma, 2015). Uncertainties and inconsistencies are more likely to surface as plurality increases. On the other hand, the permeation of change through organizational systems and subsystems creates an institutional excuse to exercise temporal and spatial tensions induced by uncertainty about the unknown future or confusion around roles/identities (Lüscher and Lewis, 2008). Finally, saliency of tensions might arise when scarcity of resources (time or money) causes actors to tend towards rationalization and cost–benefit analysis of competing choices (Miron-Spektor et al., 2018). Actor cognition refers to sensemaking in ambiguous situations according to cognitive frames (Hahn et al., 2014), that is, 'mental template[s] that individuals impose on an information environment to give it form and meaning' (Walsh, 1995, p. 281). This process often follows past experiences, knowledge structure, and what is known to the actors (or within their comfort zone) as a mechanism to mitigate ambiguity and develop certain boundaries (Ashcraft et al., 2009). As such, actor cognition intensifies the experience of contradictory demands and disregards interrelatedness due to, for example, stereotypical thinking (Hahn et al., 2014).

MANAGEMENT RESPONSES

Strategies to manage tensions should be based on an exploration of organizational responses to experienced tensions. This requires navigation of both 'vicious' and 'virtuous' cycles in order to highlight paradoxical thinking (Lewis, 2000; Smith and Lewis, 2011). Vicious cycles describe the typical responses shown by organizations/actors when faced with salient tensions. These responses are centred on consistency schemes, defensive mechanisms and inertia forces (Smith and Lewis, 2011). Consistency schemes refer to the preference of actors to exercise consistency in their cognition and action when responding to tensions. Defensive mechanisms such as repression, regression and ambivalence reduce emotional anxiety related to inconsistencies and contradiction (Lewis, 2000). Organizational inertia often reinforces actor commitment to past behaviours when dealing with tensions (Gilbert, 2005). These factors may offer a temporary sense of relief by enabling the actor to choose and stick to a single choice, but eventually exacerbate the underlying tensions by masking their interrelatedness.

Virtuous cycles, on the other hand, promote acceptance of opposing choices, which enables paradoxical resolution strategies as explained by Smith and Lewis (2011). In contrast to defensiveness, acceptance allows for comfort to motivate actor response to tensions. Cognitive and behavioural complexity, emotional composure and dynamic capabilities are indispensable in nurturing acceptance and the ability to work through paradoxical tensions (Smith and Lewis,

2011). Cognitive complexity enables development of cognitive frames that recognize dualities, while behavioural complexity legitimizes competing behaviours. Emotional composure eases fear and anxiety, giving actors room to recognize the interrelatedness of contradictory elements (Sundaramurthy and Lewis, 2003). Finally, dynamic capabilities contribute to acceptance strategies by underlining 'collective tools' (Smith and Lewis, 2011, p. 392) through which organizations can deal with tensions arising from change and uncertainty. By cultivating acceptance as a way of thinking and working through tensions, managers can exercise resolution strategies that acknowledge the coexistence of paradoxical elements. These resolution strategies should be grounded on the idea of iterative splitting and integration of contradictory choices. Smith and Lewis (2011, p. 392) elaborate this in their dynamic equilibrium model as follows: 'paradoxical resolution denotes purposeful iterations between alternatives in order to ensure simultaneous attention to them over time. Doing so involves consistent inconsistency as managers frequently and dynamically shift decisions. Actors therefore make choices in the short term while remaining acutely aware of accepting contradiction in the long term.'

Outcomes

Inherent in paradox theory are the negative outcomes of ignoring or masking the interdependencies of opposing forces encapsulated in vicious cycles. These forces may be manifested as, for example, ambivalence (Eisenhardt, 2000), myopia (Smith and Lewis, 2011), missing alternative views (Barron and Harackiewicz, 2001), unethical behaviour (Schweitzer et al., 2004) and chaos (Thiétart and Forgues, 1995). Conversely, paradoxical thinking is argued to boost creativity, augment flexibility and resilience, and foster positivity. Such mechanisms not only promote short-term achievement but also offer a pathway to long-term success. This is how paradoxical thinking generates sustainability (Smith and Lewis, 2011). Key variables of paradox theory are summarized in Figure 15.1.

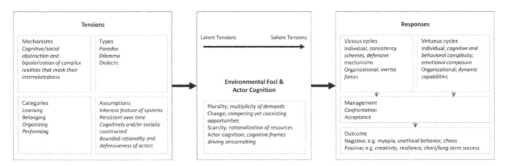

Figure 15.1   Overview of paradox theory variables

DOMAIN WHERE THE THEORY APPLIES

At the heart of paradox theory we observe contradiction and interdependence of elements/ choices with attributes of simultaneity and persistence. Paradox theory can therefore be applied whenever the subject of interest exhibits conflict of demands and oppositional forces between elements that make sense in isolation but are contradictory when coupled (Lewis,

2000). Further, the opposing elements must have 'inextricable links' (Schad et al., 2016, p. 11). The level of interdependence may vary from separable to ontologically inseparable, yet the elements should persist over time; that is, the elements must define and inform each other in a dynamic and cyclical fashion (Schad et al., 2016). Lewis and Smith (2014) identify complexity and goals as important boundary conditions of the paradox theory that substantiate its application to organizations that are complex (in terms of environment, maturity and size) and pursue multiple goals.

Paradox theory has also been considered as a meta-theory, which extends its application across a variety of contexts relating to organizational tensions and their management (Lewis and Smith, 2014; Pierce and Aguinis, 2013). Schad et al. (2016) maintain that paradox theory is suitable for meta-theorizing (Ritzer, 2001) across multiple specific organization theories, which can in turn be applied to study a diverse range of phenomena. The versatility and ubiquity of paradox theory is also manifested in its application across multiple levels of analysis, such as tensions surfacing at individual, team, organization and system levels. Studied paradoxical tensions include change–stability (Lüscher and Lewis, 2008), flexibility–control (Osono et al., 2008), exploration–exploitation (Andriopoulos and Lewis, 2009; Papachroni et al., 2015; Smith and Tushman, 2005) and collaboration–competition (Murnighan and Conlon, 1991; Stadtler and Van Wassenhove, 2016).

RELATIONSHIPS BETWEEN THE VARIABLES AND THEORETICAL PREDICTIONS

Paradox theory explains relationships between the core variables of salient paradoxical tensions, management strategies (responses), and outcomes via reinforcing cycles (vicious and virtuous), each of which follows certain iterative dynamics that affect the outcome of paradoxical thinking.

Reinforcing Cycles

Vicious cycles depict the iterative dynamics of defensive responses to paradoxical tensions by actors and organizations. These responses lead to a downward spiral because of the emphasis on one choice (for temporary relief through avoidance), which instigates pressures from its opposing choice and curtails any sustainability outcomes. Therefore, vicious cycles offer an opportunity to evaluate the short-term and long-term outputs of defensive responses to paradoxical tensions. Factors such as cognitive and behavioural forces for consistency (following actors' existing knowledge structure and lived experience), anxiety and fear of the unknown, and institutional inertia, comprise diagnostics of defensiveness and inform endeavours to turn towards embracing (rather than circumventing) paradoxes.

Virtuous cycles identify important links between paradoxes, responses and outcomes by perpetuating innovation (Andriopoulos and Lewis, 2009; Jay, 2013) and learning (Miron-Spektor et al., 2011) when actors and organizations welcome tensions. This positive reaction requires cognitive and behavioural complexity, composure and dynamic capability of organizations to encourage acceptance of paradoxes and work through tensions. In this way, organizations can foster peak performance and promote enduring, expansive sustainability outcomes. For example, Sharma and Bansal (2017) maintain that embracing financial–social paradox has the potential to furnish organizations with, for example, new forms in terms of structures and practices (Tracey et al., 2011) and improved survival (Battilana and Dorado, 2010).

HOW HAS THE THEORY BEEN USED?

We discuss selected applications of paradox theory in the organization and management literature outside and inside PSCM (see Appendix Table 15A.1). De Keyser et al. (2019) demonstrate that researchers have utilized paradox theory as a means to theorize, understand and advance, or verbalize, something puzzling. This aligns with Lewis and Smith's (2014) postulations on widening the scope of paradox theory and Schad et al.'s (2016) review of paradox research in management science. Paradox theory studies are proliferating in terms of both diversity (for example, mechanisms, types and categories) and level of applications (for example, macro and micro), which resonates with its meta-theoretical capacity.

Outside PSCM

Actor responses and cognitive frames
Paradox theory offers a promising discourse centred on actor/organization cognitive frames and their responses to tensions within and between organizations, including in cross-sector collaboration projects. For example, paradoxical cognitive frames are conceptualized as fostering ambivalent interpretations of managerial sensemaking of corporate sustainability tensions, as opposed to univalent interpretations driven by the business case frame (Hahn et al., 2014). However, this interpretation is a dynamic and temporal process subject to different framing adopted by actors at different organizational levels. Drawing on multi-level tensions of a bottom-of-the-pyramid (BoP) project, Sharma and Jaiswal (2018) argue that the differing cognitive frames adopted by organizational and project leaders are mediated by bottom-up temporal work and event-driven temporal shift. Therefore, cognitive fluidity (flexibility) is vital for the success of collaborative projects – for example, between business and non-governmental organizations (NGOs) – as it not only allows for the engagement of paradoxes, but also enables parties to find ways to work through tensions rather than being resigned to a known course of action (Sharma and Bansal, 2017). This cognitive fluidity provides interesting insights into the debates of instrumental and ecologically dominant logics in sustainability research (Montabon et al., 2016).

Employees' cognitive frames and responses to tensions are important predictors of individual performance and organizational sustenance in both internal and interfacing contexts. For example, a high paradox mindset encourages employees to accept contradictory choices without fear and anxiety, which advances their in-role job performance (Miron-Spektor et al., 2018). This is further illustrated by Stadtler and Van Wassenhove (2016) in their case study of coopetition in a complex, cross-sector partnership of logistics emergency teams supporting disaster response operations. In this study, employees navigated coopetition tensions by juxtaposing collaborative and competitive logics, and using a paradoxical mindset to develop nested identity and contextual segmentation. Employees exercised both integrating and separating responses to cope with the coopetition tensions.

Issues of managing paradoxes

Studies have taken varying approaches to explore the issue of managing paradoxical tensions, extending paradox theory and its applications for understanding various phenomena. For example, an investigation of continuous improvement (*kaizen*) projects reveals how defensiveness and acceptance relate to competing and interrelating epistemic objects between frontline employees and managerial staff through mediation of materials artifact (Aoki, 2020). Epistemic objects also serve to characterize the organizational context for actor responses to paradoxes. Moreover, differentiation and integration strategies can escalate organizational success in the management of exploitation–exploration tensions in product design innovation. Andriopoulos and Lewis (2009) demonstrate this by categorizing nested tensions of innovation – strategic intent (profit–breakthroughs), customer orientation (tight–loose coupling), and personal drivers (discipline–passion) – that explicate the interplay among innovation paradoxes, and demonstrate how their management can fuel virtuous cycles of ambidexterity.

Sustainability tensions

Sustainability entails attending to and balancing the triad of people, planet and profit. As such, sustainability is replete with tensions, which makes application of paradox theory salient to its expanding discourse (Mazutis et al., 2020; Slawinski et al., 2017). Relevant to sustainability and paradox are the part–whole and short–long (temporal) tensions relating to social systems and subsystems (Jay et al., 2017). In this regard, Hahn et al. (2015) offer a compelling conceptualization that postulates the source of sustainability to reside between multi-level (that is, individual, organizational and systemic) interactions and/or within spatial and temporal contexts. Compartmentalization and temporal splitting are put forth as response strategies to work through the paradoxical tensions of sustainability. For example, an organization may employ temporal splitting for product design tensions by pursuing efficiency and functionality parameters in the basic development phase, then considering social/environmental footprint in the production ramp-up (Jay et al., 2017).

Paradoxical leadership

Studies that focus on paradoxical leadership are concerned with the role of paradoxical thinking in high-level, strategic corporate decisions that often involve various tensions such as intuition–rationality, exploration–exploitation and stability–flexibility. This is inherent in the idea that paradoxical leadership stimulates 'practices seeking creative, both/and solutions that can enable fast-paced, adaptable decision making' (Lewis et al., 2014, p. 58). This is illustrated in a review of seven case studies of innovation projects that examines management of the intuition–rationality tension. The authors describe a process of accepting the contradictory elements of rational and intuitive approaches, making decisions through the integration of intuitive and rational practices, and embedding the resulting outcomes into the organizational context (Calabretta et al., 2017). Paradoxical leadership also informs practices used by leaders to shape lower-level managers' interpretive context of tensions (Knight and Paroutis, 2017), as well as the company's ability to foster strategic agility (Lewis et al., 2014). For example, three related contexts – instrumental, relational and temporal – are theorized to make latent exploration–exploitation tensions in the media sector salient through leader practices of diversifying, devaluing and multitasking (Knight and Paroutis, 2017).

Questioning the assumptions

An emerging stream of literature has focused on the dark side of paradoxical theory and mindset with the intention to motivate what is called a 'critical' paradox theory. In a conceptual piece, Berti and Simpson (2021) question the lack of attention to asymmetrical power relations in paradox theory by expounding the notion of organizational pragmatic paradoxes: 'contradictory demands received within the context of an intense managerial relationship, such as when a subordinate is ordered to "take initiative"'. A key argument is that paradox theory assumes actor agency for behaving paradoxically, and as such ignores the dynamics of disempowerment. Organizational pragmatic paradoxes result from an interplay between unavoidable pressure to attend to tensions, and various dimensions of power, and can lead to paralysis and other pathological consequences (Berti and Simpson, 2021). Explaining the false mastery of paradox, Gaim et al. (2019) juxtapose managing impressions against tackling emissions in the Volkswagen Dieselgate debacle, to theorize discursive (as opposed to substantive) embracing of paradox, which causes dysfunctional behaviours. These contributions make a case for including problematization approaches in the paradox discourse in order to preserve its relevance across a wide range of applications (Cunha and Putnam, 2019).

Paradox theory and its interplay with other organization theories has also been a subject of interest. For example, Keller and Sadler-Smith (2019) review paradox and dual-process theories, arguing that cognition as a basic tenet of paradox theory relates to managers' use of 'intuition' and 'analysis' for processing information. Intuition and analysis are themselves highly suggestive of a micro-level paradox given that they are contradictory yet interrelated elements. Keller and Sadler-Smith (2019) propose an integrative framework which explains how the theories of intuition and analysis inform each other, unpacking the relationship between the two seemingly paradoxical systems of thinking and reasoning. Pinto (2019) presents an application of paradox and stakeholder theory in the context of organizational performance management, arguing that such a perspective prevents short-sighted (Slawinski and Bansal, 2015), metric-oriented approaches that are prone to detrimental consequences.

Inside PSCM

PSCM scholars have shown an increasing interest in paradox theory given the complex decision choices, multi-stakeholder environments and global dynamics surrounding internal and external supply chains (Sandberg, 2017). For example, sustainability is by its very nature built around balancing priorities (Wu and Pagell, 2011). Tensions naturally arise when dealing with multiple trigger points (Seuring and Müller, 2008) associated with the differing and sometimes conflicting demands (Donaldson and Preston, 1995) of purchasing and supply chain stakeholders. In such situations, stakeholder theory (Mitchell et al., 1997) can assist with analysing the stakeholders and their salience, whether stakeholder demands are self-serving or reciprocal. The contested nature of sustainability and the power of paradox theory (as a meta-theory) to reinvigorate the sustainable supply chain discourse have been debated by Matthews et al. (2016) with the aim of motivating a paradigm shift in research and practice. A paradoxical framework is used to uncover tensions across different levels of sustainability analysis (for example, firm, network) and between various types of theories developed in the pertinent literature (Matthews et al., 2016).

Fayezi et al. (2018) characterize the interpretive context of procurement sustainability tensions by tapping into the attributes of different stakeholders and considering how they may generate tensions associated with triple bottom line sustainability in procurement. Considering managers' sensemaking of sustainability, it is argued that contextualization of sustainability standards (that is, making them workable for emerging market suppliers) shifts adversarial cognitive frames grounded on instrumentalism towards a paradoxical approach based on integration (Xiao et al., 2019). Contributions addressing sustainability tensions also include discussions of lean improvement projects (Maalouf, 2016) and practice–performance tensions for green supply chains that render supply chain position (upstream and downstream) paradoxes salient (Schmidt et al., 2017).

Researchers draw on paradox theory to investigate capabilities that circumvent defensiveness when responding to contradictory and competing choices. With regard to collaboration–competition tensions, buyer coopetition capabilities are argued to drive paradoxical resolutions, while their evaluative capabilities foster trust, triggering positive responses from suppliers (Wilhelm and Sydow, 2018). Paradox theory has also shown utility in a stream of the literature that deals with antecedents and outcomes of ambidexterity. This entails such things as exploring capabilities that augment ambidexterity (Chandrasekaran et al., 2012), and performance implications of ambidextrous strategy. For example, Kristal et al. (2010) explain that combinative competitive capabilities such as quality, delivery, flexibility and cost are affected by exploration and exploitation practices in the supply chain and coincide with business performance.

WHAT ARE THE FUTURE RESEARCH OPPORTUNITIES?

PSCM research can benefit from a diversity of paradigms and approaches being applied to the study of different phenomena (Boyer and Swink, 2008). Paradox theory can be considered as a theory (and meta-theory) to turn such diversity into a creative endeavour for pushing boundaries and challenging the theoretical and community assumptions that dominate our discipline. Paradox theory complements contingency-based narratives with paradoxical approaches that spur dynamism and change in dealing with tensions. This paradigm shift marks what we might call a 'paradox transition' in a discipline that has traditionally tended to follow instrumentalism.

Supply Chain Tensions and Design Decisions

The ideas of paradox theory encourage 'rethinking the supply chain' in terms of structure, boundaries, and issues of institution, agency and power. Paradoxical leadership has implications for the physical and support structures of supply chains (Carter et al., 2015) to both tighten and widen their visible horizon. In this context, supply chain designs must seek ambivalence to work through tensions.

PSCM research should investigate tensions that arise from shifts in supply chain products/ services, processes and systems, as these require employees and leaders to engage with new ideas and actions. Paradox theory can contribute to advancing supply chain theory relating to paradoxes of learning, and help in developing strategies for mitigating resistance to change by encouraging acceptance and integration of the new along with the old. Supply chains encompass a variety of roles and identities at multiple levels and locations within and outside of the organization, including subsidiaries and partners. This is a critical source of belonging tensions in PSCM, as individuals assume multiple roles, identities and memberships, and even work as part of cross-functional teams. PSCM research should attend to such role multiplicity tensions, particularly where belonging tensions are mixed up with performing tensions as actors pursue conflicting goals across multiple roles. For example, Fayezi et al. (2018) show a complex interpretive context for procurement professionals whereby individuals might assume functional key performance indicators (KPIs) based on cost, while also feeling pressure to fulfil demands from social stakeholders. In such cases, paradox theory's disintegration and integration approaches can be applied to allow employees and managers to circumvent anxiety by accepting paradoxes.

On the other hand, PSCM is replete with organizing tensions that research has recognized, but should pursue further. This is particularly critical to the supply chain design discourse, where arguments are shifting to promote, for example, collaboration, empowerment, flexibility and diversity. While this has helped to make PSCM an inclusive discourse that promotes outside-in thinking in theory, in practice it is not always easy to achieve these qualities in supply chains. Further, the pursuit of these qualities in supply chains might not necessarily need to be at the expense of competition, direction, control and homogeneity. Paradoxical supply chain design is a promising area of research for PSCM scholars and needs further attention (Bals and Tate, 2018). In relation to performing paradoxes, PSCM researchers are best placed to advance paradox theory and the supply chain discourse by studying the implications of a paradoxical response to the contradictory and competing demands of social, environmental and economic stakeholders in various tiers of the supply chain. This is particularly relevant for creating responsible supply chains. For example, social issues such as modern slavery, poverty alleviation and gender equality accentuate performance paradoxes that, if not systematically attended to, result in unsustainable decisions and actions (Gold et al., 2015; Trautrims et al., 2020) that favour short-termism no matter which side (social–financial) is adopted.

Supply Chain Tensions and Power Regimes

An important source of debate between PSCM and paradox scholars is the notion of using power distribution and dynamics to make sense of and respond to tensions. Given that supply chains operate across institutions, cultures and economies, they offer opportunities to explore the realities of paradoxical thinking in environments where, for example, systemic power might prevail. Hargrave and Van de Ven (2017, p. 329) define systemic power as 'institutionalized power that operates automatically through rules and routines which are seemingly independent of the interests of particular actors yet advantage some actors over others'. It is therefore important for future research to explore how such power regimes interplay with paradoxical thinking when creating system-wide changes (Schad and Bansal, 2018). If systemic power sits behind one side of a contradiction, failure to apply a paradoxical mindset can create various unintended consequences, such as what Busse et al. (2016) describe as a false sense of legitimacy in global supply chains in the context of supply chain sustainability risk. Other opportunities for future research include exploration of resource-based power differentials, as articulated by resource dependency theory (Pfeffer and Salancik, 1978), and evaluation of the dimensions of organizational power such as coercion, manipulation, domination and subjectification (Fleming and Spicer, 2014) in conjunction with (particularly lower-level) supply chain managers' agency for exercising paradoxical response strategies.

Supply Chain Tensions and Network Structures

In the context of multi-tier and networked supply chains, triadic relationships (for example, buyer–supplier–supplier), and strategies for coping with and responding to paradoxical tensions in such environments, offer a fruitful area for future research (Choi and Wu, 2009). For example, PSCM researchers have identified various governance mechanisms to diffuse sustainability in multi-tier operations (Mena et al., 2013; Tachizawa and Wong, 2014). These studies are grounded on contingent-based strategies for creating system-wide sustainability. Paradox theory can augment such perspectives by introducing paradoxical governance (Blome et al., 2013; Sundaramurthy and Lewis, 2003) through temporal and spatial separating and integrating approaches.

Supply Chain Tensions and Actor Cognitions

Finally, we invite PSCM scholars to integrate and leverage research from behavioural operations management with psychological, sociological and organizational paradox, to study the micro-foundations of the paradoxical mindset/cognition in the supply chain (Gond et al., 2017; Keller and Sadler-Smith, 2019). For example, neuroscience concepts might serve our discipline by uncovering the psychological constructs that define actor cognition and sensemaking as it relates to the construction of vicious or virtuous cycles when dealing with paradoxical supply chain tensions (Waldman et al., 2019). Attending to negative and unintended consequences of paradoxical approaches in PSCM is equally important in order to gain a balanced perspective on engaging with paradox theory for supply chain theory development.

REFERENCES

Andriopoulos, C., and Lewis, M.W. (2009). Exploitation–Exploration Tensions and Organizational Ambidexterity: Managing Paradoxes of Innovation. *Organization Science, 20*(4), 696–717. doi:10.1287/orsc.1080.0406.

Aoki, K. (2020). The Roles of Material Artifacts in Managing the Learning–Performance Paradox: The Kaizen Case. *Academy of Management Journal, 63*(4), 1266–1299. doi:10.5465/amj.2017.0967.

Ashcraft, K.L., Kuhn, T.R., and Cooren, F. (2009). Constitutional Amendments: 'Materializing' Organizational Communication. *Academy of Management Annals, 3*(1), 1–64. doi:10.5465/19416520903047186.

Bals, L., and Tate, W.L. (2018). Sustainable Supply Chain Design in Social Businesses: Advancing the Theory of Supply Chain. *Journal of Business Logistics, 39*(1), 57–79. doi:10.1111/jbl.12172.

Barron, K.E., and Harackiewicz, J.M. (2001). Achievement Goals and Optimal Motivation: Testing Multiple Goal Models. *Journal of Personality and Social Psychology, 80*(5), 706.

Battilana, J., and Dorado, S. (2010). Building Sustainable Hybrid Organizations: The Case of Commercial Microfinance Organizations. *Academy of Management Journal, 53*(6), 1419–1440. doi:10.5465/amj.2010.57318391.

Berti, M., and Simpson, A. (2021). The Dark Side of Organizational Paradoxes: The Dynamics of Disempowerment. *Academy of Management Review, 46*(2), 252–274.

Blome, C., Schoenherr, T., and Kaesser, M. (2013). Ambidextrous Governance in Supply Chains: The Impact on Innovation and Cost Performance. *Journal of Supply Chain Management, 49*(4), 59–80. doi:10.1111/jscm.12033.

Boyer, K.K., and Swink, M.L. (2008). Empirical Elephants – Why Multiple Methods are Essential to Quality Research in Operations and Supply Chain Management. *Journal of Operations Management, 26*(3), 338–344. doi:10.1016/j.jom.2008.03.002.

Burgelman, R.A. (2002). Strategy as Vector and the Inertia of Coevolutionary Lock-in. *Administrative Science Quarterly, 47*(2), 325–357. doi:10.2307/3094808.

Busse, C., Kach, A.P., and Bode, C. (2016). Sustainability and the False Sense of Legitimacy: How Institutional Distance Augments Risk in Global Supply Chains. *Journal of Business Logistics, 37*(4), 312–328. doi:10.1111/jbl.12143.

Calabretta, G., Gemser, G., and Wijnberg, N.M. (2017). The Interplay Between Intuition and Rationality in Strategic Decision Making: A Paradox Perspective. *Organization Studies, 38*(3–4), 365–401. doi: 10.1177/0170840616655483.

Carter, C.R., Rogers, D.S., and Choi, T.Y. (2015). Toward the Theory of the Supply Chain. *Journal of Supply Chain Management, 51*(2), 89–97. doi:10.1111/jscm.12073.

Chandrasekaran, A., Linderman, K., and Schroeder, R. (2012). Antecedents to Ambidexterity Competency in High Technology Organizations. *Journal of Operations Management, 30*(1–2), 134–151. doi:10.1016/j.jom.2011.10.002.

Choi, T.Y., and Wu, Z. (2009). Triads in Supply Networks: Theorizing Buyer–Supplier–Supplier Relationships. *Journal of Supply Chain Management, 45*(1), 8–25. doi:10.1111/j.1745-493X.2009.03151.x.

Cunha, M.P.e., and Putnam, L.L. (2019). Paradox Theory and the Paradox of Success. *Strategic Organization, 17*(1), 95–106. doi:10.1177/1476127017739536.

De Keyser, B., Guiette, A., and Vandenbempt, K. (2019). On the Use of Paradox for Generating Theoretical Contributions in Management and Organization Research. *International Journal of Management Reviews, 21*(2), 143–161. doi:10.1111/ijmr.12201.

Donaldson, T., and Preston, L.E. (1995). The Stakeholder Theory of the Corporation: Concepts, Evidence, and Implications. *Academy of Management Review, 20*(1), 65–91. doi:10.5465/amr.1995.9503271992.

Eisenhardt, K.M. (2000). Paradox, Spirals, Ambivalence: The New Language of Change and Pluralism. *Academy of Management Review, 25*(4), 703–705. doi:10.5465/amr.2000.3707694.

Farjoun, M. (2010). Beyond Dualism: Stability and Change As a Duality. *Academy of Management Review, 35*(2), 202–225. doi:10.5465/amr.35.2.zok202.

Fayezi, S., Zomorrodi, M., and Bals, L. (2018). Procurement Sustainability Tensions: An Integrative Perspective. *International Journal of Physical Distribution and Logistics Management, 48*(6), 586–609. doi:10.1108/ijpdlm-01-2017-0013.

Fleming, P., and Spicer, A. (2014). Power in Management and Organization Science. *Academy of Management Annals, 8*(1), 237–298. doi:10.5465/19416520.2014.875671.

Ford, J.D., and Backoff, R.W. (1988). Organizational Change in and out of Dualities and Paradox. In R.E. Quinn and K.S. Cameron (eds), *Paradox and Transformation: Toward a Theory of Change in Organization and Management*. Cambridge, MA: Ballinger, pp. 81–121.

Gaim, M., Clegg, S., and Cunha, M.P.e. (2019). Managing Impressions Rather Than Emissions: Volkswagen and the False Mastery of Paradox. *Organization Studies*, 1–22. doi:10.1177/0170840619891199.

Gilbert, C.G. (2005). Unbundling the Structure of Inertia: Resource versus Routine Rigidity. *Academy of Management Journal, 48*(5), 741–763. doi:10.2307/20159695.

Gold, S., Trautrims, A., and Trodd, Z. (2015). Modern Slavery Challenges to Supply Chain Management. *Supply Chain Management: An International Journal, 20*(5), 485–494.

Gond, J.-P., El Akremi, A., Swaen, V., and Babu, N. (2017). The Psychological Microfoundations of Corporate Social Responsibility: A Person-Centric Systematic Review. *Journal of Organizational Behavior, 38*(2), 225–246. doi:10.1002/job.2170.

Hahn, T., Pinkse, J., Preuss, L., and Figge, F. (2015). Tensions in Corporate Sustainability: Towards an Integrative Framework. *Journal of Business Ethics, 127*(2), 297–316. doi:10.1007/s10551-014-2047-5.

Hahn, T., Preuss, L., Pinkse, J., and Figge, F. (2014). Cognitive Frames in Corporate Sustainability: Managerial Sensemaking with Paradoxical and Business Case Frames. *Academy of Management Review, 39*(4), 463–487. doi:10.5465/amr.2012.0341.

Hargrave, T.J., and Van de Ven, A.H. (2017). Integrating Dialectical and Paradox Perspectives on Managing Contradictions in Organizations. *Organization Studies*, 65–171. doi:10.1177/0170840616640843.

Jarzabkowski, P., Lê, J.K., and Van de Ven, A.H. (2013). Responding to Competing Strategic Demands: How Organizing, Belonging, and Performing Paradoxes Coevolve. *Strategic Organization*, *11*(3), 245–280. doi:10.1177/1476127013481016.

Jay, J. (2013). Navigating Paradox as a Mechanism of Change and Innovation in Hybrid Organizations. *Academy of Management Journal*, *56*(1), 137–159. doi:10.5465/amj.2010.0772.

Jay, J., Soderstrom, S., and Grant, G. (2017). Navigating the Paradoxes of Sustainability. In W.K. Smith, M.W. Lewis, P. Jarzabkowski and A. Langley (eds), *The Oxford Handbook of Organizational Paradox*. Oxford University Press. https://www.oxfordhandbooks.com/view/10.1093/oxfordhb/9780198754428.001.0001/oxfordhb-9780198754428-e-18.

Keller, J., and Sadler-Smith, E. (2019). Paradoxes and Dual Processes: A Review and Synthesis. *International Journal of Management Reviews*, *21*(2), 162–184. doi:10.1111/ijmr.12200.

Kelly, G. (1955). *The Psychology of Personal Constructs*. New York: Norton.

Knight, E., and Paroutis, S. (2017). Becoming Salient: The TMT Leader's Role in Shaping the Interpretive Context of Paradoxical Tensions. *Organization Studies*, 38(3–4), 403–432. doi:10.1177/0170840616640844.

Kristal, M.M., Huang, X., and Roth, A.V. (2010). The Effect of an Ambidextrous Supply Chain Strategy on Combinative Competitive Capabilities and Business Performance. *Journal of Operations Management*, *28*(5), 415–429. doi:http://dx.doi.org/10.1016/j.jom.2009.12.002.

Lewis, M.W. (2000). Exploring Paradox: Toward a More Comprehensive Guide. *Academy of Management Review*, *25*(4), 760–776. doi:10.5465/amr.2000.3707712.

Lewis, M.W., Andriopoulos, C., and Smith, W.K. (2014). Paradoxical Leadership to Enable Strategic Agility. *California Management Review*, *56*(3), 58–77. doi:10.1525/cmr.2014.56.3.58.

Lewis, M.W., and Smith, W.K. (2014). Paradox as a Metatheoretical Perspective: Sharpening the Focus and Widening the Scope. *Journal of Applied Behavioral Science*, *50*(2), 127–149. doi:10.1177/0021886314522322.

Lüscher, L.S., and Lewis, M.W. (2008). Organizational Change and Managerial Sensemaking: Working Through Paradox. *Academy of Management Journal*, *51*(2), 221–240. doi:10.5465/amj.2008.31767217.

Maalouf, M. (2016). Managing Paradoxical Tensions During the Implementation of Lean Capabilities for Improvement. *International Journal of Operations and Production Management*, *36*(6), 687–709. doi:10.1108/IJOPM-10-2014-0471.

Matthews, L., Power, D., Touboulic, A., and Marques, L. (2016). Building Bridges: Toward Alternative Theory of Sustainable Supply Chain Management. *Journal of Supply Chain Management*, *52*(1), 82–94. doi:10.1111/jscm.12097.

Mazutis, D., Slawinski, N., and Palazzo, G. (2020). A Time and Place for Sustainability: A Spatiotemporal Perspective on Organizational Sustainability Frame Development. *Business and Society*. doi:10.1177/0007650320949843.

Meixell, M.J., and Luoma, P. (2015). Stakeholder Pressure in Sustainable Supply Chain Management. *International Journal of Physical Distribution and Logistics Management*, *45*(1/2), 69–89. doi:10.1108/ijpdlm-05-2013-0155.

Mena, C., Humphries, A., and Choi, T.Y. (2013). Toward a Theory of Multi-Tier Supply Chain Management. *Journal of Supply Chain Management*, *49*(2), 58–77. doi:10.1111/jscm.12003.

Merton, R.K., and Barber, E. (1976). Sociological Ambivalence. In R.K. Merton (ed.), *Sociological Ambivalence and Other Essays*. New York: Free Press, pp. 3–31.

Miron-Spektor, E., Gino, F., and Argote, L. (2011). Paradoxical Frames and Creative Sparks: Enhancing Individual Creativity through Conflict and Integration. *Organizational Behavior and Human Decision Processes*, *116*(2), 229–240. doi:https://doi.org/10.1016/j.obhdp.2011.03.006.

Miron-Spektor, E., Ingram, A., Keller, J., Smith, W.K., and Lewis, M.W. (2018). Microfoundations of Organizational Paradox: The Problem Is How We Think about the Problem. *Academy of Management Journal*, *61*(1), 26–45. doi:10.5465/amj.2016.0594.

Mitchell, R.K., Agle, B.R., and Wood, D.J. (1997). Toward a Theory of Stakeholder Identification and Salience: Defining the Principle of Who and What Really Counts. *Academy of Management Review*, *22*(4), 853–886. doi:10.2307/259247.

Montabon, F., Pagell, M., and Wu, Z. (2016). Making Sustainability Sustainable. *Journal of Supply Chain Management*, *52*(2), 11–27. doi: 10.1111/jscm.12103.

Murnighan, J.K., and Conlon, D.E. (1991). The Dynamics of Intense Work Groups: A Study of British String Quartets. *Administrative Science Quarterly*, *36*(2), 165–186. doi:10.2307/2393352.

Osono, E., Shimizu, N., and Takeuchi, H. (2008). *Extreme Toyota: Radical Contradictions That Drive Success at the World's Best Manufacturer*. Hoboken, NJ: Wiley.

Papachroni, A., Heracleous, L., and Paroutis, S. (2015). Organizational Ambidexterity through the Lens of Paradox Theory: Building a Novel Research Agenda. *Journal of Applied Behavioral Science*, *51*(1), 71–93. doi:10.1177/0021886314553101.

Pfeffer, J., and Salancik, G.R. (1978). *The External Control of Organizations: A Resource Dependence Perspective*. New York: Harper & Row.

Pierce, J.R., and Aguinis, H. (2013). The Too-Much-of-a-Good-Thing Effect in Management. *Journal of Management*, *39*(2), 313–338. doi:10.1177/0149206311410060.

Pinto, J. (2019). Key to Effective Organizational Performance Management Lies at the Intersection of Paradox Theory and Stakeholder Theory. *International Journal of Management Reviews*, *21*(2), 185–208. doi:10.1111/ijmr.12199.

Poole, M.S., and van de Ven, A.H. (1989). Using Paradox to Build Management and Organization Theories. *Academy of Management Review*, *14*(4), 562–578. doi:10.2307/258559.

Quinn, R.E. (2015). *The Positive Organization: Breaking Free from Conventional Cultures, Constraints, and Beliefs*. Oakland, CA: Berrett-Koehler Publishers.

Ritzer, G. (2001). *Explorations in Social Theory: From Metatheorizing to Rationalization*. London: SAGE.

Sandberg, E. (2017). Introducing the Paradox Theory in Logistics and SCM Research – Examples from a Global Sourcing Context. *International Journal of Logistics Research and Applications*, *20*(5), 459–474. doi:10.1080/13675567.2017.1280007.

Schad, J., and Bansal, P. (2018). Seeing the Forest and the Trees: How a Systems Perspective Informs Paradox Research. *Journal of Management Studies*, *55*(8), 1490–1506. doi:10.1111/joms.12398.

Schad, J., Lewis, M.W., Raisch, S., and Smith, W.K. (2016). Paradox Research in Management Science: Looking Back to Move Forward. *Academy of Management Annals*, *10*(1), 5–64. doi:10.5465/19416520.2016.1162422.

Schmidt, C.G., Foerstl, K., and Schaltenbrand, B. (2017). The Supply Chain Position Paradox: Green Practices and Firm Performance. *Journal of Supply Chain Management*, *53*(1), 3–25. doi:10.1111/jscm.12113.

Schweitzer, M.E., Ordóñez, L., and Douma, B. (2004). Goal Setting as a Motivator of Unethical Behavior. *Academy of Management Journal*, *47*(3), 422–432. doi:10.5465/20159591.

Seuring, S., and Müller, M. (2008). From a Literature Review to a Conceptual Framework for Sustainable Supply Chain Management. *Journal of Cleaner Production*, *16*(15), 1699–1710. doi:http://dx.doi.org/10.1016/j.jclepro.2008.04.020.

Sharma, G., and Bansal, P. (2017). Partners for Good: How Business and NGOs Engage the Commercial–Social Paradox. *Organization Studies*, *38*(3–4), 341–364. doi:10.1177/0170840616683739

Sharma, G., and Jaiswal, A.K. (2018). Unsustainability of Sustainability: Cognitive Frames and Tensions in Bottom of the Pyramid Projects. *Journal of Business Ethics*, *148*(2), 291–307. doi:10.1007/s10551-017-3584-5.

Slawinski, N., and Bansal, P. (2015). Short on Time: Intertemporal Tensions in Business Sustainability. *Organization Science*, *26*(2), 531–549. doi:10.1287/orsc.2014.0960.

Slawinski, N., Pinkse, J., Busch, T., and Banerjee, S.B. (2017). The Role of Short-Termism and Uncertainty Avoidance in Organizational Inaction on Climate Change: A Multi-Level Framework. *Business and Society*, *56*(2), 253–282. doi:10.1177/0007650315576136.

Smith, W., and Lewis, M. (2011). Toward a Theory of Paradox: A Dynamic Equilibrium Model of Organizing. *Academy of Management Review*, *36*(2), 381–403. doi: 10.5465/amr.2009.0223.

Smith, W.K., Lewis, M.W., and Tushman, M.L. (2016). 'Both/and' leadership. *Harvard Business Review*, *94*(5), 62–70.

Smith, W.K., and Tushman, M.L. (2005). Managing Strategic Contradictions: A Top Management Model for Managing Innovation Streams. *Organization Science*, *16*(5), 522–536. doi: 10.1287/orsc.1050.0134.

Stadtler, L., and Van Wassenhove, L.N. (2016). Coopetition as a Paradox: Integrative Approaches in a Multi-Company, Cross-Sector Partnership. *Organization Studies*, *37*(5), 655–685. doi:10.1177/0170840615622066.

Sundaramurthy, C., and Lewis, M. (2003). Control and Collaboration: Paradoxes of Governance. *Academy of Management Review*, *28*(3), 397–415. doi:10.5465/amr.2003.10196737.

Tachizawa, E.M., and Wong, C.Y. (2014). Towards a Theory of Multi-Tier Sustainable Supply Chains: A Systematic Literature Review. *Supply Chain Management: An International Journal*, *19*(5/6), 643–663. doi:10.1108/scm-02-2014-0070.

Thiétart, R.A., and Forgues, B. (1995). Chaos Theory and Organization. *Organization Science*, *6*(1), 19–31. doi:10.1287/orsc.6.1.19.

Tracey, P., Phillips, N., and Jarvis, O. (2011). Bridging Institutional Entrepreneurship and the Creation of New Organizational Forms: A Multilevel Model. *Organization Science*, *22*(1), 60–80. doi:10.1287/orsc.1090.0522.

Trautrims, A., Schleper, M.C., Cakir, M.S., and Gold, S. (2020). Survival at the Expense of the Weakest? Managing Modern Slavery Risks in Supply Chains During COVID-19. *Journal of Risk Research*, *23*(7/8), 1–6. doi:10.1080/13669877.2020.1772347.

Tushman, M.L., and O'Reilly III, C.A. (1996). Ambidextrous Organizations: Managing Evolutionary and Revolutionary Change. *California Management Review*, *38*(4), 8–30. doi: 10.2307/41165852.

Waldman, D.A., Wang, D., and Fenters, V. (2019). The Added Value of Neuroscience Methods in Organizational Research. *Organizational Research Methods*, *22*(1), 223–249. doi:10.1177/1094428116642013.

Walsh, J.P. (1995). Managerial and Organizational Cognition: Notes from a Trip Down Memory Lane. *Organization Science*, *6*(3), 280–321. doi:10.1287/orsc.6.3.280.

Wilhelm, M., and Sydow, J. (2018). Managing Coopetition in Supplier Networks – A Paradox Perspective. *Journal of Supply Chain Management*, *54*(3), 22–41. doi:10.1111/jscm.12167.

Wu, Z., and Pagell, M. (2011). Balancing Priorities: Decision-Making in Sustainable Supply Chain Management. *Journal of Operations Management*, *29*(6), 577–590. doi:10.1016/j.jom.2010.10.001.

Xiao, C., Wilhelm, M., van der Vaart, T., and van Donk, D.P. (2019). Inside the Buying Firm: Exploring Responses to Paradoxical Tensions in Sustainable Supply Chain Management. *Journal of Supply Chain Management*, *55*(1), 3–20. doi:10.1111/jscm.12170.

APPENDIX: Table 15A.1 A summary of selected articles

Author (year)/ journal	Title	Aims and research questions	Findings	Research approach and context	Level of analysis	Unit of analysis	Paradox type/ category	Paradox approach
Outside PSCM								
Aoki (2020)/ AMJ	The Roles of Material Artifacts in Managing the Learning–Performance Paradox: The Kaizen Case	'To develop a theory on the roles of material artifacts in the management of paradox focusing on the learning–performance paradox which frontline employees face when they engage in incremental innovation' *How do material artifacts contribute to transforming organizations in ways that effectively manage the learning–performance paradox?*	'Identifies four distinct roles of material artifacts (triggering, supporting, disconnecting, and connecting) and their impact on the management of paradoxes. It shows how competing and interrelating epistemic objects explain defensiveness (exclusive focus on performance) and acceptance of frontline employees in relation to learning–performance paradox'	Qualitative (two transformation projects) Manufacturing plants (China)	Teams	Continuous improvement (*Kaizen*) projects	Learning Performing	To theorize
Miron-Spektor et al. (2018)/ AMJ	Microfoundations of Organizational Paradox: The Problem Is How We Think About the Problem	'To explore why some individuals thrive with and leverage tensions (while others might struggle)' *What conditions intensify the experience of tensions? What is the impact of tensions on one's workplace efforts, such as job performance? How do individuals' approaches affect their ability to cope with, or even benefit from, these tensions?*	'Identifies employees' experience of tensions contributed positively to their in-role job performance and innovation when their mindsets encourage them to value, accept, and feel comfortable with contradictions. Experiencing tensions is detrimental for individuals with a low paradox mindset' 'Argues scarce resources intensify any surface tensions, and thus affect performance outcomes indirectly'	Quantitative and qualitative Consumer products (US, UK, Israel, China)	Individuals	In-role job (product specialists)	Performing Individual approaches	To theorize

Author (year)/ journal	Title	Aims and research questions	Findings	Research approach and context	Level of analysis	Unit of analysis	Paradox type/ category	Paradox approach
Berti and Simpson (2021)/*AMR*	The Dark Side of Organizational Paradoxes: The Dynamics of Disempowerment	'To contribute to the paradox theory by conceptualizing a neglected issue relating to the agency of actors in embracing paradoxes which itself highlights inattentiveness to this dark side of paradox due to insufficient consideration of asymmetrical relations of power'	'Draws attention to organizational pragmatic paradoxes which are contradictory demands received within the context of an intense managerial relationship, such as when a subordinate is ordered to "take initiative"' 'Develops a model which highlights how organizational pragmatic paradoxes derive from power relations restricting actors' capacities for enacting legitimate responses (agency) to tensions. The model links different organizational power dimensions to various manifestations of pragmatic paradoxes'	Conceptual	Individuals	Managerial relationship (manager–subordinate)	Pragmatic paradoxes	To theorize
Hahn et al. (2014)/*AMR*	Cognitive Frames in Corporate Sustainability: Managerial Sensemaking with Paradoxical and Business Case Frames	'To generate a better understanding of the underlying cognitive determinants of different responses to sustainability issues (economic, environmental, and social) that managers consider' *How do managers make sense of ambiguous cues concerning sustainability?*	'Proposes a business case frame and a paradoxical frame (with differences in content and structure) to influence the three stages of the sensemaking process of ambiguous issues. It argues that with the business case frame managers take a univalent interpretation of sustainability issues hence assume a pragmatic stance whereas with the paradoxical frame, this interpretation is rather ambivalent and follows a prudent stance that encourages comprehensive response'	Conceptual	Individuals	Managerial sensemaking (and decision making)	Sensemaking	To understand

Author (year)/ journal	Title	Aims and research questions	Findings	Research approach and context	Level of analysis	Unit of analysis	Paradox type/ category	Paradox approach
Sharma and Jaiswal (2018) /JBE	Unsustainability of Sustainability: Cognitive Frames and Tensions in Bottom of the Pyramid Projects	'To identify the process with which cognitive frames of different actors within organization interact and influence a sustainability initiative's survival' *Do organizational and project leaders differ in their understanding of tensions in a BoP project, and if so, how?*	'Elaborates the relationship between cognitive frames (for example paradoxical and business case) at different levels, that is, organizational and project. Also, argues that decision making horizon mediates this relationship through two mechanisms: bottom-up temporal work; and event-driven temporal shift'	Qualitative Pharmaceutical (India)	Multi (individual; organizational)	BoP projects	Learning (long-term and short-term)	To understand
Hahn et al. (2015)/JBE	Tensions in Corporate Sustainability: Towards an Integrative Framework	'To develop an integrative framework for the identification and characterization of tensions in corporate sustainability'	'Develops an integrative framework that goes beyond the traditional triad of economic, environmental, and social dimensions and argues that tensions in corporate sustainability occur between different levels (individual, organizational, systemic), in change processes, and within a temporal and spatial context'	Conceptual	Multi	Corporate sustainability	Learning	To understand

Author (year)/ journal	Title	Aims and research questions	Findings	Research approach and context	Level of analysis	Unit of analysis	Paradox type/ category	Paradox approach
Andriopoulos and Lewis (2009)/ *OrgScience*	Exploitation–Exploration Tensions and Organizational Ambidexterity: Managing Paradoxes of Innovation	'To investigate exploitation–exploration tensions and their management in practice' *How are organizations to manage paradoxes of innovation?*	'Develops a framework that explicates exploitation–exploration tensions and their management. Also, identifies nested tensions (strategic intent [profit–breakthroughs], customer orientation [tight–loose coupling], and personal drivers [discipline–passion]), posed as paradoxes of innovation, which illustrates the value of blending differentiation and integration approaches, and theorizes the potential for interwoven paradoxes, and their management to fuel virtuous cycles of ambidexterity'	Qualitative	Organizational	New product development process	Learning	To understand
Gaim et al. (2019)/ *OrgStudies*	Managing Impressions rather than Emissions: Volkswagen and the False Mastery of Paradox	'To discuss how the "embrace" of paradox can trigger dysfunctional behaviors, filling the gap between promising and practicing' 'Explores the perils (dark side) of paradoxes that are a stretch too far, being engaged through managing impressions rather than managing a reality concomitant with claims being made about practice'	'Using the Volkswagen emissions scandal, shows how paradoxical promises, embraced discursively but not substantively, created false transcendence rather than paradoxical mastery. As such it contributes to paradox theory by discussing how the illusion of paradox embrace can trigger dysfunctional behaviors'	Qualitative (secondary data)	Organizational	VW emission scandal	Performing (illusion–reality) Stretch goal	To theorize

Author (year)/ journal	Title	Aims and research questions	Findings	Research approach and context	Level of analysis	Unit of analysis	Paradox type/ category	Paradox approach
Sharma and Bansal (2017) /*OrgStudies*	Partners for Good: How Business and NGOs Engage the Commercial–Social Paradox	*How do businesses and NGOs engage the commercial–social paradox in a collaborative project?*	'Identifies that in the projects that worked well (two out of five projects), the two parties held fluid categories, that is they saw differences between business and NGO as contextual and aimed to find creative workarounds to emergent problems. In the projects that did not work well, businesses and NGOs imposed categorical imperatives, that is they saw sharp differences that they intensified by imposing standardized and familiar solutions on their partner' 'Argues that organizational cognition and actions are deeply related in engaging paradoxes. Those organizations that assumed cognitive fluidity sought to solve problems and accommodate each other's needs; those that assumed cognitive imperatives resorted to cognitive templates that were inflexible to each other's needs'	Qualitative India	Multi (cross-sector partnership)	Projects	Performing	To verbalize

Author (year)/ journal	Title	Aims and research questions	Findings	Research approach and context	Level of analysis	Unit of analysis	Paradox type/ category	Paradox approach
Stadtler and Van Wassenhove (2016)/ *OrgStudies*	Coopetition as a **Paradox**: Integrative Approaches in a Multi-Company, Cross-Sector Partnership	*How do employees cope with tensions arising from coopetition?*	'Shows how employees build on the organizational and the boundary spanning task contexts and develop paradoxical frames. Juxtaposing the competitive and collaborative logics, these frames shape the employees' understanding of who they are (a nested identity) and what they should do (contextual segmentation). This juxtaposition allows the employees to navigate emerging tensions by adopting both logics (integrating behavior) and by contextually prioritizing one logic without ignoring the other (demarcating behavior)'	Qualitative	Individuals	Logistics emergency teams	Performing	To understand

Author (year)/ journal	Title	Aims and research questions	Findings	Research approach and context	Level of analysis	Unit of analysis	Paradox type/ category	Paradox approach
Inside PSCM								
Wilhelm and Sydow (2018) /JSCM	Managing Coopetition in Supplier Networks – A Paradox Perspective	'To investigate the competitive tensions that evolve when buying firms are trying to engage both collaboration and competition simultaneously in their relations with core suppliers' *How do buying firms manage the paradox of coopetition in their supplier networks?* *Which coopetition capabilities does the buying firm need in order to trigger positive responses from suppliers and avoid negative tension dynamics?*	'Both splitting and acceptance approaches to managing the paradox of coopetition can be successful in terms of avoiding negative tension dynamics when coopetition capabilities at the level of the buying organization are present' 'When the buying firm has strong evaluative capabilities, it is better able to provide helpful cost improvement suggestions which, in turn, increases the potential for joint value creation through the creation of supplier (competence) trust' 'When the buying firm has strong evaluative capabilities, and demonstrates its intention for a fair division of value appropriation between both parties, higher levels of supplier (goodwill) trust makes open book policies more likely'	Qualitative (case study) Automotive	Interorganizational	Supply network	Collaboration– competition	To understand

Author (year)/ journal	Title	Aims and research questions	Findings	Research approach and context	Level of analysis	Unit of analysis	Paradox type/ category	Paradox approach
Xiao et al. (2019)/*JSCM*	Inside the Buying Firm: Exploring Responses to Paradoxical Tensions in Sustainable Supply Chain Management	*How do purchasing and sustainability managers within the buying firm make sense of and respond to paradoxical tensions in sustainable supply chain management (SSCM)?*	'When managers continue to apply an instrumental perspective, the underlying adversarial sensemaking will lead to a suppression response that resolves paradoxical tensions at the expense of supplier sustainability, which increases the risk of paradoxical tension escalation' 'Contextualizing sustainability standards can alleviate cost—sustainability tensions and create the necessary space for managers to change their adversarial sensemaking to a paradoxical approach by reducing, but not transcending, paradoxical tensions' 'If managers adopt paradoxical sensemaking, but systemic power is asymmetrically distributed, sustainability will be assimilated into the dominant business aims, and synergizing will not lead to true sustainability'	Qualitative (single case study) Consumer electronics	Functional	Managers' sensemaking of and responses to sustainability	Sensemaking of sustainability	To understand

Author (year)/ journal	Title	Aims and research questions	Findings	Research approach and context	Level of analysis	Unit of analysis	Paradox type/ category	Paradox approach
Fayezi et al. (2018)/ IJPDLM	Procurement Sustainability Tensions: An Integrative Perspective	*What procurement sustainability tensions (PSTs) do procurement professionals face in their stakeholder environment? How do legitimacy contexts of the stakeholders explain these PSTs and characterize their manifestation?*	'Identifies supply chain and company procurement sustainability tensions and explain their multi-level nature. Also, dissects the multi-stakeholder and multi-institutional environments where PSTs operate. It explains such environments in terms of various temporal and spatial legitimacy contexts that, through their assessment of institutional distance, can characterize the manifestation of PSTs'	Qualitative (case study)	Multi	Procurement function	Sensemaking of sustainability	To verbalize
Matthews et al. (2016)/ JSCM	Building Bridges: Toward Alternative Theory of Sustainable Supply Chain Management	'To explore what the next paradigm shift in SSCM might look like' *How can alternative theories of SSCM be developed? What assumptions need to be challenged in order for alternative theories of SSCM to emerge? What assumptions are needed to develop alternative theories of SSCM?*	'Given that sustainability is an essentially contested concept, a theory of SSCM will benefit from the adoption of paradox as its meta-theoretical lens' 'A paradoxical theory of SSCM will use the tensions between levels of analysis to stimulate theory development' 'A paradoxical theory of SSCM will need to strike a balance between the contradictory purposes of explanation and normativity'	Problematization approach	Theory	SSCM discourse / paradigms	Theoretical tensions	To understand

Author (year)/ journal	Title	Aims and research questions	Findings	Research approach and context	Level of analysis	Unit of analysis	Paradox type/ category	Paradox approach
Kristal et al. (2010)/*JOM*	The Effect of an Ambidextrous Supply Chain Strategy on Combinative Competitive Capabilities and Business Performance	'To investigate the influence of an ambidextrous supply chain strategy on manufacturers' combinative competitive capabilities – the ability to excel simultaneously on competitive capabilities of quality, delivery, flexibility, and cost – and, in turn, on business performance' *In practice, can we classify a group of manufacturers that follow an ambidextrous strategy in the context of supply chain management? Given that ambidextrous SC strategy is a viable approach, does an ambidextrous SC strategy coincide with combinative competitive capabilities and business performance?*	'Finds that an ambidextrous supply chain strategy coincides with combinative competitive capabilities and business performance. This contradicts conventional wisdom that argues for tradeoffs between exploration and exploitation'	Survey Manufacturing (US)	Organizational	Supply chain strategy	Combinative competitive capabilities	To verbalize
Maalouf (2016)/ *LJOPM*	Managing Paradoxical Tensions during the Implementation of Lean Capabilities for Improvement	'To deepen the understanding of lean implementation intricacies, and contribute to sustaining lean in companies' *What organizational paradoxes are salient during the building of lean structures of improvement and how have they been managed?*	'Identifies three types of organizational paradoxes in lean: organizing, performing, and belonging. Also, points to a range of managerial responses used for dealing with the three paradoxes and facilitating lean transformation'	Qualitative Denmark	Individual	Lean implementation projects	Organizing, performing and belonging	To understand

Author (year)/ journal	Title	Aims and research questions	Findings	Research approach and context	Level of analysis	Unit of analysis	Paradox type/ category	Paradox approach
Chandrasekaran et al. (2012)/*JOM*	Antecedents to Ambidexterity Competency in High Technology Organizations	'To advance understanding of the antecedents that lead to ambidexterity in considering its multilevel nature' *What are the antecedents to competency in ambidexterity for high-tech organizations?*	'Argues that a competency in ambidexterity involves three capabilities at different organizational levels: decision risk (strategic level), structural differentiation (project level), and contextual alignment (meso level)' 'Results indicate that decision risk and contextual alignment affect ambidexterity competency for high tech organizations. Structural differentiation does not affect ambidexterity competency but has mixed effects on R&D [research and development] project performance'	Survey	Business units	Exploration and exploitation R&D projects	Exploration and exploitation	To verbalize
Schmidt et al. (2017) / *JSCM*	The Supply Chain Position Paradox: Green Practices and Firm Performance	'To explore the contextual role of a firm's supply chain position (SCP) on the adoption of green supply chain management (GSCM) practices and their performance implications' *How does supply chain position influence the level of GSCM practices and the 'GSCM practice–performance link'?*	'Shows that firms located further downstream in the supply chain invest more in GSCM practices while they paradoxically gain decreasing performance benefits. In turn, upstream firms with generally lower GSCM practice levels gain increasingly higher performance. This phenomenon is called the SCP paradox'	Survey	Business unit	GSCM practice-performance of firms	SCP paradox	To verbalize

Note: *AMJ = Academy of Management Journal; AMR = Academy of Management Review; JBE = Journal of Business Ethics; OrgScience = Organization Science; OrgStudies = Organization Studies; JSCM = Journal of Supply Chain Management; IJPDLM = International Journal of Physical Distribution and Logistics Management; JOM = Journal of Operations Management; IJOPM = International Journal of Operations and Production Management.*

16. Contingency theory and the information processing view

Virpi Turkulainen

INTRODUCTION

Contingency theory is one of the focal theoretical lenses used to study organizations and has also been the theoretical foundation for a substantial body of empirical research in a variety of topic areas in operations and supply chain management (OSCM). The origins of contingency theory go back to the 1960s and 1970s; the theory was developed to solve some of the problems of the bureaucratic theory as well as the 'best practice view' of management (Donaldson, 2001; Sousa and Voss, 2008; Van de Ven et al., 2013). Contingency theory dominated academic conversations on organizations and organization design over those decades and still continues to be both the focus of organizational research (for example, Luo and Donaldson, 2013; Sinha and Van de Ven, 2005; Turkulainen and Ketokivi, 2013; Van de Ven et al., 2013) as well as the theoretical basis of empirical research in various disciplinary areas, including OSCM (for example, Flynn et al., 2010; Ketokivi and Schroeder, 2004; Shenhar, 2001; Tenhiälä, 2011).[1] Contingency theory also serves as the underlying foundation for several management theories and practices, such as the information processing view (Galbraith, 1973; Tushman and Nadler, 1978) and the configuration perspective (Meyer et al., 1993).

The fundamental argument of contingency theory has often been translated into the famous statement that 'there is no one best way to organize' (Galbraith, 1973). Traditional contingency theory and theorizing, however, focuses specifically on developing detailed and in-depth understanding of organization design (Burns and Stalker, 1961; Lawrence and Lorsch, 1967b; Thompson, 1967; Van de Ven et al., 1976; Woodward, 1965), subsequently being called the 'structural contingency theory' (Donaldson, 2001). This research has been developed into a more generic contingency theory argument; the basic argument of the majority of research building on contingency theory is that the relationship between two variables is impacted upon by a third variable (Donaldson, 2001). This can be interpreted in the context of organization design so that the relationship between organizational design and the contextual factors impacts upon the effectiveness of an organization, essentially comparing the effectiveness of organization design in different contextual conditions. While the focus of the foundational work on contingency theory is on organizations and organization design, essentially any proposition with a moderating variable is a contingency theory argument (Van de Ven et al., 2013). In line with this, the 'strategic contingency theory' examines relationships where strategy serves as the contextual factor (Dean and Snell, 1996; Ketokivi and Schroeder, 2004).

In the context of OSCM, similar conversations about the value of best practices are evident. While many OSCM practices, such as lean and total quality management (TQM), have traditionally been assumed to be universally applicable and beneficial, there is also criticism that these conclusions have been made based on anecdotal evidence and case studies of a very specific type of organizations (for example, 'world class manufacturing organizations' operating globally in high-tech industries) (Sousa and Voss, 2008). As a response to these conversations, research on OSCM practices has shifted to developing understanding of the contextual conditions under which those practices are applicable and valuable (Sousa and Voss, 2008). One of the earliest works in OSCM building on the foundations of contingency theory is the work of Skinner (1969); his notion of fit between the manufacturing strategy and the production system essentially forms the foundations of the strategic contingency theory of OSCM (Ketokivi and Schroeder, 2004). This was then further developed, for example, by Hayes and Wheelwright (1984). Interestingly, while the early works of contingency theory research in OSCM build mainly on the strategic contingency argument, the majority of contingency studies in OSCM as of today have built on the notion that the internal or external environment affects the effectiveness of various operations practices (Geraldi et al., 2011; Sousa and Voss, 2008). This is also evident in the review of contingency theory research in OSCM presented later in this chapter.

KEY ASSUMPTIONS AND CONSTRUCTS

Underlying Assumptions about Human Nature

Contingency theory builds on the assumption of organizations as 'open rational systems' (as opposed to closed and/or natural systems), according to the classification framework presented by Scott (1998). First, the rational systems view perceives organizations as instruments designed to attain specific goals. Thus, the goals are predetermined and the organization is designed and managed to achieve those goals. The open systems perspective, on the other hand, perceives organizations as capable of maintaining themselves because of throughput of resources from the environment.

A fundamental underlying assumption about human behaviour that contingency theory builds on is that human behaviour is 'boundedly rational' (March and Simon, 1958). This means that the decision makers are rational, but constrained by their limitations to gather, interpret and understand information, as well as to make calculations about the optimum solution (Cyert and March, 1992). Hence, while the decision makers aim at finding the optimum solution to their decision making problem, they are not necessarily able to identify the best, optimum solution; rather, for example, they simplify the decision making problem, set targets, and identify a solution that satisfy those targets (March and Simon, 1958). The concept of bounded rationality integrates the fundamental elements of rational systems: goal specificity and formalization (Scott, 1998). By focusing on cognitive limitations to rationality, contingency theory does not address, for example, opportunism in decision making.

Levels and Units of Analysis

The level of analysis in research on the foundations of contingency theory varies. Often the level of analysis in contingency theory is an organization, such as the firm (Lawrence and Lorsch, 1967a) or a work unit, which refers to the smallest formal grouping of individuals in an organization, such as a department or an organizational unit (Gresov, 1990; Van de Ven and Delbecq, 1974). In the OSCM context, contingency theory has been applied, for example, at the level of a project (Geraldi et al., 2011; Yan and Dooley, 2013), a functional

Table 16.1   Focal concepts and assumptions

	Definition	Example references
Focal concepts		
Contingency variables	Any factor or variable of the organizational context or situational characteristic, which affects the organization. Contingency variables can be but are not necessarily under the control of the organization.	Chenhall (2003); Donaldson (2001); Sousa and Voss (2008); Thompson (1967)
Organization design (or another management decision variable)	Organizational structure and internal arrangement of work, for example, organizational differentiation and integration (or any management decision variable).	Greenwood and Miller (2010); Lawrence and Lorsch (1967a, 1967b); Sousa and Voss (2008)
Effectiveness	How well the organization is able to achieve what it is trying to achieve.	Donaldson (2001); Turkulainen and Ketokivi (2013)
Fit	Congruence between the organizational context and design (selection), interaction of a pair of organizational context and design variables affects performance (interaction), and internal consistency of multiple contingencies and structural variables (systems).	Donaldson and Joffe (2014); Drazin and Van de Ven (1985); Venkatraman (1989)
Focal assumptions		
Bounded rationality	Decision makers are rational but constrained by their limitations to gather, interpret and understand information as well as to make calculations about optimal decisions.	Cyert and March (1992); March and Simon (1958)

unit, such as the purchasing function (Bals et al., 2018; Patrucco et al., 2019; Trautmann et al., 2009), a manufacturing plant (Ketokivi and Schroeder, 2004; Turkulainen and Ketokivi, 2012), a firm (Das et al., 2000; Flynn et al., 2010; Swink and Schoenherr, 2015), as well as interorganizational levels in the supply chain setting (Bensaou and Venkatraman, 1995; Song and Di Benedetto, 2008).

The unit of analysis in the classical contingency theory is an organizational dyad, such as the dyads between different functional units of production, fundamental research, applied research and sales (Lawrence and Lorsch, 1967a, 1967b). Similarly, in OSCM research focusing on organizational design aspects, such as integration, the unit of analysis is oftentimes a dyad; either intra-organizational (Turkulainen et al., 2013) or interorganizational (for example, buyer–suppliers relationships, BSRs) (Kaipia and Turkulainen, 2017; Song and Di Benedetto, 2008). However, research building on the foundations of focal contingency theory argument, and looking at a variety of moderation effects, is applied in diverse units of analysis and operations practices (for a review, see Sousa and Voss, 2008).

Focal Concepts

The focal concepts of classic contingency theory are: (1) contingency variables; (2) organization design or any other management decision variable; (3) effectiveness; and (4) fit. These are presented in Table 16.1, with explanations and references, and further discussed in the following subsections. The relationships of the focal concepts are illustrated in Figure 16.1.

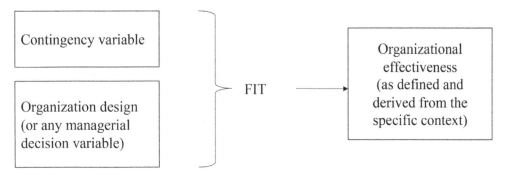

Source: Adapted from Tushman and Nadler (1978).

Figure 16.1   Relationships of the focal concepts

Contingency Variables

Contingency variables, as perceived by contingency theory, refer to variables of the organizational context, which affect the organization and can be (but are not necessarily) directly under the control of the organization (Thompson, 1967). Research has identified and examined a variety of contingencies and their impact. Some of the contingencies are external to the organization and some are internal; the external contingencies affecting the internal ones (Donaldson, 2001). Contingencies identified and examined in the classic contingency theory research include, for example, organizational size (Blau, 1970; Child, 1973; Pugh et al., 1969; Van de Ven et al., 1976), organizational age (Pugh et al., 1969), strategy (Chandler, 1962; Miles and Snow, 1978), innovation (Aiken and Hage, 1968; Burns and Stalker, 1961), technology (Pugh et al., 1969; Woodward, 1965), environmental uncertainty (Lawrence and Lorsch, 1967a), task uncertainty (Gresov, 1990; Van de Ven and Delbecq, 1974; Van de Ven et al., 1976), task interdependence (Thompson, 1967; Van de Ven et al., 1976) and dependence on other organizations (Pugh et al., 1969).

Several authors present comprehensive reviews of contingencies used in research (Chenhall, 2003; Donaldson, 2001). Furthermore, the numerous contingencies included in the plethora of studies have been classified in various ways: for example, Donaldson (2001) classifies them under the three categories of task uncertainty (for example, environmental and technological change), task interdependence (for example, strategy, technology) and size; while Sousa and Voss (2008) present a literature review on contingency theory in OSCM and divide research into four broad categories depending on the studied contingencies: national context and culture (for example, early works on operations practices in Japan versus the Western countries), firm size, strategic context (especially manufacturing strategy), and other organizational contextual variables (for example, industry, age).

Research in the PSM setting has assessed contingencies of, for example, purchase importance (Trautmann et al., 2009), product/category complexity (Schleper et al., 2020; Trautmann et al., 2009), technological newness (Hong and Hartley, 2011), strength of BSR (Fynes and Voss, 2002), level of purchasing maturity (Bals et al., 2018; Schleper et al., 2020), purchase novelty (Schleper et al., 2020; Trautmann et al., 2009), absorptive capacity (Kauppi et al., 2013), new venture's power and commitment to the supplier (Song and Di Benedetto, 2008), supply environment characteristics such as regulations and institutional environment (Patrucco et al., 2019; Richter et al., 2019; Trautmann et al., 2009), industry context (Brandon-Jones and Knoppen, 2018), environmental complexity (Bals et al., 2018; Richter et al., 2019), dynamism and volatility (Bals et al., 2018; Trautmann et al., 2009), as well as purchase and corporate strategy (Ates et al., 2018; Bals et al., 2018), and interdependence of the purchasing units (Trautmann et al., 2009).

In the broader OSCM research, studies have included, for example, contingencies such as production process type (Shou et al., 2018; Tenhiälä, 2011), process span (Swink and Schoenherr, 2015), technological uncertainty or newness (Hong and Hartley, 2011; Shenhar, 2001; Turkulainen and Swink, 2017), fit novelty (Adler, 1995), project complexity (Geraldi et al., 2011; Shenhar, 2001), fit analysability (Adler, 1995), product life cycle stage (Mahapatra et al., 2012), firm size (Jayaram et al., 2010), organizational structure (Zhang et al., 2012), cross-functional integration (Pérez-Luño et al., 2019) and industry type (Jayaram et al., 2010). Contingencies related to the surrounding environment include environmental uncertainty (Pagell and Krause, 2004), demand uncertainty (O'Leary-Kelly and Flores, 2002), dynamism of the environment (Helkio and Tenhiala, 2013; Wong et al., 2011; Zhang et al., 2012), environmental unpredictability (Wong et al., 2011), competitive intensity (Mahapatra et al., 2012), international competition (Das et al., 2000) and national context (Brush et al., 1999). Strategic contingencies used in broader OSCM research include business strategy (O'Leary-Kelly and Flores, 2002), strategic proprieties (Ketokivi and Schroeder, 2004), strategy alignment (Swink et al., 2005), emphasis on flexibility (Kathuria and Partovi, 1999), strategic role of the plant (Maritan et al., 2004) and strategic priority of the outsourced item (Kaipia and Turkulainen, 2017).

Organization Design (or Another Managerial Decision Variable)

Organization design refers to the organizational architecture and internal arrangement of work (Greenwood and Miller, 2010). The foundational work on contingency theory by Lawrence and Lorsch (1967a) conceptualizes organization design in terms of differentiation and integration: differentiation refers to segmentation of the organization into subsystems, each of which then tends to develop attributes in relation to the demands posed by its focal environment; integration, on the other hand, is the process of achieving unity and common goals among those subsystems. Examples of other organization design variables include degree of specialization (Burns and Stalker, 1961; Child, 1973; Gresov, 1990; Pugh et al., 1968), vertical span of control (Pugh et al., 1968), centralization of decision making (Burns and Stalker, 1961; Child, 1973; Pugh et al., 1968), degree of authority (Gresov, 1990; Pugh et al., 1968), formalization (Burns and Stalker, 1961; Child, 1973; Pugh et al., 1968), standardization of work (Child, 1973; Gresov, 1990; Pugh et al., 1968), level of expertise (Van de Ven and Delbecq, 1974), level of routinization of task activities (Van de Ven and Delbecq, 1974), and personal, impersonal and group coordination modes (Van de Ven et al., 1976).

In the OSCM context, contingency theory research has addressed organization design, for example, in terms of the purchasing and supply organization (PSO) and procurement organization designs (Bals et al., 2018; Bals and Turkulainen, 2017), different aspects of cross-functional and internal supply chain integration (Adler, 1995; O'Leary-Kelly and Flores, 2002; Swink and Schoenherr, 2015; Turkulainen et al., 2017), configurations of global plant network in terms of plant locations within the global plant network (Brush et al., 1999), and plant autonomy in decision making within the firm's global plant network (Maritan et al., 2004). In the broader supply chain setting, organization design has been studied, for example, in terms of supply chain integration (Flynn et al., 2010) and supplier involvement in radical innovation (Song and Di Benedetto, 2008).

However, the contingency argument has been extended to other management decision variables than just organization design. In fact, Sousa and Voss (2008) call this the 'response variable', emphasizing that the concept is essentially any organizational or managerial action, which in the OSCM area are the variety of operations management practices, such as the quality management practices (Fynes and Voss, 2002; Jayaram et al., 2010; Zhang et al., 2012), enterprise resource planning (ERP) systems (Tenhiälä and Helkio, 2015), planning methods (Tenhiälä, 2011), e-procurement practices (Kauppi et al., 2013), as well as human resource management (HRM) practices in the manufacturing setting (Ahmad and Schroeder, 2003).

Effectiveness

Performance in contingency theory refers to effectiveness, and essentially means how well the organization is able to achieve whatever it is trying to achieve; while some organizations focus on efficiency, some focus on growth or innovation (Donaldson, 2001). This highlights the perspective of rational organizations as presented above. It is important to note that effectiveness is not the same as performance, even though many scholars (for example, Donaldson, 2001) use these terms interchangeably. The key point of effectiveness is the link between organizational goals and organizational performance; performance as such can be measured, for example, by financial measures or operational measures independently of whether they are the main goals of the organization or not. Hence, effectiveness fundamentally depends on the context, and this context dependence is especially critical when the organization is embedded in a broader system, such as a supply chain (Turkulainen and Ketokivi, 2013). Classical measures of organizational effectiveness in the manufacturing context are, for example, manufacturing cost efficiency, conformance quality, flexibility and delivery (Hayes and Wheelwright, 1984). However, Turkulainen and Ketokivi (2013) suggest that the dependent variable of effectiveness should be empirically derived as it depends on the context. This means that we should not make assumptions about the organizational goals but, rather, empirically assess them to ensure that the performance measures we use are in fact the focal goals of the organization.

Fit

Fit is at the heart of contingency theory argument and theorizing. The fundamental assumption and hypothesis in contingency theory is that organizations which have a fit between organization design and contingencies are more effective (Donaldson, 2001). At the general level this can be translated to the assumption that organizations which have fit between the management decision variable under investigation and contextual variables are more effective (Donaldson, 2001). There is no common understanding and agreement about the theoretical meaning of fit; rather, it has been conceptualized and operationalized in different ways. One conceptualization makes a distinction between three types of fit: 'fit as selection' (that is, congruence between the organizational context and design), 'fit as interaction' (that is, interaction of a pair of organizational context and design variables affects performance), and 'fit as systems' (that is, internal consistency between multiple organizational contextual and design variables affects performance) (Drazin and Van de Ven, 1985). Another conceptualization identifies six different types of fit: 'fit as moderation', 'fit as mediation', 'fit as matching', 'fit as gestalts', 'fit as profile deviation' and 'fit as covariation' (Venkatraman, 1989). Clarifying the form of fit is essential in theoretical discussions and in ensuring that the empirical operationalization of fit is then in line with it (Venkatraman, 1989). Some of the critique towards contingency theory also links to the conceptualizations of fit (Meyer et al., 1993).

RELATIONSHIPS BETWEEN THE VARIABLES

The generic argument of the structural contingency theory is that the fit between the organization design and the contextual factors impacts upon the effectiveness of an organization (Donaldson, 2001). This can be divided into three simple core arguments: (1) there is a relationship between the contingency variable and the organization design; (2) the contingency variable determines the organization design; and (3) there is a fit between the contingency variable and the organization design variable that leads to higher effectiveness (Donaldson, 2001). Taken together, contingency theory views organization design as a constrained optimization problem: at the organizational level, this involves maximizing the effectiveness by minimizing the misfit between the environmental demands and internal organization design (Van de Ven et al., 2013). This in turn requires maximizing the benefits of differentiation, while minimizing the costs of integration (Lawrence and Lorsch, 1967a). As we can see here, the contingency theory notion that organizations should adapt their structures to the requirements posed by the environment follows the rationality argument as presented above. Moreover, the notion that organizations and units within organizations face different contextual conditions and environments, and subsequently different challenges, is fundamentally the open systems perspective as presented above.

Considering the contingency variable of environmental stability, the classic studies on organization design make a distinction between two contrasting organizational designs of mechanistic (high degree of specialization, centralization of decision making, and formalization) and organic (low specialization, decentralization of decision making, and low level of formalization), suggesting that they are suitable for different environments. The mechanistic structure is effective in stable conditions; and the organic structure in changing conditions, as it is able to respond quickly to new problems and unforeseen requirements (Burns and Stalker, 1961). Organizational size then has been suggested to be associated with higher concentration of authority (Pugh et al., 1969), and that in effective larger organizations, the levels of decentralization of decision making, formalization and specialization are higher (that is, bureaucratic structure) (Donaldson, 2001). Moreover, organizational age has been suggested to be negatively related to concentration of authority (Pugh et al., 1969).

Important to note here is that typically empirical research considers the relationships between the contingency and the organization design as bivariate relationships (reductionist approach), looking at one set of variables at a time. Furthermore, the second argument above is linked with the assumption that a change in a contingency enforces a change in the design. To further clarify the relationship between the environment and the organization design, Donaldson (2001) presents the SARFIT (structural adaptation to regain fit) model. It states that an organization is initially in a state of fit; fit positively affects performance. A change in the contingency variable then implies a misfit between the organization design and the contingency, leading to lower effectiveness. When effectiveness becomes so low that it is less than satisficing, then the organization adapts its design to regain fit and again achieve higher effectiveness. However, the organization is not considered merely responsive to the environment; rather, the organization also has strategic choice (Child, 1972), and the relationship between the environment and the organization is essentially reciprocal. While this is the underlying argument, most empirical research, however, takes a static perspective and merely assumes that the organization adapts to reach fit. Recent research further elaborates the notion of fit and proposes a 'compensatory misfit theory', suggesting that over-fitting the organization design (that is, the level of a specific organization design variable is too high to fit the contingencies) can compensate for an under-fitting design (that is, the level of another organization design variable is too low and hence a misfit) (Luo and Donaldson, 2013), and also brings up for further discussion fit to multiple contingencies (Donaldson and Joffe, 2014).

Information Processing Perspective

The information processing perspective further develops the contingency theory argument, proposing the conceptualizing of organizations as information processing systems (Galbraith, 1973; Tushman and Nadler, 1978). It was developed partly to respond to the lack of clarify in terms of the concept of fit of contingency theory (Tushman and Nadler, 1978). Information processing refers to gathering, interpreting and synthesizing information and, hence, is different from mere data as it means a change in knowledge (Tushman and Nadler, 1978). As organizations are open systems, they are assumed to face uncertainty from their environment and subsequently need to develop information processing capacity to manage those information processing requirements in order to be effective. Furthermore, due to bounded rationality, dividing the organization into a hierarchical structure implies that different organizational levels possess different stocks of knowledge, increasing the challenge of information processing (Conner and Prahalad, 1996; Galbraith, 1973). In addition, also increasing task complexity, for example in terms of strategic scope, is suggested to require more complex information flows (Turkulainen and Ketokivi, 2013). Organizations facilitate information processing capacity by their structure and variety of integration mechanisms, which vary both in their capacity to facilitate information processing as well as in their costs. The information processing perspective has been used extensively in research in OSCM (for a review, see Busse et al., 2017). While the original idea of the information processing perspective was developed within the context of an organization, it has also been later extended to the interorganizational level to develop understanding of buyer–supplier relationships and supply chains (Bensaou and Venkatraman, 1995; Busse et al., 2017). The information processing perspective is illustrated in Figure 16.2.

Configurational Perspective

The configurational perspective builds on contingency theory, especially aiming to address the criticism on contingency theory in terms of the organizations' need to fit the contingencies, reductionism and multivariatism (Donaldson, 2001; Meyer et al., 1993). Rather, it takes a more holistic perspective, suggesting that organizations cannot be understood by analysing distinct organizational characteristics in isolation. Configurations refer to a 'constellation

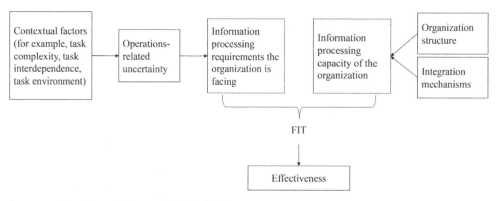

Source: Adapted from Tushman and Nadler (1978).

Figure 16.2   Information processing perspective

of conceptually distinct characteristics that commonly occur together' (Meyer et al., 1993, p. 1175). According to the configuration perspective, organizations can be classified into a few configurations in terms of a combination of several variables (for example, strategy and structure; Miller, 1986). The variables need to fit each other in order for the organization to be effective, assuming that there are a few potential fits. This links to conceptualizing fit as system (Drazin and Van de Ven, 1985) or fit as gestalts (Venkatraman, 1989). Configurations can be based on typologies (Ahmad and Schroeder, 2003; Burns and Stalker, 1961; Miles and Snow, 1978) or empirically based taxonomies (Adler, 1995; Bensaou and Venkatraman, 1995; Flynn et al., 2010), though the latter approach has sometimes been criticized due to lack of theory (Miller, 1996). Some of the configuration research does not even focus on finding fit with any contingencies, presenting a contrasting view to contingency theory (Donaldson, 2001).

Few studies have built on the configuration perspective within the OSCM. Research has, for example, empirically identified configurations of design-manufacturing coordination (Adler, 1995), configurations of BSRs (Bensaou and Venkatraman, 1995), configurations of internal, customer and supplier integration, and their operational and business performance (Flynn et al., 2010), as well as configurations of internal supply chain integration mechanisms and how they are associated with different integration needs (Turkulainen et al., 2017). In the purchasing and supply management (PSM) setting, research has identified configurations of organization designs in the context of public procurement (Patrucco et al., 2019).

OSCM RESEARCH BUILDING ON CONTINGENCY THEORY AND THE INFORMATION PROCESSING VIEW

Contingency theory is valuable for OSCM research because it provides an opportunity to explain OSCM phenomena and advance the understanding of, for example, the use of various operations management practices and their implications in different operational contexts. Interestingly, while the early works building on contingency theory in OSCM focus on the strategic contingency argument (Hayes and Wheelwright, 1984; Skinner, 1969), the main bulk of contingency studies in OSCM have built on the notion that the environment in which the organization operates affects the effectiveness of various operations practices (Sousa and Voss, 2008). Research in OSCM has also abundantly built on the information processing view (IPV) (for a review, see Busse et al., 2017); the IPV is useful for OSCM for multiple reasons, including the boundary spanning nature of supply chain management (SCM) as well as increasing uncertainty due to the shortening of product life cycles and increasing customer expectations and competition (Swink et al., 2007). Research has also continued to see advances in the contingency theory arguments by elaborations in the OSCM context (Turkulainen and Ketokivi, 2013), or elaboration of IPV in the OSCM context (Busse et al., 2017; Flynn and Flynn, 1999).

As in general in research building on contingency theory, theoretical and practical contributions of OSCM contingency research can be achieved by: (1) identifying important contingency variables that distinguish between contexts; (2) grouping different contexts based on these contingency variables; and (3) determining the most effective internal organization designs or responses in each major group (Sousa and Voss, 2008). When building on the foundations of generic contingency theory arguments, it is important to note that contextualizing the generic contingencies is crucial; development of the hypothesis requires elaboration of the theoretical arguments in a specific context. Hence, for example, hypothesizing that environmental uncertainty acts as a contingency in any practice–performance link is not universally established.

In the following, I present an overview of some of the research in the OSCM context that builds on contingency theory. On one hand, research is divided into studies focusing specifically on the PSM context, and studies in the more generic OSCM setting. And on the other hand, research is divided into studies focusing on organization designs (mainly following the line of the structural contingency theory; Donaldson, 2001) and studies on the generic contingency relationships (Sousa and Voss, 2008; Van de Ven et al., 2013).

Research on Organization Design in the PSM Context

Several studies have focused on organization design within the PSM context, building on the foundations of the structural contingency theory. These include developing a comprehensive contingency framework of PSO structures and identifying external and internal contingencies affecting the choice of PSO structure (Bals et al., 2018), and developing a conceptual framework for organization design in the specific context of public procurement and the dependence of organization design on several internal and external contextual factors (Patrucco et al., 2019).

In the global sourcing area, studies have addressed integration in the global sourcing organization, proposing that ways to manage integration in global sourcing organizations depend on three contingencies of category characteristics, supply environment characteristics and interdependence of the purchasing units (Trautmann et al., 2009), and how companies actually make global sourcing decisions, and the effect of contextual conditions of sourcing maturity, product complexity and purchase novelty on the use of these archetypes of decision making (Schleper et al., 2020). Within the sustainable supply chain management setting, research has addressed how different types of sustainability-related uncertainties can be managed by applying a fitting configuration of processing mechanisms in the context of sustainable supply management (Foerstl et al., 2018).

Research on Generic Contingency Relationships in the PSM Context

A more generic contingency argument has also served as the foundation in PSM research. These studies include the contingency effect of the strength of the BSR on the relationship between quality practices and performance (Fynes and Voss, 2002), how buyers manage the interface among the interdependent first-tier suppliers and the contingency effect of techno-logical newness (Hong and Hartley, 2011), and the contingent effect of absorptive capacity on the relationship between e-purchasing tools and category performance (Kauppi et al., 2013). Research has also addressed the influence of the BSR on the performance of the service supplier and the contextual effect of the contractual support and service site size (Karatzas et al., 2016), as well as the relationships between the purchasing recognition, purchasing involvement, and dynamic capability and its impact on cost and innovation performance and the contingent effect of the industry context (Brandon-Jones and Knoppen, 2018).

In the new product development (NPD) setting, research has assessed the contingent value of specific integrative devices on project performance under various conditions of uncertainty (Yan and Dooley, 2013), and supplier involvement in radical NPD, as well as the contingency effects of new venture power and commitment to the supplier (Song and Di Benedetto, 2008). In the international purchasing context, Richter et al. (2019) test the performance implications of a variety of organization design dimensions under different conditions of complexity and uncertainty of a specific national institutional context. And finally, building on the strategic contingency theory, research has addressed how the strategic priority of cost versus quality is associated with organizational integration of the BSR in an outsourcing context (Kaipia and Turkulainen, 2017), as well as to what extent the (mis)fit between cost of innovation purchas-ing strategy and purchasing structure (centralization, formalization and cross-functionality) impacts upon purchasing performance (Ates et al., 2018).

Research on Organization Design in the Broader OSCM Context

Research has also built on the structural contingency theory to address various aspects of organization design within the broader OSCM context. Research has developed understanding of the mediating role of supply chain process variability on the relationship between organi-zation structure and performance, as well as the effect of predictability of demand (Germain et al., 2008). Several studies have built on contingency theory to develop contextualized understanding of organizational integration; for example, to identify configurations of design–manufacturing coordination and the effect of fit novelty and analysability (Adler, 1995), to identify different configurations of supply chain integration (Flynn et al., 2010), to understand how integration of operations–sales in global project operations in project sales versus project execution phases is managed, as well as how the contingencies of project uniqueness, ambi-guity, complexity and geographical dispersion are associated with how integration is managed (Turkulainen et al., 2013), and to identify different patterns of internal supply chain integration and the associated reasons for why integration is needed (Turkulainen et al., 2017).

Furthermore, contingency theory-based organization design research in the broader OSCM context has examined the effect of fit and misfit in the use of HRM practices in an operations setting (Ahmad and Schroeder, 2003), the links between the dynamism and competitiveness of the business environment and various supply chain strategies, as well as their relationships with the various supply management practices (Prajogo et al., 2018), and lately, turning focus to sustainability, has identified how different forms of sustainability-related uncertainty can be managed with different types of sustainability-driven supply chain modification mechanisms (Busse et al., 2017).

In the international operations context, research has addressed how plant location decisions are affected by the choice of whether the plant is integrated or independent in the focal network, and domestic or foreign as compared to the headquarters (Brush et al., 1999), and whether the strategic role of the plant has implications on organization design in terms of plant autonomy on planning, control and production decisions (Maritan et al., 2004).

Finally, in the project operations context, Davies and Frederiksen (2013) elaborate the volume–variety matrix (Hayes and Wheelwright, 1979) and the linkage between the product and the organization design, suggesting that at the project level, high-variety, unique project products are to be matched with one-off project organizations to develop and complete the product. This has been further elaborated at the level of product and organization subsystem components in the context of major projects (Artto and Turkulainen, 2018).

Research on Generic Contingency Relationships in the Broader OSCM Context

Research building on the generic contingency argument in the broader OSCM context is vast and varied. While Ketokivi and Schroeder (2004) study both the strategic and the structural contingency arguments on the value of variety of manufacturing practices, only a few build on the strategic contingency argument. These include the contingent effect of the emphasis on flexibility priority on the link between workforce management practices and performance (Kathuria and Partovi, 1999), the contingent effect of the manufacturing strategy alignment on the link between various manufacturing practices and capabilities (Swink et al., 2005), and the contingent effects of the financial leverage, internationalization and diversification strategies on the link between chief supply chain officer (CSCO) appointment to the top management team and firm performance (Roh et al., 2016).

The main bulk of these studies assess the effect of the external and internal environment. The value of flexibility strategy in the manufacturing context is suggested to be contingent on environmental uncertainty (Pagell and Krause, 2004). Research on the fundamental OSCM practices has addressed, for example, contextual factors affecting the use of quality management practices, suggesting that their value depends on dynamism of the operating environment and organization structure (Zhang et al., 2012) and that the value of the quality system design is contingent on firm size, TQM duration and industry type (Jayaram et al., 2010), or international competition (Das et al., 2000). Research has also addressed the contingent use of planning methods, suggesting that the effectiveness of sophisticated planning methods depends on process type (Tenhiälä, 2011), the contextual value of ERP systems in dynamic and stable environments (Tenhiälä and Helkio, 2015), as well as the contextualized value of information sharing in the sales and operations planning (S&OP) process (Kaipia et al., 2017).

Topic-wise, the majority of OSCM studies building on contingency theory have focused on contextualizing the value of internal and external integration. The value of internal, cross-functional integration has been suggested to be contingent on, for example, process span (Swink et al., 2007; Swink and Schoenherr, 2015), operations performance dimension (Turkulainen and Ketokivi, 2012), strategic scope (Turkulainen and Ketokivi, 2013), level of differentiation (Turkulainen and Ketokivi, 2013), as well as the level of supplier and customer integration (Flynn et al., 2010). Furthermore, the performance value of marketing–

manufacturing integration has been suggested to be contingent on business strategy and demand uncertainty (O'Leary-Kelly and Flores, 2002). Supply chain integration, on the other hand, has been suggested to provide contextual value depending on unpredictability and change (Wong et al., 2011), and type of production systems (Shou et al., 2018). Research has analysed the proactive management of the critical suppliers and the influence of competitive intensity and product life cycle stage (Mahapatra et al., 2012). And linked to these, a study has contextualized the value of involving internal supply chain personnel in a firm's product innovation activities, suggesting that it depends on the organization's technology context and the level of operational supplier integration, as well as the interaction of these two contingency factors (Turkulainen and Swink, 2017).

In the broader SCM setting, research building on contingency theory has also developed a contingent resource-based view to understand the relationship between specific resources (information sharing and connectivity), capabilities and performance, as well as the contingent effect of supply chain complexity (Brandon-Jones et al., 2014).

And finally, the classical contingency theory statement of 'one size does not fit all projects' was brought to the project operations context when Shenhar (2001) studied projects and their differences under two contingencies – technological uncertainty and complexity in terms of system scope – suggesting than when planning for projects and their management, project characteristics need to be considered, calling for a project-specific approach to project management. The contingency variable of project complexity has been further elaborated by Geraldi et al. (2011).

Avenues for Future Research

As the review above shows, contingency theory has served as the foundation in a vast variety of studies in OSCM over the past decades, as well as in a number of studies in the more specific area of PSM. Interestingly, however, based on their review of 23 years of sourcing literature, Giunipero et al. (2019) conclude that contingency theory is rarely used in studies on sourcing: only 3 per cent of articles were identified as using it as the underlying theory, though the number of these studies has been increasing in the twenty-first century. This provides ample opportunities for future research in PSM.

Overall, as can be seen in the review of existing contingency studies presented above, contingency theory provides an opportunity to engage in theory-based empirical research to develop elaborated and more detailed understanding of a variety of managerial practices in PSM or other topic areas. For example, future research could engage in a detailed discussion of the focal concepts of contingency theory in a specific area of PSM. This would mean elaborating and contextualizing, first, the broader organizational contingencies and further developing those to a specific managerial decision making area in PSM. Second, research could engage in an in-depth conversation of conceptualizing and empirically assessing effectiveness in that specific PSM setting. Research could then further study the effectiveness of a variety of the specific managerial areas in PSM, utilizing these elaborated contingencies and established effectiveness measures. Moreover, considering different forms of fit also provides opportunities for future research. Overall, engaging in empirical research building, for example on data collected by case studies, provides ample opportunities to develop more in-depth, contextualized understanding of the managerial challenges in PSM. This would also facilitate developing understanding of the contextual richness of the organizations under investigation and subsequently facilitate better understanding of the effects that organizational context may have on the practice–performance relationships.

NOTE

1. In the OSCM context, research on management practices with the contingency theory lens is sometimes referred to as 'OM practice contingency research' (OM PCR) (Geraldi et al., 2011; Sousa and Voss, 2008).

REFERENCES

Adler, P.S. (1995). Interdepartmental Interdependence and Coordination: The Case of the Design/ Manufacturing Interface. *Organization Science*, *6*(2), 147–167.

Ahmad, S., and Schroeder, R.G. (2003). The Impact of Human Resource Management Practices on Operational Performance: Recognizing Country and Industry Differences. *Journal of Operations Management*, *21*(1), 19–43.

Aiken, M., and Hage, J. (1968). Organizational Interdependence and Intra-organizational Structure. *American Sociological Review*, *33*(6), 912–930.

Artto, K., and Turkulainen, V. (2018). It Takes Two to Tango: Product–Organization Interdependence in Managing Major Projects. *International Journal of Operations and Production Management*, *38*(6), 1312–1339.

Ates, M.A., van Raaij, E.M., and Wynstra, F. (2018). The Impact of Purchasing Strategy–Structure (Mis) fit on Purchasing Cost and Innovation Performance. *Journal of Purchasing and Supply Management*, *24*.

Bals, L., Laine, J., and Mugurusi, G. (2018). Evolving Purchasing and Supply Organizations: A Contingency Model for Structural Alternatives. *Journal of Purchasing and Supply Management*, *24*, 41–58.

Bals, L., and Turkulainen, V. (2017). Achieving Efficiency and Effectiveness in Purchasing and Supply Management: Organization Design and Outsourcing. *Journal of Purchasing and Supply Management*, *23*(4), 256–267.

Bensaou, M., and Venkatraman, N. (1995). Configurations of Interorganizational Relationships: A Comparison between U.S. and Japanese Automakers. *Management Science*, *41*(9), 1471–1492.

Blau, P.M. (1970). A Formal Theory of Differentiation in Organizations. *American Sociological Review*, *35*(2), 201–218.

Brandon–Jones, A., and Knoppen, D. (2018). The Role of Strategic Purchasing in Dynamic Capability Development and Deployment – A Contingency Perspective. *International Journal of Operations and Production Management*, *38*(2), 446–473.

Brandon–Jones, E., Squire, B., Autry, C.W., and Petersen, K.J. (2014). A Contingent Resource-Based Perspective of Supply Chain Resilience and Robustness. *Journal of Supply Chain Management*, *50*(3), 55–73.

Brush, T., Maritan, C., and Karnani, A. (1999). The Plant Location Decision in Multinational Manufacturing Firms: An Empirical Analysis of International Business and Manufacturing Strategy Perspectives. *Production and Operations Management*, *8*(2), 109–132.

Burns, T., and Stalker, G.M. (1961). *The Management of Innovation* (3rd edn). London: Tavistock Publications.

Busse, C., Meinlschmidt, J., and Foerstl, K. (2017). Managing Information Processing Needs in Global Supply Chains: A Prerequisite to Sustainable Supply Chain Management. *Journal of Supply Chain Management*, *53*(1), 87–113.

Chandler, A.D. (1962). *Strategy and Structure: Chapters in the History of American Enterprise*. Cambridge, MA: MIT Press.

Chenhall, R.H. (2003). Management control systems design within its organizational context: findings from contingency–based research and directions for the future. *Accounting, Organizations, and Society, 28*(2–3), 127–168.

Child, J. (1972). Organization Structure, Environment, and Performance: The Role of Strategic Choice. *Sociology, 6*(1), 1–22.

Child, J. (1973). Predicting and Understanding Organization Structure. *Administrative Science Quarterly, 18*(2), 168–185.

Conner, K.R., and Prahalad, C.K. (1996). A Resource–based Theory of the Firm: Knowledge versus Opportunism. *Organization Science, 7*(5), 477–501.

Cyert, R.M., and March, J.G. (1992). *The Behavioral Theory of the Firm* (2nd edn). Oxford: Blackwell Publishers.

Das, A., Handfield, R.B., Calantone, R.J., and Ghosh, S. (2000). A Contingent View of Quality Management – The Impact of International Competition on Quality. *Decision Sciences, 31*(3), 649–690.

Davies, A., and Frederiksen, L. (2013). Project–based Innovation: The World after Woodward. In Phillips, N., Sewell, G., and Griffiths, D. (eds), *Technology and Organization: Essays in Honour of Joan Woodward* (Research in the Sociology of Organizations, Vol. 29). Bingley: Emerald, pp. 177–215.

Dean, J.W., Jr, and Snell, S.A. (1996). The Strategic Use of Integrated Manufacturing: An Empirical Examination. *Strategic Management Journal, 17*(6), 459–480.

Donaldson, L. (2001). *The Contingency Theory of Organizations*. Thousand Oaks, CA: SAGE Publications.

Donaldson, L., and Joffe, G. (2014). Fit – The Key to Organizational Design. *Journal of Organization Design, 3*(3), 38–45.

Drazin, R., and Van de Ven, A.H. (1985). Alternative Forms of Fit in Contingency Theory. *Administrative Science Quarterly, 30*(4), 514–539.

Flynn, B.B., and Flynn, E.J. (1999). Information-Processing Alternatives for Coping with Manufacturing Environment Complexity. *Decision Sciences, 30*(4), 1021–1052.

Flynn, B.B., Huo, B., and Zhao, X. (2010). The Impact of Supply Chain Integration on Performance: A Contingency and Configuration Approach. *Journal of Operations Management, 28*(1), 58–71.

Foerstl, K., Meinlschmidt, J., and Busse, C. (2018). It's a Match! Choosing Information Processing Mechanisms to Address Sustainability-Related Uncertainty in Sustainable Supply Management. *Journal of Purchasing and Supply Management, 24.*

Fynes, B., and Voss, C. (2002). The Moderating Effect of Buyer–Supplier Relationships on Quality Practices and Performance. *International Journal of Operations and Production Management, 22*(6), 589–613.

Galbraith, J.R. (1973). *Designing Complex Organizations*. Reading, MA: Addison–Wesley.

Geraldi, J., Maylor, H., and Williams, T. (2011). Now Let's Make It Really Complex (Complicated): A Systematic Review of the Complexities of Projects. *International Journal of Operations and Production Management, 31*(9), 966–990.

Germain, R., Claycomb, C., and Dröge, C. (2008). Supply Chain Variability, Organizational Structure, and Performance: The Moderating Effect of Demand Unpredictability. *Journal of Operations Management, 26*(5), 557–570.

Giunipero, L.C., Bittner, S., Shanks, I., and Cho, M.H. (2019). Analyzing the sourcing literature: Over two decades of research. *Journal of Purchasing and Supply Management, 25.*

Greenwood, R., and Miller, D. (2010). Tackling Design Anew: Getting Back to the Heart of Organizational Theory. *Academy of Management Perspectives, 24*(4), 78–88.

Gresov, C. (1990). Effects of Dependence and Tasks on Unit Design and Efficiency. *Organization Studies, 11*(4), 503–529.

Hayes, R.H., and Wheelwright, S.C. (1979). Link Manufacturing Process and Product Life Cycles. *Harvard Business Review, 57*(1), 133–140.

Hayes, R.H., and Wheelwright, S.C. (1984). *Restoring Our Competitive Edge: Competing Through Manufacturing*. New York: John Wiley & Sons.

Helkio, P., and Tenhiala, A. (2013). A contingency theoretical perspective to the product-process matrix. *International Journal of Operations and Production Management, 33*(2), 216–244.

Hong, Y., and Hartley, J.L. (2011). Managing the Supplier–Supplier Interface in Product Development: The Moderating Role of Technological Newness. *Journal of Supply Chain Management*, *47*(3), 43–62.

Jayaram, J., Ahire, S.L., and Dreyfus, P. (2010). Contingency Relationships of Firm Size, TQM Duration, Unionization, and Industry Context on TQM Implementation – A Focus on Total Effects. *Journal of Operations Management*, *28*(4), 345–356.

Kaipia, R., Holmström, J., Smaros, J., and Rajala, R. (2017). Information sharing for sales and operations planning: Contextualized solutions and mechanisms. *Journal of Operations Management*, *52*, 15–29.

Kaipia, R., and Turkulainen, V. (2017). Managing Integration in Outsourcing Relationships – The Influence of Cost and Quality Priorities. *Industrial Marketing Management*, *61*(2), 114–129.

Karatzas, A., Johnson, M., and Bastl, M. (2016). Relationship Determinants of Performance in Service Triads: A Configurational Approach. *Journal of Supply Chain Management*, *52*(3), 28–47.

Kathuria, R., and Partovi, F.Y. (1999). Work Force Management Practices for Manufacturing Flexibility. *Journal of Operations Management*, 18(1), 21–39.

Kauppi, K., Brandon-Jones, A., Ronchi, S., and van Raaij, E.M. (2013). Tools Without Skills – Exploring the Moderating Effect of Absorptive Capacity on the Relationship between E–Purchasing Tools and Category Performance. *International Journal of Operations and Production Management*, *33*(7), 828–857.

Ketokivi, M.A., and Schroeder, R.G. (2004). Strategic, Structural Contingency and Institutional Explanations in the Adoption of Innovative Manufacturing Practices. *Journal of Operations Management*, *22*(1), 63–89.

Lawrence, P.R., and Lorsch, J.W. (1967a). Differentiation and Integration in Complex Organizations. *Administrative Science Quarterly*, *12*(1), 1–47.

Lawrence, P.R., and Lorsch, J.W. (1967b). *Organization and Environment – Managing Differentiation and Integration*. Boston, MA: Harvard Business School Press.

Luo, B.N., and Donaldson, L. (2013). Misfits in Organization Design. *Journal of Organization Design*, *2*(1), 2–10.

Mahapatra, S.K., Das, A., and Narasimhan, R. (2012). A Contingent Theory of Supplier Management Initiatives: Effects of Competitive Intensity and Product Life Cycle. *Journal of Operations Management*, *30*(5), 406–422. doi:10.1016/j.jom.2012.03.004.

March, J.G., and Simon, H.A. (1958). *Organizations*. Cambridge, MA: Blackwell.

Maritan, C.A., Brush, T.H., and Karnani, A.G. (2004). Plant Roles and Decision Autonomy in Multinational Plant Networks. *Journal of Operations Management*, *22*(5), 489–503.

Meyer, A.D., Tsui, A.S., and Hinings, C.R. (1993). Configurational Approaches to Organizational Analysis. *Academy of Management Journal*, *36*(6), 1175–1195.

Miles, R.E., and Snow, C.C. (1978). *Organizational Strategy, Structure, and Process*. Stanford, CA: Stanford University Press.

Miller, D. (1986). Configurations of Strategy and Structure: Towards a Synthesis. *Strategic Management Journal*, *7*(3), 233–249.

Miller, D. (1996). Configurations Revisited. *Strategic Management Journal*, *17*(7), 505–512.

O'Leary–Kelly, S.W., and Flores, B.E. (2002). The Integration of Manufacturing and Marketing/Sales Decisions: Impact on Organizational Performance. *Journal of Operations Management*, *20*(3), 221–240.

Pagell, M., and Krause, D.R. (2004). Re-exploring the Relationship between Flexibility and the External Environment. *Journal of Operations Management*, *21*(6), 629–649.

Patrucco, A.S., Walker, H., Luzzini, D., and Ronchi, S. (2019). Which Shape Fits Best? Designing the Organizational Form of Local Government Procurement. *Journal of Purchasing and Supply Management*, *25*(3), 100504.

Pérez–Luño, A., Bojica, A., and Golapakrishnan, S. (2019). When More is Less – The Role of Cross-Functional Integration, Knowledge Complexity and Product Innovation in Firm Performance. *International Journal of Operations and Production Management*, *39*(1), 94–115.

Prajogo, D., Mena, C., and Nair, A. (2018). The Fit Between Supply Chain Strategies and Practices: A Contingency Approach and Comparative Analysis. *IEEE Transactions on Engineering Management*, *65*(1).

Pugh, D.S., Hickson, D.J., Hinings, C.R., and Turner, C. (1968). Dimensions of Organization Structure. *Administrative Science Quarterly, 13*(1), 65–105.

Pugh, D.S., Hickson, D.J., Hinings, C.R., and Turner, C. (1969). The Context of Organization Structures. *Administrative Science Quarterly, 14*(1), 91–114.

Richter, N.F., Schlaegel, C., Midgey, D.F., and Tressin, T. (2019). Organizational Structure Characteristics' Influences on International Purchasing Performance in Different Purchasing Locations. *Journal of Purchasing and Supply Management, 25*(4), 100523.

Roh, J., Krause, R., and Swink, M. (2016). The Appointment of Chief Supply Chain Officers to Top Management Teams: A Contingency Model of Firm-Level Antecedents and Consequences. *Journal of Operations Management, 44*, 48–51.

Schleper, M.C., Blome, C., and Stanczyk, A. (2020). Archetypes of Sourcing Decision-Making: The Influence of Contextual Factors on Consensus, Argumentation and Cabal. *International Journal of Operations and Production Management, 40*(2), 117–143.

Scott, W.R. (1998). *Organizations: Rational, Natural, and Open Systems* (5th edn). Upper Saddle River, NJ: Prentice Hall.

Shenhar, A.J. (2001). One Size Does Not Fit All Projects: Exploring Classical Contingency Domains. *Management Science, 47*(3), 394–414.

Shou, Y., Li, Y., Park, Y., and Kang, M. (2018). Supply Chain Integration and Operational Performance: The Contingency Effects of Production Systems. *Journal of Purchasing and Supply Management, 24*(4), 352–360.

Sinha, K.K., and Van de Ven, A.H. (2005). Designing Work Within and Between Organizations. *Organization Science, 16*(4), 389–408.

Skinner, W. (1969). Manufacturing – Missing Link in Corporate Strategy. *Harvard Business Review, 47*(3), 136–145.

Song, M., and Di Benedetto, C.A. (2008). Supplier's Involvement and Success of Radical New Product Development in New Ventures. *Journal of Operations Management, 26*(1), 1–22.

Sousa, R., and Voss, C.A. (2008). Contingency Research in Operations Management Practices. *Journal of Operations Management, 26*(6), 697–713.

Swink, M., Narasimhan, R., and Kim, S.W. (2005). Manufacturing Practices and Strategy Integration: Effects on Cost Efficiency, Flexibility, and Market-Based Performance. *Decision Sciences, 36*(3), 427–457.

Swink, M., Narasimhan, R., and Wang, C. (2007). Managing Beyond the Factory Walls: Effects of Four Types of Strategic Integration on Manufacturing Plant Performance. *Journal of Operations Management, 25*(1), 148–164.

Swink, M., and Schoenherr, T. (2015). The Effects of Cross–Functional Integration on Profitability, Process Efficiency, and Asset Productivity. *Journal of Business Logistics, 36*(1), 69–87.

Tenhiälä, A. (2011). Contingency Theory of Capacity Planning: The Link between Process Types and Planning Methods. *Journal of Operations Management, 29*(1–2), 65–77. doi:10.1016/j.jom.2010.05.003.

Tenhiälä, A., and Helkio, P. (2015). Performance Effects of Using an ERP System for Manufacturing Planning and Control under Dynamic Market Requirements. *Journal of Operations Management, 36*(5), 147–164.

Thompson, J.D. (1967). *Organizations in Action – Social Science Bases of Administrative Theory* (Transaction edn). New Brunswick, NJ: Transaction Publishers.

Trautmann, G., Turkulainen, V., Hartmann, E., and Bals, L. (2009). Integration in the Global Sourcing Organization – An Information Processing Perspective. *Journal of Supply Chain Management, 45*(2), 57–74.

Turkulainen, V., and Ketokivi, M. (2008). Cross-Functional Integration – What are the Real Benefits? Paper presented at the Academy of Management Annual Conference, Anaheim, CA.

Turkulainen, V., and Ketokivi, M. (2012). Cross–functional Integration and Performance – What are the Real Benefits? *International Journal of Operations and Production Management, 32*(4), 447–467.

Turkulainen, V., and Ketokivi, M. (2013). The Contingent Value of Organizational Integration. *Journal of Organization Design, 2*(2), 31–43.

Turkulainen, V., Kujala, J., Artto, K., and Levitt, R. (2013). Organizing in the Context of Global Project-based Firm – The Case of Sales–Operations Interface. *Industrial Marketing Management*, *42*(2), 223–233.

Turkulainen, V., Roh, J., Whipple, J., and Swink, M. (2017). Managing Internal Supply Chain Integration: Integration Requirements and Mechanisms. *Journal of Business Logistics*, *38*(4), 290–309.

Turkulainen, V., and Swink, M.L. (2017). Supply Chain Personnel as Knowledge Resources for Innovation – A Contingency View. *Journal of Supply Chain Management*, *53*(3), 41–59. doi:10.1111/jscm.12133

Tushman, M.L., and Nadler, D. (1978). Information Processing as an Integrating Concept in Organizational Design. *Academy of Management Review*, *3*(3), 613–624.

Van de Ven, A.H., and Delbecq, A.L. (1974). A Task Contingent Model of Work-Unit Design. *Administrative Science Quarterly*, *19*(2), 183–197.

Van de Ven, A.H., Delbecq, A.L., and Koenig, R., Jr (1976). Determinants of Coordination Modes within Organizations. *American Sociological Review*, *41*(2), 322–338.

Van de Ven, A.H., Ganco, M., and Hinings, B. (2013). Returning to the Frontier of Contingency Theory of Organizational and Institutional Designs. *Academy of Management Annals*, *7*(1), 393–440.

Venkatraman, N. (1989). The Concept of Fit in Strategy Research: Toward Verbal and Statistical Correspondence. *Academy of Management Review*, *14*(3), 423–444.

Wong, C.Y., Boon-itt, S., and Wong, C.W.Y. (2011). The Contingency Effects of Environmental Uncertainty on the Relationship between Supply Chain Integration and Operational Performance. *Journal of Operations Management*, *29*(6), 604–615.

Woodward, J. (1965). *Industrial Organization: Theory and Practice* (2nd edn). London: Oxford University Press.

Yan, T., and Dooley, K.J. (2013). Communication Intensity, Goal Congruence, and Uncertainty in Buyer–Supplier New Product Development. *Journal of Operations Management*, *31*(7–8), 523–542.

Zhang, D., Linderman, K., and Schroeder, R. (2012). The Moderating Role of Contextual Factors on Quality Management Practices. *Journal of Operations Management*, *30*(1–2), 12–23.

FURTHER READING

Some Seminal Papers and Books

Galbraith, J.R. (1973). *Designing Complex Organizations*. Reading, MA: Addison–Wesley.

Lawrence, P.R., and Lorsch, J.W. (1967a). Differentiation and Integration in Complex Organizations. *Administrative Science Quarterly*, *12*(1), 1–47.

Lawrence, P.R., and Lorsch, J.W. (1967b). *Organization and Environment – Managing Differentiation and Integration*. Boston, MA: Harvard Business School Press.

Thompson, J.D. (1967). *Organizations in Action – Social Science Bases of Administrative Theory* (Transaction edn). New Brunswick, NJ: Transaction Publishers.

Tushman, M.L., and Nadler, D.A. (1978). Information Processing as an Integrating Concept in Organizational Design. *Academy of Management Review*, *3*(3), 613–624.

Woodward, J. (1965). *Industrial Organization: Theory and Practice* (2nd edn). London: Oxford University Press.

More Recent Advances of Contingency Theory

Burton, R.M., DeSanctis, G., and Obel, B. (2006). *Organizational Design – A Step-by-Step Approach*. New York: Cambridge University Press.

Donaldson, L. (2001). *The Contingency Theory of Organizations*. Thousand Oaks, CA: SAGE Publications.

Joseph, J., and Gaba, V. (2020). Organizational Structure, Information Processing, and Decision-Making: A Retrospective and Road Map for Research. *Academy of Management Annals*, *14*(1), 267–302.

Turner, K.L., and Makhija, M.V. (2012). The Role of Individuals in the Information Processing Perspective. *Strategic Management Journal*, *33*(6), 661–680.
Van de Ven, A.H., Ganco, M., and Hinings, B. (2013). Returning to the Frontier of Contingency Theory of Organizational and Institutional Designs. *Academy of Management Annals*, *7*(1), 393–440.

17. Social exchange theory

Carl Marcus Wallenburg and Robert Handfield

INTRODUCTION

Social exchange theory (SET) views exchange as consisting of interactions that generate obligations, and is valuable in understanding close interfirm collaboration. SET is built on a theoretical framework that provides insight into social components that govern exchange relationships, emphasized by social exchange involving 'give-and-take' between entities, reciprocity and cooperation (Blau, 1964). The author of the theory was not happy with the name 'social exchange theory', noting:

> As I might have anticipated, my theory therefore got stuck with the name of 'exchange theory'. This was too bad, not only because the theory is not limited to social behavior that looks like exchange but also because it suggested that the theory was a special kind of theory, whereas it is a general behavioral psychology, admittedly applied to a limited range of social situations. (Homans, 1984, p. 338)

Nonetheless, SET proposes that individuals or collectives of actors engage in exchange relationships with other actors, expecting that the economic and social rewards will be greater than the costs of the interaction. When this turns out to be the case, the exchange tends to be repeated and, over time, increases trust and commitment and produces relational exchange norms that govern the relationship (Lambe et al., 2001). The underlying assumption is that the actors in a supply chain will try to maximize their net outcome when choosing their exchange partners and deciding how to interact with them.

SET has been extensively applied by supply chain management (SCM) scholars to explain interfirm exchange relationships. Despite its usefulness and influence in our understanding of business-to-business (B2B) exchange, several theoretical ambiguities within SET remain in the supply chain field. To guide future research in the specific domain of purchasing and supply management as well as the broader field of SCM, this chapter first describes SET, then provides an overview of prior applications, and concludes with several avenues for future research for utilizing and extending the theory.

The roots of SET may be traced to 'one of the oldest theories of social behavior', namely that any interaction between individuals is an exchange of resources (Homans, 1958, p. 597). The essence of SET lies in that interactions are motivated by parties seeking rewards and avoiding punishment (Emerson, 1976). The exchanged resources can be not only tangible, such as goods or money, but also intangible, such as social amenities or friendship. As such, SET's origins lie in sociology (especially Homans, 1958, 1961; Gouldner, 1960; Blau, 1964; Emerson, 1976), and social psychology (Thibaut and Kelley, 1959).

An example by Redmond (2015) provides a good illustration of how SET works:

> A friend, who does not own a car, needs a ride home on Saturday to attend his sister's wedding; it is a ninety-mile round-trip. He offers to pay for gas and give you five dollars. You have tentative plans for Saturday, and two hours of driving for five bucks does not seem that appealing, but this is

a friend in need. After you hesitate, your friend offers ten dollars and lunch, so you finally agree. In this exchange, both parties reach an agreement based on comparing how much something will cost relative to the level of reward or benefit that something will provide (a ride home for the friend, and ten dollars and lunch for you).

Sociologist George Homans (1950, 1958, 1961) proposed examining such interaction as an exchange that follows principles revolving around rewards and costs. For you, the costs include wear and tear on your car and giving up two hours of your time; the rewards are $10, a free lunch, and providing support for a friend and gaining his appreciation. Since your friend is desperate for a ride, you probably could have asked for $20 or $30, but such a demand could raise questions about what kind of a friend you are. Homans argued that, in general, two or more parties try to get something that is of greater value to them than the cost they incur. In this example, you and your friend probably both feel good about the exchange: you both feel that you are getting more out of the exchange than you have to forfeit.

SET has a long history in the field of business research and has been advanced in two fairly distinct domains:

1. Organizational behaviour (OB): with an intrafirm perspective on employers and employees, based on the notion that a workplace entails not only economic exchange where wages are paid for the execution of tasks, but also social exchange which provides additional value to employees; a typical application of this would be a worker's organizational citizenship behaviour that is influenced by the supervisor–worker relationship.
2. B2B relationships: with an interfirm perspective involving buyers and sellers, based on the notion that relationship-based exchange (between the theoretical poles of market and hierarchy) also entails more than a purely monetary dimension. Parameters such as the degree of commitment and trust in B2B relationships feature prominently in supply chain research that employs SET as a theoretical foundation (Morgan and Hunt, 1994).

This chapter's focus is on the latter form of SET relationships viewed in the context of SCM research. Starting in the 1980s and coined by supply chain and marketing scholars, SET has provided the foundation (whether explicitly or implicitly) for much of the work proposing closer buyer–seller relationships. A large share of the papers published on SET has historically appeared in two journals: *Industrial Marketing Management* and *Journal of Business and Industrial Marketing*.

Morris et al. (2001) note that for several years industrial marketing took 'a back seat' to consumer marketing and coined the term 'The Sleeping Giant' for the field of industrial marketing (Morris et al., 2001; Webster and Wind, 1980). The establishment of the *Industrial Marketing Management* journal in 1971 was instrumental in promoting closer buyer–seller relationships in industrial buying and selling. In addition, the first special issue on industrial marketing in the 1984 autumn edition of the *Journal of Marketing* represented a good introduction to the current theoretical foundation for industrial marketing and buyer–seller relationships (Wilson and Cunningham, 1984).

In the mid-2000s, the application and further development of SET also heavily expanded into different areas of SCM, such as logistics, and purchasing and supply management. Against this background, SET can be considered one of the grand theories developed outside the SCM realm, but has evolved to have a growing and lasting impact within SCM (Spina et al., 2016).

Table 17.1   Overview of SET variables

Key variable	Explanation	References
Exchange	Refers to a series of sequential but interrelated interactions in which one party receives something via the (in)activity of the exchange counterpart.	Mitchell et al. (2012)
Rewards	Essentially anything that a recipient values. This includes tangible elements (for example, goods or money), intangible elements such as information, and hedonic elements such as pride and joy. The value is subjective; it may also be negative.	Cropanzano et al. (2017); Homans (1961)
Costs	The tangible and intangible inputs (for example, working time) invested by the exchange counterpart.	Homans (1958)
Credit/indebtedness	The difference between the incurred costs and the received rewards.	Schoenherr et al. (2015)
Rules of reciprocity	Specifies in which form, which time frame, and to whom a received reward is expected to be reciprocated.	Goulder (1960)
Comparison level	The net outcome an actor expects to receive over time from a certain type of exchange relationship.	Thibaut and Kelly (1959)
Comparison level for alternatives	The maximum net outcome that the actor could receive from any alternative exchange relationship that the actor could engage in instead of the current one.	Thibaut and Kelly (1959)
Satisfaction	The result when the net outcome of the exchange exceeds the comparison level.	Thibaut and Kelly (1959)
Dependence	The result when the exchange's net outcome exceeds the comparison level for alternatives (that is, the second-best option).	Thibaut and Kelly (1959)
Relational norms	The mutual understanding among exchange partners concerning what behaviour is appropriate.	Heide and John (1992); Macneil (1980); Noordewier et al. (1990)

Despite its name, SET is not a single, concise theory. It is better understood as a family of conceptual models that share one underlying paradigm (Cropanzano et al., 2017). The broad context of SET may help to explain why its theoretical applications often differ from author to author. Nevertheless, there is consensus that the basic premise of SET is that individual and organizational actors enter into and maintain relationships in order to derive a net positive value, based on both economic and social elements of the relationship. The relationships are treated as a series of sequential but interrelated interactions (Mitchell et al., 2012). These interactions, which typically involve dyads as well as multilateral settings, lead to obligations between the exchange parties through the concept of reciprocity (Blau, 1964; Emerson, 1976; Homans, 1958). When one party through its (in)activity provides value to the second party, this creates an obligation for the second party to reciprocate. Moreover, SET proposes that repeated beneficial interactions over time generate relationship norms that enhance a relationship's efficiency and effectiveness.

KEY VARIABLES AND DEFINITIONS

Because SET is not a single theory, there is no fixed set of variables that are included in all specific instances of SET. An overview of common variables associated with the application of SET is provided in Table 17.1. These variables are also depicted as 'Element 1 – Variables' in Figure 17.1.

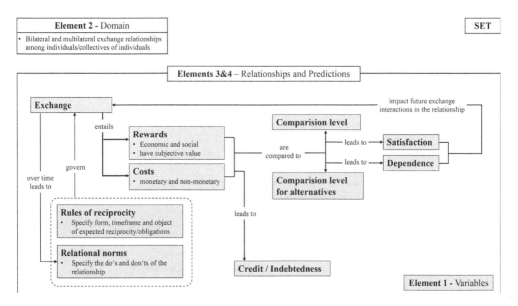

Figure 17.1   Overview of SET elements

Exchange

In SET, exchange relationships are typically treated as a series of sequential but interrelated exchange interactions (Mitchell et al., 2012). In this respect, one could expect exchange to refer to a situation where actor A provides something of value to actor B in direct return for something else of value. However, in SET, the concept of exchange is more ambiguous than this 'upfront' scenario, for several reasons.

First, in SET, what is returned is not always specified up front (Masterson et al., 2000) (that is, in our upfront example, you could have taken your friend to his sister's wedding without directly getting $10 and a free lunch, instead expecting that your favour will be returned in some form in the future). Second, depending on the rules of reciprocity, the return may be delayed (that is, when you take your friend to his sister's wedding, you do not know when in the future your favour may be returned). Third, in SET, the boundaries of the exchange are often unclear (that is, when your friend subsequently takes you out for lunch twice, it could be that both times are in exchange for you taking him to his sister's wedding; however, it could also be that the second lunch already is part of a new exchange for which your friend expects something in exchange). Fourth, in SET, the exchange is not necessarily bilateral, but could be multilateral (that is, if your friend subsequently helps your spouse with some work in the garden, it may be unclear whether this is in exchange for your favour or whether this is part of a second, independent exchange relationship). Fifth, SET not only views the active process of providing something but also the inactive process of withholding something as a potential element of the exchange (Crompanzano et al., 2017). And finally, SET not only views things of positive value but also takes into account when one actor receives something that is of negative value (Crompanzano et al., 2017).

Rewards

Rewards are the reason why actors enter into and maintain exchange relationships (Lambe et al., 2001). However, within the SET framework, rewards have no exact price but are defined in terms of value to each actor. What constitutes a reward, and the relative size of the reward, lies in the eye of the beholder. A reward may be anything economic or non-economic that one actor receives through the (in)activity of the exchange counterpart. This includes tangible elements such as goods or money, but also intangible elements such as information, providing references, or access to new suppliers. Depending on the type of exchange relationship, rewards can also include hedonic elements such as pride and joy. Homans's (1961) definition of comparison of rewards allows for an extensive assortment of things to be considered rewards; essentially, anything we put value on. One implication of this is that what is valuable to one person may not be considered valuable to another. The value of those rewards also fluctuates over time; the rewards may not always remain at the same value. When you are hungry, food has value and can be a reward, but eating more is no longer rewarding once you are full. 'A man emits a unit of activity, however that unit is defined, and this unit is either reinforced or punished by one or more units of activity he receives from another man or by something he receives from the non-human environment' (Homans, 1961).

As SET views relationships between actors over time, it can also account for instances where the actual value an actor receives deviates from the actor's initial assessment of the value. For example, an actor may gain access to information that is hardly noticed initially but later turns out to be of high value. This could be information about what a certain supplier is planning to do. In such instances, the reward is not what the actor initially thought it to be, but is equal to the actual realized value. While exchange partners expect positive rewards over time, this does not mean that every exchange element has a positive value. For example, the value may shift as a function of time-consuming contract negotiations (Rinehart et al., 2004), bullying tactics in negotiations, or hierarchical behaviour in which the supplier's leeway is restricted (Steinbach et al., 2018). While SET traditionally has viewed the value an actor receives as one-dimensional (ranging from positive to negative), Crompanzano et al. (2017) offered a useful extension through a second dimension: the activity dimension, with the polar values of exhibit and withhold. This emphasizes that positive and negative value can result from both activity and inactivity of the counterpart.

Costs

Within the SET framework, the cost variable is also not well defined. Homans (1961) originally defined costs as something of value that is given up; it can also be a punishment or the withdrawal of a reward. Money is the most obvious 'cost' exchanged for some product or service, but a cost can also refer to the time and energy devoted to a relationship with a particular business or supplier. Then, it refers to the subjective perception and cost estimation of the tangible and intangible inputs (for example, working time) provided by an actor into the relationship. Thus, costs are not an objectively quantifiable datum within SET. Ambiguity may exist concerning both which inputs are actually made and how to value these inputs. (For example, results of exchange may differ when using a full costing versus a marginal costing approach). Also, some inputs are non-economic (for example, management attention, stress or emotional effort) and are, therefore, subjective. Further, Blau (1964) emphasized that in selecting to spend time in one relationship, we forfeit the opportunity to spend time in another relationship, alluding to the concept of opportunity cost.

Credit/Indebtedness

As rewards and costs unfold over time, both parties' net outcome (that is, the rewards minus the costs) may become skewed, as in the case where one actor has built up capital to which the second actor is indebted (Schoenherr et al., 2015).

As such, the variation of credit/indebtedness may shift the current balance between rewards and costs at any given point in time. As both components are perceptional and subjective, the balance will inevitably vary based on perceptions. Within the SET framework, the value balance is typically formed as the pure difference between the rewards and the costs. Moreover, SET also allows for actors both to attach a higher value to earlier inputs (which equates to an interest rate on value over time), and the converse, which attaches greater value to more recent inputs (due to a recency bias).

Rules of Reciprocity

SET typically focuses on relationships in which the inputs of the actors are exchanged asynchronously. After one actor provides something to the other actor, this action is reciprocated later. The rules of reciprocity refer first to the time frame within which the reciprocal activity is expected. This time frame may vary from the short term, in which the response is expected instantaneously, to the long term, where capital can be built up over a longer period before it needs to be repaid. Second, the rules of reciprocity determine to the parties to whom the rewards are reciprocated. In dyadic relationships, this is the respective counterpart. However, in multilateral relationships, the target of reciprocity could also be other actors or even a group of actors. For example, if a member in a purchasing alliance supports another member, the expectation could be that, in return, the second company helps any member in the alliance, not necessarily the original party which provided the initial support.

Comparison Level

Based on Thibaut and Kelly's (1959) work, some SET conceptualizations include the comparison level for the status quo. This variable refers to the net outcome an actor expects to receive over time from a certain type of exchange relationship. It is necessarily larger than zero, because SET assumes that actors enter and maintain relationships to receive rewards that exceed the costs.

Comparison Level for Alternatives

Originating from Thibaut and Kelly (1959), this variable refers to the maximum net outcome that the actor could receive from any alternative exchange relationship that the actor could engage in instead of the current one. This includes alternative buyer–seller relationships that are non-negative. While this variable is not explicitly included in most conceptualizations of SET, it is frequently implicitly present through power and/or dependence. Conceptually, dependence is the difference between the current relationship's net outcome and the net outcome of the best alternative relationship.

Satisfaction

Some versions of SET entail the concept of satisfaction. It is one of the key outcomes of an exchange relationship, and refers to whether the individual actor is satisfied with the relationship, reducing the likelihood of change.

Dependence

In SET, dependence refers to whether alternative exchange relationships would yield similar outcomes or not. It is most commonly conceptualized as the difference in outcome between current exchange relationships and the next best alternative. As the current relationship's outcome is already highly subjective (because both rewards and costs are subjective in nature), there is no objective measure or proxy for dependence within SET.

Relational Norms, Including Trust and Commitment

As contracts do not fully govern many exchange relationships, relational norms are a vital element of SET. While norms are influenced by the context of the exchange relationship (for example, national cultures or industry standards), they are specific to the individual relationship and are developed over time. They refer to a mutually accepted understanding of the do's and don'ts within the relationship (that is, how the relationship is to be operated). As such, they can be both implicit and explicit in nature. These norms may relate to the rules of reciprocity (for example, within which time frame, in which form, and to whom an (in)activity is reciprocated). But they also include norms on communication and information sharing (for example, what information is shared with whom). Norms may also cover the relative domain for relationship autonomy, the degree to which trust and commitment is expected, and specify routines applied under various circumstances.

ASSUMPTIONS OF SET

SET focuses on the behaviour of individuals or collectives of individuals. Generally speaking, applying SET at levels beyond the individual level (for example, dyads or triads of companies) assumes that companies' or organizational subunits' behaviour is rooted in the behaviour of individuals comprising these organizational units.

The most basic assumption of SET is that the actors involved in the exchange behave rationally, in that they seek to maximize their rewards and minimize their costs during any form of exchange (Blau, 1964; Homans, 1958; Thibaut and Kelley, 1959). Therefore, 'individuals take part in an exchange only when they expect their rewards from the activity to justify the cost of taking part in it' (Gefen and Ridings, 2002, p. 50). However, when the SET literature refers to rational actors, this does not imply *Homo economicus* (for example, an individual who behaves perfectly rationally), but rather an actor with bounded rationality (see Simon, 2000, as well as Chapter 7 in this book on transaction cost economics, regarding the concept of bounded rationality) that considers not only economic elements of the exchange, but also social and psychological elements.

Additionally, SET assumes that actors learn from the past and consider their experiences in the relationship between current and future decision making. Further, SET assumes the confines of a cultural context. That means that rules of reciprocity and norms of engagement are also shaped by others outside the relationship and will vary depending on the relationship's specific set-up. In this regard, the context is, for example, impacted upon by national cultures and industry cultures, but will also differ depending on the tier within the supply chain and whether the relationship is vertical, horizontal or lateral.

Besides these central assumptions, different variations of SET assume that actors dislike being indebted, and therefore prefer building credit over time. The fear in many cases is that excessive indebtedness may result in default or that the 'credits' may expire or be forgotten beyond a given future horizon.

DOMAIN WHERE THE THEORY APPLIES

SET is fairly vague in what constitutes an exchange or an interaction among actors. Therefore, this theory applies to any form of relationship where humans interact, both business and non-business relationships. It can be applied to all higher-level relationships among organizational entities as long as these entities are viewed as collectives of individuals.

While SET is most often applied to dyadic relationships, it is equally applicable to multilateral relationships of more than two actors, and also when the actors are at different levels; for example, the interaction among two workers (individual level) and their employer (organizational level).

SET is generally applied to two instances: the relationship perspective and the individual actor perspective. The first instance is top-down, where the relationship is shaped by rules of reciprocity, relational norms, and other elements such as routines. These elements impact upon how the actors within the relationship act and think. The second perspective is bottom-up and views the relationship between two actors from the individual's perspective. Therefore, the relationship is nothing more than what the actors do and how they think about one another. In SCM research, both perspectives have been applied across many studies; whereas in OB research, the latter clearly dominates.

RELATIONSHIPS BETWEEN THE VARIABLES

The relationships between the key variables in SET are fairly straightforward. Actors engage in relationships with other actors to receive a positive net outcome in the form of economic and social rewards versus costs of the exchanges within the relationship. The exchange is based on rules of reciprocity. They specify bilateral obligations, which the actors in the relationship are expected to fulfil. As the exchange of rewards is typically asynchronous, one party in the relationship will build credit against which the other party is indebted. Each party estimates the net outcome from the relationship as the balance of rewards and costs. When this net outcome exceeds the comparison level, the actor is satisfied; when it exceeds the comparison level for alternatives, the actor is dependent on the exchange counterpart and will strive to maintain the relationship.

Over time, positive exchanges result in trust and commitment, and relational norms that govern the relationship (Lambe et al., 2001), which generally continue to grow in value.

THEORETICAL PREDICTIONS (FACTUAL CLAIMS)

One of the greatest strengths of SET is its applicability to a broad array of settings, which unfortunately also presents one of its greatest weaknesses. The predictions made by SET are vague and imprecise (Compranzano et al., 2017). While SET posits that (in)activity which provides positive value to the exchange partner will be positively reciprocated, and (in)activity which provides negative value will be negatively reciprocated, the theory is limited in its ability to make any predictions regarding which specific behaviours will result in reciprocation on behalf of the counterpart. As an example, if a company provides its supplier with useful information, SET does not predict whether the supplier will reciprocate by also providing useful information, or by putting more effort into improving the components it supplies, or by reducing its order lead time, or any other (in)activity. In a similar vein, SET also does not predict when a supplier will reciprocate. Reciprocation could occur immediately but may also occur after a considerable time delay.

Moreover, SET also does not predict exactly to whom the supplier will reciprocate. A supplier could reciprocate to the individual they received the information from, as they feel indebted to them. Alternatively, they could reciprocate to a specific department as the person may be viewed as the department's representative, or to somebody else in the company when the person is viewed as a representative of the company.

SET also does not establish propositions regarding what factors will be impacted upon (that is, moderation or mediation), when, to whom, and through which (in)activity the supplier will reciprocate. Consequently, all SET's theoretical predictions pertain to a higher level of abstraction, and are thus more generic. This makes it a useful framework in which to position hypothesized relationships that exist amongst buyers and sellers. Exemplary predictions that arise from the application of SET to buyer–seller relationships emerge as follows.

The costs that one party is willing to expend on a relationship increase with the rewards that can be or are received from the relationship. This is the case because actors expect a positive net outcome, and therefore incurred costs will not exceed expected rewards.

Interactions that occur early in the relationship are more decisive for the development of relationship (especially trust and commitment) than later interactions. Early impressions are made during these first few interactions. The initial interactions are crucial in determining whether the B2B relationship will expand, diminish, remain stable or dissolve. If the net outcome is deemed acceptable, future interactions are likely to occur. In other words, trust is established through a series of 'small promises kept' that set the stage for a deeper relationship. Later interactions will occur in the context of the relationship's whole history, and against relational norms and precedents that have already been established.

For the (in)activity of one actor, the more often this (in)activity is rewarded, and the more valuable the reward, the higher the likelihood that the actor will perform the same (in)activity again (Griffith et al., 2006). In contrast, when an actor's (in)activity does not yield the expected reward or unexpected punishment, the actor will scrutinize the (in)activity and typically aggressively avoid the action in the future (Homans, 1961).

Obligations are difficult to evaluate on a transaction-by-transaction basis (Masterson et al., 2000). The calculation of rewards derived from interactions with others consists of both short- and long-term and explicit and implicit elements (Lind and Tyler, 1988). Social exchange rewards do not have an exact price in terms of a single quantitative medium of exchange. To complicate the SET analysis, when explicit short-term rewards are deemed inadequate, this can be offset, to a degree, by long-term implicit rewards.

HOW HAS THIS THEORY BEEN USED?

To explore the possibility of future research, we reflect on the current topical issues in SCM and posit how SET can be beneficial for these research areas. This includes the classical challenge between purchasing research that considers all actors to be rational and like-minded, reflecting a largely Western bias regarding contracting, and what can be considered behavioural SCM (Schorsch et al., 2017). By extending our lens to consider that supply chains are, in fact, systems involving complex motives, desires, wishes or interactions of and between individual people, we enable a more holistic view of SET.

Examples in Purchasing and Supply Management

SET provides a useful lens for viewing global buyer–seller relationships, espousing a view that interpersonal links between firm boundary spanners and the concomitant links between firms are mutually affected (Emerson, 1976; Ouchi, 1980).

A seminal application of SET can be found in Anderson and Narus (1991) who note that buyer–seller norms are a function of the 'industry bandwidth' of working relationships, which can be used by managers to segment, target and position each relationship according to the expected customer value.

A second seminal piece is Dwyer et al. (1987), who establish the notion of exchange as a 'critical event in the marketplace', which leads to antecedent conditions and processes for developing buyer–seller social exchange. They distinguished between 'discrete transactions' (for example, spot contracts) and 'relational exchange', and established a 'hypothesized realm of buyer–supplier relationships' dependent on the seller's and the buyer's motivational invest-ment in the relationship.

Another important set of insights from Cousins et al. (2006) emphasizes the 'social' nature of relational norm development in buyer–seller relationships. Results from their study of 111 manufacturing organizations in the United Kingdom suggest that informal socialization pro-cesses are important in the creation of relational capital, which in turn can lead to improved supplier relationship outcomes. What is interesting is that these informal socialization conduits play a more important role in deriving benefits rather than formal, social interactions deriving these benefits. Many such 'informational' benefits originate from the Japanese automotive industry. For instance, Dyer and Nobeoka (2000) provide evidence that suppliers were able to learn more quickly when participating in Toyota's knowledge sharing network. Toyota's network relied on methods such as: (1) motivating members to participate and openly share valuable knowledge (while preventing undesirable spillovers to competitors); (2) preventing free riders; and (3) reducing the costs associated with finding and accessing different types of valuable knowledge. Other research examines the longitudinal benefits of safeguarding relationships to preserve performance outcomes, wherein results from over 300 buyers and suppliers suggest that lower levels of opportunism occur through bilateral investments and interpersonal trust, which leads to enhanced performance outcomes and future expectations (Jap and Anderson, 2003). Similar research exists in applying SET to help explain the role that positive buyer–supplier relationships plays in explaining buyers' cost and innovation improvement (Carey et al., 2011), as well as improved customer satisfaction (Shiau and Luo, 2012). Another stream of research (for example, Thomas et al., 2013) utilizes SET to show how negotiations strategies impact upon different aspects of the ongoing exchange relationships, for example, information exchange.

Examples in Operations Management

In operations literature, relational norms are seen as a key governing force in mitigating opportunism and examining opportunism through an organization-level analytical lens (Tangpong et al., 2010). This line of research seems to implicitly assume that human agents operating in buyer–supplier relationships are subdued to the exchange norms, and therefore the role of human agents in operational relationships is largely overlooked and understudied. For instance, Tangpong et al. (2010) found in a series of replicated experiments that relational norms and agent cooperativeness interact with each other in mitigating opportunism, and that the interactionist perspective yielded the highest explained variance in opportunism. Opportunism can even result in production disruptions, causing supply chain inefficiencies and significant negative economic impacts due to disruptions in production environments (Morgan et al., 2007).

A study by Pagell and Handfield (2000) found that the relationship between unions and management can significantly impact upon the company's operations strategy. Plant managers in a union environment are often unwilling to explore the adoption of innovations if they believe that adoption success is contingent on a human resource policy that is at odds with their existing workforce's nature. These results suggest that relational norms may produce improved management–union partnerships that allow work practices that increase flexibility and improve response times.

Examples in Logistics Management

Most SET applications in the logistics context apply an interfirm perspective that is closely related to the research in supply management and industrial marketing. An early example of this is by Moore and Cunningham (1999), who find that pronounced social exchange is associated with higher effectiveness in logistics outsourcing. Other examples which view the effectiveness of logistics outsourcing utilize survey data from companies that outsource to investigate how relationship-specific improvement activities related to costs and performance (Wallenburg, 2009) and just behaviour (Hofer et al., 2012) of logistics service providers positively impact upon the reciprocity by the service provider's customer.

Examples in Marketing

A seminal article in the analysis of buyer–seller relationships stemming from SET was by Morgan and Hunt (1994), who established the commitment–trust theory of relationship marketing. Their model, using data from over 200 automotive tyre retailers, is based on two key mediating variables – commitment and trust – as enablers for cooperation in relational exchanges with customers and suppliers, as well as with internal and other external stakeholders. They identified successful partnership cooperators:

> by (1) providing resources, opportunities, and benefits, that are superior to the offerings of alternative partners; (2) maintaining high standards of corporate values and allying oneself with exchange partners having similar values; (3) communicating valuable information, including expectations, market intelligence, and evaluations of the partner's performance; and (4) avoiding malevolently taking advantage of their exchange partners. (Morgan and Hunt, 1994, p. 34)

Another key formative article was by Anderson and Narus (1991), who suggested that each supplier 'must systematically decide which customer firms are in their firm's best interests to have collaborative relationships with, and then, actively work to keep them delighted', while in other cases 'transactional relationships offer the supplier the opportunity to prune elements of the product offering that customers deem superfluous' (Anderson and Narus 1991, pp. 112–113). Thus, they recommended, depending on the 'industry bandwidth' of working relationships, to segment, target and position each relationship according to the expected customer value.

Examples in Management

The application of SET in management, and specifically the realm of organizational behaviour, typically differs considerably from the above fields of application. First, the primary focus is intrafirm, on the relationships between the employer and employees (often focused on organizational citizenship behaviour, OCB) as well as between superior and subordinate employees (often focused on leader member exchange, LMX). Second, the focus is not on effective and ineffective relational norms, but mostly on three sequential aspects (Cropanzano et al., 2017): (1) an activity of one actor towards another actor; which (2) directly results in reciprocal responses; and (3) when repeated over time, the sequence of activity and reciprocal response will change the nature of the relationship (for example, turning low-quality relationships into high-quality relationships).

One study that applies SET and relates to both the OCB and the LMX domains is by Anand et al. (2018). Based on survey data of 60 managers and 289 employees, they show that work arrangements that are individualized to the single employee (that is, idiosyncratic deals) positively impact upon the exchange relationship between managers and employees. This relationship, in turn, positively affects the OCB of the individual employees. In addition, they show that the link between idiosyncratic deals and LMW is weaker when the value congruence among employees is high.

OUTLOOK ON FUTURE RESEARCH OPPORTUNITIES

There are several areas where SET provides a promising base for future research. For instance, collaboration in a velocity-driven digital era requires a different set of norms for managing industrial buyer–seller relationships, requiring differentiated approaches for managing event transparency, visibility material flows and a time-defined component (Chen et al., 2015; Oliveira and Handfield, 2019). These relational objectives may differ in an ecosystem where digital linkages create greater transparency over interactions between internal and external parties to exchanges with the buyer and seller firms. Such emerging exchange systems may require new forms of governance over buyer and seller relationships, which now often consist of multiple stakeholders that are often linked in networked multilateral supply chains. Prior industrial marketing research established that individuals are no longer the sole decision makers in B2B relationships, but that multiple stakeholders often play a role (Rinehart et al., 2004). Supply management executives themselves recognize that they cannot operate in a void, and have begun to establish contractual performance objectives that extend to total cost models spanning multiple entities in supply chain networks. In this respect, it will also be fruitful to investigate how rules of reciprocity are changing over time. It can, for example, be expected that timespans of reciprocity will shrink in times of instant gratification and customer impatience (Daugherty et al., 2019) and that companies will increase their focus on short-term tangible rewards at the expense of long-term intangible rewards.

Internal dynamics that require purchasing to mediate the internal relationships with stakeholders and external relationships with sellers provide another important set of research themes for exploration. This may relate to aspects such as internal fragmentation of companies, where relational norms between companies differ depending on which specific departments interact (that is, purchasing may interact completely differently with the sales department of the supplier compared to how the operations department interacts with the supplier's research and development department (Brattström and Faems, 2020).

Supply management alignment can create synergistic effects derived through strong internal lines of communication combined with external supply relationships based on defined metrics and processes (Handfield et al., 2015, p. 12). This alignment concept presents an intriguing approach for what an executive we interviewed called a 'virtual integrated company' where 'an organization is willing to manage the standards, discipline, execution, fixed capital investments, and so on of the "make" decision, versus the sourcing, negotiation, contracting, and supplier signals associated with the "buy" decision'. As the primary boundary spanning interface between the internal and external domains of the enterprise, purchasing has a mandate to ensure alignment in performance outcomes between the stakeholder's expectations and the supplier's resulting performance, and the elements of SET provide an important theoretical basis for mapping and understanding the relative forms of value among multiple engaged parties.

Finally, contracting behaviours in Eastern cultures are often not well explained in the context of Western buyer–seller relationships. SET provides a useful lens for viewing global buyer–seller relationships, espousing a view that interpersonal links between firm boundary spanners and the concomitant links between firms are mutually affected. When one overlays the cultural artifacts that exist, for example, in the Chinese culture and the role of *guanxi*, comparatively little research specifies how such relationships unfold. Recent research calls for a deeper set of explanations that translates the typical Western pragmatic business relationships into different cultural contexts and provides substantive guidance for how to build effective business relationships.

SET provides a compelling theoretical foundation, that can serve to explore a number of important research areas that lie ahead. Some of the many areas where SET can be applied include aligned relational norms that create greater product innovation and technology development (Cousins et al., 2006), knowledge sharing and new process capability development (Dyer and Nobeoka, 2000), improved multi-tier supplier integration (Choi and Yunsook, 2002), risk mitigation (Ellis et al., 2011), supplier performance improvement and capability augmentation (Terpind et al., 2008), supplier financial disruption avoidance (Wagner et al., 2009) and sustainable supply chain improvements (Wieland et al., 2016). Because SET encompasses such a broad array of conceptual models, it provides a very flexible theoretical foundation for many research inquiries in SCM.

REFERENCES

Anand, S., Hu, J., Vidyarthi, P., and Liden, R.C. (2018). Leader–member exchange as a linking pin in the idiosyncratic deals–performance relationship in workgroups. *Leadership Quarterly*, 29(6), 698–708.
Anderson, J., and Narus, J. (1991). Partnering as a focused market strategy. *California Management Review*, 33(1), 95–113.
Blau, P.M. (1964). *Exchange and Power in Social Life*. New York: Wiley.
Brattström, A., and Faems, D. (2020). Interorganizational relationships as political battlefields: how fragmentation within organizations shapes relational dynamics between organizations. *Academy of Management Journal*, 63(5), 1591–1620.
Carey, S., Lawson, B., and Krause, D.R. (2011). Social capital configuration, legal bonds and performance in buyer–supplier relationships. *Journal of Operations Management*, 29(4), 277–288.
Chen, D., Preston, D. and Swink, M. (2015). How the use of big data analytics affects value creation in supply chain management. *Journal of Management Information Systems*, 32 (4), 4–39.
Choi, T.Y., and Yunsook, H. (2002). Unveiling the structure of supply networks: case studies in Honda, Acura, and DaimlerChrysler. *Journal of Operations Management*, 20(5), 469–493.
Cousins, P., Handfield, R., Lawson, B., and Peterson, K. (2006). Creating supply chain relational capital: the impact of formal and informal socialization processes. *Journal of Operations Management*, 24(6), 851–864.
Cropanzano, R., Anthony, E.L., Daniels, S.R., and Hall, A.V. (2017). Social exchange theory: a critical review with theoretical remedies. *Academy of Management Annals*, 11(1), 479–516.
Daugherty, P.J., Bolumole, Y., and Grawe, S.J. (2019). The new age of customer impatience. *International Journal of Physical Distribution and Logistics Management*, 49(1), 4–32.
Dwyer, F.R., Schurr, P.H., and Oh, S. (1987). Developing buyer–seller relationships. *Journal of Marketing*, 51(2), 11–27.
Dyer, J., and Nobeoka, K. (2000). Creating and managing a high performance knowledge network: the Toyota case. *Strategic Management Journal*, 21(3), 345–367.
Ellis, S.C., Shockley, J., and Henrey, R.M. (2011). Making sense of supply disruption risk research: a conceptual framework grounded in enactment theory. *Journal of Supply Chain Management*, 47(2), 65–96.
Emerson, R.M. (1976). Social exchange theory. *Annual Review of Sociology*, 2(1), 335–362.
Gefen, D., and Ridings, C.M. (2002). Implementation team responsiveness and user evaluation of customer relationship management: a quasi-experimental design study of social exchange theory. *Journal of Management Information Systems*, 19(1), 47–69.
Gouldner, A.W. (1960). The norm of reciprocity: a preliminary statement. *American Sociological Review*, 25(2), 161–178.

Griffith, D.A., Harvey, M.G., and Lusch, R.F. (2006). Social exchange in supply chain relationships: the resulting benefits of procedural and distributive justice. *Journal of Operations Management*, 24(2), 85–98.

Handfield, R., Cousins, P., Lawson, B., and Petersen, K., (2015). How can supply management really improve performance? A knowledge-based model of alignment capabilities. *Journal of Supply Chain Management*, 51(3), 3–17.

Heide, J.B., and John, G. (1992). Do norms matter in marketing relationships? *Journal of Marketing*, 56(2), 32–44.

Hofer, A.R., Knemeyer, A.M., and Murphy, P.R. (2012). The roles of procedural and distributive justice in logistics outsourcing relationships. *Journal of Business Logistics*, 33(3), 196–209.

Homans, G.C. (1950). *The Human Group*. New York: Harcourt Brace.

Homans, G.C. (1958). Social behavior as exchange. *American Journal of Sociology*, 63(6), 597–606.

Homans, G.C. (1961). *Social Behavior: Its Elementary Forms*. New York: Harcourt Brace.

Homans, G.C. (1984). *Coming to My Senses: The Autobiography of a Sociologist*. New Brunswick, NJ: Transaction Publishers.

Jap, S., and Anderson, E. (2003). Safeguarding interorganizational performance and continuity under ex post opportunism. *Management Science*, 49(12), 1684–1701.

Lambe, C.J., Wittmann, C.M., and Spekman, R.E. (2001). Social exchange theory and research on business-to-business relational exchange. *Journal of Business-to-Business Marketing*, 8(3), 1–36.

Lind, E.A., and Tyler, T.R. (1988). *The Social Psychology of Procedural Justice*. Basel: Springer Science and Business Media.

Macneil, I.R. (1980). *The New Social Contract*. New Haven, CT: Yale University Press.

Masterson, S.S., Lewis, K., Goldman, B.M., and Taylor, M.S. (2000). Integrating justice and social exchange: the differing effects of fair procedures and treatment on work relationships. *Academy of Management Journal*, 43(4), 738–748.

Mitchell, M.S., Cropanzano, R.S., and Quisenberry, D.M. (2012). Social exchange theory, exchange resources, and interpersonal relationships: a modest resolution of theoretical difficulties. In K. Törnblom and A. Kazemi (eds), *Handbook of Social Resource Theory* (pp. 99–118). New York: Springer.

Moore, K.R. and Cunningham, W.A. (1999), Social exchange behavior in logistics relationships: a shipper perspective. *International Journal of Physical Distribution and Logistics Management*, 29(2), 103–121.

Morgan, R., and Hunt, S., (1994) The commitment–trust theory of relationship marketing. *Journal of Marketing*, 58(3), 20–38.

Morgan, N.A., Kaleka, A., and Gooner, R.A. (2007). Focal supplier opportunism in super-market retailer category management. *Journal of Operations Management*, 25(2), 512–527.

Morris, M.H., Pitt, L.F., and Honeycutt, E.D. (2001). *Business-to-Business Marketing: A Strategic Approach*. Thousand Oaks, CA: SAGE.

Noordewier, T.G., John, G., and Nevin, J.R. (1990). Performance outcomes of purchasing arrangements in industrial buyer–vendor relationships. *Journal of Marketing*, 54(4), 80–93.

Oliveira, M., and Handfield, R. (2019). Analytical foundations for development of real-time supply chain capabilities. *International Journal of Production Research*, 57(5), 1571–1589.

Ouchi, W. (1980). Markets, bureaucracies and clans. *Administrative Science Quarterly*, 25(1), 129–141.

Pagell, M., and Handfield, R. (2000). The impact of unions on operations strategy. *Production and Operations Management*, 9(2), 141–157.

Redmond, M.V. (2015). Social exchange theory. Dissertation, Iowa State University, Ames.

Rinehart, L.M., Eckert, J.A., Handfield, R.B., Page Jr, T.J., and Atkin, T. (2004). An assessment of supplier–customer relationships. *Journal of Business Logistics*, 25(1), 25–62.

Schoenherr, T., Narayanan, S., and Narasimhan, R. (2015). Trust formation in outsourcing relationships: a social exchange theoretic perspective. *International Journal of Production Economics*, 169, 401–412.

Schorsch, T., Wallenburg, C.M., and Wieland, A. (2017). The human factor in SCM. *International Journal of Physical Distribution and Logistics Management*, 47(4), 238–262.

Shiau, W.L., and Luo, M.M. (2012). Factors affecting online group buying intention and satisfaction: a social exchange theory perspective. *Computers in Human Behavior*, 28(6), 2431–2444.

Simon, H.A. (2000). Bounded rationality in social science: today and tomorrow. *Mind and Society*, 1(1), 25–39.

Spina, G., Caniato, F., Luzzini, D., and Ronchi, S. (2016). Assessing the use of external grand theories in purchasing and supply management research. *Journal of Purchasing and Supply Management*, 22(1), 18–30.

Steinbach, T., Wallenburg, C.M. and Selviaridis, K. (2018). Me, myself and I: non-collaborative customer behavior in service outsourcing – the key role of outcome orientation and outcome attributability. *International Journal of Operations and Production Management*, 38(7), 1519–1539.

Tangpong, C., Hug, K., and Ro, Y., (2010). The interaction effect of relational norms and agent cooperativeness on opportunism in buyer–supplier relationships. *Journal of Operations Management*, 28(5), 398–414.

Terpind, R., Krause, D., Handfield, R., and Tyler, B. (2008). Buyer–supplier relationships: derived value over two decades. *Journal of Supply Chain Management*, 44(2), 22–55.

Thibaut, J.W., and Kelley, H.H. (1959). *The Social Psychology of Groups*. New York: Wiley.

Thomas, S.P., Thomas, R.W., Manrodt, K.B., and Rutner, S.M. (2013). An experimental test of negotiation strategy effects on knowledge sharing intentions in buyer–supplier relationships. *Journal of Supply Chain Management*, 49(2), 96–113.

Wagner, S., Bode, C., Kozmol, P. (2009). Supplier default dependencies: empirical evidence from the automotive industry. *European Journal of Operational Research*, 198, 150–161.

Wallenburg, C.M. (2009). Innovation in logistics outsourcing relationships: proactive improvement by logistics service providers as a driver of customer loyalty. *Journal of Supply Chain Management*, 45(2), 75–93.

Webster, F., and Wind, J. (1980). Industrial marketing: the sleeping giant. *Journal of Marketing*, 44(4), 6–7.

Wieland, A., Handfield, R., and Durach C. (2016). Mapping the landscape for future research topics in SCM. *Journal of Business Logistics*, 37(3), 205–212.

Wilson, D., and Cunningham, W. (1984). From the Editor. *Journal of Marketing*, 48(4), 5–6

SUGGESTED FURTHER READING

For an overview:

Cropanzano, R., and Mitchell, M.S. (2005). Social exchange theory: an interdisciplinary review. *Journal of Management*, 31(6), 874–900.

Lambe, C.J., Wittmann, C.M., and Spekman, R.E. (2001). Social exchange theory and research on business-to-business relational exchange. *Journal of Business-to-Business Marketing*, 8(3), 1–36.

For an excellent review of the current state of SET application in organizational behaviour:

Cropanzano, R., Anthony, E.L., Daniels, S.R., and Hall, A.V. (2017). Social exchange theory: a critical review with theoretical remedies. *Academy of Management Annals*, 11(1), 479–516.

18. The relational view

Feigao (Kelly) Huang, Eugenia Rosca, Lydia Bals and Wendy L. Tate

INTRODUCTION

The dynamics of competition have been changing; competition is taking place more between pairs or networks of partnering firms rather than between single firms (Slone, 2004). Organizations are increasingly recognizing the need to stop solely focusing on the internal resources and look outside for critical external resources from the networks, as evidenced by the rapid proliferation of strategic interfirm alliances (Powell et al., 1996). The relational view (RV), introduced in the seminal paper by Dyer and Singh (1998), was advanced against this background to provide insights for companies to gain benefits from interfirm relationships. In the past two decades, the RV lens has been used to explain why and how firms form strategic alliances (Kale et al., 2002; Kale et al., 2000), and in the context of supply chain management (SCM) why and how supply chain partners collaborate (Chen et al., 2013; Dyer and Nobeoka, 2000) to achieve value creation and interorganizational competitive advantage.

Various theories were advanced to explain why firms perform differently. One of the theories is the resource-based view (RBV). According to the RBV, companies possess a portfolio of internal resources and capabilities, which can lead to a long-term competitive advantage if they are rare, valuable and hard to imitate or substitute (Barney, 1991). Hence, the level of analysis in the RBV is a single firm. The RV complements the RBV and proposes that a firm's critical resources and capabilities may extend beyond a firm's boundaries and may be embedded in interfirm relations. The central argument of the RV is that 'idiosyncratic inter-firm linkages may be a source of relational rents and competitive advantage' (Dyer and Singh, 1998, p. 661). In essence, a pair or network of firms can develop interfirm relationships that can produce relational rents, which firms need to collectively generate rather than working individually, and can lead to interorganizational competitive advantage (Esper and Crook, 2014). Therefore, companies can build competitive advantage not only from the internal resources owned by a firm itself but also from the external resources embedded in the relational networks (Lavie, 2006). The level of analysis in the RV is a firm dyad or network, and this has made the RV particularly relevant for empirical research in supply chain management.

KEY VARIABLES AND DEFINITIONS

The focus of the RV is on common benefits that collaborative partners cannot generate independently. The outcome variable in the RV is relational rent, which refers to 'a supernormal profit jointly generated in an exchange relationship that cannot be generated by either firm in isolation and can only be created through the joint idiosyncratic contributions of the specific alliance partners' (Dyer and Singh, 1998, p. 662). Partnering firms can generate relational rents through the following four sources: (1) relation-specific assets; (2) knowledge-sharing routines; (3) complementary resources and capabilities; and (4) effective governance (Dyer and Singh, 1998). These four mechanisms require joint contribution of the exchange partners and generate interorganizational resources and capabilities which are very difficult for the competitors to imitate or replicate due to their idiosyncrasy (Dyer and Singh, 1998). The four potential sources of relational rents are described in detail in the following subsections.

Relation-Specific Assets

Dyer and Singh (1998) proposed that investment in relation-specific assets is a determinant of relational rent. Relation-specific assets refer to those assets that are tailored toward the needs of a specific relationship (Dyer and Singh, 1998). Williamson (1985) differentiated three types of asset specificity. For example, the geographical proximity of plants of the partnering firms – what Williamson (1985) called site specificity – can lead to greater productivity because it reduces exchange time and improves communication quality and problem solving. In addition, the customized capital investments for particular partners such as machinery and tools – what Williamson (1985) called physical asset specificity – can lead to product differentiation and improved quality. What is more, partner-specific know-how and talents such as dedicated personnel to specific partners – what Williamson (1985) called human asset specificity – can lead to more efficient communication and increase speed to market. Partner-tailored assets can have better fit with the assets owned by the partner, and the fit can create more synergy effects for both parties (Weber et al., 2016). And the specialized investment makes it hard for outsiders to comprehend how asset specificity contributes to superior performance; hence, the outsiders are less likely to imitate or replicate the combination of relation-specific assets to achieve similar performance (Dyer and Singh, 1998). As a result, investment in relation-specific assets has the potential to create long-term interorganizational competitive advantage.

Dyer and Singh (1998) pointed out that there are two key subprocesses that influence interconnected firms' gains from relation-specific assets. The first is the duration of safeguard to protect against opportunism. Typically, relation-specific assets involve upfront costs, and some assets are more durable and more costly, such as dedicated plants. Partners need to have safeguards to be committed to costly investment (Williamson, 1985). So, a long-term safeguard against opportunism is positively associated with partner-specific investment. The second is the volume of exchange between interfirm partners. In line with the logic of scale economy that a bigger volume increases productivity, the more transactions with the exchange partners, the more incentivized the partners are to invest in specialized assets.

Knowledge-Sharing Routines

Knowledge-sharing routine is another determinant of relational rents. It is defined as 'a regular pattern of interfirm interactions that permits the transfer, recombination, or creation of specialized knowledge' (Dyer and Singh, 1998, p. 665). These mechanisms are purposefully designed to accumulate, integrate and exchange relevant interorganizational knowledge. They can facilitate interorganizational learning, which is critical to competitive success (Grant, 1996; Powell et al., 1996). For example, Dyer and Nobeoka (2000) examined how Toyota and its suppliers learn faster than the competitors. They found that an important factor is Toyota's Operations Management Consulting Division, which is a special unit of knowledge transfer consultants designed to centrally coordinate and share valuable production knowledge throughout Toyota's supplier network.

Dyer and Singh (1998) named two subprocesses of how partners create knowledge-sharing routines. The first is partner-specific absorptive capacity, which represents a firm's ability of identifying and assimilating valuable information from a particular partner. Several factors influence this absorptive capacity, for example, the extent of overlapping knowledge bases between the partners, the ability of identifying the 'what' and 'where' of critical information, and the creation of interorganizational processes that facilitate information sharing and socio-technical interactions across firm boundaries. The second is the alignment of incentives to encourage transparency and discourage free-riding (Eisenhardt, 1989). Partners need to dedicate required resources to ensure knowledge transfer, which can be a big commitment in the case of valuable production knowledge. So, formal and/or informal incentives should be put into place to govern information sharing and create a transparent environment. Also, free-riding is detrimental to the collective good of this particular relationship. Free-riders enjoy the benefits of knowledge acquisition from the partnership, but refuse to share their knowledge, which hurts the generation of relational rents (Dyer and Nobeoka, 2000).

Complementary Resources and Capabilities

Dyer and Singh (1998) proposed complementary resources and capabilities as a determinant of relational rent, and they defined complementary resource endowments as 'distinctive resources of alliance partners that collectively generate greater rents than the sum of those obtained from the individual endowments of each partner' (p. 666). They argued that the firm leverages the partner's resources and capabilities in conjunction with the complementary resources of its own to generate supernormal profits by accessing scarce resources that would otherwise be difficult to obtain in a secondary market. The example of Coca-Cola and Nestlé working together to distribute hot canned drinks through vending machines is a case in point (Dyer and Singh, 1998). Nestlé brought competence in product development and Coca-Cola brought a strong distribution network to this collaboration, and the combination of complementary capabilities creates synergy effects and collaborative advantage for both parties.

Dyer and Singh (1998) talked about two types of complementarities. The first is strategic resource complementarity. It should be noted that not all the resources of a potential partner are complementary. Firms need to think about the strategic complementarity of potential resources. An important factor is the ability to recognize the value in potential resources. Given imperfect information, it is very challenging for firms to place a value on potential resources and have a correct judgement on the potential strategic resource complementarity of the partnership. The second is organizational complementarity, which refers to the compatibility in the organizational systems, processes and cultures of exchange partners. These mechanisms facilitate coordination in the partnership and are necessary for the partners to realize the benefits coming from strategic resource complementarity.

Effective Governance

Finally, Dyer and Singh (1998) proposed effective governance as a determinant of relational rent, arguing that good governance lowers transaction costs and incentivizes exchange partners to work toward value creation initiatives. Research in transaction cost economics

(TCE) also suggests that firms apply governance in a discriminating way, namely, governing different types of transactions (with different attributes) with different modes of governance to minimize transaction costs and improve efficiency (Williamson, 1991).

In the context of collaborative relationships, Dyer and Singh (1998) suggested that it is more effective to rely on self-enforcing governance mechanisms than to use third-party enforcement mechanisms such as legal contracts. For example, self-enforcement removes contracting costs and reduces monitoring costs. Besides, unlike contracts which are fixed and have limited space in outlining all possible contingencies, self-enforcing agreements provide more flexibility for exchange partners to adapt and respond to unforeseen changes. Within self-enforcing governance mechanisms, informal safeguarding such as trust or embeddedness (Uzzi, 1997) is preferred over formal safeguarding such as economic hostages (Williamson, 1983) because of its effectiveness of curbing opportunism in the partnership featuring relation-specific assets and of facilitating complex exchanges (Dyer and Chu, 2003; Uzzi, 1997). In addition to lower costs incurred, informal safeguards are more difficult to be imitated by competitors than formal safeguards, which is conducive to relational rent generation. Table 18.1 and Figure 18.1 help to clarify and define the variables and relationships of RV.

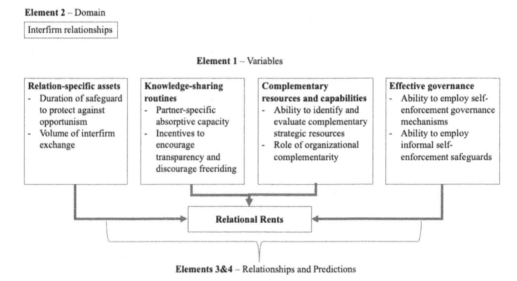

Figure 18.1   Overview of RV elements

DOMAIN WHERE THE THEORY APPLIES

The core argument of the RV is that a firm's critical resources and capabilities may extend beyond a firm's boundaries and may be embedded in interfirm linkages (Dyer and Singh, 1998; Lavie, 2006). So, the domain of the RV ranges from dyadic relationships to network linkages (Dyer, 1997). These interfirm resources and capabilities can create joint competitive advantage and common benefits for collaborative firms. The RV provides four mechanisms that firms can use to create exclusive, partner-specific rents, namely: investing in relation-specific assets; setting up knowledge-sharing routines; combining complementary

Table 18.1   *Definitions of RV variables*

Element	Explanation	Supporting references
Unit of analysis	Relationships between or among organizations.	Dyer, 1997; Dyer and Nobeoka, 2000; Dyer and Singh, 1998
Level of analysis	Firm dyad or network.	Dyer, 1997; Dyer and Nobeoka, 2000; Dyer and Singh, 1998
Key variables/definitions		
Relational rent	Surplus profits that can only be generated through joint relation-specific contributions from both partners.	Dyer and Singh, 1998; Mesquita et al., 2008; Weber et al., 2016
Relation-specific assets	Asset specificity facilitates collaboration. The more partnering firms invest in relationship-specific assets, the greater the potential will be for relational rents. The two subprocesses that affect the investment in specific assets are the duration of safeguards to protect against opportunism, and the volume of interfirm exchange.	Chen et al., 2013; Dyer, 1996; Dyer and Singh, 1998; Jap, 1999; Mesquita et al., 2008; Weber et al., 2016; Williamson, 1985
Knowledge sharing routines	Interorganizational learning is critical. Knowledge sharing routines are institutionalized processes that facilitate interfirm knowledge exchanges. The more partnering firms engage in knowledge sharing and exchange, the greater the potential will be for relational rents. The two subprocesses that can improve knowledge sharing are partner-specific absorptive capacity, and incentives to encourage transparency and discourage freeriding.	Chen et al., 2013; Dyer and Hatch, 2006; Dyer and Nobeoka, 2000; Dyer and Singh, 1998; Grant, 1996; Kale et al., 2002; Mesquita et al., 2008; Weber et al., 2016
Complementary resources and capabilities	Complementary resources refer to distinctive resources owned by individual firms which combined can generate greater rents than the sum of individual gains. The more partnering firms combine complementary resources and capabilities in a unique way, the greater the potential will be for relational rents. The two subprocesses that can improve resource combination are the ability to identify and evaluate complementary strategic resources, and the role of organizational complementarity.	Dyer and Singh, 1998; Jap, 1999; Weber et al., 2016
Effective governance	Governance affects transaction costs and partners' willingness to collaborate. The more partnering firms use effective governance, the greater the potential will be for relational rents. The two subprocesses that can influence governance are the ability to employ self-enforcement governance mechanisms, and the ability to employ informal self-enforcement safeguards.	Chen et al., 2013; Dyer, 1996; Dyer and Chu, 2003; Dyer and Singh, 1998; Kale et al., 2000; Mesquita et al., 2008; Poppo and Zenger, 2002; Weber et al., 2016; Williamson, 1985

resources and capabilities; and having effective governance in place (Dyer and Singh, 1998; Weber et al., 2016). The primary domain of the RV includes alliances and supply chains. It provides guidance on managing partner cooperation, including interorganizational processes and routines and governance structures.

RELATIONSHIPS BETWEEN THE VARIABLES

First, relation-specific assets can positively impact the relationship performance. Comparing automaker–supplier relationships in the United States (US) and Japan, Dyer (1997) found that the Japanese transaction relationships have a higher level of asset specificity. For example, a Nissan seat supplier built a plant close to a Nissan assembly plant (site specificity) and the two parties jointly built a conveyor (physical asset specificity) to carry the seats to enhance performance. Second, setting up knowledge-sharing routines has a positive impact on relational rents. The importance of knowledge sharing and organizational learning has been established in the literature (Grant, 1996; Powell et al., 1996). In a study of suppliers selling to both Toyota and US automakers, Dyer and Hatch (2006) found that even using the same supplier network firms can still achieve a competitive advantage and enjoy quality and productivity benefits if they have more knowledge transfers with the suppliers.

Third, complementary resources and capabilities are positively related to the generation of relational rents. A major reason for strategic alliances is that firms want to access external resources in conjunction with internal resources to create synergy effects (Gulati, 1995). As the previous example of Coca-Cola and Nestlé shows, it is difficult for a single firm's resources to generate the benefits that can outweigh the common benefits coming from the collaboration (Dyer and Singh, 1998). Finally, effective governance can positively influence relationship performance. The central proposition of TCE is that the mode of governance needs to match the transaction attributes so as to minimize coordination costs (Williamson, 1991). Using longitudinal data of three industries over a 20-year period, Gulati and Singh (1998) found that firms use different types of alliance types (governance structures) to address coordination costs and appropriation concerns in the relationship.

In the original framework (Dyer and Singh, 1998), the four key variables are directly related to relational rents, although the authors talked about the interactions among the four determinants in the argument. For instance, with effective governance in place, exchange partners are more likely to invest in relation-specific assets, employ knowledge sharing routines and combine complementary resources and capabilities. However, the interactions between those four variables were not made explicit at that time.

Yet, scholars started to make efforts on theory refinement, and research shows that the four determinants are interconnected while generating relational rents. For example, Mesquita et al. (2008) indicated a positive relationship between investment in partner-specific assets and relational governance mechanisms. And Chen et al. (2013) suggested that specialized assets create value partly through knowledge exchange. Weber et al. (2016) took a step further and examined the interrelations among all the four determinants. Specifically, in the context of corporate venture capital, the authors proposed that in addition to the direct effect on relational rents, complementary resources and capabilities also indirectly influence relationship performance via the other three determinants, namely, relation-specific assets, knowledge sharing routines and informal self-enforcing governance mechanisms (Weber et al., 2016).

THEORETICAL PREDICTIONS (FACTUAL CLAIMS)

The original framework (Dyer and Singh, 1998) is a direct model depicting the four determinants of relational rents; namely, the more exchange partners invest in relation-specific assets, engage in knowledge sharing and exchange, combine complementary resources and capabilities in a unique way, and use effective governance, the greater the potential will be for relational rents. Twenty years after the theory was advanced, Dyer et al. (2018) extended the RV and offered a dynamic perspective (see Figure 18.2). The authors argued that the original model was a static model and did not consider the unfolding of cooperation over time (Dyer et al., 2018). For example, in line with the original predictions, researchers find that a high level of trust leads to lower transaction costs and superior relationship performance (Dyer and Chu, 2003). However, some studies show a negative association between trust and relationship performance (Villena et al., 2011). Dyer et al. (2018) argued that an evolutionary lens can explain the inconsistent results, saying that trust increases over time in partnership, and may lead to complacency and hence relationship deterioration.

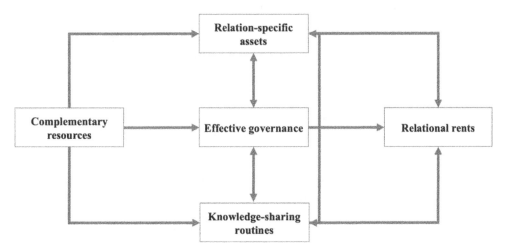

Figure 18.2   A dynamic RV model

Similarly to Weber et al. (2016), Dyer et al. (2018) argued that complementary resources are a precondition for the other three determinants because complementarity motivates firms to seek partnership. As seen from the dynamic model, complementary resources can generate relational rents on their own. As mentioned earlier, Coca-Cola and Nestlé brought distinctive resources to the cooperation of marketing hot drinks. The two partnering firms may be able to create value without investing in relation-specific assets or knowledge sharing routines. However, this is only likely to happen when the combined resources are of low interdependence.

Thompson (1967) differentiated three types of interdependence – pooled or modular interdependence, sequential interdependence, and reciprocal interdependence – with the coordination needs involved in an ascending order. For instance, reciprocal interdependence requires exchange partners to closely and continuously coordinate with each other to generate synergies. The complexity of coordination requires partnering firms to make subsequent investments in relation-specific assets and knowledge sharing routines. And investment in one tends to increase investment in the other because of interconnectedness of the investments. Therefore, Dyer et al. (2018) proposed that relation-specific assets and knowledge sharing routines mediate the relationship between complementary resources and relational rents in the case of a high level of resource interdependence, and that the two types of investments reinforce each other.

In addition, resource interdependence also influences the choice of governance mechanisms. High resource interdependence is positively associated with high investments in relation-specific assets and knowledge sharing routines, which entail higher coordination costs (Williamson, 1991) and require proper governance to address appropriation concerns (Williamson, 1985). If exchange partners anticipate appropriation concerns and high coordination costs, they are more likely to use more hierarchical governance structures to facilitate coordination and align incentives, hence ensuring cooperation (Gulati and Singh, 1998). Thus, governance plays the role of a mediator in the relationship between complementary resources and relational rents, and is interconnected with relation-specific assets and knowledge sharing routines.

It can be seen from above that resource interdependence plays an important role in the dynamic RV model. Besides the effect on the relationships between the four determinants, it also affects the generation of relational rents, which also demonstrates the evolutionary perspective. When resource interdependence is low, the rent generation will be quick, since exchange partners are less likely to invest in relation-specific assets, knowledge sharing routines or deploying appropriate governance mechanisms, which all take time. Likewise, the relational rents generated will also disappear rather quickly because the partnership is more decomposable. Hence, Dyer et al. (2018) proposed an inverted U shape for the generation of relational rents in the case of low resource interdependence. On the other hand, the case would be different when the complementary resources are of high interdependence. The partners will spend time to devise plans to exploit and combine the highly interdependent resources. Initially, the rent generation will be slow because it takes time for the partners to learn to learn and for the investments to develop and contribute to value creation (Dyer and Nobeoka, 2000). Similarly, after relational rents reach their peak, they decline slowly because the relationship is less decomposable due to the goodwill trust developed through close interactions. Therefore, for the rent generation in the context of high resource interdependence both the upward curve and the downward curve are smoother than those in the inverted U shape in the case of low resource interdependence (Dyer et al., 2018).

HOW HAS THIS THEORY BEEN USED?

The RV was proposed when there was an 'explosion of alliances' (Dyer and Singh, 1998). An alliance refers to a strategic agreement between or among firms to pool resources to tap market opportunities, such as joint ventures, research and development (R&D) alliances and direct investment (Gulati, 1995). The RV has been extensively used to understand the strategic alliances and under which conditions they can lead to relational rents. Some research suggests that firms with past alliance experiences are more likely to have a better market performance and enjoy greater alliance success (Anand and Khanna, 2000). Building on this logic, Kale et al. (2002) surveyed 78 firms and their 1572 alliances, and found that firms which set up a dedicated alliance function to disseminate alliance knowledge and coordinate alliance activities realize greater alliance success. In addition to know-how acquisition, alliance partners also want to protect their own core proprietary assets. Kale et al. (2000) suggested that relational capital fosters learning due to the wide-ranging and continuous contact between alliance members, and protects against leakage of core proprietary assets due to its ability to curb partner opportunism. This shows the importance of informal self-enforcing governance in helping firms balance 'trying to learn and trying to protect' and increase potential relational rents.

The level of analysis in the RV has made this theory particularly attractive for supply chain scholars to explore why and how firms collaborate across the supply chain. Supply chain management is essentially systemic and strategic collaboration within the focal firm and across firms in the supply chain (Mentzer et al., 2001). Information sharing, resource sharing, joint knowledge creation and collaborative communication are essential to supply chain collaboration and good supply chain performance (Cao and Zhang, 2011). Wieland and Wallenburg (2013) found that the relational competencies such as communication and cooperation have a positive effect on improved resilience; which, in turn, enhances the supply chain's customer value. Chen et al. (2013) indicated that hospital–supplier information technology integration and knowledge exchange positively influence the level of hospital–supplier integration, which contributes to superior supply chain performance. And Gölgeci et al. (2019) suggested that relational capability or the capability to manage and leverage firm relationships helps to enhance environmental collaboration between supply chain partners, which has a positive impact on environmental performance.

Specifically in the context of purchasing and supply management, Inemek and Matthyssens (2013) found that suppliers' innovativeness may benefit from collaboration in new product development and close relational ties with buyers. Socialization mechanisms between buyers and suppliers, such as joint teamwork and supplier conferences, enable firms to develop relation-specific assets and facilitate the exchange of information and ideas, thus enhancing suppliers' operational and communication performance (Cousins and Menguc, 2006). Exploring how to make collaboration in purchasing in the public sector more effective, Walker et al. (2013) found that effective governance is a great enabler of collaborative procurement; specifically, forming a governing board improves governance and reduces transaction costs because organizations can enjoy greater economies of scale and lessen costs associated with supplier search and negotiations.

Supply chain scholars have often used the RV in combination with other theoretical lenses, namely the RBV, social network theory, social capital theory or TCE (Hitt et al., 2016). For instance, Mesquita et al. (2008) compared the RBV and the RV and suggested that suppliers' investment in partner-specific assets and capabilities is more positively associated with exclusive, dyad-specific performance benefits than with redeployable benefits in other partnerships. Johnson et al. (2007) combined insights from the RV and TCE to show how the adoption of e-business technologies can decrease dyadic coordination costs and shift resources toward more strategic and productive areas, such as supplier development and strategic sourcing.

OUTLOOK ON FUTURE RESEARCH OPPORTUNITIES

As mentioned in the previous section, the RV has been used to explain alliance performance and supply chain performance in the past two decades. Many studies examine the rent generating effects of only one of the determinants (Dyer and Nobeoka, 2000), and few researchers deal with more than one determinant (Mesquita et al., 2008). Weber et al. (2016) is a notable exception that operationalizes and empirically tests all four sources of relational rents. Further efforts to expand the RV can be undertaken in newly emerging research contexts, such as alliances and partnerships in the context of organizations undergoing digital transformations. Previous studies have already explored how e-business technologies can reduce dyadic coordination costs and lead to improved financial performance (Johnson et al., 2007). Yet, the phenomenon of digital transformation provides an interesting context for theoretical advancements of established views (Hanelt et al., 2021). How do the four RV determinants enable the creation of relational rents for digitally transformed alliances and organizations? It is worthwhile to explore how digital technologies and new software solutions reshape alliances, collaborations and the resulting relational rents.

Extant literature has focused exclusively on using the RV to understand commercial and traditional alliances, while recent research suggests that non-traditional partners can have an important role in addressing key sustainable development challenges (Heuer et al., 2020). In this context, a fruitful direction for further research is to apply the RV to new contexts, namely, different types of partners (for example, non-governmental organizations, community associations) and different types of relational rents (for example, social impact, environmental value). As firms need to transition toward more sustainable organizations and supply chains, and embrace principles of social equity, inclusion and environmental awareness, the RV can be further elaborated to explain and predict how firms can collaborate with support actors (for example, brokers) to enhance the sustainability impact of their supply chains.

Also, in the context of moving toward a circular economy, questions regarding a more systemic perspective of relational rents arise. Therefore, the incorporation of sustainability considerations requires a novel definition and conceptualization of 'relational rents' beyond traditional economic measures, and might unravel new variables, beyond the four proposed by Dyer and Singh (1998). Another context worth highlighting is resilience research (Wieland and Wallenburg, 2013), as it also requires a broader understanding of rents as well as the actors involved. With global issues such as potential supply disruptions due to climate change, political issues or crises such as the ongoing COVID-19 pandemic, there is ample opportunity for relevant research. In terms of domain, sustainability and resilience issues may require a systemic or at least network perspective, regarding the interfirm linkages in scope. Moreover, considering a broader range of stakeholders, there could even be a domain adaption from interfirm to interorganizational linkages, deliberately taking into account the aforementioned different types of partners (for example, non-governmental organizations) beyond corporations.

In addition, the majority of the RV research has examined the direct model as outlined in the original framework (Dyer and Singh, 1998). The interrelationships between the four sources of relational rents remain underexplored. Notable exceptions include Mesquita et al. (2008) and Weber et al. (2016). The dynamic model proposed by Dyer et al. (2018) offers opportunities to study the interconnectedness of the variables. Specifically, the resource interdependence concept and the life cycle of partnerships entailed by the evolutionary lens provide researchers with tools to dig deeper into firm differential performance.

Competition is increasingly taking place at the level of the supply chain. Individual firms compete with each other, and at the same time supply chains also compete with each other (Slone, 2004). So, firms need to shift focus from firm-level competitive advantage to supply chain or network competitive advantage. And the RV provides this lens for a closer examination.

REFERENCES

Anand, B., and Khanna, T. (2000). Do firms learn to create value? The case of alliances. *Strategic Management Journal*, *21*(3), 295–316.

Barney, J.B. (1991). Firm resources and sustained competitive advantage. *Journal of Management*, *17*(1), 99–120.

Cao, M., and Zhang, Q. (2011). Supply chain collaboration: Impact on collaborative advantage and firm performance. *Journal of Operations Management*, *29*(3), 163–180.

Chen, D.Q., Preston, D.S., and Xia, W. (2013). Enhancing hospital supply chain performance: A relational view and empirical test. *Journal of Operations Management*, *31*(6), 391–408.

Cousins, P.D., and Menguc, B. (2006). The implications of socialization and integration in supply chain management. *Journal of Operations Management*, *24*(5), 604–620.

Dyer, J.H. (1996). Does governance matter? Keiretsu alliances and asset specificity as sources of Japanese competitive advantage. *Organization Science*, *7*(6), 649–666.

Dyer, J.H. (1997). Effective interfirm collaboration: How firms minimize transaction costs and maximize complements. *Strategic Management Journal*, *23*(8), 707–725.

Dyer, J.H., and Chu, W. (2003). The role of trustworthiness in reducing transaction costs and improving performance: Empirical evidence from the United States, Japan, and Korea. *Organization Science*, *14*(1), 57–68.

Dyer, J.H., and Hatch, N.W. (2006). Relation-specific capabilities and barriers to knowledge transfers: Creating advantage through network relationships. *Strategic Management Journal*, *27*(8), 701–719.

Dyer, J.H., and Nobeoka, K. (2000). Creating and managing a high-performance knowledge-sharing network: The Toyota case. *Strategic Management Journal*, *21*(3), 345–367.

Dyer, J.H., and Singh, H. (1998). The relational view: Cooperative strategy and sources of interorganizational competitive advantage. *Academy of Management Review*, *23*(4), 660–679.

Dyer, J.H., Singh, H., and Hesterly, W.S. (2018). The relational view revisited: A dynamic perspective on value creation and value capture. *Strategic Management Journal*, *39*(12), 3140–3162.

Eisenhardt, K.M. (1989). Agency theory: An assessment and review. *Academy of Management Review*, *14*(1), 57–74.

Esper, T.L., and Crook, T.R. (2014). Supply chain resources: Advancing theoretical foundations and constructs. *Journal of Supply Chain Management*, *50*(3), 3–5.

Gölgeci, I., Gligor, D.M., Tatoglu, E., and Arda, O.A. (2019). A relational view of environmental performance: What role do environmental collaboration and cross-functional alignment play? *Journal of Business Research*, *96*, 35–46.

Grant, R.M. (1996). Toward a knowledge-based theory of the firm. *Strategic Management Journal*, *17*, 109–122.

Gulati, R. (1995). Does familiarity breed trust? The implications of repeated ties for contractual choice in alliances. *Academy of Management Journal*, *38*, 85–112.

Gulati, R., and Singh, H. (1998). The architecture of cooperation: Managing coordination costs and appropriation concerns in strategic alliances. *Administrative Science Quarterly*, *43*, 781–814.

Hanelt, A., Bohnsack, R., Marz, D., and Antunes Marante, C. (2021). A systematic review of the literature on digital transformation: Insights and implications for strategy and organizational change. *Journal of Management Studies*, *58*(5), 1159–1197.

Heuer, M.A., Khalid, U., and Seuring, S. (2020). Bottoms up: Delivering sustainable value in the base of the pyramid. *Business Strategy and the Environment*, *29*(3), 1605–1616.

Hitt, M.A., Xu, K., and Carnes, C.M. (2016). Resource based theory in operations management research. *Journal of Operations Management*, *41*, 77–94.

Inemek, A., and Matthyssens, P. (2013). The impact of buyer–supplier relationships on supplier innovativeness: An empirical study in cross-border supply networks. *Industrial Marketing Management*, 42(4), 580–594.

Jap, S.D. (1999). Pie-expansion efforts: Collaboration processes in buyer–supplier relationships. *Journal of Marketing Research*, 36(4), 461–475.

Johnson, P.F., Klassen, R.D., Leenders, M.R., and Awaysheh, A. (2007). Utilizing e-business technologies in supply chains: The impact of firm characteristics and teams. *Journal of Operations Management*, 25(6), 1255–1274.

Kale, P., Dyer, J.H., and Singh, H. (2002). Alliance capability, stock market response, and long-term alliance success: the role of the alliance function. *Strategic Management Journal*, 23(8), 747–767.

Kale, P., Singh, H., and Perlmutter, H. (2000). Learning and protection of proprietary assets in strategic alliances: Building relational capital. *Strategic Management Journal*, 21(3), 217–237.

Lavie, D. (2006). The competitive advantage of interconnected firms: An extension of the resource-based view. *Academy of Management Review*, 31(3), 638–658.

Mentzer, J.T., DeWitt, W., Keebler, J.S., Min, S., Nix, N.W., et al. (2001). Defining supply chain management. *Journal of Business Logistics*, 22(2), 1–25.

Mesquita, L.F., Anand, J., and Brush, T.H. (2008). Comparing the resource-based and relational views: Knowledge transfer and spillover in vertical alliances. *Strategic Management Journal*, 29(9), 913–941.

Poppo, L., and Zenger, T. (2002). Do formal contracts and relational governance function as substitutes or complements? *Strategic Management Journal*, 23(8), 707–725.

Powell, W.W., Koput, K.W., and Smith-Doerr, L. (1996). Interorganizational collaboration and the locus of innovation: Networks of learning in biotechnology. *Administrative Science Quarterly*, 41, 116–145.

Slone, R.E. (2004). Leading a supply chain turnaround. *Harvard Business Review*, 82(10), 114–121.

Thompson, J.D. (1967). *Organizations in Action: Social Science Bases of Administrative Theory*. New York: Sharpe.

Uzzi, B. (1997). Social structure and competition in interfirm networks: The paradox of embeddedness. *Administrative Science Quarterly*, 42(1), 35–67.

Villena, V.H., Revilla, E., and Choi, T.Y. (2011). The dark side of buyer–supplier relationships: A social capital perspective. *Journal of Operations Management*, 29(6), 561–576.

Walker, H., Schotanus, F., Bakker, E., and Harland, C. (2013). Collaborative procurement: A relational view of buyer–buyer relationships. *Public Administration Review*, 73(4), 588–598.

Weber, C., Bauke, B., and Raibulet, V. (2016). An empirical test of the relational view in the context of corporate venture capital. *Strategic Entrepreneurship Journal*, 10(3), 274–299.

Wieland, A., and Wallenburg, C.M. (2013). The influence of relational competencies on supply chain resilience: A relational view. *International Journal of Physical Distribution and Logistics Management*, 43(4), 300–320.

Williamson, O.E. (1983). Credible commitments: Using hostages to support exchange. *American Economic Review*, 73(4), 519–540.

Williamson, O.E. (1985). *The Economic Institutions of Capitalism: Firms, Markets and Relational Contracting*. New York: Free Press.

Williamson, O.E. (1991). Strategizing, economizing, and economic organization. *Strategic Management Journal*, 12(S2), 75–94.

19. Supply networks: dyads, triads and networks

Zhaohui Wu and Thomas Y. Choi

INTRODUCTION

Research into supply chain relationships arose from the increasing needs of buyers to manage suppliers. Often assuming the perspective of a focal buyer, researchers have explored the dyadic relationship between a buyer and its supplier on the upstream side (Ellram and Hendrick, 1995; Helper, 1991) or between a manufacturer and its distributor on the downstream side (Anderson and Narus, 1990). In studies of supply management, scholars often resort to transaction cost economics to understand the nature of the relationships (for example, voice versus arm's-length) (Ellram and Hendrick, 1995; Helper, 1991) and how a focal buyer can help and evaluate suppliers to improve operational performance (Choi and Hartley, 1996; Hartley and Choi, 1996). Supply chain managers understand that their suppliers, in turn, work with other suppliers in the next tier, where there are relationships among these suppliers. Many relationships in the extended supply chains may not be visible to the focal buyers but would affect their operations performance in ways they may not have anticipated (Choi et al., 2021).

The natural extension of buyer–supplier relationship studies in the dyadic context is to extend out to the next tier and include one additional supplier. Here enter triads and triadic relationships. Triads are the smallest functional and analytical unit of a network (Choi and Wu, 2009a; Simmel, 1950; Wasserman and Faust, 1994). One familiar type of triadic relationship takes place in a dual sourcing or parallel sourcing setting where a focal buyer uses two suppliers. To the buyer, the practical issue is whether and how to influence the relationship between the two suppliers. Prominent among this research is the work of Choi and colleagues. One of their first studies in this genre (Choi et al., 2002) begins with the observation that as firms reduce the number of direct suppliers that they use, they seek to influence the relationships between suppliers more actively. This study looks at how dual sourcing and parallel sourcing scenarios with interactions, or lack thereof, between two suppliers can affect the operations performance of the common buyer. The study specified three archetypal supplier–supplier

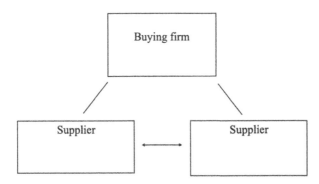

Figure 19.1   Buyer–supplier–supplier relationship triad

Table 19.1   Summary of research on triads

Unit of analysis	Supporting references
Relationships among individuals	Alessio, 1990; Cartwright and Harary, 1956; Davis, 1963, 1970; Heider, 1958; Obstfeld, 2005
Relationships among social groups (for example, departments) and production plants	Gimeno, 1999; Wu and Choi, 2005
Relationship among firms	Gimeno, 1999; Madhavan et al., 2004; Wuyts et al., 2004
Theoretical argument	
Sentiment and cognitive balance	Homans, 1950; Streufert and Streufert, 1978
Power balance and relational dependence	Bastl et al., 2013; Caplow, 1968; Homans, 1950
Structural holes	Burt, 1992; Rossetti and Choi, 2005
Mediation and network change	Finne and Holmström, 2012; Li and Choi, 2009; Obstfeld, 2005

relationships: competitive, cooperative and coopetitive, and develops propositions regarding how each of these archetypes affects the performance outcomes for both suppliers and their common buyer. A simple illustration of the buyer–supplier–supplier triad is shown in Figure 19.1.

From there, the interest in triads received a strong boost among supply chain management scholars around 2008–2009, with various conceptual papers, empirical studies and essays, and a debate between Choi and Wu (2009b, 2009c) and Dubois (2009) in the *Journal of Purchasing and Supply Management*. In this debate, Choi and Wu argue: 'We need to study how in a network, a dyad is affected by another dyad. Therefore, to study a network, studying triads becomes imperative ... Simply, dyads are inadequate in capturing the interactive nature inherent in a network' (Choi and Wu, 2009b, p. 265). Dubois (2009) agrees, but advances that triads also fall short of adequately depicting network processes. In a rejoinder, Choi and Wu (2009c) try to clarify that 'a triad is the smallest network unit where we can observe how a link affects a link or a node affects a link either directly or indirectly ... there is nothing arbitrary about studying triads. If we say that we study networks, we have to begin by studying triads.' Table 19.1 summarizes the key theoretical arguments and unit of analysis of studies on triads.

THEORETICAL FOUNDATION OF TRIADS

George Simmel, a sociologist and philosopher, was the first to contemplate the conceptual difference between a dyad and a triad. He studied and wrote about several subjects, but his work on triadic societal relationships (that is, kinships and other settings in economics and trade) is of immediate relevance (Simmel, 1950). He saw the shift from dyad to triad as a fundamental transformation, and identified two possible roles for the third member of a triad. The first is the role of a mediator, who acts impartially, quells conflict between the other two members, and perhaps ensures the triad's continued existence. Simmel called this role the *tertius iungens* or the third who channels. The second and perhaps more interesting role is the third who profits or exploits the other two. Simmel referred to this third as the *tertius gaudens*. As an extension, a third possible role may be one who divides and rules, a member who actively foments conflict between the other two in order to further their own interests, but this can be viewed as an extreme case of *tertius gaudens*. By acting as *tertius gaudens*, the third in the bridge position exerts control over the disconnected firms by actively separating the other two and nurturing the structural hole. This bridge or broker benefits from information or resource asymmetry between the two disconnected nodes.

Structural Hole Theory

Burt (1992) draws on Simmel's notion of *terius gaudens* to explain the relational behaviour of nodes in a social network. He coins the term 'structural hole' to refer to a state of disconnect between two nodes in a triad, without direct links except through a common third. This common node is a bridge between the two nodes without the direct link, and plays the role of a broker. This structural arrangement is referred to as a triad with a structural hole (Burt, 1992). A structural hole embeds tension (Burt, 1992, p. 32), implying 'no tension, no *tertius*'. Here, the absence of a direct link leads to competitive tensions between the disconnected nodes within the triad. Baker and Obstfeld (1999) refer to the *tertius gaudens* as a strategy that focuses on disunion between two disconnected nodes in a triad. In such a triadic arrangement, the disconnected nodes may be aware of each other but do not directly interact (Burt, 1997; Choi and Wu, 2009c; Madhavan et al., 2004). The notion of a structural hole is consistent with Granovetter's (1973) 'weak tie' concept where the *tertius* connects two different networks; they are networks of distinct knowledge sets or social groups.

The *tertius iungens*, the other mechanism deliberated by Simmel, received less attention in management research until the mid-2000s. We acknowledge Obstfeld (2005) as among the first to bring attention to this concept. *Tertius iungens* focuses on the union of the two disconnected nodes by a non-partisan third node in a triad. Obstfeld (2005) argues that by applying the *tertius iungens* relational strategy, the broker joins the disconnected firms to facilitate interaction between them. The broker relinquishes its power and control in exchange for synergy, cooperation and self-coordination in the triad (Obstfeld, 2005). When an agent (that is, individual or firm) continuously enacts the *tertius iungens* strategy, the agent becomes a matchmaker. This role requires generalist knowledge and the development and maintenance of a wide range of connections. A *tertius iungens* strategy also implicates the mechanism of network evolution beyond the triad. Obstfeld (2005, p. 122) presents a sequence of recursive steps based on the *tertius iungens* strategy to explain how reciprocity as a result of 'making the connection' could lead to more connections and correspondingly create more structural holes. This mechanism sheds light on the micro-processes of creating cooperation and competition dynamics in networks.

Balance Theory

Balance theory came from behavioural psychology and has been developed by researchers since the 1950s, focusing on relationships among individuals in social groups (Alessio, 1990; Cartwright and Harary, 1956; Davis, 1963, 1970; Davis and Leinhardt, 1972; Heider, 1958; Taylor, 1967). The theory was developed largely by considering the relationships among individuals in teams or social groups. Management researchers have elevated the unit of analysis from social groups to firms (Gimeno, 1999; Litwak and Meyer, 1966; Madhavan et al., 2004; Monge and Contractor, 2001). With respect to business triads, balance theory examines how firms seek to establish equitable relationships.

The key concepts of balance theory address how individual entities in a triad deal with the cognitive tension in an unbalanced relationship state, and how an unbalanced state would move toward a balanced state (Anderson, 1975; Morrissette, 1958; Newcomb, 1961; Rodrigues, 1967; Rodrigues and Coleta, 1983). This is the 'structural theorem' (see Cartwright and Harary, 1956). Simply put, the enemy of my friend is my enemy, and the friend of my enemy is my enemy. In a balanced triad, there would be either three positive (that is, friendly, cooperative) relationships or one positive with two negative (that is, adversarial, confrontational) relationships. Accordingly, entities in an unbalanced triad would attempt to address the relational inequity or mistrust that causes the unbalance, until it is resolved and the triad achieves balance. As a general rule, an unbalanced triad tends to transform into a balanced state, and a new relationship arrangement often results (Heider, 1958). This characteristic lets us predict relationship formation patterns and the nature of the new relationships.

For instance, a buyer works hard to establish cooperative relationships with both of its suppliers in a triad. The buyer asks the two suppliers to share capacity together; however, the two suppliers cannot bring themselves to cooperate. As such, this triad with two positive and one negative relationship is in a state of unbalanced relationship. Per balance theory, this unbalanced state will try to move toward a balanced state. One possible outcome is the buyer working hard to change the relationship between the two suppliers into a positive one, thus reaching a balanced state of all positive relationships. Otherwise, if the negative relationship between two suppliers remains negative, what will likely happen is one of the positive relationships with two suppliers the buyer has worked hard to establish will likely turn into a negative relationship. See Choi and Wu (2009a) for similar examples. Figure 19.2 provides illustrations of balanced and imbalanced relational states.

Balance theory has conceptual connection to other theories in behavioural psychology, such as cognitive dissonance theory (Festinger, 1957; Scott, 1963; Streufert and Streufert, 1978), exchange and dependency theory (Blau, 1964; Emerson, 1962; Homans, 1950), theories on sentiments (Homans, 1950) and equity theory (Adams, 1963; Hatfield et al., 1979; Walster et al., 1978). Sociologists have recognized that individual behavioural principles in a group can be generalized (Alessio, 1990). They have applied these individual-level theories to examine social processes in groups and organizations (see Gimeno, 1999; Litwak and Meyer, 1996; Madhavan et al., 2004; Monge and Contractor, 2001; Moore, 1979; Ritter, 2000; Wuyts et al., 2004).

Besides the balance of relational sentiments, another form of balance is the balance of power. Caplow (1968) proposes a coalition theory for triads. Simply stated, the two weaker members of a triad are likely to form a coalition to counterbalance the strongest member among the three. He enumerates several assumptions concerning the use of power, as well as six possible triadic power distributions. Surprisingly, Caplow also contends that 'the nature of the triadic situation often favors the weak over the strong'. Bastl et al. (2013) look more closely at such coalitions in triads. They examine relationships among buyers and suppliers in triads involving weaker players, and develop archetypal arrangements that can result. They compare coalitions and strategic alliances in such circumstances along six dimensions, including purpose, focus and duration. They offer a quote from Caplow (1956) that: 'the formation of given coalitions depends upon the initial distribution of power in the triad and ... may be predicted to some extent when the initial distribution of power is known' (p. 489).

Triads in supply chain management studies help to describe the relational dynamics among three firms in various triadic settings (for example, buyer–supplier–supplier; supplier–buyer–end customer). Triadic dynamics also describe the larger-scale dynamics of industry sectors. Rossetti and Choi (2005) find that when aerospace original equipment manufacturers (OEMs)

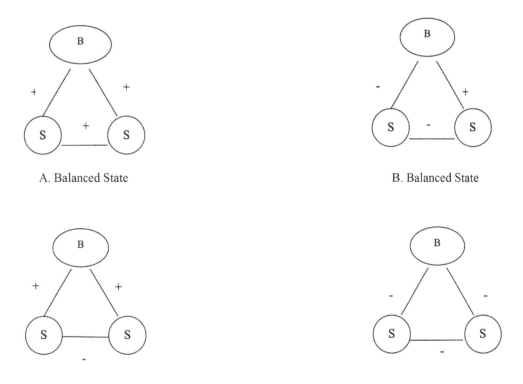

Figure 19.2   Illustrations of balanced and imbalanced relational state

choke their suppliers with short-term, cost-driven decisions, they become competitors in the aftersales market. The suppliers seek out the end customers (airlines) to sell after-market parts, and by doing so they disintermediate the OEMs, ultimately altering the triad and breaking the linear chain. Here, the triadic framework clarifies industry dynamics.

In recent years, researchers have leveraged the triadic framework to answer some very practical supply management issues. One salient development is service triads, in which firms focus on what they do best and outsource the remaining tasks to outside suppliers (Wynstra et al., 2016). The ensuing relationships between supplier, buyer and end customer can be viewed as a 'service triad', in which the buyer (the middleman) contracts with a supplier to deliver services directly to the buyer's customer (Li and Choi, 2009; Niranjan and Metri, 2008). Li and Choi (2009) focus on shifting relationship structures and in particular on the position of the (services) buyer vis-à-vis that of the supplier and end customer. In this case, the bridge position of the buyer between supplier and customer, providing information and monitoring benefits, may decay as the supplier comes into direct contact or interaction with the customer, leading to erosion of those benefits. They warn that 'left unmanaged, this state of transferred bridge position has serious performance implications for the buyer'.

As service operations become ever more prominent in operations management research, scholars have begun to assess various forms of service triad to gain insights on service performance and management strategy. For instance, Finne and Holmström (2012) analyse the process by which subsystem suppliers bypass system integrators (buyers) and directly build relations with customers. Their study demonstrates that triadic cooperation among supplier, buyer and customer improves the value to the customer 'by improving service quality', and it also 'aligns the interests and capabilities of supplier and intermediary'. Menor and Johnson (2012) elaborate on various aspects of service quality and the roles that service triad actors have in managing quality, and Peng et al. (2010) use a triadic approach to study maintenance services.

SUPPLY NETWORKS

A supply network refers to an interconnected system of firms engaged in the manufacture and assembly of parts to create a finished product (Choi and Hong, 2002). As supply chain management practitioners and researchers, we often conceive of a supply network as an 'ego network'. The focal firm functions as the ego as it looks upstream and downstream in a supply chain to understand how it is connected to others through the flow of information, materials and contractual relationships. The network perspective finds both intellectual heritage and analytical tools in social network analysis (see Wasserman and Faust, 1994, for an overview). This approach facilitates the investigation of the structural characteristics of supply networks.

The network perspective has rapidly gained traction across several sciences, from anthropology to physics. Borgatti and Li (2009) provide a comprehensive overview of social network analysis, covering both specific concepts, such as structural holes or betweenness centrality, and the generic explanatory mechanisms that network theorists often employ to relate network variables to outcomes. They point out that many network concepts provide potential starting points for supply chain management (SCM) research. Scholars over the past two decades have often looked to social network research for both theories and methodology. In response, Kim et al. (2011) offer physical meaning to various centrality measures; for instance, they consider a node with high indegree centrality as one that handles high supply load.

Supply Network Structure, Network Position and Performance

One of the earliest studies of supply networks is a structural depiction of three vehicle subassemblies (Choi and Hong, 2002). These networks supply the parts for the centre consoles of three different automobiles: the Honda Accord, Acura CL/TL and DaimlerChrysler (DCX) Grand Cherokee. Based on these supply networks, the study examines the supply network structures and how they operate. Using the existing literature, the authors frame structure in three dimensions: formalization, centralization and complexity. They conclude that the three structural dimensions affect one another progressively, and cost considerations appear to be the most significant factor shaping supply network structure. Later, Kim et al. (2011) applied the social network analysis to the supply network structures compiled in Choi and Hong (2002). See Figure 19.3 for an example.

Both the structure of a supply network and the positions of its constituent firms influence individual firms' innovativeness and influence over others. Carnovale and Yeniyurt (2015) utilize a manufacturing joint venture network dataset to identify the effects of various network constructs such as betweenness, density, brokerage and weakness on network innovation.

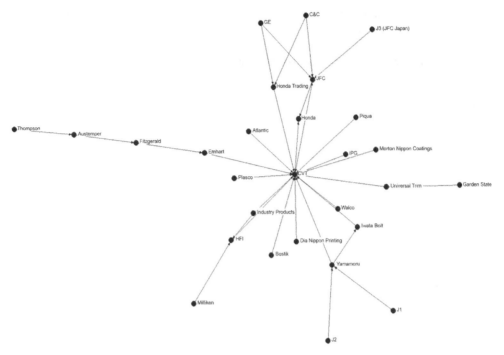

Source: Adapted from Lin et al. (2014).

Figure 19.3   *US domestic food flows (in tons) by county*

They find support for the idea that innovation in a supply chain depends heavily on the structure of the interfirm network. Bellamy et al. (2014) examine the structural characteristics of supply networks and investigate the relationship between a firm's supply network accessibility and interconnectedness, and its innovation output. Their results also indicate that interconnected supply networks strengthen the association between supply network accessibility and innovation. Moreover, the influence of the two structural characteristics on innovation output can be enhanced by a firm's absorptive capacity and the level of innovation of its supply network partners.

Archetypes of Supply Network

Supply networks can capture different business activities such as agricultural, manufacturing, information-based services and product development processes (Harland et al., 2001; Miles and Snow, 2007; Pathak et al., 2014). Pathak et al. (2014) identify four supply network archetypes. Their archetypes include communities that work toward similar goals without direct competition. Communities may partner temporarily for activities such as logistics or promotion. Federations work to manufacture parts (or subassemblies) or develop technologies to satisfy a customer's demands. A consortium develops knowledge; it performs research and development. In a hierarchy, firms perform separate tasks but may cooperate in some operational activities while competing over access to common resources or even over price. The researchers discuss how a supply network could shift from one type into another, and propose the possibility of additional network archetypes.

Supply Networks as Complex Adaptive Systems

An agent (individuals or collective entities such as businesses) as a node in a supply chain can look toward its suppliers and its customers, but visibility in either direction is invariably going to be limited. What lies beyond the realm of its visible range simply emerges for the focal firm. Choi et al. (2001) propose the notion that supply networks need to be understood as a complex adaptive system (CAS). The CAS perspective highlights the emergent nature of an open system, implying that decision makers should allow for autonomous network activity, and balance control and emergence to induce both stability and flexibility. This CAS perspective has been adopted by many researchers. For instance, applying an agent-based simulation model, Giannoccaro et al. (2017) find that the relationship between scope of control and supply network performance follows an inverted U shape.

The Complex Adaptive Supply Network research group initiated by Choi and Dooley has drawn supply chain scholars across the world to collaborate, and has produced many distinctive research papers in the past decade (see https://research.wpcarey.asu.edu/supply-networks/what-we-do/), as evidenced in many recent supply network research studies. We review some of them in the following sections.

Nexus Suppliers

Yan et al. (2015) propose the theory of nexus suppliers to emphasize the importance of hidden critical suppliers, where a nexus supplier is defined as 'any supplier in a multi-tiered supply network that potentially exerts a profound impact on a buyer's performance due to its network position'. A nexus supplier may be several tiers removed in the supply network, and may not be immediately visible to the focal buying firm. According to Yan et al. (2015), nexus suppliers can be categorized into three types: operational, monopolistic and informational. While managing strategic players among top-tier suppliers is well understood, we have only recently begun to recognize nexus suppliers.

The idea of creating an index for nexus suppliers is first proposed in a *Harvard Business Review* Online Forum by Choi et al. (2015). Subsequently, Shao et al. (2018) then demonstrate one possible way to compute nexus supplier indexes through a business analytics approach. They build a mathematical model which they call the nexus supplier index (NSI), through data envelopment analysis (DEA). The NSI incorporates various network centrality measures (that is, degree, betweenness, eigenvector and closeness) to provide a combined metric to evaluate a supplier's potential for being a critical supplier based on its network position; that is, a nexus supplier.

Competition Network

Historically, a link between two firms would be considered non-existing unless they have a direct relationship, such as a buyer–supplier relationship or new venture relationship. However, Skilton and Bernardes (2014) argue otherwise. They argue that a competitive relationship is a link: if two firms are in a competitive context and are aware of each other, their actions are interdependent and their competitive relationship, albeit without a direct interaction, constitutes a link. Skilton and Bernardes propose and test a theory of the effects of competition network structure on product market entry. Competition networks are defined as the patterns of interdependence between rivals that emerge from direct competition. By studying networks based on competitive interdependence, they extend social network theory and improve the understanding of product market entry. Based on data drawn from the aircraft modification industry, they find that the size, interconnectedness and diversity of competition networks systematically influence subsequent product entry into a market.

Network Resiliency

Kim et al. (2011) are among the first to examine supply chain disruption at the network level. They conceptualize supply network disruption and resilience by examining the structural relationships among networked entities. They compare four fundamental supply network structures to help understand supply network disruption and resilience. Their analysis show that node/arc-level disruptions do not necessarily lead to network-level disruptions, and demonstrate the importance of differentiating a node/arc disruption from a network disruption. Their results also indicate that network structure significantly determines the likelihood of disruption. Their work suggests that resilience improves when the structural relationships in a network follow the power law. Their work also addresses a useful analytical approach to assessing the resilience of supply network structures. More recently, Durach et al. (2020) describe a supply chain resilience study in a tetradic context involving a buyer, two first-tier suppliers, and a common second-tier supplier. Their study shows how the two first-tier suppliers in a coopetitive relationship actually help the resilience of the focal buyer coming from a source not visible to the focal buyer: the second-tier supplier.

RESEARCH OPPORTUNITIES

Recent sustainability studies focus on large supply networks. They differ from previous work in their scale. Specifically, the supply networks under investigation are not necessarily product- or firm-specific; rather, the research is concerned with the flow of resources and processes in a broad economic system. For instance, Lin et al. (2014) analyse the structure of the virtual water trade associated with the global food commerce, and observe a hierarchy in which nations that trade large volumes of water are more likely to link up and associate with other similar nations, particularly when the trade directionality is considered. Lin et al. (2019) study domestic food flows within the United States of America (USA) (see Figure 19.4). The network properties indicate potential vulnerability to the disturbance of key nodes. By examining the transportation and logistics infrastructure of a country, this analysis offers insights to national policy beyond the typical research focus and interests that focus on firms and for-profit supply chains. Dooley et al. (2019) examine how the structural and functional characteristics of a product's process network impact upon the network's collective greenhouse gas emissions. Collectively, these studies suggest a different conception, scale of sustainability beyond the firm level, to tackle the much larger network structures and designs of our overall economic systems.

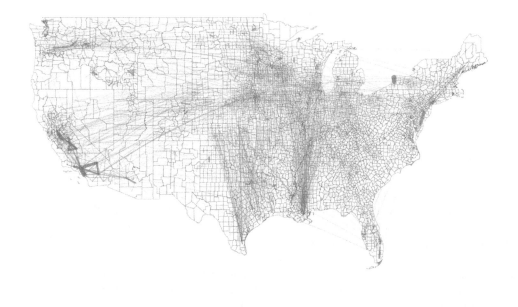

Source: Adapted from Lin et al. (2014).

Figure 19.4   US domestic food flows (in tons) by county

Another opportunity exists when considering combining supply network research and institutional theory research. Supply networks act as the carriers of institutions and institutional dynamics (Bhakoo and Choi, 2013). Supply network researchers have made inroads into analysing structural embeddedness (Choi and Kim, 2008) and cultural embeddedness (Wu and Pullman, 2015). Structural embeddedness refers to the importance of framing suppliers as being economically and contractually committed to other participants in larger supply networks rather than in isolation. Cultural embeddedness looks at behavioural norms based on shared (or mutually understood) political systems, values and ideologies.

By adopting the concept of structural embeddedness, we learn that a buying company needs to look at a supplier's extended supply network to more fully understand a supplier's performance (Kim and Choi, 2021). Emphasizing the concept of structural embeddedness, Choi and Kim (2008) suggest that firms consider network structural characteristics when evaluating suppliers. A supplier's structural embeddedness refers to the extent to which its criticality depends on its extended supply network. Choi and Kim argue that supplier performance is influenced by other companies in their supply networks, so a supplier's structural embeddedness can be as important as their internal capabilities.

Borgatti and Li (2009) call for more development of network perspectives, and suggest that social network concepts such as ego-network structure, structural holes, node centrality, network cohesion and structural equivalence might be applied to supply chain management. These concepts can be applied to examine the structural characteristics and efficacy of logistics networks (Carter et al., 2007). Li et al. (2021) explore the impact of financial squeeze on supply chain network structure and operational outcomes. They find that financial squeeze affects the stability of the supply chain network, and the effect varies depending on the location of the suppliers. Kim et al. (2011) apply several key social network analysis metrics to supply networks. They examine individual supply network members in terms of their structural position in the network, and suggest that buying firms consider the potential roles of suppliers based on their network centrality measures such as degree, closeness, betweenness and eigenvector. Mazzola et al. (2018) explore how firms reconcile the dichotomy between central and structural holes network positions, by dynamically shifting from a central to a structural holes position (and vice versa) over time. This study suggests that a dynamic perspective employed increases the ability of a firm to develop new products. In recent development, companies such as Resilinc (www.resilinc.com/) are using supplier and transportation data to carry out network mapping for the purpose of monitoring real-time global movements of goods. Such supply networks mapping leveraging dynamic big data will raise interesting research questions on supply network traceability, transparency and real-time decision-making. Those buying companies that had done the network mapping had a clear advantage over those that did not when the COVID-19 pandemic first struck China (Choi et al., 2020).

Cultural embeddedness provides insight into why individuals and firms, imprinted with values, norms and logic, behave as they do, and how their behaviours can influence network structure and structural change. Because supply networks operate within the broader context of industry sectors, the analysis of supply networks offers a meso-theory of the mechanisms, patterns and processes of institutional change. Wu and Jia (2018) point out that the institutional lens broadens the scope of what we consider as supply networks by considering the roles of government, non-profit organizations in supply chain management.

Lastly, the focus and context of supply networks are changing, and so are the nodes and boundary of supply networks. As evidenced through the COVID-19 pandemic and trade war between the USA and China, government entities, and non-governmental organizations (NGOs) and intergovernmental organizations (IGOs), are becoming important players in a focal firm's research and development and production networks. Likewise, we need to study the supply networks of the government entities. The shortage of personal protection equipment (PPE) requires private and public partnership. Understanding network structure and structuring, collaboration and network governance gains urgency as we tackle new challenges in this new political and economic setting.

CONCLUDING REMARKS

In this chapter we have taken stock of the evolution of supply network research. We began by considering dyads and triads. We highlighted the key concepts, including *tertius gaudens*, *tertius iungens*, structural hole and balance theory. These concepts constitute the theoretical underpinning of triads. We then expanded out to supply networks. Our review suggests that the supply network has become an established area of inquiry, and researchers have made great strides in understanding supply network structure, embeddedness, competition networks and nexus suppliers. These studies provide practical insights on performance at both firm and network levels. Lastly, we pointed out the opportunities and directions of supply network research by highlighting the broadening scope of supply networks that include institutional actors and new ways of conceiving supply networks to tackle sustainability challenges.

REFERENCES

Adams, J.S. (1963). Toward an understanding of inequity. *Journal of Abnormal Psychology*, *67*, 422–436.

Alessio, J.C. (1990). A synthesis and formalization of Heiderian balance and social exchange. *Social Forces*, *68*(4), 1267–1285.

Anderson, B. (1975). Cognitive balance theory and social network analysis. In: Holland, P. and Leinhardt, P.W.S. (eds), *Perspectives on Social Network Research*. Academic Press, New York.

Anderson, J.C., and Narus, J.A. (1990). A model of distributor firm and manufacturer firm working partnerships. *Journal of Marketing*, *54*(1), 42–58.

Bastl, M., Johnson, M., and Choi, T.Y. (2013). Who's seeking whom? Coalition behavior of a weaker player in buyer–supplier relationships. *Journal of Supply Chain Management*, *49*(1), 8–28.

Baker W.E., Obstfeld D. (1999), Social capital by design: structures, strategies, and institutional context. In: Leenders, R.T.A.J. and Gabbay, S.M. (eds), *Corporate Social Capital and Liability*. Springer, Boston, MA.

Bellamy, M.A., Ghosh, S., and Hora, M. (2014). The influence of supply network structure on firm innovation. *Journal of Operations Management*, *32*(6), 357–373.

Bhakoo, V., and Choi, Y. (2013). The iron cage exposed: institutional pressures and heterogeneity across the healthcare supply chain. *Journal of Operations Management*, *31*(6), 432–449.

Blau, P.M. (1964). *Exchange and Power in Social Life*. Wiley, New York.

Borgatti, S.P., and Li, X. (2009). On social network analysis in a supply chain context. *Journal of Supply Chain Management*, *45*(2), 5–22.

Burt, R.S. (1992). *Structural Holes*. Harvard University Press, Boston, MA.

Burt, R.S. (1997). The contingent value of social capital. *Administrative Science Quarterly*, *42*(2), 339–365.

Caplow, T. (1956). A theory of coalitions in the triad. *American Sociological Review*, *21*(4), 489–493.

Caplow, T. (1968). *Two Against One: Coalitions in Triads*. Prentice-Hall, Englewood Cliffs, NJ.

Carnovale, S., and Yeniyurt, S. (2015). The role of ego network structure in facilitating ego network innovations. *Journal of Supply Chain Management*, *51*(2), 22–46

Carter, R.C., Ellram, L.M., and Tate, W. (2007). The use of social network analysis in logistics research. *Journal of Business Logistics*, *28*(1), 137–168.

Cartwright, D., and Harary, F. (1956). Structural balance: a generalization of Heider's theory. *Psychological Review*, *63*(5), 277–292.

Choi, T., Dooley, K., and Rungtusanatham, M. (2001). Supply networks and complex adaptive systems: control versus emergence. *Journal of Operations Management*, *19*(3), 351–366.

Choi, T.Y., and Hartley, J.L. (1996). An exploration of supplier selection practices across the supply chain. *Journal of Operations Management*, *14*(4), 333–343.

Choi, T.Y., and Hong, Y. (2002). Unveiling the structure of supply networks: case studies in Honda, Acura, and Daimler Chrysler. *Journal of Operations Management*, *20*(5), 469–493.

Choi, T.Y., and Kim, Y. (2008). Structural embeddedness and supplier management: a network perspective. *Journal of Supply Chain Management*, *44*(4), 5–13.

Choi, T.Y., Narayanan, S., Novak, D., Olhager, J., Sheu, J-B., and Wiengarten, F. (2021). Managing extended supply chains. *Journal of Business Logistics*, *42*(2), 200–206.

Choi, T.Y., Rogers, D., and Vakil, B. (2020). Coronavirus is a wake-up call for supply chain management. *Harvard Business Review*, March 27.

Choi, T., B. Shao, and Shi, Z. (2015). Hidden suppliers can make or break your operations. *Harvard Business Review*, 'Future of Operations' online forum. https://hbr.org/2015/05/hidden-suppliers-can -make-or-break-your-operations.

Choi T.Y., and Wu, Z. (2009a). Triads in supply networks: interpretation through balance theory and structural-hole concept. *Journal of Supply Chain Management*, *45*(1), 8–25.

Choi, T.Y., and Wu, Z. (2009b). Taking the leap from dyads to triads: buyer–supplier relationships in supply network. *Journal of Purchasing and Supply Management*, *14*(4), 263–266, 269–270.

Choi T.Y., and Wu, Z. (2009c). Go ahead, leap: triads and their practical and theoretical import: In response to 'To leap or not to leap: Triads as arbitrary subsets of networks of connected dyads' by Anna Dubois. *Journal of Purchasing and Supply Management*, *15*(4), 269–270.

Choi, T.Y., Wu, Z., Ellram, L.M., and Koka, B. (2002). Supplier–supplier relationships and their implications for buyer–supplier relationships. *IEEE Transactions on Engineering Management*, *42*(2), 119–130.

Davis, J.A. (1963). Structural balance, mechanical solidarity, and interpersonal relations. *American Journal of Sociology*, *68*(4), 444–462.

Davis, J.A. (1970). Clustering and hierarchy in interpersonal relations: testing two graph theoretical models on 742 sociomatrices. *American Sociological Review*, *35*(5), 843–851.

Davis, J.A., and Leinhardt, S. (1972). The structure of positive interpersonal relations in small groups. In: Berger, J., Zelditch Jr, M., and Anderson, B. (eds), *Sociological Theories in Progress*. Houghton Mifflin, Boston, MA.

Dooley, K., Pathak, S., Kull, T.J., Wu, Z. Johnson, J., and Rabinovich, E. (2019). Process network modularity, commonality, and greenhouse gas emissions. *Journal of Operations Management*, *65*(2), 1–21.

Dubois, A. (2009). Comment on 'Taking the leap from dyads to triads: Buyer–supplier relationships in supply networks' by Choi and Wu: to leap or not to leap: triads as arbitrary subsets of networks of connected dyads. *Journal of Purchasing and Supply Management*, *15*(4), 267–268.

Durach, C., Wiengarten, F., and Choi, T.Y. (2020). Supplier–supplier co-opetition and supply chain disruption: first-tier supplier resilience in the tetradic context. *International Journal of Operations and Production Management*, *40* (7/8), 1041–1055.

Ellram, L.M., and Hendrick, T.E. (1995). Partnering characteristics: a dyadic perspective. *Journal of Business Logistics*, *16*(1), 41–64.

Emerson, R.M. (1962). Power–dependence relations. *American Sociological Review*, *27*(1), 31–41.

Festinger, L. (1957). *A Theory of Cognitive Dissonance*. Row, Peterson & Co., Evanston, IL.

Finne, M., and Holmström, J. (2012). A manufacturer moving upstream: triadic collaboration for service delivery. *Supply Chain Management: An International Journal*, *18*(1), 21–33.

Giannoccaro, I., Nair, A., and Choi, T. (2017). The impact of control and complexity on supply network performance: an empirically informed investigation using NK simulation analysis. *Decision Sciences Journal*, *49*(4), 625–659.

Gimeno, J. (1999). Reciprocal threats in multimarket rivalry: staking out 'spheres of influence' in the U.S. airline industry. *Strategic Management Journal*, *20*(2), 101–128.

Granovetter, M. (1973). The strength of weak ties. *American Journal of Sociology*, *78*(6), 1360–1380.

Harland, C.M., Lamming, R.C., Zheng, J., and Johnsen, T.E. (2001). A taxonomy of supply networks. *Journal of Supply Chain Management*, *37*(3), 21–27.

Hartley, J.L., and Choi, T.Y. (1996). Supplier development: customers as a catalyst of process change. *Business Horizons*, *39*(4), 37–44.

Hatfield, E., Utne, M.K., and Traupmann, J. (1979). Equity theory and intimate relationships. In: Burgess, R.L. and Huston, T.L. (eds), *Social Exchange in Developing Relationships*. Academic Press, New York.

Heider, F. (1958). *The Psychology of Interpersonal Relations*. John Wiley & Sons, New York.

Helper, S. (1991). How much has really changed between U.S. automakers and their suppliers? *Sloan Management Review*, *32*(4), 15–28.

Homans, G.C. (1950). *The Human Group*. Harcourt, Brace & Co., New York.

Kim, Y., and Choi, T.Y. (2021). Supplier relationship strategies and outcome dualities: an empirical study of embeddedness perspective. *International Journal of Production Economics*, *232*, 1–19.

Kim, Y., Choi, T.Y., Yan, T., and Dooley, K. (2011). Structural investigation of supply networks: a social network analysis approach. *Journal of Operations Management*, *29*(3), 194–211.

Li., M., Alam, Z., Bernardes, E., Giannoccaro, I., Skilton, P.F., and Rahman, M.S. (2021). Out of sight, out of mind? Modeling the impacts of financial squeeze on extended supply chain networks. *Journal of Business Logistics*, *42*(2), 233–263.

Li, M., and Choi, T.Y. (2009). Triads in services outsourcing: bridge, bridge decay and bridge transfer. *Journal of Supply Chain Management*, *45*(3), 27–39.

Lin, X, Dang Q., and Konar, M. (2014). A network analysis of food flows within the United States of America. *Environmental Science and Technology*, *48*(10), 5439–5447.

Lin, X., Ruess, O.J., Martson, L., and Komnar, M. (2019). Food flows between counties in the United States. *Environmental Research Letter*, *14*(8), 084011. doi.org/10.1088/1748-9326/ab29ae.

Litwak, E., and Meyer, H.J. (1966). A balance theory of coordination between bureaucratic organizations and community primary groups. *Administrative Science Quarterly, 11*(1), 31–58.

Madhavan, R., Gnyawali, D.R., and He, J. (2004). Two's company, three's a crowd? Triads in cooperative–competitive networks. *Academy of Management Journal, 47*(6), 918–927.

Mazzola, E., Giovanni, P., and Robert, H. (2018). Change is good but not too much: dynamic positioning in the interfirm network and new product development. *Journal of Product Innovation Management, 35*(6), 960–982.

Menor, L.J., and Johnson, P.F. (2012). Service operations management and service supply network triadic arrangements. 4th World Conference Production and Operations Management, Amsterdam.

Miles, R.E., and Snow, C.C. (2007). Organization theory and supply chain management: an evolving research perspective. *Journal of Operations Management, 25*(3), 459–463.

Monge, P.R., and Contractor, N.S. (2001). Emergence of communication networks. In: Jablin, F.M. and Putman, L.L. (eds), *Handbook of Organizational Communication*. SAGE, Beverly Hills, CA.

Moore, M. (1979). Structural balance and international relations. *European Journal of Social Psychology, 9*(3), 323–326.

Morrissette, J.O. (1958). An experimental study of the theory of structural balance. *Human Relations, 11*, 239–254.

Newcomb, T.M. (1961). *The Acquaintance Process*. Holt, Rinehart & Winston, New York.

Niranjan, T.T., and Metri, B.A. (2008). Client–vendor–end-user triad: a service quality model for IS/ITES outsourcing. *Journal of Services Research, 8*(1), 123–138.

Obstfeld, O. (2005). Social networks, the tertius iungens orientation, and involvement in innovation. *Administrative Science Quarterly, 50*, 100–130.

Pathak, S., Wu, Z., and Johnson, D. (2014). Towards a structural view of co-opetition in supply networks. *Journal of Operations Management, 32*(5), 245–267.

Peng, T.J.A., Lin, N.J., Martinez, V., and Yu, C.-M.J. (2010). Managing triads in a military avionics service maintenance network in Taiwan. *International Journal of Operations and Production Management, 30*(4), 398–422.

Ritter, T. (2000). A framework for analyzing interconnectedness of relationships. *Industrial Marketing Management, 29*(4), 317–326.

Rodrigues, A. (1967). Effects of balance, positivity, and agreement in triadic social relations. *Journal of Personality and Social Psychology, 5*(4), 472–476.

Rodrigues, A., and Coleta, J.A.D. (1983). The prediction of preferences for triadic relations. *Journal of Social Psychology, 121*(1), 73–80.

Rossetti, C., and Choi, T.Y. (2005). On the dark side of strategic sourcing: experiences from the aerospace industry. *Academy of Management Executive, 19*(1), 1–15.

Scott, W.A. (1963). Cognitive complexity and cognitive balance. *Sociometry, 26*(1), 66–74.

Shao, B.M., Zhan, S., Choi, T.Y., and Chae, S. (2018). A data-analytics approach to identifying hidden critical suppliers in supply networks: development of nexus supplier index. *Decision Support Systems, 114*, 37–48. https://doi.org/10.1016/j.dss.2018.08.008.

Simmel, G. (1950). The Triad. In: Wolff, K.H. (transl., ed.), *The Sociology of George Simmel*. Free Press, Glencoe, IL.

Skilton, P.F., and Bernardes, E. (2014). Competition network structured product market entry. *Strategic Management Journal, 36*(11), 1688–1696.

Streufert, S., and Streufert, S.C. (1978). *Behavior in the Complex Environment*. V.H. Winston & Son, Washington, DC.

Taylor, H.F. (1967). Balance and change in the two-person group. *Sociometry, 30*(3), 262–279.

Walster, E., Walster, G.W., and Berscheid, E. (1978). *Equity: Theory and Research*. Allyn & Bacon, Boston, MA.

Wasserman, S., and Faust, K. (1994). *Social Network Analysis: Methods and Applications*. Cambridge University Press, New York.

Wu, Z., and Choi, T.Y. (2005). Supplier–supplier relationships in the buyer–supplier triad: building theories from eight case studies. *Journal of Operations Management, 24*(1), 27–52.

Wu, Z., and Jia, F. (2018). Toward a theory of supply chain fields – understanding the institutional process of supply chain localization. *Journal of Operations Management, 58–59*, 27–41.

Wu, Z., and Pullman, M.E. (2015). Cultural embeddedness in supply networks. *Journal of Operations Management*, *37*(1), 45–58.

Wuyts, S., Stremersch, S, Van Den Bulte, C., and Franses, P.H. (2004). Vertical marketing systems for complex products: A triadic perspective. *Journal of Marketing Research*, *41*(4), 479–487.

Wynstra, F., Spring, M., and Schoenherr, T. (2016). Service triads: a research agenda for buyer–supplier–customer triads in business services. *Journal of Operations Management*, *35*, 1–20.

Yan, T., Choi, T.Y., Kim, Y., and Yang, Y. (2015). A theory of the nexus supplier: a critical supplier from a network perspective. *Journal of Supply Chain Management*, *51*, 52–66.

20. Stakeholder theory

Gyöngyi Kovács

INTRODUCTION

Stakeholder theory helps in the structuring and management of societal problems, and in bringing people together to solve them. Yet it is not always that clear what is at stake, nor who has a stake, or an interest, in the problem at hand. Second to that is the question of who an organisation should prioritise among all the stakeholders when it comes to solving a problem.

Originally, much of the debate centred around widening the view from a focus of a firm's stockholders to wider interest groups, which then were called stakeholders. This comes from the problem companies have started to face when everything they did boiled down to how their shares fared on the stock exchange. Quarterly earnings reports became the norm, with good financial results required in ever shorter time periods. Yet the paradox is that good financial results alone are not enough; the market also reacts to other news, good or bad. A good return on investment in an operation can quickly be overshadowed by a scandal, as the expectation is for the company's customers (where financial flows originate from) to vote with their feet and turn away from scandal-ridden suppliers. But if that is the case, and if the neoclassical economic view does not suffice, who shall a company listen to, and who is it accountable to?

ONE, OR SEVERAL STAKEHOLDER THEORIES?

In spite of a common focus to identify interest groups beyond shareholders, stakeholder theory has a few different origins. Most prominent is the economist versus stakeholder theorist debate, sometimes called 'Friedman vs Freeman' (Agle et al., 2008). While Friedman, coming from a focus on markets, focuses on the various groups and companies a business needs to take into account and align for being able to operate, and what it means to manage a company well and indeed maximise profit, Freeman focuses on whether business and ethics can be separated from one another (they cannot), and the responsibilities of business.

Importantly, while Friedman considers stakeholder theory as a theory of the firm, Freeman as a pragmatist views it as a theory of strategic management, and an idea of how to create value (Agle et al., 2008). This distinction, and the underlying question of the normative value of stakeholder theory, is in fact its most contested point (Donaldson and Preston, 1995). After all, if a theory is not normative, is it still a theory? Stakeholder theory has been much criticised for not being able to come to more than descriptions of why any firm outperforms another. On the other hand, many of stakeholder theory's suggestions for 'better' decision-making are seen as normative (Freeman et al., 2020). What is more, stakeholder theory offers a view that does not focus on short-term solutions only, but can also consider the long-term impact of decisions.

DOMAIN WHERE THE THEORY APPLIES

Stakeholder theory (ST) can be applied to many different types of problems. It has been used extensively in business ethics, and corporate social responsibility, when focusing on moral problems and dilemmas. It has also been used as a new way to see corporate governance.

How ST is being used depends very much on what is at stake, and whose perspective is taken. Problem framing is also key to determining the unit of analysis. Is the management of a company concerned with who they are accountable to in general? Or is there a specific problem that would need to be discussed, wanting to get public opinion behind a potential way forward? Conversely, is there a problem that a potential stakeholder wants to raise with the firm?

From the company perspective, much of the focus is on determining who are the company's, or the specific problem's, stakeholders in the first place. And while there are always many potential ones, it also becomes a question of prioritising between them. This is a matter of both the alignment of a stakeholder with the company, and its salience.

Key Variables and Their Definitions

Stakeholder theory is first and foremost concerned with something that is at stake. This is usually a problem or topic that is of interest to various interest groups; in fact, it is this that brings them together. These interested parties, called stakeholders, may not share their reasons, motives or agenda with regard to what is at stake, and often they would not engage in any interaction with one another if it was not for this problem at hand. Yet, depending on the problem and perspective, they are not of equal importance to the problem owner, and may not have the same means to push for their agenda. Therefore, ST distinguishes between a few important notions about stakeholders (Table 20.1).

The alignment of a stakeholder refers to the degree of internalisation of a stakeholder; that is, whether any of them are internal stakeholders such as employees or owners, or external ones. Among external ones, there is a further distinction between suppliers and customers in the input–output environment – that is, the supply chain – versus competitors from the competitive environment, various layers of government and even trade organisations in a regulatory environment; versus non-governmental organisations that can be seen as in a further external (sometimes called lateral; Polsa, 2002) relationship to the firm (Achrol et al., 1983; Carter and Ellram, 1998; Friedman and Miles, 2004). Arguably, the interdependencies of the input–output environment place those stakeholders in a prime position to exert pressure on the firm. This is inherent also in supply chain management, to the extent that once extending the unit of analysis to the supply chain, these stakeholders become internalised (Kovács et al., 2006); also in light of supply chain versus supply chain competition (Christopher, 1998). Yet this is not what distinguishes stakeholder theory from other theories; rather, its unique proposition lies in the very notion of also considering others than owners and the supply chain.

A stakeholder's salience to some extent stems from its degree of internalisation and alignment, but there are a few additional factors that have been highlighted in the literature. Mitchell et al. (1997) suggest that stakeholder salience is a matter of their power, legitimacy and urgency. Friedman and Miles (2004), on the other hand, focus on their necessity and compatibility. From a supply chain perspective, the necessity of suppliers and customers is engrained in their contractual relationships with the firm; thus supply chain members are

Table 20.1   Definitions of ST variables

Element	Explanation	Supporting references
Stake	The key common issue or problem that brings different groups together.	Friedman and Miles (2002)
Stakeholder	An interested party with a specific view or agenda about the problem at hand. It is their interest that defines them as being a stakeholder, and not whether the problem owner acknowledges their interest.	Friedman and Miles (2002)
Key variables/definition		
Stakeholder salience	The relative importance of an interested party to a problem owner. This is defined in terms of stakeholder attributes, such as: (1) power, legitimacy, and urgency; or (2) necessity and compatibility.	Mitchell et al.(1997); Friedman and Miles (2004)
Stakeholder pressure	The demands of an interested party on the problem owner with regard to the issue at hand.	Kovács (2008)
Key assumptions		
Perspective of the problem owner	There is a specific problem owner (for example company, chief executive officer) from whose perspective stakeholder salience can be assessed, and on whom pressure may be exerted.	Friedman and Miles (2002)
Voice of the stakeholder	Stakeholders are active parties that can engage in a dialogue with the problem owner and/or one another.	Friedman and Miles (2002)
Purpose of business	Corporations focus on their self-interest and on generating short-term shareholder value.	Donaldson and Preston (1995)

a priority from the perspectives of both their alignment with the firm as belonging to its input–output environment, as well as their salience due to their necessity. Not surprisingly, the customer being king (or queen) is reiterated in many topics to which stakeholder theory has been applied, including that of green purchasing (Carter and Jennings, 2004). Stakeholders that are not contractually bound are seen as contingent; yet they can also exert stakeholder pressure on the firm, as for example governments do through legislation, regulation and policy (Sarkis et al., 2010). Importantly, however, stakeholder salience is not static, and the problem owner (company) may perceive a stakeholder differently over time (Friedman and Miles, 2002). Yet their perception of a stakeholder's salience will impact on how they address the common issue or problem (see Figure 20.1).

Stakeholder salience aside, there are different ways of relating to stakeholders. Stakeholders exerting pressure on the company, and the company responding to such pressure, is just one of these ways. The pressure perspective would see companies acting in self-interest in their decision of whose pressure and on which matter they choose to react to. In other words, companies develop their capabilities to respond to stakeholder pressure while facing it (Sarkis et al., 2010). This is, though, also a very passive view of companies, which can themselves initiate stakeholder dialogue, and where the spectrum in these dialogues can vary from reciprocity to co-creation. As Freeman et al. (2020) say, at the end, we are in this boat together.

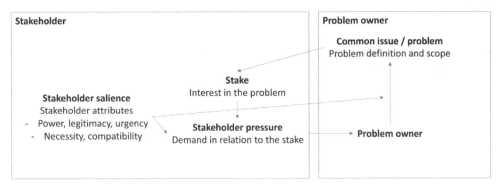

Figure 20.1   Overview of ST elements

Levels of Analysis

Let us quickly revisit the matter of the level of analysis. Stakeholder theory has been used as a lens through which to look at a common problem or a particular company. In supply chain management, stakeholder theory has even been applied to end-to-end supply chains, with the supply chain being the level of analysis.

Delineating and also delimiting a common problem can be very useful, not just to see problems beyond companies, such as the protection of a species in a specific region, or a problem that is common to a city or indeed an industry or a supply chain, but also to identify stakeholders that would be salient to this problem. Any company may also be part of many different types of problems depending on their location: from employment-related issues in one country, to health and safety-related ones at another facility; to pollution prevention ones in their supply chain.

Problems that are typically looked at through the lens of stakeholder theory rarely focus on the economic bottom line of the firm, however. Rather, the question is geared towards ecological, social, health and safety, or ethical questions; and issues that firms rarely tackle alone (Sarkis et al., 2010). That said, shareholders and financiers are included amongst the stakeholders of a company, and ST does not exclude economic questions by definition.

Apart from defining a common problem, the level of analysis can also be that of the link between stakeholders and the firm, or stakeholders and the supply chain; that is, with questions focusing on how to manage such relationships. This is also different from the mainstream relationship management literature on the supply chain, as few of these relationships are based on commercial, or frequent, transactions. Thus, as opposed to most other theories of the firm, the common denominator for a relationship between stakeholders is not an economic transaction but a shared interest in a common issue.

Furthermore, the level of analysis may differ for different problems. Some problems are bound to specific locations or regions, whereby the location of a company, its headquarters or its production facilities may matter. Other problems extend to, for example, questions of pollution overall, in which case the production facilities and the product chain, or the life cycle of a product, can be the level of analysis. Problems that focus on labour issues can be geographically bound, or addressed on the supply chain level. Increasingly, the level of analysis is the supply chain, whether it is focused on conflict minerals or human rights or modern slavery, for example.

RELATIONSHIP BETWEEN THE VARIABLES AND THEORETICAL PREDICTIONS

If there is one thing stakeholder theory is much criticised for, it is for not being able to make any theoretical predictions. Its strength lies in seeing problems beyond economic firm performance, and in being able to identify the interest groups that have a stake in these problems. This widens the owner and shareholder focus to that of the interest group and stakeholders.

Conceptually, the main question becomes not just how to define a stakeholder, but also how important, or salient, any given stakeholder is to the problem, or to a company. Here, the frameworks vary, and look at stakeholder salience from the perspective of either power, legitimacy and urgency, or a stakeholder's necessity and compatibility. The outcome of their salience, and the relationship with them, can then be measured in terms of the time and resources spent on the management of that relationship (Chen et al., 2018). This is to take a convergent view on stakeholders, where they all play a role together to tackle a problem.

Mitchell et al.'s (1997) framework further defines seven types of stakeholders with varying degrees of power, legitimacy and urgency, and the eighth type of the non-stakeholder. In this vein:

1. Dormant stakeholders have power but lack legitimacy and urgency.
2. Discretionary stakeholders have legitimacy but neither power nor urgency.
3. Demanding stakeholders have urgency but neither power nor legitimacy.
4. Dominant stakeholders have power and legitimacy but no urgency.
5. Dangerous stakeholders have power and urgency but no legitimacy.
6. Dependent stakeholders have legitimacy and urgency but no power.
7. Definitive stakeholders have all three.
8. Non-stakeholders have none.

Conversely, those that possess all three attributes are also seen as 'highly salient', those with two out of three as 'expectant', and those with one of the three as 'latent' stakeholders. This framework is very useful in identifying who to engage with when it comes to a particular problem, but also how to engage with them. If the unit of analysis is the relationship between a stakeholder and the firm, the salience of the stakeholder can guide the firm in whether to engage a particular stakeholder in one question only, or whether to engage with them in an advisory manner, involve them on the board of a decision making group, or lobby with or through them. This is also called the 'instrumental view' on stakeholders (see Donaldson and Preston, 1995). On this basis, Aapaoja and Haapasalo (2014) distinguish between the stakeholders that have responsibilities for a project or problem, those to keep informed, the next level to keep satisfied, versus those to use minimum effort to engage with. The scale they use includes the combination of stakeholder attributes of power, legitimacy and urgency, and combines these with the stakeholder's assessed probability to impact upon or ability to contribute to the matter at hand. Importantly, however, the way a company chooses to engage with particular stakeholders bears further implications for how their legitimacy is perceived henceforth, which may then become a self-fulfilling prophecy for their future prioritisation (Chen et al., 2018).

From a global supply chain perspective, however, it is worth noting that any stakeholder's attributes will vary across the various locations in the supply chain. Multinational corporations, for example, are more likely to focus on stakeholders that exhibit higher stakeholder salience in the location of their headquarters, as Kovács (2008) also confirmed across the supply chain. This brings some interesting new questions to the forefront, such as how stakeholders can contribute to the development and implementation of global environmental standards (Sarkis et al., 2011).

EXAMPLES IN PURCHASING AND SUPPLY CHAIN MANAGEMENT

Purchasing and supply chain management literature has primarily used stakeholder theory in the sphere of greening, from environmental purchasing, to greening operations, life cycle assessment, to green and reverse logistics. One of the most interesting articles that compares the merits of stakeholder theory to that of others is Sarkis et al.'s (2011) review of various organisational theories and their current versus potential contribution to green supply chain management.

From a different perspective, Pålsson and Kovács (2014) attribute the drivers and motives for greening the supply chain to either the resource-based view (RBV) or to stakeholder theory, though focusing mostly on external stakeholders that would not be encompassed by RBV.

But while they see the two as fundamentally different, albeit complementary theories, one of the fathers of the RBV has since himself argued that the RBV needs to encompass a stakeholder perspective as well (see Barney, 2018). A different merger of the two can be seen in procurement literature, where stakeholder theory has been used to determine who a purchasing manager should listen to when developing their own purchasing competence (Kern et al., 2011).

While suppliers and customers are often regarded as external stakeholders, in supply chain management, they are internal to the supply chain (see Kovács et al., 2006). Interesting differences in supply chain management literature can be seen with regard to the alignment of stakeholders, with who to include in supply chain decisions beyond suppliers and customers (Pullman and Wikoff, 2017), but also with bringing forward non-organisational stakeholders such as 'society' and 'the environment' (Oliveira et al., 2020). The former is the more prevalent in public procurement literature, where the importance of society at large is the more critical.

Apart from greening, stakeholder theory has also been used in supply chain management literature concerning public health, or even disaster management and humanitarian supply chains. Overall, also in supply chain management, stakeholder theory is used most often where profit is not the only driving objective.

STAKEHOLDER THEORY IN HUMANITARIAN SUPPLY CHAINS

With regard to humanitarian supply chains, the article by Heaslip et al. (2012) highlights the difference in identifying the stakeholders of disaster relief as opposed to the network of actors that had been discussed in earlier literature. Whilst not strictly adhering to the stakeholder attributes as described earlier, Heaslip et al. (2012) identify primary and secondary stakeholders, or in other terms, overt and latent stakeholders. From a supply chain perspective, it is interesting to see that the primary stakeholders are again those that are involved with material flows. What remains debatable is the role of donors as the origins of monetary flows in this supply chain, versus that of beneficiaries as aid recipients, without any purchasing power in the original sense. In fact it is donors and the headquarters of humanitarian organisations that are the stakeholders here (Schiffling and Piecyk, 2014), even if beneficiaries are sometimes put at the core of humanitarian stakeholder models (as in Fontainha et al., 2017).

Addressing the imbalance between donors being powerful stakeholders, while beneficiaries are legitimate and urgent but powerless stakeholders, humanitarian supply chains are moving towards cash-based interventions, in which it is not goods or services in-kind but rather money that is delivered to beneficiaries. Thereby beneficiaries are to regain their purchasing power and, with that, the possibility to influence what they are about to get, as well as to regain their dignity in this process. This is rather similar to the thinking in social welfare programmes. From a stakeholder theoretical perspective, it importantly redistributes the power to beneficiaries, elevating their stakeholder salience.

Fontainha et al. (2017) argue that stakeholders vary, depending on whose perspective one takes in a disaster, as well as depending on the phase of disaster relief. They find a staggering 41 different ways of how disaster management and humanitarian supply chain literature views stakeholders and their alignment. As Schiffling and Piecyk (2014) put it, there is no single key stakeholder in humanitarian supply chains that would focus on their economic bottom line, which makes it somewhat more confusing and also complex to analyse stakeholder attributes in relation to any potential performance measure. Most interestingly, this is an area of supply chain management where there are at times not one but several focal organisations, with all sorts of hierarchical to fuzzy relationships with one another (Fontainha et al., 2017). This is an important notion, as it ascertains the possibilities of stakeholders engaging with one another, and not just the problems, or focal organisations at hand. Also considering stakeholders' relationships to one another, Heaslip et al. (2012) further comment on the role of secondary, latent stakeholders, as those having the means to influence primary stakeholders in their ways of engaging with the humanitarian sector.

Furthermore, stakeholder theory has been used in humanitarian supply chain management to structure the various challenges that different humanitarian organisations face in disaster relief (Kovács and Spens, 2009). There are important differences here between international humanitarian organisations – which the bulk of humanitarian logistics literature focuses on – and local or governmental ones. On a more detailed level, Schiffling and Piecyk's (2014) article is the most comprehensive in analysing the stakeholder attributes of the many different types of stakeholders of a humanitarian supply chain.

FUTURE RESEARCH OPPORTUNITIES

Many of the future research opportunities stem from stakeholder theory itself. Freeman et al. (2020) problematise how to describe the contribution of a company in the future, how to account for any contributions beyond profit, and how to account for stakeholders being human (that is, not economic). Economics has even started to include accounting for the value of human happiness, which has been embraced by the Organisation for Economic Co-operation and Development's (OECD) 'Better Life Index' on the scale of nation states. And while the pursuit of happiness has been criticised for fuelling discontent (Delhey and Kroll, 2013), 'happiness' as a concept in the happiness index in fact measures 'being content' with what one has. How else would Finland be the happiest country on earth for so many times in a row?

An interesting avenue for further research is in the combination of stakeholder theory with other theories (Freeman et al., 2020). This lends itself to considering the dimension of people and their voices, for example in the resource-based view as 'stakeholder resource dependence' (Frooman, 1999), in agency theory as 'stakeholder agency theory' (Hill and Jones, 1992), or Barney's (2018) renewed resource-based view that incorporates stakeholders as well. While not actually new, these developments have yet to find their way into supply chain management research.

Following Sarkis et al.'s (2011) suggestions, it is high time to use stakeholder theory beyond stakeholder classification in supply chain management, to embrace its full potential when analysing global supply chains. We are yet to understand how, for example, very local stakeholders of very specific problems can influence global supply chains in their operations. For example, local environmental groups have a better understanding of the pollution-related problems in their immediate environment, but companies with headquarters far away tend not to heed them much attention until their relationship becomes a destructive one. Yet, looking at stakeholders in various locations, and in the global supply chain, could indeed contribute to the rise of global product, process, but also environmental and social standards.

Learning from humanitarian supply chains, one could also consider multiple focal organisations and their stakeholders in supply chain management. What is more, there is much to learn from looking at the relationships between stakeholders to understand how they influence one another, and how that influence contributes to the dynamics of their salience.

Newer trends also need a different lens to understand them. The sharing economy could be much better understood if it incorporated more than just the economic incentives for different groups engaging in such activities. New business models would definitely benefit from understanding not just existing but also future users' and non-users' perspectives on what they intend to do. In addition, it is high time to move away from the outspoken stakeholders with a voice to indeed consider the environment, or society at large, as stakeholders. After all, the Lorax is not always there to speak for the trees.

REFERENCES

Aapaoja, A. and Haapasalo, H. (2014), 'A framework for stakeholder identification and classification in construction projects', *Open Journal of Business and Management*, 2 (1), article 42090.

Achrol, R.S., Reve, T. and Stern, L.W. (1983), 'The environment of marketing channel dyads: a framework for comparative analysis', *Journal of Marketing*, 47 (4), 55–67.

Agle, B.R., Donaldson, T., Freeman, R.E., Jensen, M.C., Mitchell, R.K. and Wood, D.J. (2008), 'Dialogue: toward superior stakeholder theory', *Business Ethics Quarterly*, 18 (2), 153–190.

Barney, J.B. (2018), 'Why resource-based theory's model of profit appropriation must incorporate a stakeholder perspective', *Strategic Management Journal*, 39 (13), 3305–3325.

Carter, C.R. and Ellram, L.M. (1998), 'Reverse logistics: a review of the literature and framework for future investigation', *Journal of Business Logistics*, 19 (1), 85–102.

Carter, C.R. and Jennings, M.M. (2004), 'The role of purchasing in corporate social responsibility: a structural equation analysis', *Journal of Business Logistics*, 25 (1), 145–186.

Chen, J., Harrison, G. and Jiao, L. (2018), 'Who and what really count? An examination of stakeholder salience in not-for-profit service delivery organizations', *Australian Journal of Public Administration*, 77 (4), 813–828.

Christopher, M. (1998), *Logistics and Supply Chain Management. Strategies for Reducing Cost and Improving Service*, 2nd edn. London: Prentice Hall.

Delhey, J. and Kroll, C. (2013), 'A "happiness test" for the new measures of national well-being: how much better than GDP are they?' In: Brockmann, H. and Delhey, J. (eds), *Human Happiness and the Pursuit of Maximization*. Dordrecht: Springer, pp. 191–210.

Donaldson, T. and Preston, L.E. (1995), 'The stakeholder theory of the corporation: concepts, evidence, and implications', *Academy of Management Review*, 20 (1), 65–91.

Fontainha, T.C., Leiras, A., de Mello Bandeira, R.A. and Scavarda, L.F. (2017), 'Public–private–people relationship stakeholder model for disaster and humanitarian operations', *International Journal of Disaster Risk Reduction*, 22, 371–386.

Freeman, R.E., Phillips, R. and Sisodia, R. (2020), 'Tensions in stakeholder theory', *Business and Society*, 59 (2), 213–231.

Friedman, A.L. and Miles, S. (2002), 'Developing stakeholder theory', *Journal of Management Studies*, 39 (1), 1–21.

Friedman, A.L. and Miles, S. (2004), 'Stakeholder theory and communication practice', *Journal of Communication Management*, 9 (1), 89–97.

Frooman, J. (1999), 'Stakeholder influence strategies', *Academy of Management Review*, 24 (2), 191–205.

Heaslip, G., Sharif, A.M. and Althonayan, A. (2012), 'Employing a systems-based perspective to the identification of inter-relationships within humanitarian logistics', *International Journal of Production Economics*, 139 (2), 377–392.

Hill, C.W. and Jones, T.M. (1992), 'Stakeholder-agency theory', *Journal of Management Studies*, 29 (2), 131–154.

Kern, D., Moser, R., Sundaresan, N. and Hartmann, E. (2011), 'Purchasing competence: a stakeholder-based framework for chief purchasing officers', *Journal of Business Logistics*, 32 (2) 122–138.

Kovács, G. (2008), 'Corporate environmental responsibility in the supply chain', *Journal of Cleaner Production*, 16 (15), 1571–1578.

Kovács, G. and Spens, K. (2009), 'Identifying challenges in humanitarian logistics', *International Journal of Physical Distribution and Logistics Management*, 39 (6), 506–528.

Kovács, G., Spens, K.M. and Korkeila, R. (2006), 'Stakeholder response to future changes in the reverse supply chain', *International Journal of Logistics Systems and Management*, 2 (2), 160–176.

Mitchell, R.K., Agle, B.R. and Wood, D.J. (1997), 'Toward a theory of stakeholder identification and salience: Defining the principle of who and what really counts', *Academy of Management Review*, 22 (4), 853–886.

Oliveira, M.V.D.S.S., Simão, J. and da Silva Caeiro, S.S.F. (2020), 'Stakeholders' categorization of the sustainable public procurement system: the case of Brazil', *Journal of Public Procurement*, 20 (4), 423–449.

Pålsson, H. and Kovács, G. (2014), 'Reducing transportation emissions: a reaction to stakeholder pressure or a strategy to increase competitive advantage', *International Journal of Physical Distribution and Logistics Management*, 44 (4), 283–304.

Polsa, P. (2002), 'Power and distribution network structure in the People's Republic of China – the case of an inland city in transition', Doctoral Thesis, Helsinki: Swedish School of Economics and Business Administration.

Pullman, M. and Wikoff, R. (2017), 'Institutional sustainable purchasing priorities: stakeholder perceptions vs environmental reality', *International Journal of Operations and Production Management*, 37 (2), 162–181.

Sarkis, J., Gonzalez-Torre, P. and Adenso-Diaz, B. (2010), 'Stakeholder pressure and the adoption of environmental practices: the mediating effect of training', *Journal of Operations Management*, 28 (2), 163–176.

Sarkis. J., Zhu, Q. and Lai, K.-H. (2011), 'An organizational theoretic review of green supply chain management literature', *International Journal of Production Economics*, 130 (1), 1–15.

Schiffling, S. and Piecyk, M. (2014), 'Performance measurement in humanitarian logistics: a customer-oriented approach', *Journal of Humanitarian Logistics and Supply Chain Management*, 4 (2), 198–221.

21. Institutional theory

Katri Kauppi

INTRODUCTION

Institutional theory is focused on explaining similarity, not variety, in organizational practices: what causes organizations within an industry to become very much like each other in the practices and structures they have as time passes (DiMaggio and Powell, 1983). The theory explains how organizations conform to institutional rules in how they work to gain public acceptance, access to various resources and to improve their likelihood of survival (Meyer and Rowan, 1977). These institutional rules are argued to spread through three specific institutional pressures: coercive, mimetic and normative (DiMaggio and Powell, 1983). In conforming to these pressures, organizations gradually become similar (isomorphic); which then increases the legitimacy of these organizations (Deephouse, 1996). As legitimacy (general acceptance of how the organization operates) is seen as necessary to compete, organizations adopt those practices perceived as most legitimate. This eventually leads to similarity in how organizations operate and how, for example, supply chains are structured. Another key construct related to the theory, though surprisingly rarely incorporated into empirical studies (see Kauppi, 2013), is uncertainty. High environmental uncertainty particularly encourages the need to strive for legitimacy by imitating other parties (DiMaggio and Powell, 1983). When there is high uncertainty due to, for example, economic instability or the visibility one organization has to its supply chain, it can be safer to use similar operating practices that everyone else uses rather than test new ones (which potentially could be more effective).

Where institutional theory perhaps differs from many other organizational theories is the logic that organizations adopt structures and practices not due to their effectiveness or efficiency in producing outcomes, but due to the legitimacy and public acceptance that their adoption grants to the organization (Alvesson and Spicer, 2019). It is thus geared towards explaining behaviours that may defy rational economic explanation (Suddaby et al., 2013). According to institutional theory, organizational success rests not (only) on how efficient an organization is, but also on whether the organization is accepted by its institutional environment, and thus receives the resources it needs for survival (Meyer and Rowan, 1977; Tolbert and Zucker, 1999) such as financing, stakeholder acceptance and customer orders. This can create conflicts between what might be the most efficient way to handle operations given the practical realities of the operating environment, and the structures and practices that should be adopted based on institutional rules and myths (Meyer and Rowan, 1977; Scott, 2008). Such conflicts can be solved by ceremonial conformity; loose coupling and decoupling between the actual operations and the formal structures and practices that arise from institutional demands (Meyer and Rowan, 1977). An example of decoupling would be a supplier making cosmetic changes in its sustainability practices after a failed audit in order to pass the next one, but in practice returning to old unsustainable habits in between the audits (Wilhelm et al., 2016).

When talking to an organizational theorist, institutional theory can take on various meanings as presented, for example, by Scott (1987). When institutional theory is applied in purchasing and supply chain research, however, it usually relates to the study of isomorphism, that is, similarity in organizational practices and forms. An example of isomorphism in a supply chain context would be that most organizations use a code of conduct as their key tool in achieving supply chain sustainability. More specifically, what is often studied are the causes of such isomorphism, focusing thus particularly on what is also known as neo-institutional theory. This chapter will focus on this theoretical perspective when explaining institutional theory, building on the key references of Meyer and Rowan (1977) and DiMaggio and Powell (1983), most often credited for the birth of this (neo)-institutional theory. Towards the end of the chapter, a brief overview of some of the other variants of institutional theory is also presented.

KEY VARIABLES AND DEFINITIONS

DiMaggio and Powell (1983), in their seminal work, have presented three mechanisms, or forms of pressure, towards institutional isomorphism: coercive, mimetic and normative. These pressures drive organizations towards isomorphism, which in turns increases their legitimacy. These and other key variables of the theory are defined in Table 21.1.

In their founding work, DiMaggio and Powell (1983) present testable hypotheses for both organizational and field-level behaviour. An organizational field is defined as 'organizations that, in the aggregate, constitute a recognized area of institutional life: key suppliers, resource and product consumers, regulatory agencies, and other organizations that produce similar services or products' (DiMaggio and Powell, 1983, p. 148). Early on, much sociological neo-institutional research focused on higher levels than the individual organization (Scott, 2008). Later, many review studies of institutional theory in subfields of management show the organizational-level unit of analysis to be the most typical approach (see Kauppi, 2013; Weerakkody et al., 2009). This is likely because subfields of management often focus on functional practices within an organization, and the research tradition has not been to examine the behaviour and process of fields and industries overall. The theory can be applied at both levels.

Institutional Isomorphism

Institutional isomorphism is a process through which organizations conform to institutional rules, becoming homogeneous over time (DiMaggio and Powell, 1983). Three types of isomorphism are introduced by DiMaggio and Powell (1983): coercive, mimetic and normative isomorphism. Institutional theory focuses on institutional isomorphism, but other forms of isomorphism exist. Specifically, competitive isomorphism is often discussed in population ecology models (see Hannan and Freeman, 1977); competitive isomorphism explains similarity based on selection and survival of the fittest organizational forms in a particular environment.

Coercive Pressure

Coercive pressures are requirements imposed from outside the organization, by parties the organization relies on for resources or support (DiMaggio and Powell, 1983). Sources of coercive pressure include, for example, dominant suppliers and buyers, investors and governmental parties. According to Mizruchi and Fein (1999), coercive pressures are driven by two

Table 21.1   Definitions of institutional theory variables

Element	Explanation	Supporting references
Unit of analysis	Most typically organizational or field-level analysis, but also individual, organizational function, supply relationship or society level analysis, for example.	DiMaggio and Powell, 1983; Scott, 2008; Weerakkody et al., 2009; Kauppi, 2013; Svejvig, 2013
Level of analysis	Macro-level, looking at how organizational fields become isomorphic; or micro-level, looking at how organizations conform to institutional pressures.	DiMaggio and Powell, 1983; Aksom et al., 2020
Key variables	*Definition*	
Institutional isomorphism	Constraining process that impels one organization to become similar to others in a population under similar conditions.	DiMaggio and Powell, 1983
Coercive pressure	Coercive pressures are caused by entities an organization depends on, for example powerful suppliers or customers, or regulatory bodies which demand the use of certain practices.	DiMaggio and Powell, 1983
Mimetic pressure	Mimetic pressures, or imitative pressures, describe the pressure to imitate successful organizations when faced with uncertainty between means and ends.	DiMaggio and Powell, 1983
Normative pressure	Normative pressures are a result of professional norms and standards within industries and functions, spread by professional associations and educational bodies, for example.	DiMaggio and Powell, 1983
Legitimacy	Perception or assumption that the actions of an organization (or, for example, purchasing function or a supply chain) are desirable and appropriate in the institutional environment the organization operates within.	Suchman, 1995; Meyer and Rowan, 1977
Decoupling	The process of an organization adopting strategies and practices based on institutional expectations and pressures without properly implementing such practices. In this instance, the organization practices 'ceremonial conformity', appearing publicly as if changing its practices, but actually not changing how it operates on a daily basis.	Meyer and Rowan, 1977
Assumptions about human nature	Individuals are assumed to be 'oversocialized', accepting and following social norms without questioning their rationality. Human behaviour is seen as unreflective and routine.	DiMaggio and Powell, 1991, p. 14; Tolbert and Zucker, 1999

forces: (1) pressures from other organizations which an organization is dependent on; and (2) pressure to conform to the cultural expectations of the larger society. Examples would include a buying organization demanding International Organization for Standardization (ISO) standards from its suppliers, or pressure from stakeholders for consumer goods manufacturers to present sustainability certificate labels for their products.

Mimetic Pressure

Mimetic isomorphism occurs within industry groups to maintain legitimacy by imitating successful strategies. Organizations will ascribe competitors' success to their strategic choices and imitate the practices of these competitors (Liu et al., 2010). A classic example is the spread of lean manufacturing practices from Toyota, which were credited to be behind their success in the automotive industry and since adopted across industries. Mimetic pressures can be very strong in situations with uncertainty between actions and outcomes, or overall environmental uncertainty (DiMaggio and Powell, 1983).

Normative Pressure

Normative pressures are about sharing of norms and values among people who belong to same networks through, for example, their work or profession (Basaglia et al., 2009). Employees with comparable educational backgrounds, linked to same institutions, and with similar industry experiences, often define problems and filter information in the same way (DiMaggio and Powell, 1983). DiMaggio and Powell (1983) discuss two main sources of isomorphism through professionalization: formal education through universities, and professional networks spanning organizations and diffusing new practices (examples in the supply chain management domain would include the Institute of Supply Management in the United States and Chartered Institute of Procurement and Supply in the United Kingdom).

Legitimacy

Legitimacy is a key element in institutional theory, as striving for it leads to adoption of particular structures and practices. Meyer and Scott (1983, p. 201) present organizational legitimacy as the degree of cultural support for an organization. A widely cited definition by Suchman (1995, p. 574) provides a more detailed description of this concept as: 'a generalized perception or assumption that the actions of an entity are desirable, proper, or appropriate within some socially constructed system of norms, values, beliefs and definitions'. Suchman (1995) further defines three different forms of legitimacy: pragmatic, moral and cognitive. While Deephouse et al. (2017, p. 33) suggest that there are four states of organizational legitimacy resulting from legitimacy evaluations: accepted, proper, debated and illegitimate.

Decoupling

Preferably, the alignment between structures and activities in an organization is tight (Meyer and Rowan, 1977). But in the presence of conflicting institutional pressures, or when faced with institutional pressures that are in conflict with their task environments, organizations will decouple their formal structure from actual production activities (Boxenbaum and Jonsson, 2008, p. 86). This means, for example, that an organization can symbolically adopt some ISO standards but only 'go through the motions' related to them rather than truly integrate the associated practices into their performance improvement systems. Some later studies distinguish between policy–practice decoupling (adopting a practice symbolically without proper implementation) and means–ends decoupling (complying with a policy but failing to achieve the goals of such a policy) (Haack and Schoeneborn, 2015).

DOMAIN WHERE THE THEORY APPLIES

Institutional theory seeks to explain homogeneity, not variation (DiMaggio and Powell, 1983). It predicts how organizations and, as a result, organizational fields become similar, and the processes through which organizational structures are adopted (Aksom et al., 2020;

Donaldson, 2008, p. 5). The emphasis of the theory is thus on the causes of organizational structure, but it also includes the idea of consequences: adoption of the correct structure as approved in the institutional environment leads to legitimacy and support (DiMaggio and Powell, 1983; Donaldson, 2008, p. 7). The theory can thus be used to explain the adoption decisions of an organization, a supply chain or, for example, the purchasing function: what makes these units adopt similar practices, technologies or structures. Further, the theory can explain how adoption of such practices, technologies and structures impacts upon performance through increased legitimacy and access to, for example, financial resources. A relevant example is sustainability practices: organizations not demonstrating the use of sustainable supply chain practices to their stakeholders are at risk of being negatively portrayed in (social) media, and may also be subject to less advantageous loan terms by financial institutions.

RELATIONSHIPS BETWEEN THE VARIABLES

Figure 21.1 presents the key variables of the theory and their relationships with each other. The relationships between the variables take place within an organizational field. In a particular field, the three types of institutional pressures lead to isomorphism of practices at the field level, and to adoption decisions at an organizational level. Increased environmental uncertainty in the field moderates this relationship, increasing particularly the impact of mimetic pressures. The adoption of the institutionalized practices gives the adopting organizations legitimacy and increased survival prospects. The actual performance of such institutionally adopted practices, however, is also contingent on the extent to which they are coupled or decoupled with actual operations. Several studies in, for example, quality management have shown that institutionally motivated adoptions of ISO certifications tend to lead to weaker implementation of the associated practices and hence also the performance of such practices.

THEORETICAL PREDICTIONS (FACTUAL CLAIMS)

Both seminal articles, Meyer and Rowan (1977) and DiMaggio and Powell (1983), present a set of theoretical predictions, the former as propositions and the latter as hypotheses. These predictions follow what is presented in Figure 21.1 concerning the relationships between key variables in the theory.

Specifically, Meyer and Rowan (1977, p. 352) predict that 'organizations that incorporate socially legitimated rationalized elements in their formal structures maximize their legitimacy and increase their resources and survival capabilities'. But as the institutional demands can be at odds with the demands of the business context, they further theorize that 'elements of structure are decoupled from activities and from each other' (Meyer and Rowan, 1977, p. 357).

DiMaggio and Powell (1983) postulate in more detail the processes leading to organizational isomorphism through coercive, mimetic and normative pressures. Higher dependence on another organization is expected to lead to higher resemblance to that organization. Higher levels of uncertainty between means and ends, as well as higher levels of goal ambiguity, increase the likelihood that an organization will imitate others that it perceives as successful. Higher reliance on academic credentials in hiring, as well as higher levels of participation in professional organizations, increase the likelihood that an organization will start to resemble

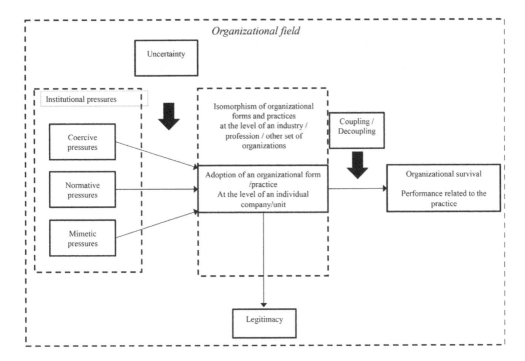

Figure 21.1   Overview of institutional theory key variables and their relationships

other organizations in its field. Most other articles follow a similar logic, suggesting that the three types of pressure (which take on particular characteristics, given the phenomena studied) lead to increased levels of adoption of a particular form, structure or practice. DiMaggio and Powell (1983) further specify field-level hypotheses, theorizing the factors that make an organizational field likely to become highly homogenous. These include, for example, dependence on a single source of vital resources, the extent of transactions with the state, the limited number of alternative organizational models, and technological uncertainty.

HOW HAS THIS THEORY BEEN USED?

In the 1980s, institutional theory started to gather empirical support as organizational scientists, mainly through large quantitative datasets, explored the processes of institutionalization (Alvesson and Spicer, 2019). In operations management, as well as in supply chain management, the theory was a late emerger in the early 2000s (compared to, for example, contingency theory, the resource-based view and agency theory).

Kauppi (2013) provides a review of institutional theory usage in operations and supply chain management (OSCM) research up to 2012 in eight key journals in the area (*Journal of Operations Management, International Journal of Operations and Production Management, Manufacturing and Service Operations Management, Production and Operations Management, International Journal of Production Economics, International Journal of Production Research, Supply Chain Management: International Journal* and the *Journal of*

Table 21.2   Overview of institutional theory usage in OSCM journals

Application area	Authors	Overview of timeline and methods
Environmental sustainability	Adebanjo et al., 2016b; Agarwal et al., 2018; Dubey et al., 2015, 2017; Glover et al., 2014; Gonzalez et al., 2008; Grekova et al., 2014; Heras-Saizarbitoria et al., 2011; Hoejmose et al., 2014; Huang et al., 2016; Li et al., 2019; Lo and Shiah, 2016; Miemczyk, 2008; Seles et al., 2016; Shi et al., 2012; Simpson, 2012; Tachizawa et al., 2015; Wu et al., 2012; Yang et al., 2019; Ye et al., 2013; Zhu, 2016; Zhu and Sarkis, 2007; Zhu et al., 2013	A total of 23 articles, with the peak of publications (15) appearing between 2012 and 2016. 20 of the articles use the survey methodology, 1 is a conceptual study, and 2 are qualitative studies.
Social sustainability	Adebanjo et al., 2013; Castka and Balzarova, 2008; Flynn, 2019; Kauppi and Hannibal, 2017; Lo et al., 2014; Mani and Gunasekaran, 2018; Moxham and Kauppi, 2014; Venkatesh et al., 2020; Yawar and Kauppi, 2018	A total of 9 articles, with 8 published after 2012. A variety of methods: 1 survey, 3 qualitative studies, 2 conceptual studies, 2 secondary data analyses, and 1 mixed methods.
Quality management	Adebanjo et al., 2016a; Boiral and Roy, 2007; Braunscheidel et al., 2011; Dubey et al., 2018; Lo et al., 2011; Lo and Yeung, 2018; Martinez-Costa et al., 2008; Nair and Prajogo, 2009; Prajogo, 2011; Sila, 2007	A total of 10 articles, with most published between 2007 and 2011. Most (6) are surveys, with 2 secondary data analyses and 2 qualitative studies.
Supplier integration	Cai et al., 2010; Huo et al., 2013; Wong and Boon-itt, 2008; Yeung et al., 2006	A total of 4 articles between 2006 and 2013. 3 surveys and 1 case study.
Information technology/ information systems	Barratt and Choi, 2007; Bhakoo and Choi, 2013; Hew et al., 2020; Liu et al., 2010; Saldanha et al., 2015; Sodero et al., 2013; Xie et al., 2016; Zhang and Daliwal, 2009	A total of 8 articles between 2006 and 2013. A mix of methods with 4 qualitative studies, 3 surveys, and 1 secondary data analysis.
Sustainability in general	Grosvold et al., 2014; Sancha et al., 2015; Sayed et al., 2017; Wilhelm et al., 2016	A total of 4 studies between 2014 and 2017. 4 case studies, 1 combining survey and secondary data.
Other topics (1 article per topic area)	Cheng and Chen, 2016; Dobrzykowski, 2019; Gopal and Gao, 2009; Hirschinger et al., 2016; Howard et al., 2007; Meehan et al., 2016; Munir and Baird, 2016; Rogers et al., 2007; Tate et al., 2009; Wang et al., 2018; Wu et al., 2013; Zsidisin et al., 2005	A total of 12 studies spread throughout 2005–2019. A mix of methods including survey, secondary data, delphi study, qualitative studies and mixed methods. Topics include, for example, outsourcing, modularity and supplier development.

Supply Chain Management). For this chapter, an abstract-based keyword search of institutional theory usage in the same operations and supply chain management journals, and also the *Journal of Purchasing and Supply Management*, was conducted to provide a more updated usage of the theory in our field. The combined overview based on this review and that of Kauppi (2013) in these nine OSCM journals is provided in Table 21.2.

This overview demonstrates that sustainability-related topics have received by far the most attention in the use of institutional theory. Such articles represent 36 out of the total 66 articles using the theory published between 2005 and 2020. While earlier applications of the theory focused mostly on explaining the adoption of quality management practices and different information technology and systems and supplier integration (the bulk of this work conducted between 2006 and 2013), environmental, social and overall sustainability-related topics dominated in the following years (mostly post-2012). Surveys have been the dominant methodological choice, with 37 out of 66 articles using survey instruments. Kauppi (2013) criticized the item formation for surveys looking at institutional pressures, noting that most studies only use a single construct for external pressures overall. Such a grouped construct for all the institutional pressures, however, does not provide a detailed explanation on how exactly supply chain practices are influenced: are they shaped by education or legislative pressure or, for example, by mimicking leading multinational organizations. In this respect, some improvements have been made. While single construct studies still continue to be published, there are also several using separate constructs for each of the institutional pressures (see for example Dubey et al., 2017; Dubey et al., 2018; Hew et al., 2020; Huo et al., 2013; Munir and Baird, 2016; Zhu et al., 2013; Zhu, 2016). Surveys have been the dominant method particularly in examining environmental sustainability-related issues (20/23). Other application areas show a more varied use of methods, including qualitative methods, conceptual studies and secondary data. Most reviewed studies use the company or organization as their unit of analysis; that is, the entity being impacted upon by institutional pressures.

The results of this review are in line with those of, for example, Walker et al. (2015), who note supply chain management, sustainability and total quality management as the top areas in which institutional theory has been applied. Institutional theory has also been subject to comparative studies of explanatory value with other theories (see for example Adebanjo et al., 2016b; Rogers et al., 2007; Tate et al., 2009; Zsidisin et al., 2005), particularly in recent years in relation to the natural resource-based view (Grekova et al., 2014; Li et al., 2019).

A BRIEF LOOK ON THE OTHER VARIANTS OF INSTITUTIONAL THEORY AND THEIR USE IN THE FIELD

While institutional theory examines isomorphism, ironically the theory itself has many variants (Tolbert and Zucker, 1999). For a detailed discussion on these, the reader is referred to the works of Scott (1987, 2008). In this chapter the focus has been on the stream that relies heaviest on Meyer and Rowan's (1977) and DiMaggio and Powell's (1983) seminal works; this has also been the stream of institutional theory most applied in OSCM (and in other fields such as enterprise systems research; see Svejvig, 2013). There are, however, several other streams of the theory, which have seen limited use in OSCM so far but are equally important in explaining phenomena in our field. A brief overview of three such streams is provided here, along with key references for interested readers.

Economic Variant of Institutional Theory

Similarly to the institutional theory stemming from the works of DiMaggio and Powell (1983) discussed above, the economic variant of institutional theory emphasizes the role of uncertainty in driving isomorphism in organizational practices (Kauppi, 2013). This stream builds on the work of Haunschild and Miner (1997). The main difference in argumentation is that organizations are not seeking legitimacy; rather, they are economically motivated to mimic each others' practices (Haunschild and Miner, 1997). Particularly, organizations engage in three types of imitation: frequency-based (mimicking practices adopted by many), trait-based (mimicking practices from organizations of prestige, high performance and large size) and outcome-based (mimicking practices appearing to have resulted in success) (Haunschild and Miner, 1997). This economic variant of institutional theory is used by, for example, Ketokivi and Schroeder (2004), Huang et al. (2010) and Turkulainen et al. (2017) in explaining the adoption of operations and supply chain management practices.

Institutional Work

A second, relatively new stream of institutional studies deals with institutional work. This theoretical stream moves the focus from the structures as outcomes of institutionalization to the processes of institutionalization: what creates, maintains and disrupts institutions (Lawrence and Suddaby, 2006, pp. 215–216; Suddaby et al., 2013). This stream builds on the key works of DiMaggio (1988), Oliver (1991, 1992) and Lawrence and Suddaby (2006). DiMaggio (1988, p. 14) introduces the concept of institutional entrepreneurship: actors with sufficient resources who cause new institutions to arise. Oliver (1991) provides a typology of responses to institutional pressures, ranging from passive conformity to proactive manipulation, along with antecedents to each of the strategic responses. Oliver (1992) presented antecedents to deinstitutionalization, that is, factors that can lead to erosion or rejection of an institutionalized organizational practice. This stream has so far seen extremely limited use in our field. Notable exceptions include Wu and Jia (2018) who investigate supply chain localization as a process of institutional change, arguing that multinational enterprises in China build new institutional infrastructure to deal with institutional voids.

Institutional Logics

Institutional logics are seen as 'a set of material practices and symbolic constructions linking institution and action'; they explain how a particular social world works (Svejvig, 2013, p. 7). The seminal piece in this stream of institutional theory is that by Friedland and Alford (1991, p. 232), which introduces capitalist market, bureaucratic state, democracy, family and religion as the central institutions of Western societies, each with their own logic. This, along with other key pieces in this stream, brought institutional logics as a key element in defining the content and meaning of institutions (Thornton and Ocasio, 2008, p. 100). This stream has moved the focus from isomorphism to the effect of these (and other, later defined) institutional logics on organizations, as well as to how organizational actors can shape these institutional logics (Thornton and Ocasio, 2008, p. 100). A key tenet in this stream is that to understand organizational behaviour, it needs to be examined in an institutional context with its logics, which both regulates such behaviour and provides the opportunity for change (Thornton and Ocasio, 2008, pp. 101–102). Example applications include Longoni et al.'s (2019) work on managing tensions between conflicting logics in a migrant integration supply chain, and Pemer and Skjølsvik's (2016) work on examining the institutional logics of actors involved in purchases of knowledge-intensive services.

OUTLOOK ON FUTURE RESEARCH OPPORTUNITIES

While several studies using institutional theory, particularly neo-institutional theory with its focus on institutional pressures and conformity, have already been conducted in our field, many opportunities remain to contribute to both theory and practice. Kauppi (2013) provided an extensive research agenda for institutional theory in operations and supply chain management, with a focus on three areas: (1) increased examination of the role of uncertainty in how organizations react to institutional pressures and imitate practices of other organizations; (2) examining the relationships between the three types of institutional pressures themselves; and (3) understanding the role of academia as a source and target of institutional pressures. These and other interesting avenues are briefly discussed below.

First, including uncertainty as a variable in empirical studies on institutional theory was encouraged due to its key role in the theory but limited appearance in practice so far (Kauppi, 2013). Still, only a handful of papers (Yang et al., 2019; Yawar and Kauppi, 2018; Reusen et al., 2020; Lo and Shiah, 2016) explicitly discuss the role of uncertainty and/or include it as a variable in survey research, leaving room to examine its impact between pressure and adoption. Second, a more detailed examination of the three pressures and their linkages was suggested, for example, to understand which of the pressures takes precedence under which conditions in a supply chain environment. With the increased use of separate measures for the three pressure constructs since then, some progress in understanding this has been made already. Yet, few studies investigate what happens if the three institutional pressures are in conflict with each other in terms of the practices they push onto supply chains. Relatedly, a more detailed look at the parties exerting pressure (which actually falls more under the domain of institutional work) was also suggested by Kauppi (2013). Studies such as that by Kauppi and Hannibal (2017) examining how social sustainability assessment initiatives instigate and use institutional pressures to drive third-party accreditation in supply chains are still rare, meaning that there is much scope to understand the institutional work shaping modern supply chains. The third suggestion of Kauppi (2013), of OSCM academics trying to understand our own role as a source of institutional pressure, is also a research avenue to be examined.

While in the 1980s management scholars had already begun using large quantitative secondary datasets to explore institutionalization of practices (Alvesson and Spicer, 2019), we are yet to see secondary data being used extensively to understand the institutionalization of particular practices in the supply chains of different industries. The concept of decoupling has also been examined in only a handful of studies (see Grosvold et al., 2014; Wilhelm et al., 2016; Yang et al., 2019). Further opportunities thus exist to understand the extent to which, for example, different sustainability practices (codes of conduct, sustainability certifications, and so on) actually bring about changes in the day-to-day operations of global supply chains, or whether they are used more as a tool to improve an organization's supply chain image. Overall, Greenwood et al. (2017, p. 17) argue that future institutional theory research should focus on the outcomes and consequences of institutions: does their maintenance or destruction bring benefit or harm to organizations and societies?

REFERENCES

Adebanjo, D., Ojadi, F., Laosirihongthong, T., and Tickle, M. (2013). A case study of supplier selection in developing economies: a perspective on institutional theory and corporate social responsibility. *Supply Chain Management: An International Journal*, 18(5), 553–566.

Adebanjo, D., Samaranayake, P., Mafakheri, F., and Laosirihongthong, T. (2016a). Prioritization of six-sigma project selection: a resource-based view and institutional norms perspective. *Benchmarking: An International Journal*, 23(7), 1983–2003.

Adebanjo, D., Teh, P.L., and Ahmed, P.K. (2016b). The impact of external pressure and sustainable management practices on manufacturing performance and environmental outcomes. *International Journal of Operations and Production Management*, 36(9), 995–1013.

Agarwal, A., Giraud-Carrier, F.C., and Li, Y. (2018). A mediation model of green supply chain management adoption: the role of internal impetus. *International Journal of Production Economics*, 205, 342–358.

Aksom, H., Zhylinska, O., and Gaidai, T. (2020). Can institutional theory be refuted, replaced or modified? *International Journal of Organizational Analysis*, 28(1), 135–159.

Alvesson, M., and Spicer, A. (2019). Neo-institutional theory and organization studies: a mid-life crisis? *Organization Studies*, 40(2), 199–218.

Barratt, M., and Choi, T. (2007). Mandated RFID and institutional responses: cases of decentralized business units. *Production and Operations Management*, 16(5), 569–585.

Basaglia, S., Caporarello, L., Magni, M., and Pennarola, F. (2009). Environmental and organizational drivers influencing the adoption of VoIP. *Information Systems and E-Business Management*, 7(1), 103–118.

Bhakoo, V., and Choi, T. (2013). The iron cage exposed: Institutional pressures and heterogeneity across the healthcare supply chain. *Journal of Operations Management*, 31(6), 432–449.

Boiral, O., and Roy, M.J. (2007). ISO 9000: integration rationales and organizational impacts. *International Journal of Operations and Production Management*, 27(2), 226–247.

Boxenbaum, E., and Jonsson, S. (2008). Isomorphism, diffusion and decoupling. In: *The SAGE Handbook of Organizational Institutionalism*, edited by Greenwood, R., Oliver, C., Sahlin, K., and Suddaby, R. London: SAGE Publications, pp. 78–98.

Braunscheidel, M.J., Hamister, J.W., Suresh, N.C., and Star, H. (2011). An institutional theory perspective on Six Sigma adoption. *International Journal of Operations and Production Management*, 31(4), 423–451.

Cai, S., Jun, M., and Yang, Z. (2010). Implementing supply chain information integration in China: the role of institutional forces and trust. *Journal of Operations Management*, 28(3), 257–268.

Castka, P., and Balzarova, M. (2008). ISO 26000 and supply chains – on the diffusion of the social responsibility standard. *International Journal of Production Economics*, 111(2), 274–286.

Cheng, J.H., and Chen, M.C. (2016). Influence of institutional and moral orientations on relational risk management in supply chains. *Journal of Purchasing and Supply Management*, 22(2), 110–119.

Deephouse, D.L. (1996). Does isomorphism legitimate?. *Academy of Management Journal*, 39(4), 1024–1039.

Deephouse, D.L., Bundy, J., Tost, L.P., and Suchman, M.C. (2017). Organizational legitimacy: six key questions. In: *The SAGE Handbook of Organizational Institutionalism*, edited by Greenwood, R., Oliver, C., Lawrence, T., and Meyer, R. London: SAGE Publications, pp. 27–54.

DiMaggio, P.J. (1988). Interest and agency in institutional theory. In: *Institutional Patterns and Organizations: Culture and Environment*, edited by Zucker, L. Cambridge, MA: Ballinger, pp. 3–22.

DiMaggio, P.J., and Powell, W.W. (1983). The iron cage revisited: institutional isomorphism and collective rationality in organizational fields. *American Sociological Review*, 48(2), 147–160.

DiMaggio, P.J., and Powell, W.W. (1991). Introduction. In: *The New Institutionalism in Organizational Analysis*, edited by DiMaggio, P. and Powell, W. Chicago, IL: University of Chicago Press, pp. 1–40.

Dobrzykowski, D. (2019). Understanding the downstream healthcare supply chain: Unpacking regulatory and industry characteristics. *Journal of Supply Chain* Management, 55(2), 26–46.

Donaldson, L. (2008). The conflict between contingency and institutional theories of organizational design. In: *Designing Organizations*, edited by Burton, R., Eriksen, B., Håkonsson, D., Knudsen, T. and Snow, W. Boston, MA: Springer, pp. 3–20.

Dubey, R., Gunasekaran, A., and Ali, S.S. (2015). Exploring the relationship between leadership, operational practices, institutional pressures and environmental performance: a framework for green supply chain. *International Journal of Production Economics*, 160, 120–132.

Dubey, R., Gunasekaran, A., Childe, S.J., Papadopoulos, T., Hazen, B., et al. (2017). Examining the effect of external pressures and organizational culture on shaping performance measurement systems (PMS) for sustainability benchmarking: some empirical findings. *International Journal of Production Economics*, 193, 63–76.

Dubey, R., Gunasekaran, A., Childe, S.J., Papadopoulos, T., Hazen, B.T., and Roubaud, D. (2018). Examining top management commitment to TQM diffusion using institutional and upper echelon theories. *International Journal of Production Research*, 56(8), 2988–3006.

Flynn, A. (2019). Determinants of corporate compliance with modern slavery reporting. *Supply Chain Management: An International Journal*, 25(1), 1–16.

Friedland, R., and Alford, R. (1991). Bringing society back in: symbols, practices, and institutional contradictions. In: *The New Institutionalism in Organizational Analysis*, edited by Powell, W. and DiMaggio, P. Chicago, IL and London: University of Chicago Press, pp. 232–263.

Glover, J.L., Champion, D., Daniels, K.J., and Dainty, A.J. (2014). An institutional theory perspective on sustainable practices across the dairy supply chain. *International Journal of Production Economics*, 152, 102–111.

Gonzalez, P., Sarkis, J., and Adenso-Diaz, B. (2008). Environmental management system certification and its influence on corporate practices: evidence from the automotive industry. *International Journal of Operations and Production Management*, 28(11), 1021–1041.

Gopal, A., and Gao, G. (2009). Certification in the Indian offshore IT services industry. *Manufacturing and Service Operations Management*, 11(3), 471–492.

Greenwood, R., Oliver, C., Lawrence, T.B., and Meyer, R. (2017). Introduction: into the fourth decade. In: *The SAGE Handbook of Organizational Institutionalism*, edited by Greenwood, R., Oliver, C., Lawrence, T. and Meyer, R. London: SAGE Publications, pp. 1–24.

Grekova, K., Bremmers, H.J., Trienekens, J.H., Kemp, R.G.M., and Omta, S.W.F. (2014). Extending environmental management beyond the firm boundaries: an empirical study of Dutch food and beverage firms. *International Journal of Production Economics*, 152, 174–187.

Grosvold, J., Hoejmose, S.U., and Roehrich, J.K. (2014). Squaring the circle: management, measurement and performance of sustainability in supply chains. *Supply Chain Management: An International Journal*, 19(3), 292–305.

Haack, P., and Schoeneborn, D. (2015). Is decoupling becoming decoupled from institutional theory? A commentary on Wijen. *Academy of Management Review*, 40(2), 307–310.

Hannan, M.T., and Freeman, J. (1977). The population ecology of organizations. *American Journal of Sociology*, 82(5), 929–964.

Haunschild, P., and Miner, A. (1997). Modes of interorganizational imitation: the effects of outcome salience and uncertainty. *Administrative Science Quarterly*, 42(3), 472–500.

Heras-Saizarbitoria, I., Landin, G., and Molina-Azorin, J. (2011). Do drivers matter for the benefits of ISO 14001? *International Journal of Operations and Production Management*, 31(2), 192–216.

Hew, J.J., Wong, L.W., Tan, G.W.H., Ooi, K.B., and Lin, B. (2020). The blockchain-based Halal traceability systems: a hype or reality? *Supply Chain Management: An International Journal*, 25(6), 863–879.

Hirschinger, M., Spickermann, A., Hartmann, E., von der Gracht, H., and Darkow, I. (2016). The future of logistics in emerging markets – fuzzy clustering scenarios grounded in institutional and factor-market rivalry theory. *Journal of Supply Chain Management*, 51(4), 73–93.

Hoejmose, S.U., Grosvold, J., and Millington, A. (2014). The effect of institutional pressure on cooperative and coercive 'green' supply chain practices. *Journal of Purchasing and Supply Management*, 20(4), 215–224.

Howard, M., Lewis, M., Miemczyk, J., and Brandon-Jones, A. (2007). Implementing supply practice at Bridgend engine plant: the influence of institutional and strategic choice perspectives. *International Journal of Operations and Production Management*, 27(7), 754–776.

Huang, X., Gattiker, T.F., and Schroeder, R.G. (2010). Do competitive priorities drive adoption of electronic commerce applications? Testing the contingency and institutional views. *Journal of Supply Chain Management*, 46(3), 57–69.

Huang, Y.C., Yang, M.L., and Wong, Y.J. (2016). Institutional pressures, resources commitment, and returns management. *Supply Chain Management: An International Journal*, 21(3), 398–416.

Huo, B., Han, Z., Zhao, X., Zhou, H., Wood, C.H., and Zhai, X. (2013). The impact of institutional pressures on supplier integration and financial performance: evidence from China. *International Journal of Production Economics*, 146(1), 82–94.

Kauppi, K. (2013). Extending the use of institutional theory in operations and supply chain management research: Review and research suggestions. *International Journal of Operations and Production Management*, 33(10), 1318–1345.

Kauppi, K., and Hannibal, C. (2017). Institutional pressures and sustainability assessment in supply chains. *Supply Chain Management; An International Journal*, 22(5), 458–472.

Ketokivi, M.A., and Schroeder, R.G. (2004). Strategic, structural contingency and institutional explanations in the adoption of innovative manufacturing practices. *Journal of Operations Management*, 22(1), 63–89.

Lawrence, T.B., and Suddaby, R. (2006). Institutions and Institutional Work. In: *Handbook of Organization Studies*, edited by Clegg, S.R., Hardy, C., Lawrence, T.B., and Nord, W.R. London: SAGE, pp. 215–54.

Li, Y., Ye, F., Dai, J., Zhao, X., and Sheu, C. (2019). The adoption of green practices by Chinese firms. *International Journal of Operations and Production Management*, 39(4), 550–572.

Liu, H., Ke, W., Wei, K., Gu, J., and Chen, H. (2010). The role of institutional pressures and organizational culture in the firm's intention to adopt internet-enabled supply chain management systems. *Journal of Operations Management*, 28(5), 372–384.

Lo, C.K., Pagell, M., Fan, D., Wiengarten, F., and Yeung, A.C. (2014). OHSAS 18001 certification and operating performance: the role of complexity and coupling. *Journal of Operations Management*, 32(5), 268–280.

Lo, S.M., and Shiah, Y.A. (2016). Associating the motivation with the practices of firms going green: the moderator role of environmental uncertainty. *Supply Chain Management: An International Journal*, 21(4), 485–498.

Lo, C.K., and Yeung, A.C. (2018). Quality management standards, institutionalization and organizational implications: a longitudinal analysis. *International Journal of Production Economics*, 200, 231–239.

Lo, C., Yeung, A., and Cheng, T. (2011). Meta-standards, financial performance and senior executive compensation in China: an institutional perspective. *International Journal of Production Economics*, 129(1), 119–126.

Longoni, A., Luzzini, D., Pullman, M., and Habiague, M. (2019). Business for society is society's business: tension management in a migrant integration supply chain. *Journal of Supply Chain Management*, 55(4), 3–33.

Mani, V., and Gunasekaran, A. (2018). Four forces of supply chain social sustainability adoption in emerging economies. *International Journal of Production Economics*, 199, 150–161.

Martinez-Costa, M., Martinez-Lorente, A., and Choi, T. (2008). Simultaneous consideration of TQM and ISO 9000 on performance and motivation: an empirical study of Spanish companies. *International Journal of Production Economics*, 113(1), 23–39.

Meehan, J., Ludbrook, M.N., and Mason, C.J. (2016). Collaborative public procurement: Institutional explanations of legitimised resistance. *Journal of Purchasing and Supply Management*, 22(3), 160–170.

Meyer, J., and Rowan, B. (1977). Institutionalized organizations: formal structure as myth and ceremony. *American Journal of Sociology*, 83(2), 340–363.

Meyer, J., and Scott, R. (1983). Centralization and the legitimacy problems of local government. In: *Organizational Environments: Ritual and Rationality*, edited by Meyer, J., and Scott, R. Beverly Hills, CA: SAGE Publishers, pp. 199–215.

Miemczyk, J. (2008). An exploration of institutional constraints on developing end-of-life product recovery capabilities. *International Journal of Production Economics*, 115(2), 272–282.

Mizruchi, M.S., and Fein, L.C. (1999). The social construction of organizational knowledge: a study of the uses of coercive, mimetic, and normative isomorphism. *Administrative Science Quarterly*, 44(4), 653–683.

Moxham, C., and Kauppi, K. (2014). Using organisational theories to further our understanding of socially sustainable supply chains. *Supply Chain Management: An International Journal*, 19(4), 413–420.

Munir, R., and Baird, K. (2016). Influence of institutional pressures on performance measurement systems. *Journal of Accounting and Organizational Change*, 12(2), 106–128.

Nair, A., and Prajogo, D. (2009). Internalisation of ISO 9000 standards: the antecedent role of functionalist and institutionalist drivers and performance implications. *International Journal of Production Research*, 47(16), 4545–4568.

Oliver, C. (1991). Strategic responses to institutional processes. *Academy of Management Review*, 16(1), 45–79.

Oliver, C. (1992). The antecedents of deinstitutionalization. *Organization Studies*, 13(4), 563–88.

Pemer, F., and Skjølsvik, T. (2016). Purchasing policy or purchasing police? The influence of institutional logics and power on responses to purchasing formalization. *Journal of Supply Chain Management*, 52(4), 5–21.

Prajogo, D. (2011). The roles of firms' motives in affecting the outcomes of ISO 9000 adoption. *International Journal of Operations and Production Management*, 31(1), 78–100.

Reusen, E., Stouthuysen, K., Roodhooft, F., Van den Abbeele, A., and Slabbinck, H. (2020). Imitation of management practices in supply networks: relational and environmental effects. *Journal of Supply Chain Management*, 56(1), 54–72.

Rogers, K., Purdy, L., Safayeni, F., and Duimering, P. (2007). A supplier development program: rational process or institutional image construction? *Journal of Operations Management*, 25(2), 556–572.

Saldanha, J.P., Mello, J.E., Knemeyer, A.M., and Vijayaraghavan, T.A.S. (2015). Implementing supply chain technologies in emerging markets: an institutional theory perspective. *Journal of Supply Chain Management*, 51(1), 5–26.

Sancha, C., Longoni, A., and Giménez, C. (2015). Sustainable supplier development practices: drivers and enablers in a global context. *Journal of Purchasing and Supply Management*, 21(2), 95–102.

Sayed, M., Hendry, L.C., and Bell, M.Z. (2017). Institutional complexity and sustainable supply chain management practices. *Supply Chain Management: An International Journal*, 22(6), 542–563.

Scott, W. (1987). The adolescence of institutional theory. *Administrative Science Quarterly*, 32(4), 493–511.

Scott, W. (2008). Approaching adulthood: the maturing of institutional theory. *Theory and Society*, 37(5), 427–442.

Seles, B.M.R.P., de Sousa Jabbour, A.B.L., Jabbour, C.J.C., and Dangelico, R.M. (2016). The green bullwhip effect, the diffusion of green supply chain practices, and institutional pressures: evidence from the automotive sector. *International Journal of Production Economics*, 182, 342–355.

Shi, G.V., Koh, L.S.C., Baldwin, J., and Cucchiella, F. (2012). Natural resource based green supply chain management. *Supply Chain Management: An International Journal*, 17(1), 54–67.

Sila, I. (2007). Examining the effects of contextual factors on TQM and performance through the lens of organizational theories: an empirical study. *Journal of Operations Management*, 25(1), 83–109.

Simpson, D. (2012). Institutional pressure and waste reduction: the role of investments in waste reduction resources. *International Journal of Production Economics*, 139(1), 330–339.

Sodero, A.C., Rabinovich, E., and Sinha, R.K. (2013). Drivers and outcomes of open-standard interorganizational information systems assimilation in high-technology supply chains. *Journal of Operations Management*, 31(6), 330–344.

Suchman, M. (1995). Managing legitimacy: Strategic and institutional approaches. *Academy of Management Review*, 20(3), 571–610.

Suddaby, R., Seidl, D., and Lê, J.K. (2013). Strategy-as-practice meets neo-institutional theory. *Strategic Organization*, 11(3), 329–344.

Svejvig, P. (2013). Using institutional theory in enterprise systems research: developing a conceptual model from a literature review. *International Journal of Enterprise Information Systems (IJEIS)*, 9(1), 1–30.

Tachizawa, E.M., Gimenez, C., and Sierra, V. (2015). Green supply chain management approaches: drivers and performance implications. *International Journal of Operations and Production Management*, 35(11), 1546–1566.

Tate, W., Ellram, L., Bals, L., and Hartmann, E. (2009). Offshore outsourcing of services: an evolutionary perspective. *International Journal of Production Economics*, 120(2), 512–524.

Thornton, P.H., and Ocasio, W. (2008). Institutional logics. In: *The SAGE Handbook of Organizational Institutionalism*, edited by Greenwood, R., Oliver, C., Sahlin, K., and Suddaby, R. London: SAGE Publications, pp. 99–128.

Tolbert, P.S., and Zucker, L.G. (1999). The institutionalization of institutional theory. In: *Studying Organization. Theory and Method*, edited by Clegg, S., and Hardy, C. London and Thousand Oaks, CA: SAGE, pp. 169–184.

Turkulainen, V., Kauppi, K., and Nermes, E. (2017). Institutional explanations missing link in operations management? Insights on supplier integration. *International Journal of Operations and Production Management*, 37(8), 1117–1140.

Venkatesh, V.G., Zhang, A., Deakins, E., and Mani, V. (2020). Drivers of sub-supplier social sustainability compliance: an emerging economy perspective. *Supply Chain Management: An International Journal*, 25(6), 655–677.

Walker, H., Chicksand, D., Radnor, Z., and Watson, G. (2015). Theoretical perspectives in operations management: an analysis of the literature. *International Journal of Operations and Production Management*, 35(8), 1182–1206.

Wang, S., Li, J., Song, J., Li, Y., and Sherk, M. (2018). Institutional pressures and product modularity: do supply chain coordination and functional coordination matter? *International Journal of Production Research*, 56(20), 6644–6657.

Weerakkody, V., Dwivedi, Y.K., and Irani, Z. (2009). The diffusion and use of institutional theory: a cross-disciplinary longitudinal literature survey. *Journal of Information Technology*, 24(4), 354–368.

Wilhelm, M.M., Blome, C., Bhakoo, V., and Paulraj, A. (2016). Sustainability in multi-tier supply chains: Understanding the double agency role of the first-tier supplier. *Journal of Operations Management*, 41, 42–60.

Wong, C.Y., and Boon-itt, S. (2008). The influence of institutional norms and environmental uncertainty on supply chain integration in the Thai automotive industry. *International Journal of Production Economics*, 115(2), 400–410.

Wu, T., Daniel, E.M., Hinton, M., and Quintas, P. (2013). Isomorphic mechanisms in manufacturing supply chains: a comparison of indigenous Chinese firms and foreign-owned MNCs. *Supply Chain Management: An International Journal*, 18(2), 161–177.

Wu, G., Ding, J., and Chen, P. (2012). The effects of GSCM drivers and institutional pressures on GSCM practices in Taiwan's textile and apparel industry. *International Journal of Production Economics*, 135(2), 618–636.

Wu, Z., and Jia, F. (2018). Toward a theory of supply chain fields–understanding the institutional process of supply chain localization. *Journal of Operations Management*, 58, 27–41.

Xie, Y., Breen, L., Cherrett, T., Zheng, D., and Allen, C.J. (2016). An exploratory study of reverse exchange systems used for medical devices in the UK National Health Service (NHS). *Supply Chain Management: An International Journal*, 21(2), 194–215.

Yang, Y., Lau, A.K., Lee, P.K., Yeung, A.C., and Cheng, T.E. (2019). Efficacy of China's strategic environmental management in its institutional environment. *International Journal of Operations and Production Management*, 39(1), 138–163.

Yawar, S.A., and Kauppi, K. (2018). Understanding the adoption of socially responsible supplier development practices using institutional theory: dairy supply chains in India. *Journal of Purchasing and Supply Management*, 24(2), 164–176.

Ye, F., Zhao, X., Prahinski, C., and Li, Y. (2013). The impact of institutional pressures, top managers' posture and reverse logistics on performance – evidence from China. *International Journal of Production Economics*, 143(1), 132–143.

Yeung, A., Cheng, T., and Lai, K. (2006). An operational and institutional perspective on total quality management. *Production and Operations Management*, 15(1), 156–170.

Zhang, C., and Dhaliwal, J. (2009). An investigation of resource-based and institutional theoretic factors in technology adoption for operations and supply chain management. *International Journal of Production Economics*, 120(1), 252–269.

Zhu, Q. (2016). Institutional pressures and support from industrial zones for motivating sustainable production among Chinese manufacturers. *International Journal of Production Economics*, 181, 402–409.

Zhu, Q., and Sarkis, J. (2007). The moderating effects of institutional pressures on emergent green supply chain practices and performance. *International Journal of Production Research*, 45(18), 4333–4356.

Zhu, Q., Sarkis, J., and Lai, K.H. (2013). Institutional-based antecedents and performance outcomes of internal and external green supply chain management practices. *Journal of Purchasing and Supply Management*, 19(2), 106–117.

Zsidisin, G., Melnyk, S., and Ragatz, G. (2005). An institutional theory perspective of business continuity planning for purchasing and supply management. *International Journal of Production Research*, 43(16), 3401–3420.

22. Complex adaptive systems

Kevin J. Dooley

INTRODUCTION

'Complex adaptive systems' is a general term referring to a meta-theory. It is not one theory, but rather a broad set of assumptions, constructs, theories, models and methodologies. At its core, complexity adaptive systems theories, or complexity science, is a subset of systems theory. Traditional reductionist science held that systems could be described by the elements inside them and how they interacted. Reductionist science tends to assume causal linearity and unidirectionality.

Systems theory posits that complexity or non-linearity arises when system variables interact and when variables have feedback mechanisms; for example, X causes Y, and Y causes X. Systems theory was initially created in the 1940s as a means to control mechanical systems. Weiner (1948) proposed that the concepts of feedback and interactions were critical to understanding or designing any biological or social system. Von Bertalanffy developed general systems theory in 1951 (von Bertalanffy, 1951), and systems theory developed rapidly in depth and application through the following decades. In social systems applications, including management, systems theory influenced new theories concerning evolutionary processes and learning within organizations, control mechanisms and contingency theory, namely how a system's external environment shapes its behaviour (for example, Simon, 1957; Forrester, 1961; Bateson, 1972).

The concepts of complexity and complex adaptive systems first emerged from these systems theory roots in the 1980s. Gleick's (1987) *Chaos: Making of a New Science* popularized chaos theory and fractals. Chaos theory had been discovered at several points in history, but the book introduced the topic to a broad public. In operations management, desktop software allowed people to look for chaos in various types of operational time series data (Dooley and Van de Ven, 1999). Attempts were made to use chaos theory to predict stock market prices (Guastello, 1995). Concurrent with that, Prigogine and Stengers (1984) published *Order Out of Chaos*, which illustrated the conditions under which small changes in the external environment can lead to adaptive change by the system. To many management scholars, Prigogine and Stenger's work introduced them for the first time to the concept of emergence, whereby orders and patterns in an organizational or supply chain emerge from interactions from within the system, as opposed to being mechanically preplanned and controlled. Prigogine and Stenger's work influenced many of the early organizational science applications (for example, Chiles et al., 2004).

KEY VARIABLES AND DEFINITIONS

General Concepts

The standard definition of a system is that any system contains other systems, and any system is a part of other systems (Bateson, 1972). This embeddedness is not de facto hierarchical, but it represents the nesting nature of systems. A complex adaptive system is a system that: (1) behaves in complex ways because of the multitude of interactions between components of the system, including causality that is nonlinear and multidirectional; and (2) through such interactions is adaptive to environment changes in order to maintain, satisfice or optimize particular needs or desires.

For example, if we consider an organization as a complex adaptive system:

1. The organization is a system in that it is composed of other systems; for example, production, purchasing or human resources. It is also a part of larger systems; for example, a supply chain, an industry sector, a community, and so on.
2. The organization's behaviour is complex in that its actions are the result of interactions between people and teams inside and outside the organization, and outcomes from the organization emerge in sometimes unpredictable and dynamic ways.
3. The organization makes changes through its internal processes to adapt to the environment; in other words, market conditions, competitor actions, supply chain failures, and so on.

It is worthwhile to note that organizational theorists have traditionally associated the term 'complexity' with a description of the inner workings of an organization (Dooley, 2021), often related to size or variety. For example, a firm with many specialists is considered more complex than a firm with few specialists. In the case of a complex adaptive system, complexity refers to the manner in which the system behaves relative to its internal structure. A complex adaptive system's aggregate behaviour is emergent, in that it is not predictable from and cannot be reduced or understood from its component parts (Holland, 1995).

The conceptual formulation of a complex adaptive system is significantly influenced by the limitations we have in making predictions or understanding how it works. Since the 'rules' of a complex adaptive system are not deducible from observing behaviour and outcomes alone, scientists wished to construct mathematical models, in the form of computer simulations. The first widely adopted definition of a complex adaptive system was simultaneously a specification for a computer simulation language.

Table 22.1 shows the definitions of concepts or constructs associated with complex adaptive systems. A common source for all of these is Holland (1995).

Agents are the basic element of a complex adaptive system. In organization contexts, agents can represent individual people, teams, divisions or whole firms. Agents seek to maximize their fitness by evolving over time. The fitness of the agent is often modelled as a multi-attribute utility function. Agents scan their internal and external environment and interpret these observations via their schemata. Schemata are mental models and heuristic rules that define how observations are interpreted and what are appropriate responses for given stimuli. Schemata often evolve from smaller, more basic schemata. Agents are assumed to be rationally bounded, in that they have limited and perhaps biased access to information within the system, and schemata may differ across agents due to differences in how people make decisions. Within an agent, multiple and contradictory schemata may exist, competing

Table 22.1   *Definitions of complex adaptive systems concepts*

Element	Explanation
Unit of analysis	Can be applied at any level of a living system, from a microbe to the Earth as a whole. In organizational sciences, the unit of analysis is typically the firm or a collection of firms; for example, an industry sector or supply network.
Level of analysis	In organizational sciences, the level of analysis is typically the firm or a collection of firms.
Key constructs/concepts	
Agents	The people who constitute an organization, or the organizations that constitute a collection of organizations.
Schemata	Mental models and heuristic rules that define how an agent observes the current system state and identifies actions to improve its fitness.
Fitness function	A (typically) multidimensional utility function that represents how system state conditions relate to fitness of the agent.
Resources	Agents exchange resources with one another or with the environment. Resources may be physical (tangible: for example, money) or non-physical (intangible: for example, information).
Agent interactions	Agents communicate with one another and exchange resources.
Agent tags	Agents have labels that other agents use to interpret their role in the system.
Assumptions about human nature and reality	
Bounded rationality	Agents will act rationally according to their fitness function, but will be bounded by cognitive limitations.
Satisficing	Agents will satisfice or optimize their fitness function.
Nonlinearity	Agent interactions lead to causal relations and outcomes that may be non-linear.
Dynamism	Agent interactions lead to causal relations and outcomes that are dynamic; in other words, they change over time.
Emergence	The behaviours and outcomes of a complex adaptive system emerge from the interactions of its components; the system's collective behaviour cannot be explained by its components alone.

via a selection–enactment–retention process. Schemata evolve through learning actions that improve agent fitness.

Actions between agents involve the exchange of information and/or resources, occurring through lines of connectivity. These flows may be non-linear. The impact of information or resources can undergo multiplier effects based on the nature of connectivity between agents in the system. An action by one agent can be considered information for other agents that are connected to it. Agent tags help to identify what other agents are capable of transacting with a given agent. For example, in an organizational complex adaptive system, tags may identify agents belonging to different functions or business units, or on particular project teams. Figure 22.1 shows how the concepts of complex adaptive systems theory relate to one another.

Example

Given that the complex adaptive systems concepts are a meta-theory, it is useful to examine a specific organizational theory that draws from complex adaptive systems concepts. Consider Prigogine and Stenger's (1984) model of dissipative systems as an example of how to apply complex adaptive systems theory to operations and supply chain management. Their model addresses the process question of how complex adaptive systems adapt to environmental changes. The theory fundamentally draws from a thermodynamic model of what happens when a system absorbs energy from an external source; in applications to organizations, we substitute 'energy' by 'information and resources', but the mechanisms are the same. Under

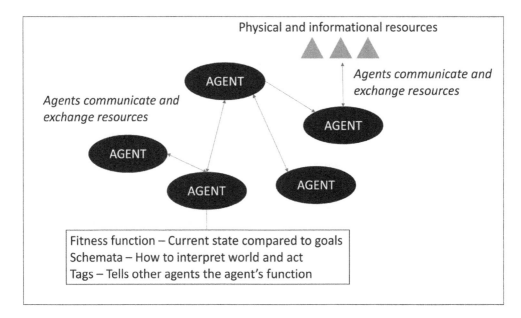

Figure 22.1   A complex adaptive system

normal loads, the system balances the import and processing (dissipation) of that energy; as energy absorbed into the system increases, the system is pushed far from equilibrium, where small perturbations can shift the structure of the system. This new structure performs the same function as the original structure, but is structurally different, more able to dissipate the energy being imported.

As a specific example of this dissipative model of adaption, consider Chiles et al. (2004). In this article the authors use a dissipative model to analyse the emergence of the entertainment cluster in Branson, Missouri. Their case study maps historical events to four dimensions of the complexity model: fluctuation, positive feedback, stabilization and recombination:

1. Fluctuation. Agents within the system innovate in response to internal or external changes, leading to small experiments, by plan or by chance.
2. Positive feedback. Fluctuations that improve fitness are amplified.
3. Stabilization. New structures emerge and are stabilized by feedback.
4. Recombination. The system continues to make small-scale adaptations through combining agents, schemata and resources.

Table 22.2 shows the mapping of the Branson case into the complex adaptive systems framework.

ASSUMPTIONS REGARDING REALITY

Any theory or model that draws from complex adaptive systems theory will make certain assumptions about reality. Drawing upon Choi et al. (2001), which applies complex adaptive systems concepts to supply networks, any such theory should assume the following.

Table 22.2   Example of dissipative systems model

Element	Explanation
Unit, level of analysis	Industry cluster of entertainment businesses in Branson, Missouri beginning around 1955
Key constructs/concepts	
Agents	Theatres within the Branson area; other related service providers and government organizations
Schemata	Collective vision to use scales of economy and audience focus to drive economic growth
Fitness function	Decisions by theatres primarily made to secure short and long-term economic gain through growth
Resources	As one example, financial resources for growth flowed in from country music labels who saw an opportunity to increase demand for their products
Agent interactions	As one example, theatres interacted other media channels like television shows to enhance awareness of Branson and co-brand
Agent tags	In this case perhaps the most important tags were the names of the artists who were associated with different theatres
Process model	
Fluctuation	Small changes in the local system of Branson lead to theatre owners recognizing the entrepreneurial opportunity of an entertainment cluster
Positive feedback	Popular live musical events acted as positive feedback, enhancing confidence of initial investors and attracting more
Stabilization	Branson reinvented itself several different times during the next several decades, each time making structural changes to achieve growth after it had flattened
Recombination	Theatres 'reused' human and reputational capital amongst themselves as part of on-going innovation

Source: Chiles et al. (2004).

First, do not assume that organizations within the supply network are rational. Organizations will act in a boundedly rational way. In a supply network, in practice this means that an organization will preface its own fitness (for example, economic health) over other organizations' fitness, and that the information available for it to sense the state of the system and make decisions will be limited because of lack of traceability and transparency in supply chains. The complex adaptive systems perspective of a supply network also recognizes that within the 'organization as agent' is another complex adaptive system of 'people as agents', thus the behavioural aspects of human behaviour have to be taken into account to understand the emergent behaviour of an organization.

Second, do not assume that organizations optimize. Organizations rarely have the desire or opportunity to optimize towards a given goal. Instead, organizations within a supply network make decisions that lead to 'good enough' outcomes, and that balance many, sometimes conflicting, objectives.

Third, do not assume (only) linear causality. While many of our research methods and thus theories tend to represent linear causality between cause and effect, theories and models of causality in a complex adaptive system should consider:

- Causality may be nonlinear; or may be linear in a region but non-linear otherwise.
- Causality may be contingent on one or many other causes or states of the system.
- Causality may be bidirectional.
- Causality may be present but unobservable.

Fourth, do not assume that supply networks remain the same over time. Any complex adaptive systems model or theory should, at least in part, be a process model (Poole et al., 2000), in that it describes how the system changes over time. In supply networks, new organizations enter while some leave, and new transactional connections are made or broken. Even if all the organizations within a supply network are the same at two points in time, the supply network will be different, because those organizations and their interrelations will be different.

Fifth, do not assume that order within a supply network is created by a single company. There is a tendency to believe that a strong downstream buyer 'designs' a supply network and controls it like a mechanism. Instead, order in the supply network emerges from the actions and interactions of numerous organizations. Sometimes a change in a supply network can be triggered by a single company, but it is the collective that determines, via the actions of its members, what happens.

HOW HAS THIS META-THEORY BEEN USED?

Dooley (2021) examines how much complex adaptive systems concepts (as well as other complexity science-related concepts) have been adopted by scholars in organization science, management, operations management and supply chain management. The search for relevant articles was confined to the top-reputation journals as per the *Financial Times* journal list. Over a 20-year period from 1999 to 2018, the journals *Administrative Science Quarterly, Journal of Management, Manufacturing and Service Operations Management, Operations Research, Organizational Behavior and Human Decision Processes, Production and Operations Management, Sloan Management Review* and *Strategic Entrepreneurship Journal* had zero relevant articles. The journals *Academy of Management Journal, Academy of Management Review, Entrepreneurship Theory and Practice, Journal of Business Ethics, Journal of Business Venturing, Journal of Management Studies, Journal of Operations Management, Management Science, Organization Science, Organization Studies* and *Strategic Management Journal* had a total of 50 relevant articles over the 20 years. In sum, complex adaptive systems theory has been a niche topic.

Dooley (2021) reports that there were three theories or models most drawn from by these articles: Kauffman's (1995) NK rugged landscape model, Prigogine and Stenger's (1984) model of change when dissipative systems are in a far from equilibrium state, and Ashby's (1956) law of requisite variety. Some articles also drew from Bak's (1996) sandpile model of self-organized criticality, and the modelling techniques of non-linear dynamical systems (Guastello, 1995).

Lack of presence within journals in the *Financial Times* list does not mean, however, that complexity-inspired papers are not being written and published: it again reflects more of the niche versus mainstream nature of these concepts. For example, only two articles in the *Financial Times* sample address complexity and leadership. Painter-Morland (2008) uses complex adaptive systems (CAS) concepts to argue that leadership is relational and distributed throughout the organization; while Tourish (2018) posits that while many leadership papers have adopted a new language of complexity, the mechanisms they posit are still simple and grounded in the historical 'leader as hero' meme. Concurrent with this, though, much scholarly activity was occurring around the topic. Uhl-Bien et al. (2007, p. 298) proposed that 'three entangled leadership roles (adaptive leadership, administrative leadership, and enabling leadership) reflect a dynamic relationship between the bureaucratic, administrative functions of the organization and the emergent, informal dynamics of complex adaptive systems'. The article was part of a special issue on Leadership and Complexity, and other articles included the application of catastrophe theory (Guastello, 2007), agent-based models (Hazy, 2007), and edge of chaos (Osborn and Hunt, 2007). The work also led to a number of conference special sessions, and an edited book (Uhl-Bien and Marion, 2008).

Similarly, only one article in the *Financial Times* sample concerned complex adaptive supply networks. Choi et al. (2001) propose that supply chains are better conceptualized as supply networks that act as complex adaptive systems. They posit that supply networks are not controlled or designed by any single organization, but rather are the evolutionary result of a set of make–buy and supplier selection decisions that are made locally by buying organizations within the network. Further, they suggest that the traditional dyad of buyer–supplier is insufficient to understand real-world behaviour in supply networks. The article has over 1300 citations after almost 20 years. Some articles have drawn from the general framework to develop complexity-specific models (Pathak et al., 2007a). For example, Pathak et al. (2007b) model the evolution of supply network using multi-agent simulation modelling. Kauffman et al. (2018) develop the concept of 'tinkering' in a complex supply network design in order to accommodate 'unknown-unknowns'. Most of these articles that cite Choi et al. (2001), though, have appropriated the term 'supply network' as an alternative to 'supply chain', and have done empirical investigations using social network (graph) theory and methods (Kim et al., 2011). In this case, the concept of a supply network as a complex adaptive system is attractive, but the concept is merged back into more familiar theoretical constructs and empirical methods.

OUTLOOK ON FUTURE RESEARCH OPPORTUNITIES

Complex adaptive systems-related theories describe both the 'how' and the 'why' of an organization's or collection of organizations' change over time. They show how local change can lead to global change, and how the likelihood for a system to realize significant change differs depending on its current state. As systems are pushed farther from their stable state, small fluctuations may be amplified through feedback and lead to structural change. These models explicitly consider how timing, chance and non-linearity can lead to emergent patterns of the whole that are not predictable for observing behaviour of the entities (agents) inside the system.

As discussed, academic application of complex adaptive systems theory in management, operations management and supply chain management has been low relative to its broader adoption in other areas of the physical and social sciences. This is surprising given its perceived applicability to studying organizational and interorganizational change, and its ability to create novel theory and insight.

One barrier to using complexity science is that, whether using empirical methods or mathematical modelling, application of these theories or models requires methodological skills that many organizational scientists do not naturally obtain in their research methods training. Any individual researcher can learn these skills if desired, but more generally there is the opportunity for organizational scholars to partner with researchers from other disciplines that do have these skills.

Perhaps more importantly, though, complexity science can be a common language that creates a bridge for interdisciplinary research. For example, when considering an agricultural supply network, supply chain scholars can readily examine the network and its structure and evolution from a complexity science perspective. At the same time, a conservation biologist can look at that same system from the perspective of biodiversity and complex systems; and an agronomist can study the soil system from a complex adaptive systems perspective. In reality, supply chains and landscapes and soil all are part of the same system. Together, integration of these multiple disciplines via a complexity science lens offers potential for novel insight, theory and practice.

Specific to supply chain management, logistics and procurement researchers, there are different units of analysis that can be relevant to future studies. Aligned with supply network research over the last decade, complexity science is most readily applied to interorganizational networks. When examining behaviours and actions at the 'strategic' level, such as supplier selection or supplier innovation, then a complex adaptive system model treats each organization as a boundedly rational agent. In the past, supply chain scholars have studied these supply networks much more from a structural versus dynamic perspective. In a way, we have emphasized the 'system' rather than the 'adaptive' part of 'complex adaptive system'. Thus, one need we have is for more process theories of supply network evolution and adaptation.

When examining behaviours and actions at the 'tactical' level, such as inventory placement or supply risk at a transaction level, then a complex adaptive system model treats each processing unit (for example, factory, warehouse, vehicle) as an agent; and in some contexts, can even treat the work-in-process inventory as an agent. This aligns with the emerging discipline of data science, which combines operations research, statistical modelling and artificial intelligence methods to explain and manage complex systems. These applications yield 'big data' that is voluminous and longitudinal in nature. Complexity science models of change may help data science researchers to explain the changes they are observing in the systems they are monitoring and managing.

Related to supply chain management in practice, innovators and markets are constantly borrowing from complex adaptive systems concepts in the creation and development of their products and services. For example, shared services such as ride sharing conceptualize operations as a distributed set of agents, who are incentivized in various ways to take action, and who use simple heuristics to make decisions. Order within the system is not planned or predetermined, but rather emergences from the interaction of drivers and customers, and the structure and rules that define the sharing platform. In these applications, scholars might help to create innovative solutions and new services for practice by deploying complex adaptive systems theories and models.

REFERENCES

Ashby, W.R. (1956). *An Introduction to Cybernetics*, Chapman & Hall: London.
Bak, P. (1996). *How Nature Works*. Springer-Verlag: New York.
Bateson, G. (1972). *Steps to an Ecology of Mind: Collected Essays in Anthropology, Psychiatry, Evolution, and Epistemology*. University of Chicago Press: Chicago, IL.
Chiles, T., Meyer, A., and Hench, T. (2004). Organizational emergence: The origin and transformation of Branson, Missouri's musical theaters. *Organization Science*, 15, 499–519.

Choi, T., Dooley, K., and Rungtusanatham, M. (2001). Supply networks and complex adaptive systems: Control versus emergence. *Journal of Operations Management*, 19, 351–366.

Dooley, K. (2021), Complexity science and the organization sciences: 1999–2018. In E. Elliott and L. Kiel (eds), *Complex Systems in the Social and Behavioral Sciences*, Ann Arbor, MI: University of Michigan Press, pp. 64–82.

Dooley, K., and Van de Ven, A. (1999). Explaining complex organizational dynamics. *Organization Science*, 10(3), 358–372.

Forrester, J. (1961). *Industrial Dynamics*. MIT Press: Portland, OR.

Gleick, J. (1987). *Chaos: The Making of a New Science*. Heinemann: London.

Guastello, S. (1995). *Chaos, Catastrophe, and Human Affairs*. Erlbaum: Mahwah, NJ.

Guastello, S. (2007). Non-linear dynamics and leadership emergence. *Leadership Quarterly*, 19(4), 357–369.

Hazy, J. (2007). Computer models of leadership: Foundations for a new discipline or meaningless diversion? *Leadership Quarterly*, 18(4), 391–410.

Holland, J. (1995). *Hidden Order: How Adaptation Builds Complexity*. Basic Books: New York.

Kauffman, S. (1995). *At Home in the Universe*. Oxford University Press: Oxford.

Kauffman, S., Pathak, S., Sen, P., and Choi, T. (2018). Jury rigging and supply network design: Evolutionary 'tinkering' in the presence of unknown-unknowns. *Journal of Supply Chain Management*, 54, 51–63.

Kim, Y., Choi, T., Yan, T., and Dooley, K. (2011). Structural analysis of supply networks. *Journal of Operations Management*, 29(3), 194–211.

Osborn, R., and Hunt, J. (2007). Leadership and the choice of order: Complexity and hierarchical perspectives near the edge of chaos. *Leadership Quarterly*, 18(4), 319–340.

Painter-Morland, M. (2008). Systemic leadership and the emergence of ethical responsiveness. *Journal of Business Ethics*, 82, 509–524.

Pathak, S., Day, J., Nair, A., Sawaya, W., and Kristal, M. (2007a). Complexity and adaptivity in supply networks: Building supply network theory using a complex adaptive systems perspective. *Decision Sciences*, 38(4), 547–580.

Pathak, S., Dilts, D., and Biswas, G. (2007b). On the evolutionary dynamics of supply network topologies. *IEEE Transactions on Engineering Management*, 54, 662–672.

Poole, M., Van de Ven, A., Dooley, K., and Holmes, M. (2000). *Organizational Change and Innovation Processes: Theory and Methods for Research*. Oxford University Press: New York.

Prigogine, I., and Stengers, I. (1984) *Order out of Chaos: Man's New Dialogue with Nature*. Flamingo Edition: London.

Simon, H. (1957). *Administrative Behavior*. Macmillan: New York.

Tourish, D. (2018). Is complexity leadership theory complex enough? *Organization Studies*, 40(2), 219–238.

Uhl-Bien, M., and Marion, R. (2008). *Complexity Leadership, Vol. 1*. IAP: Charlotte, NC.

Uhl-Bien, M., Marion, R., and McKelvey, B. (2007). Complexity leadership theory: Shifting leadership from the industrial age to the knowledge era. *Leadership Quarterly*, 18(4), 298–318.

von Bertalanffy, L. (1951). General system theory – A new approach to unity of science. *Human Biology*, 23, 303–361.

Wiener, N. (1948). *Cybernetics: Or Control and Communication in the Animal and the Machine*. MIT Press: Cambridge, MA.

SUGGESTED FURTHER READING

For more information on the general nature of complexity adaptive systems, see:
Holland, J. (1995). *Hidden Order: How Adaptation Builds Complexity*. Basic Books: New York.
For an overview of complexity science applied to supply networks, see:
Choi, T., Dooley, K., and Rungtusanatham, M. (2001). Supply networks and complex adaptive systems: Control versus emergence. *Journal of Operations Management*, 19, 351–366.

Pathak, S., Day, J., Nair, A., Sawaya, W., and Kristal, M. (2007). Complexity and adaptivity in supply networks: Building supply network theory using a complex adaptive systems perspective. *Decision Sciences*, 38(4), 547–580.

23. Factor market rivalry: a general theory of supply chain management

Peter M. Ralston, Matthew A. Schwieterman and John E. Bell

INTRODUCTION

Supply chain competition has become more intense as organizational boundaries blur between firms and companies choose to focus on core competencies while allowing partners to provide necessary functions to help drive customer value (Chen and Miller 2015; Handley 2012). Supply chain research often focuses on modifying downstream supply chain service delivery through improving speed, providing innovation, utilizing sales promotion activities, or even lowering prices (Bell et al. 2015). While a customer orientation has obvious benefits, the competitive supply chain landscape also extends to supply side activities. The upstream competition for supply chain resources is known as factor market rivalry (FMR).

As supply chain scholars seek to apply a general theory to create deductive research hypotheses or make abductive observations from empirical research, they need to determine which theory is best to apply, how to apply it, and how to build on that theory through newly generated research findings (Ketokivi and Choi 2014). Therefore, as supply chain scholars, it is important to understand the tenets of FMR theory, since it is relevant to the upstream competition for resources between firms and supply chains in today's markets.

Perhaps a brief pause is warranted to discuss FMR and its connection to supply chain management (SCM). One issue that may arise is that supply chains are often viewed as greater than a simple buyer–supplier exchange. How can FMR, dealing with factor markets and the perception of individual firms competing in those factor markets seeking access to constrained factors, apply to SCM? We believe that the answer lies in the formation of supply chains which usually result from purposeful firm action to create link-by-link dyads resulting in emergent networks.

LeMay et al. (2017) defined SCM as the design and coordination of a network through which organizations and individuals get, use, deliver and dispose of material goods; acquire and distribute services; and make their offerings available to markets, customers and clients (LeMay et al. 2017, p. 1446). While supply chains are noted to be comprised of networks of firms (Carter et al. 2015), these networks are often a series of relationships between individual firms (Fawcett and Magnan 2004). In fact, supply chain participation is an individual firm-level decision (Ralston et al. 2020). Firms balance between their needs for self-interest and interdependency, especially in long-term collaborative or integrated relationships (Richey et al. 2010). A realization of the importance and totality of supply chains is important, but firms (and others) need to realize that individual companies have a relatively nuanced view of the supply chain (Bowersox et al. 2000). This vantage point allows one to view FMR, the intense rivalry that develops over resource positions (Markman et al. 2009), as a general theory that is core to the study of SCM. FMR holds such a place due to the supply-side implications of the theory, and the resulting impacts of dyadic FMR activity across the supply chain network, from exchanges surrounding raw materials all the way to end customer purchasing behaviour.

Overall, theoretical discussions and theory development can be conceptualized as having four elements: foundational domain, variables, relationships and predictions (Wacker 1998). The scope of this chapter will be to offer suggestions as to when to apply FMR in research, as well as how to apply the theory. We also offer a broad range of future research suggestions where the use of FMR in SCM research makes sense and provides an excellent lens for the type of problems faced in the management of supply chains. Therefore, we not only contribute to this scholarly effort by identifying the structure of FMR and the most important work in the literature, but we also provide motivations and avenues for expanding on the use of FMR theory in the discipline.

DOMAIN OF FMR

As Markman et al. (2009) note in their seminal work on the phenomenon, FMR is defined as competition over resource positions. Factors of production include anything a firm requires to produce or deliver a good or service for consumption. This includes components of or inputs to a finished good, or access to a good for resale, as well as necessary capital (for example human, financial, technical) and services required to produce and provide a good for consumption. While it may be easy to envision strategic resources as critical factors of production, other resources necessary for customer value creation and delivery can be critical as well when their source is constrained (Ellram et al. 2013). For example, if a firm that utilizes a third-party logistics (3PL) firm to fulfil and ship customer orders, and a separate firm that also utilizes the 3PL, each experience an increase in demand at nearly the same time, the 3PL firm's capacity may become constrained, causing one or both firms to experience a decrease in delivery service level. An additional aspect to consider when thinking about factors of production is the value of these factors to a company's competitive advantage. If an input or factor of production is critical to the competitive advantage of multiple firms, competition is created between these firms, knowingly or unknowingly, to acquire the necessary factors of production (Obloj and Capron 2011; Pulles et al., 2014).

The genesis of FMR occurs from a combination of competitive dynamics theory (Baum and Korn 1996; Chen and Hambrick 1995; Chen and Miller 2015) and resource-based theory (the resource-based view, RBV) (Barney 1991; Penrose 1959; Wernerfelt 1984). Penrose (1959) is an early proponent of firms being comprised of various resources which contribute to firm growth. Wernerfelt (1984) notes the power of this view by offering a series of propositions centred around viewing firms as bundles of resources. One specific proposition suggests identifying resources which can lead to high firm profits, and then taking appropriate steps to protect these valuable resources. Finally, Barney (1991) suggests that access to heterogenous firm resources can lead to sustained competitive advantage, especially if these resources are valuable, inimitable, rare and non-substitutable. Additional work suggests that access to needed resources may span organizational boundaries and include transacting or working with external partners (Barney et al. 2011; Dyer and Singh 1998).

Baum and Korn (1996) provide a detailed look at competition and interfirm rivalry. The authors suggest that competition can occur due to macroeconomic effects over which firms have limited control. Competition also occurs when firms vie for limited resources (Hannan

Table 23.1   *Key variables of FMR*

Variable	Definition	Example citations
Resource competition	A resultant clash when two or more parties seek to secure access or utilize a given input.	Markman et al. 2009
Scarcity of input	A resource for which demand exceeds present supply at a particular location.	Markman et al. 2009; Bell et al. 2012; Ellram et al. 2013
Factor market myopia (FMM)	Limiting the perceived sources of resources or too narrowly focusing on solutions to needs.	Ellram et al. 2013; Ralston et al. 2017: Opengart et al. 2018
Factor market response	Firm action originating from factor market rivalry.	Capron and Chatain 2008; Schwieterman and Miller 2016
Factor market interdiction	Firm action resulting from factor market rivalry to improve competitive position and weaken rivals.	Bell et al. 2015

and Freeman 1989). Rivalry is what occurs when firms compete for incompatible positions (that is, limited asset stocks or a finite customer base) and feel the need to proactively manage a resource or react to a competitor's moves in regard to that resource (Baum and Korn 1996; Caves 1984; Porter 1980). A competitive action is defined as a specific and detectable move that a firm undertakes to impact upon the position of a competitor, while a reaction is a specific and detectable countermove (Chen and Hambrick 1995). The specific act to impair the position of a competitor for a resource is the root of rivalrous behaviour (Chen and Miller 2015).

Competition over customers commonly exists between industry players, but a firm may also actively try to compete with rivals over a supply-side resource. Supply limits cause firms to take note of their inventory or access to valuable resources (Grewal and Slotegraaf 2007). These constrained resource stocks also may cause firms to note other users of the same resources. The unique distinction of FMR is that battles for resource positions can occur outside of a focal firm's industry, and even position within a supply chain (Markman et al. 2009). Ellram et al. (2013) detail that competitors for supply-side resources usually occur in three general scenarios: (1) product market competitors which also compete for the same supply-side resources; (2) firms which compete in similar industries, but might not have a significant product market overlap; and (3) firms that are not in similar industries, but still utilize the same supply-side resources in either the same or a different manner. An example of scenario three would be two manufacturers that produce completely different goods, but compete for the same limited supply of transportation because both manufacturers are located geographically near each other. Thus, a key variable of FMR is the competition for resources, divided between resource rivals that are also product market competitors, and resource rivals that only compete in factor markets. As such, the domain of FMR includes resource positions broadly, while also analysing sources of constrained supply, and rivals for that constrained supply. Table 23.1 summarizes the key variables of FMR.

RELATIONSHIPS AMONGST VARIABLES

Ellram et al. (2013) bring the idea of FMR to the SCM literature. The authors suggest that FMR can occur for resources, even those not traditionally viewed as strategic, that are versatile in function, mobile and seemingly ubiquitous. The challenge with a resource that is seemingly ubiquitous is when a firm quickly and unexpectedly realizes that a resource is constrained, and the firm lacks strategic planning and alternatives for how to respond. The primary condition which creates FMR is scarcity of a valuable resource needed to provide a good or service to a customer (Bell et al. 2012; Ellram et al. 2013: Markman et al. 2009). Without scarcity or constraint, there is no reason for rivalry to exist.

While scarcity is a baseline condition to drive FMR, a firm's perception of which resources exist in a competitive space is also an area of great interest within this theory. FMR research in the supply chain has focused on two related aspects of this variable. Ellram et al. (2013) provide a rationale for the impact of FMR and also how FMR may develop unexpectedly between firms. The fact that firms face unexpected competition hints at limitations to firms' conceptualization of which resources fit within a competitive arena. Ralston et al. (2017) further this idea by discussing one cause of FMR, namely factor market myopia (FMM). This view supports the conjecture that firms are likely to experience a myopic view of competition, which limits their propensity to sense and act on the competitive aspects of the resource base. The root of myopia may come from bounds around knowledge of alternative sources of supply, a lack of substitutable resources, or even selective attention to the competitive market (Gavetti et al. 2007; Simon 1997). Whatever the cause, knowledge limits around a given resource and the resource's potential users can create a singular focus and help to spur FMM (Ralston et al. 2017). The primary detrimental result of FMM is intense FMR. Firms begin to believe that the only avenue to firm success is through securing access to this constrained factor. This myopia leads to firms locking-in on the specific factor, which may become even more constrained, instead of looking at alternative sources for that resource or a substitute solution altogether.

Once firms become aware of the possibility of FMR impacting upon their environment, the possibility for firm-level action comes to the forefront of the theory. This has spawned a separate research stream on FMR which centres on the ability to use advantageous positions of limited factors for a firm's benefit. Limiting the effectiveness of a resource, or controlling access to a resource, could be another way to generate a competitive advantage (Capron and Chatain 2008). In the first supply chain research dealing with this variable, Bell et al. (2015) coined the term 'supply chain interdiction' to discuss the dual benefits of a firm holding access to a resource stock for operational gain, and so that a competing supply chain could not use that same resource. Schwieterman and Miller (2016) discuss internal and external actions that firms can take under periods of supply-side competition, such as improving resource access or reducing specific resource importance as ways to move forward from FMR. Opengart et al. (2018) discuss breaking down barriers to FMM by looking at non-traditional sources of supply for labour. Instead of fighting for the same limited labour supply of truck drivers, the authors suggest that firms could expand the labour pool by seeking non-traditional populations of drivers. Alternatively, firms could replace their need for truck drivers by substituting the drivers with an automated trucking fleet. This practice of substituting resources may reduce the reliance on a constrained factor of production, and is a viable solution to lessen FMR (Schwieterman and Miller 2016).

PREDICTIONS OF FMR

FMR produces a set of theoretical predictions for how a firm's actions will impact upon firm-level outcomes. Additionally, FMR outlines how the actions a firm may take are impacted upon by the firm's ability to conceptualize the resource as existing in a competitive arena under conditions of scarcity. As such, FMR seems reliant on firm-specific character-istics and specific characteristics of the resource for which rivalry exists. For example, note the potential difference in rivalry between competitors from the same product markets versus resource rivalry which exists between competitors without product market overlap. If a firm only views resource competition in a downstream direction or from direct competitors, that firm may experience a blind spot caused by ignoring resource competitors without product market overlap. This boundary can exacerbate the negative consequences of FMR when it limits a firm's ability to take corrective action (Ellram et al. 2013; Ralston et al. 2017).

Further, the awareness of potential rivals has a direct impact on the types of competitive actions a firm will be able to take. When viewing Schwieterman and Miller's (2016) typology of actions, the ability of a firm to take actions on the external environment is heavily dependent upon its ability to identify rivalry. Moreover, if a firm feels that it is unable to spot rivalry, it may elect to focus more inwardly, and take steps to reduce the importance of, or reliance upon, the resource in question. When we consider the possibility of firms utilizing FMR activities as a competitive weapon (Bell et al. 2015), it becomes apparent that a firm may utilize this strategy if it also competes with the resource rivals in product markets, because harming the resource base of a competitor is only attractive if the resource rival also competes for customers.

The preceding discussion of firm-level awareness and motivation underscores how a firm may regard FMR from two perspectives. First, firms may take an active approach in the presence of FMR in order to seek benefits. This would include steps taken to use supply chain interdiction in order to improve access to a scarce resource, but also knowing that this could hinder a rival and therefore improve the focal firm's competitive position (Bell et al. 2015). A passive approach in the presence of FMR would be undertaken to avoid harm caused by reduced access to resources. Firms want to secure access to the resource needed to operate, and may take actions designed to maintain a long-term source of the said resources. Moreover, if the resource in question is sufficiently scarce to make the firm concerned over a long-term horizon, firms may look elsewhere for substitutable resources or work to reduce their reliance on the constrained resource altogether (Schwieterman and Miller 2016).

FMR AS A GENERAL THEORY FOR SUPPLY CHAIN MANAGEMENT

FMR theory has specific characteristics that drive the framework's applicability to certain supply-side investigations. Unequivocally, FMR exists on the supply side of exchanges (Markman et al. 2009). FMR occurs for resources of production or service delivery. This distinction separates FMR from demand-side competition which exists for customers, shelf space, or where a company appears on a website search. Promotion wars, price battles and market share struggles can absolutely be activities that drive competition; however, these activities occur on the demand side of a supply chain (Jaworski and Kohli 1993).

Another core characteristic of FMR is the idea of resource scarcity. There has to be some level of scarcity that causes supply constraints for a needed resource (Markman et al. 2009). Without supply restrictions, the idea of resource access, acquisition and accumulation would take on a different meaning (Barney 1991; Maritan and Peteraf 2011). There may be a natural inclination to compete for resources because they are scarce, and not necessarily due to the fundamental contribution of the resource to a firm's good or service delivery.

Realizing that supply-side competition and resource scarcity are necessary requirements for FMR, we can begin to broadly define the theory's place within other paradigms utilized in SCM research. Ellram et al.'s (2013) piece is the seminal work on FMR within SCM. The authors introduce the concept of FMR to SCM and show how the theory applies within the field. Future researchers utilized FMR to investigate battles for resource positions within SCM. These investigations led to ideas such as FMM (Ralston et al., 2017), factor market responses (Schwieterman and Miller 2016) and supply chain interdiction (Bell et al. 2015).

In moving FMR forward, researchers showed the applicability of FMR to SCM, often through middle-range theorizing. Middle-range theorizing utilizes accumulated evidence to build contextualized understanding of a phenomenon (Merton and Merton 1968; Pellathy et al. 2018). This grounding in real-world scenarios and observable events creates practical business implications that can offer guidance to managers. While one should not doubt the value of offering general guidance in the specific context of SCM, there exists an opportunity to broaden the applicability of FMR to SCM research. It is our belief that FMR extends beyond solely being a middle-range theory for certain situations, to being one of the general theories underlying SCM.

A key consideration for viewing FMR as a general supply chain theory is the exclusivity to supply chain contexts. Just as middle-range theory may take a general theory and apply it to a context such as SCM, so would a general SCM theory need to be rooted in supply chain phenomena exclusively. This is to say, FMR would not exist outside the context of SCM, given that the supply base is the domain of the theory.

General theories are typically frameworks focused on common antecedents with broad applicability (Pellathy et al. 2018; Stank et al. 2017; Swanson et al. 2020). This is where the greatest opportunity with FMR may lie. Understanding that scarcity helps to drive FMR, researchers have done a good job of showing how resource competition can exist within the supply chain (Ellram et al. 2013). Researchers such as Bell et al. (2015) and Ralston et al. (2017) have taken accumulated evidence grounded in past events to provide contextualized outcomes or counters to FMR. Schwieterman and Miller (2016) offer general responses to FMR, but the starting point is still centred around resource competition. Competition creates battles. Competition costs money. Competition creates suboptimal situations and disequilibriums as one firm seeks advantage over another. However, instead of competition immediately generating FMR activities for firms or supply chains, we suggest that firms first assess the value of the resource to the firm in delivering customer value and generating firm profits, before waging factor market battles. Table 23.2 reframes ideas surrounding FMR to bridge the gap between middle-range theorizing and a general theory.

Instead of immediately competing for a constrained resource, firms need to determine the value of the resource to the firm, no matter whether the resource is a strategic or supporting input. The value of the resource should be established in terms of the resource's importance as a strategic input, as an input necessary for customer value creation, or as an input important to a firm's overall business strategy at the current point of resource competition (Maritan and Peteraf 2011). If a firm deems the value of the resource to be critical to the firm's business, and there are no substitutes, a company passes the first internal test as to whether the firm should engage in factor market rivalry.

Table 23.2   *Framing FMR to bridge the gap between middle-range theory and general theory*

	Supply side competition *	
	Resource scarcity *	
Resource competition	→	Resource value
Static scarcity of input	→	Temporal (Dynamic) nature of scarcity
Factor market myopia, factor market response, and supply chain interdiction	→	Optimal factor market myopia, optimal factor market response, optimal supply chain interdiction

Note: * necessary condition for FMR.

After a firm assesses the value of the resource to a firm, and if the firm decides the resource is valuable, the next step is to assess the nature of the scarcity of the input. How long will the scarcity be in effect? Is there a viable substitute to the resource in question? How long might it take to identify a possible substitute? These questions addressing both time and opportunity are important for a firm to ask no matter what the context of the scenario. This further places FMR in general theory status. Perhaps moving from 'static' scarcity of a resource to 'dynamic' scarcity of a resource will also prevent immediate surprise if a product becomes scarce over time (Bell et al. 2013). In other words, companies may be able to see constraints develop, which can prevent the deleterious effects of intense FMR and instead lead to the optimal level of FMM, optimal factor market response and optimal supply chain interdiction. Specifically, as firms possess limited time and managerial bandwidth to scan the environment, the decision of how much time to allocate to known FMR issues versus scanning for unexpected resource competition may be critical.

Finally, if a firm determines that there is a long-term possibility of a scarce resource with no viable substitutes, that is also a valuable resource to a firm's operation, then the firm needs to examine appropriate responses. FMM, an intense focus on securing access to a resource, may be appropriate (Ralston et al. 2017). However, firms need to be ready to quickly pivot to another opportunity if one appears. Firms also need to establish plans to seek substitutes or internally develop options as an additional response to FMR (Schwieterman and Miller 2016). FMR should not lead firms down a path of never-ending competition for a resource. Only when firms understand their resource position in comparison to direct market competitors should firms use FMR activities to change their competitive position amongst rivals (Bell et al. 2015; Insead and Chatain 2008). Ultimately, a competitive advantage may result if a firm can secure access to a resource when a competitor cannot.

These tests are important because of the costs FMR generates. FMR activities may be a necessary step to compete for a resource. For example, rare natural resources or permanently constrained assets may lead to perpetual FMR. A firm must also understand the characteristics of the limited resource and the value of the resource to the company's business to ensure that it is making a sound business decision and has exhausted all other possible avenues before engaging in FMR activities. Why is this the case? FMR is an expensive endeavour. Strategies to limit the length of time FMR activities exist between supply-side competitors should be a dual goal along with securing access to a valuable resource.

One of the benefits to considering FMR as a general theory of SCM is the way FMR differentiates and extends other underlying theoretical foundations of the discipline. For example, Mentzer et al. (2000, 2001) discuss the value of managing supply chains. In other words, a key focus within SCM is the coordination of product or service delivery between entities within a supply chain. This coordination can lead to information sharing, improved demand information and reduced costs. This perspective shares similarities with Lambert et al. (1998) as well as Lambert and Cooper (2000) who discuss supply chain formation between partners focused on process management. FMR differs inasmuch as temporal scarcity of a valuable resource could drive increased collaboration between supply chain partners. Alternatively, Lambert and Cooper (2000) astutely point out that creating in-depth relationships with all supply chain members could be counterproductive, if not impossible. The authors suggest separating supply chain members into primary and supporting members. A key difference afforded by the consideration of FMR is that constrained and valuable resources provided by supporting members within a supply chain may lead to the development of a supply chain relationship with these providers. Viewing supply chain relationships through an FMR lens may actually lead to a different understanding and classification of the benefits and value of certain supply chain relationships. In FMR, relationships may be used to bridge capabilities between parties in order for a firm to properly secure, or lessen the impact of, a constrained resource.

FMR is a firm-level phenomenon. As early as 1969, Donald Bowersox advocated for thinking about products within a firm as the combination of form, place, possession and time utilities (Bowersox 1969). While Bowersox realized the value of partners to effectively manage supply chains, he also recognized the role that individual firms had in deciding why and whether or not to be a supply chain participant. Researchers later recognized that the utility decision also applied to resources a firm might utilize (Bowersox and Closs 1996). Where FMR distinguishes itself in this utility discussion is the realization that resource access is influenced by other users of the resource as well. The competition aspect extends FMR beyond solely accessing and providing a product or a resource in the right form at the right place and time. It extends this idea with the realization that providing utility to customers through the access and use of resources is done so in a competitive upstream environment where utility creation can be limited by FMR with other firms.

FMR's contribution to the supply chain literature is different from other resource- or competition-based theories. For example, resource-dependence (R-D) theory clearly specifies the importance of resource access to a firm, and discusses the dependencies firms can develop upon the providers of resources (Pfeffer and Salancik 1978). However, R-D theory also discusses the power imbalance that may result between a buyer and supplier. Without a doubt, this power imbalance may exist; but FMR actually centres around the competition for resource access. A proper response to hardships stemming from securing resource access (that is, a power imbalance between firms) would be to seek alternative sources of supply for the resource, or substitutes to the resource altogether (Schwieterman and Miller 2016). A competition-based theory such as the awareness–motivation–capability (AMC) perspective suggests that competitive actions of firms are driven by the firm's awareness, motivation and capability to compete (Chen et al. 2007). AMC is most often focused on rivals downstream in the supply chain and any competitive actions that result. As FMR is focused on supply-side competition, the theory further distinguishes itself as focused on competition that is developed around resources.

Discussing FMR within the context of other theoretical paradigms is important so that we can understand the framework's role within SCM. This discussion also helps us to realize that FMR is in fact a supply chain theory. This, along with the further conceptualization of characteristics of factor market rivalry activities, lead us to identifying FMR as a general theory of SCM. Because of the further refinement of theory, the following section identifies future research areas for exploration.

FUTURE RESEARCH DIRECTIONS: FACTOR MARKET RIVALRY AND SUPPLY CHAIN MANAGEMENT

Future research could build upon the temporal nature of resource scarcity. Some resources, such as various natural resources, are scarce based on the absolute amount available for commercial purposes (Bell et al. 2013). Other resources experience scarcity temporarily. An example of this is Ellram et al.'s (2013) description of transportation services scarcity based on increased demand at various points in time. The fact that scarcity can be generated by temporal factors is one of the ways in which FMR presents challenges for managers to identify problems before they occur. In addition to temporal scarcity caused by unexpected increases in demand, scarcity may also be driven by unexpected decreases in supply caused by exogenous circumstances. One salient example is the decrease in packing plant capacity during the COVID-19 pandemic. Due to the lack of capacity at facilities, a large amount of livestock was not processed according to schedule (Hein 2020). This led to many being euthanized without entering the food supply chain, due to ageing past the desirable point of processing. A possible research area for FMR involves sequential demand for resource capacity. In the case of the COVID-19 packing plant capacity shortage, the livestock resources that were ageing out of the supply chain were unable to be inventoried, due to the processing capacity being utilized for livestock at the prime age. Research is needed to identify and provide guidance for FMR situations stemming from capacity shortages, and industries with sequencing and perishability issues that lead to waste if capacity is temporarily scarce.

Another avenue for future research is to examine the role that FMR plays in the development of exclusivity agreements between trading partners. Exclusivity can imply that a customer will only deal with a certain supplier, or that a supplier will only sell to a certain customer in a given area (González Hernando et al. 2003). Exclusivity has traditionally been studied in the context of marketing, where the parties want exclusive distribution to take advantage of access to customers in a given geographic area via a sole distributorship agreement. The primary focus is typically on buyers agreeing to only utilize a particular supplier for a given input (USLegal Inc. 2021). In the context of FMR, the exclusivity agreement would likely include provisions limiting a supplier's ability to serve competitors of the buyer. Separately, motivational behaviour and individual integrity (Maak 2008; McGregor 1960) can impact upon the actions of a firm and hence the supply chain (Castillo et al. 2018). Are exclusivity arrangements negotiated because firms are actively pursuing FMR with a competitor? While future research could examine the role that exclusivity agreements play in maintaining access to resources for a focal firm, research could explore the role to which exclusivity agreements are used to limit the resource access of rivals. This research could shed light on how firms utilize these tactics as an alternative to vertical integration and M&A activity with suppliers.

FMR actions can also be executed through the use of mergers and acquisitions (M&A), where the initiating firm attempts to actively capture and control supply of a resource by acquiring an upstream or lateral firm (Bell et al. 2015). For example, the merger of Turner Broadcasting and Time Warner resulted in a disruption to Turner Broadcasting's rivals because they could no longer distribute content through Time Warner (Schwieterman and

Miller 2016; Suzuki 2009). Therefore, future research on M&A activities, and vertical and horizontal integration in the supply chain, could be posited through the lens of FMR to better understand how competition for resources is executed using M&A in the supply chain. This can include how M&A can be used as a competitive supply chain tool to increase supply chain performance and competitive advantage (Gupta 2012). Or in a different perspective, research could focus on how a firm might use M&A to minimize or overcome resource dependencies and improve its organizational autonomy (Kalaitzi et al. 2019). Similarly, FMR could be used as a guiding theory in research about how M&A can be leveraged as a bridging strategy to overcome natural resource scarcity and prevent competitors from controlling scarce resources (Bell et al. 2012; Kalaitzi et al. 2018).

Additional future research using FMR as a guiding theory could extend into the academic area of legal scholarship where antitrust laws and the litigated competition over resources is documented in lawsuits. For example, in the United States, antitrust laws may prevent companies from disrupting and controlling the supply of resources in an industry. In fact, the practices of Standard Oil in the early twentieth century to control the upstream supply chain in the oil industry are cited as motivation for the passing of the Sherman Anti-Trust Act (Bell et al. 2015; Williamson and Daum 1959). Therefore, an avenue of research and source of data exists in legal cases where violations and testing of the Sherman Anti-Trust Act are documented. These legal precedents should define the exact boundaries (which may be dynamic) of what supply chain interdiction and FMR actions are considered legal and ethical in the United States. However, since most supply chains extend globally, research is also needed on the legal and ethical application of FMR theory and supply chain competition for resources across national boundaries, where antitrust laws differ or may not be enforced (Bell et al. 2015).

Another fruitful avenue of research could lie in a more technical approach to defend firms from FMR, by making them less reliant on scarce resources. For example, Bell et al. (2015) identify that most firms stop short of proactively defending their key supply resources and simply rely on supplier relationships and contract incentives, similar to the bridging strategies identified by Kalaitzi et al. (2018). Instead, firms should consider more proactive ways to build defences against FMR activities by avoiding the use of scarce resources in product design, finding substitute materials and resources, and developing ways to create utility through the use of new innovations that eliminate the need for scarce resources. For example, General Electric (GE) has evaluated its scarce material dependencies in the metals industry and encourages its design engineers to avoid the use of rare metals such as rhenium in new product designs (Duclos et al. 2010). Unfortunately, research has shown that many design engineers lack the needed data to know what materials might be vulnerable to rivalry as they design new products (Kohler 2013; Kohler et al. 2013). Therefore, better information is needed upstream in the supply chain at the design level to ensure that product design decisions do not make firms vulnerable to FMR activities during the product life cycle. Finally, technical innovations and how they relate to FMR defence strategies may be another opportunity for future research. For example, the ability of autonomous vehicles to potentially relieve transportation companies and shippers from needing more scarce driver resources could help firms to defend against driver losses to competitors in the future.

Research on resource competition (Bell et al. 2015; Markman et al. 2009) is focused primarily on the access to resources that are vital to a firm's strategy. Indeed, Barney (1991) outlined that valuable, inimitable, rare and non-substitutable resources are likely to be the most strategic for a firm. However, little research in the FMR domain has examined the role that preferred resources play in the development of rivalry and resource competition. Just as some resources are more valuable than others, so a firm may have suppliers that are more desirable than others for various reasons. Researchers focusing on FMR may be able to contribute by delineating the scope and intensity of FMR activities stemming from firms' preferences for specific suppliers or specific resources. Moreover, this may be a fruitful research area for scholars to explore the role that consumer brand awareness plays in retailers desiring access to products to sell. While much of the FMR work looks at the possibility of substitutes, in a retail environment the ability of one good to substitute for another is heavily based on consumers' willingness to consider the products as substitutes. This would possibly be a bridge between FMR and the marketing research focusing on customer market competition.

While global economies have cyclical ebbs and flows over time directly affecting labour markets, there appear to be certain supply chain positions which are always in need. Occupations such as truck drivers, pilots, certified maintenance technicians and warehouse workers have recently experienced severe shortages. These shortages increase firm costs as organizations must consistently find new workers or replace existing ones. Yes, there are alternatives to human resources such as improved efficiencies, task replacement/reduction, or even automation. However, these alternatives can be expensive, and certain roles require special certifications that cannot be replaced. Instead, the response may be intense FMR for these positions. While previous work has identified the FMM which results from 'feeling' the need to compete for constrained workers (Opengart et al. 2018; Ralston et al. 2017), future work should consider which factors can break down FMM and lessen the negative impact of FMR activities. In terms of labour shortages, perhaps identifying non-traditional labour pools would be one way to lower costs associated with FMR. Non-traditional labour pools could include demographics not traditionally represented within the workforce (that is, by gender or race). Additionally, perhaps there are alternatives which exist for underserved populations such as those with criminal records, or hybrid part-time job sharing for early retirees. All of this is to say that FMR activities may drive firm action and increase costs over and above looking for other sources of workers which could represent a critical partnership between SCM and human resource managers within firms.

While industries that have labour needs and associated FMR has been previously discussed, there are certain vocations which require a perceived high level of talent associated with a simultaneous competitive component. FMR may exacerbate the competition for perceived high-talent workers who have limited substitutes. Talent markets for corporate executives or professional athletes may have a different competitive marketplace for their services due to the real possibility that hiring one employee may serve as a detriment to a competing firm (that is, supply chain interdiction). The issue here is that the factor market will elicit interesting behaviours between industry players. Obviously, there could be competitive bidding between firms for an athlete or executive. However, another real possibility is the perception of interest by one party to pique the interest of a separate party, or to artificially inflate the price one party has to pay to attain a resource. If the price to attain an asset is higher than expected, the firm cannot spend that money elsewhere. In this regard, the strategic competition aspect of FMR can be further developed.

Finally, firms may collude with other users of the constrained resource to limit competition or secure equitable access to the resource for all parties. This collusion on the supply side shares similarities to the marketplace forbearance that Chen and Miller (2012) describe for service competitors which compete in multiple markets. During factor market activities, firms

Table 23.3   *Future research topics*

Overarching category	FMR research topics	Example research questions
Supply chain structure	Supply chain sequence of activities; temporal nature of supply chain activities	How do supply chains cope with factors of production which are either perishable or which cannot be processed due to a processing glut (for example, food inputs or commodity refining)?
Supply chain relationships	Exclusivity between supply chain members	Do exclusive relationships drive factor market rivalry over and above competing for factors in an open market? Is exclusivity a catalyst for competitors to develop substitutes to constrained factors?
	Supply chain mergers and acquisitions	Are mergers and acquisitions a competitive weapon within SCM, or more so an act of survival? Does factor access improve competitive positioning or does more access contribute to a loss of innovation?
Resource litigation	Supply chain legal battles	Does factor market rivalry spur legal battles? In what way do supply chain legal battles impact upon competitive behaviour within intense factor markets?
Resource availability	Factor ubiquity	What steps can firms take to minimize the use of constrained factors in production? What role does planned obsolescence play in factor market rivalry?
	Preferred, specific factors	Does the utilization of specific types (i.e., brand or component manufacturer) of factors contribute to more intense factor market rivalry? Is the lock-in from specific factors of production quantifiable and worthwhile?
	Factor market collusion	What is the optimal level of coordination between resource users to ensure access to a constrained factor? Does factor market collusion represent an industry-level interdiction?
Human resources	Factor market extension	How can factor market myopia (FMM) be broken through expanding factor market pools when considering constrained labour markets?
	Factor market perception	What role does supply chain interdiction play when competing for a perceived high-talent, limited resource?

may coordinate the use of and access to resources in short supply across resource users, that could be more rightly considered collusion with potential opportunistic characteristics. What happens is that firms find a way to lessen intense FMR actions. However, this forbearance still results in some costs. What is the appropriate balance for firms when it comes to factor market collusion, and what characteristics of constrained resources are better suited to forbearance?

Table 23.3 summarizes the general research categories which underscore the presented future research areas. The overarching research topics are displayed, and example research questions are provided.

CONCLUSION

FMR activities are an area ripe for research within the SCM discipline. With the realization that FMR looks at supply-side competition for constrained resources, the theory is truly a general theory of SCM. This chapter serves to delineate the theoretical foundation of FMR and explain how the theory applies to SCM. Variables specific to FMR are defined and predictions of the theory are provided. With the understanding that intense competition can exist for constrained resources, a number of future research avenues are provided and discussed.

REFERENCES

Barney, J.B. (1991), 'Firm resources and sustained competitive advantage', *Journal of Management*, 17 (1), 99–120.

Barney, J.B., Ketchen D.J. and Wright, M. (2011), 'The future of resource-based theory: Revitalization or decline?', *Journal of Management*, 37 (5), 1299–1315.

Baum, J.A. and Korn, H.J. (1996), 'Competitive dynamics of interfirm rivalry', *Academy of Management Journal*, 39 (2), 255–291.

Bell, J.E., Autry, C.W. and Griffis, S.E. (2015), 'Supply chain interdiction as a competitive weapon', *Transportation Journal*, 54 (1), 89–103.

Bell, J.E., Autry, C.W., Mollenkopf, D.A. and Thornton, L.M. (2012), 'A natural resource scarcity typology: Theoretical foundations and strategic implications for supply chain management', *Journal of Business Logistics*, 33 (2), 158–166.

Bell, J.E., Mollenkopf, D.A. and Stolze, H.J. (2013), 'Natural resource scarcity and the closed- loop supply chain: A resource advantage view', *International Journal of Physical Distribution and Logistics Management*, 43 (5–6), 351–379.

Bowersox, D.J. (1969), 'Physical distribution development, current status, and potential', *Journal of Marketing*, 33 (1), 63–70.

Bowersox, D.J. and Closs, D.J. (1996), 'Logistical management: The integrated supply chain process', McGraw-Hill College.

Bowersox, D.J., Closs, D.J. and Stank, T.P. (2000), 'Ten mega-trends that will revolutionize supply chain logistics', *Journal of Business Logistics*, 21 (2), 1–15.

Capron, L. and Chatain, O. (2008), 'Competitors' resource-oriented strategies: Acting on competitor's resources through interventions in factor markets and political markets', *Academy of Management Review*, 33 (1), 97–121.

Carter, C.R., Rogers, D.S. and Choi, T.Y. (2015), 'Toward the theory of the supply chain', *Journal of Supply Chain Management*, 51 (2), 89–97.

Castillo, V.E., Mollenkopf, D.A., Bell, J.E. and Bozdogan, H. (2018), 'Supply chain integrity: A key to sustainable supply chain management', *Journal of Business Logistics*, 39 (1), 38–56.

Caves, R.E. (1984), 'Economic analysis and the quest for competitive advantage', *American Economic Review*, 74 (2), 127–132.

Chen, M.J. and Hambrick, D.C. (1995), 'Speed, stealth, and selective attack: How small firms differ from large firms in competitive behavior', *Academy of Management Journal*, 38 (2), 453–482.

Chen, M.J., Su, K.H. and Tsai, W. (2007), 'Competitive tension: The awareness–motivation–capability perspective', *Academy of Management Journal*, 50 (1), 101–118.

Chen, M.J. and Miller, D. (2012), 'Competitive dynamics: Themes, trends, and a prospective research platform', *Academy of Management Annals*, 6 (1), 135–210.

Chen, M.J. and Miller, D. (2015), 'Reconceptualizing competitive dynamics: A multidimensional frame-work', *Strategic Management Journal*, 36 (5), 758–775.

Duclos, S.J., Otto, J.P. and Konitzer, D.G. (2010), 'Design in an era of constrained resources', *Mechanical Engineering*, 132 (9), 36–40.

Dyer, J. and Singh, H. (1998), 'The relational view: Cooperative strategy and sources of interorganiza-tional competitive advantage', *Academy of Management Review*, 23 (4), 660–679.

Ellram, L.M., Tate, W.L. and Feitzinger, E.G. (2013), 'Factor-market rivalry and competition for supply chain resources', *Journal of Supply Chain Management*, 49 (1), 29–46.

Fawcett, S.E. and Magnan, G.M. (2004), 'Ten guiding principles for high-impact SCM', *Business Horizons*, 47 (5), 67–74.

Gavetti, G., Levinthal, D. and Ocasio, W. (2007), 'Neo-Carnegie: The Carnegie School's past, present, and reconstructing for the future', *Organization Science*, 18 (3), 523– 536.

González-Hernando, S., Argüelles, V.I. and Gutierrez, J.A.T. (2003), 'Exclusivity and relationalism in marketing channels', *Journal of Business and Industrial Marketing*, 18 (1), 22–39.

Grewal, R. and Slotegraaf, R.J. (2007), 'Embeddedness of organizational capabilities', *Decision Sciences*, 38 (3), 451–488.

Gupta, S. (2012), 'Mergers and acquisitions for enhancing supply chain competitiveness', *Journal of Marketing and Operations Management Research*, 2 (3), 129–147.

Handley, S.M. (2012), 'The perilous effects of capability loss on outsourcing management and performance', *Journal of Operations Management*, 30 (1–2), 152–165.

Hannan, M.T. and Freeman, J. (1989), *Organizational Ecology*. Boston, MA: Harvard University Press.

Hein, Treena (2020), 'COVID-19: US pig backlog may rise to 10 million', *PigProgress*. https://www.pigprogress.net/Health/Articles/2020/5/Covid-19-US-pig-backlog-may-rise-to-10-million-587253E. Accessed 5 July 2020.

Insead, L.C. and Chatain, O. (2008), 'Competitors' resource-oriented strategies: Acting on competitors' resources through interventions in factor markets and political markets', *Academy of Management Review*, 33 (1), 97–121.

Jaworski, B.J. and Kohli, A.K. (1993), 'Market orientation: Antecedents and consequences', *Journal of Marketing*, 57 (3), 53–70.

Kalaitzi, D., Matopoulos, A., Bourlakis, M. and Tate, W. (2018), 'Supply chain strategies in an era of natural resource scarcity', *International Journal of Operations and Production Management*, 38 (3), 784–809.

Kalaitzi, D., Matopoulos, A., Bourlakis, M. and Tate, W. (2019), 'Supply chains under resource pressure: Strategies for improving resource efficiency and competitive advantage', *International Journal of Operations and Production Management*, 39 (12), 1323–1354.

Ketokivi, M. and Choi, T. (2014), 'Renaissance of case research as a scientific method', *Journal of Operations Management*, 32 (5), 232–240.

Kohler, A.R. (2013), 'Material scarcity: A reason for responsibility in technology development and product design', *Science and Engineering Ethics*, 19 (3) 1165–1179.

Kohler, A.R, Bakker, C. and Peck, D. (2013), 'Critical materials: A reason for sustainable education of industrial designers and engineers', *European Journal of Engineering Education*, 38 (4), 441–451.

Lambert, D.M. and Cooper, M.C. (2000), 'Issues in supply chain management', *Industrial Marketing Management*, 29 (1), 65–83.

Lambert, D.M., Cooper, M.C. and Pagh, J.D. (1998), 'Supply chain management: Implementation issues and research opportunities', *International Journal of Logistics Management*, 9 (2), 1–20.

LeMay, S., Helms Marilyn, M., Kimball, B. and McMahon, D. (2017), 'Supply chain management: The elusive concept and definition', *International Journal of Logistics Management*, 28 (4), 1425–1453.

Maak, T. (2008), 'Undivided corporate responsibility: Towards a theory of corporate integrity', *Journal of Business Ethics*, 82, 353–368.

Maritan, C.A. and Peteraf, M.A. (2011), 'Building a bridge between resource acquisition and resource accumulation', *Journal of Management*, 37 (5), 1374–1389.

Markman, G.D., Gianiodis, P.T. and Buchholtz, A.K. (2009), 'Factor-market rivalry', *Academy of Management Review*, 34 (3), 423–441.

McGregor, D.M. (1960), *The Human Side of Enterprise*. New York: McGraw-Hill.

Mentzer, J.T., DeWitt, W., Keebler, J.S., Min, S., Nix, N.W., et al. (2001), 'Defining supply chain management', *Journal of Business Logistics*, 22 (2), 1–25.

Mentzer, J.T., Min, S. and Zacharia, Z. G. (2000), 'The nature of interfirm partnering in supply chain management', *Journal of Retailing*, 76 (4), 549–568.

Merton, R.K. and Merton, R.C. (1968), *Social Theory and Social Structure*. New York: Simon & Schuster.

Obloj, T. and Capron, L. (2011), 'Role of resource gap and value appropriation: Effect of reputation gap on price premium in online auctions', *Strategic Management Journal*, 32 (4), 447–456.

Opengart, R., M. Ralston, P. and LeMay, S. (2018), 'Labor markets: Preventing rivalry and myopia through HRM', *Journal of Organizational Effectiveness: People and Performance*, 5 (4), 346–360.

Pellathy, D.A., In, J., Mollenkopf, D.A. and Stank, T.P. (2018), 'Middle-range theorizing on logistics customer service', *International Journal of Physical Distribution and Logistics Management*, 48 (1), 2–18.

Penrose, E.T. (1959), *The Theory of the Growth of the Firm*. New York: John Wiley.

Pfeffer, J. and Salancik, G. (1978), *The External Control of Organizations: A Resource Dependence Perspective*. New York: Harper & Row.

Porter, M.E. (1980), *Competitive Strategy: Techniques for Analyzing Industries and Competitors*. New York: Free Press.

Pulles, N.J., Veldman, J., Schiele, H. and Sierksma, H. (2014), 'Pressure or pamper? The effects of power and trust dimensions on supplier resource allocation', *Journal of Supply Chain Management*, 50 (3), 16–36.

Ralston, P.M., Keller, S.B. and Grawe, S.J. (2020), 'Collaborative process competence as an enabler of supply chain collaboration in competitive environments and the impact on customer account management', *International Journal of Logistics Management*, 31 (4), 905–929.

Ralston, P., LeMay, S. and Opengart, R. (2017), 'Factor market myopia: A driver of factor market rivalry', *Transportation Journal*, 56 (2), 167–183.

Richey, R.G., Jr., Roath, A.S., Whipple, J.M. and Fawcett, S.E. (2010), 'Exploring a governance theory of supply chain management: Barriers and facilitators to integration', *Journal of Business Logistics*, 31 (1), 237–256.

Schwieterman, M. and Miller, J. (2016), 'Factor market rivalry: Toward an integrated understanding of firm action', *Transportation Journal*, 55 (2), 97–123.

Simon, H. (1997), *Administrative Behavior*, 4th edn. New York: Free Press

Stank, T.P., Pellathy, D.A., In, J., Mollenkopf, D.A. and Bell, J.E. (2017), 'New frontiers in logistics research: Theorizing at the middle range', *Journal of Business Logistics*, 38 (1), 6–17.

Suzuki, A. (2009), 'Market foreclosure and vertical merger: A case study of the vertical merger between Turner Broadcasting and Time Warner', *International Journal of Industrial Organization*, 27 (4), 532–543.

Swanson, D., Goel, L., Francisco, K. and Stock, J. (2020), 'Understanding the relationship between general and middle-range theorizing', *International Journal of Logistics Management*, 31 (3), 401–421.

USLegal Inc. (2021) 'Exclusivity Agreement Law and legal definition.' https://definitions.uslegal.com/e/exclusivity-agreement. Accessed 7 May 2021.

Wacker, J.G. (1998), 'A definition of theory: Research guidelines for different theory-building research methods in operations management', *Journal of Operations Management*, 16 (4), 361–385.

Wernerfelt, B. (1984), 'A resource-based view of the firm', *Strategic Management Journal*, 5 (2), 171–180.

Williamson, H.F. and Daum, A.R. (1959), *The American Petroleum Industry: The Age of Illumination, 1859–1899*. Evanston, IL: Northwestern University Press.

24. The industrial network approach and purchasing and supply management research

Björn Axelsson, Lars-Erik Gadde and Finn Wynstra

THE INDUSTRIAL NETWORK APPROACH: ORIGIN AND EVOLUTION

The industrial network approach seeks to analyse the interaction between actors in business networks. The approach was initially developed by a group of European researchers in the 1970s. In fact, the industrial network approach encompasses two core models: the interaction model, which pertains to bilateral exchange episodes and long-term relations between firms; and the network model (or activities–resources–actors model), which considers the relations between a set of actors (three or more) and their interdependencies. The emphasis on collaboration and the interdependence between different business relationships may not seem very distinctive today in the 2020s, but some 50 years ago this was a significant deviation from the then-current models of business relations in general, and of procurement and business marketing in particular. Still today, the industrial network approach (INA) stands out in that it considers interaction, and interdependence, as a given condition in the overwhelming majority of business exchanges.

The INA view on business marketing and purchasing originates in an international research project starting in 1976, on international marketing and purchasing of industrial goods. This project involved researchers from five European countries with ambitions to investigate the business processes between firms, which in this particular project involved buying and selling firms. These researchers – collectively referred to as the Industrial Marketing and Purchasing (IMP) Group – were dissatisfied with the descriptions, conceptualizations and analyses of interorganizational relations in the mainstream literature. Contemporary purchasing models, for instance, considered the occurrence of close relations with suppliers to be a market failure because these features would impose unwanted dependences (Westing et al., 1969). In contrast, prior empirical observations made by this group of researchers pointed out the central role of long-term business relationships; a phenomenon neglected in established frameworks at the time. The project members concluded that more realistic conceptualizations had to be based on systematic empirical data. In their joint project, more than 1000 face-to-face interviews were conducted in Sweden, the United Kingdom, France, Italy and (what was then) West Germany. The interviews covered around 800 customer–supplier relationships in the five countries. The empirical results were similar across firms and countries, and confirmed the widespread existence of long-term, close buyer–supplier relations. These findings strongly contrasted with the mainstream view of (business marketing and) purchasing processes (Robinson et al., 1967; Westing et al., 1969).

After six years, the project was reported in a joint publication edited by Håkansson (1982). In the 'Introduction' (p. 1), the authors started by challenging the contemporary perspective in several respects. They challenged the concentration of the industrial buyer behaviour literature 'on a narrow analysis of a single discrete purchase', and the view of industrial marketing 'as the manipulation of marketing mix variables', as well as the analysis of 'either the process of industrial purchasing or of industrial marketing'. Instead, they emphasized the importance of the relationships between buyers and sellers, and the interaction between the two parties 'where either firm may be the more active part'. The main contribution of this first step in INA theory development was the interaction model portraying the interplay between buyer and seller. The model and its constructs are further described in the following two sections.

The next step was initiated in the second half of the 1980s, also through the launch of a multinational project. IMP1 was focused on interaction in dyadic relationships. The analysis of these relationships indicated that they were connected to, and significantly impacted by, other relationships. Therefore, the environment of the relationship in the interaction model was far from a diffuse or anonymous context, but featured specific other firms and relationships. Thus, the new project (IMP2) aimed at conceptualizing the embeddedness of the individual relationship in its contextual setting of other interdependent relationships. IMP2 extended the geographical coverage by also involving researchers from the United States, Australia and Japan. The project is reported in Håkansson and Snehota (1995). The study showed that understanding of business interaction requires that the individual relationship is seen as an element embedded in a network of other relationships. As such, the IMP definition of networks closely follows that by Cook and Emerson (1978, p. 725): 'An exchange network is a set of two or more connected exchange relations ... Two exchange relations are connected to the degree that exchange in one relation is contingent upon exchange (or nonexchange) in the other relation.'

The main contribution from the IMP2 study is a matrix scheme for network analysis building on the ARA model (activities–resources–actors). The model and its constructs are further described in the section on core constructs.

In both the IMP1 and IMP2 projects, the impact of the network is considered, but at the relationship level. These conditions called for a publication taking the network level as the starting point for analysis: Håkansson et al. (2009a). This book is not based on a specific research project, but still heavily grounded in empirics. Firstly, the authors rely on their own field studies conducted for more than 40 years. Secondly, they draw on the numerous dissertations and papers presented by researchers in the expanding IMP community. Again, the central role of interaction is emphasized, and its features and effects are explored in relation to the three ARA layers. In addition to the spatial network impact, specific attention is directed to dynamic conditions. Furthermore, the authors discuss the implications for management and public policy.

FROM RELATIONSHIPS TO NETWORKS: THE INTERACTION AND ARA MODELS

In the following we describe the INA's two central models. The INA perspective on business relationships constituted a watershed between established conceptualizations and the observations of reality made by the IMP pioneers. As noted, contemporary economic theory perceived the occurrence of close relations with suppliers to be a market failure, because such features imposed unwanted dependencies. This view of relationships was probably one of the main triggers of the INA since its early advocates had identified the existence of long-term and close relationships, as well as the benefits they provided (Håkansson et al., 1977; Ford,

1980). The relationships with suppliers were economically significant for buying firms, since studies showed that a limited number of suppliers accounted for a large portion of their costs (and correspondingly for their income). Moreover, suppliers were often important sources of technology and knowledge, implying that small suppliers could also be significant business partners. For these reasons, the INA perspective claims that what takes place in the relationships between companies is more important than what takes place within the individual firms. These conditions have supported the argument that a firm's business relationships are its most valuable resource, which in turn makes the interaction within such relations highly important (see Ford et al., 2003).

The Interaction Model

Figure 24.1 portrays the original interaction model evolving from the IMP1 project. Interaction occurs on both the organizational level and the individual level. The interaction processes build on the aims and experiences of the parties and is impacted upon by features such as technology, organizational structure and the strategies of the parties. Interaction contains two processes: short-term exchange episodes, and long-term relationships involving adaptations and thus institutionalization of the interaction. The processes were found to be affected by the atmosphere of the interaction, which can be either cooperative or confrontative through the exploitation of power. Interaction is also affected by various aspects of the environment of the two parties, such as internationalization and market structure. In the coming discussion of central constructs, we will return to adaptations, closeness and dynamism.

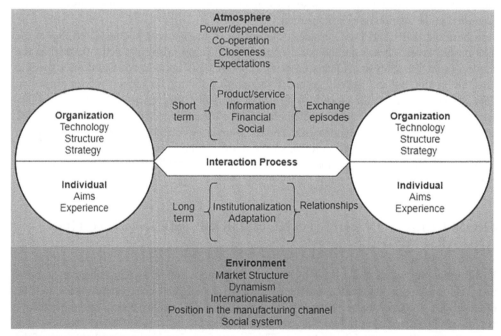

Source: Based on Håkansson (1982).

Figure 24.1   Interaction model

The significance of interaction has been increasingly emphasized over time. In Håkansson (1982), interaction was primarily considered a process ongoing between individuals or between organizations, as illustrated in Figure 24.1. Håkansson et al. (2009a) extended the analysis of interaction to involve the three network layers, thus exploring interaction in relation to activities, actors and resources. Finally, even greater attention to interaction is provided by the subtitle of the book celebrating 40 years of IMP (Håkansson and Snehota, 2017): *Making Sense of the Interactive Business World.*

The ARA Model

The initial ARA model (Håkansson, 1987) portrayed the business reality as a network containing three layers. In relation to the terminology of Wacker (1998), this network was defined by its ongoing activities, the resources exploited in the undertaking of activities, and the actors controlling resources and conducting activities. In reality, the three layers are completely intertwined, but combined they offer three separate lenses on the network, thus enabling the holistic perspective required for analysis of complex realities.

Through IMP2, the conceptualization of the INA was further developed as a means for better understanding of interaction and dyadic constellations (see Figure 24.2). One extension regards the content of a business relationship that is defined by three central constructs: the links between the activities of the two parties, the ties between their respective resources, and the bonds that evolve between the two. Activities are linked through coordinative efforts; resources become tied through the successive combining and recombining of the resources of the parties. Finally, actors are bonded through their joint coordination and combining, as well as through the personal connections between people. The second extension relates to the function of a relationship. What is ongoing in a business relationship does not only impact upon the specific dyad. There is also a function for the two individual companies, as well as for the larger setting – the network – where the two parties reside. In this way, the links, ties and bonds in the relationship impact upon the activity, resource and actor features of the two companies and the other firms connected to them. Central constructs subject to further discus-

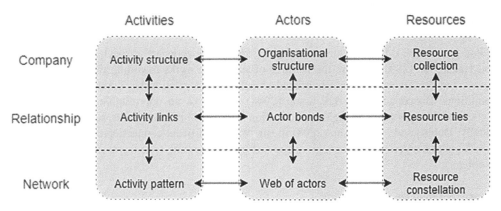

Source: Based on Håkansson and Snehota (1995, p. 45).

Figure 24.2   *The ARA model*

sion regard interdependencies between activities, heterogeneity of resources, and adaptations among actors.

THE CORE CONSTRUCTS IN THE INA

In the following, we describe the core constructs of the two INA models: one of the four main elements of a theory according to Wacker (1998). The constructs presented are those most central and distinctive for INA's conceptualization of interorganizational relationships and networks: network embeddedness, interdependencies, heterogeneity of resources, involvement and interfaces (related to closeness in the interaction model), adaptations, and network dynamics.

Network Embeddedness

Following the ARA model, business relationships are embedded in networks, implying that what happens in one relationship tends to affect what happens, and what can be done, in other relationships. In the ARA terminology one significant assumption is that the 'total' network of activities, resources and actors is boundless, since it is always possible to identify further connections in any direction. This network constitutes a complex setting, also including 'technological, logistical, and administrative systems as well as legal structures; it is a mirror and source of the multiple interdependencies arising between companies with permeable and fuzzy boundaries' (Håkansson and Snehota, 2017, p. 11). These conditions impose severe analytical and managerial difficulties.

Any analysis of network conditions must therefore be based on limitations of the total network, such as subnetworks related to logistics, technology, industries, or those developed around single companies. An important feature of the INA is that the research boundaries become set as the study progresses, based on the evolving findings, while most other theories tend to rely on preset system boundaries. Moreover, since the total network is boundless and changing, it is unknowable for those involved in managerial action. Decision makers must act on their knowledge of the limited part of the network they consider relevant for their actions, identified as their 'network pictures' (Ford et al., 2003) or 'network horizon' (Holmen and Pedersen, 2003).

For this review, IMP publications related to supplier networks are of special interest. Gadde and Håkansson (2001) explore the features of supply networks regarding the three network layers, and discuss strategic issues related to outsourcing, relationship features and network conditions. Bocconcelli and Håkansson (2008) show how an unprofitable company made a successful turnaround through the activation and transformation of its supplier network. Finally, Dubois and Fredriksson (2008) illustrate the significant connection between the relationship and network levels through a study of triadic sourcing (one buyer in relation to two suppliers).

Interdependencies

Interdependence is a central feature of the activity layer because no activity is isolated from others; it is linked to activities undertaken previously and simultaneously, as well as those that will be undertaken later. These interdependencies occur between manufacturing, logistics, and service activities as well as in relation to design and research and development. The myriad of interdependent activities must be integrated within firms to secure efficient in-house operations. However, over time, increasing outsourcing has made integration across the boundaries of firms even more significant for performance improvements in supply chains and supply networks. These efforts require analytical tools for investigation of the potential effects of the coordination mechanisms applied for integration of activities.

Dubois (1998) developed such tools regarding serial and parallel interdependencies. Activities that must be undertaken in a specific order are serially related. The relevant mechanism for coordination depends on the standardization or customization of what is exchanged between the parties. Parallel interdependence occurs for activities that are undertaken at the same time and exploit the same resources. In this situation the central task in coordination is to secure effective use of resources. This framing was further developed to analyse interfirm interdependencies within and among supply chains (Dubois et al., 2004; Håkansson and Persson, 2004). An overview of the role of interdependence in INA research is presented in Freytag et al. (2017).

Heterogeneity of Resources

One of the central assumptions in the INA is resource heterogeneity, implying that the value of a resource is dependent on its connections to other resources. In today's interactive business landscape, the economic feature of a resource is not a given: it is determined by the effects of its ties to other resources. In this way, the combining and recombining of resources are central issues in supplier networks (Gadde and Håkansson, 2001). Baraldi (2008) shows how a buying company (IKEA) is provided with substantial benefits through the long-term resource combining with its suppliers.

The conditions for efficient and effective combining of resources change over time, thus making recombining a crucial issue. Håkansson and Waluszewski (2002) show, in another IKEA case, the significance of resource recombining in relation to suppliers when network conditions change. This book also presents the 'four resources' (4R) framework, useful for analysis of resource development. According to this framework, the evolvement of a specific resource is determined by its interplay with other resources representing four categories. The framework distinguishes between physical and organizational resources. The physical resources are represented by the products exchanged and the facilities utilized (involving, for example, production resources and the transportation infrastructure). The organizational resources contain the business units where the knowledge and capabilities of the actors reside, as well as the business relationships providing access to external resources.

Involvement and Interfaces

'Closeness' is one of the concepts in the interaction model. This relatively broad concept was further refined by, for example, Gadde and Snehota (2000) in their analysis of how to 'make the most of supplier relationships'. They distinguished between high and low involvement relationships and their respective contributions to relationship performance. Araujo et al. (1999) presented a more fine-tuned distinction based on the buying firm's resource interfaces with suppliers, and the accompanying consequences for productivity and innovation.

Four interface categories were identified: from standardized interfaces without adjustments between resources, to interactive interfaces based on intense interaction and collaboration involving mutual adjustments on the two sides of the dyad. In-between the two we find specified interfaces where the buyer prescribes the features of what is exchanged and how it should be produced. When translation interfaces are at hand, the buyer describes the features of what to exchange and leaves it to the supplier to decide how to comply with these requests.

This framing was further extended by Gadde and Wynstra (2017), who analysed the consequences of the various interfaces in relation to rationalization and development efforts on the supply side of a company. Based on this exploration they present strategic alternatives for the leveraging of these two strategic roles and the interfaces, as well as the organizing issues related to each type of interface.

Adaptations

Integration of activities, combining of resources, and involvement among actors are examples of adaptations between business partners. Adaptations provide benefits by improving operational performance but are also costly. Therefore, the financial consequences of adaptations in activity links, resource ties and actor bonds need to be scrutinized both before and after such investments are undertaken. Moreover, adaptations impose dependencies in relation to business partners. Historically, firms were recommended to avoid adaptations to individual suppliers, because such conditions would imply lock-in effects and make it difficult to exploit market forces.

In today's business landscape, however, firms deliberately enter situations leading to interdependencies. They do so because in order to survive and progress in the interactive business world, organizations cannot escape the interdependencies accompanying adaptations in terms of well-functioning activity links, resource ties and actor bonds. However, these adaptations in relation to specific business partners will constrain the opportunities for prosperous engagement with other firms, because these potential partners have adapted their resources and activities to their current business partners.

Changing business conditions impact upon the perceptions and effects of interdependencies. In these situations, firms may consider modifying their adaptations, since adaptations are important means for handling interdependencies. But any attempt to reduce certain interdependencies through changes in the pattern of adaptations will induce other forms of interdependencies, which in turn must be handled.

Network Dynamics

Network conditions are in continuous flux. They evolve successively through the interaction among the actors in their attempts to improve network performance. In these efforts technological developments represent significant enablers for reconfiguring activity coordination and resource combining. Somewhat paradoxically, however, networks also feature considerable stability. Modifications and renewal normally tend to occur within the basic building blocks, constituted by the interdependencies and adaptations within established activity patterns, resource constellations and webs of actors. The embeddedness within this broad setting favours changes that are in line with contemporary network structures and processes, while constraining other forces for modification.

The same conditions make it difficult for individual firms in isolation to change the basic structure. Over time, other firms in the network have made substantial investments in the current setting. Therefore, it is not likely that they would be motivated to engage in modifications that might threaten their network positions. Rather, they can be expected to prefer the status quo and thus counteract change initiatives. This means that major modifications require the unified efforts of several actors in interaction, because the action space of a single firm is severely constrained. For these reasons there is a network saying that has become classical: 'If the network is against you; you can do nothing. But if the network is with you; you can do almost anything.'

THE DOMAINS AND UNITS OF ANALYSIS OF THE INA

The second element of any theory, according to Wacker (1998), is its domain.

Above we illustrated some central constructs used in INA research. The starting point for this conceptual evolution was that the IMP founders were dissatisfied with the framing of the processes in business marketing and purchasing. In their efforts to improve this situation they were able to rely on constructs developed within other research disciplines (for example, sociology and organization theory). It is beyond the scope of this chapter to elaborate on the various theories that the INA has drawn on; for a review we refer the reader to Easton (1992).

For this reason, the concepts applied – such as relationships and networks – are broader than those established before (for example, marketing mix and models of organizational buying behaviour). These conditions, in combination with the generality of the ARA model's basic concepts, make it possible to use the INA frameworks for many research problems and in many different empirical settings. When issues related to activities, resources and actors are significant, the INA provides a relevant alternative.

This relevance is illustrated by the fact that INA models have been applied to other phenomena than business marketing and purchasing. In the initiation phase, research in international business provided important input to the development of the approach, and over time, contributions have been made to research on innovation and technological development (Håkansson and Waluszewski, 2002: Håkansson et al., 2009b). Moreover, the INA models have been used for reinterpretation of prerequisites and effects of public policy (Guercini and Tunisini, 2017; Hoholm and Araujo, 2017). Finally, in recent years, enhanced attention has been paid to issues dealing with start-ups and various forms of new ventures (see Baraldi et al., 2019).

Domains related to purchasing and supply management where the INA perspective does not really apply would involve atomistic markets with anonymous trading partners, such as pure commodity markets. It would be a misunderstanding to think that this means that the INA perspective applies only to technologically complicated goods and services; even the development and production of IKEA's famous Lack table can be effectively understood in terms of integration of activities, combining of resources, and involvement of different business actors (Baraldi, 2008).

GENERAL DIFFUSION OF THE INA IN PURCHASING AND SUPPLY MANAGEMENT RESEARCH

As the name already suggests, IMP and the INA have been extensively used in studying phenomena in the field of purchasing and supply management (PSM), but by a relatively small community. To illustrate this, we draw on a study that reviewed some 2522 journal articles dealing with PSM, from the period 1995–2014 (Wynstra et al., 2019). These articles are published in a set of 18 international journals across the marketing, operations management and strategy/organization disciplines, plus the two specialist PSM journals *Journal of Purchasing and Supply Management* (*JPSM*) and *Journal of Supply Chain Management*. Of these 2522 publications, 50 articles (2 per cent) explicitly apply the industrial network approach. Of these, 42 articles are published in *Industrial Marketing Management* (*IMM*) and *JPSM*. The INA has been particularly popular in the period 2000–2010; before and after this period (that is, 1995–1999 and 2011–2014), the PSM studies in our set did not apply the INA.

There may be several factors explaining this somewhat limited diffusion of the INA in PSM research published in (top) journals. First, many of the original or at least early IMP contributors were initially focusing on publishing in books, and in some journals not covered in this dataset (such as the *Journal of Business-to-Business Marketing* and *Journal of Business Research*). Part of this focus may be explained by the fact that many of the top journals in marketing and operations management, especially those that have their roots in North America, are not a natural home to the mainly qualitative, in-depth studies that IMP research would typically involve. Another factor explaining the limited focus on top journals may be the institutional context in the academic institutions of the early IMP contributors. In many cases, these universities (especially in Scandinavia) did not steer researchers so strongly towards publications in top journals – for better or for worse.

The second plausible reason for the somewhat limited diffusion of the INA is the consequence of the first; since relatively few IMP studies were published in top journals, fewer people outside the IMP community (be they readers or reviewers) have become familiar with it, and those that have seen it may not have deemed it a very productive avenue for getting published.

A third reason may be that regarding Wacker's third and fourth elements of theory – specific relationships between constructs and predictions – INA research tends to be more ambiguous than, for instance, transaction cost economics. One central postulate in INA theory is that any action and any outcome in a network is highly context specific. Therefore, findings and conclusions generated in one business relation or network should not be generalized to another one without careful consideration.

Despite this apparent limited diffusion of the INA in PSM research, one should not draw the conclusion that the impact or significance of the industrial network approach is limited. Just considering relative quantities of journal publications is a narrow metric, which disregards the impressive series of books that have been published, for instance. Also, the impact – implicit or explicit – of the INA on PSM research cannot be completely gauged in this way. In fact, Wynstra (2010) demonstrates that a relatively high share (10 per cent) of the most-cited articles published in *JPSM* by then had been authored by researchers associated with IMP (Dubois, Gadde, Harrison, Håkansson, Wynstra).

APPLICATIONS OF THE INA PERSPECTIVE

We have identified ten themes central to PSM research, which include studies that have adopted the INA. For each of the chosen themes, we briefly describe the theme and review some illustrative examples of studies that have adopted the INA. In this review of applications of the INA perspective, we draw on the set of articles described above (Wynstra et al., 2019), the review by Johnsen (2018), and additional publications from other journals and books.

Strategic Role of Procurement

The seminal article by Kraljic (1983) directed attention to the strategic role of procurement. While the category sourcing strategies from that article have received most attention (see below), the article also suggested the contingencies under which organizations should adopt a more strategic focus on procurement ('supply management') and when they could continue to rely on a predominantly operational focus ('purchasing'). At the same time, IMP researchers pointed out the strategic importance of purchasing in Axelsson and Håkansson (1984). This book was based on an interview study involving a broad selection of purchasing managers, aiming at identifying their 'best examples' where procurement efforts made significant strategic impact. These illustrations were then discussed around three themes, each one portraying a strategic role of procurement: the rationalization role, the development role, and the supply network design role. While the first two roles were to some extent comparable to Kraljic's notions of purchasing versus supply management, respectively, the supply network role had not explicitly been defined. Moreover, Axelsson and Håkansson (1984) emphasized that there are trade-offs in fulfilling these different roles.

Gadde and Håkansson (2001) returned to these roles and integrated them systematically in their analysis of the interconnections between purchasing, on the one hand, and the network's activities, resources and actors on the other. The authors concluded that the strategic role of purchasing is manifested through the buying firm's approaches and actions in relation to three specific areas: make-or-buy decisions, the relationships with individual suppliers, and the design of the entire supplier base.

Supplier Relations

Early studies in business marketing adopting the INA strongly emphasized the importance of business relationships and the role of interaction between buyers and sellers. Several subsequent studies from the buying firm perspective were 'mirror images' of those made from the selling party's perspective (see Håkansson, 1982). Studying the general as well as specific aspects of a great number of interactive settings demonstrated, among others, how interactive processes differed for a firm supplying raw materials or semi-assembly products relative to components and production equipment. These studies have been extended by Van der Valk et al. (2009), for example, who studied various kinds of services based on the same idea (notably, how the product is used by the buyer: as a product to process further, as a part of a bigger product, or operatively as a working method). Other studies focusing on business relationships have looked at the durability of relationships (Dubois et al., 2021) and reasons for terminating relations (Halinen and Tähtinen, 2002).

As organizations have several supplier relationships, there is an interest in how to best segment them. Ever since the seminal article by Kraljic (1983), companies have struggled with sorting supplier relationships into categories. IMP research has looked into this theme too. Pedersen and Dubois (2002) expressed criticism of all-too-simple classifications, which is obvious from the title of their work: 'Why relationships do not fit into portfolio models'. Their critique is twofold. First, buyer–supplier relations are not just to be seen from a power balance perspective; interdependence is the natural consequence of adaptations and concerns virtually all relationships. Second, specific buyer–supplier relations should not be seen in isolation. Grouping suppliers based on the product or service delivered disregards interdependencies and synergies with other products and services, and limits the viewpoint of buying firms to the current exchange, with the danger that the overall potential of the supplier in innovation is overlooked.

Persson and Håkansson (2007) also challenge the Kraljic matrix, and specifically the recommended strategies that are indicated based on a supplier's position in the matrix. They demonstrate that in each of the four matrix quadrants a relationship-oriented approach – contrary to the conventional view – could be an effective choice. This is not to say that cooperation is the sole way to leverage supplier relations. The earlier-mentioned study by Dubois and Fredriksson (2008) demonstrates how cooperative and competitive measures could go hand-in-hand. For instance, a company can capture the benefits of long-term cooperation by alternating or shifting volumes between parallel suppliers.

Supplier Base Configurations

The supplier (supply) base has been identified as one of the most strategic assets of a firm (Ford et al., 2003). One distinction in relation to other theories is the explicit view of the INA that supplier networks become established through evolutionary processes that are not fully under control of the buying firm. Other approaches tend to consider these networks as predominantly created and managed by the buying firm. Within the IMP Group, however, there are also some studies that adopt such a more voluntaristic perspective (Möller and Rajala, 2007). At the same time, supplier bases are often characterized by a high degree of stability. In a longitudinal study, building on data covering more than 50 years, it is demonstrated how the supplier base of a company evolves through entries and exits of suppliers, as well as modifications of their relative positions (Dubois et al., 2021). Other studies illustrating the features and dynamics of supplier bases include the previously mentioned papers by Araujo et al. (1999), Baraldi (2008), Bocconcelli and Håkansson (2008) and Persson and Håkansson (2007).

One of the central INA constructs is embeddedness, implying that what takes place in one relationship impacts on – and is impacted upon by – what is ongoing in the surrounding network. The obvious implication is that activities directed towards one business partner also need to bring other relationships into the picture. Numerous studies make clear that firms do take specific other relationships into consideration when deciding and acting in relation to a focused counterpart (Blankenburg and Johanson, 1992). Following this notion of embeddedness, the INA has traditionally avoided the term supply 'chains', but has consistently referred to supplier networks (see Gadde and Håkansson, 2001). Relations with and between suppliers can be interconnected in multiple ways; not just those between the different tiers in a supply chain for a specific component.

Organizing Procurement

Historically, PSM organizing focused on intra-organizational issues such as the choice between centralization and decentralization, the organizing of the purchasing department and its connections to other corporate functions. Over time, outsourcing, specialization, and the need for supplier resources required increasing attention to organizing across the boundaries of firms. From the INA perspective this external organizing was a primary focus from the very beginning, since the early studies indicated that business marketing and purchasing to a large extent could be characterized as organizational issues in relation to important business partners.

External organizing is significant for the features of the exchange processes in a relationship. The outcomes of efforts to mobilize and motivate suppliers are contingent on the organizational arrangements applied between the firms. Moreover, the content of a relationship, in terms of activity linking, resource combining and actor bonding, are all features determined by the forms of organizing across the borders of firms. The four types of interfaces in buyer–supplier relationships discussed in previous sections rely on different organizational constellations (Araujo et al., 1999; Gadde and Wynstra, 2017). Moreover, the basic conditions in the supplier base regarding, for example, collaboration between the various suppliers are generated through the organizing forms established.

The most crucial issue in the organizing at the supply side of companies are the linkages between internal and external organizing (Gadde and Håkansson, 2001). Dubois and Wynstra (2005) developed a framework for analysis of the connection between the two. The internal dimension characterizes the relationship between purchasing and other company departments regarding the internal decision-making processes. For the external dimension the authors distinguish between different levels of mutual adjustments between buyer and supplier, from market-based transactions to intense collaboration. Hessel and Gadde (2013) also developed a framework for analysis of internal–external linkages. In this case the interplay between internal organizing, relationship organizing, and supplier base organizing is related to each of the three ARA dimensions.

Offshoring and International Sourcing

There are rather few INA studies specifically addressing international procurement. Many of the studies addressing other topics, however, naturally deal with buying and selling firms located in different countries (Håkansson, 1982; Håkansson and Snehota, 1995). Thus, the international aspect has in many studies been treated as a contextual factor. Still, some studies specifically highlight the international dimension. Hallén (1982) investigated the extent to which international purchasing in industrial firms is influenced not only by the market conditions, but also by the attitudes toward buying from abroad and the firm's competence in international transactions. Other studies include Salmi and Sharafutdinova (2008) and Andersson and Salmi (2001). Agndal (2006) addressed international sourcing, primarily related to small and medium-sized firms, focusing on issues such as the role of personal relationships as venues into new markets, and the degree of rational planning relative to seemingly serendipitous events in and around relationships are addressed.

Service Procurement

Procuring business-to-business services has over time attracted more attention by IMP-oriented researchers. Axelsson and Wynstra (2002) nuance the traditionally perceived specifics of service procurement by connecting INA models to theories of service management and marketing. The INA and in particular the service-dominant logic (SDL) have quite a lot in common. One element is the emphasis on co-creation of solutions by the buyer and seller, as well as by other actors. Another is the emphasis on relationships as valuable assets enabling firms to co-produce solutions. The specific contribution from the INA encompasses the concepts to systematically describe and analyse individual relationships as well as broader business networks (or ecosystems) (Ford, 2011).

Most traditional procurement literature treats service procurement as indirect procurement: items that do not enter the buying firm's final customer offerings. To address this shortcoming, the aforementioned work by Van der Valk et al. (2009) distinguishes between procurement of so-called consumption and instrumental services (indirect), versus semi-manufactured and component services (direct), and related interaction patterns.

Another major area is procurement of solutions and outcome (performance)-based procurement. The INA perspective has emphasized two aspects here. One is the new relationship challenges that tend to follow from solution procurement: a broader set of suppliers are involved, higher degrees of responsibility are delegated to (some) suppliers, and the collaboration of procurement with sales and marketing is intensified (Andersson et al., 2018). The other aspect is the business network (or ecosystem) and the complexities in manoeuvring therein when building a system of cooperating suppliers to enable the solution offerings (Spring and Araujo, 2009).

Logistics and Distribution Channels

Regarding distribution channel research, Alderson (1957) argued that the activities in distribution are related in an 'ecological network'. This holistic perspective was later undermined by the evolving producer-oriented channel management approach. Over time, however, changes in the business reality called for alternative models of distribution constellations, and made INA theory a relevant framing, as pointed out by, for example, Gadde and Ford (2008). Specific application areas regard, for instance, food supply, recycling and recovery in waste handling, supply to construction sites, as well as distribution systems for mobile phones and personal computers.

The business reality of logistics and distribution channels has become more complex, increasingly characterized by substantial interdependencies. For this reason, the holistic features of INA theory provide relevant frameworks for analysis. Jahre et al. (2006) is one example of comprehensive case studies of logistics issues. The book is based on a major Norwegian research project where the four resources (4R) framework is applied. The relevance of the INA is also acknowledged outside the IMP Group for research dealing with logistics service providers, since the models offer insights regarding the dynamics of outsourcing. For example, Marasco (2008, p. 16) claims that the INA represents 'a robust structure that enables a comprehensive understanding of TPL relationships'.

Collaborative Innovation

Collaborative innovation has been a hallmark of IMP research from the beginning. One important contribution is a joint publication based on studies in the middle of the 1980s (Håkansson, 1987). Chapters in the book are devoted to process and product development, as well as to the significance of supplier relationships and to the role of personal networks among technicians.

Later, Håkansson and Eriksson (1993) adopted the interaction approach to identify and analyse four key processes in managing supplier involvement in product development: prioritizing, mobilizing, coordinating, and timing of activities and resources. This classification has subsequently been adapted and refined by Wynstra et al. (1999) and Van Echtelt et al. (2008) to identify sets of specific activities that are, on the one hand, related to short-term, project-based collaborative innovation for specific products and services; and on the other hand, to long-term technology development.

In these and other IMP-related studies on buyer–supplier collaboration in innovation, it is noteworthy that these studies typically consider multiple cycles or time horizons of collaboration forms. This can be related back to the emphasis of the original interaction model that considers both individual, short-term exchange episodes, and the more long-term relationship development process.

Public Sector Procurement

Public procurement is a significant part of economic activity in society. IMP researchers have looked into this field from a variety of angles. A general theme in IMP studies of public procurement is the consequences for good and bad – but most of all bad – of the dominant market view. This criticism is frequently followed by requests for a modernized legal structure for public procurement which would allow for bringing in more of a relationship-based work mode (or governance mode).

Axelsson and Torvatn (2017) demonstrate how the theoretical points of departure from microeconomic theory have been translated into policies and practices in public procurement. They confront these practices to the five basic governance modes identified by Gereffi et al. (2005) to find out whether – and to what extent – the policies and practices are in line with these different governance modes. In doing so they point to efforts in policies and regulations to 'repair' shortcomings due to the points of departure by adding 'exceptions' and 'special cases' to the dominant (version of) market governance. In a follow-up study, Håkansson and Axelsson (2020) look into public sector outsourcing from two empirical cases. They utilize the four types of buyer–seller interfaces from Araujo et al. (1999) as well as a general model of when to outsource or not. These two tools are used to systematically identify when outsourcing in the public sector could be considered a relatively straightforward option, and when it would be more challenging. Other studies of public procurement applying the INA include studies such as Waluszewski et al. (2019).

Research Methods

On a final note, several IMP scholars have substantially contributed to the debate on research methods. Some of these contributions have dealt with research methods regarding interorganizational relations and networks in general (Halinen and Törnroos, 2005), while some have focused on methods for PSM research in particular (Dubois and Araujo, 2007). The publications usually deal with the qualities and requirements of qualitative research and longitudinal fieldwork, while some articles specifically address the so-called abductive approach to research (Dubois and Gadde, 2002). Such an abductive approach, or 'systematic combining', relies on 'a continuous movement between an empirical world and a model world' (Dubois and Gadde, 2002, p. 554). Such continuous iterations between theory and observation would maximally leverage the qualities of case research, whereas received wisdom typically relates case research to a predominantly exploratory or inductive approach.

CONCLUSION

The industrial network approach, and the interaction and actors–resources–activities models that it incorporates, have been applied in numerous studies in PSM. In fact, one could argue that the INA is one of the few theoretical perspectives that is so specifically rooted in observations on buyer–supplier relations. At the same time, a distinguishing feature is that the INA has been used to study both the supply side and the buy side of buyer–supplier relations, and often in a more holistic fashion than most other theories.

As the discussion of the central concepts has illustrated, the INA is distinct from other perspectives that deal with interorganizational relations in that it provides a conceptualization of what is the substance of relations (activity links, actor bonds, resource ties) that is deeply rooted in the primary processes of development, production and exchange of goods and services. Other approaches, such as social exchange theory (Blau, 1964; Thibaut and Kelly, 1959) and the relational view (Dyer and Singh, 1998) focus more on the governance of relations through norms (equity, reciprocity) and atmosphere (trust, commitment).

The industrial network approach is also in other respects an atypical theory. First of all, this approach has been used to study different phenomena where firms (and other organizational actors) interact, either bilaterally or in network settings. Second, the approach has been developed by a group of researchers. It is not uncommon for a theoretical perspective to be initiated and/or propagated by a team of researchers, but in the case of the Industrial Marketing and Purchasing (IMP) Group, the collective nature of the efforts is remarkable. The IMP Group has not only conducted large-scale field studies together and published many books as a collective, but has also organized an annual conference (since 1984) and many research manuscript workshops in connection with its dedicated journal, the *IMP Journal* (since 2019 part of the *Journal of Business and Industrial Marketing*).

The INA and its specific models (the interaction model and the ARA model) have been applied in a multitude of procurement contexts. It has enabled systematic descriptions and analyses and, as a result, has enabled researchers to identify patterns of behaviour as well as providing insightful lessons learned. Still, it has been criticized for not being very concrete in guiding managers in their creation of action plans and effecting strategies. This criticism has been countered by IMP researchers who have argued against the often sparser theoretical models that are more ambitious in offering prescriptive guidance. The IMP philosophy emphasizes the contextual dependency of procurement and supplier relations in business markets and, thus, the importance of performing a thorough description and analysis before moving towards prescription.

REFERENCES

Agndal, H. (2006), 'The purchasing market entry process – A study of 10 Swedish industrial small and medium-sized enterprises', *Journal of Purchasing and Supply Management*, 12 (4), 182–196.

Alderson, W. (1957), *Marketing Behavior and Executive Action*, Homewood, IL: Richard D. Irwin.

Andersson, P., B. Axelsson and C. Rosenqvist (2018), *Organizing Marketing and Sales: Mastering Contemporary B2B Challenges*, Bingley: Emerald Publishing.

Andersson, H. and A. Salmi (2001), 'Can you buy a business relationship? On the importance of customer and supplier relationships in acquisitions', *Industrial Marketing Management*, 30 (7), 575–586.

Araujo, L., A. Dubois and L-E. Gadde (1999). 'Managing interfaces with suppliers', *Industrial Marketing Management*, 28 (5), 497–506.

Axelsson, B. and H. Håkansson (1984), *Inköp för konkurrenskraft*, Lund, SE: Studentlitteratur.

Axelsson, B. and T. Torvatn (2017), 'Public purchasing in an interactive world', in Håkansson, H. and I. Snehota (eds), *No Business is an Island: Making Sense of the Interactive Business World*, Bingley: Emerald Insight, pp. 173–194.

Axelsson, B. and F. Wynstra (2002). *Buying Business Services*, Chichester: John Wiley & Sons.

Baraldi, E. (2008), 'Strategy in industrial networks: Experiences from IKEA', *California Management Review*, 50 (4), 99–126.

Baraldi, E., M. Ingemansson Havenvid, Å. Linné and C. Öberg (2019), 'Start-ups and networks: Interactive perspectives and a research agenda', *Industrial Marketing Management*, 80, 58–67.

Blankenburg, D. and J. Johanson (1992), 'Managing network connections in international business', *Scandinavian International Business Review*, 1 (1), 5–19.

Blau, P. (1964), *Exchange and Power in Social Life*, New York: Wiley.

Bocconcelli, R. and H. Håkansson (2008), 'External interaction as a means of making change in a company: The role of purchasing in a major turn-around for Ducati', *IMP Journal*, 2 (2), 25–27.

Cook, K.S. and R.M. Emerson (1978). 'Power, equity and commitment in exchange networks', *American Sociological Review*, 43, 721–739.

Dubois, A. (1998), *Organizing Industrial Activities across Firm Boundaries*, London: Routledge.

Dubois, A. and L. Araujo (2007), 'Case research in purchasing and supply management: Opportunities and challenges', *Journal of Purchasing and Supply Management*, 13 (3), 170–181.

Dubois, A. and P. Fredriksson (2008), 'Cooperating and competing in supply networks: Making sense of a triadic sourcing strategy', *Journal of Purchasing and Supply Management*, 14 (3), 170–179.

Dubois, A. and L.-E. Gadde (2002), 'Systematic combining: An abductive approach to case research', *Journal of Business Research*, 55 (7), 553–560.

Dubois, A., L-E. Gadde and L-G. Mattsson (2021), 'Purchasing behavior and supplier base evolution – A longitudinal case study', *Journal of Business and Industrial Marketing*, 36 (5), 689–705.

Dubois, A., K. Hulthén and A-C. Pedersen (2004), 'Supply chains and interdependence: A theoretical analysis', *Journal of Purchasing and Supply Management*, 10 (1), 3–9.

Dubois, A. and F. Wynstra (2005), 'Organizing the purchasing function as an interface between internal and external networks', in F. Wynstra, K. Dittrich and F. Jaspers (eds), *Dealing with Dualities. Proceedings of the 21 IMP Conference*, Rotterdam: Erasmus University.

Dyer, J.H. and H. Singh (1998), 'The relational view: Cooperative strategy and sources of interorganizational competitive advantage', *Academy of Management Review*, 23 (4), 660–679.

Easton, G. (1992). 'Industrial Networks: A Review', in Axelsson, B. and G. Easton (eds.), *Industrial Networks: A New View of Reality*. London: Routledge, pp. 1–27.

Ford, D. (1980), 'Development of buyer–seller relationships in industrial markets', *European Journal of Marketing*, 14 (5–6), 339–353.

Ford, D. (2011), 'IMP and service-dominant logic: Divergence, convergence and development', *Industrial Marketing Management*, 40 (2), 231–239.

Ford, D., L-E. Gadde., H. Håkansson and I. Snehota (2003), *Managing Business Relationships*, Chichester: Wiley.

Freytag, P., L-E. Gadde and D. Harrison (2017), 'Interdependencies – blessings and curses', in H. Håkansson and I. Snehota (eds), *No Business is an Island. Making Sense of the Interactive Business World*, Bingley: Emerald Publishing, pp. 235–252.

Gadde, L-E. and D. Ford (2008), 'Distribution research and the industrial network approach', *IMP Journal*, 2 (3), 36–52.

Gadde, L-E. and H. Håkansson (2001), *Supply Network Strategies*, Chichester: Wiley.

Gadde, L-E. and I. Snehota (2000), 'Making the most of supplier relationships', *Industrial Marketing Management*, 29 (4), 305–316.

Gadde, L-E. and F. Wynstra (2017), 'Purchasing and supply management: on strategic roles and supplier interfaces', in H. Håkansson and I. Snehota (eds), *No Business is an Island: Making Sense of the Interactive Business World*, Bingley: Emerald Publishing, pp. 67–86.

Gereffi, G., J. Humphrey and T. Sturgeon (2005), 'The governance of global value chains', *Review of International Political Economy*, 12 (1), 78–104.

Guercini, S. and A. Tunisini (2017), 'Regional Development Policies', in H. Håkansson and I. Snehota (eds), *No Business is an Island: Making Sense of the Interactive Business World*, Bingley: Emerald Publishing, pp. 141–156.

Håkansson, H. (ed.) (1982), *International Marketing and Purchasing of Industrial Goods – An Interaction Approach*, Chichester: John Wiley & Sons.

Håkansson, H. (ed.) (1987), *Industrial Technological Development – An Interaction Approach*, London: Croom Helm.

Håkansson, H. and B. Axelsson (2020), 'What is so special with outsourcing in the public sector?', *Journal of Business and Industrial Marketing*, 35 (12), 2011–2021.

Håkansson, H. and A-C. Eriksson (1993), 'Getting innovations out of supplier networks', *Journal of Business-to-Business Marketing*, 1 (3), 3–34.

Håkansson, H., D. Ford, L-E. Gadde, I. Snehota and A. Waluszewski (2009a), *Business in Networks*, Chichester: Wiley.

Håkansson, H. and L-E. Gadde (2018), 'Four decades of IMP research – The development of a research network', *IMP Journal*, 12 (1), 6–36.

Håkansson, H., J. Johanson and B. Wootz (1977), 'Influence tactics in buyer–seller processes', *Industrial Marketing Management*, 5 (6), 319–332.

Håkansson, H. and G. Persson (2004), 'Supply chain management: The logic of supply chains and networks', *International Journal of Logistics Management*, 15 (1), 11–26.

Håkansson, H. and I. Snehota (1995), *Developing Relationships in Business Networks*, London, UK and New York, USA: Routledge.

Håkansson, H. and I. Snehota (eds) (2017), *No Business is an Island. Making Sense of the Interactive Business World*, Bingley: Emerald Publishing.

Håkansson, H. and A. Waluszewski (2002), *Managing Technological Development: IKEA, the Environment and Technology*, New York: Routledge.

Håkansson, H., A. Waluszewski, F. Prenkert and E. Baraldi (2009b), *Use of Science and Technology in Business: Exploring the Impact of Using Activity for Systems, Organizations, and People* (International Business and Management), Cheltenham, UK and Northampton, MA, USA: Edward Elgar Publishing.

Halinen, A. and J. Tähtinen (2002), 'A process theory of relationship ending', *International Journal of Service Industry Management*, 13 (2), 163–180.

Halinen, A. and J-Å. Törnroos (2005), 'Using case methods in the study of contemporary business networks', *Journal of Business Research*, 58 (9), 1285–1297.

Hallén, L. (1982), 'International purchasing in a small country: An exploratory study of five Swedish firms', *Journal of International Business Studies*, 13, 99–112.

Hessel, I. and L.E. Gadde (2013), 'Supply side organizing – Linking three overlapping domains', *IMP Journal*, 7 (1), 24–45.

Hoholm, T. and L. Araujo (2017), 'Innovation Policy in an Interacted World – The Critical Role of the Context', in H. Håkansson and I. Snehota (eds), *No Business is an Island. Making Sense of the Interactive Business World*, Bingley: Emerald Publishing, pp. 105–122.

Holmen, E. and A-C. Pedersen (2003), 'Strategizing through analyzing and influencing the network horizon', *Industrial Marketing Management*, 32 (5), 409–418.

Jahre, M., L-E. Gadde., D. Harrison., H. Håkansson and G. Persson (2006), *Resourcing in Business Logistics: The Art of Systematic Combining*, Lund, SE: Liber.

Johnsen, T.E. (2018), 'Purchasing and supply management in an industrial marketing perspective', *Industrial Marketing Management*, 69, 91–97.

Kraljic, P. (1983), 'Purchasing must become supply management', *Harvard Business Review*, 61 (5), 109–117.

Marasco, A. (2008), 'Third-party logistics: A literature review', *International Journal of Production Economics*, 113 (1), 127–147.

Möller, K. and A. Rajala (2007), 'Rise of strategic nets – New modes of value creation', *Industrial Marketing Management*, 36 (7), 895–908.

Pedersen, A-C. and A. Dubois (2002), 'Why relationships do not fit into purchasing portfolio models – A comparison between the portfolio and industrial network approaches', *European Journal of Purchasing and Supply Management*, 8, 35–42.

Persson, G. and H. Håkansson (2007), 'Supplier segmentation when supplier relationships matter', *IMP Journal*, 1 (3), 26–41.

Robinson, P.J., Faris, Ch.W. and Wind, Y. (1967). *Industrial Buying and Creative Marketing*. Boston, MA: Allyn & Bacon.

Salmi, A. and E. Sharafutdinova (2008), 'Culture and design in emerging markets: The case of mobile phones in Russia', *Journal of Business and Industrial Marketing*, 23 (6), 384–394.

Spring, M. and L. Araujo (2009), 'Service, services and products: Rethinking operations strategy', *International Journal of Operations and Production Management*, 29 (5), 444–467.

Thibaut, J.W. and H.H. Kelley (1959), *The Social Psychology of Groups*, New York: Wiley.

Van der Valk, W., F. Wynstra and B. Axelsson (2009), 'Effective buyer–seller interaction patterns in ongoing service exchange', *International Journal of Operations and Production Management*, 29 (8), 807–833.

Van Echtelt, F.E.A., F. Wynstra, A.J. van Weele and G. Duysters (2008), 'Managing supplier involvement in new product development: A multiple-case study', *Journal of Product Innovation Management*, 25 (2), 180–201.

Wacker, J.G. (1998), 'A definition of theory: Research guidelines for different theory-building research methods in operations management', *Journal of Operations Management*, 16 (4), 361–385.

Waluszewski, A., H. Håkansson and I. Snehota (2019), 'The public–private partnership (PPP) disaster of a new hospital – Expected political and existing business interaction patterns', *Journal of Business and Industrial Marketing*, 34 (5), 1119–1130.

Westing. J., Fine, I. and Zens, G. (1969) *Purchasing Management: Materials in Motion*. New York: John Wiley & Sons.

Wynstra, F. (2010), 'What did we do, who did it and did it matter? A review of fifteen volumes of the (European) Journal of Purchasing and Supply Management', *Journal of Purchasing and Supply Management*, 16 (4), 279–292.

Wynstra, F., R. Suurmond and F. Nullmeier (2019), 'Purchasing and supply management as a multidisciplinary research field: Unity in diversity?', *Journal of Purchasing and Supply Management*, 25(5), 100578.

Wynstra, J.Y.F., A.J. van Weele and B. Axelsson (1999), 'Purchasing involvement in product development: A framework', *European Journal of Purchasing and Supply Management*, 5 (3–4), 129–141.

25. Dynamic capabilities theory

Anna Land, Tim Gruchmann, Erik Siems and Philip Beske-Janssen

INTRODUCTION

Organizations face continuous challenges associated with disturbing familiar practices by replacing them with new ones (Fallon-Byrne and Harney, 2017). Thus, the emergence of dynamic capabilities theory is considered an important step in framing and conceptualizing organizational change processes by building upon concepts such as organizational learning and knowledge management (Easterby-Smith et al., 2009). Introduced in the seminal paper by Teece et al. (1997), the body of literature on dynamic capabilities has grown rapidly in the last two decades, leading to an intensively studied and complex management theory (Barreto, 2010), also conceptualized and applied in supply chain management (SCM) research today. Furthermore, dynamic capabilities theory has been extended for various industry contexts, such as the automotive, food and logistics industries (for example, Beske et al., 2014; Land et al., 2015; Gruchmann and Seuring, 2018).

The concept of dynamic capabilities was derived from the transformation of the resource-based view (RBV) and the natural resource-based-view (NRBV) and proposed for more dynamic settings and applied to more complex systems such as supply chains (Beske, 2012). The (N)RBV considers firms to consist of a bundle of resources, which if rare, valuable, hard to imitate and non-substitutable, can lead to a long-term competitive advantage, assuming that the firm's environment stays relatively unchanged (Barney, 1991). However, most firms do not operate in such stable environments and need to adapt to changes. The core underlying phenomenon to be studied through dynamic capabilities theory is thus the interaction between the resource base of a company and its capabilities to extend and modify existing resources or create new ones (Helfat et al., 2007). Defined by Teece et al. (1997, p. 516) as 'the firm's ability to integrate, build, and reconfigure internal and external competences to address rapidly changing environments', dynamic capabilities provide a relatively new lens to study strategic renewal (Kindström et al., 2013).

This chapter presents an overview of dynamic capabilities theory, shedding light on its origins and evolution in the SCM context. Key variables for dynamic capabilities theory, such as their nature, role, context, building, outcome and heterogeneity, are introduced (Teece et al., 1997). The chapter also focuses on three of the most relevant research topics in SCM and how dynamic capabilities are employed in these contexts. These lie within the domains of supply chain resilience (Brusset and Teller, 2017), business models (Teece, 2018) and sustainable supply chain management (SSCM) (Beske, 2012). Relationships between key variables are discussed, and theoretical predictions for future applications are made. A particular focus is on the theoretical applications for SSCM, as sustainability has become a business imperative. We posit that key SSCM practices, such as orientation, continuity, collaboration, risk management and proactivity, might be more successfully implemented through dynamic capabilities related to knowledge management, partner development, co-evolvement, supply chain reconceptualization and reflexive control.

DYNAMIC CAPABILITIES MICROFOUNDATIONS AND KEY STRUCTURAL DIMENSIONS

Based on Teece's (2007) theoretical underpinnings, dynamic capabilities can be aggregated into three distinct analytical activities: (1) sensing opportunities and threats (for example, from changed consumption patterns or technological innovations); (2) shaping/seizing opportunities (for example, through the design of new sustainable business models); and (3) maintaining competitiveness by the reconfiguration and transformation of the resource base. Labelled as 'microfoundations', these corporate-level activities build the organizational basis of dynamic capabilities theory.

Sensing Opportunities and Threats

Even though sensing for new opportunities (and threats) means having access to knowledge, it also embraces the ability to recognize, sense and shape the development of new opportunities (Kırcı and Seifert, 2015). Hence it is, on one hand, a process of understanding the relationship between the users' needs and existing as well as potential solutions, which are identified or detected within a continuous process of scanning the narrow and broad environment (Helfat and Peteraf, 2015; Teece, 2018). On the other hand, sensing new opportunities is related to direct (research and development, R&D) resources and specific processes such as changing the customers' behaviour (Teece, 2007).

Shaping/Seizing Opportunities

According to Teece (2007), the traditional elements of business models such as tangible asset ownership, cost control and inventory optimizations are not sufficient for long-term competitive performance. Thus, seizing opportunities through novel solutions (products, processes or services) can require the adaptation of the underlying business model. Despite pure financial investments in the right physical assets and technologies, organizational adaptation of routines is required to exploit the identified chances (Helfat and Peteraf, 2009). In staying competitive, the ability to recognize and to steer essential resources and competences, so-called 'choke points', along the value chain is thus a critical strategic element (Teece, 2007).

Maintaining Competitiveness by Reconfiguration and Transformation

Transformation processes, in turn, embrace capabilities to orchestrate existing resources (tangible and intangible assets) and organizational routines towards new patterns and, hopefully, a superior resource configuration (Teece, 2018). Therefore, the company actively and intentionally works for the modification of the resource base to gain and retain a higher economic value than the competitors (Helfat and Peteraf, 2009).

Key Structural Dimensions

Complemented by the dynamic capabilities microfoundations, Teece et al. (1997, p. 516) define dynamic capabilities as 'the firm's ability to integrate, build, and reconfigure internal and external competences to address rapidly changing environments'. To date, however, several authors have offered alternative definitions and conceptualizations (Barreto, 2010). Based on Teece et al.'s (1997) main structural dimensions of dynamic capabilities – namely, nature, role, context, building, outcome and heterogeneity – the alternative perspectives of dynamic capabilities in the literature are introduced in Table 25.1.

These structural dimensions from Gruchmann and Seuring (2018) are presented as 'Element 1 – Variables' in Figure 25.1. Elements 2–4 are presented in the following sections. The unit of analysis is the organization, as dynamic capabilities can be uniform across the firm; however, they might also differ between functions depending on the capabilities being reconfigured (Pavlou and Sawy, 2011).

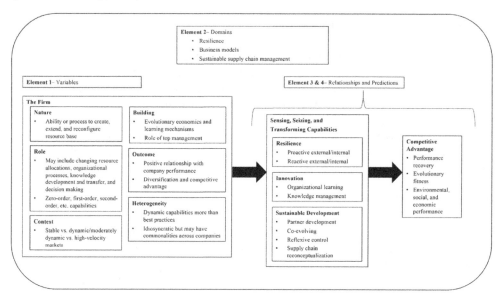

Figure 25.1   Overview of dynamic capabilities theory elements

DYNAMIC CAPABILITIES IN THE RESILIENCE DOMAIN

Resilience

The concept of resilience emerged from ecology in the early 1970s (Holling, 1973) and has since evolved across many disciplines (Manfield and Newey, 2018). In Holling's (1973) study focused on ecological stability, resilience was proposed as the ability of a system to maintain and adapt its essential structure, function and relationships in the face of disturbance or change. In the context of organizations, Luthar et al. (2000) have defined organizational resilience as the capability to resist and recover from shocks or disasters that could affect an organization

Table 25.1   *Dynamic capabilities: structural dimensions*

Structural dimensions	Explanation	Supporting references
Nature	Several authors followed Teece et al.'s (1997) argumentation, describing the nature of dynamic capabilities as ability (i.e., capacity) or process (i.e., routine) to create, extend and reconfigure the firm's resource base. Others, such as Makadok (2001), see dynamic capabilities rather as a special type of resource responsible for the improvement of the productivity of other resources. Accordingly, resources do not by themselves lead to an improved outcome, since the performance is dependent on how they are leveraged.	Eisenhardt and Martin, 2000; Helfat et al., 2007; Makadok, 2001; Teece et al., 1997; Winter, 2003; Zahra et al., 2006
Role	According to Easterby-Smith et al. (2009), dynamic capabilities can take on different roles in the firm, such as changing resource allocations and organizational processes, knowledge development and transfer, as well as decision making. In this line, some authors have introduced a certain hierarchy of capabilities. For instance, Wang and Ahmed (2007) describe a similar hierarchical order distinguishing between zero-order, first-order, second- and third-order capabilities. Similarly, Winter (2003) distinguishes between ordinary capabilities allowing a firm to run its business in the short term which can be seen more as 'administrative' routines and operations, substantive capabilities to solve problems, and dynamic capabilities to change ordinary capabilities.	Easterby-Smith et al., 2009; Teece, 2018; Wang and Ahmed, 2007; Winter, 2003
Context	According to Eisenhardt and Martin (2000), dynamic capabilities vary depending on the context, particularly depending on the degree of market dynamics. Here, some researchers see dynamic capabilities as being exclusively valuable in rapidly changing or unpredictable market environments, while others acknowledge their relevance in both stable and dynamic market environments. Eisenhardt and Martin (2000) suggest analytical routines relying on existing knowledge in rather moderately dynamic markets with predictable changes, while experiential routines relying on situation-specific or new knowledge are more appropriate in high-velocity markets with non-linear changes.	Barreto, 2010; Eisenhardt and Martin, 2000; Zahra et al., 2006
Building	According to Makadok (2001), dynamic capabilities creation and development can be distinguished. Considering the creation of dynamic capabilities, many authors follow an evolutionary economics perspective emphasizing learning mechanisms such as structuring R&D, information technology support, as well as problem-solving and knowledge-sharing processes. Additionally, top management can guide the building and creation of dynamic capabilities. Considering the development of dynamic capabilities, existing operational capabilities can be shaped to obtain more mature dynamic capabilities.	Easterby-Smith et al., 2009; Makadok, 2001; Newey and Zahra, 2009; Winter, 2003

Structural dimensions	Explanation	Supporting references
Outcome	In line with Teece et al. (1997), many authors assume a direct relationship between dynamic capabilities and company performance, explaining business success particularly through achieving competitive advantages. In contrast, other researchers question such a direct relationship, stressing that company performance depends on the specific resource configuration. Nevertheless, the creation of a new resource base might affect intermediate outcomes on company performance, such as related and unrelated diversification.	Barreto, 2010; Eisenhardt and Martin, 2000; Helfat et al., 2007; Makadok, 2001; Teece et al., 1997; Zollo and Winter, 2002
Heterogeneity	According to Barreto (2010), there are generally two perspectives in respect of the degree of heterogeneity. On the one hand, it is assumed that dynamic capabilities are essentially company-specific and unique. On the other hand, some authors assume that dynamic capabilities have at least a few commonalities across companies. Most of the authors are sceptical about these commonalities, arguing that dynamic capabilities are more than just best practices.	Barreto, 2010; Easterby-Smith et al., 2009; Eisenhardt and Martin, 2000; Makadok, 2001; Teece et al., 1997

Source: Adapted from Gruchmann and Seuring (2018, p. 1261).

or system either internally or externally. It should be noted that the concept has been portrayed quite differently across various studies Linnenluecke (2017). Based on the literature review of Ma et al. (2018) that analysed the conceptual similarities and differences of organizational resilience across streams, a common understanding about organizational resilience should include that: (1) 'organizational resilience is a capability to cope with crisis under discontinuous and emergent environment'; (2) it 'emphasizes on survival, adaptability, the ability to bounce back, and improvement under disruptive situations'; and (3) it 'is a multi-level concept and is related to organizational resources, routines, and processes' (p. 255). Ma et al. (2018) explicitly define organizational resilience as 'a multi-level, dynamic capability' (p. 255). Others have argued for supply chain resilience, which may be an additional level added to Ma et al.'s (2018) propositions. Ponomarov and Holcomb (2009) and Ponis and Koronis (2012) dedicate their entire studies to defining supply chain resilience.

Resilience in Supply Chain Management

The concept of supply chain resilience emerged around the early 2000s (Jüttner et al., 2003). Since then, supply chain resilience has received great attention from both practitioners and scholars because of promising approaches to cope with disruptions, caused by external events (for example, pandemic diseases, natural disasters) or internal events (for example, human error or machine failure) (Ma et al., 2018). Ponomarov and Holcomb define supply chain resilience as 'the adaptive capability of the supply chain to prepare for unexpected events, respond to disruptions, and recover from them by maintaining continuity of operations at the desired level of connectedness and control over structure and function' (Ponomarov and Holcomb, 2009, p. 131). Therefore, contrasting with ordinary supply chains, more resilient supply chains contain the continual readiness to be prepared for unanticipated events and have the resources to respond to them, due to purposefully managed, agile and flexible processes, also considered adaptive capabilities (Ponomarov and Holcomb, 2009).

To build supply chain resilience, Christopher and Peck (2004) propose four core elements: (1) a purposeful supply chain design (that is, re-engineering); (2) a high degree of collaboration between the supply chain members to detect and treat risks; (3) an agile supply chain network to respond quickly to a changing environment; and (4) risk management awareness in the entire organization. Within this approach, attributes such as visibility, agility, availability, efficiency, flexibility, redundancy and velocity were considered as secondary factors. However, other studies have identified that those secondary factors are critical for building supply chain resilience and should be classified as higher-order capabilities, also known as dynamic capabilities, rather than lower-level capabilities (Hendry et al., 2019; Mwangola, 2018). Therefore, we argue that analysing supply chain resilience through the lens of the dynamic capabilities theory provides fruitful insights.

Resilience as a Dynamic Capability in Supply Chain Management

There are particular parallels between dynamic capabilities theory and the resilience approach. For example, the latter assumes that the possession of adaptive capabilities, which enable an organization to prepare for, to counter and to recuperate from disruptions, can lead to resilience and hence a competitive advantage (Hendry et al., 2019; Ponis and Koronis, 2012). Similarly, dynamic capabilities are concerned with the continuous process of sensing threats and opportunities and exploiting them with a reconfiguration of the existing resources or the creation of new ones. While Brusset and Teller (2017) stated that resilience is an operational capability than a dynamic capability, Eltantawy (2016) framed resilience as a higher-level, multifaceted, dynamic capability.

In fact, multiple studies indicate that the concept of resilience includes various capabilities and dimensions. For example, Mwangola (2018) has proposed agility and visibility as two dimensions of resilience. Furthermore, the empirical study by Chowdhury and Quaddus (2017) showed that resilience could be grouped into: (1) proactive capabilities, such as flexibility, visibility, redundancy, integration, financial strength or efficiency; and (2) reactive capabilities, such as supply chain response (that is, mitigating disruptions as fast as possible while seeking low impact) or recovery (that is, minimizing recovery time, cost, disruption absorption and impact). Brusset and Teller (2017) confirmed that 'integration and flexibility capabilities' have a positive impact on supply chain resilience. Dabhilkar et al. (2016) take these two classifications a step further by positing supply-side resilience as four dynamic capabilities: proactive-internal, proactive-external, reactive-internal and reactive-external. However, Golgeci and Ponomarov (2013) posit supply chain resilience as a 'crucial, responsive capability' (p. 606) and, therefore, more reactive than proactive. Nevertheless, we would argue that more recent literature recognizes both the proactive and reactive routines of supply chain resilience, and adapt Dabhilkar et al.'s (2016) table to show examples of dynamic resilience capabilities from updated sources (see Table 25.2).

Resilience capabilities are considered to be bundles of practices. Similar to Dabhilkar et al.'s (2016) findings, Table 25.2 reveals that most of the recent papers on supply chain resilience belong to more than one practice bundle category. It is also noteworthy that many studies apply supply chain resilience dynamic capabilities as the dependent variable (for example, Jiang et al., 2019; Golgeci and Ponomarov, 2013), while others view it as a precursor or independent variable for other constructs, such as weighted performance (Birkie et al., 2017; Mandal et al., 2017) and supply management sustainability performance (Eltantawy, 2016).

DYNAMIC CAPABILITIES IN THE BUSINESS MODELS DOMAIN

Business models have been extensively discussed and defined in the literature (Zott et al., 2011). Linked to the strategy and innovation literature, the business model concept describes the ways in which a business 'creates, delivers, and captures value' (Osterwalder and Pigneur, 2009, p. 14). The elements of business model design generally include features embedded in the product/service, that is, determination of the benefit to the customer from consuming/using the product/service, identification of targeted market segments, and confirmation of the revenue streams and design of the mechanisms to capture value (Teece, 2018). Business model innovation is a key activity to innovate value creation, delivery and capture mechanisms in order to stay competitive (Baden-Fuller and Morgan, 2010; Teece, 2009). Relevant dynamic capabilities should create, refine and transform the business models leading to new customer offerings and revenue streams (Bocken and Geradts, 2019; Teece, 2007). While lower-level dynamic capabilities as repeatable actions allow the operationalization of the current business model (Winter, 2003), higher-level capabilities enable companies to adjust, recombine and create ordinary capabilities (Teece, 2018). Although the link between dynamic capabilities to sense, seize and transform business strategy and related resources clearly points to business

Table 25.2   *Examples of proactive and reactive resilience capabilities from the literature*

Resilience routines		Source									
	Eltantawy (2016)	Hendry et al. (2019)	Souza et al. (2017)	Birkie et al. (2017)	Mwangola (2018)	Brusset and Teller (2017)	Ma et al. (2018)	Chowdhury and Quaddus (2017)	Su and Linderman (2016)	Golgeci and Ponomarov (2013)	Mandal et al. (2017)
Proactive capability routines											
Internal											
Trained/experienced employees			X	X			X	X		X	X
Learning from previous disruptions and near misses	X	X	X	X	X		X				
Established recovery process		X	X	X	X	X	X	X	X	X	
External											
Alternative sourcing bases		X		X		X	X	X		X	
Scanning environment for detection of symptoms of disruption				X	X	X	X		X	X	
Customer–supplier long-term relationship cooperation		X	X	X	X	X	X	X			X
Reactive capability routines											
Internal											
Task force for recovery				X				X			
Clear identification of responsibility				X		X					
Coordination within a firm	X		X	X			X			X	X
Support from top management	X			X							

Resilience routines	Eltantawy (2016)	Hendry et al. (2019)	Souza et al. (2017)	Birkie et al. (2017)	Mwangola (2018)	Source Brusset and Teller (2017)	Ma et al. (2018)	Chowdhury and Quaddus (2017)	Su and Linderman (2016)	Golgeci and Ponomarov (2013)	Mandal et al. (2017)
External											
Coordination among firms	X	X		X	X	X	X	X	X	X	X
Information dissemination to relevant organizations		X	X	X	X	X		X			X

Source: Adapted from Dabhilkar et al. (2016).

model innovation, the business model literature only recently started to address the question on how organizational designs and business models affect dynamic capabilities, and vice versa (Fjeldstad and Snow, 2018; Teece, 2018). As organizational (co-)evolution builds on components such as strategy, structures, processes, incentives and people (Bocken and Geradts, 2019), dynamic capabilities theory uses overlapping constructs such as routines, capabilities and resources (Barreto, 2010; Eisenhardt and Martin, 2000; Teece et al., 1997). To illustrate sweet spots between business model innovation and dynamic capabilities, this section elaborates on organizational learning and knowledge management as well as (open) innovation capabilities from both perspectives.

Impact of Business Model Design on Dynamic Capabilities' Development and Vice Versa

Organizational design is found to be an antecedent for dynamic capabilities building, and vice versa (Teece, 2018; Zahra et al., 2006; Zollo and Winter, 2002). For instance, Zahra et al. (2006) proposed a link between organizational age, knowledge and dynamic capabilities, pointing to knowledge management as an important feature of mature organizations. In turn, Zollo and Winter (2002) studied how dynamic capabilities contribute to the co-evolution of organizational learning mechanisms. More recently, researchers have claimed that change and innovation requirements concerning the development of an organization encompass not only managerial capabilities but also individual and collective (learning) capabilities. For instance, Bocken and Geradts (2019) empirically found the development of individual capabilities through training and development programmes as operational drivers for sustainable business models. Fallon-Byrne and Harney (2017) conceptualized learning opportunities as an element of the organizational innovation strategy to foster an innovation climate and related dynamic capabilities building. Accordingly, organizational structures enabling innovation – for example, through incentives – can be seen as antecedents for capability development within human resources which mobilize necessary forces for business model transformation (Bocken and Geradts, 2019).

Generally, the firm's dynamic capabilities help to leverage the profitability of a business model design, while a lack of dynamic capabilities limits the feasibility of particular strategies (Teece, 2018). Accordingly, companies have to develop higher-level capabilities beyond operational routines which help to integrate, build and reconfigure internal competences (Teece et al., 1997; Teece, 2007). For instance, capabilities that foster managerial decision making under uncertainty are seen as among these higher-order capabilities which guide the reconfiguration of business models to better suit a changing business environment and, at the same time, to support the realization of a certain corporate strategy (Teece, 2018). Taking the theoretical stance of sensing and seizing, the learning function of an organization supports the successful incorporation of new technologies into the business model; for example, using artificial intelligence algorithms in platform business models of sea freight brokers (Gruchmann et al., 2020). Taking the theoretical stance of transforming an organization's overall design and structure, so-called strong or higher-order capabilities support the freeing up of resources which can be devoted to developing future business models (Teece, 2018).

Dynamic Capabilities for Market and Supply Chain Transformations

Taking an evolutionary economics perspective and, thus, the theoretical stance of transforming, the processes of varying, selecting and retaining business models through dynamic capabilities, may also induce market transformation (Schaltegger et al., 2016). Accordingly, dynamic capabilities also have to tackle meso and macro factors in supply chains and entire industries (at least indirectly), as most of the factors combined into the scenarios lie outside the control of the organization itself. Thus, meso and macro factors not only describe the current trends from an economic or technological point of view, but also cover social and environmental aspects, which must be incorporated in current business models. Hence, dynamic capabilities support potential pathways for the diffusion of businesses models in the industry promoted by retention processes and strategies of growth, replication, mimicry and mergence (Schaltegger et al., 2016). In order to grow quickly and, thereby, capture a sufficient share of the available profits, pioneers with new and innovative business models have to be fast learners accompanied by monitoring capabilities, as imitation by others might occur (Teece, 2018). Therefore, pioneering new business models through start-up initiatives is just one possible option. In particular, mimicry strategies of copying business model elements of niche businesses and incorporating them in a modified way into a mass-market player's business models are often applied. For the logistics industry, for instance, start-up businesses with a city logistics focus provide the potential for replication and mimicry as they allow for alternative transportation modes such as cargo bikes or public transportation. Accordingly, pioneers have to couple their business models with strategies and capabilities that make imitation difficult such as through new (digital) technologies as well as consumer empowerment (Gruchmann et al., 2018).

More generally, companies may use strategic management to enhance their innovation potential for (sustainable) transformations of their business model (Kindström et al., 2013). In this line, competitive advantage is linked with internal and external innovation processes, while dynamic capabilities can have a significant effect on the innovation performance (Lee and Yoo, 2019). Moreover, open innovation capabilities allow companies to overcome internal barriers and quickly respond to external changes by absorbing external knowledge (Chesbrough, 2003). Therefore, knowledge management capabilities transform the information gained from the outside by fusing it with existing, internal knowledge. By collecting information on market and technological changes, open innovation capabilities enhance the evolutionary fitness to the environment, utilizing existing resources as new resources (Pavlou and El Sawy, 2011).

DYNAMIC CAPABILITIES IN THE SSCM DOMAIN

Since social and environmental issues have become a major concern to the public, companies face the challenge to integrate sustainability into their supply chains (Busse et al., 2017); hence the interest of both practitioners and scholars in SSCM has increased (Touboulic and Walker, 2015). Even though there have already been answers to the calls for strengthening the robustness of developed frameworks and for promoting the building of more comprehensive theory in (S)SCM, the need for theoretical, grounded research in SSCM is still not saturated (Touboulic and Walker, 2015).

Seuring and Müller (2008, p. 1700) define SSCM as 'the management of material, information and capital flows as well as cooperation among companies along the supply chain while taking goals from all three dimensions of sustainable development, that is, economic, environmental and social, into account which are derived from customer and stakeholder requirements'. This definition takes up the established view of a supply chain as linking several parties through upstream and downstream material, financial and information flows. Moreover, the three dimensions of sustainability are included, as well as both the market perspective, through customer requirements, and stakeholder theory. These additions have several consequences. First of all, adding the sustainability requirements of various stakeholders leads to much greater uncertainties. Additionally, stakeholders interested in sustainability are more likely to penalize a company whose sustainability claims are not fulfilled, than the stakeholder base of more conventional companies where sustainability initiatives are of lower priority. Furthermore, the requirements of stakeholders are time-sensitive and can shift dynamically in unpredictable directions, potentially leading to highly dynamic markets for which dynamic capabilities have been proposed (Eisenhardt and Martin, 2000). Finally, both SCM and SSCM are prone to the dynamics of business environments in a globalized world with complex logistics networks and global competition (Carter and Rogers, 2008; Seuring and Müller, 2008), which can lead to non-transparent business environments where change may come suddenly and unpredictably. This forms a clear link, firstly, between the dynamic business environments of sustainable supply chains and dynamic capabilities to maintain or achieve competitiveness in such environments and dynamic markets; and secondly, to supply chain resilience, as discussed earlier in this chapter, as SSCM has also been discussed as a strategy for managing supply chain risk (Gouda and Saranga, 2018).

Another linkage between both perspectives – dynamic capabilities and SSCM – lies in the perception of performance. The assessment of 'performance' in dynamic capabilities theory has been linked to the perceived value a good or service offers to customers and, therefore, goes beyond a one-dimensional financial performance assessment (Easterby-Smith et al., 2009; Helfat et al., 2007; Kumar et al., 2018). Similarly, as can be deduced from the SSCM definition, performance in SSCM is assessed against the three dimensions of sustainability, also going beyond the economic perspective and stakeholder requirements. Finally, dynamic capabilities and SSCM practices alike are employed by companies to purposefully influence and change their business environments to match their own business models and strategies (for example, Defee and Fugate, 2010; Eisenhardt and Martin, 2000; Winter, 2003). Dynamic capabilities are used to change the resource combinations, while SSCM is used to develop sustainable suppliers, products, or to create awareness of sustainability.

Key Dynamic Capabilities for Sustainable Supply Chain Management

While dynamic capabilities may be based on widespread routines, the specific design and implementation of these routines can be very different in various companies or supply chain settings based on, for instance, employee behaviour, management styles or corporate culture. In the following, we will describe core dynamic capabilities which can be observed in the SSCM domain.

Knowledge and information play a pivotal role in today's business environments (Handoko et al., 2018). This can be in the form of specific patents, knowledge about specific materials with sustainable qualities or production processes, or even specific local circumstances.

Knowledge management in the form of a dynamic capability allows companies to access, understand, integrate or even acquire relevant knowledge and information. Accordingly, in the supply chain domain, Defee and Fugate (2010, p. 188) define it as 'a capability held by two or more parties that fosters an understanding of the current knowledge resources possessed by each party'. By evaluating the current knowledge base and potentially reconfiguring it, such a capability is also of great importance to shape future resource configurations or to help in transforming the current ones.

Supply chain partner development, in turn, is of high value to be able to steer current routines towards new patterns, and thus a more competitive resource configuration, that is, transforming the resource base (Teece, 2018). This is critical, as many now argue that competition is no longer between companies but rather between supply networks. Hence, developing the partners in a supply chain can have a high impact, especially in a sustainability setting where more sustainable practices need to be continuously developed and implemented throughout the supply network in order to reach a higher overall sustainability performance (Liu et al., 2018). This capability is also employed to reach higher supply chain resilience. Such a capability involves sensing and seizing opportunities and threats in the form of understanding and evaluation of current abilities of supply chain partners, and means to potentially develop them further for improved sustainability performance (Pagell and Wu, 2009) and resilience. Hence, such a dynamic capability is closely linked to the knowledge management capability.

Co-evolution allows the development and implementation of new capabilities and business practices (Defee and Fugate, 2010). Eisenhardt and Martin (2000, p. 1107) describe co-evolution as 'the routines by which managers reconnect webs of collaborations among various parts of the firm to generate new and synergistic resource combinations among businesses'. The same holds true in the SSCM domain when transforming the current resource base, or even shaping it by adding new patterns.

A reflexive supply chain control capability encompasses information gathering, evaluation and sharing and, therefore, is again related to knowledge management. However, this capability continuously evaluates the system's functionality in relation to the supply chain's requirements in the form of a management accounting system which goes beyond purely financial data (Beske, 2012). Such a capability can thus be understood to help sense threats and also, to a limited account, sense opportunities.

Supply chain reconceptualization is used to shape the supply chain (SC) by, for example, including new actors who have become valuable for the SC due to dynamically changing circumstances. These new actors can be partners from related industries, or even completely new partners previously outside of the scope of the supply network such as non-governmental organizations or other stakeholders (Busse et al., 2017; Liu et al., 2018). When realizing new business models, such a capability is also of high importance, as this will potentially require the inclusion of new and different partners in the SC (Beske et al., 2014).

Implementing such capabilities can also, of course, lead to the development of new capabilities. Specifically, one purpose of the co-evolving dynamic capability is the design and implementation of new capabilities. This particular topic will be further discussed in the following section.

RELATIONSHIPS AND PREDICTIONS

In order to provide an overview of the relationships between the key variables and domains of dynamic capabilities, Table 25.3 is presented. One notable commonality among all domains is the emphasis on the knowledge management capability, the development of which has inherent impacts on other routines and capabilities, such as training and retaining experienced employees, developing long-term relationships and cooperation with partners, and co-evolving to build and develop further capabilities. The outcomes linked to firms' abilities to reconfigure and adapt their resource base as the business environment changes has direct effects on their competitive advantage in the traditional sense of financial performance, but also in terms of social and environmental performance.

Based on the relationships shown in Table 25.3, some predictions can be established for dynamic capabilities theory in the wider supply chain context. Future threats due to pandemics, economic crises or natural disasters for supply chains seem inevitable. For example, global supply disruptions caused by COVID-19 have raised awareness of supply chain vulnerabilities. As a result, the debate around achieving more resilient supply chains has received increasing attention not only from academics (for example, evident by the number of calls for papers on the topic) but also from politicians, practitioners and the media. Because studies have indicated that certain dynamic capabilities are the prerequisites for supply chain resilience as an outcome, it can be assumed that scholars and managers are interested in more research on how those can be created or further developed to build a more resilient supply chain. Instead of developing more conceptual frameworks, a longitudinal research design with empirical data should be favoured, to shed light on the underlying development as well as transformation processes and the (business) context (Mandal et al., 2017).

Furthermore, future research should analyse how dynamic capabilities, which build resilience, can be strengthened in the long term. The identification of specific capabilities to facilitate and accelerate organizational learning for either avoiding disruptions or being able to respond faster can be targeted by future studies (Brusset and Teller, 2017). While some studies indicate that supply chain resilience might have a positive impact on a firm's competitive advantage (Hendry et al., 2019; Ponomarov and Holcomb, 2009), further research should explore the relationship between resilience and the (sustainable) performance of a company by taking into account the mitigating effect of dynamic capabilities (Mwangola, 2018).

In the sustainable supply chain context, future dynamic capabilities research should foster the more profound implementation of sustainability in supply chains. As the world is currently experiencing a climate catastrophe with greater impact and higher frequency of natural disasters, such a development should be a high priority. To date, a truly sustainable supply chain hardly exists (Montabon et al., 2016; Pagell and Shevchenko, 2014). Research should identify dynamic capabilities which can help to spread sustainability into the wider supply network, and those that proactively shape the business environment, identify non-compliant suppliers or such dynamic capabilities which enhance resilience in more fragile supply chains with a sustainability focus.

Another path for future sustainable development lies in the circular economy, where the linear production system of current supply chains is transformed to a circular one. The whole concept of circularity, while not new, has only recently received attention by a greater number of researchers and practitioners. Accordingly, few established routines and standards exist and developments in the market are very dynamic. Additionally, very little research in dynamic

Table 25.3   Relationships between key variables and domains

Domains / Key variables	Resilience	Business models	SSCM
Nature	Dynamic capabilities enable the continual readiness to be prepared for unanticipated events and having the resources to respond to and recuperate from them (Chowdhury and Quaddus, 2017; Ponomarov and Holcomb, 2009).	Business model innovation is achieved through value creation, delivery and capture to stay competitive over time (Bocken and Geradts, 2019); while dynamic capabilities refine and transform business models, leading to new customer offerings and revenue streams (Teece, 2007, 2009).	Dynamic capabilities have been discussed as internal, firm-focused capabilities for managing the supply chain, as well as supply chain-wide dynamic capabilities to gain competitive advantage through and for the supply chain as a whole (Defee and Fugate, 2010).
Role	Some capabilities, such as flexibility or redundancy, are seen as more reactive and allow recovery from a threat or disruption (Hendry et al., 2019). For example, building visibility or developing supply chain partners are considered to be more proactive capabilities, and enable the avoidance of disruptions beforehand (Dabhilkar et al., 2016; Souza et al., 2017).	Lower-level dynamic capabilities as repeatable actions allow the operation of the current business model (Winter, 2003); while higher-level capabilities enable companies to adjust, recombine and create ordinary capabilities and related resources leading to business model innovation (Teece, 2018).	Dynamic capabilities in SSCM are used to embed sustainability into the supply chain; for higher sustainability performance and also for risk management purposes (Reuter et al., 2010). They are employed to strategically select and develop suppliers, that is, to (re) configure the supply base (Beske et al., 2014).
Context	The higher the expected impact caused by disruption, the higher is the need for adaptive capabilities to be ready to respond and recover from such disruption (Mwangola, 2018; Ponomarov and Holcomb, 2009).	Dynamic capabilities do not just react on a volatile environment, but may also induce market transformation and the evolution of business models (Teece, 2018).	Dynamic capabilities are employed in dynamic markets, but also with a more general scope, to be able to develop timely responses to changes in the business environment and embedded in the overall context of the supply chain (Kırcı and Seifert, 2015).
Building	Supply-side resilience can be clustered into a combination of four different dynamic capabilities specifications: proactive-internal, proactive-external, reactive-internal, and reactive-external (Dabhilkar et al., 2016; Hendry et al., 2019; Souza et al., 2017).	Organizational design is found to be an antecedent for dynamic capabilities building (for example, business model innovation facilitated through learning incentives) (Bocken and Geradts, 2019; Teece, 2018). Business model innovation requirements encompass not only managerial capabilities, but also individual and collective (learning) capabilities (Zahra et al., 2006; Zollo and Winter, 2002).	Firms that adopt SSCM practices reap the benefits, as this helps them build sustainability in their supply chains: 'SSCM practices are the platform for developing dynamic capabilities which directly influence the firm's performance' (Mathivathanam et al., 2017, p. 638). As proposed by Reuter et al. (2010, p. 54), 'the content of sustainable global supplier management processes is dependent on previous paths of sustainable capability building within the organizations'.

Key variables	Domains Resilience	Business models	SSCM
Outcome	There is a significantly positive correlation between resilience capabilities and performance recovery after disruption (Birkie et al., 2017; Dabhilkar et al., 2016).	Competitive advantage is linked with internal and external innovation processes; while dynamic capabilities can have a significant effect on the innovation performance (Teece et al., 1997). Open innovation capabilities enhance the evolutionary fitness to the environment, utilizing existing resources as new resources (Lee and Yoo, 2019; Pavlou and El Sawy, 2011).	The extent of risk, uncertainty and dynamism of the business environment is more intense with SSCM than the conventional SCM. Hence, building dynamic capabilities is critical in order to achieve sustainable performance across the triple bottom line (Kumar et al., 2018). Dynamic capabilities are a prime source for sustained competitive advantage, and serve as antecedents gained by implementing SSCM practices (Beske, 2012; Mathivathanan et al., 2017).
Heterogeneity	Holling (1973) concludes his seminal work by stating that a management approach based on resilience 'would emphasize the need to keep options open, the need to view events in a regional rather than a local context, and the need to emphasize heterogeneity' (p. 21). Random events over time causing supply chain disruptions will be unexpected, the impact on each firm and supply chain will vary, and the resilience resources and capabilities will be heterogeneous among firms and supply chains.	As argued by Jacobides and Winter (2012, p. 1376), 'business models, in principle, are imitable; once established, they can be emulated, with no such setup costs, by others'. However, heterogeneity and distinction may come in the form of a 'superior skill or knowledge or simply an ability to implement the business model' (p.1376).	Even though dynamic capabilities might be observable to an extent, and only idiosyncratic in specific details, they are often relationship-specific and socially complex. As such, they are deeply embedded in the individual organizational and supply chain context and can be heterogeneous (Beske et al., 2014; Reuter et al., 2010).

capabilities for circular economy has been published to date (for example, Khan et al., 2020). Building circular supply networks from the ground up requires dynamic engagement with suppliers, competitors or even new partners. Especially in the beginning, circular supply chains will need to be able to dynamically adapt to possibly unforeseen changes, for example due to lack of experience. Inevitably, this will also influence the business models of companies.

With regard to business model research, only a minority of sustainable business models reach international benchmarks of multinational enterprises, since most of them still operate in a niche and often lack integrated business designs combined with approaches for building dynamic capabilities. For instance, necessary logistics capabilities can help local food networks to achieve a higher sustainability performance by leveraging the companies' embedded sustainability potentials in their core business (Gruchmann et al., 2019). While the food sector shows a high potential for especially regional patterns of production and consumption, resilience can be further built by co-evolution and partner development capabilities to allow for integrated and consolidated services on the operational levels of the supply chain. How such potentials can be transferred into other branches (material and chemical industry, fashion, electronic sector, and so on) is a matter for further research. However, it can be predicted that co-evolution and partner development capabilities for sustainability might also enable a higher resilience in other industry sectors.

Moreover, digital technologies offer the possibility to move from conventional asset ownership to product-as-a-service models (Porter and Heppelmann, 2015). This development can already be seen in logistics business models, in which the ownership of physical assets, such as warehouses or trucks, is less important for offering transportation services to the customer (Gruchmann et al., 2020). Configuring advanced services based on digital platforms can provide significant opportunities for value creation capability development accordingly (Parida et al., 2019). Having developed related organizational learning and knowledge management capabilities to use such technologies, digital business models drive collaborative value creation, where value is created beyond company boundaries and across networks and supply chains (Gruchmann et al., 2020). Here, it can be predicted that dynamic capabilities towards digital technologies might enable cross-company supply chain optimization in various industry sectors.

CONCLUSION

In this chapter we provide a brief introduction to dynamic capabilities theory. We focus on three distinctive domains in the realm of SCM, namely: (1) supply chain resilience; (2) business models; and (3) sustainability in supply chains. For each of the domains we highlight their relationships with key structural variables according to Teece et al. (1997).

Each of these domains has very strong linkages to the theory of dynamic capabilities. The main connection lies naturally in the dynamic changes that the domains all encompass, and its strategic importance for a competitive advantage. In terms of supply chain resilience, it is the sudden and possibly entirely unforeseen supply chain disruption which needs to be mitigated and eventually rectified. Implementing dynamic capabilities to sense threats, especially, is of high importance in this regard and can be considered a higher-order capability (Eltantawy, 2016). For business models, dynamic capabilities are implemented to create, refine and even transform the business models (Bocken and Geradts, 2019), or to even transform the market

(Schaltegger et al., 2016). For the third domain, SSCM, related dynamic capabilities can, for example, come in the form of adding new resources; that is, reconfiguring the supply chain by changing or developing the supply chain partners (Kırcı and Seifert, 2015). But it can also be based on capabilities which leverage and reconfigure the current resource base, for example, by developing partners into better-fitting ones.

An important common factor for all three domains lies in the management of knowledge. Using knowledge management capabilities, for example, to create transparency throughout the supply chain is an invaluable way to help sense threats and to coordinate across firm boundaries, which is of high importance for supply chain resilience. Knowledge management has also been discussed as an important capability, especially for mature organizations dynamically adopting their business models. According to Bocken and Geradts (2019), the development of individual capabilities through training and development are important for developing new business models, especially with a sustainability focus. Generally, knowledge management and learning can be viewed as having high importance for sensing and seizing opportunities by developing new or adapting existing business models (Teece, 2018); for example, when implementing new technologies (Gruchmann et al., 2020). The same holds true for SSCM, where the sharing of knowledge and information is of great importance when developing partners, finding new partners, and sensing and seizing opportunities for new practices or technologies. Additionally, such knowledge management capabilities help to develop new business models for the overall supply chain to help cater to the needs of the supply chain partners and their stakeholders.

Generally, the SSCM domain can also be seen as a link for all three domains discussed here. Sustainable supply chains are even more prone to sudden supply chain disruptions due to high demands related to sustainability, and due to the smaller supplier and customer base compared with conventional supply chains. Therefore, supply chain resilience and its related dynamic capabilities are of high importance in this domain as well. Additionally, involving supply chain partners globally when developing business models also helps in sensing global threats and opportunities as well as seizing opportunities.

This chapter can only show a very brief glimpse of what dynamic capabilities theory has to offer. Clearly, with the rapidly accelerating change and dynamics of global markets, largely driven by technological advances, and with the climate catastrophe leading to higher frequency of natural disasters with potential high impacts on supply chains, dynamic capability theory will be of high relevance in the future. Much has been achieved since Winter wrote in 2003 about the 'the mystery and confusion surrounding the concept of dynamic capabilities' (Winter, 2003, p. 994). Nevertheless, as we have shown in detail above, future research is still very much required, gradually shifting from the conceptual work to empirical studies investigating the validity of the theory; for example, through longitudinal research.

REFERENCES

Baden-Fuller, C. and M.S. Morgan (2010), 'Business models as models', *Long Range Planning*, 43 (2–3), 156–171.

Barney, J. (1991), 'Firm resources and sustained competitive advantage', *Journal of Management*, 17 (1), 99–120.

Barreto, I. (2010), 'Dynamic capabilities: a review of past research and an agenda for the future', *Journal of Management*, 36 (1), 256–280.

Beske, P. (2012), 'Dynamic capabilities and sustainable supply chain management', *International Journal of Physical Distribution and Logistics*, 42 (4), 372–387.

Beske, P., Land, A., and S. Seuring (2014), 'Sustainable supply chain management practices and dynamic capabilities in the food industry: a critical analysis of the literature', *International Journal of Production Economics*, 152, 131–143.

Birkie, S., Trucco, P., and P. Campos (2017) 'Effectiveness of resilience capabilities in mitigating disruptions: leveraging on supply chain structural complexity', *Supply Chain Management: An International Journal*, 22 (6), 506–521.

Bocken, N.M. and T.H. Geradts (2019), 'Barriers and drivers to sustainable business model innovation: organization design and dynamic capabilities', *Long Range Planning*, 53 (4), 101950.

Brusset, X. and C. Teller (2017), 'Supply chain capabilities, risks, and resilience', *International Journal of Production Economics*, 184, 59–68.

Busse, C., Schleper, M.C., Weilenmann, J., and S.M. Wagner (2017), 'Extending the supply chain visibility boundary, utilizing stakeholders for identifying supply chain sustainability risks', *International Journal of Physical Distribution and Logistics Management*, 47 (1), 18–40.

Carter, C. and D. Rogers (2008), 'A framework of sustainable supply chain management: moving toward new theory', *International Journal of Physical Distribution and Logistics Management*, 38, 360–387.

Chesbrough, H.W. (2003). *Open Innovation: The New Imperative for Creating and Profiting from Technology*, Boston, MA: Harvard Business School Printing Corporation.

Chowdhury, M.M.H. and M. Quaddus (2017), 'Supply chain resilience: conceptualization and scale development using dynamic capability theory', *International Journal of Production Economics*, 188, 185–204.

Christopher, M. and H. Peck (2004), 'Building the resilient supply chain', *International Journal of Logistics Management*, 15 (2), 1–14.

Dabhilkar, M., Birkie, S., and M. Kaulio (2016), 'Supply-side resilience as practice bundles: a critical incident study', *International Journal of Operations and Production Management,* 36 (8), 948–970.

Defee, C. and B. Fugate (2010), 'Changing perspective of capabilities in the dynamic supply chain era', *International Journal of Logistics Management*, 21, 180–206.

Easterby-Smith, M., Lyles, M.A., and M.A. Peteraf (2009), 'Dynamic capabilities: current debates and future directions', *British Journal of Management*, 20, 1–8.

Eisenhardt, K.M. and J.A. Martin (2000), 'Dynamic capabilities: what are they?', *Strategic Management Journal*, 21 (10–11), 1105–1121.

Eltantawy, R.A. (2016), 'The role of supply management resilience in attaining ambidexterity: a dynamic capabilities approach', *Journal of Business and Industrial Marketing*, 31 (1), 123–134.

Fallon-Byrne, L. and B. Harney (2017), 'Microfoundations of dynamic capabilities for innovation: a review and research agenda', *Irish Journal of Management*, 36 (1), 21–31.

Fjeldstad, Ø.D. and C.C. Snow (2018), 'Business models and organization design', *Long Range Planning*, 51 (1), 32–39.

Golgeci, I. and S.Y. Ponomarov (2013), 'Does firm innovativeness enable effective responses to supply chain disruptions? An empirical study', *Supply Chain Management: An International Journal*, 18 (6), 604–617.

Gouda, S. and H. Saranga (2018), 'Sustainable supply chains for supply chain sustainability: impact of sustainability efforts on supply chain risk', *International Journal of Production Research*, 56 (17), 5820–5835.

Gruchmann, T., Melkonyan, A., and K. Krumme (2018), 'Logistics business transformation for sustainability: assessing the role of the lead sustainability service provider (6PL)', *Logistics*, 2 (4), 25.

Gruchmann, T., Pratt, N., Eiten, J., and A. Melkonyan (2020), '4PL digital business models in sea freight logistics: the case of FreightHub', *Logistics*, 4 (2), 10.

Gruchmann, T. and S. Seuring (2018), 'Explaining logistics social responsibility from a dynamic capabilities perspective', *International Journal of Logistics Management*, 29 (4), 1255–1278.

Gruchmann, T., Seuring, S., and K. Petljak (2019), 'Assessing the role of dynamic capabilities in local food distribution: a theory-elaboration study', *Supply Chain Management: An International Journal*, 24 (6), 767–783.

Handoko, I., Bresnen, M., and Y. Nugroho (2018), 'Knowledge exchange and social capital in supply chains', *International Journal of Operations and Production Management*, 38 (1), 90–108.

Helfat, C.E., Finkelstein, S., Mitchell, W., Peteraf, M.A., Singh, H., et al. (2007), *Dynamic Capabilities: Understanding Strategic Change in Organizations*, Malden, MA: Blackwell Publishing.

Helfat, C.E. and M.A. Peteraf (2009), 'Understanding dynamic capabilities: progress along a developmental path', *Strategic Organization*, 7 (1), 91–102.

Helfat, C.E. and M.A. Peteraf (2015), 'Managerial cognitive capabilities and the microfoundations of dynamic capabilities', *Strategic Management Journal*, 36 (6), 831–850.

Hendry, L.C., Stevenson, M., MacBryde, J., Ball, P., Sayed, M., and L. Liu (2019), 'Local food supply chain resilience to constitutional change: the Brexit effect', *International Journal of Operations and Production Management*, 39 (3), 429–453.

Holling, C.S. (1973), 'Resilience and stability of ecological systems', *Annual Review of Ecology and Systematics*, 4, 1–23.

Jacobides, M.G. and S.G. Winter (2012), 'Capabilities: structure, agency, and evolution', *Organization Science*, 23 (5), 1365–1381.

Jiang, Y., Ritchie, B., and M. Verreynne (2019), 'Building tourism organizational resilience to crises and disasters: a dynamic capabilities view', *International Journal of Tourism Research*, 21, 882–900.

Jüttner, U., Peck, H., and M. Christopher (2003), 'Supply chain risk management: outlining an agenda for future research', *International Journal of Logistics Research and Applications*, 6 (4), 197–210.

Khan, O., Daddi, T., and F. Iraldo (2020), 'Microfoundations of dynamic capabilities: Insights from circular economy business cases', *Business Strategy and the Environment*, 29, 1479–1493.

Kindström, D., Kowalkowski, C., and E. Sandberg (2013), 'Enabling service innovation: a dynamic capabilities approach', *Journal of Business Research*, 66 (8), 1063–1073.

Kırcı, M. and R. Seifert (2015), 'Dynamic capabilities in sustainable supply chain management: a theoretical framework', *Supply Chain Forum: An International Journal*, 16 (4), 2–15.

Kumar, G., Subramanian, N., and R.A. Arputham (2018), 'Missing link between sustainability collaborative strategy and supply chain performance: role of dynamic capability', *International Journal of Production Economics*, 203, 96–109.

Land, A., Nielsen, H., Seuring, S., and D.M. Neutzling (2015), *Sustainable Supply Chain Management Practices and Dynamic Capabilities in the Automotive Industry*, Briarcliff Manor, NY: Academy of Management.

Lee, K. and J. Yoo (2019), 'How does open innovation lead competitive advantage? A dynamic capability view perspective', *PloS one*, 14 (11), e0223405.

Linnenluecke, M.K. (2017), 'Resilience in business and management research: a review of influential publications and a research agenda', *International Journal of Management Reviews*, 19 (1), 4–30.

Liu, L., Zhang, M., Hendry, L.C., Bu, M., and S. Wang (2018), 'Supplier development practices for sustainability: a multi-stakeholder perspective', *Business Strategy and the Environment*, 27, 100–116.

Luthar, S.S., Cicchetti, D., and B. Becker (2000), 'The construct of resilience: a critical evaluation and guidelines for future work', *Child Development*, 71 (3), 543–562.

Ma, Z., Xiao, L., and J. Yin (2018), 'Toward a dynamic model of organizational resilience', *Nankai Business Review International*, 9 (3), 246–263.

Makadok, R. (2001), 'Toward a synthesis of the resource-based and dynamic-capability views of rent creation', *Strategic Management Journal*, 22, 387–401.

Mandal, S., Bhattacharya, S., Korasiga, V., and R. Sarathy (2017), 'The dominant influence of logistics capabilities on integration', *International Journal of Disaster Resilience in the Built Environment*, 8 (4), 357–374.

Manfield, R. and L. Newey (2018), 'Resilience as an entrepreneurial capability: integrating insights from a cross-disciplinary comparison', *International Journal of Entrepreneurial Behavior and Research*, 24 (7), 1155–1180.

Mathivathanan, D., Govindan, K., and A.N. Haq (2017), 'Exploring the impact of dynamic capabilities on sustainable supply chain firm's performance using Grey-Analytical Hierarchy Process', *Journal of Cleaner Production*, 147, 637–653.

Montabon, F., Pagell, M., and Z. Wu (2016), 'Making sustainability sustainable', *Journal of Supply Chain Management*, 52 (2), 11–27.

Mwangola, W. (2018), 'Conceptualizing supply chain resilience: an alternative dynamic capabilities perspective', *American Journal of Management*, 18 (4), 76–88.

Newey, L. and S. Zahra (2009), 'The evolving firm: how dynamic and operating capabilities interact to enable entrepreneurship', *British Journal of Management*, 20, 81–100.

Osterwalder, A. and Y. Pigneur (2009), *Business Model Generation: A Handbook for Visionaries, Game Changers, and Challengers*, Amsterdam: Modderman Drukwerk.

Pagell, M. and A. Shevchenko (2014), 'Why research in sustainable supply chain management should have no future', *Journal of Supply Chain Management*, 50 (1), 44–55.

Pagell, M. and Z. Wu (2009), 'Building a more complete theory of sustainable supply chain management using case studies of 10 exemplars', *Journal of Supply Chain Management*, 45, 37–56.

Parida, V., Sjödin, D., and W. Reim (2019), 'Reviewing literature on digitalization, business model innovation, and sustainable industry: past achievements and future promises', *Sustainability*, 11, 391.

Pavlou, P.A. and O.A. El Sawy (2011), 'Understanding the elusive black box of dynamic capabilities', *Decision Sciences*, 42 (1), 239–273.

Ponis, S.T. and E. Koronis (2012), 'Supply chain resilience: definition of concept and its formative elements', *Journal of Applied Business Research*, 28 (5), 921–930.

Ponomarov, S.Y. and M.C. Holcomb (2009), 'Understanding the concept of supply chain resilience', *International Journal of Logistics Management*, 20 (1), 124–143.

Porter, M.E. and J.E. Heppelmann (2015), 'How smart, connected products are transforming companies', *Harvard Business Review*, 93 (10), 96–114.

Reuter, C., Foerstl, K., Hartmann, E., and C. Blome (2010), 'Sustainable global supplier management: the role of dynamic capabilities in achieving competitive advantage', *Journal of Supply Chain Management*, 46 (2), 45–63.

Schaltegger, S., Lüdeke-Freund, F., and E.G. Hansen (2016), 'Business models for sustainability: a co-evolutionary analysis of sustainable entrepreneurship, innovation, and transformation', *Organization and Environment*, 29 (3), 264–289.

Seuring, S. and M. Müller (2008), 'From a literature review to a conceptual framework for sustainable supply chain management', *Journal of Cleaner Production*, 16, 1699–1710.

Souza, A., Alves, M., Macini, N., Cezarino, L., and L. Liboni (2017), 'Resilience for sustainability as an eco-capability', *International Journal of Climate Change Strategies and Management*, 9 (5), 581–599.

Su, H. and K. Linderman (2016), 'An empirical investigation in sustaining high-quality performance', *Decision Sciences*, 47 (5), 787–819.

Teece, D.J. (2007), 'Explicating dynamic capabilities: the nature and microfoundations of (sustainable) enterprise performance', *Strategic Management Journal*, 28 (13), 1319–1350.

Teece, D.J. (2009), *Dynamic Capabilities and Strategic Management: Organizing for Innovation and Growth*, New York: Oxford University Press on Demand.

Teece, D.J. (2018), 'Business models and dynamic capabilities', *Long Range Planning*, 51 (1), 40–49.

Teece, D.J., Pisano, G., and A. Shuen (1997), 'Dynamic capabilities and strategic management', *Strategic Management Journal*, 18 (7), 509–533.

Touboulic, A. and H. Walker (2015), 'Theories in sustainable supply chain management: a structured literature review', *International Journal of Physical Distribution and Logistics Management*, 45 (1–2), 16–42.

Wang, C. and P. Ahmed (2007), 'Dynamic capabilities: a review and research agenda'. *International Journal of Management Reviews*, 9, 31–51.

Winter, S. (2003), 'Understanding dynamic capabilities', *Strategic Management Journal*, 10, 991–995.

Zahra, S., Sapienza, H., and P. Davidsson (2006), 'Entrepreneurship and dynamic capabilities: a review, model and research agenda', *Journal of Management Studies*, 43, 917–955.

Zollo, M. and S. Winter (2002), 'Deliberate learning and the evolution of dynamic capabilities', *Organization Science*, 13, 339–351.

Zott, C., Amit, R., and L. Massa (2011), 'The business model: recent developments and future research', *Journal of Management*, 37, 1019–1104.

26. Supply chains as complex adaptive systems
Anurag Tewari and Richard Wilding

INTRODUCTION

Contemporary supply chain researchers have become increasingly interested in conceptualising supply chain networks as complex systems (Choi et al., 2001; Nair et al., 2009; Nair and Reed-Tsochas, 2019; Pathak et al., 2007; Surana et al., 2005). Their interest spans from the fact that traditionally supply chains are viewed as a linear structure of simplistic organisations. This linear tree-like structure is assumed to have sequentially organised transactions leading to successive value creation (Mabert and Venkataramanan, 1998), an assumption that might not be consistent with reality. In reality, supply networks are an ensemble of an interconnected network of multiple organisations, spanning several scales and with an overwhelming number of interactions and interdependencies of decisions and processes (Surana et al., 2005). Furthermore, organisations of this complex supply network constantly form adaptive strategies and processes as a response to changes encountered in the strategy of other network entities/firms or the global environment (Nair and Reed-Tsochas, 2019). As a result, the network evolves and self-organises, producing complex dynamical, disorderly and non-linear behaviours that are hard to explain using conventional supply chain wisdom (Pathak et al., 2007).

The complex supply chain behaviours encountered in reality are comparable to the non-linear dynamical system behaviours commonly observed in many natural and artificial complex systems such as the ecosystems, immune systems, communication networks, infrastructure networks, the internet, stock markets and the global economy (Amaral and Ottino, 2004; Cohen and Axelrod, 1984; Holland, 2006). Modelling these system behaviours or generating predictive capabilities for such systems has proved challenging, as these systems are impermeable to conventional reductionist approaches. Under the name of 'complexity science', a growing field of interdisciplinary studies represents a cluster of ideas that provides concepts, principles and tools to interrogate such systems (Newman, 2011).

Prominent complexity researchers Holland (1995) and Kauffman (1993) argue that some characteristics are common to all complex systems. These characteristics are: (1) a high degree of interconnectedness and interdependency among components; (2) the existence of feedback loops among subsystems; (3) inherent difficulty in the study of these systems in isolation; (4) the presence of emergent behaviours where the system's outcomes manifest out of small-scale interactions among its subsystems; (5) non-linear and dynamical responses to minor perturbations; (6) sensitivity to initial conditions; and (7) a seemingly unpredictable response (Holland, 1995; Kauffman, 1993; Varga et al., 2009). These systems are often argued to be at the edge of chaos, self-organising, and coevolutionary (Varga et al., 2009). A particular case of such systems is those that have an additional characteristic of being dominated by agent or agency-related interactions. These complex systems with a multitude of heterogeneous interacting agents or entities are categorised as complex adaptive systems (CASs) and are studied using the complex adaptive systems theory.

A CAS view of complexity is most suited to investigate and compare the actions and interactions of agents, individual groups, species, or the formulation of response strategies against their competitors and environment (Gell-Mann, 2002; Holland, 2006; Newman, 2011). The CAS perspective is particularly useful to explain agent adaption, self-organisation, coevolution and system-level emergence. In CASs, the diversity of agents and a seemingly simple looking set of localised rules of their engagement can result in complicated structures and patterns (Levin, 1998). In the wider domain of social and natural science, the CAS view has been used to explain self-organised coevolution of many peculiar stochastic micro events concerning agents such as molecules, genes, neurons, particles, organisations or individuals, into emergent structures (McKelvey, 1999). Since supply chain networks are systems with a diverse array of organisations and human agents involved in a multitude of dynamical and parallel interactions, a CAS view is particularly relevant for deciphering the complex nature of the supply chain networks. The theoretical underpinning for this approach is that systems comprising of a diverse and independent set of agents will demonstrate non-linear and complex system behaviour generated bottom-up from a multitude of interactions happening among agents and between agents and environment.

KEY VARIABLES AND DEFINITIONS

Complex Adaptive Systems

CASs are a class of complex systems dominated by a diverse population of interconnected and adaptive agents. The actions and interactions of these agents cause non-linear, emergent, and dynamical system behaviours. CASs can exist, far from equilibrium, in an unstable and dynamic environment through adaptation, self-organisation and coevolution. The term 'adaptation' comes from evolutionary biology. Evolutionary biology argues that every species has a survival mechanism of responding to changes in its environment, or to the changes in the nature of threats faced by the species. Adaptation is that response.

From a system perspective, adaptation refers to a system's ability to progressively modify or improve the fitness or survivability of its agents through the formulation of success strategies to tackle threats and the dynamism of the environment it operates within. Defining adaptation in organisations, Levinthal writes, 'Adaptation is interpreted here to mean a change in significant attribute of the organisation' (Levinthal, 1997, p. 934). In response to environmental signals and other agents' behaviour, every individual agent of a CAS flexibly and proactively seeks to continually revise its behaviours, actions and strategies, and continuously improve its survival or fitness against predefined organisational or system objectives. It is a kind of evolutionary process in which a system feeds back into itself the outcomes of its adopted strategies and learns from them. The system works on a simple set of rules or schemas to implement this learning and revise its future course of action. The system changes introduced through adaptation continually create newer opportunities and novel future states and courses for the system. Thus, a CAS can exhibit system-wide emergent patterns without being externally imposed on the system.

Typical characteristics of a CAS are threefold. First, it is a nested system of a large number of a diverse set of agents (Holland, 2006). Here 'nested' implies that it is a system of systems where a set of loosely coupled agents with a high degree of connectedness and evolving pattern of non-linear interactions are embedded in a larger system (Punzo et al., 2020). These agents of a CAS seek to maximise their fitness through evolutionary and self-organising behaviour (Dooley, 1996; Gell-Mann, 1994; Newman, 2011). Second, to be able to respond to their environment, to various stimuli and environmental conditions, these agents develop fluid mental models, schemas or rules (Dooley, 1996; Gell-Mann, 1994, 2002). Third, the agent diversity is a result of continuous adaptation, which never lets the system stabilise; instead, it takes the system towards perpetual novelty. In other words, these systems exhibit evolutionary characteristics (Holland, 2006).

The key objective of an agent within a complex system is to maximise its fitness, and the fitness function of an agent in a complex aggregate is determined by many global and local factors, including the mental models or schemas maintained by each individual agent. Often synonymously used by complexity researchers, the terms 'schemas', 'mental models', 'agent internal mechanisms' and 'mind frames' convey the same meaning in the field of complexity science. These are the lowest fundamental units that influence an agent's interactions and in turn provide emergent and self-organising capabilities to the system at a macro level.

The basic unit of a CAS is its agents. Agents are a diverse set of semi-autonomous units engaged in actions and interactions with each other, system components and the environment. From a supply chain perspective, agents could be taken as individual firms that are nested in a larger network or system of product, information and financial flow (Pathak et al., 2007). The objective of these agents is to maximise their fitness by evolving over time, using adaptive strategies. When these agents encounter stimuli from the environment and other agents, these agents respond to these stimuli according to a set of internal models/schemas or rules. These internal models help the agents to interpret reality and their surroundings. Thus, one could infer that the fitness of the agent is a complex aggregate of many factors, both local and global.

Emergence and Self-Organisation

An important phenomenon of a CAS is 'emergence'. Goldstein presented a glossary of terms where he conceptualised emergence to be: 'a process ... whereby new emergent structures, patterns, and properties arise without being externally imposed on the system' (Goldstein, in Zimmerman et al., 1998, p. 270).

Emergence as a concept has a long history in natural sciences and ecosystems research. In recent times, complex science has contributed the most to the phenomenon of emergence, with many valuable contributions looking at it from various perspectives. Emergence from a complexity perspective has been studied in natural sciences (Bak, 1996; Kauffman, 1993; Nicolis and Prigogine, 1989), in organisations (Maguire and McKelvey, 2002; McKelvey, 1999, 2002; Stacey, 1996) and also in the sphere of social inquiries (Buckley, 1998; Eve et al., 1997; Goldspink and Kay, 2003).

Emergence is not a new abstraction to organisational researchers. It has been studied at various levels (Lichtenstein and Plowman, 2009). Plowman et al. (2007) conducted a study about the amplification of small effects into emergent structures at an organisational level. In their investigation of a religious organisation, Plowman et al. (2007) found that small changes led to the emergence of radical changes at the system level. Lichtenstein (2000) uses a CAS framework to study and compare self-organised emergence at two firms. Chiles et al. (2004) use the dissipative structure's model to argue the emergence of collective organisations. The authors use a longitudinal case study to collectively study the emergent dynamics of a musical theatre and the collective community and other associated organisations.

The CAS view posits that adaptation driven by local rules and schemas leads to the creation of order due to emergent system behaviours. However, the system could attain order through another CAS phenomenon of self-organisation. Self-organisation is an exhibited system behaviour in which a system naturally evolves or emerges to a new state without interference or influence of any outside force or agent (Bak, 1996).

Self-organisation is a structural rearrangement that occurs when a system is in a far from equilibrium condition or is in a state of high entropy. During this process of self-organisation, the system moves to or attains a structure that allows the system to function in far from equilibrium conditions in a much more energy-efficient manner. Outside stimuli or agents do not enforce these structural or system changes; rather, they emerge from within the system. Since the order emerges from within the system, the process of self-organisation is suggested to be 'order for free' (Kauffman, 1993). Self-organisation in a CAS has been suggested to rely upon feedback loops or information flows among system agents and all interconnected system components. The process of self-organisation in natural systems is often observed over a very long duration or interval.

In complex systems theory, self-organisation has been linked to four mechanisms or models: rugged landscape, synergetics, multiple basin dynamics and the sandpile. However, the Kauffman (1993) rugged landscape mechanism is most suited to explain self-organisation in supply chain networks from a supply chain standpoint.

Rugged/Fitness Landscape

The rugged/fitness landscape model of self-organisation was theorised in ecosystem research by Kauffman and colleagues (Kauffman, 1993; Kauffman and Johnsen, 1991; Kauffman and Levin, 1987) to explain the complex adaptive behaviours of species. Discussing a theoretical scenario about some sort of cataclysm destroying the habitat and available food source of an ecological niche, Kauffman (1993) argues that any species adapted to living in this given ecological niche must find a new ecological niche, habitat and food source. A survival response to this would be that the species would disperse out into a surrounding rugged landscape to look for other niches that may support survival. Some of the newly accrued niches will work well, as the species located in those niches share traits required to survive there. Kauffman (1993) argues that different locally stable niches and ecosystems are fitness peaks requiring varying degrees and nature of adaptation. This model has found its usefulness in arguing how a diverse population of people might end up clustering in some meaningful groupings (Trofimova and Mitin, 2002).

Generalising the rugged landscape model, one can view landscape being analogous to a mountain range with peaks and valleys, where peaks represent multiple, low-entropy, optimal states for the objective or performance function of the system (Kauffman, 1993). By drawing this parallel between the rugged peaks of a mountain range and the alternative performance peak/levels available to a system, Kauffman (1993) succeeds in arguing against the Darwinian logic of selection. Kauffman (1993) posits that, depending upon the system's ongoing energy or fitness level, the system will move from one peak of performance to another without adhering to the Darwinian logic of selection. Darwinian evolution is replaced by an adaptive search that may land the system in one of the multiple suboptimal peaks available due to the ruggedness of the landscape.

The ruggedness of the landscape or the number of available fitness peaks is linked to the system's complexity. On one end of the spectrum, we could have a less complex system, having gently rolling hills of fitness peaks; and on the opposite end of the spectrum, there could be a system with a jagged landscape of multiple suboptimal peaks. Kauffman (1993) presented a coevolutionary cellular automata model, the 'NKC model', to calculate the fitness and peaks of a complex adaptive landscape. In the model, N represents the number of diverse variations in the population of agents. K represents the number of interconnections per element, and C is the number of agents external to the system.

In the model, K indicates the ruggedness and fitness of the available peaks to the system. When $K = 0$, it signifies a smooth landscape with a single peak, while for $K = N - 1$, the landscape is completely rugged with an exponentially high number of peaks. At $K = 0$, it is argued that the agents are not dependent on each other, or their individual traits do not play a role in their survivability. However, as K increases, the interdependence and nature of connections among agents put a constraint on the system, and multiple suboptimal system states, analogues to fitness peaks, are created. The model is essential as it diverts attention from individual agent traits to a combined fitness function of the species. The search for fitness function is driven by the existing agent diversity of the species and the interactions the species has with its environment. The NKC model succeeds in demonstrating that when an organisation pursues local or incremental perspectives, this could be highly disadvantageous in a rugged landscape or complex scenarios. Due to the existence of multiple fitness peaks, the organisation can get trapped in a local performance peak and lose out on fitter and more beneficial possibilities that may exist elsewhere in higher performance peaks (Allen and Varga, 2006). In simple words, global optima are easier to achieve when the organisations are simple systems with lesser complexity. However, as the organisational system grows in complexity and there is an increase in interdependence among system agents and components, global optima become an elusive reality (Choi et al., 2001).

From a supply chain perspective, the fitness landscape view compels supply chain researchers to acknowledge the impact of distributed decision making on the complexity of the system and its potential to achieve global optima. Since distributed decision making can be linked to the number and nature of interactions and interconnections among system components and system agents, it would impact upon the system's complexity. Choi et al. (2001) argue that in a supply chain context, the ruggedness of the landscape could be reduced by limiting the interactions among system processes, components and agents. For example, if an organisation chose to modularise its design or manufacturing by combining parts, activities and processes, the organisation would reduce the system complexity and the number of system interconnections. This will reduce the K value and thus reduce the number of peaks in the rugged landscape of the system.

Coevolution

Coevolution is a phenomenon where interactions between two diverse sets of population or species bring about a reciprocal evolutionary change in each other (Eaton, 2008). CASs are known to demonstrate coevolutionary characteristics. It is often argued that order in a CAS emerges from the coevolutionary interactions among heterogeneous agents and between agents and the environment. For example, in the fitness landscape model, settling down of a system into suboptimal peaks represents new order emerging from reciprocatory interactions among agents and the environment. During this process of order creation, species can simultaneously react to and influence their environment (Kauffman, 1993). Thus, one may infer that CASs are coevolutionary, where system entities and the environment are bound together in a mutually constituting relationship of change.

Coevolution in CASs represents the recursive and self-constituting nature of influence between heterogeneous agents and the environment. Discussing coevolution from a supply chain perspective, Choi et al. (2001) explain that when the entities of a CAS respond to the changes in the environment, this interaction may result in the entities changing, which in turn will also bring about changes in the environment. Coevolution is an essential phenomenon of CASs and can be used to explain non-linear, path-dependent and evolutionary system changes.

The agent, environment and system properties of a CAS are condensed into a visual representation (Figure 26.1). The visual model emphasises that a CAS should be approached using the following: (1) the characteristic of agents or entities that constitute the CAS; (2) the nature of coupling or interconnectedness among these agents; (3) the environment in which these agents are embedded; and (4) the system properties or phenomena that are a characteristic of the CAS. The arrows among the agents, environment and agent coupling symbolise the recursive, self-constituting and coevolutionary dynamism among these system constituents.

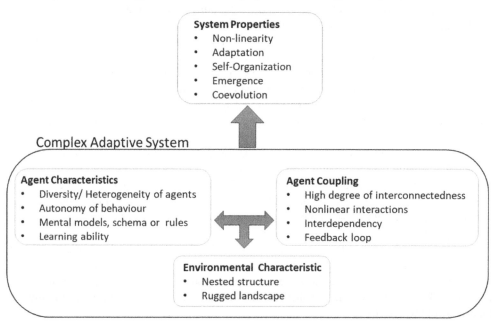

Figure 26.1   Agents, environment and system properties of a complex adaptive system

Supply Chain Networks as CASs

Defining a CAS in a supply chain context, Pathak et al. (2007) posit that it is a: 'system of interconnected autonomous firms that make choices to survive and, as a collective, the system evolves and self-organises over time' (Pathak et al., 2007, p. 562).

This definition helps to connect supply network ontology to the ontological assumptions of CASs. Furthermore, theorising a supply chain network as an interorganisational network system of buyers, suppliers, retailers, logistics providers, financial institutions, governmental organisations, and a diverse array of human actors within these subsystems, makes the supply chain network an ideal candidate for being a CAS.

Like any other CAS, supply chain networks also demonstrate dynamism, where the network topology continues to evolve in a non-linear and heterogeneous fashion (Pathak et al., 2007; Varga et al., 2009). Like other CASs, the supply chain network also exhibits parallelism, modularity, adaptation and self-organisation (Choi et al., 2001; Nilsson and Darley, 2006; Pathak et al., 2007; Surana et al., 2005).

Nilsson and Darley (2006) argue that the complexity in a supply chain network arises out of the agent's interaction in the network. The authors view these interactions as reactive, and also as often leading to deliberately proactive behaviour affecting other entities or subsystems in the network environment, giving rise to the complex behaviour of the network. Surana et al. (2005) attribute the complexity in the supply chain network to the vast span of a supply network over several tiers, with bi-level hierarchy and heterogeneity in the network. Surana et al. (2005) further suggest that non-linear network behaviour emerges from the complex nature of interactions between various supply chain agents such as customers, supply chain executives or truck drivers. Surana et al. (2005) recognise that these agents are autonomous individuals with their individual targets and goals, yet on aspects of collective performance goals these agents act in a highly interdependent manner, resulting in a coevolutionary behaviour. They state: 'at present, networks are largely controlled by humans, the complexity, diversity and geographic distribution of the networks make it necessary for networks to maintain themselves in a sort of evolutionary sense' (Surana et al., 2005, p. 4243)

Supply chain networks' emergent and self-organising behaviour result from the micro interactions among supply chain network agents (Choi et al., 2001). The outcomes of these interactions are contingent upon the agents' internal models or schemas, the dimensionality of agent behaviours, the self-organising and emergent properties of their relationships, and the connectivity among agents. Choi et al. (2001) view agent schemas as norms, beliefs and values, while dimensionality is the degree of freedom or kinds of behaviours that an agent can demonstrate. The authors argue that these behaviours, or agent dimensionality, could be altered by system aspects such as managerial interventions, rule regulations or institutional pressure.

Schemas in a CAS and its Status in Supply Chain Research

Holland (1993) argues that a less obvious, but essential, aspect of a CAS is the set of internal rules or models that an agent uses to predict the outcomes of their actions. Driven by local and global stimuli, the agents develop, update and modify these rules, also referred to as agent schemas, to interpret reality or respond to stimuli (Dooley, 1996; Gell-Mann, 1994). In a supply chain context, Choi et al. (2001) were the first to point out that aggregation of several such non-linear agent schemas and mental models can aggregate into internal mechanisms leading to complex supply chain behaviours. Mental models of agents have been studied in the context of cooperation and opportunism among network firms (Nair et al., 2009); in the context of internal decision making and supply chain resilience (Datta et al., 2007); and for evolutionary aspects of supply chains (Varga et al., 2009).

DOMAIN WHERE THE THEORY APPLIES

To Model Network-Level Dynamism and Interdependencies

The functioning of every individual firm or entity within a supply chain is ultimately dependent upon the material, information and financial flows that transpire in the network. A supply chain firm's ability to compete, coordinate and survive in its supply chain ecosystem will depend upon the nature and structure of its embeddedness in the network, and the overall complexity of the network. CAS theory is an appropriate theoretical foundation to study firms' embeddedness and network-level interdependencies. Nair et al. (2009) used a CAS view to model how an individual firm's exit strategy could influence network level behaviours. The underlying assumption that necessitated the use of the CAS view was that individual behaviours at the agent level could manifest in network-level outcomes; or one could say that there are network-level interdependencies that shape cooperation, coordination and defection strategies of individual actors in a CAS. Similarly, to account for a nested system's view in the study of sustainable supply chain practices in the aerospace sector, Varga et al. (2009) proposed to examine supply chains using a CAS perspective. Another study by Dhanorkar et al. (2019) also commits to a CAS view to model the dynamism, uncertainties and interdependencies that shape the functioning of online material and waste exchanges.

It is worth mentioning that the CAS perspective is restricted to interorganisational networks, with individual firms acting as the network agents/nodes. However, the CAS view could be extended to an intrafirm network, with people or business functions/units acting as nodes/ agents of the network. For example, Nilsson and Darley (2006) used a CAS perspective to study firm-level tactical and operational decision making in the manufacturing and logistics environment. The authors considered different organisational functions, such as sales, operations planning, warehouse and capacitated machines, as the CAS network agents, along with the organisation's customers.

To Study Adaptation

Agent adaptation is a fundamental tenet of a CAS. Supply chain researchers have effectively used a CAS perspective to study and model adaptive agent behaviours in a supply network. It has been argued that supply chain and logistic systems adapt, reconfigure or evolve to their environment and to other signals originating from agent interactions. The adaptive behaviour is demonstrated in reconfiguration or alteration of network structure, operational processes, or by a shift in agent strategies or behaviours (Wycisk et al., 2008).

To study the adaptive response of firms against hostile buyer/customer behaviours, Giannoccaro et al. (2018) have used Kauffman's (1993) NK fitness landscape framework. NK models are mathematical models based upon Kauffman's (1993) fitness landscape view, where

N represents the number of diverse variations in the population of agents, and K represents the number of interconnections per element. In this study, agents seek to follow an adaptive strategy to discover fitness/performance peaks that may maximise their payoffs. This adaptive strategy is in response to prescriptive recommendations or changes in stocking decisions advocated by their buyer firms.

HOW HAS THIS THEORY BEEN USED?

The CAS view on the supply chain networks has been progressively used to model adaptation, non-linearity and dynamism. Dhanorkar et al. (2019) used a CAS perspective to study buyer–supplier transactions at a node, dyad and network level. The study focuses on how node-level buyer strategies and the effect of dyadic-level buyer–supplier affinities could influence network-level competitive effects. Nilsson and Darley (2006) adopt a CAS view to improve tactical and operational decision making in the manufacturing and logistics scenario.

Giannoccaro et al. (2018) employed a CAS-driven NK simulation to investigate the relationship between the performance of a supply chain network and the degree of control exerted by individual agents on their connections. Espinosa et al. (2019) adopted CAS theory to study the process of product returns. The study researched the impact of returns handling employee behaviours on the overall adaptability of the reverse supply chain. Using a CAS, the study was able to argue that firms with autonomous decision making agents can adapt better in handling the process of product returns. Day (2014) used a CAS lens to study disaster relief supply chains. The CAS framework helped Day to focus on understanding how the collective resilience of a disaster relief operation emerges in a non-linear and dynamic manner due to the exogenous environmental factors and aggregation of interactions among multiple stakeholders associated with the disaster relief supply chain. Johnsen et al. (2019) use two case studies from the offshore wind power industry to explore supply network strategies necessary to manage network complexity. In this study, a CAS viewpoint is used to conceptualise and model network complexity.

Hou et al. (2018) modelled the influence of trust on shaping the supply network's resilience to random and targeted disruption. The study used the CAS view to theorise interdependent and agent interactions. The CAS view was adopted by Statsenko et al. (2018) to create a framework for governing regional supply chain networks and for improving the resilience and adaptability of these industrial regions. Nair et al. (2016) develop a theory using the CAS perspective to explain the emergence and proliferation of environmental innovations. In their study of adaptive strategies against disruptions, Zhao et al. (2019) visualise supply chain firms to be a CAS where these firms adapt and restructure if the system experiences a disruption.

OUTLOOK ON FUTURE RESEARCH OPPORTUNITIES

The use of CAS theory in supply chains is still at an early stage of maturity. Key variables, methodologies and concepts from the wider domain of CASs need further refinement to establish their comparable supply chain counterparts.

The CAS view is an appropriate theoretical foundation for evaluating cascading outcomes or phenomena linked to agent adaptation. However, a limited number of studies have investigated such network-level cascading processes or discussed supply chain phenomena linked to agent adaptation. There are opportunities to investigate how local interactions, driven by a simple set of rules, could alter network properties. Such studies can lay a foundation for expanding our understanding of supply chain resilience. The complexity perspective has been effectively used to study resilience in many engineering and infrastructure systems, such as transport networks, aerospace systems and complex engineering systems (Punzo et al., 2020). In these studies, network properties such as connectedness, relational interdependencies and agents' adaptive search for fitness peaks have been highlighted as the determinants of systems' resilience. Our understanding of supply chain resilience can be refined using these CAS studies from other domains.

The CAS view could be useful for establishing indirect causalities linked to supply chain performance. For instance, local performance improving strategies, such as financial choices, cooperative or competing strategies, exercising power or pressure tactics, structural choices, and so on, adopted at an agent level, could have far-reaching consequences for network performance. From a conventional standpoint, these agent strategies might not seem apparent candidates for evaluation; however, when aggregated over the entire network using a CAS perspective, these agent strategies may prove to exert a dominant causal influence on several dimensions of network performance. For example, norms and trust across a network are often shaped by an aggregation of buyer–supplier relationships across the network. The CAS view helps to explain how local interactions and behaviours at one network location would impact upon the whole, such as how a part influences the whole. The search for local adaptive strategies at an agent/individual level could inform the emergence of collective patterns at a network level.

Another vital area for future supply chain research is to expand our understanding of entropy in a supply network context. Entropy is an important concept of complexity research that finds its origin in the second law of thermodynamics. In simple terms, entropy conveys disorder, randomness and uncertainty in a system, and the entropy of a system cannot decrease; a system will continue to become progressively disorderly. However, this does not restrict localised order from emerging through self-organisation. In his theory of 'dissipating structures', Prigogine (1955) argues that emergent localised self-organisation, or breaking and reappearing of localised system structures, can speed up the entropy production. Suppose this assertion is combined with the argument that at the edge of chaos, the rate of entropy production is increased (Latora et al., 2000). In that case, it can have interesting implications for supply chains. In supply chains, the concept of entropy takes an information-theoretic view that information is measurable and a good proxy for defining the system's complexity. The more information that is needed to define a system, the greater is its complexity. Leaning on this view, one can say that for open systems, such as supply chains, energy enters the system at low entropy and is dissipated through self-organisation. As a result, the system can attain order at a local level, and information quantity in the supply chain might be isomorphic to negative entropy.

REFERENCES

Allen, P.M., and Varga, L. (2006). A co-evolutionary complex systems perspective on information systems. *Journal of Information Technology*, *21*(4), 229–238. https://doi.org/10.1057/palgrave.jit .2000075.

Amaral, L.a.N., and Ottino, J.M. (2004). Complex networks. *European Physical Journal B – Condensed Matter*, *38*(2), 147–162. https://doi.org/10.1140/epjb/e2004-00110-5.

Bak, P. (1996). *How Nature Works: The Science of Self-Organized Criticalit.* New York: Copernicus.

Buckley, W.F. (1998). *Society – A Complex Adaptive System: Essays in Social Theory.* Amsterdam: Gordon & Breach.

Chiles, T.H., Meyer, A.D., and Hench, T.J. (2004). Organizational emergence: The origin and transformation of Branson Missouri's musical theatres. *Organization Science*, *15*(5), 499–519. https://doi.org/10.1287/orsc.

Choi, T.Y., Dooley, K.J., and Rungtusanatham, M. (2001). Supply networks and complex adaptive systems: control versus emergence. *Journal of Operations Management*, *19*(3), 351–366. https://doi.org/10.1016/S0272-6963(00)00068-1

Cohen, M.D., and Axelrod, R. (1984). Coping with complexity: The adaptive value of changing utility. *American Economic Review*, *74*(1), 30–42.

Datta, P.P., Christopher, M., and Allen, P. (2007). Agent-based modelling of complex production/distribution systems to improve resilience. *International Journal of Logistics Research and Applications*, *10*(3), 187–203. https://doi.org/10.1080/13675560701467144.

Day, J.M. (2014). Fostering emergent resilience: The complex adaptive supply network of disaster relief. *International Journal of Production Research*, *52*(7), 1970–1988.

Dhanorkar, S., Kim, Y., and Linderman, K. (2019). An empirical investigation of transaction dynamics in online surplus networks: A complex adaptive system perspective. *Journal of Operations Management*, *65*(2), 160–189. https://doi.org/10.1002/joom.1006.

Dooley, K. (1996). A nominal definition of complex adaptive systems. *Chaos Network*, *8*(1), 2–3.

Eaton, C.D. (2008). Coevolutionary Research. In S.E. Jørgensen and B.D. Fath (eds), *Encyclopedia of Ecology* (pp. 659–663). Elsevier. https://doi.org/10.1016/B978-008045405-4.00777-1.

Espinosa, J.A., Davis, D., Stock, J., and Monahan, L. (2019). Exploring the processing of product returns from a complex adaptive system perspective. *International Journal of Logistics Management*, *30*(3), 699–722. https://doi.org/10.1108/IJLM-08-2018-0216.

Eve, R.A., Horsfall, S., and Lee, M.E. (1997). *Chaos, Complexity, and Sociology: Myths, Models, and Theories.* Thousand Oaks, CA: SAGE.

Gell-Mann, M. (1994). *The Quark and the Jaguar.* New York: W.H. Freeman & Company.

Gell-Mann, M. (2002). What is complexity? In A.Q. Curzio and M. Fortis (eds), *Complexity and Industrial Clusters* (pp. 13–24). Heidelberg: Physica-Verlag.

Giannoccaro, I., Nair, A., and Choi, T. (2018). The impact of control and complexity on supply network performance: An empirically informed investigation using NK simulation analysis. *Decision Sciences*, *49*(4), 625–659. https://doi.org/10.1111/deci.12293.

Goldspink, C., and Kay, R. (2003). Organizations as self-organizing and sustaining systems: A complex and autopoietic systems perspective. *International Journal of General Systems*, *32*(5), 459–474. https://doi.org/10.1080/0308107031000135017.

Holland, J.H. (1993). Echoing emergence: Objectives, rough definitions, and speculations for echo-class models. No. 1993-04-023. Santa Fe institute, Santa Fe, NM.

Holland, J.H. (1995). *Hidden Order: How Adaptation Builds Complexity.* New York: Addison Wesley Publishing Company.

Holland, J.H. (2006). Studying complex adaptive systems. *Journal of Systems Science and Complexity*, (November), 1–8.

Hou, Y., Wang, X., Wu, Y., and He, P. (2018). How does the trust affect the topology of supply chain network and its resilience? An agent-based approach. *Transportation Research Part E: Logistics and Transportation Review*, *116*(July), 229–241. https://doi.org/10.1016/j.tre.2018.07.001.

Johnsen, T.E., Mikkelsen, O.S., and Wong, C.Y. (2019). Strategies for complex supply networks: Findings from the offshore wind power industry. *Supply Chain Management*, *24*(6), 872–886. https://doi.org/10.1108/SCM-11-2018-0410.

Kauffman, S.A. (1993). *The Origins of Order: Self-Organization and Selection in Evolution.* New York: Oxford University Press.

Kauffman, S.A., and Johnsen, S. (1991). Coevolution to the edge of chaos: Coupled fitness landscapes, poised states, and coevolutionary avalanches. *Journal of Theoretical Biology*, *149*(4), 467–505. https://doi.org/10.1016/S0022-5193(05)80094-3.

Kauffman, S.A., and Levin, S. (1987). Towards a general theory of adaptive walks on rugged landscapes. *Journal of Theoretical Biology*, *128*(1), 11–45.

Latora, V., Baranger, M., Rapisarda, A., and Tsallis, C. (2000). The rate of entropy increase at the edge of chaos. *Physics Letters, Section A: General, Atomic and Solid State Physics*, *273*(1–2), 97–103. https://doi.org/10.1016/S0375-9601(00)00484-9.

Levin, S. a. (1998). Ecosystems and the biosphere as complex adaptive systems. *Ecosystems*, 1(5), 431–436. https://doi.org/10.1007/s100219900037.

Levinthal, D. (1997). Adaptation on rugged landscapes. *Management Science*, 43(7), 934–950. https://doi.org/10.1287/mnsc.43.7.934.

Lichtenstein, B.B. (2000). Self-organized transitions: A pattern amid the chaos of transformative change. *Academy of Management Perspectives*, *14*(4), 128–141. https://doi.org/10.5465/ame.2000.3979821.

Lichtenstein, B.B., and Plowman, D.A. (2009). The leadership of emergence: A complex systems leadership theory of emergence at successive organizational levels. *Leadership Quarterly*, *20*(4), 617–630. https://doi.org/10.1016/j.leaqua.2009.04.006.

Mabert, V.A., and Venkataramanan, M.A. (1998). Special research focus on supply chain linkages: Challenges for design and management in the 21st century. *Decision Sciences*, *29*(3), 537–552. https://doi.org/10.1111/j.1540-5915.1998.tb01353.x.

Maguire, S., and McKelvey, B. (2002). Complexity and management: Moving from fad to firm foundations. *Emergence*, *1*(2), 1–19. https://doi.org/10.1207/s15327000em0102_3.

McKelvey, B. (1999). Self-organization, complexity catastrophe, and microstate models at the edge of chaos. In J.A.C. Baum and B. McKelvey (eds), *Variations in Organization Science. In Honor of Donald T. Campbell* (pp. 279–307). Thousand Oaks, CA: SAGE.

McKelvey, B. (2002). Emergent order in firms: Complexity science vs. the entanglement trap. *Complex Systems and Evolutionary Perspectives of Organizations: Applications of Complexity Theory to Organizations*, *1*, 1–15.

Nair, A., Narasimhan, R., and Choi, T.Y. (2009). Supply networks as a complex adaptive system: Toward simulation-based theory building on evolutionary decision making. *Decision Sciences*, *40*(4), 783–815. https://doi.org/10.1111/j.1540-5915.2009.00251.x.

Nair, A., and Reed-Tsochas, F. (2019). Revisiting the complex adaptive systems paradigm: Leading perspectives for researching operations and supply chain management issues. *Journal of Operations Management*, *65*(2), 80–92. https://doi.org/10.1002/joom.1022.

Nair, A., Yan, T., Ro, Y.K., Oke, A., Chiles, T.H., and Lee, S.Y. (2016). How environmental innovations emerge and proliferate in supply networks: A complex adaptive systems perspective. *Journal of Supply Chain Management*, *52*(2), 66–86. https://doi.org/10.1111/jscm.12102.

Newman, M.E.J. (2011). Complex systems: A survey. *American Journal of Physics*, *79*(8), 800. https://doi.org/10.1119/1.3590372.

Nicolis, G., and Prigogine, I. (1989). *Exploring Complexity: An Introduction*. New York: Freeman.

Nilsson, F., and Darley, V. (2006). On complex adaptive systems and agent-based modelling for improving decision-making in manufacturing and logistics settings: Experiences from a packaging company. *International Journal of Operations and Production Management*, *26*(12), 1351–1373. https://doi.org/10.1108/01443570610710588.

Pathak, S.D., Day, J.M., Nair, A., Sawaya, W.J., and Kristal, M.M. (2007). Complexity and adaptivity in supply networks: Building supply network theory using a complex adaptive systems perspective. *Decision Sciences*, *38*(4), 547–580. https://doi.org/10.1111/j.1540-5915.2007.00170.x.

Plowman, D.A., Baker, L.T., Beck, T.E., Kulkarni, M., Solansky, S.T., and Travis, D.V. (2007). Radical change accidentally: The emergence and amplification of small change. *Academy of Management Journal*, *50*(3), 515–543. https://doi.org/10.5465/AMJ.2007.25525647.

Prigogine, I. (1955). *An Introduction to Thermodynamics of Irreversible Processes*. Springfield, IL: Thomas.

Punzo, G., Tewari, A., Butans, E., Vasile, M., Purvis, A., et al. (2020). Engineering resilient complex systems: The necessary shift toward complexity science. *IEEE Systems Journal*, *14*(3), 3865–3874. https://doi.org/10.1109/JSYST.2019.2958829.

Stacey, R.D. (1996). *Complexity and Creativity in Organizations*. San Francisco, CA: Berrett-Koehler Publishers.

Statsenko, L., Gorod, A., and Ireland, V. (2018). A complex adaptive systems governance framework for regional supply networks. *Supply Chain Management*, *23*(4), 293–312. https://doi.org/10.1108/SCM-08-2017-0279.

Surana, A., Kumara, S., Greaves, M., and Raghavan, U.N. (2005). Supply-chain networks: A complex adaptive systems perspective. *International Journal of Production Research*, *43*(20), 4235–4265. https://doi.org/10.1080/00207540500142274.

Trofimova, I., and Mitin, N. (2002). Self-organization and resource exchange in EVS modeling. *Nonlinear Dynamics, Psychology and Life Sciences*, *6*, 351–362.

Varga, L., Allen, P.M., Strathern, M., Rose-Anderssen, C., Baldwin, J.S., and Ridgway, K. (2009). Sustainable supply networks: A complex systems perspective. *Emergence: Complexity and Organization*, *11*(3), 16–36.

Wycisk, C., McKelvey, B., and Hülsmann, M. (2008). 'Smart parts' supply networks as complex adaptive systems: Analysis and implications. *International Journal of Physical Distribution and Logistics Management*, *38*(2), 108–125. https://doi.org/10.1108/09600030810861198.

Zhao, K., Zuo, Z., and Blackhurst, J.V. (2019). Modelling supply chain adaptation for disruptions: An empirically grounded complex adaptive systems approach. *Journal of Operations Management*, *65*(2), 190–212. https://doi.org/10.1002/joom.1009.

Zimmerman, B., Lindberg, C., and Plsek, P. (1998). *Edgeware*. Irving, TX: VHA.

27. Cluster theory and purchasing science: geographical proximity as a strategic decision factor in sourcing

Holger Schiele

HISTORY: INDUCTIVE THEORY CONSTRUCTION BASED ON A LONG TRADITION

'Clusters' refer to regional-sectoral agglomerations of firms and institutions, that is, localised supply chains generating a specific product and its components, which they offer to economic actors located outside that agglomeration. The slow down of growth in international trade in the last decade and events such as the Covid-19 crisis exposing the vulnerability of global supply chains have re-emphasised the discussion on locational choices in supplier selection. However, cluster theory and the cluster phenomenon are older than that. Numerous clusters give structure to economic activities; not only famous ones such as Silicon Valley or Hollywood, but also plenty more specialised clusters such as golf equipment in Carlsbad (California); light aircraft in Wichita and pharmaceuticals in Pennsylvania (United States); tufted carpets in northern Belgium; the seed valley in Hoorn (Netherlands); or kitchen furniture in Eastern Westfalia and cutlery in Solingen (Germany); and many others (Porter, 1998a; Schiele, 2003). The Chinese economy is strongly characterised by extreme forms of clusters, one-product towns, whose implementation may offer an explanation for the successful industrialisation of the country (Barbieri et al., 2019). Cluster theory, discussing localised supply chains, also leads to a series of implications for purchasing science and practice.

Two constitutional elements are central to the cluster theory: (1) being a phenomenon at the meso level of analysis; and (2) having a geographical component. We can distinguish between micro, meso and macro level. The micro level refers to individual actors (persons, single firms), while the macro level refers to all actors (typically of a nation). The meso level is in between, referring to groups of actors which consist of smaller units (in this case the firms), which form an interconnected group (the cluster) and are nested in a larger unit (the economy). The analysis of industries and their dynamics is a meso-analytical approach. Cluster theory differs from classical industrial economics approaches in that it adds a second analytical lens, the proximity (geographical and, in function of that, cultural and organisational proximity among organisations).

The regional agglomeration of economic activities has been observed for a long time. Several different theory streams have tried to make sense out of the phenomenon, mainly rooted in industrial economics and in economic geography. The Porterian cluster theory, which will be described in detail below, is the most influential and recent of these theories, but historically anteceding it are several French theories (*filière* and *milieu innovateur*) and the industry district model.

The economist Alfred Marshall was the first to publish a discussion on regional-sectoral agglomerations in his textbook (Marshall, 1961 [1890]). Trying to explain observations of small-scale co-location of entire industries, he identified three explanatory mechanisms, privileging these regions as compared to isolated actors, which Krugman (1991) summarised as follows:

1. The presence of a labour pool in industrial agglomerations allows workers to specialise at lower risk, because multiple employers are present. Firms in an agglomeration, in turn, can draw on a better-educated labour force than their isolated competitors.
2. The creation of 'intermediate inputs', that is specialised suppliers, enables firms in agglomerations to externalise more work than their isolated competitors which, in the absence of good suppliers, have to rely on less efficient in-house production.
3. Technology spillover occurs through the intensive exchange among actors in proximity, including tacit knowledge, which can hardly be codified and is not accessible to actors located outside the agglomeration. Marshall summarised it as: 'The mysteries of the trade become no mystery; but are as it were in the air' (Marshall, 1961 [1890], p. 225).

From a purchasing perspective, the hypothesis would be that the best and most specialised suppliers can be found in industrial agglomerations.

However, Marshall's explanation for agglomeration did not find much resonance during his lifetime. The industrial district model was only rediscovered almost 100 years later in Italy, when Becattini (1979, 1991) searched for an explanation for the observation of surprising firm success in North-East Italy, as opposed to less successful firms from the same industries, but located in other parts of the country. It was then noticed that often the competitive Italian firms are located in 'one-product towns', classical cases of very small-scale regional-sectoral supply chains. In Italy they became known as 'industrial districts' and represent as much as 35 per cent of the value added (Tunisini et al., 2011). Much current literature on agglomerations uses the term 'industrial district', which shows substantial overlap with Porter's cluster theory.

In parallel, French literature on the *filière* and the 'innovative milieu' developed. From a purchasing perspective, the *filière* literature proposes an interesting hypothesis, according to which the dominance in a supply chain moves according to the product life cycle. Hence, in well-established supply chains, suppliers would achieve lower margins; in innovative chains, on the other hand, manufacturers are more dependent on their suppliers (Malsot, 1980). This life cycle character would imply more importance of agglomeration effects in young, innovative supply chains. The innovative milieu approach, in turn, tries to explain the success of regional innovation systems by localised relational capital (Pumain and Torre, 2020), observing the coincidence of collaboration and competition in such regions, which is made possible through an intensive knowledge flow propelled through shared sets of norms and a vision of collaboration (Steinle et al., 2007). The milieu approach alerts that many of the alleged agglomeration effects are not occurring automatically, but depend on the local actor's specific interaction.

Finally, and referring to the industrial district theory and the *filière* approach (Porter, 1998b, p. 789), Porter developed his cluster theory, summarised in the 'diamond of competitive advantage'. Like the previous models, it is not derived from conceptual thoughts, but inductively emerged out of an empirical analysis. Porter was not originally aiming at understanding regional agglomerations, but joined a committee installed by President Reagan targeted at understanding competitive advantage, that is, a firm's ability to compete in world markets.

Eventually, large tables of internationally competitive industries were compiled for a set of nations. A multitude of case studies provided detailed data, which were then aggregated in the diamond model, summarising that the regional coincidence of trend-anticipating customers, competing producers, leading suppliers and supporting industries was typically found to stand at the core of competitive industries. Porter concludes: 'For companies, a central message ... is that many of a company's competitive advantages lie outside the firm and are rooted in locations and industry clusters' (Porter, 1998b, p. xiii). Considering purchasing's responsibility to manage the external embedding of a firm in its supply network, which Porter's research identified as a main source of competitive advantage, it is therefore worth describing the cluster theory in some detail, elaborating the empirical findings supporting it, and then discussing recommendations for supply management, as well as research targets for purchasing science.

CLUSTER THEORY: MUTUALLY SUPPORTIVE LOCALISED VALUE CHAINS

'Clusters are geographic concentrations of interconnected companies and institutions in a particular field' (Porter, 1998a, p. 78). Following cluster theory, such agglomerations are more innovative, more productive and generate more start-ups than dispersed businesses, eventually ensuring competitive advantages understood as 'the set of institutions, policies, and factors that determine the level of productivity of a country' (Lacal-Arántegui, 2019, p. 623). The most visible outcome of competitive advantage of a country is that its firms are successfully exporting their products.

Even though it was criticised (Moon et al., 1995; Waverman, 1995), Porter's 'diamond of competitive advantage' constitutes the most influential theory on clusters. It represents the results of a four-year study based on the statistical evaluation of input–output analyses and more than 100 case studies. Following Porter's theory, though, agglomeration per se is not the source of the sketched benefits. An agglomeration could only be called a cluster, with the associated benefits, if a set of conditions are met: trend-anticipating customers must be present in a region ('demand conditions' in Porter's terminology), and competing producers of a good ('firm strategy, structure and rivalry'), which rely on local suppliers ('related and supporting industries') and are embedded in a net of supportive institutions such as in education and associations ('factor conditions'). Following cluster theory, firm success depends to a large extent on the environment it is embedded in and, from a managerial perspective, on how the firm can make use of this environment (Figure 27.1).

The diamond of competitive advantage – the core of Porter's cluster theory – describes the four key elements of a company's national and often even regional environment (roughly defined as an area within one hour's reach) that influence its potential for international competitiveness (Porter, 1990).

First, trend-anticipating customers (demand conditions, the nature of home demand) are particularly reflected by the amount and the sophistication of local demand. Highly sophisticated customers who anticipate international trends influence quality standards, the number of innovations, as well as the technological progress of a nation. Sophisticated and demanding customers, a large volume and – in industrial markets – the availability of a substantial number of independent buyers are favourable conditions for international success, provided the nature of home demand is anticipating or at least similar to the international trend. Producers facing

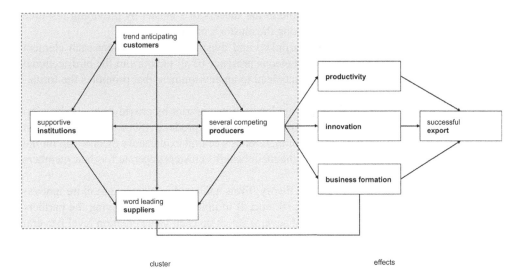

Figure 27.1   *Cluster theory*

tough requirements from their most important customers are forced to improve their products. The availability of several different customers allows them to innovate and try out different solutions; as opposed to national champions which only ask for one particular solution.

Second, several competing producers (firm strategy, structure and rivalry: the nature of domestic rivalry) play a significant role in Porter's diamond model. A strong base of local competitors is one of the major stimulations for innovation and upgrading; national champions are characteristic of the opposite. The pivotal importance of domestic rivalry is explained as forcing firms to permanently update their products and services; that is, to innovate and to cut costs, increasing productivity. In the absence of local competition, complacency can occur, eventually leading to a lack of international competitiveness. In the presence of local rivals, on the other hand, managers have limited excuses for poor performance and cannot blame macroeconomic disadvantages compared to their competitors from other countries.

Third, competitive suppliers (related and supporting industries) can be used to share ideas, knowledge and skills. The presence of local suppliers and firms that use similar or identical technologies to produce a complementary good enables cost-effective collaborations, for example in new product development projects. The diamond distinguishes between direct suppliers and related industries, which may share second-tier suppliers, even though delivering into a different final product. Again, the availability of competing domestic suppliers which are internationally competitive is of importance, as opposed to 'captive' suppliers serving just a local champion. A purely domestic supply industry is not conductive to the upgrading of a cluster.

Fourth, educational and professional infrastructure (factor conditions) can be divided into: 'basic factors', such as natural resources and an unskilled labour force; and 'advanced factors', such as highly qualified manpower, for example engineers and academics. A nation's competitive advantage strongly relies on the existence and maintenance of the advanced factors which are unique to a cluster and consequently hard to imitate by other actors not rooted in the same system. The advanced factors, in particular educational institutions and professional associations and institutes, play an important role in the success of a cluster by providing resource input and establishing the social glue among the cluster's members.

These four determinants form an interlinked and dynamic complex where each element is affected by the other three. The simultaneous presence of all factors and the bi-directional interdependencies between all determinants lead to an environment that promotes the formation of clusters.

The cluster theory differs from simple agglomeration empirics by providing an explanation for competitive success, being a product of innovation and productivity in a dynamic context with repeated new business formation. Competition is a central explanatory mechanism for the innovation, productivity and start-ups as the main benefits clusters generate for their members (DeWitt et al., 2006; Leontiades, 1990).

First, innovation: according to cluster theory, firms anchored in clusters are more innovative because of: (1) having the incentive (the need) to innovate; and (2) having the partners required to achieve that. The existence of several actors on each value creation level (several customers, several competitors, several alternative suppliers) propels competition – that is, the need to upgrade own performance – and offers alternatives. In a cluster, both are present: customers demanding different solutions, as well as suppliers offering alternative solutions. The process of discovery, as a trial-and-error process, can take place. Trend-anticipating customers, at the same time, ensure that the direction of innovation is profitable and that sunk costs are avoided. The proximity of the actors allows partners to be identified and competitors' progress to be monitored, thus reinforcing the pressure to innovate, while at the same time providing information on solutions.

Second, productivity: competitive pressure, as in the case of innovation, also drives firms in clusters to be more productive, as both: (1) the need to increase productivity; and (2) the availability of resources to achieve that are present. The availability of a labour pool of skilled and specialized workforce allows productivity to be improved through higher specialisation. Likewise, the abundance of specialised suppliers makes it possible for clustered firms to externalise more work, concentrate on their core competencies, and thus achieve productivity benefits. Again, like in the case of the mechanism for innovation, better access to knowledge and thus knowledge exchange on best practices accelerates the collective learning process of the cluster firms.

Third, new business formation: in clusters, the 'knowledge is in the air', and also the knowledge on new business opportunities. Therefore, actors cannot expect to keep a business idea for themselves and after a long preparation surprise the world with a new firm. Instead: (1) they feel under pressure to quickly execute the idea, so that nobody else comes first; and (2) in a cluster, several customers are present, some of which might want to try out the new product. At the same time, the intensive knowledge flow allows potential founders to identify the business needs of the incumbent firms. New ventures, then, provide a growth dynamic for clusters, allowing them to expand continuously.

Importantly, cluster theory also explains what clusters are not. A single large firm establishing a supplier park in its neighbourhood statistically accounts as being a regional-sectoral agglomeration. However, in the absence of rivalry between several competing producers it does not fulfil the conditions to be termed a cluster. In such a case, few of the above described competitive mechanisms responsible for the upgrading of cluster companies would be effective. Note, finally, that in the Porterian view, clusters are confined to a region or appear on a national level.

Providing a theoretical explanation for a testable phenomenon, the cluster theory is a strong theory according to Wacker's (2008) model of theory building (reflecting definition domain, relationship and prediction as necessary elements of a good theory): all elements of the theory can clearly be defined and contribute to a model of relationships, which make testable predictions. However, a certain – also operational – limitation of Porter's cluster theory may rest in its limited parsimony. All constitutive elements are supposed to be interlinked and to influence each other, which creates substantial complexity and might obscure cause and effect; this makes it difficult to measure causality (Leontiades, 1990). A multitude of possible connections and different emphases explain the predicted benefits of clusters, which ultimately present a highly competitive environment (Martínez-Marín et al., 2020). In terms of domain generalisability, cluster theory claims a high level of abstraction and wide application, with only a few limitations, such as the need for a divisible production process and a transportable good, as otherwise the productivity enhancing labour division cannot take place, nor would it make any contribution to competitiveness, if the good is not exportable (Steinle and Schiele, 2002).

A critique of Porter's cluster theory stems from the level of analysis: 'While Porter understands that only firms make decisions and therefore only firms can sustain competitive advantage, he chose industries as his basic unit of analysis' (Leontiades, 1990, p. 31). The logical consequence of this view is that the managerial discretion is seen as reduced; as opposed to, for instance, the view of the classical 'great men' theory of entrepreneurial leadership. In fact, the implication is that firms might be successful if embedded in a competitive environment, that is, in a strong industry in their home country, and management's action is to recognise the quality of the local environment and anchor the company there, while not being completely free in its decisions (Schiele et al., 2014). In Porter's words, leaders 'do not work separately from the determinants … of the diamond of competitive advantage, [but] It is often leadership that determines which of the firms from a favorably situated nation will succeed or fail' (Porter, 1998b, p. 129). Other criticisms of Porter's theory refer to its scope, neglecting the social component of clusters, relying predominantly on the competition argument (Steinle et al., 2007). Porter can be interpreted in a way to assume that when the requested actors are present in a region in sufficient number, beneficial agglomeration effects always take place. However, relying on the milieu approach, it has been argued that, as a fifth element, a supportive and unifying social system explicitly needs to be present in a region, as a necessary condition.

With a view on firms' environmental embedding emphasised by cluster theory and related agglomeration theories, it becomes clear that purchasing and supply chain design requires special attention from a cluster theory perspective.

CLUSTER AND PURCHASING: BENEFITING FROM WORLD-LEADING DOMESTIC SUPPLIERS

Manzini and Di Serio (2017) conducted a literature review on clusters, strategy and operations. They concluded that the overwhelming part of the literature relying on cluster theory is in economic geography, mainly targeted at understanding and improving regional agglomerations. There is some literature applying the cluster theory in strategic management, as part of the larger set of 'ecosystem theory', which tries to explain competitive advantage by a firm's position in its business ecosystem (Jarzabkowski and Wilson, 2006). Less than 5 per cent of the articles Manzini and Di Serio identify use cluster theory in operations management, that is, not only purchasing, but also production and logistics. While their analysis can be criticised on the grounds of relying on a preselected set of journals, using keyword research a similar picture emerges. Likewise, Tolossa et al.'s (2013) review only identified 17 papers dealing with clusters and the supply chain in the broader sense. Most of these papers report cases, such as the Amish furniture cluster's supply chain (DeWitt et al., 2006), New England cotton industry (Bozarth et al., 2007), United States petrochemicals (Patti, 2006), German rail and steel (Schiele, 2008), Chinese textiles (Ikram et al., 2018) and machine building (Xue et al., 2012).

In his original book, though, Porter derives some key propositions for purchasing managers, which can be summarised as follows: 'Having a competitive domestic supplier industry is far preferable to relying even on well-qualified foreign suppliers' (Porter, 1998b, p. 103). This translates into a clear request: 'Source from the most advanced and international home-based suppliers' (Porter, 1998b, p. 586). Five arguments are derived from cluster theory to substantiate the claim to prefer cluster sourcing: (1) in clusters more intensive buyer–supplier working relationships can develop; (2) suppliers serve as transmitters of information from one producer to the next, thus strengthening all; (3) due to physical and cultural proximity, the information flow is superior; (4) transaction costs are lower; and (5) privileged innovation access for customers close to the core research facilities of the supplier, that is, being a preferred customer.

Considering purchasing, the cluster theory has different implications for firms located somewhere in the periphery and for those located in the industry centre, the cluster: 'The implications of the cluster approach for global sourcing are twofold. Firstly, knowledge of the existence and location of particular clusters can support the search process in sourcing. Secondly, the availability of suppliers in a local cluster may be a reason not to globalise sourcing' (Steinle and Schiele, 2008, p. 5). More specifically, cluster theory generates theses on location decisions, supplier innovation, risk assessment, clustering and corporate strategy.

Location

Given the superior power of innovation of clustered suppliers, their superior productivity and more advanced level of specialization due to new business formation, cluster theory recommends a firm to give preference to local suppliers, in order to achieve competitive advantage compared to firms which are forced to rely on a global supply base, in case they do not have a domestic cluster. The larger the local supplier base a company can rely on is, the higher the share of cluster sourcing in the total purchasing volume is recommended (Jin, 2004). Local sourcing reduces lead time and inventory, and may increase quality (Patti, 2006). Local pooling may become possible, even bundling demands with other (small) firms in the cluster (Landinez Lamadrid et al., 2018). Cluster theory also supports the idea of reshoring, understood as 'a return of manufacturing activities in national factories owned by the company or carried out from suppliers present in the same country of the parent company' (Talamo and Sabatino, 2018, p. 383). However, cluster theory links this recommendation to the condition of the presence of a home cluster. Hence, the theory is more sophisticated than a simple 'source locally' call, for in the absence of local competition the cluster benefits are not expected to materialise. In the same way, and relying on the assumption of an endemic benefit of proximity, cluster theory does not recommend to restrict local suppliers and prevent them from selling globally, in order to gain advantages of scale. Porter forwards two propositions (Porter, 1998b):

Proposition 1: Having a competitive domestic supplier industry is far preferable to relying even on well-qualified foreign suppliers.

Proposition 2: Source from the most advanced and international home-based suppliers.

Innovation

Given the superior innovation power of cluster suppliers, due to their drive to innovate induced for competitive reasons, and the benefit of these suppliers, in their turn, relying on a multitude of supportive organisations and subsuppliers, from cluster theory it is derived that in particular for innovation and new product development with early supplier integration, cluster suppliers are recommended. Depending on the competitive strategy of the firm, in the case of a differentiation strategy, a cluster-oriented reconfiguration of the supply chain is recommended. The same is true for niche firms relying on customised components (Grandinetti and Tabacco, 2015). Clustered supply chains may have particular strengths in incremental rather than radical innovation (Dankbaar, 2007). Companies that are not embedded in the leading-edge cluster can be disconnected from the development of innovations. In conclusion, cluster theory proposes:

Proposition 3: In case a company pursues an innovation strategy, the reliance on cluster suppliers is suggested.

Risk and Resilience

Shorter supply chains present a lower probability of physical interruptions. At the same time, cluster companies have been found to be more profitable due to higher productivity and innovation, and hence show less vulnerability to crises. In addition, a cluster containing several actors on each value chain level can better reconfigure itself should one actor face problems. As opposed to this, a captive supply chain, similar to an integrated company, has more difficulty in reconfiguring if one chain member falls out. Hence, and in addition to the classical suggestions put forward by Porter, the hypothesis emerges that clusters are more resilient and firms anchored in clusters are better risks (Talamo and Sabatino, 2018). On the other hand, if an entire cluster is affected by the occurrence of a risk, a firm solely relying on suppliers from it may suffer problems (Lee, 2014). At the same time, proximity reduces uncertainty, which stands at the core of risk (Lorentz et al., 2018). Based on cluster theory it can therefore be assumed that:

Proposition 4: 'Cluster-suppliers are less risky and more resilient than a globally dispersed supply chain.'

Strategy

Following the traditional strategic management view, the purchasing function could hardly contribute to establishing competitive advantage of a firm, because the assumption was of perfect factor mobility. Every competitor would rely on the same suppliers in the same way, especially in paying the same price and getting the same product (Ramsay, 2001). If buying goods and components did not allow differentiatiation, it would be hard to argue for achieving strategic benefits through purchasing. Cluster theory, however, contests this assumption: 'a resource-based view of regional clusters posits an additional category of resources that are internal to a region, but external to any single firm. In other words, there are spatial asymmetries in the presence of, and the market for, certain critical resources' (Enright, 1998, p. 321). Following the cluster theory's assumption that clusters are regionally interconnected mutually dependent social systems, buyers external to the cluster face more difficulties in accessing cluster-based suppliers and in achieving preferred customer status compared to local buyers (Steinle and Schiele, 2008). Clusters have been interpreted as clubs, that is, exclusive groups whose members internally act differently than they do towards external partners. As such, buyers are requested to analyse each important supplier to establish whether the firm is: (1) hosted in the same cluster; (2) hosted in a foreign cluster; or (3) in an industry which does not show any clustering phenomenon. In case (1) the cluster-based supplier is more eligible for exclusive bonding; that is, the buying firm gaining privileged access to the supplier's resources and – provided these resources are valuable and rare – gaining competitive advantage. The conclusion of this line of reasoning is that firms which have a so-called inverted supply structure (Figure 27.2) – that is, predominantly relying on international suppliers for their strategic goods, to which they have less privileged access – may strategically be vulnerable and uncompetitive, if confronted with competitors which can rely on a strong supply network in their local cluster (Steinle and Schiele, 2008).

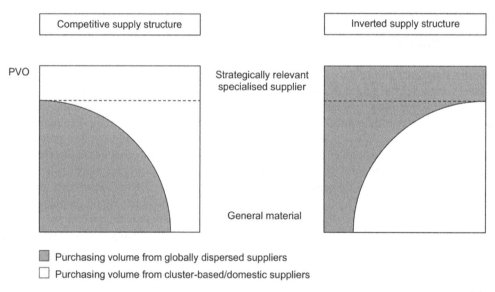

Figure 27.2   *'Inverse' supply structure as an indicator of firm failure due to an uncompetitive supply network*

If cluster embedded suppliers offer distinctive advantages in terms of innovation, productivity and specialisation through start-up formation, then it follows that a firm with a strong background as preferred customer in a cluster has competitive advantages compared to a firm without its own domestic network, being a second-class customer with dispersed suppliers. The more specialised the supplier is, the more likely it is that it can contribute to establishing competitive advantage. Hence, following the cluster theory, successful firms rely on special-ised suppliers from their home cluster. On the other hand, if the best suppliers are clustered in another country, which is home to major competitors of a producer, then cluster theory would predict such a producer to be strategically vulnerable. The expectation would be that such a peripheral firm would be a candidate to leave the market in a cyclical downturn. Eventually, in a free market economy, cluster theory expects regions to specialize and industries to con-centrate at particular locations. Highlighting the importance of supplier connections, cluster theory attributes a strategic role to purchasing, by shaping the supply structure, which may be a strategic asset or a strategic liability. Cluster theory, then, conceptually paves the way to enable purchasing to join strategic management and positions:

Proposition 5: 'Employing cluster suppliers allows purchasing to strategically contribute to increasing the competitive advantage of the firm by being these suppliers' preferred customer.'

CONCLUSION: CLUSTER THEORY AS LINK BETWEEN PURCHASING SCIENCE AND STRATEGIC MANAGEMENT

The cluster theory is the most-used theory explaining the phenomenon of regional-sectoral industry agglomeration, which was found to lead to higher productivity, innovation and enterprise formation in such centres. At its core is the assumption of a regional coincidence of a self-reinforcing system of several competing producers, their suppliers, supportive institutions and trend-anticipating customers leading to the competitive advantage of firms, which enables them to export more. Given the importance that the cluster theory attributes to the proximate environment of a firm, it is of great relevance for purchasing, providing both practical guidance and conceptual backing.

Cluster theory supports the locational choice as part of sourcing strategies, arguing in favour of local suppliers. Cluster theory also contributes to the emergent topic of innovation from and with suppliers, emphasising the benefits of regional collaboration. From a risk management perspective, cluster suppliers are expected to be better risks than remote suppliers. All these conclusions from cluster theory are empirically testable. However, less than 5 per cent of all papers on cluster research refer to supply chain issues, leaving a large and rewarding space for purchasing and supply scholars to contribute. In addition, research so far is mainly conceptual and case study based, while large empirical quantitative studies are still needed to test the generalisability of cluster relevance (Tolossa et al., 2013). Of particular importance is that contingency factors may be relevant, since not all industries show clustering effects (Steinle and Schiele, 2002).

At the same time, cluster theory feeds the avenue of research and practice establishing purchasing as a strategically relevant function in the firm. In fact, cluster theory argues that a firm's strategy might not be discussed purely based on internal strength and assumed market requirements, but as a basic precondition, which fundamentally requires the strategical analysis of the proximate (meso) environment, in particular the supply network that a firm can access or build. Cluster theory provides a specification for the relational view of the firm (Dyer and Singh, 1998). Here, future research at the intersection of purchasing and strategic management has the potential to provide great benefit for both fields.

Last not least, it is worth recalling that most literature on clusters actually focuses on the public side in particular – despite the many cases of failed state-induced cluster policies (Hospers et al., 2009) – exploring how governments can foster the formation of regional clusters (Manzini and Di Serio, 2017). Here, public procurement could serve as an instrument (Elola et al., 2017). The feasibility of this, however, depends to some extent on the respective legislation. However, the increasing interest in public procurement for innovation could benefit from employing the cluster concept, embedding the stimulation of innovation through demand-side measures in a wider context, namely cluster development.

REFERENCES

Barbieri, E., Di Tommaso, M.R., Pollio, C., and Rubini, L. (2019). Industrial policy in China: the planned growth of industrial towns in the Cantonese region. *Cambridge Journal of Regions, Economy and Society, 12*(3), 401–422. doi:10.1093/cjres/rsz012.

Becattini, G. (1979). Dal 'settore' industriale al 'distretto' industriale. Alcune considerazioni sull'unità di indagine dell'economia industriale. *Rivista di economia e politica industriale, 4*(1), 7–21.

Becattini, G. (1991). Italian industrial districts: problems and perspectives. *International Studies of Management and Organisation, 21*(1), 83–90.

Bozarth, C., Blackhurst, J., and Handfield, R.B. (2007). Following the thread: industry cluster theory, the New England cotton textile industry, and implications for future supply chain research. *Production and Operations Management, 16*(1), 154–157.

Dankbaar, B. (2007). Global sourcing and innovation: the consequences of losing both organizational and geographical proximity. *European Planning Studies, 15*(2), 271–288.

DeWitt, T., Giunipero, L.C., and Melton, H.L. (2006). Clusters and supply chain management: the Amish experience. *International Journal of Physical Distribution and Logistics Management, 36*(4), 289–308. doi:10.1108/09600030610672055

Dyer, J.H., and Singh, H. (1998). The relational view: cooperative strategy and sources of interorganizational competitive advantage. *Academy of Management Review, 23*(4), 660–679.

Elola, A., Valdaliso, J.M., Franco, S., and López, S.M. (2017). Public policies and cluster life cycles: insights from the Basque Country experience. *European Planning Studies, 25*(3), 539–556. doi:10.1080/09654313.2016.1248375

Enright, M.J. (1998). Regional clusters and firm strategy. In A.D. Chandler (ed.), *The Dynamic Firm* (pp. 315–342). Oxford: Oxford University Press.

Grandinetti, R., and Tabacco, R. (2015). A return to spatial proximity: combining global suppliers with local subcontractors. *International Journal of Globalisation and Small Business, 7*(2), 139–161. doi:10.1504/IJGSB.2015.071189.

Hospers, G.J., Desrochers, P., and Sautet, F. (2009). The next Silicon Valley? On the relationship between geographical clustering and public policy. *International Entrepreneurship and Management Journal, 5*(3), 285–299. doi:10.1007/s11365-008-0080-5.

Ikram, A., Su, Q., Fiaz, M., and Rehman, R.U. (2018). Cluster strategy and supply chain management: the road to competitiveness for emerging economies. *Benchmarking, 25*(5), 1302–1318. doi:10.1108/BIJ-06-2015-0059.

Jarzabkowski, P., and Wilson, D.C. (2006). Actionable strategy knowledge: a practical perspective. *European Management Journal, 24*(5), 348–367.

Jin, B. (2004). Achieving an optimal global versus domestic sourcing balance under demand uncertainty. *International Journal of Operations and Production Management, 24*(12), 1292–1305. doi:10.1108/01443570410569056.

Krugman, P. (1991). *Geography and Trade*. Leuven and London: Leuven University Press.

Lacal-Arántegui, R. (2019). Globalization in the wind energy industry: contribution and economic impact of European companies. *Renewable Energy, 134*, 612–628. doi:10.1016/j.renene.2018.10.087.

Landinez Lamadrid, D., Ramirez Rios, D., Neira Rodado, D., Crespo, F., Ramirez, L., and Jimenez Manjarres, W. (2018). Cooperation in clusters: a study case in the furniture industry in Colombia. In

K. Saeed and W. Homenda (eds), *Computer Information Systems and Industrial Management*. CISIM 2018. Lecture Notes in Computer Science, vol 11127. Springer, Cham, 181–192. doi:10.1007/978-3-319-99954-8_16.

Lee, S.H. (2014). Determining the optimal number of cluster suppliers under supply failure risks. *International Journal of Supply Chain Management, 3*(3), 16–23.

Leontiades, M. (1990). The competitive advantage of nations – reviewed by Milton Leontiades. *Planning Review, 18*(5), 30–32.

Lorentz, H., Kumar, M., and Srai, J.S. (2018). Managing distance in international purchasing and supply: a systematic review of literature from the resource-based view perspective. *International Business Review, 27*(2), 339–354.

Malsot, J. (1980). Filières et effets de domination dans le système productif. *Annales des Mines, 186*(1), 29–40.

Manzini, R.B., and Di Serio, L.C. (2017). Current thinking on cluster theory and its translation in economic geography and strategic and operations management: is a reconciliation possible? *Competitiveness Review, 27*(4), 366–389. doi:10.1108/CR-11-2015-0088.

Marshall, A. (1961 [1890]). *Principles of Economics. An Introductory Volume* (9th Variorum edn). London: Macmillan.

Martínez-Marín, S., Puello-Pereira, N., and Ovallos-Gazabon, D. (2020). Cluster competitiveness modeling: an approach with systems dynamics. *Social Sciences, 9*(2). doi:10.3390/socsci9020012.

Moon, H.C., Rugman, A.M., and Verbeke, A. (1995). The generalized double diamond approach to international competitivness. *Research in Global Strategic Management, 5*, 97–114.

Patti, A.L. (2006). Economic clusters and the supply chain: a case study. *Supply Chain Management: An International Journal, 11*(3), 266–270.

Porter, M.E. (1990). *The Competitive Advantage of Nations*. London: Macmillan.

Porter, M.E. (1998a). Clusters and the new economics of competition. *Harvard Business Review, 12*, 77–90.

Porter, M.E. (1998b). *The Competitive Advantage of Nations* (8th edn). London: Macmillan.

Pumain, D., and Torre, A. (2020). Regional science: economy and geography in France and French-speaking countries. *Papers in Regional Science, 99*(2), 293–313. doi:10.1111/pirs.12513.

Ramsay, J. (2001). Purchasing's strategic irrelevance. *European Journal of Purchasing and Supply Management, 7*(4), 257–263. doi:10.1016/S0969-7012(01)00007-7.

Schiele, H. (2003). *Der Standort-Faktor: wie Unternehmen durch regionale Cluster ihre Produktivität und Innovationskraft steigern* (1. Aufl. ed.). Weinheim: Wiley-VCH.

Schiele, H. (2008). Location, location: the geography of industry clusters. *Journal of Business Strategy, 29*(3), 29–36.

Schiele, H., Harms, R., and Banerjee, S. (2014). A national competitiveness-based portfolio approach for international strategic management: illustrated with the case of the TATA industries. *European Journal of International Management, 8*(1), 106–125.

Steinle, C., and Schiele, H. (2002). When do industries cluster? A proposal on how to assess an industry's propensity to concentrate at a single region or nation. *Research Policy, 31*, 849–858.

Steinle, C., and Schiele, H. (2008). Limits to global sourcing? Strategic consequences of dependency on international suppliers: cluster theory, resource-based view and case studies. *Journal of Purchasing and Supply Management, 14*(1), 3–14.

Steinle, C., Schiele, H., and Mietzner, K. (2007). Merging a firm-centred and a regional policy perspective for the assessment of regional clusters: concept and application of a 'dual' approach to a medical technology cluster. *European Planning Studies, 15*(2), 235–251.

Talamo, G., and Sabatino, M. (2018). Reshoring in Italy: a recent analysis. *Contemporary Economics, 12*(4 Special Issue), 381–398. doi:10.5709/ce.1897-9254.284.

Tolossa, N.J., Beshah, B., Kitaw, D., Mangano, G., and De Marco, A. (2013). A review on the integration of supply chain management and industrial cluster. *International Journal of Marketing Studies, 5*(6), 164–174.

Tunisini, A., Bocconcelli, R., and Pagano, A. (2011). Is local sourcing out of fashion in the globalization era? Evidence from Italian mechanical industry. *Industrial Marketing Management, 40*(6), 1012–1023. doi:10.1016/j.indmarman.2011.06.011.

Wacker, J.G. (2008). A conceptual understanding of requirements for theory-building research: guidelines for scientific theory building. *Journal of Supply Chain Management, 44*(3), 5–15.

Waverman, L. (1995). A critical analysis of Porter's framework on the competitive advantage of nations. *Research in Global Strategic Management, 5*, 67–95.

Xue, X., Wei, Z., and Liu, Z. (2012). The impact of service system on the implementation of cluster supply chain. *Service Oriented Computing and Applications, 6*(3), 215–230.

28. Organizational learning theory and its application to purchasing management and supply chain management research

Arash Azadegan and Javad Feizabadi

INTRODUCTION

The quest for organizational intelligence is the essence of strategic management (Levinthal and March, 1993). Intelligent organizations can be developed either by calculated rationality[1] (Porter, 1980) or by organizational learning (Gavetti and Levinthal, 2000; Senge, 1990). In the first path, the linkages between organizational actions and performance outcomes is guided by existing routines and past experience while in the second path the intelligence is developed by the mental model/belief and landscape cognitive representation of the linkages between actions and performance outcomes. Practitioners and academics alike observed a persistent performance heterogeneity across firms and industries that could be attributed, among other sources of performance heterogeneity, to the firm's experiential learning capabiliy (Balasubramanian and Lieberman, 2010; Senge, 1990). Organizational learning is a key resource for organizational adaptation, success and survival (Fiol and Lyles, 1985; Levitt and March, 1988; March, 1991). It could contribute to developing organizational intelligence by either replacing the long-term planning, or supplementing and augmenting it (Levinthal and March, 1993). The learning capability of an organizations influences its average performance as well as diminishing performance variability (that is, improving performance reliability[2]) (Levinthal and March, 1993; March, 1991). It's argued that learning effect on average performane is always instrumental to attain competitive advantage by the organization, however, its effect on performance variability may not be perceived desirable especially in contexts of intense competition (Levinthal and March, 1993). In the turbulent performance landscape, the firms may need to engage in long-jumps and quantum changes (O'Reilly and Tushman, 2004).

It is well established that how well organizations learn depends on how well they are able to enact a learning environment (that is, scan their business environment and obtain information, then develop an interpretation and convert information and data into knowledge, and repeatedly apply it to their operations) (Daft and Weick, 1984). The engagement of the learners with the environment is influenced by a variety of environmental stimuli perceived by organizations, and subsequently crafting the adaptive strategic schemas to respond to the perceived stimuli. The response, in turn, hinges on the way an organization perceives the dynamics of its operating environment. Organizations relying on their cognitive resources could view their environment either linear and additive, or multiplicative, interdependent and positive feedback events (Boisot and McKelvey, 2011). Depending on these organizational ontological assumptions, they can form their interpretation of the events; develop adaptive schemes and actions; and learn from them differently.

Regrettably, the notion of organizational learning is often used interchangeably with knowledge generation, where data, information and past experiences are combined to develop an understanding of the relationship between external events. Clearly, organizational learning is related to data, information and experience. However, we clarify what may be missing from the literature: that organizational learning theory (OLT) is distinct from organizational knowledge management. Our stance is that knowledge management is concerned more with the consequences of learning. OLT focuses on the process alongside the outcomes based on which learning takes place. Indeed, without organizational learning, it can be difficult to effectively develop knowledge (be it in tacit or explicit forms) to conform and adjust to changes in one's environment.

Organizational learning is the process by which data (that is, dots) are linked up (that is, information) and transformed into knowledge (that is, different patterns linking up the dots) and expertise (Huber, 1991; March, 1991). This distinction is how we differentiate between OLT (and associated conceptual subsets) from a knowledge-based view (KBV), arguably an extension of the resource-based view (RBV) (Barney, 2001; Grant, 2002). Whereas the KBV focuses on how the outcome of the learning process (knowledge) can be beneficial to the firm, OLT dives more deeply into how individuals in the organizations could engage with the environment, develop their mental models, interact with others and generate organizational experience. Indeed, organizational learning theories move beyond mere information and data as inputs, to consider factors such as intuition, mental schemas, ideas, perspectives, patterns and even organizational culture into the process (Crossan and Berdrow, 2003; Skilton and Dooley, 2010).

Let us be clear in differentiating key terms used to differentiate the two theories. While data refers to a set of objective facts associated with events, information refers to a value-added form of data that augments the meaning of the data through contextualization, categorization, calculation, correction or condensation (Argote, 2013). Again, the emphasis on OLT is in the interaction between organizational task experience and the context that creates one's learning. This learning process, at the individual, group, department, or organizational level, in turn, could be described by two mechanisms of declarative and explicit knowledge; as well as procedural and implicit knowledge reflected in routines and skills respectively (Levitt and March, 1988). Eventually, such learning can become embedded within the organization as memories in repositories, routines, processes, practices, tools and norms (Moorman and Miner, 1997). The activities that organizations adopt over time, and deciphering and reinforcing the interactions among the activities to develop core elements in organizations and their evolution over time, are influenced by organizational learning (Senge, 1990; Siggelkow, 2002).

There are other key distinctions between OLT and the KBV. The first is in the fact that OLT differentiates the forms of processes by which learning is done (which eventually leads to knowledge). Literature in OLT also offers a distinction between context and content of learning (Fiol and Lyles, 1985), and the notion of culmination (learning curve) and diminishing in learning (forgetting) (Blackler et al., 1999; Rao and Argote, 2006). Perhaps more importantly, since OLT is rooted in behavioural theories and concepts of experimentation (Cyert and March, 1963) it offers practical explanations that are useful to the learning process. These characteristics make OLT a feasible choice of theory in explaining organizational phenomena and behaviour, particularly in complicated contexts such as that related to purchasing and supply management. As we will further explain, organizational learning can offer a strong theoretical framework for the supply chain management (SCM) and purchasing and supply management (PSM) fields, that are looking for the 'how' and 'why' relating to which organizations perform better.

In this chapter we provide an overview of past works in organizational learning, and how it relates to supply chain and supply management. We decipher streams of literature in OLT by reviewing the conceptual subsets, and offer insights on how they can be of use to SCM/PSM researchers. Finally, the chapter offers a literature review on how OLT has been applied to date in supply chain management, and where potential shortcomings in the use of theory are visible. Throughout the chapter, our aim is to offer explanations that can be of benefit to researchers who plan to leverage the theory and associated conceptual frameworks in explaining SCM/PSM.

DEFINING ORGANIZATIONAL LEARNING: WHAT THE LITERATURE SUGGESTS

As is common among many overarching concepts in management, there is no general consensus on how organizational learning is defined. Some define organizational learning as a change in cognition and behaviour (Cyert and March, 1963; Levitt and March, 1988). This body of research considers changes in knowledge reflected in organizational routines and practices as reflective of the change in organizational knowledge. In a separate behavioural approach, and relying on learning curve research, researchers consider changes in the characteristics of organizational performance such as quality, speed, efficiency and productivity as a result of organizational knowledge change (Dutton and Thomas, 1984). Others believe that organizational learning should be defined as the change in the organization's knowledge which results from the interaction between task performance experience and its contextual factors (Argote, 2013). Interestingly, Huber (1991) takes an opposing stance, arguing that organizations can acquire knowledge without changing their behaviour. In fact, Huber goes as far as refuting the idea that organizational learning is an actual change in the organization. Huber does offer some notable insights. Taking a behavioural approach in organizational learning, it must be noted that many variables may need to be controlled by measuring changes in the behaviour to isolate the effect of the change in knowledge. For example, change in behaviour might be because of introducing a new policy by the organization, and not a result of experience.

If effectively managed, what organizations learn can become memories. These can be embedded in organizational processes, member cognition, tasks and standard operating procedures. The learning embedded in transactive memory systems (that is, member–tool, member–task and task–tool networks) and routines (that is, task–task networks) are codifiable and explicit. Such memories are more readily transferable and less depreciable than the memory embedded in member and member–member network (that is, social network) repositories, which is tacit and difficult to articulate (Argote and Miron-Spektor, 2011). The memory repositories can be organizational members (for example, member–tool, member–task, member–task–tool) and are considered as sources of competitive advantage (Argote, 2013).

OVERVIEW AND CONCEPTUAL SUBSETS TO ORGANIZATIONAL LEARNING THEORY

The origins of OLT date back to the 1930s and the research work of a philosopher who highlighted the importance of 'experiential' and 'progressive' learning (Dewey, 1986). Focusing on the operating context of an educational organization, Dewey (1986) argued that effective learning must have two virtues: continuity and interactions. Continuity conveys the idea that when an experience is created for someone in an organization, it has to be stored and carried on into the future. Interaction refers to the interdependencies between past experience and the current situation.

Since then, a number of conceptual subsets have considered the potential explanation that learning at the organizational level can enhance performance. As we will note below, there are at least four streams of research in OLT, and one particular extension worthy of consideration. Interestingly, the original ideas of Dewey, as related to progressive and experiential learning, have gained much less attention in the literature; the revival of seminal and original works could be an area that is useful for research. In this case, considering the notions of continuity and interaction can be a viable source of explanation for research in SCM/PSM. For instance, related to interaction, of note is the work of Gavetti and Levinthal (2000), who analyzed the interplay between two mechanisms of wisdom generation: in backward-looking, the wisdom is enacted based on the positive or negative reinforcement of linkage between action and outcomes while in forward-looking the linkage between choices and outcomes is based on the actor's belief and mental model of the performance landscape. Reviewing their work can be of particular value to young researchers, because the authors offer interesting insights into the benefits of the interaction between experiential and cognitive perspectives of learning on adaptation to the environment. In other words, whereas experiential learning relates to what has been stored in organizational memory, cognitive learning is based on managerial ability to conceptualize mental schemas or frameworks. Combined, this particular view can be of benefit to researchers in the field of SCM/PSM. In the next section, we offer further explanation of different conceptual subsets related to OLT. Table 28.1 provides an overview of the key definitions related to OLT, the conceptual subsets and assumptions of the theory.

Conceptual Subset 1: The Adaptation and Routines Stream

A key conceptual subset of organizational learning relates to the work of Cyert and March (1963). In their book, these authors define organizational learning as the adaptive behaviour of organizations over time. Huber (1991) argues that organizations can acquire knowledge without any changes in their behaviour, and defines organizational learning as a change in the range of potential behaviour. Other works in this stream have added more nuance and detail to the concept of adaptation and routine (Levinthal and March, 1993; Levitt and March, 1988). Three dimensions of adaptation are highlighted across these works: (1) adaptation of goals; (2) adaptation of attention rules; and (3) adaptation in search rules. An explanation of each of the three dimensions seems merited at this point.

As related to the adaptation of goals, Cyert and March (1963) consider organizations as open systems that interact with their endogenous and exogenous environment. Contingent upon the magnitude of change in their environment, they may need to adapt their goals. This goal adaptation exercise is affected by three factors: the organization's past goals, the organ-

Table 28.1   *Key elements, unit of analysis and assumptions of organizational learning theory streams*

Element	Explanation	References
Unit of analysis	Change in: behaviours, routines, knowledge and experience	Argote (2013); Crossan et al. (1999); Cyert and March (1963); Huber (1991)
Level of analysis	Individual, group, organizational, interorganizational, triads, networks	Argote (2013); Crossan et al. (1999); Dyer and Hatch (2004); Hult et al. (2003); Jones and Macpherson (2006)
Key variables/definitions *The adaptation and routines stream*		
Adaptive behaviour, range and potential behaviour	Adaptation of goals, adaptation of attention rules, and adaptation in search rules of organizations over time	Cyert and March (1963); Huber (1991)
Routine	An overarching notion including the rules, forms, procedures, conventions, strategies and technologies	Levitt and March (1988); Nelson and Winter (1982)
Explorative and exploitative learning		
Experiential (that is, exploitative) and innovative (that is, explorative) learning	Exploitative learning considers data information and knowledge in the short run, from the immediate surroundings and in limited areas of inquiry and more shallow considerations; explorative learning considers data, information and knowledge in the long run, from a broader set of fields, by combining information from distant knowledge sources and by using more in-depth assessment and evaluation	Argyris and Schön (1978); Dodgson (1991); Fiol and Lyles (1985); March (1991)
Learning curves and forgetting		
Experiential knowledge generation	The knowledge creation is the result of interaction between organizational task experience and its endogenous and exogenous contextual factors	Argote (2013)
Learning curve	The lowering of costs of production on a per-unit basis based on the experience and volume of production	Argote (2013); Barndt (1985); Epple et al. (1991)
Learning forgetting	In classic learning curve research, it is assumed that the knowledge an organization acquires is going to persist indefinitely; however, what is learned can diminish and depreciate over time based on factors such as employee turnover, product/process technology change, and simply change in organizational strategy	Blackler et al. (1999); Rao and Argote (2006)

Element	Explanation	References
Organizational learning as a process: the '4-I' framework		
Intuiting	The pre-conscious recognition of the pattern and/or possibilities inherent in a personal stream of experience	Crossan et al. (1999); Jones and Macpherson (2006)
Interpreting	The explaining of an insight or idea, to oneself or others; this process goes from pre-verbal to verbal and requires the development of language	Crossan et al. (1999); Jones and Macpherson (2006)
Integrating	The process of developing shared understandings and coordinated action through mutual adjustment	Crossan et al. (1999); Jones and Macpherson (2006)
Institutionalizing	The process of embedding individual and group learning into the organization's systems, structures, procedures and strategy	Crossan et al. (1999); Jones and Macpherson (2006)
Ambidextrous learning		
Ambidexterity	Instead of optimizing the trade-offs between experiential and innovative learnings, ambidexterity rests upon the idea of complementarity and the synergic effect of exploitative and explorative learnings	O'Reilly and Tushman, (2004); Tushman and O'Reilly (1996)
Assumptions about human and organization nature		
Bounded rationality	The organizations are shaped by environmental forces mediated by human minds; the human mind mediation refers to the learning process in which humans acquire increasing insights and continuous restructuring of the problem as the problems arise, and they reflect themselves in organizations' structural elements; the human mind's information processing capacity is bounded	Simon (1991)
Uncertainty avoidance	Organizations avoid uncertainty by: (1) solving pressing problems rather than developing long-term strategy; (2) avoiding the requirements that they anticipate future reactions of other parts of their environment by arranging a negotiated environment	Cyert and March (1963)
Problemistic search	Organizations conduct the search that is stimulated by a problem (usually a rather specific one) and are directed towards finding a solution to that problem; problemistic search can be distinguished from random curiosity and search for understanding	Cyert and March (1963)

ization's past performance, and the performance of other comparable organizations (Cyert and March, 1963). Adaptation in attention rules requires the organization to determine which part of the changing (endogenous and exogenous) environment needs the most attention. Adaptation in attention is particularly important for managers because of the limited extent to which they can concentrate on a particular issue or organizational problem. As such, adaptation in attention allows for prioritizing time and cognitive effort of managers, which in turn can help with organizational adaptation. Lastly, the adaptation in search rules refers to the organization's ability to find solutions as a new problem arises (Cyert and March, 1963). The term 'routines' is an overarching notion including the rules, forms, procedures, conventions, strategies and technologies around which an organization is established and through which the organization is run (Levitt and March, 1988; Nelson and Winter, 1982).

Organizational routines are changes in response to direct organizational experience through two mechanisms: trial-and-error experimentation, and organizational search (Levitt and March, 1988). Certain disturbances might affect the process of changing the routines based on organizational experiences, such as false interpretation of events and the impediment of the realization of personal insights (March and Olsen, 1975).

Given the heavy involvement of SCM/PSM managers in all aspects of organizational decision making, considering the adaptation model can be a useful approach to explaining research in this field (Feizabadi et al., 2019). For instance, purchasing managers often have to decide on whether to extend contracts to a mediocre supplier or search for a new supplier. This particular responsibility can be explained by the adaptation model. Another example of responsibility by purchasing managers is in clearly defining user requirements, item specifications and contract details across a number of purchased items and services. The adaptation and routines model helps to explain how allocating the right level of attention on purchases with more value potential or risk concerns may be the reason behind the behaviour of many purchasing managers.

Conceptual Subset 2: Explorative and Exploitative Learning

Some of the most important and highly cited works on OLT go back to the late 1970s and the seminal work of Argyris and Schön (1978) on behavioural psychology and organizational development. From this perspective, organizational learning is based on its response to changes in its external environment, be they incremental or radical. In general, this body of research explicates two learning processes related to the change magnitude in the organizations: (1) adaptive learning, which explains the learning process in reaction to endogenous and exogenous changes; and (2) proactive learning, which is the learning process that is based on a more purposeful approach rather than a reactive approach.

Specific to this conceptual subset, a number of researchers have used distinctive terms describing these two organizational learning processes. For instance, March (1991) distinguishes between explorative and exploitative learning. Fiol and Lyles (1985) label them as lower-level versus higher-level learning, and Dodgson (1991) refers to them as tactical versus strategic learning. Argote (2013) labels them as experiential and innovative learning. No matter the labelling, the two forms of learning are essentially differentiated based on the scope and extent to which they consider data, information and knowledge to be combined. Exploitative learning offers more immediate results in the short run. It considers data, information and knowledge from the immediate surroundings and in limited areas of inquiry and more shallow considerations. Instead, explorative learning considers data, information and knowledge from a broader set of fields, by combining information from distant knowledge sources and by using more in-depth assessment and evaluation. More recent studies, such as that of Garvin (2003), differentiate learning into groups that are somewhat different from exploration and exploitation. Garvin considers organizational learning to consist of intelligence, experience and experimentation.

The above differentiations are particularly important to research in SCM/PSM. During the past three decades, the role of purchasing and supply managers has expanded beyond what are considered routine, daily or tactical activities. Instead, supply managers are considered as trusted advisors to executives on strategic matters related to how well the supply chain is managed. In short, both strategic and tactical learning is within the purview of what professionals in SCM/PSM are responsible for. Leveraging the distinction can therefore offer interesting explanations on decision making and planning in organizations.

Conceptual Subset 3: Learning Curves and Forgetting

'Learning curve' is the common label placed on the rate of learning by an organization as related to routine and repetitive tasks. Learning curves explain the lowering of costs of production on a per-unit basis based on the experience and volume of production. The learning curve is at times referred to by other labels, including progress curve (at the level of firm), learning curve, experience curve (at the level of industry) (Barndt, 1985), or simply learning by doing (Epple et al., 1991) (at the level of the individual employee).

What is important to consider in studying learning curves is that there is a diminishing marginal return for production efficiency. When graphically represented, learning curves often show a concave pattern, such that after a certain level, there is only limited (to no) additional learning. Recognizing the optimal level of learning can help purchasing managers in better estimating the cost of production with suppliers without short-changing suppliers.

Another important consideration about learning curves is related to the (limited) extent to which an organization's learning can be measured and assessed by learning curves. Learning curves vary by individuals, by the type of processes in place, and by the incentives and motivation set forth at the individual and organizational level. Yet a third important consideration – the rate at which an organization generates knowledge from experience – varies across functions, organizations in the same industry, as well as across organizations in different industries. The literature has pointed to several areas with varying learning rates, generally categorized into three groups: (1) increased proficiency of individuals, including direct production workers, managers and engineers; (2) improvement in organizational technology; and (3) advances in its structure, routines and methods of coordination. Clearly, the larger the proportion of labour involved in the production, the more important the learning curve becomes (Monczka et al., 2015). There are key distinctions between continuous and discrete production processes in terms of learning rates.

Researchers in SCM/PSM should be cognizant of the limitations to which their assessment of learning curves is generalizable. For instance, in order to effectively assess the extent of organizational learning, many variables should be controlled, such as the technology type or economies of scale. Also, there would still be variation across firms in the same industry in terms of the learning rate. Analytical models that elaborate further on the pattern and the variation of learning pace across firms (Fang, 2012; Huberman, 2001) could be of use here.

Here, a discussion on 'forgetting' seems necessary. In classic learning curve research, it is assumed that the knowledge an organization acquires will persist indefinitely over time. However, what is learned can diminish and depreciate over time, based on factors such as employee turnover, product/process technology change, and simply change in organizational strategy. Depending on where organizational learning is stored (organizational routines, memory systems and standard operating procedures) the rate of depreciation in learning can vary. It follows that forgetting to account for 'forgetting' in productivity analysis and planning can lead to mistakes and miscalculations (Blackler et al., 1999; Rao and Argote, 2006).

The organizational learning curve and the diminishing effect of learning (forgetting) can offer interesting perspectives on the study of SCM/PSM phenomena, particularly as related to longitudinal studies. Let us take an example from a prevalent and recent global concern from 2020. The sudden onset of the COVID-19 pandemic caught many organizations by surprise. Many had to implement new and different operating procedures internally and in working with their suppliers. How well the lessons learned from 2020 are maintained to prevent future disruptions in managing supply management relationships is one example of the potential application of research related to the learning curve and forgetting.

Conceptual Subset 4: Organizational Learning as a Process – The 4-I Framework

A fourth and less applied perspective on organizational learning is based on the work of Crossan and colleagues (Crossan and Berdrow, 2003; Crossan et al., 1999). These authors view organizational learning as a process of combining thought and action that is formed by organizational mechanisms. Crossan and colleagues differentiate the process based on four psychological and sociological micro-processes that occur at the individual, group and organizational levels (Jones and Macpherson, 2006): that is, intuition, interpretation, integration and institutionalization. The framework is based on the earlier works of Daft and Weick (1984), who consider organizations as interpretation systems that engage in modes of interpretation, including enacting, discovering, undirected viewing and conditioned viewing. How the modes are used is contingent on management's beliefs about the environment and organizational intrusiveness.

More specific to the Crossan model, intuiting occurs at the individual level; intuiting is the 'pre-conscious recognition of the pattern and/or possibilities inherent in a personal stream of experience' (Jones and Macpherson, 2006). Intuiting is likely to influence the individual's behaviour, but is only relevant to organizational learning if the individual interacts with others and attempts to share the patterns and possibilities recognized. At this level (group), what the individual has considered is interpreted across a number of organizational members, most likely at the group level. Interpreting involves further elaborating and detailing an idea, pattern recognition or perception. Crossan and colleagues suggest that the interpretation process offers means to take the more tacit insight into a more explicit form. The process may involve evolving the thoughts from preverbal to verbal, and at times even developing the necessary language to explain it. The third step in the process is integrating. In this stage, a shared understanding of the concept is developed, and at times coordinated action to adjust firm behaviour or understanding is developed. More dialogue, along with a larger group of individuals and groups and coordinated actions across them, is formed at this stage. Finally, in the institutionalization stage, actions or thoughts become more routinized across the organization. Tasks, actions and mechanisms to ensure repeated compliance with the new way of thinking are implemented.

Institutionalizing allows for individual and group learning to be embedded across systems and procedures of the organization.

The key distinction of the Crosson 4-I model from other conceptual subsets is in explaining how the notion of organizational learning is intertwined between individual learning (where intuiting occurs), group learning (where interpreting and integrating occur), and organization (where institutionalizing occurs). This perspective is notably distinct from other perspectives. Arguably, the Crosson 4-I model offers a thorough perspective on the process of organizations (and interorganizational learning); its validation can be difficult.

Complementing the idea of iterating across different organizational levels, Argote (2013) illustrates organizational learning as a recurring cycle in which experience is converted to knowledge. She also notes how environmental context (competitors, customers, institutions, volatility, complexity and munificence) affects the experiences that an organization acquires, and indirectly influences the learning process and outcomes. Organizational context (for example, culture, technology, structure, identity, memory, goals, incentives, absorptive capacity) being influenced by environmental context affects the learning process and outcomes more directly.

Nevertheless, for researchers in SCM/PSM, the process-based perspective can be quite useful. For instance, the 4-I model can help to explain how an individual purchasing manager intuitively considers the external environment and the organization's effective response to it. Through interpretation and integration, such perspectives can be validated or refuted in the department or across functions. Beyond the functional level and on to the executive level, decision-makers can then consider how to institutionalize original (and modified) intuition and interpretations to develop a viable response. Regrettably, this type of explanation and extension of the 4-I model is absent in SCM. Barring a few notable exceptions (Bell et al., 2014; Esper et al., 2010; Manuj et al., 2014), most studies merely mention Crosson et al. and set aside its rich applicability to the field. A final note on the 4-I model is that it can be easily extended to consider the notion of institutionalizing to the supply chain and beyond the four walls of the organization itself. Topics such as technology transfer, supplier development and supplier innovation, and shared product development, can benefit from the use of the 4-I framework to explain the process by which interorganizational learning occurs.

Conceptual Extension: Ambidextrous Learning

Beyond the conceptual subsets mentioned above, it may be important to highlight an extension to organizational learning that has gained notable leverage in the literature. Ambidextrous organizations have been the topic of much research and have offered a novel way of explaining firm behaviour that can offer a competitive advantage. From an OLT perspective, ambidexterity consists of the combination of explorative and exploitative learning, which was elaborated on in an earlier section (O'Reilly and Tushman, 2004; Tushman and O'Reilly, 1996). The origin of the notion dates back to Duncan (1976), who argues that exploitation (that is, discipline) is associated with alignment, and exploration (that is, creativity and innovation) with adaptation. March (1991, p. 102) clarifies the meaning of the two terms: 'exploration refers to activities related to experimentation, discover, search, and variation whereas exploitation represents activities associated with refinement, efficiency, selection, implementation'.

A short explanation of the underlying reasons for the effectiveness of ambidexterity seems necessary at this point. Levinthal and March (1993) identify three significant limitations of learning organizations. These include the tendency to overlook distant times, distant places, and organizational failures. An effective learning organization should be able to overcome the learning myopia. By considering the effect of one's decisions on the future, on distant places (distant departments, distant business partners, suppliers, and so on) one can minimize the effects of imperfect decisions. Organizations also fail to learn from their mistakes. Arguably, the lack of a feedback loop in reconsidering what did not work in the past leads to making the same mistakes in the future.

The learning myopia engenders an imbalance between exploitative and exploratory activities in the organizations to shape organizational actions. The argument behind ambidexterity is that organizational learning and, by extension, organizational performance is improved by minimizing the trade-offs between exploration and exploitation (Azadegan and Dooley, 2010; Azadegan et al., 2008). The essence of March's (1991) argument is the tendency of organizations, as adaptive systems, to emphasize exploitation because of the certain and predictable returns that lead from them, which in turn help in improving performance reliability. Arguably, improved reliability (or the reduction of performance variability) is not the same as raising performance.

March (1991) argues that organizational learning could enhance both performance reliability and average. However, performance mean is more helpful than reliability in improving an organization's competitive advantage because trained and experienced personnel actually perform at higher levels (Levinthal and March, 1993). Moreover, trained and experienced personnel create conditions in which average knowledge and mutual learning being enhanced over the long run is a desirable outcome. The effects are also important in terms of the organization's adaptability to its operating environment.

Higher emphasis on exploitation and accumulating experience on existing routines, technologies, procedures would put the organization in a competency or success trap (Levitt and March, 1988). On the other hand, more concentration on exploration and generating completely new knowledge might put the existence and short-term survival of the firm into danger, and tip the organization into an endless search or failure trap (Levinthal and March, 1993; Raisch and Birkinshaw, 2008). A key dimension of useful organizational experience is in their novelty. While organizational experience and the learning created from them are more certain when there is a lower degree of novelty (that is, exploitation), the associated returns are tangible and more deterministic. However, as an organization embarks on experiences beyond its routine in developing radically new knowledge (that is, exploration), the expected return becomes temporally and spatially more uncertain (Levinthal and March, 1993).

It follows that finding a healthy balance between exploitation and exploration is necessary for the long-term survival and viability of the organization. Levinthal and March (1993) explain this in terms of learning myopia. Often exploitative activities are overemphasized by organizations because of the more immediate results. On the other hand, exploration takes time to show results and is often riskier. Balancing between exploitation and exploration often requires placing closer attention to exploration and adding efforts in this area.

A notable line of work on organizational learning is that offered by Peter Senge and his work related to learning organizations (Senge, 2014). In the book *The Fifth Discipline*, Senge explains learning organizations as those 'where people continually expand their capacity to create the results they truly desire, where new and expansive patterns of thinking are nurtured, where collective aspiration is set free, and where people are continually learning how to learn together'. The definition applies to both explorative learning and exploitative learning.

Whether the learning is focused on the short run, and with immediate feedback and less risk (that is, exploitation), or is focused on the long run, without much immediate feedback and higher risks, the ability of a group of individuals to learn how to learn together can be a competitive advantage. Senge goes on to explain the components that entail a learning organization. These include systems thinking, personal mastery, mental models, shared vision and team learning. A full explanation of the components of the fifth discipline is outside the scope of this chapter, but the reader is encouraged to review and apply the combination of March's (1991) concepts with that of *The Fifth Discipline.*

However, balancing between the two can be quite challenging, since organizations tend to stick with proven experiences that yield more apparent returns in the short term, and certainty, as compared to engaging in explorative experience in which their returns are long-term, uncertain and slower to come to fruition. Since then, studies on ambidexterity and ambidextrous organizations have moved to consider the concept in interorganizational settings such as network clusters (Ferrary, 2011), sustainability (Du et al., 2013), process and project management (Leybourne and Sainter, 2012; Rialti et al., 2018), public utilities (Gieske et al., 2020) and other contexts. The trade-off between exploitative and explorative learning in organization science is described as managing the tension between creativity and discipline.

Specific to operations and supply management research, the work of Fisher (1997) on conceptualizing and linking ambidexterity to the field is worthy of note. Fisher (1997) considers two categories of products with two configurations of the supply chain. In line with the ambidexterity concept, an efficient supply chain resonates with exploitation, and a responsive supply chain resembles exploration orientation. Although Fisher (1997) focused on the fit, alignment, and congruence of the two types of products with two supply chain configurations, the work is an intriguing point for supply chain scholars to reflect on the supply chain set of activities, bypassing the duality and simultaneously embodying a high extent of efficiency and flexibility. While Fisher focused on the dichotomy across types of learning, recent research is looking into having the two supply chain configurations simultaneously, in line with the notion of ambidexterity (Aslam et al., 2018; Ojha et al., 2018b).

SCM/PSM researchers interested in pursuing ambidexterity as a theoretical explanation for their studies need to be cognizant of different levels of learning and, thus, levels of balance in learning. Stated otherwise, ambidexterity can occur at the individual, group, department, organization or supply chain level. At each level, routines and learning behaviours can create imbalances. More importantly, levels of learning can affect one another. For instance, an organization that tends to recruit individuals with an exploratory style of learning in all of its functions and departments may find it difficult to create ambidexterity at the firm level. On the other hand, an organization that tends to focus just on exploratory learning as a corporate strategy may find it difficult to effectively utilize individual or group learning skills that are focused on exploration. Indeed, the interaction between individual and organization has implications for managing the trade-offs between exploration and exploitation. Beyond the organization, the interaction between the organization and its business partners (that is, suppliers and customers) can also influence its ability to be ambidextrous. This offers challenges, but also opportunities, for researchers in SCM/PSM. For instance, studying how an exploitative focus on supply management fits with an explorative organizational learning style could be a very interesting topic of research. Within procurement, whether and how ambidexterity at the department level is beneficial can also be a viable area of research.

Table 28.2 Literature on organizational learning in supply chain and supply management

Authors	Year	Application of organizational learning and key findings	Methodology
West and Burnes	2000	Offers challenges and benefits of applying organizational learning through case studies in the automotive industry.	Conceptual
Hult et al.	2000	Organizational learning has a positive effect on information processing in the purchasing system, and cycle time of the purchasing process.	Survey-based
Hult et al.	2000	Organizational learning has a positive influence on customer orientation and relationship commitment.	Survey-based
Hult et al.	2003	Organizational learning has consequences on supply management, and firm's performance consequences.	Survey-based
Tucker	2004	Focuses on hospital operations and finds that learning from failures requires careful understanding of their nature.	Case study
Wu et al.	2006	Organizational learning has a positive effect on minimizing the bullwhip effect, but requires effective communication between parties.	Survey-based
Panayides	2007	Organizational learning has a positive effect on improved relations, logistics services and firm performance.	Survey-based
Azadegan et al.	2008	Different combination of learning styles, which leads to ambidexterity, enhances how well supplier innovativeness improves buyer performance.	Survey-based
Cha et al.	2008	Interorganizational learning in the form of knowledge transfer reduces the firm's internal operational costs.	Modeling
Richey et al.	2009	A strong organizational learning orientation exacerbates the inverse relationship between technological readiness and interfirm collaboration.	Survey-based
Azadegan and Dooley	2010	Offers empirical evidence of how combination of learning styles between supplier and buyer enhances performance.	Survey-based
Ferrary	2011	Exploitative learning is particularly effective in managing exploitative learning styles for acquisition and development firm strategies.	Case study
Yu et al.	2013	Leverages organizational learning theory to explain how internal integration is an enabler of external integration.	Survey-based
Yao et al.	2013	Offers explanation of how learning curves improves organizational learning in the context of collaborative planning, forecasting and replenishment (CPFR).	Survey-based
Bell et al.	2014	Applies arguments from organizational learning theory on how external technology integration is applicable to the development of logistics information systems.	Case study
Manuj et al.	2014	Applies organizational learning theory to third-party logistics providers by offering an explanation of the learning stages (Intuition, interpretation, integration, and institutionalization).	Case study
Bouncken et al.	2015	Offers explanations of why innovation timing and market entry strategy are ambiguous for small and medium-sized enterprises, based on interorganizational learning.	Survey-based
Dobrzykowski	2015	Offers explanation of how developing innovative products requires effective use of learning from external sources.	Survey-based
Cai et al.	2016	Extends how organizational learning can be viewed as outside-in and inside-out organizational learning, which affect supply chain collaborations differently.	Survey-based
Hall and Johnson-Hall	2017	Differentiates how internal and industry-wide product recalls, as forms of failure, provide the impetus for organizational learning.	Archival data
Ojha et al.	2018a	Learning orientations have a strong effect on how leadership style (transformational) affects the ability of the firm to reach ambidexterity.	Survey-based
Saenz et al.	2018	Interorganizational learning facilitates development of manufacturing flexibility and customer satisfaction.	Survey-based
Azadegan et al.	2019	Uses explanations from the double-loop learning concept to explain how near-miss events lead to stronger focus on procedural versus flexible response strategies.	Survey-based

APPLICATION OF OLT IN SCM/PSM

Table 28.2 offers a select review of literature that has leveraged OLT (and its various subsets of conceptual streams) in SCM/PSM. Several interesting observations can be made from these articles. To start, despite the fact that OLT has been used in other disciplines for decades, SCM/PSM researchers seem to have discovered the concept in the early 2000s. A second important observation is in the fact that researchers often use OLT and the concept of the knowledge-based view or knowledge management interchangeably (Bouncken et al., 2015; Richey and Autry, 2009; Yu et al., 2013). We noted above how the concepts are distinguishable and how the actual merits of OLT are in its ability to explain the process, rather than the mere outcome of learning.

Another, and perhaps more important observation, is that the OLT can be applied in varying extent to theorize and explain organizational and supply chain phenomena. In most cases, organizational learning is simply used as a platform (or even a mere placeholder) for how organizational experiences lead to improved performance. In these and similar articles, the depth and richness of the varied streams of theories in organizational learning seem to not be leveraged. In other words, in such cases, organizational learning is used to mention what is used to improve performance, rather than how performance is improved (Cai et al., 2016; Hult et al., 2000; Panayides, 2007; West and Burnes, 2000; Wu and Katok, 2006).

The concept of ambidexterity (or the combination of exploratory and exploitative learning styles) seems to have drawn many SCM/PSM researchers to use its explanations in more depth (Ferrary, 2011; Ojha et al., 2018a). This is beyond the scope of this chapter; nevertheless, we highlight some key literature on the topic. Of note is the relationship between ambidexterity, flexibility and adaptation, and performance (Krishnan and Pertheban, 2017; Kristal et al., 2010; Rojo et al., 2016; Tamayo-Torres et al., 2014). The stream of work by Azadegan (2011), Azadegan and Dooley (2010) and Azadegan et al. (2008) explains and empirically validates how buyers with differentiated learning styles (explorative or exploitative) may be better off with suppliers that have different learning styles, to effectively improve their performance. Interestingly, Hult et al. (2003) offer the notion of learning orientation and memory orientation as a means to enhance organizational learning as a strategic resource. While not related to any of the conceptual definitions or streams mentioned earlier, the attempt to differentiate organizational learning into different subsets in this study is commendable.

A few studies have looked at failures as a means for organizations to learn (Hall and Johnson-Hall, 2017). An interesting study which can be related to forgetting is that by Tucker (2004), who breaks down potential reasons for operational failures into lack of controls and inability of personnel to restore functions. The work of Azadegan et al. (2019) offers explanations of how 'near-misses' (failures that were prevented) offers a means to learn from and, in turn, change an organization's approach to future disruptions. As we noted earlier, a handful of studies have considered the 4-I theoretical concept (Manuj et al., 2014). Of note is the work of Bell et al. (2014), who not only leverage the notions of intuiting, interpreting, integrating and institutionalizing into their exploratory assessment of external technology integration, but also carefully infuse the concepts of 'feed-forward' and 'feedback' explanations offered by Crosson et al. in their study.

FINAL THOUGHTS

Despite the rich and diverse theoretical explanations offered by OLT and the several sub-set of streams in theory; a true and effective explanation of research phenomena using the theory seems scant in SCM/PSM literature. In this chapter we have provided potential means by which researchers can more effectively leverage this interesting and potent theory to explain their area of work.

The supply chain and purchasing management activities have become core elements in determining the firm's success across a wide range of industries, and warrant strategic management. The strategic management research attempts to address three problems (Levinthal and March, 1993): (1) the ignorance problem: uncertainty about the past and future, and the causal structure of relationships; (2) the conflict problem: multiple nested agents with several time preferences and a complex incentive structure; and (3) the ambiguity problem: lack of clarity, instability and endogeneity in agents' choices and their identity. Considering the shift in the competition basis from firms to the supply chains, the three strategy problems get amplified in developing intelligence in the supply chain domain. Long-term planning and designing a learning organization both have considerable limitations to address the strategy problems. In particular, organizational learning is restricted by myopic views of temporal, spatial, and overlooked failure. Other theories such as the RBV and its extension the KBV should also be considered as developing intelligence through learning from experience. Given the complex nature of strategic problems, both calculated rationality and organizational learning should be used as complementary approaches to influence organizational actions.

Considering the increasing attention in recent years on artificial intelligence and machine learning, they merit research attention. More research is required to shed light on how and under what conditions artificial intelligence and machine learning could impact upon organizational learning (Choudhury et al., 2020; Feizabadi, 2020). For example, Balasubramanian et al. (2020) developed a conceptual argument on the risks for organizational learning of substituting human learning by machine learning. They highlighted two potential risks – of reducing routine organizational diversity, and diminishing the knowledge richness – as possible issues related to replacing human learning by machine learning, which could mute or amplify the learning myopia. Machine learning might be beneficial when the system is loosely coupled, to facilitate the problem diagnostics, but it is not effective in a tightly coupled system with dense interdependencies to facilitate problem detection. Both problems – diagnosis facilitated in loosely coupled systems, and problem detection in tightly coupled systems – are recognized as essential elements of organizational learning (Levinthal and March, 1993). Future research needs to investigate theoretically and empirically the implications of artificial intelligence and machine learning adoptions by firms and supply chains for organizational learning and for developing intelligent organizations, which is the essence of strategic management.

Here we note that among the benefits of organizational learning is its applicability across several units and levels of analysis. Indeed, the unit of analysis for studies that are conceptualized based on OLT can be behaviours, routines, knowledge or experience. Similarly, since learning occurs at a multitude of levels, the use of OLT can be viable at the individual, group, organizational or interorganizational levels. This is in contrast to other theories commonly used in SCM/PSM, such as the resource-based view (RBV) and transaction cost economics (TCE), which are essentially limited to firm-level explanations (Azadegan et al., 2020). Analysis at different levels in organizational learning, and their interaction type, are often critical for developing research that is truly reflective of the real world, especially for SCM/PSM researchers. However, special care needs to be taken in designing and developing the research questions. For instance, whether group learning complements the organizational-level learning, acts as a substitute, or is independent, is important to consider in multi-level studies. Moreover, the properties of coordination, communication and influence occur at the group level in the organization. We hope that researchers in SCM/PSM ensure that they are properly differentiating their use of organizational learning from knowledge-based views, and consider the nuances associated with different types, contexts, combinations and processes to which organizational learning applies. As the supply chain complexity expands, the importance of the transfer of learning and integration across the firm's boundaries becomes more of a consideration.

We highlighted the key notable characteristics of OLT and its differences in use and applicability to other related intellectual areas such as supply chain management. Such features of OLT make it unique from an ontological and epistemological perspective and thus require careful consideration when used (Edmondson and McManus, 2007; Wacker, 1998). Given the focus on the process and the underlying reasons for learning, researchers should recognize that certain types of methodologies are better suited for the use of OLT. Whereas survey research is commonly applied for explaining OLT, perhaps there is a limit to the extent that this methodology can be used, simply because of its inability to determine causality (versus correlation). Instead, methodologies that can dive deeper into explaining the phenomenon (in-depth theory validation qualitative methods), or those that offer evidence of causality (vignette-based experiments or simulations) could be viable methodologies. By recognizing the richness offered by OLT and effectively reflecting it in their research design, SCM/PSM researchers can be assured that their work would be a stronger contribution to the field.

NOTES

1. Organizational intelligence is developed by specifying well-defined objectives, pursuing the objectives by collecting information to assess alternative course of actions in terms of their expected returns, and choosing the best future-oriented course of action. Calculated rationality is subject to several limitations: availability of information, organizational information processing capacities, and the assumption of preferences following axioms of rationality.
2. More trained and experienced individuals and groups in the organization enhance its average performance compared to organizations with lower learning levels; also, experienced and knowledgeable individuals and groups in the organization engender fewer surprises, hence improving performance reliability.

REFERENCES

Argote, L. (2013). Organizational learning: Creating, retaining and transferring knowledge. Springer, NY. doi:10.1007/978-1-4614-5251-5.
Argote, L., and Miron-Spektor, E. (2011). Organizational learning: From experience to knowledge. Organization Science, 22(5), 1123–1137.
Argyris, C., and Schön, D. A. (1978). Organizational learning: A theory of action perspective. Boston, MA: Addison-Wesley Publishing Company.
Aslam, H., Blome, C., Roscoe, S., and Azhar, T. M. (2018), Dynamic supply chain capabilities: How market sensing, supply chain agility and adaptability affect supply chain ambidexterity. International

Journal of Operations & Production Management, 38(12), pp. 2266–2285. https://doi.org/10.1108/IJOPM-09-2017-0555.

Azadegan, A. (2011). Benefiting from supplier operational innovativeness: the influence of supplier evaluations and absorptive capacity. Journal of Supply Chain Management, 47(2), 49–64.

Azadegan, A., and Dooley, K. J. (2010). Supplier innovativeness, organizational learning styles and manufacturer performance: An empirical assessment. Journal of Operations Management, 28(6), 488–505.

Azadegan, A., Dooley, K. J., Carter, P. L., and Carter, J. R. (2008). Supplier innovativeness and the role of interorganizational learning in enhancing manufacturer capabilities. Journal of Supply Chain Management, 44(4), 14–35.

Azadegan, A., Srinivasan, R., Blome, C., and Tajeddini, K. (2019). Learning from near-miss events: An organizational learning perspective on supply chain disruption response. International Journal of Production Economics, 216, 215–226.

Azadegan, A., Syed, T. A., Blome, C., and Tajeddini, K. (2020). Supply chain involvement in business continuity management: effects on reputational and operational damage containment from supply chain disruptions. Supply Chain Management: An International Journal, 25(6), 747–772.

Balasubramanian, N., and Lieberman, M. B. (2010). Industry learning environments and the heterogeneity of firm performance. Strategic Management Journal, 31(4), 390–412.

Balasubramanian, N., Ye, Y., and Xu, M. (2020). Substituting human decision-making with machine learning: Implications for organizational learning. Academy of Management Review.

Barndt, W. D. (1985). Experience curve. Harvard Business Review, 63(5), 218–218.

Barney, J. B. (2001). Resource-based theories of competitive advantage: A ten-year retrospective on the resource-based view. Journal of Management, 27(6), 643–650.

Bell, J. E., Bradley, R. V., Fugate, B. S., and Hazen, B. T. (2014). Logistics information system evaluation: Assessing external technology integration and supporting organizational learning. Journal of Business Logistics, 35(4), 338–358.

Blackler, F., Crump, N., and McDonald, S. (1999). Organizational learning and organizational forgetting: Lessons from a high technology company. Organizational Learning and the Learning Organization. Developments and Theory and Practice, M. Easterby-Smith, L. Araujo, and J. Burgoyne (eds). SAGE Publications, London, 194–216.

Boisot, M., and McKelvey, B. (2011). Connectivity, extremes, and adaptation: A power-law perspective of organizational effectiveness. Journal of Management Inquiry, 20(2) 119–133.

Bouncken, R. B., Pesch, R., and Kraus, S. (2015). SME innovativeness in buyer–seller alliances: effects of entry timing strategies and inter-organizational learning. Review of Managerial Science, 9(2), 361–384. doi:10.1007/s11846-014-0160-6.

Bouncken, R. B., Pesch, R., and Kraus, S. (2015). SME innovativeness in buyer–seller alliances: effects of entry timing strategies and inter-organizational learning. Review of Managerial Science, 9(2), 361–384.

Cai, Z., Huang, Q., Liu, H. F., and Liang, L. (2016). The moderating role of information technology capability in the relationship between supply chain collaboration and organizational responsiveness: Evidence from China. International Journal of Operations & Production Management, 36(10), 1247–1271. doi:10.1108/ijopm-08-2014-0406.

Cha, H. S., Pingry, D. E., and Thatcher, M. E. (2008). Managing the knowledge supply chain: An organizational learning model of information technology offshore outsourcing. Mis Quarterly, 32(2), 281–306.

Choudhury, P., Starr, E., and Agarwal, R. (2020). Machine learning and human capital complementarities: Experimental evidence on bias mitigation. Strategic Management Journal, 41(8), 1381–1411.

Crossan, M. M., and Berdrow, I. (2003). Organizational learning and strategic renewal. Strategic Management Journal, 24(11), 1087–1105.

Crossan, M. M., Lane, H. W., and White, R. E. (1999). An organizational learning framework: From intuition to institution. Academy of Management Review, 24(3), 522–537. doi:10.2307/259140.

Cyert, R. M., and March, J. G. (1963). A behavioral theory of the firm. Englewood Cliffs, NJ: Blackwell.

Daft, R. L., and Weick, K. E. (1984). Toward a model of organizations as interpretation systems. Academy of Management Review, 9(2), 284–295.

Dewey, J. (1986). Experience and education. Paper presented at The Educational Forum.

Dobrzykowski, D. D., Leuschner, R., Hong, P. C., and Roh, J. J. (2015). Examining absorptive capacity in supply chains: Linking responsive strategy and firm performance. Journal of Supply Chain Management, 51(4), 3–28. doi:10.1111/jscm.12085.

Dodgson, M. (1991). Technology learning, technology strategy and competitive pressures. British Journal of Management, 2(3), 133–149.

Du, W. Y., Pan, S. L., and Zuo, M. Y. (2013). How to balance sustainability and profitability in technology organizations: An ambidextrous perspective. IEEE Transactions on Engineering Management, 60(2), 366–385. doi:10.1109/tem.2012.2206113.

Duncan, R. B. (1976). The ambidextrous organization: Designing dual structures for innovation. The Management of Organization, 1(1), 167–188.

Dutton, J. M., and Thomas, A. (1984). Treating progress functions as a managerial opportunity. Academy of Management Review, 9(2), 235–247. doi:10.2307/258437.

Dyer, J. H., and Hatch, N. W. (2004), Human capital and learning as a source of sustainable competitive advantage. Strategic Management Journal, 25: 1155–1178.

Edmondson, A. C., and McManus, S. E. (2007). Methodological fit in management field research. Academy of Management Review, 32(4), 1246–1264.

Epple, D., Argote, L., and Devadas, R. (1991). Organizational learning curves: A method for investigating intra-plant transfer of knowledge acquired through learning by doing. Organization Science, 2(1), 58–70. doi:10.1287/orsc.2.1.58.

Esper, T. L., Ellinger, A. E., Stank, T. P., Flint, D. J., and Moon, M. (2010). Demand and supply integration: A conceptual framework of value creation through knowledge management. Journal of the Academy of Marketing Science, 38(1), 5–18. doi:10.1007/s11747-009-0135-3.

Fang, C. (2012). Organizational learning as credit assignment: A model and two experiments. Organization Science, 23(6), 1717–1732. doi:10.1287/orsc.1110.0710.

Feizabadi, J. (2020). Machine learning demand forecasting and supply chain performance. International Journal of Logistics Research and Applications, 1–24. doi.org/10.1080/13675567.2020.1803246.

Feizabadi, J., Maloni, M., and Gligor, D. (2019). Benchmarking the triple-A supply chain: Orchestrating agility, adaptability, and alignment. Benchmarking – An International Journal, 26(1), 271–295. doi: 10.1108/bij-03-2018-0059.

Ferrary, M. (2011). Specialized organizations and ambidextrous clusters in the open innovation paradigm. European Management Journal, 29(3), 181–192. doi:10.1016/j.emj.2010.10.007.

Fiol, C. M., and Lyles, M. A. (1985). Organizational learning. Academy of Management Review, 10(4), 803–813.

Fisher, M. L. (1997). What is the right supply chain for your product? Harvard Business Review, 75, 105–117.

Garvin, D. A. (2003). Learning in action: A guide to putting the learning organization to work. Harvard Business Review Press. Boston, MA.

Gavetti, G., and Levinthal, D. (2000). Looking forward and looking backward: Cognitive and experiential search. Administrative Science Quarterly, 45(1), 113–137.

Gieske, H., Duijn, M., and van Buuren, A. (2020). Ambidextrous practices in public service organizations: innovation and optimization tensions in Dutch water authorities. Public Management Review, 22(3), 341–363. doi:10.1080/14719037.2019.1588354.

Grant, R. M. (2002). The knowledge-based view of the firm. The Strategic Management of Intellectual Capital and Organizational Knowledge, 17(2), 133–148.

Hall, D. C., and Johnson-Hall, T. D. (2017). Learning from conformance quality failures that triggered product recalls: The role of direct and indirect experience. Journal of Supply Chain Management, 53(4), 13–36.

Huber, G. P. (1991). Organizational learning: The contributing processes and the literatures. Organization Science, 2(1), 88–115

Huberman, B. A. (2001). The dynamics of organizational learning. Computational & Mathematical Organization Theory, 7(2), 145–153.

Hult, G. T. M., Ketchen, D. J., and Nichols, E. L. (2003). Organizational learning as a strategic resource in supply management. Journal of Operations Management, 21(5), 541–556. doi:10.1016/j.jom.2003.02.001.

Hult, G. T. M., Hurley, R. F., Giunipero, L. C., and Nichols, E. L. (2000). Organizational learning in global purchasing: A model and test of internal users and corporate buyers. Decision Sciences, 31(2), 293–325. doi:10.1111/j.1540-5915.2000.tb01625.x.

Hult, G. T. M., Hurley, R. F., Giunipero, L. C., and Nichols, E. L. J. (2000). Organizational learning in global purchasing: A model and test of internal users and corporate buyers. Decision Sciences, 31(2), 293–325.

Hult, G. T. M., Ketchen, D. J. J., and Nichols, E. L. J. (2003). Organizational learning as a strategic resource in supply management. Journal of Operations Management, 21(5), 541–556.

Hult, G. T. M., Nichols, E. L., Giunipero, L. C., and Hurley, R. F. (2000). Global organizational learning in the supply chain: A low versus high learning study. Journal of International Marketing, 8(3), 61–83. doi:10.1509/jimk.8.3.61.19628.

Jones, O., and Macpherson, A. (2006). Inter-organizational learning and strategic renewal in SMEs – Extending the 4I framework. Long Range Planning, 39(2), 155–175. doi:10.1016/j.lrp.2005.02.012.

Krishnan, S., and Pertheban, T. (2017). Enhancing supply chain ambidexterity by adapting resiliency. Journal of Logistics Management, 6(1), 1–10.

Kristal, M. M., Huang, X., and Roth, A. V. (2010). The effect of an ambidextrous supply chain strategy on combinative competitive capabilities and business performance. Journal of Operations Management, 28(5), 415–429.

Levinthal, D. A., and March, J. G. (1993). The myopia of learning. Strategic Management Journal, 14(S2), 95–112.

Levitt, B., and March, J. G. (1988). Organizational learning. Annual Review of Sociology, 14(1), 319–338.

Leybourne, S. A., and Sainter, P. (2012). Advancing project management: Authenticating the shift from process to 'nuanced' project-based management in the ambidextrous organization. Project Management Journal, 43(6), 5–15. doi:10.1002/pmj.21306.

Manuj, I., Omar, A., and Pohlen, T. L. (2014). Inter-organizational learning in supply chains: A focus on logistics service providers and their customers. Journal of Business Logistics, 35(2), 103–120. doi:10.1111/jbl.12044.

Manuj, I., Omar, A., and Pohlen, T. L. (2014). Inter-organizational learning in supply chains: A focus on logistics service providers and their customers. Journal of Business Logistics, 35(2), 103–120.

March, J. G. (1991). Exploration and exploitation in organizational learning. Organization Science, 2(1), 71–87.

March, J. G., and Olsen, J. P. (1975). Uncertainty of past – Organizational learning under ambiguity. European Journal of Political Research, 3(2), 147–171. doi:10.1111/j.1475-6765.1975.tb00521.x.

Monczka, R. M., Handfield, R. B., Giunipero, L. C., and Patterson, J. L. (2015). Purchasing and Supply Chain Management: Cengage Learning.

Moorman, C., and Miner, A. S. (1997). The impact of organizational memory on new product performance and creativity. Journal of Marketing Research, 34(1), 91–106.

Nelson, R. R., and Winter, S. G. (1982). The Schumpeterian tradeoff revisited. American Economic Review, 72(1), 114–132.

O'Reilly, C. A., and Tushman, M. L. (2004). The ambidextrous organization. Harvard Business Review, 82(4), 74–81.

Ojha, D., Acharya, C., and Cooper, D. (2018a). Transformational leadership and supply chain ambidexterity: Mediating role of supply chain organizational learning and moderating role of uncertainty. International Journal of Production Economics, 197, 215–231.

Ojha, D., Struckell, E., Acharya, C., and Patel, P. C. (2018b). Supply chain organizational learning, exploration, exploitation, and firm performance: A creation-dispersion perspective. International Journal of Production Economics, 204, 70–82. doi:10.1016/j.ijpe.2018.07.025.

Panayides, P. M. (2007). The impact of organizational learning on relationship orientation, logistics service effectiveness and performance. Industrial Marketing Management, 36(1), 68–80.

Porter, M. E. (1980). Industry structure and competitive strategy: Keys to profitability. Financial Analysts Journal, 36(4), 30–41.

Raisch, S., and Birkinshaw, J. (2008). Organizational ambidexterity: Antecedents, outcomes, and moderators. Journal of Management, 34(3), 375–409.

Rao, R. D., and Argote, L. (2006). Organizational learning and forgetting: The effects of turnover and structure. European Management Review, 3(2), 77–85. doi:10.1057/palgrave.emr.1500057.

Rialti, R., Marzi, G., Silic, M., and Ciappei, C. (2018). Ambidextrous organization and agility in big data era: The role of business process management systems. Business Process Management Journal, 24(5), 1091–1109. doi:10.1108/bpmj-07-2017-0210.

Richey, R. G., and Autry, C. W. (2009). Assessing interfirm collaboration/technology investment tradeoffs: The effects of technological readiness and organizational learning. International Journal of Logistics Management, 20(1), 30–56. doi:10.1108/09574090910954837.

Rojo, A., Llorens-Montes, J. and Perez-Arostegui, M. N. (2016), The impact of ambidexterity on supply chain flexibility fit. Supply Chain Management, 21(4), 433–452. https://doi.org/10.1108/SCM-08-2015-0328.

Saenz, M. J., Knoppen, D. and Tachizawa, E. M. (2018). Building manufacturing flexibility with strategic suppliers and contingent effect of product dynamism on customer satisfaction. Journal of Purchasing and Supply Management, 24(3), 238–246.

Senge, P. M. (1990). The art and practice of the learning organization. New York: Doubleday.

Senge, P., Ross, R., Kleiner, A., and Roberts, C. (2011). The fifth discipline fieldbook: Strategies and tools for building a learning organization. London: Nicholas Brealey Publishing.

Siggelkow, N. (2002). Evolution toward fit. Administrative Science Quarterly, 47(1), 125–159. doi:10.2307/3094893.

Simon, H. A. (1991). Bounded rationality and organizational learning. Organization Science, 2(1), 125–134.

Skilton, P. F., and Dooley, K. J. (2010). The effects of repeat collaboration on creative abrasion. Academy of Management Review, 35(1), 118–134.

Tamayo-Torres, J., Gutierrez-Gutierrez, L., and Ruiz-Moreno, A. (2014). The relationship between exploration and exploitation strategies, manufacturing flexibility and organizational learning: An empirical comparison between non-ISO and ISO certified firms. European Journal of Operational Research, 232(1), 72–86.

Tucker, A. L. (2004). The impact of operational failures on hospital nurses and their patients. Journal of Operations Management, 22(2), 151–169.

Tushman, M. L., and Oreilly, C. A. (1996). Ambidextrous organizations: Managing evolutionary and revolutionary change. California Management Review, 38(4), 8–29. doi:10.2307/41165852.

Wacker, J. G. (1998). A definition of theory: research guidelines for different theory-building research methods in operations management. Journal of Operations Management, 16(4), 361–385.

West, P. and Burnes, B. (2000). Applying organizational learning: Lessons from the automotive industry. International Journal of Operations and Production Management, 20(10), 1236–1252. https://doi.org/10.1108/01443570010343762.

Wu, D. Y., and Katok, E. (2006). Learning, communication, and the bullwhip effect. Journal of Operations Management, 24(6), 839–850.

Yao, Y., Kohli, R., Sherer, S. A., and Cederlund, J. (2013). Learning curves in collaborative planning, forecasting, and replenishment (CPFR) information systems: An empirical analysis from a mobile phone manufacturer. Journal of Operations Management, 31(6), 285–297. doi:10.1016/j.jom.2013.07.004.

Yu, W., Jacobs, M. A., Salisbury, W. D., and Enns, H. (2013). The effects of supply chain integration on customer satisfaction and financial performance: An organizational learning perspective. International Journal of Production Economics, 146(1), 346–358.

Yu, W. T., Jacobs, M. A., Salisbury, W. D., and Enns, H. (2013). The effects of supply chain integration on customer satisfaction and financial performance: An organizational learning perspective. International Journal of Production Economics, 146(1), 346–358. doi:10.1016/j.ijpe.2013.07.023.

29. Signalling theory

Christian von Deimling, Michael Eßig and Andreas H. Glas

INTRODUCTION

There is evidence that signalling theory is becoming increasingly popular in several management research areas (Bergh et al., 2014; Connelly et al., 2011a). Although the theory was initially developed in the labour market by Spence (1973, 2002), signalling is seen as a general phenomenon applicable in any market suffering information asymmetry (Morris, 1987, p. 47; Spence, 1973, p. 356). Therefore, studies citing signalling theory are available, for example, in the literature on strategy, corporate governance, mergers and acquisitions, entrepreneurship, quality management, marketing, investment and finance decisions, and human resources management (Connelly et al., 2011a; Taj, 2016). Signalling theory has also found its way into research on buying decisions, mostly related to a business-to-consumer context and often discussed from a marketing point of view (Etzion and Pe'er, 2014; Hossain et al., 2018; Kirmani and Rao, 2000; Rao et al., 1999; Wells et al., 2011).

Adoption of signalling theory for purchasing decisions in a business-to-business environment or in the broader supply chain context seems to follow a far slower pace (Bakshi et al., 2015; Cheng et al., 2020; Stump and Heide, 1996; Terlaak and King, 2006). Also, recent activities to provide a compendium of applied theories in supply chain management, and in purchasing and supply management, indicate that signalling theory, as compared to other theories, has not gained much attention (Chicksand et al., 2012; Defee et al., 2010; Halldórsson et al., 2015; Kembro et al., 2014; Shook et al., 2009; Spina et al., 2016; Touboulic and Walker, 2015; Walker et al., 2015; Wynstra et al., 2019). In their investigation of 2522 purchasing and supply management articles from a set of 18 high-impact management journals published in the period 1995–2014, signalling theory does not seem to play a significant role, while other theories in the area of information economics such as agency theory or game-theoretical approaches gained momentum (Wynstra et al., 2019).

This chapter proceeds in six further sections, following Wacker's suggestions for a more detailed description of a theory (Wacker, 1998). The first section is concerned with defining the scope of signalling theory and its key variables. The second section renders the conditions for when signalling theory can be effectively applied. The third section provides insights into the domain of signalling theory and deals with the question of where to apply signalling theory (in general terms). The fourth section covers the signalling theory predictions. The fifth section sheds light on how the theory has been used particularly in the field of purchasing and supply management. The sixth section deals with an outlook on future research opportunities (Wacker, 1998).

KEY VARIABLES AND DEFINITIONS

Deeply rooted in information economics, signalling theory addresses how parties in a potential transaction try to react to the asymmetrical information structure of markets (Rao et al., 2018). In essence, signalling theory diverts attention to a key challenge facing decision-makers, namely how they can use signals in situations that have incomplete and asymmetrically distributed information (Bergh et al., 2014). Information asymmetry describes a condition where one party in a relationship has more or better information than another (Bergh et al., 2019). In a decision-making situation, this information asymmetry (if not addressed) can lead to opportunistic behaviour, both before (*ex ante*) and after the decision to be made (*ex post*). Hence, involved parties are vulnerable to adverse selection (*ex ante*) and to moral hazard (*ex post*) (Bergh et al., 2019; Kirmani and Rao, 2000). In this context, signals are considered as informational cues sent out by the better-informed party to influence decisions by the less-informed party (Taj, 2016, p. 339). Signals are mainly considered to address adverse selection problems, *ex ante* to a decision (Kirmani and Rao, 2000, p. 67). A signal is considered as effective if it is costly, if it is difficult to imitate, if a particular asset or wealth is at risk, if it is credible, and if it can be confirmed after the contract has been signed (Bergh et al., 2014; Connelly et al., 2011a; Connelly et al., 2011b; Ippolito, 1990). As a result of sending out observable signals, senders and receivers can distinguish between – or separate – high- from low-quality actors (Bergh et al., 2014). Hence, signalling helps to influence *ex ante* resource allocation decisions on both sides (sender and receiver) (Spence, 1973, 1976). Hence, at the core, the dyadic relationship between the sender and the receiver serves as the unit of analysis in the signalling theory. In this dyadic relationship, particular attention is paid to the exchange of information and the decisions based on it. In order to separate high- from low-quality actors, it can be assumed that several of these dyadic exchange relationships exist (dyadic relationship between a high-quality sender and a receiver, and dyadic relationship between a low-quality sender and a receiver). Signalling theory then takes a look at the different dyadic relationships in their entirety so that a meaningful (investment) decision can be made between alternatives.

The incentive for the better-informed party to invest in sending signals is that one can credibly convey one's hidden qualities through the signal to the receiver (Connelly et al., 2011a; Rao et al., 1999; Riley, 2001; Spence, 1973, 2002). This allows the sender of the signal to stand out from its peers or competitors. The sender weighs whether and how much effort to invest in the signal by maximizing potential pay-offs (Kirmani and Rao, 2000; Spence, 1973, 2002). The incentive for the recipient of the signal (the less-informed party) is that the signal enables them to make informed decisions about hidden properties that would otherwise be difficult to evaluate from the recipient's point of view before signing the contract (Spence, 1973, 2002). The advantage for the receiver is that the signal helps to identify and select the most suitable option that has (most likely) the desired quality properties. Future confidence in the credibility of the signal increases if it can be confirmed after the contract has been concluded, and first-hand experience proves the existence of the hidden qualities (Spence, 1973, 2002). For the recipient, a credible signal can also pay off in terms of saving *ex ante* and *ex post* transaction costs (Kirmani and Rao, 2000). Spence argues that senders and receivers strive towards situations in which signalling equilibria are realized (Spence, 1973, 2002). These signalling equilibria are Pareto-optimal if there exists no other feasible solution for which an improvement for one party does not lead to a simultaneous degradation in one (or more) of the other parties (Bergh et al., 2014, p. 1337).

The essential predictive mechanism that drives the different explanations associated with signalling theory is the existence of a 'separating equilibrium' (Bergh et al., 2014, p. 1335), and that investing in the signal especially pays off for the party with high-quality attributes (also called 'sheepskin effect'). Against this background, signalling theory helps to stipulate answers to questions such as: (1) How much time, energy and money should be invested by the signalling entity into the signal? (2) How far can the receiving entity trust the signal to be credible? and (3) Under what circumstances will the signalling equilibrium break down? Signalling theory provides a unique, practical and empirically testable perspective on problems of social selection under conditions of imperfect information (Connelly et al., 2011a, p. 63). Signalling always requires active action on the market and thus planning, organization and control. Signal-theoretic approaches always consider pre-contractual signalling (and related decisions). The contribution of signalling theory is the prediction that higher-quality firms will choose signals which allow their superior quality to be revealed. In comparison, lower-quality firms will choose signals which attempt to hide their poor quality (Morris, 1987). It is claimed that the prediction of choices can at least be improved by adding together the predictions from other theories grounded in information economics, such as agency or transaction cost theory (Morris, 1987).

To illustrate the basic idea behind signalling theory in more detail, Spence shared a model ('the most simple one' that he could devise) that he developed from observations on the job market (Spence, 2002, p. 436). His original observations will be the departure point, as there is also some criticism that the central constructs of signalling theory got blurred over time (Connelly et al., 2011a, p. 39; Rao et al., 2018, p. 296). Following Spence, signalling theory is based on eight key constructs. It is assumed that (1) a signalling entity (or signaller) and (2) a receiving entity (or receiver) are exchanging (3) a signal to alleviate information asymmetry in a potential transaction. In more complex models, signals occur in conjunction with (4) indices, and hence form a set of signals and indices that are exchanged between signallers and receivers. Creating a signal is associated with (5) signalling costs that in conjunction with payment schedules determine payoff-structures for the signalling entity. Signals gain credibility if they can be confirmed after a certain decision has been taken concerning the transaction in question. This (6) signal confirmation is embedded (together with the afore-mentioned constructs) in (7) an informational feedback loop that is not run through once, but several times. The exchange of the signal between the signaller and the receiver results in (8) a variety of Pareto-optimal signalling equilibria. While the key constructs 'signaller', 'receiver' and 'signal' have received considerable attention so far (Connelly et al., 2011a; Taj, 2016) the other constructs often remain in the shadows. Over time, a ninth concept has been added, namely (9) 'signalling environment'. The key constructs and their definitions are briefly provided in Table 29.1.

As a starting point, Spence assumes that in most job markets, the employer is not sure of the productive capabilities and capacities of potential employees at the time they are hired (Spence, 1973, p. 356). Also, a confirmation of those productive capabilities and capacities will not necessarily become available right after hiring, as it often takes time for employees to learn and to get accustomed to the (new) job in question (Spence, 1973, p. 356). While the productive capabilities and capacities of job applicants remain mostly unknown to employers before hiring (and even remain unknown for a certain time after hiring), the potential employees are well aware of their own productive capabilities and capacities. Against this background, Spence concludes that for the employer, the hiring decision is one under uncer-

Table 29.1   *Key constructs of signalling theory*

Constructs	Explanation	References
(1) Signalling entity (or signaller)	*Original:* Signallers possess information concerning individuals, products/services or organizations, which can be transformed into signals delivered to receivers. As the signallers expect to benefit from reduced information asymmetry, they are willing to invest in signals to reveal less observable qualities.	(Cheng et al., 2020, p. 219; Spence, 2002, p. 436; Taoketao et al., 2018, p. 1040)
	Examples: Signallers as individuals (employees, recruiters, managers, individual entrepreneurs, individual leaders), Signallers as groups (specific groups of managers), Signallers as products, Signallers as firms (sellers, suppliers, young firms), Signallers as networks of firms (an alliance of multiple firms)	(Connelly et al., 2011a, pp. 47–51; Ozmel et al., 2012; Taj, 2016, p. 339)
	Discussion: Signallers might exhibit characteristics that in addition to the signals they send determine the perception and interpretation process on the receiver's side (for example, signallers honesty/dishonesty, signallers credibility, signallers behaviour).	(Cheng et al., 2020; Connelly et al., 2011a; Gomulya and Mishina, 2017)
(2) Receiving entity (or receiver)	*Original:* The receivers lack information about the individual, product or organization in question and would like to receive this information in order to make an informed decision. The receiver holds beliefs on the hidden qualities of the signaller and interprets the incoming signals.	(Connelly et al., 2011a; Spence, 1973, 2002; Taj, 2016)
	Examples: Receivers as individuals (stakeholders, consumers, investors, employers, acquirers), Receivers as groups (specific groups of managers, stakeholder, investors, the board of directors). Receivers as firms (buying firms, competitors). Receivers as networks of firms (an alliance of multiple firms)	(Connelly et al., 2011a, pp. 47–51; Ozmel et al., 2012)
	Discussion: The characteristics exhibited by the receiver might (at least in part) determine the effectiveness of signalling. The signalling process is thought to have a limited impact if the receiver is not actively looking for the signal. The extent to which receivers scan their environment is termed 'receiver attention'. In addition, 'receiver interpretation' is of key importance as they may interpret signals differently from what signallers have intended. Also, the cognitive abilities of receivers are discussed and how they deal with the vast numbers of signals available to them.	(Connelly et al., 2011a, p. 52; Drover et al., 2018; Taj, 2016, p. 340)

Constructs	Explanation	References
(3) Signal (or market signal)	*Original*: Signals are things one does that are visible and that are in part designed to communicate. Signals are composed out of observable characteristics that are subject to manipulation. Signals are informational cues sent out by one party to another in order to influence desired outcomes.	(Spence, 1973, p. 357; Spence, 2002, p. 434; Taj, 2016)
	Examples: Reputation of the firm, board structure, earnings claims, consultant surveys, branding, advertisements, number of patents, certified management standards, education and experience of human resources, investments in memberships, investments in specific assets, pricing structure, the prestige of a third party (such as a venture capitalist), third-party endorsements, pre-announcing a particular behaviour (for example, in the case of new product release/introduction).	(Bergh et al., 2014, p. 1339; Bergh et al., 2019; Cheng et al., 2020, p. 219; Connelly et al., 2011a, pp. 47–51; Courtney et al., 2017; Eliashberg and Robertson, 1988; Moratis, 2018; Terlaak and King, 2006; Xu et al., 2018; Yasar et al., 2020, p. 4)
	Discussion: Different properties of signals are discussed (for example, intensity, strength, clarity and visibility of a signal; signal fit; signal bonding; ease/difficulty to imitate signal; the effectiveness of signals in different markets). Attempts are made to develop different signal typologies (for example, 'default independent signals' vs. 'default contingent signals'; intentional vs. unintentional signals; positive vs. negative signals; easy-to-verify vs. difficult-to-verify; low- vs. high-cost signal). It is discussed how sets of signals (mixed vs. unmixed signals, or mix of conflicting signals) or signal dynamics (signals at different points in time; signal consistency; efficient balance of signal rates and durations; value of signals over time) might help to alleviate information asymmetry.	(Cheng et al., 2020, p. 220; Connelly et al., 2011a; Connelly et al., 2011b; Drover et al., 2018, p. 218; Etzion and Pe'er, 2014, p. 1607; Ippolito, 1990, p. 42; Kirmani and Rao, 2000, p. 69; Mavlanova et al., 2012; Moratis, 2018; Stern et al., 2014; Wu et al., 2013)
(4) Indices	*Original*: Indices are attributes over which one has no control, and that cannot be altered. However, indices might alter the receiver's perception (in conjunction with signals) and are assumed to have an impact on informed decisions. Indices represent publicly available information on an individual, product or firm.	(Spence, 1973, p. 357; Spence, 2002, p. 434)
	Examples: Age, sex, gender, race (as far as individuals are concerned, examples taken from Spence, 1973); Examples in a company/supplier context are rare. It can be assumed, that publicly available knowledge of companies/suppliers can be interpreted as indices. Hence, the name of a supplier, its brands/product portfolio, location, size, turnover, profit, etc., can be employed as indices.	(Spence, 1973, pp. 368–374)
	Discussion: While the informational influence of indices on decisions seems well examined in the job market, it seems as though indices are rarely discussed in other market situations. Indices are often not addressed or are even neglected in studies in management research.	-

Constructs	Explanation	References
(5) Signal costs	*Original:* Costs associated with obtaining a signal (time, energy and money). Signalling costs are to be interpreted broadly even to include psychic and other costs, as well as the direct monetary ones. The cost of the signal is negatively correlated with the unseen characteristic that is valuable to the receiver. The amount of signalling costs should be just high enough to dissuade the low-quality signaller from signalling, yet low enough to make signalling attractive for the high-quality signaller.	(Kirmani and Rao, 2000, p. 73; Spence, 1973, p. 359; Spence, 2002, p. 436)
	Examples: All costs concerned with obtaining a college degree (tuition fees plus all opportunity costs during that time); costs concerned with obtaining a certain certification (obtaining such a certification would be more costly for a firm with poor quality practices than for a firm that already has high standards).	(Bergh et al., 2014, p. 1338; Spence, 1973, 2002)
	Discussion: In general, signalling costs are defined broadly and are difficult to determine. An alternative to the costliness of a signal may exist when there is a penalty associated with false signalling. Future research might explore the extent to which signal costs and penalty costs serve as substitutes or complements. Spence raised another set of issues concerning signalling costs, namely, whether signallers distinguish among receivers at the time that the investment decision into the signal is made (and whether they are investing different signalling costs for different receivers).	(Bergh et al., 2014, p. 1338; Connelly et al., 2011a, p. 61; Spence, 1976, p. 596)
(6) Signal confirmation	*Original:* Signal confirmation refers to whether the expected attributes transported by the signal are realized (or is at least not disconfirmed) through subsequent experience.	(Spence, 1973, p. 368; Spence, 2002, p. 437)
	Examples: Warranty (as an *ex ante* signal of superior product quality) without the (*ex post*) occurrence of a warranty claim.	(Etzion and Pe'er, 2014)
	Discussion: Since signal confirmation is rarely examined, it is discussed how to include and empirically test signal confirmation. This would require to link the receiver's *ex ante* expectation of a signal to *ex post* experience. Against this background, it also seems critical to account for confirmation bias. Confirmation bias occurs when individuals may weigh signals that agree with their current position greater than those that will contradict their prior held knowledge.	(Bergh et al., 2014, p. 1348; Yasar et al., 2020, p. 8)

Constructs	Explanation	References
(7) Informational feedback loop	*Original*: As new signals are received over time, both the signaller and receiver may adjust their expectations for future transactions. Receivers' conditional probabilistic beliefs are modified (receivers make and learn from mistakes, adjust their expectations, and then try again), offered return schedules are adjusted, signaller behaviour concerning signal choice changes (as payoff structures also change), and after a decision has been made, new data become available to the receiver. Each feedback loop generates the next one. *Examples*: Information exchange, that occurs early in the procurement process (market analysis, supplier evaluation). *Discussion*: Recent discussions in management research assume that information asymmetry works in two directions: receivers desire information about signallers, but signallers also desire information about receivers in order to know which signals are most effective. Hence, there is feedback in terms of information cues sent from the receiver to the signaller (countersignals). In such situations, it might be necessary to distinguish between different types of information asymmetry (I and II), where I is the information asymmetry between sender and receiver (requiring a signal) and II stands for the information asymmetry that is occurring by a reverse distribution of roles (requiring a countersignal)	(Bergh et al., 2014, p. 1352; Spence, 1973, p. 360) - (Connelly et al., 2011a, p. 55; Taj, 2016)
(8) Signalling equilibria/separating equilibria	*Original*: A separating equilibrium occurs when signallers with different hidden attributes always choose to invest in different signals. Hence, the signal always reveals the signaller with a certain set of attributes, so that the receiver's beliefs become deterministic over time. There are multiple different signalling equilibria (separating, pooling and semi-separating). *Examples*: – *Discussion*: The separating equilibrium concept is seen as the essential predictive mechanism that drives the unique explanations associated with signalling theory. Hence, the current discussion centres on how to test for and assure the presence of and means for establishing a separating equilibrium. Bergh et al. argue that, lacking the equilibrium concept, researchers may be at risk to identify various behaviours or characteristics as signals in the generic sense, that are not consistent with signalling theory's signals. Other equilibria are also discussed, such as the episodic equilibrium that occurs in competitive and dynamic markets.	(Bergh et al., 2014, p. 1336; Spence, 1973, p. 361) – (Bergh et al., 2014; Etzion and Pe'er, 2014)
(9) Signalling environment	*Original*: Not addressed directly. However, Spence is aware of the fact that the perception of a signal and its credibility is influenced by the number of signallers on the market, and the occurrence of credible signals that are confirmed after the decision has been made. *Examples*: Industry characteristics in which the relationship is examined. *Discussion*: Signalling environment is an underresearched area. For instance, a volatile environment tends to introduce distortion and noise into the signalling process and, thus, may diminish specific signals' visibility.	(Spence, 1973, 1976, 2002) – (Bergh et al., 2014, p. 1335; Cheng et al., 2020, p. 220; Connelly et al., 2011a, p. 55; Park and Patel, 2015; Taj, 2016)

tainty, and is characterized by an asymmetric distribution of information. While information asymmetry can basically take two forms – information asymmetry of quality, and information asymmetry of intentions (Stiglitz, 2000) – Spence focused on information asymmetry of latent and unobservable quality (Connelly et al., 2011a, p. 42). The potential employee is usually better informed on their own productive capabilities and capacities than the employer (Spence, 1973, p. 356). It is assumed that those with high ability will try to separate themselves from those with lower ability by reducing the information asymmetry if incentives are high enough. Both employer and employee are vulnerable to adverse selection and moral hazards associated with incomplete information about the other party (Bergh et al., 2014, p. 1337). This can be adapted to purchasing and supply management problems: suppliers – who are more capable about their capabilities and capacities not only before being selected but even after signing the contract – must be selected from buyers dealing with this information asymmetry.

(1) Signallers and (2) Receivers

In order to overcome the above-mentioned information problem, Spence introduced two interacting roles: signalling entities and signal receiving entities. Signallers (for example, job applicants or, in purchasing and supply management: suppliers) possess information concerning individuals, products/services or organizations, which can be transformed into signals delivered to receivers (for example, potential employers or, in purchasing and supply management: buyers). As the signallers expect to benefit from reduced information asymmetry, they are willing to invest in signals to reveal less observable quality attributes. The receivers lack information about the individual, product or organization in question and would like to receive this information in order to make an informed decision. The receiver holds beliefs on the hidden qualities of the signaller and interprets the incoming signals (Bergh et al., 2014; Connelly et al., 2011a; Spence, 1973, 1976, 2002).

(3) Signals and (4) Indices

While the employer (receiver) cannot be sure of the productive capabilities and capacities, he can alternatively observe the image the job applicant (signaller) presents beforehand (Spence, 1973, p. 357). Spence assumes that this image is composed of a set of signals and indices (Spence, 1973, p. 357). He reserves the term 'signal' to those attributes of the image that are observable and that can be intentionally altered by the applicant (Spence, 1973, p. 357). It is critical to note that if the better-informed side (employee or supplier) takes the active role in conveying information about hidden attributes, this is qualified as signalling (or as sending a 'market signal'). In contrast, 'market screening' would require the less-informed side to actively provide a set of different contractual agreements from which the better-informed side can select (Riley, 2001, p. 438). Moreover, signals can be defined as snapshots pointing to unobservable signaller qualities at a given point in time (Moratis, 2018, p. 3). Indices are attributes that are not generally thought to be alterable, and they are not a matter of individual choice, such as race, gender or age of the applicant (Spence, 1973, p. 357). Indices are considered as the publicly available information. It is assumed that indices have an impact on job applicants' overall image (Spence, 1973, p. 368). The various sets of signals and indices are assumed to not only define the employers' beliefs on the productive capabilities and capacities of potential employees, but also determine the employers' decision on what wage to offer for what set of signals and indices (Spence, 1973, p. 358). In purchasing and supply, images could, for example, refer to suppliers' attributes such as name, location or manufacturing programme.

(5) Signalling Costs

The effort to obtain a particular signal by the signalling entity is termed 'signalling costs', which are to be interpreted broadly (more in terms of opportunity costs) (Spence, 1973, p. 359). The potential job applicant invests in a signal if there is sufficient return as defined by the offered wage (or payment) schedule (Spence, 1973, p. 358). Hence it is assumed that individuals make rational investment choices concerning education, and that they select signals to maximize the difference between the signalling cost and the offered wages (Spence, 1973, p. 437). To obtain and send a signal, the job applicant (signaller) can, for example, invest time, energy and money to improve their educational standing in the market by acquiring certificates or a college degree. The corresponding signal (the college degree) contains information suggesting specific qualities about the potential employee that would otherwise be nebulous to the employers (Cheng et al., 2020, p. 219).

(6) Signal Confirmation

Besides, employers have beliefs about the rationale between the selected signal and the individual's underlying productivity (Spence, 2002, p. 437). If the high ability of the applicant is confirmed after hiring, the corresponding signal is considered as effective (Spence, 2002, p. 437). Hence, numerous confirmations can increase the effectiveness of a certain signal. Also, those confirmed signals help to shape the employer's conditional beliefs (in terms of the relation of a signal and the underlying productivity) (Spence, 1973, p. 360). The credibility of a signal is also important for a signal to be effective. High signal credibility is said to occur when the employer believes that sending a certain signal requires a significant investment, and that the investment is at risk if the signal is not in line with the underlying qualities of the potential applicant (Wells et al., 2011, p. 376). In summary, signalling cost and return structures and their credibility provide the basis for a selection process whereby employers can use the signal to select an employee from among a larger set of employees (Bergh et al., 2014, p. 1337).

(7) Informational Feedback Loop

Spence points out that signalling is not to be seen as a static activity but, in contrast, as one embedded into a closed, 'self-confirming' (Spence, 2002, p. 437) feedback loop (Spence, 1973, p. 359). This feedback-loop consists of four elements: (1) employers' conditional probabilistic beliefs; (2) offered wage schedules (as a function of signals and indices); (3) signalling decisions by applicants; and (4) hiring decisions and observations of the relationship between productivity and signal (also called 'signal confirmation'). Spence assumes that new market information comes in to the employer through hiring and subsequent observation of productive capabilities as they relate to signals (4). This information alters the employer's conditional probabilistic beliefs on the relation of signals and productivity (1). The conditional probabilistic beliefs determine the offered wage schedule (2). This leads to a situation in which applicant behaviour for signal choice and corresponding investments changes (3). The information conveyed to the employers leads to new incoming market information which after a certain time lag is confirmed or disconfirmed (4), and a new round starts (Spence, 2002, p. 437). It is critical to note that conditional beliefs (1), offered wage schedules (2), signal choice (3), and hiring decisions and confirmed signals (4), generally differ from the ones facing the previous feedback loop (Spence, 1973, p. 359). Hence, Spence included a time-based, evolutionary perspective in his model that consists of multiple feedback iterations. The feedback loop is illustrated in Figure 29.1. While conditional beliefs (1), offered wage schedules (2), and hiring decisions/confirmed signals (4), represent actions on the employer's side (receiving entity), the signalling decision is reserved to the job applicant's side (signalling entity).

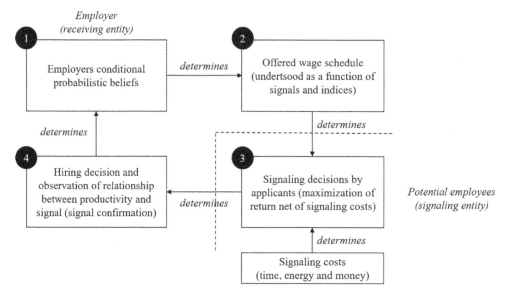

Figure 29.1   *Informational feedback loop in the job market as proposed by Spence (1973, p. 359)*

Spence's basic ideas about the informational feedback loop on the labour market can also be applied to the relationship between buyers and suppliers in very early stages in a procurement process. Following Spence's idea, new market information on potential suppliers comes in to the buyer, for example through market analysis and subsequent observation of productive capabilities of potential suppliers (4). This market information may alter the buyer's conditional probabilistic beliefs on the relation of signals and productivity (1). The conditional probabilistic beliefs determine the assumptions on planned contract specifications and contract values (2). This leads to a situation in which supplier behaviour for signal choice and corresponding investments changes (3). The information conveyed to the buyers leads to new incoming market information that, after a certain time lag, gets confirmed or disconfirmed (4), and a new round starts.

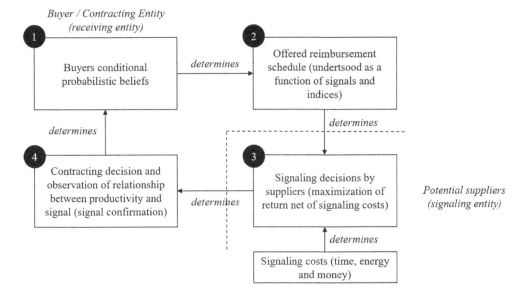

Figure 29.2   Feedback loop adopted to a buyer–supplier relationship

(8) Signalling Equilibria (as Signalling Outcome)

Many signalling equilibria can be the result of the above-mentioned feedback loop; in fact, Spence points out that there is a continuum of signalling equilibria, that can be sorted by the Pareto criterion between the poles' 'pooling equilibria' and 'separating equilibria' (Spence, 2002, p. 437). An equilibrium is best thought of as a situation in which beliefs (in terms of the relation between the productive capabilities and capacities and the signal) are confirmed or at least not contradicted by the new data at the end of the feedback loop. Spence assumes that such beliefs will tend to persist over time as new entrants into the market flow through (Spence, 1973, p. 368). In the job market example, this means that the observed signal corresponds to the underlying productivity, and that the employee is offered the appropriate wage (based on the signal sent). This situation is considered Pareto optimal if there exists no other feasible solution for which an improvement for one party does not lead to a simultaneous degradation in one (or more) of the other parties (Bergh et al., 2014, p. 1337).

A pooling equilibrium is created when the employer believes that they cannot distinguish between low- and high-ability applicants. In this situation, all potential applicants would be treated the same. Hence, all applicants would be offered the same (weighted average) wage schedule. In this situation, there is no incentive for additional investment into a signal for high-ability applicants to separate from the low-ability applicants. It is clear that the group of low-ability applicants benefits from this situation to a larger extent (in terms of free-riding behaviour). Hence, pooling can occur when high-quality actors are not able to recoup the greater costs they must invest in attaining separation. So, in essence, they allow low-quality actors to free-ride on the signal (Etzion and Pe'er, 2014, p. 1609). It needs to be noted that this situation is only tolerable for high-ability employees if the group of low-ability workers is relatively small in size. Hence, they would not lose too much in accepting the lower weighted average wage schedule (Spence, 1973, p. 437).

A separating equilibrium, in contrast, is created when employers believe that they can distinguish between low- and high-ability applicants. In this situation, there is an observable relation between ability and corresponding signal. Offered wage schedules display the employers' beliefs on different ability levels concerning received signals. Hence, an applicant with a college degree is offered a distinctively higher wage than an applicant without a college degree. It needs to be remembered that low-ability applicants need to invest more time, energy and money in obtaining a signal (such as a college degree). A separating equilibrium occurs when the cost of a signal is sufficiently high to prevent low-quality actors from attaining one, thereby yielding demarcated subpopulations: high-quality actors that generate the signal, and low-quality actors that do not (Etzion and Pe'er, 2014, p. 1608). High-ability applicants will only invest in obtaining a college degree if the earnings for going to college (equals the wage offered to those holding a degree), less the signalling costs, outweigh the earnings of not going to college. Low-ability applicants will not invest in going to college if the earnings for not going to college exceed the earnings for going to college less the signalling costs. Morris states that low-ability employees will then choose different signals which attempt to hide their poor productivity (Morris, 1987, p. 53). This gives room for moral hazard.

Spence also introduces the term 'lower-level equilibrium trap' (Spence, 1973, p. 374). Spence notes that the combination of signals (for example, college degree) with indices (for example, gender) might lead to altered (and unfair) beliefs about productivity on the employer's side. This may result in different offered wage schedules; for example, men with college degrees are offered higher wages than women with college degrees. Spence argues that the combination of signals and indices leads to a separation of beliefs into two independent groups (that are in themselves homogenous). Due to the embodied mechanisms in the model, albeit informationally based, there is no chance for the disadvantaged group to obtain the same standing as the other group (Spence, 1973, pp. 373–374).

(9) Signalling Environment

While Spence does not explicitly address the influence of the signal environment on the outcomes of signalling, there seems to be a growing interest in the signalling environment and its outcomes (Connelly et al., 2011a; Park and Patel, 2015; Taj, 2016). Park and Patel argue that in situations where decision makers lack clear information due to environmental distortion or noise, they often rely on information about signal senders in conjunction with other information from the environment in order to establish discernible patterns to evaluate the signal senders (Park and Patel, 2015). It is assumed, for example, that the signalling environment, either within an organization or between organizations, can affect the extent to which signalling reduces information asymmetry (Connelly et al., 2011a). More specifically, how far environmental distortions may occur and in how far those environmental distortions have the potential to lower the observability of a signal are discussed (Connelly et al., 2011a). Environmental distortions may occur in situations where, for example, the medium for propagating the signal reduces the observability of the signal. Also, the presence of other signal receivers (external referents, third parties), who also interpret the signals and publish their interpretation results (for example, university rankings for evaluating educational quality) may influence or distort signalling. Distortion occurs when a signal is interpreted by others in a particular way, and an individual who is unsure about how to interpret the signal may look to imitation as a means of decision making (also known as the 'bandwagon effect') (Connelly et al., 2011a). Also, the share of more honest signallers or more deceptive signallers on the market may increase or decrease signal reliability (Connelly et al., 2011a). In addition, unintended signals may increase the number of signals to evaluate and interpret (from the receiver's point of view). Hence, providing countersignals (signals issued by the receiver) may help to reduce noise, to sort out relevant signals and improve their interpretation (Taj, 2016)

KEY CONDITIONS AND ASSUMPTIONS

The application of signalling theory requires a thorough understanding of key conditions and assumptions (Wacker, 1998). These conditions and assumptions can be broken down into conditions and assumptions related to behavioural aspects, those referring to fundamental mechanisms rooted in signalling, and those related to the market structure. Behavioural elements are concerned with: (1) rational; and (2) risk-neutral human behaviour in decision making. Conditions and assumptions targeting fundamental mechanisms rooted in signalling theory include the existence of: (3) *ex ante* information asymmetry; (4) *ex post* observability of hidden quality attributes; (5) (*ex ante*) payoff transparency; (6) bond vulnerability; and (7) inverse relation of signalling costs to hidden quality attributes. Also, in Spence's job market model, markets consist of: (8) numerous (competing) signallers with varying hidden attributes; (9) repeated feedback loops; and (10) a receiving entity that persists in the market over time. Signalling theory is most effectively applied under those strict conditions. Hence, these conditions must be carefully examined in each case. Although the conditions under which signalling may be an appropriate strategy are well described in the literature, it seems as though there is a lack of testing those conditions and describing those tests (Bergh et al., 2014; Connelly et al., 2011a). The conditions and assumptions are presented in Table 29.2.

Rational (a) and Risk-Neutral Behaviour (b)

It is assumed that all market participants are rational wealth maximisers (Morris, 1987). Hence, individuals are acting in their own interest, trying to realize the highest possible benefit for themselves. One might criticize that this behaviour is at least complemented by behaviour in which individuals also act in the interest of their organizations or investors (Morris, 1987). In the Spence job market example, this would mean that individuals are rationally investing in education. If they did not invest in the signal, they would incur lower wages (Spence, 1973). Also, potential applicants will rationally select themselves out of certain job markets. As a consequence, certain signal configurations will never appear in these markets and will never reach the receivers. This situation might result in informationally based discrimination (Spence, 1973).

It is also assumed that the receivers make risk-neutral decisions (Spence, 1973). This means that the market participants (and especially the receivers) are indifferent to risk when making an investment decision. Hence, they would exclusively invest in assets with the highest expected yield. Risk-averse receivers would prefer lower yields with known risks, as opposed to high-risk receivers who would prefer higher yields with unknown risks. While Spence is aware of the influence of risk on the outcome of the investment decision, he explicitly excludes risk and its influence from further considerations (Spence, 1973).

Table 29.2   Conditions for applying signalling theory

Conditions	Explanation (remark)	References
Overall conditions; human behavioural aspects		
Rational behaviour (wealth maximization)	It is assumed that all market participants are striving for the highest possible benefit with limited alternative courses of action.	(Morris, 1987; Spence, 1973)
Risk-neutral behaviour	It is assumed that the market participants (and especially the receivers) are indifferent to risk when making an investment decision.	(Spence, 1973)
Conditions related to fundamental mechanisms		
Ex ante information asymmetry	It is assumed that information asymmetry exists between interacting parties (between signalling and receiving entities) before a decision is to be taken. The signaller is better informed than the receiver. There needs to be an information problem and information scarcity.	(Bergh et al., 2014, 2019; Kirmani and Rao, 2000; Morris, 1987)
Ex post observability of hidden quality attributes	It is assumed that hidden quality attributes are discernible after a decision has been taken. It needs to be noted that there may be a certain time lag before hidden quality attributes can be revealed and confirmed.	(Kirmani and Rao, 2000; Spence, 1973, 2002)
Ex ante payoff transparency	It is assumed that signallers and receivers have sufficient knowledge of costs (for example, signalling costs) and other payoffs (for example, signalling costs compared to any payments/return on invest).	(Kirmani and Rao, 2000)
Bond vulnerability	It is assumed that 'bonding' occurs when some asset or wealth is forfeited under specified conditions. For bonding to be effective, market conditions must allow firms to acquire a bond that is sufficiently large to alter the incentives to cheat. Costs of signals must be structured in such a way that dishonest signals do not pay.	(Connelly et al., 2011a; Ippolito, 1990; Kirmani and Rao, 2000)
Signalling costs are inversely related to quality	It is assumed that signalling costs are lower for those signallers with high-quality/high-ability attributes and that signalling costs are significantly higher for those signallers with low-quality/low-ability attributes.	(Morris, 1987; Spence, 1973, 2002)
Conditions related to the market structure		
Multiple competing signalling entities	It is assumed that there are competing signalling entities on the market, which exhibit varying hidden qualities. Hence, markets consist of signallers with heterogenous hidden qualities or abilities and thus competing interests.	(Connelly et al., 2011a; Morris, 1987; Spence, 1973, 1976, 2002)
Repeated signalling cycles (feedback loops)	It is assumed that successive waves of new signallers come into the market. This alters receivers' conditional probabilistic beliefs, and leads to a change in offered payment structures. This leads to changes in signalling behaviour with respect to signal choice changes (on the signaler's side). After a decision has been taken, new data become available to the receivers through confirmed signals. Each cycle, then, generates the next one.	(Spence, 1973)
Persistence of receiving entity in the market over time to gather experience	It is assumed that there is a certain continuity provided by the receiver's persistent presence in the market.	(Spence, 1973)

Ex Ante Information Asymmetry (c)

It is assumed that information asymmetry exists between interacting parties (between signalling and receiving entities) before a decision is to be taken. Typically, the signaller is better informed than the signal receiver. Information asymmetry occurs when one party has access to privileged or private information. This information may be proprietary, be legally protected, or arise from specialized assets or expertise, and can be the source of acquisition gains and competitive advantage (Bergh et al., 2019). There are two types of information where asymmetry is of particular interest. First, information asymmetry is important when one party is not fully aware of the characteristics or attributes of another party. Second, information asymmetry is important when one party is not fully aware of the behaviour or the intentions of another party. Connelly and colleagues highlight that studies which explicitly invoke signalling theory focus on the role of signalling in understanding how parties resolve information asymmetries about latent and unobservable quality attributes (Connelly et al., 2011a). More specifically, this information asymmetry only persists *ex ante* to a decision, since Spence assumes that those hidden quality attributes can be conveyed through a signal, and can be confirmed *ex post* to a decision. It needs to be noted that signalling mostly refers to actions that should influence desired outcomes conveying positive signals. Hence, there is an implicit assumption of positive intentions on the signaller's side (Reuer et al., 2012; Taj, 2016; Wells et al., 2011). In purchasing and supply situations *ex ante* information asymmetry is a typical characteristic before entering into contractual relationships.

Ex Post Observability of Hidden Quality Attributes (d)

If the *ex post* inspection does not unambiguously observe and confirm hidden quality attributes, receivers will not be able to form or advance their conditional probabilistic beliefs with respect to the question of how credible a signal conveys information on hidden quality attributes. Hence, signalling is less useful for situations in which violations of quality claims cannot be unambiguously established after the investment decision has been made. Also, signalling seems less feasible, for example, for credence products or services, as their quality is not discernable after the investment decision and is not discernable even after use (Kirmani and Rao, 2000). However, there seems to be no suggestion of how much effort to 'invest' in signal confirmation.

Ex Ante Payoff Transparency (e)

Signalling models are often exposed to criticism when it comes to payoff transparency. Payoff transparency occurs when the signaller not only knows the required signalling costs to obtain a specific signal, but also knows the potential payment structures of signal receivers. In Spence's example, the job applicant would not only be aware of investments required in educational advancements but would also know the offered wage schedules of potential employers (Kirmani and Rao, 2000).

Bond Vulnerability (f)

'Bond vulnerability' occurs when some asset or wealth is forfeited under specified conditions (Ippolito, 1990). The asset or wealth that is at risk is often referred to as a bond (Ho and Wei, 2016). For bonding to be effective, market conditions must allow firms to acquire a bond that is sufficiently large to alter the incentives to cheat (Ippolito, 1990). In other words, costs of signals must be structured in such a way that dishonest signals do not pay (Connelly et al., 2011a). Hence the receiver's belief that the signaller made a significant investment by sending the signal; and the investment is at risk if a false signal is sent. Wells et al. (2011) argue that a false signal is thus prohibitively expensive for a signaller with low-quality products.

Signalling Costs are Inversely Related to Quality (g)

For a signal to help alleviate asymmetric information, it needs to be effective (Spence, 1973, p. 367). Spence points out that a critical assumption in his model is that effective signalling depends upon the negative correlation of costs and productivities (Spence, 1973, p. 358). He emphasizes that if this condition fails to hold, every applicant will invest in the signal in the same way, and as a consequence applicants cannot be distinguished from one another (Spence, 1973, p. 358). In his model, potential employees with low productive capabilities and capacities need to invest at a level disproportionately higher than job applicants with high productive capabilities and capacities (Bergh et al., 2014, p. 1337). As previously stated, individuals make rational investment choices concerning education and they select signals to maximize the difference between the signalling cost and the offered wage schedule. Due to a different cost structure and lower expected returns, low-ability employees will most likely not invest in the same signal as high-ability employees. Consequently, one can conclude that there are signals that fall in different cost and return structures (Karasek and Bryant, 2015). Spence added that effective signalling depends not only upon the negative correlation of costs and productivities but also upon there being a 'sufficient' number of signals within the appropriate cost and return structures (Spence, 2002, p. 437).

Multiple Competing Signalling Entities (h)

Spence points out that multiple signalling entities that exhibit varying hidden qualities should be competing for the investment decision of the receiving entity. In Spence's model, at least two different groups of signallers with different hidden quality attributes (high ability versus low ability) are distinguished from one another. This condition is crucial for creating a separating equilibrium and for helping to derive and explain investment decisions in one option over the other option (Spence, 1973, 1976, 2002). However, the sources of signals and the specific signals sent imply that receivers need to cope with a vast number of signals in a particular decision making situation. While signalling theory implicitly implies that receivers can deal with an endless number of signals, it seems more realistic that receivers rely on a smaller subset of these signals and must make sense of these subsets (Drover et al., 2018). Also, being confronted and having to select between multiple competing signalling entities, namely suppliers, is a common situation in purchasing and supply management decisions.

Repeated Signalling Cycles (Feedback Loops) (i)

It is assumed, that successive waves of new signallers come into the market, which alters receivers' conditional probabilistic beliefs, changes offered payment structures, changes signalling behaviour with respect to signal choice changes, and after a decision has been taken, new data become available to the receivers through confirmed signals. Each cycle, then, generates the next one (Spence, 1973, 1976, 2002).

Persistence of Receiving Entity in the Market Over Time to Gather Experience (j)

In order to confirm a signal, Spence assumes that the receiver of the signal needs to stay active in the market over time. The persistence of the receiver in the market over time (Spence, 1973) will not only help to confirm incoming signals, but also determine and develop the receiver's conditional beliefs about signal credibility. This will then lead to adjustments in offered payment structures and will thus have the potential to alter selected signals. Hence, staying active in the market will help the receiver to enter subsequent learning cycles. This might also lead to a situation in which the receiving entity can compare a wide variety of signals in order to enhance decisions with experience.

DOMAIN WHERE THE THEORY APPLIES

Although the theory was initially developed in the labour market by Spence (1973, 2002), signalling is seen as a general phenomenon applicable in any market suffering information asymmetry (Morris, 1987, p. 47; Spence, 1973, p. 356). Therefore, studies citing 'signalling theory' are (for example) available in the literature on strategy, corporate governance, entrepreneurship, quality management, marketing, investment and finance decisions and human resources management (Connelly et al., 2011a; Taj, 2016). Signalling theory also found its way into research on buying decisions, mostly related to a business-to-consumer context and often discussed from a marketing point of view. Hence, signalling is often employed by those who offer products and services to the market, and signals are interpreted and used for buying decisions by consumers (Atkinson and Rosenthal, 2014; Cheung et al., 2014; Eliashberg and Robertson, 1988; Etzion and Pe'er, 2014; Hossain et al., 2018; Kirmani and Rao, 2000; Mavlanova et al., 2012; Rao et al., 1999; Wells et al., 2011). Adoption of signalling theory for purchasing decisions in a business-to-business environment or in the broader supply chain context seems to follow a far slower pace (Bakshi et al., 2015; Cheng et al., 2020; Ho and Wei, 2016; Jones et al., 2010; Shao et al., 2020; Simaens and Koster, 2013; Terlaak and King, 2006; Wolters and Schuller, 1997). Besides applying signalling theory in management research, there is also extensive use of signalling theory in biology, anthropology and economics (Connelly et al., 2011a).

THEORETICAL PREDICTIONS (FACTUAL CLAIMS)

The essential predictive mechanism that drives the different explanations associated with signalling theory is the existence of a 'separating equilibrium' (Bergh et al., 2014, p. 1335), and that investing in the signal pays off for the high-ability applicant (also called the 'sheepskin effect'). Against this background, signalling theory helps to stipulate answers to questions such as: (1) How much time, energy and money should be invested by the signalling entity into the signal? (2) How far can the receiving entity trust the signal to be credible? and (3) Under what circumstances will the signalling equilibrium break down? Signalling theory provides a unique, practical and empirically testable perspective on problems of social selection under conditions of imperfect information (Connelly et al., 2011a, p. 63). Thus, signalling theory can help to find ways to reduce *ex ante* transaction costs by employing effective signals. Also, signalling theory can be seen as helpful in lowering *ex post* transaction costs through confirmed signals over time.

HOW HAS THIS THEORY BEEN USED?

As already pointed out, signalling is most effective under conditions in which prepurchase information about quality attributes is scarce, post-contract information about quality attributes is unambiguous, parties are informed about the payoffs, and the bond is vulnerable (Kirmani and Rao, 2000). In the articles on purchasing and supply chain management, three content-related directions have so far been taken in the application of signal theory.

The first direction focuses on building long-term relationships between suppliers and buyers (Jones et al., 2010; Wolters and Schuller, 1997). Wolters and Schuller examine how signals can be used for building trust and commitment *ex ante* to enter a long-term buyer–supplier relationship in the automotive industry. They assume signals such as joint targets, agreements on cost sharing mechanisms, modelling lifetime contracts, dual and single sourcing, early supplier involvement and supplier coaching. They argue that the original equipment manufacturer (OEM) is signalling its desire and willingness for a long-term cooperative partnership with its counterpart. The aim of signalling in this context would be to influence the decision of a supplier to enter into such a long-term collaboration. The findings are based on two selected case studies (Wolters and Schuller, 1997). Jones et al. also examine trust-related signals, their manifestation and their influence on entering into a long-term partnership. Signals creating trust and that are sent by the potential suppliers to a buyer could be, for example, a promise to perform (quality and on-time delivery), a professional relationship (agent-to-agent dialogue and communications), openness (sharing schedules, forecasts, cost information), benevolent collaboration (process investment, relationship investment and sharing risks/rewards) and empathy (actions to aid a partner, actions to include a partner in decision making). Jones et al. argue that measuring these five signals not only creates a more holistic view on trust but also provides some guidance regarding where efforts need to be made to improve trust. Their findings are based on a large-scale survey designed to cover the manufacturing industry in North America (Jones et al., 2010). Both publications employ multiple signals that need to be employed in conjunction with one another to realize a long-term partnership.

The second strand deals with the procurement of services, performance-oriented contracts and recovery actions after a poorly performed service (Bakshi et al., 2015; Cheng et al., 2020; Ho and Wei, 2016). Bakshi et al. examine the signal reliability of a newly developed product and related after-sales services. Therefore, they are investigating the interaction between reliability signalling (private information) and the vendor's discretionary investment in spares inventory (private action). Their findings are based on a more formal, mathematical modelling approach (Bakshi et al., 2015). Ho and Wei investigate how far past experience in information technology (IT) services outsourcing serves as cues that affect perceived service quality. The empirical findings validate the importance of dissemination and investment of past experiences for IT provider companies and give a cue of utilizing providers' experiences to alleviate uncertainty when assessing. The results are based on a survey issued and collected in Taiwan (Ho and Wei, 2016). Cheng et al. frame supplier-induced disruptions as negative signals from suppliers (signallers) to buyers (receivers) and suppliers' recovery actions as positive signals. Using the critical incident technique to capture disruption events, they find that the messages of suppliers conveyed through their recovery actions may or may not be 'loud and clear', depending on the context (Cheng et al., 2020).

The third direction is devoted to signalling that entails certificates of quality or is concerned with sustainability reporting or socially conscious purchasing (Shao et al., 2020; Simaens and Koster, 2013; Terlaak and King, 2006; Thomas et al., 2021). Terlaak and King use an 11-year panel of United States manufacturing facilities to test whether certification with the ISO 9000 quality management standard generates a competitive advantage. Their results suggest that certified facilities grow faster after certification, and that operational improvements do not account for this growth. Results also indicate that the growth effect is greater when buyers have greater difficulty in acquiring information about suppliers (Terlaak and King, 2006). Simaens and Koster deal with the growing awareness of (un)sustainable operations. Through the lens of signalling theory, and based on document analysis, they examine the influence of sustainability reporting (as a signal) to stakeholders and buyers (Simaens and Koster, 2013). Shao et al. explore two mechanisms – signalling and disclosure – which a firm can use to communicate its sourcing decisions to consumers in a setting where only some consumers care about the firm's sourcing practices. Their findings highlight the importance of transparency and socially conscious consumption in driving responsible sourcing (Shao et al., 2020). Thomas et al. decompose social sustainability into dimensions of employee welfare and philanthropy to determine their effects on supplier selection. The results, derived from a vignette-based experiment in a transportation context, show that buyers have significant preferences to select, trust and collaborate with suppliers which have desirable levels of employee welfare, philanthropy and pricing. Thomas et al. assume that these findings help to refine the understanding of social sustainability conceptualizations and supplier selection criteria (Thomas et al., 2021).

If one focuses exclusively on dyadic relationships (as done by Spence), the above-mentioned constructs and the existing contributions to signalling in the purchasing and supply management research can be transferred into the graphic in Figure 29.3. The representation summarizes the signalling activities (signalling) of buyers (receivers) and suppliers (signallers), that are interacting on supply markets (signalling environment). The graphic indicates that signals also require a certain communication channel (not originally part of Spence's theory) to transmit the signal. In the age of digitization and digitalization those means of communication are assumed to have an impact on the signalling activities (for example, in terms of availability of information, increased information asymmetry, signalling frequency, and noise and distortions from the signalling environment). The visual representation also points out the different types of information asymmetries (I and II) that occur, depending on which organizations are taking on the role of the signalling and/or the receiving entity. The examples provided in the graphic refer to efforts to signal one's efforts and one's commitment to sustainability in a buyer–suppler relationship.

OUTLOOK ON FUTURE RESEARCH OPPORTUNITIES

What seems interesting to note, when considering the above-mentioned three research strands, is that they all seem to focus on dyadic relationships between a signalling entity (supplier) and a buying entity (buyer). While this dyadic interaction is deeply rooted in Spence's signalling theory, it does not consider a supply chain perspective or an industrial network perspective (Miemczyk et al., 2012). The supply chain perspective would extend the focus to multiple,

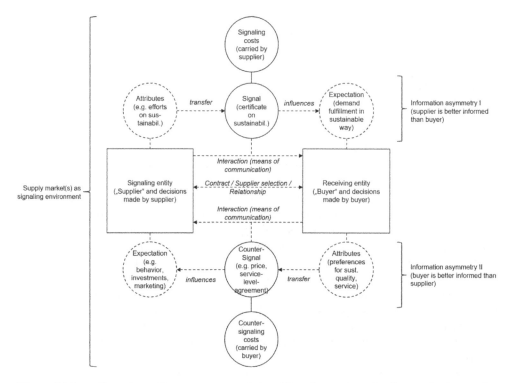

Figure 29.3   *Overview of key constructs of signalling theory in a dyadic purchasing and supply management context*

interconnected buyer–supplier dyads, with the supply chain ultimately spanning from original raw material extractors to a focal organization and down to final end customers. This supply chain perspective could enhance the current view on signalling by questioning whether and how signals are passed and treated in a supply chain. From the buyer's point of view (for example, as the focal organization in a supply chain) this would result in receiving and processing direct signals from its suppliers and indirect signals from its suppliers' suppliers. This would not only help to alleviate direct information asymmetry with its immediate suppliers, but would also help to alleviate information asymmetry further upstream in the supply chain. From the suppliers' point of view (tier 1 to n) this would also pose the question of which signal to invest in (in terms of signal choice) and how much (in order to improve individual buyer–supplier relationships) or if there is a way to collectively invest in a signal (in terms of risk or burden-sharing strategy in a supply chain, and in order to gain the contract with other competing supply chains). Additional questions arise when considering the perspective of industrial networks, that involve additional stakeholders (other than already involved in the supply chain), and their potential influence on signalling (for example, as signal coordinators on behalf of multiple suppliers, or as entities imposing noise in the signalling environment). Expanding the level of analysis seems promising to advance signalling theory and seems relevant, for example, in the area of sustainable supply chains and sustainable supply chain management, where a company's sustainability profile requires a view of not only the company's direct suppliers but also its extended supply chain or even the wider network in which it operates (Miemczyk et al., 2012; Simaens and Koster, 2013; Taoketao et al., 2018).

Expanding the level of analysis from dyadic to network-like arrangements (supply chains) might also include examining signalling in buyer–buyer relationships or in supplier–supplier relationships. In this context, signalling theory can be used to examine the formation of buyer–buyer cooperations (or supplier–supplier cooperations). Against this background one could more closely examine what signals would help to distinguish suitable from unsuitable partners in order to create win–win relationships. At this point, it would be particularly interesting to see whether not only cost savings (as a counterpart to Spence's offered wage schedules) can drive the investment in signals for joint purchasing activities, but also 'softer' factors, such as shared market knowledge, risk sharing or pooling of the supplier base (as far as buyer–buyer relationships are concerned) (Schotanus and Telgen, 2007; Schotanus et al., 2010; Walker et al., 2013).

At the next lower level, the overview developed by Wynstra et al. (2019) for the most critical topics in the area of purchasing and supply management can be employed. They distinguish four major research areas on the basis of a large-scale literature review: strategic purchasing and supply management activities; tactical/operational purchasing and supply management activities; enablers for successful purchasing and supply management activities; and benefits/competitive priorities of purchasing and supply management (Wynstra et al., 2019). These activities all require investment decisions and the alleviation of potential information asymmetries. In the area of strategic purchasing and supply management, decisions related to make-or-buy, global versus localized sourcing, supplier relationship management, supplier involvement (also in new product development), supplier development or strategic cost management all offer interesting starting points for future research. For example, one could examine the use of life cycle costs when tendering contracts and obtaining offers, to determine whether life cycle costs are suitable as a signal for more innovative, more sustainable and less maintenance-intensive products and services, and what influence they have on decision making and the reduction of information uncertainties.

In the area of tactical/operational purchasing and supply management activities, topics that occur *ex ante* to a contractual relationship could be of interest. This relates to the signals that are used on both sides of the aisle to make an informed decision. Such signals could be declarations on the economic and technical performance of suppliers, self-declarations in terms of sustainability activities, or risk management activities, labels and certificates. Those signalling activities gain additional importance when the potential supplier is offering highly innovative products (where, for example, other signals such as references are absent).

In the area of enablers for successful purchasing and supply management activities, topics such as human resources (HR), development and training, information and communication technologies, or performance measurement systems are suitable entry points. In HR one could investigate what signals are sent by potential job applicants when it comes to different required competence profiles in purchasing and supply management (Bals et al., 2019). Information and communication technology is especially interesting against the background of digitization and digitalization. While digitization may transform previously analogous information into data objects, digitalization refers to new business models that employ and exploit data. In a purchasing and supply management context, this could result in new and automated decision making algorithms on the buyer's side. On the supplier's side the question arises of how far investments in signals (for example, into signalling good data quality) may make sense, and how far digitization and digitalization introduce noise and distortions in the signalling environment. In terms of performance management systems, signalling becomes relevant when considering the condition of *ex post* signal confirmation that is unambiguous.

In the area of competitive priorities of purchasing and supply management one could question how to ensure the realization of these priorities by also using supplier-induced signals. Empirical research in all of these areas could focus on determining whether and under what conditions organizations would consider different signalling or signal-enhancing strategies, the efficacy of (combinations of) these strategies, and the perceptions of involved parties. Also, decisions may be supported by providing insights into how much to invest, in which signal, with what signal outcome. These strategies are, again, not limited to the adoption of standards, but also include the application of reporting frameworks and engaging in other types of sustainability-related disclosures (Moratis, 2018). Hence, signalling theory may be informative for understanding organizational activities with respect to purchasing and supply management, and may help to improve the understanding of how to allocate resources (in terms of signalling costs).

In terms of theoretical advancements, it could be beneficial, similarly to what Connelly et al. and Bergh et al. are proposing, to investigate each of the constructs in more detail in the context of purchasing and supply management in a business-to-business (B2B) environment. Answers to the questions: How can signallers manage a portfolio of (different) signals to maximize collective effectiveness?, How can receivers meaningfully aggregate signals in sequences and patterns?, What different types of signals are used?, How does feedback-seeking behavior improve the signalling process?, Under which circumstances are signalling equilibria realized?, When do noisy environments diminish signal observability?, How can competing receivers inject noise into the signalling environment? could advance the understanding of each of the constructs (Bergh et al., 2014; Connelly et al., 2011a). Moreover, what changes arise if the information asymmetry assumption is relaxed? In the case of agency theory, its primary mechanisms for safeguarding against the hazards of information asymmetry, such as monitoring behaviour and outcome-based incentives, become less important, and information signals might become the main basis for guiding *ex ante* contractual agreements (Bergh et al., 2019, p. 149). What also seems interesting in this context is if one changes the underlying (classic) agency relationship from supplier to buyer. Hence, in a supply and purchasing context, the buyer would be the better-informed actor and the supplier would suffer information asymmetry. This could very well be the case, when buying services, such as IT or management consulting services. In those cases, the buyer would need to decide to invest in a certain signal in order to alleviate the information asymmetry, and to subsequently steer the application of required, specialized competences (of the service providers) (Axelsson and Wynstra, 2002; Lusch, 2006; Vargo and Akaka, 2009).

REFERENCES

Atkinson, L., and Rosenthal, S. (2014). Signaling the green sell: The influence of eco-label source, argument specificity, and product involvement on consumer trust. *Journal of Advertising*, 43(1), 33–45. Retrieved from https://doi.org/10.1080/00913367.2013.834803.
Axelsson, B., and Wynstra, F. (2002). *Buying Business Services*. Chichester: John Wiley & Sons.

Bakshi, N., Kim, S.H., and Savva, N. (2015). Signaling new product reliability with after-sales service contracts. *Management Science*, 61(8), 1812–1829. Retrieved from https://doi.org/10.1287/mnsc .2014.2029.

Bals, L., Schulz, H., Kelly, S., and Stek, K. (2019). Purchasing and supply management (PSM) competencies: Current and future requirements. *Journal of Purchasing and Supply Management*, 25(5), 100572.

Bergh, D.D., Connelly, B.L., Ketchen, D.J., and Shannon, L.M. (2014). Signalling theory and equilibrium in strategic management research: An assessment and a research agenda. *Journal of Management Studies*, (December). Retrieved 25 October 2014 from https://doi.org/10.1111/joms.12097.

Bergh, D.D., Ketchen, D.J., Orlandi, I., Heugens, P.P.M.A.R., and Boyd, B.K. (2019). Information asymmetry in management research: Past accomplishments and future opportunities. *Journal of Management*, 45(1), 122–158. Retrieved from https://doi.org/10.1177/0149206318798026.

Cheng, L., Craighead, C.W., Wang, Q., and Li, J.J. (2020). When is the supplier's message 'loud and clear'? Mixed signals from supplier-induced disruptions and the response. *Decision Sciences*, 51(2), 216–254. Retrieved from https://doi.org/10.1111/deci.12412.

Cheung, C.M.K., Xiao, B.S., and Liu, I.L.B. (2014). Do actions speak louder than voices? The signaling role of social information cues in influencing consumer purchase decisions. *Decision Support Systems*, 65(C), 50–58. Retrieved from https://doi.org/10.1016/j.dss.2014.05.002.

Chicksand, D., Watson, G., Walker, H., Radnor, Z., and Johnston, R. (2012). Theoretical perspectives in purchasing and supply chain management: An analysis of the literature. *Supply Chain Management: An International Journal*, 17(4), 454–472. Retrieved 6 June 2013 from https://doi.org/10.1108/ 13598541211246611.

Connelly, B.L., Certo, S.T., Ireland, R.D., and Reutzel, C.R. (2011a). Signaling theory: A review and assessment. *Journal of Management*, 37(1), 39–67. Retrieved 16 July 2014 from https://doi.org/10 .1177/0149206310388419.

Connelly, B.L., Ketchen, D.J., and Slater, S.F. (2011b). Toward a 'theoretical toolbox' for sustainability research in marketing. *Journal of the Academy of Marketing Science*, 39(1), 86–100. Retrieved from https://doi.org/10.1007/s11747-010-0199-0.

Courtney, C., Dutta, S., and Li, Y. (2017). Resolving information asymmetry: Signaling, endorsement, and crowdfunding success. *Entrepreneurship: Theory and Practice*, 41(2), 265–290. Retrieved from https://doi.org/10.1111/etap.12267.

Defee, C.C., Williams, B., Randall, W.S., and Thomas, R. (2010). An inventory of theory in logistics and SCM research. *International Journal of Logistics Management*, 21(3), 404–489. Retrieved 5 June 2013 from https://doi.org/10.1108/09574091011089817.

Drover, W., Wood, M.S., and Corbett, A.C. (2018). Toward a cognitive view of signalling theory: Individual attention and signal set interpretation. *Journal of Management Studies*, 55(2), 209–231. Retrieved from https://doi.org/10.1111/joms.12282.

Eliashberg, J., and Robertson, T.S. (1988). New product preannouncing behavior: A market signaling study. *Journal of Marketing Research*, 25(3), 282. Retrieved from https://doi.org/10.2307/3172530.

Etzion, D., and Pe'er, A. (2014). Mixed signals: A dynamic analysis of warranty provision in the automotive industry, 1960–2008. *Strategic Management Journal*, 35, 1605–1625. Retrieved from https:// doi.org/10.1002/smj.

Gomulya, D., and Mishina, Y. (2017). Signaler credibility, signal susceptibility, and relative reliance on signals: How stakeholders change their evaluative processes after violation of expectations and rehabilitative efforts. *Academy of Management Journal*, 60(2), 554–583. Retrieved from https://doi .org/10.5465/amj.2014.1041.

Halldórsson, Á., Hsuan, J., and Kotzab, H. (2015). Complementary theories to supply chain management revisited – From borrowing theories to theorizing. *Supply Chain Management: An International Journal*, 20(6), 574–586. Retrieved from https://doi.org/10.1108/SCM-06-2015-0228.

Ho, C.T., and Wei, C.L. (2016). Effects of outsourced service providers' experiences on perceived service quality: A signaling theory framework. *Industrial Management and Data Systems*, 116(8), 1656–1677. Retrieved from https://doi.org/10.1108/IMDS-01-2016-0015.

Hossain, M.A., Rahman, S., Chowdhury, T.A., Chan, C., Yang, X., and Su, Q. (2018). How signaling mechanisms reduce 'lemons' from online group buying (OGB) markets? A study of China.

International Journal of Physical Distribution and Logistics Management, 48(7), 658–681. Retrieved from https://doi.org/10.1108/IJPDLM-02-2017-0113.

Ippolito, P.M. (1990). Bonding and nonbonding signals of product quality. *Journal of Business*, 63(1), 41–60.

Jones, S.L., Fawcett, S.E., Fawcett, A.M., and Wallin, C. (2010). Benchmarking trust signals in supply chain alliances: Moving toward a robust measure of trust. *Benchmarking*, 17(5), 705–727. Retrieved from https://doi.org/10.1108/14635771011076452.

Karasek, R., and Bryant, P. (2015). Signaling theory: Past, present, and future. *Electronic Business Journal*, 14(12), 550–558.

Kembro, J., Selviaridis, K., and Näslund, D. (2014). Theoretical perspectives on information sharing in supply chains: A systematic literature review and conceptual framework. *Supply Chain Management: An International Journal*, 19(5/6), 609–625. Retrieved from https://doi.org/10.1108/SCM-12-2013 -0460.

Kirmani, A., and Rao, A.R. (2000). No pain, no gain: A critical review of the literature on signaling unobservable product quality. *Journal of Marketing*, 64(2), 66–79. Retrieved from https://doi.org/10 .1509/jmkg.64.2.66.18000.

Lusch, R.F. (2006). Service-dominant logic: Reactions, reflections and refinements. *Marketing Theory*, 6(3), 281–288. Retrieved 12 August 2013 from https://doi.org/10.1177/1470593106066781.

Mavlanova, T., Benbunan-Fich, R., and Koufaris, M. (2012). Signaling theory and information asymmetry in online commerce. *Information and Management*, 49(5), 240–247. Retrieved from https://doi .org/10.1016/j.im.2012.05.004.

Miemczyk, J., Johnsen, T.E., and Macquet, M. (2012). Sustainable purchasing and supply management: A structured literature review of definitions and measures at the dyad, chain and network levels. *Supply Chain Management: An International Journal*, 17(5), 478–496. Retrieved from https://doi.org/ 10.1108/13598541211258564.

Moratis, L. (2018). Signalling responsibility? Applying signalling theory to the ISO 26000 standard for social responsibility. *Sustainability (Switzerland)*, 10(11), 1–20. Retrieved from https://doi.org/10 .3390/su10114172.

Morris, R.D. (1987). Signalling, agency theory and accounting policy choice. *Accounting and Business Research*, 18(69), 47–56. Retrieved from https://doi.org/10.1080/00014788.1987.9729347.

Ozmel, U., Reuer, J.J., and Gulati, R. (2012). Signals across multiple networks: How venture capital and alliance networks affect interorganizational collaboration. *Academy of Management Journal*, 56(3), 852–866. Retrieved from https://doi.org/10.5465/amj.2009.0549.

Park, H.D., and Patel, P.C. (2015). How does ambiguity influence IPO underpricing? The role of the signalling environment. *Journal of Management Studies*, 52(6), 796–818. Retrieved from https://doi .org/10.1111/joms.12132.

Rao, A.R., Qu, L., and Ruekert, R.W. (1999). Signaling unobservable product quality through a brand ally. *Journal of Marketing Research*, 36(2), 258–268. Retrieved from https://doi.org/10.1017/ CBO9781107415324.004.

Rao, S., Lee, K.B., Connelly, B., and Iyengar, D. (2018). Return time leniency in online retail: A signaling theory perspective on buying outcomes. *Decision Sciences*, 49(2), 275–305. Retrieved from https://doi.org/10.1111/deci.12275.

Reuer, J.J., Tong, T.W., and Wu, C.-W. (2012). A signaling theory of acquisition premiums: Evidence from IPO targets. *Academy of Management Journal*, 55(3), 667–683.

Riley, J.G. (2001). Silver signals: Twenty-five years of screening and signaling. *Journal of Economic Literature*, 39(2), 432–478. Retrieved from https://doi.org/10.1257/jel.39.2.432.

Schotanus, F., and Telgen, J. (2007). Developing a typology of organisational forms of cooperative purchasing. *Journal of Purchasing and Supply Management*, 13(1), 53–68. Retrieved 30 May 2013 from https://doi.org/10.1016/j.pursup.2007.03.002.

Schotanus, F., Telgen, J., and de Boer, L. (2010). Critical success factors for managing purchasing groups. *Journal of Purchasing and Supply Management*, 16(1), 51–60. Retrieved from https://doi.org/ 10.1016/j.pursup.2009.10.002.

Shao, L., Ryan, J.K., and Sun, D. (2020). Responsible sourcing under asymmetric information: Price signaling versus supplier disclosure. *Decision Sciences*, 1–28. Retrieved from https://doi.org/10.1111/ deci.12482.

Shook, C.L., Adams, G.L., Ketchen, D.J., and Craighead, C.W. (2009). Towards a 'theoretical toolbox' for strategic sourcing. *Supply Chain Management: An International Journal*, 14(1), 3–10. Retrieved 24 March 2013 from https://doi.org/10.1108/13598540910927250.

Simaens, A., and Koster, M. (2013). Reporting on sustainable operations by third sector organizations: A signalling approach. *Public Management Review*, 15(7), 1040–1062. Retrieved from https://doi.org/10.1080/14719037.2012.757350.

Spence, M. (1973). Job market signaling. *Quarterly Journal of Economics*, 87(3), 355–374.

Spence, M. (1976). Informational aspects of market structure: An introduction. *Quarterly Journal of Economics*, 90(4), 591–597.

Spence, M. (2002). Signaling in retrospect and the informational structure of markets. *American Economic Review*, 92(3), 434–459.

Spina, G., Caniato, F., Luzzini, D., and Ronchi, S. (2016). Assessing the use of external grand theories in purchasing and supply management research. *Journal of Purchasing and Supply Management*, 22(1), 18–30. Retrieved from https://doi.org/10.1016/j.pursup.2015.07.001.

Stern, I., Dukerich, J.M., and Zajac, E. (2014). Unmixed signals: How reputation and status affect alliance formation. *Strategic Management Journal*, 35, 512–531. Retrieved from https://doi.org/10.1002/smj.

Stiglitz, J.E. (2000). The contributions of the economics of information to twentieth century economics. *Quarterly Journal of Economics*, 115, 1441–1478.

Stump, R.L., and Heide, J.B. (1996). Controlling supplier opportunism in industrial relationships. *Journal of Marketing Research*, 33(4), 431–441. Retrieved from https://doi.org/10.2307/3152214.

Taj, S.A. (2016). Application of signaling theory in management research: Addressing major gaps in theory. *European Management Journal*, 34(4), 338–348. Retrieved from https://doi.org/10.1016/j.emj.2016.02.001.

Taoketao, E., Feng, T., Song, Y., and Nie, Y. (2018). Does sustainability marketing strategy achieve payback profits? A signaling theory perspective. *Corporate Social Responsibility and Environmental Management*, 25(6), 1039–1049. Retrieved from https://doi.org/10.1002/csr.1518.

Terlaak, A., and King, A.A. (2006). The effect of certification with the ISO 9000 quality management standard: A signaling approach. *Journal of Economic Behavior and Organization*, 60(4), 579–602. Retrieved from https://doi.org/10.1016/j.jebo.2004.09.012.

Thomas, R., Darby, J.L., Dobrzykowsk, D., and van Hoek, R. (2021). Decomposing social sustainability: Signaling theory insights into supplier selection decisions. *Journal of Supply Chain Management*, 57(4), 117–136. Retrieved from https://doi.org/10.1111/jscm.12247.

Touboulic, A., and Walker, H. (2015). Theories in sustainable supply chain management: A structured literature review. *International Journal of Physical Distribution and Logistics Management*, 45(1/2), 16–42.

Vargo, S.L., and Akaka, M.A. (2009). Service-dominant logic as a foundation for service science: Clarifications. *Service Science*, 1(1), 32–41. Retrieved from https://doi.org/10.1287/serv.1.1.32.

Wacker, J.G. (1998). A definition of theory: Research guidelines for different theory-building research methods in operations management. *Journal of Operations Management*, 16(4), 361–385. Retrieved from https://doi.org/10.1016/S0272-6963(98)00019-9.

Walker, H., Chicksand, D., Radnor, Z., and Watson, G. (2015). Theoretical perspectives in operations management: An analysis of the literature. *International Journal of Operations and Production Management*, 35(8), 1182–1206. Retrieved from https://doi.org/10.1108/IJOPM-02-2014-0089.

Walker, H., Schotanus, F., Bakker, E., and Harland, C. (2013). Collaborative procurement: A relational view of buyer–buyer relationships. *Public Administration Review*, (August), 588–598. Retrieved from https://doi.org/10.1111/puar.12048.studies.

Wells, J.D., Valacich, J.S., and Hess, T.J. (2011). What signal are you sending? How website quality influences perceptions of product quality and purchase intentions. *MIS Quarterly: Management Information Systems*, 35(2), 373–396.

Wolters, H., and Schuller, F. (1997). Explaining supplier–buyer partnerships: A dynamic game theory approach. *European Journal of Purchasing and Supply Management*, 3(3), 155–164. Retrieved from https://doi.org/10.1016/S0969-7012(97)00011-7.

Wu, C.W., Reuer, J.J., and Ragozzino, R. (2013). Insights of signaling theory for acquisitions research. *Advances in Mergers and Acquisitions*, 12(2013), 173–191. Retrieved from https://doi.org/10.1108/ S1479-361X(2013)0000012010.

Wynstra, F., Suurmond, R., and Nullmeier, F. (2019). Purchasing and supply management as a multidisciplinary research field: Unity in diversity? *Journal of Purchasing and Supply Management*, 25(5), 100578. Retrieved from https://doi.org/10.1016/j.pursup.2019.100578.

Xu, X., Zeng, S., and Chen, H. (2018). Signaling good by doing good: How does environmental corporate social responsibility affect international expansion? *Business Strategy and the Environment*, 27(7), 946–959. Retrieved from https://doi.org/10.1002/bse.2044.

Yasar, B., Martin, T., and Kiessling, T. (2020). An empirical test of signalling theory. *Management Research Review*, 1–27. Retrieved from https://doi.org/10.1108/MRR-08-2019-0338.

SUGGESTED FURTHER READING

For more information on information asymmetry:

Bergh, D.D., Ketchen, D.J., Orlandi, I., Heugens, P.P.M.A.R., and Boyd, B.K. (2019). Information asymmetry in management research: Past accomplishments and future opportunities. *Journal of Management*, 45(1), pp. 122–158. Retrieved from doi: 10.1177/0149206318798026.

Good literature reviews on the application of signaling theory:

Bergh, D.D., Connelly, B.L., Ketchen, D.J., and Shannon, L.M. (2014). Signalling theory and equilibrium in strategic management research: An assessment and a research agenda. *Journal of Management Studies*, (December). Retrieved 25 October 2014 from doi: 10.1111/joms.12097.

Connelly, B.L., Certo, S.T., Ireland, R.D., and Reutzel, C.R. (2011). Signaling theory: A review and assessment. *Journal of Management*, 37(1), pp. 39–67. Retrieved 16 July 2014 from doi: 10.1177/0149206310388419.

Taj, S.A. (2016). Application of signaling theory in management research: Addressing major gaps in theory. *European Management Journal*, 34(4), pp. 338–348. doi: 10.1016/j.emj.2016.02.001.

30. Portfolio theory

Cees J. Gelderman

INTRODUCTION

The work of Markowitz in the early 1950s is the origin of portfolio theory for investment purposes. Portfolio approaches are used for management problems in various fields and disciplines. For business purposes, portfolio approaches have been developed for applications in investment theory, strategic management, marketing and purchasing management. Managing supplier relations is increasingly considered as a strategically important activity for the firm. In theory, there are many different types of buyer–supplier relationships. In practice, companies need a variety of relationships, each providing its different benefits. Purchasing professionals should have the capacity to cope with a variety of relationships, to be handled in differentiated ways. Companies need a variety of relationships, each providing its different benefits, where no general best type of relationship exists (Young and Wilkinson, 1997; Gadde and Snehota, 2000). Obviously, not all suppliers are to be dealt with in the same way. This gives purchasing managers the task of developing and executing a set of differentiated supplier strategies. The need for differentiated supplier strategies requires some sort of classification (Lilliecreutz and Ydreskog, 1999). Purchasing portfolio analysis is considered as a particularly useful tool, developing and selecting differentiated purchasing and supplier strategies.

KEY CONCEPTS AND DEFINITIONS

A portfolio refers to a collection of different but connected items. The items may be objects or subjects. In general, the portfolio concept focuses on the interdependencies among the objects/subjects and emphasizes an integrated approach (Turnbull, 1990). The portfolio concept stresses the importance of the whole rather than the parts. It reflects the importance for balance in a collection of individual elements. As a consequence, it allows for differentiation and diversification, in an aim for balance and an optimal use of limited resources. We define a portfolio model as 'a tool that combines two or more dimensions into a set of heterogeneous categories for which different (strategic) recommendations are provided' (Gelderman, 2003, p. 21).

Three basic elements are to be recognized in this definition: dimensions, categories and strategic recommendations. The use of the portfolio model implies the classification of objects/subjects, usually presented in the form of a two-dimensional matrix. The basic idea is that the positions of the units on the grid or in the matrix should determine the formulation of the most appropriate strategy (Yorke and Droussiotis, 1994). Models and tools that do not provide guidance for management decisions are merely classification schemes, not portfolio models. In purchasing, classification tools can be seen as the predecessors of the actual portfolio models.

PORTFOLIO THEORY

Portfolio theory is essentially concerned with the collective returns from the use of assets together with their possible redistribution over various options at the discretion of management. How 'assets', 'returns' and 'options' are defined depends on the area of application (Yorke, 1984, p. 9), Portfolio theory has its roots in investment theory. The work of Markowitz in the early 1950s is the origin of modern portfolio theory for investment purposes. Balancing the objectives of high yield and low risk, the portfolio approach focuses on the efficient allocation of limited resources. Further development from Markowitz's portfolio theory gave rise to what is known as modern portfolio theory (Sharpe, 1963; 1964). Portfolio theory has been considered both a normative method (providing recommendations for portfolio selection) and a positive method (providing hypotheses about investment behaviour) (Castro et al., 2015).

In the early 1950s the investment community talked about risk, but there was no specific measure for this key concept. Investors had to quantify risk for investment decisions. Markowitz (1952) derived the expected rate of return for a portfolio of assets and an expected risk measure. He showed that the variance of the rate of return was a useful measure of portfolio risk, and he derived a formula for computing the variance of a portfolio. Markowitz showed that:

- The expected rate of return of a portfolio is the weighted average of the expected return for the individual investments.
- The standard deviation of a portfolio is a function not only of the standard deviation for the individual investment, but also the covariance between the rates of return for all the pairs of assets in the portfolio. In a large portfolio, these covariances are the important factors. Markowitz's formula not only indicated the importance of diversifying investments to reduce the total risk of a portfolio, but also showed how to diversify.

The Markowitz model is based on several assumptions regarding investor behaviour (Reilly and Norton, 2017):

1. Investors consider each investment alternative as being presented by a probability distribution of expected returns over some holding period.
2. Investors maximize one-period expected utility, and their utility curves demonstrate diminishing marginal utility of wealth.
3. Investors estimate the risk of the portfolio on the basis of the variability of expected returns.
4. Investors base decisions solely on expected return and risk, so their utility curves are a function of expected return and the expected variance of returns only.
5. For a given risk level, investors prefer higher returns to lower returns. Similarly, for a given level of expected return, investors prefer less risk to more risk.

Under these assumptions, a portfolio of assets is considered to be efficient if no other portfolio offers higher expected return with the same or lower risk, or lower risk with the same (or higher) expected return. Markowitz's conclusion is that rational investors would (or should) want to select 'efficient portfolios', that is portfolios with a minimum of risk (variance) for a given expected return, or with a maximum expected return for a given risk (variance).

Nowadays the Markowitz formula is still being used as the basis for modern investment theory and investment practice. The consequences are far-reaching and provide much guidance for investment decisions. The most important implication is that diversification reduces variability and risk. The greatest payoff to diversification comes when stocks (or other assets) are negatively correlated (Brealy and Myers, 2012). When there is a perfect negative correlation (–1) between two assets, the overall variance of the portfolio is zero (0). This would be a risk-free portfolio (Reilly and Norton, 2017). Investors are advised not to invest all their money into one stock, but to reduce their risk by diversification. Investors should be interested in the effect that each stock has on the risk of the portfolio as a whole. It is therefore not decisive how risky an investment is, but what the impact will be on the risk of the entire portfolio. One of the simplest ways for an individual to diversify is to buy shares in a mutual fund which holds a diversified portfolio. Software programs, called 'optimizers', are used to determine 'efficient portfolios'. Financial planners use information on past returns and manager performance, in addition to optimizers, to make recommendations to their clients (Reilly and Norton, 2017).

RELEVANCE FOR PURCHASING AND SUPPLY MANAGEMENT

Investment theory basically deals with the choice of investments between an infinite number of potential portfolios, resulting in 'yes' or 'no' types of recommendations. It is all about the composition of an investment portfolio by reducing risks and optimizing returns. In purchasing management, however, it is a matter of choice of strategies for a given number of items (usually products), resulting in a set of differentiated purchasing and supplier strategies. This means that there are important differences in scope and perspective.

Another major difference regards the existence of another party and the factor of social interaction (Yorke, 1984). Here lies a sharp contrast with the application of portfolio theory to investment purposes and to purchasing purposes. There is always an unpredictable element in a purchasing context, due to the dynamics of business and human behaviour. The risk-factor is of another order. In the investment theory the variable 'risk' is measurable in a rather easy and unambiguous way, based on a mathematical formula. It is clear that such a formula does not exist for the determination of risk in a purchasing context.

The main similarity, however, is that any portfolio approach focuses on the efficient allocation of limited resources. In a general sense this problem is relevant for investment decisions and for purchasing decisions. Another similar characteristic refers to the trade-off between risks and rewards. For instance, there are benefits in spreading purchases among a number of suppliers. However, there is a trade-off involved. The net effect of dealing with a large number of suppliers can be to shift the balance of power towards the seller rather than towards the buyer. Just as in the financial world, risks and rewards are closely linked. Buyers should therefore be aware of the balance between risk and return. Nicholson (1993) points out that buyers should ask themselves:

1. If the overall business risk increases due to a purchasing strategy, is that increased risk matched by an increased return or benefit?
2. If the buyer obtains an increased reward for the firm, has it been achieved by exposing the business to a higher level of risk?

Smeltzer and Siferd (1998) argued that proactive purchasing management is concerned with risk management. It should mitigate risk and, at the same time, provide a higher return. To conclude, purchasing management has to deal with issues of risks and rewards, albeit that the context of decision making is different in comparison to investment problems.

HISTORY OF PURCHASING PORTFOLIO MODELS

In the 1983 Purchasing Conference in Copenhagen, Kraljic, director in the Düsseldorf office of McKinsey Company, presented a new and promising instrument for the determination of a set of differentiated purchasing strategies, and a policy for the more fundamental restructuring of the portfolio as a whole. The *Harvard Business Review* (*HBR*) published his seminal paper, 'Purchasing must become supply management' (Kraljic, 1983) which pointed at the need for companies to progress toward more effective supply management, accompanied by a practical portfolio tool for shaping the supply strategy. The Kraljic portfolio approach can be considered as an important breakthrough in the development of theory in the field of purchasing and supply management. The portfolio approach is considered a powerful tool, to be used for diagnostic and prescriptive purposes, that goes far beyond the rather simplistic classification models such as the ABC analysis (Syson, 1992). Although other models have been developed, Kraljic's approach subsequently became the dominant approach to what the profession regards as operational professionalism. Purchasing portfolio models have gained ground in both academic research as well as in practice (Nellore and Söderquist, 2000).

By now the *HBR* 1983 contribution has probably become the most cited and referred to article in the field of purchasing and supply (chain) management. It is noted that Kraljic (1977) presented exactly the same concepts and ideas much earlier, albeit in a German business journal (*Beschaffung Aktuell*), that did not get much attention in the international business and academic community. The matrix was developed for BASF in the early 1970s (c. 1973, 1974), within the context of a large cash management project. Purchasing management was just one of the business functions involved. As a McKinsey consultant he was asked to develop a new tool for purchasing, similar to the then recently introduced marketing matrices, for example the Boston Consulting Group (BCG) matrix (Gelderman and Van Haaster, 2002).

THE KRALJIC PURCHASING PORTFOLIO APPROACH

Kraljic (1983) introduced the first comprehensive portfolio approach for the determination of a set of differentiated purchasing strategies and a policy for the more fundamental restructuring of the portfolio as a whole. Some 20 years ago he advised managers to guard their firms against disastrous supply interruptions, and to cope with changing economics and new technologies. His message was 'purchasing must become supply management'. Kraljic (1983, p. 112) proposed a four-stage approach as a framework for 'shaping the supply strategy':

1. Classify all the purchased materials or components in terms of profit impact and supply risk.
2. Analyze the supply market for these materials.
3. Determine the overall strategic supply position.

4. Develop materials strategies and actions plans.

Kraljic's approach includes the construction of a portfolio matrix which allows for a classification of products on the basis of two dimensions: profit impact and supply risk ('low' and 'high'), 'The profit impact of a given item could be defined in terms of the volume purchased, percentage of total cost, or impact on product quality or business growth. Supply risk is a more complex, composite dimension. It might be assessed in terms of availability, number of suppliers, competitive demand, make-or-buy opportunities, and storage risks and substitution possibilities. It should be noted that these are merely examples. Kraljic introduced matrices and dimensions that are described in general terms, allowing for customized use. Kraljic (1983, p. 113) clearly stated that 'no list of evaluation criteria is equally applicable to every industry'. Kraljic's portfolio approach allows for sufficient customization (Gelderman, 2003).

The result is a 2x2 matrix and a classification in four categories: bottleneck, non-critical, leverage and strategic items. Each of the four categories requires a distinctive approach towards suppliers (see Figure 30.1), Gelderman and Van Weele (2002, p. 31) concluded: 'Non-critical items require efficient processing, product standardization, order volume and inventory optimization. Leverage items allow the buying company to exploit its full purchasing power, for instance through tendering, competitive bidding, target pricing and product substitution.' Bottleneck items present significant problems and risks. Volume assurance, vendor control, security of inventories and backup plans are recommended here. For the strategic items a further analysis is recommended. By plotting the buying strengths against the strengths of the supply market, three basic power positions are identified and associated with three different supplier strategies: balance, exploit and diversify. Each of the three strategic thrusts has distinctive implications for the individual elements of the purchasing strategy, such as volume, price, supplier selection, material substitution, inventory policy, and so on.

Companies could consolidate their supply position by concentrating fragmented volumes in a single supplier, accepting high prices, and covering the full volume requirements through supply contracts. To reduce the long-term risk of dependence on a single source, however, companies could also search for alternative suppliers or materials, or even consider backward integration (diversify). 'When bargaining from weakness the company may have to offer longer-term contract obligations or accept higher prices in order to ensure an adequate supply' (Kraljic, 1983, p. 114). On the other hand, if the buying company is stronger than the suppliers, it can bargain and act from a position of strength. The company could press for preferential treatment. It can spread volume over several suppliers, exploit price advantages, increase spot purchases and reduce inventory levels. With no dominant party at hand, a well-balanced intermediate strategy is advised.

Kraljic's purchasing portfolio approach is still the dominant approach in the profession. After its introduction in 1983, many variations have been introduced, proposing new dimensions, values and segments. Scholars have introduced variations of the original Kraljic matrix (Elliott-Shircore and Steele, 1985; Syson, 1992; Hadeler and Evans, 1994; Olsen and Ellram, 1997; Lee and Drake, 2010; Luzzini et al., 2012; Drake et al., 2013; Bildsten, 2014; Gangurde and Chavan, 2016; Ghanbarizadeh et al., 2019; Rezaei and Lajimi, 2019). However, the proposed matrices are very similar to the Kraljic matrix in that they use practically the same dimensions and categories, and suggest some of the same recommendations (Gelderman and Van Weele, 2005). These contributions build on the original with more similarities than differences (cf. Ekström et al., 2021). A notable refinement is the model developed by Gelderman

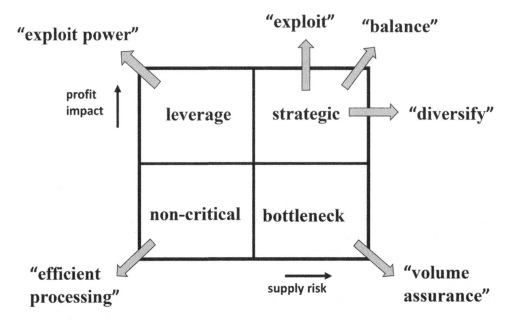

Figure 30.1   The Kraljic matrix: categories and strategic recommendations

(2003) that explicitly includes purchasing strategies to pursue other positions in the matrix. Practitioners can select appropriate strategies to move an item or product into another matrix quadrant (Pagell et al., 2010; Bianchini et al., 2019). If we take a look at the bottleneck and the strategic quadrant at the right side of the matrix, those movements are pursued that reduce the supply risk. In terms of the matrix, this means moving to the left. In certain instances, non-critical items can be moved upwards, and leverage positions could be exchanged for strategic positions (Gelderman and Van Weele, 2003).

DOMAIN WHERE THE THEORY APPLIES

The domain of purchasing portfolio approaches applies to the development of purchasing and supplier strategies by a (buying) company. Still, purchasing portfolio analysis allows for different levels of analysis. The level of aggregation refers to the question whether individual items, smaller or broader product groups will be positioned in the matrix. What is the unit of analysis? Usually products or product groups are positioned in the matrix; however, suppliers or supplier relationships can also be positioned in the matrix (Åhman, 2002). The portfolio analysis might be restricted to certain types of products, for instance raw materials, logistical services or non-product related products. Individual items can be positioned in a matrix, but also product groups. Portfolio analysis can be connected to different organizational units: the corporate level, the level of area business units, and the level of a major customer. To conclude, the purchasing portfolio analysis allows for very different units and levels of analysis.

RELATIONSHIPS BETWEEN THE VARIABLES

Portfolio theory, as developed for investment purposes, intends to provide recommendations to investors in their quest to assemble an asset portfolio that maximizes the expected return for a given level of risk. The expected return of an investment portfolio is the weighted average of the individual expected returns of the assets in the portfolio. The risk of a portfolio is measured by its standard deviation, which depends on the standard deviation of each asset in the portfolio, the weights of each asset and the correlation between each asset. Diversification is a common allocation strategy aimed at minimizing risks by holding assets that are not perfectly positively correlated. The core idea is that a portfolio of assets from different classes is less risky than a portfolio of similar assets. Portfolio theory focuses on the relationship between assets in a portfolio in addition to the individual risk of each asset. These are the key concepts and ideas of portfolio theory in a nutshell. The key variables of portfolio investment theory are risks and returns of individual assets as well as risks and returns of the portfolio of assets.

Purchasing portfolio models are similar in the sense that they are aimed at minimizing (supply) risks while maximizing the potential effect of using buying power. A notable difference, however, is the operationalization of variables and the nature of the strategic recommendations. In the Kraljic matrix, the profit impact of a supply item is determined by:

1. the volume purchased;
2. the percentage of total purchase cost;
3. impact on product quality;
4. impact on business growth.

The supply risk is determined by:

1. the availability/scarcity of the item;
2. the number of suppliers;
3. the competitive demand;
4. make-or-buy opportunities;
5. storage risks;
6. substitution possibilities.

Items are classified according to the level of their profit impact and supply risk. A set of differentiated purchasing strategies are provided for each of the four categories. The selection and elaboration of strategic recommendations is key to any (purchasing) portfolio model. In addition to the various factors that constitute the two dimensions of the Kraljic matrix, Gelderman and Van Weele (2003) found that experienced portfolio users always included additional information on:

1. the overall business strategy (related situations on end markets);
2. the specific situations on supply markets (that is power positions); and
3. the intentions and competences of individual suppliers.

The elements of the Kraljic approach are summarized in Figure 30.2.

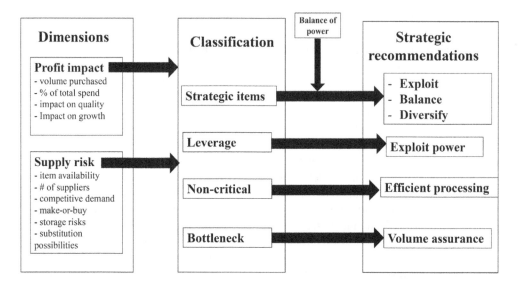

Figure 30.2   Overview of elements and relationships in the Kraljic matrix

CRITIQUES AND SUPPORT

Organizations usually have a large number of products and a variety of suppliers, which generally necessitates different treatment. For quite some time, ABC analysis (or Pareto analysis) was the only tool for differentiating between important and less important purchases. However, ABC analysis concentrates on the financial value of items, ignoring the cost of poor quality, performance risk, social risk, and other components (Hartmann et al., 2001). Moreover, ABC analysis does not provide strategic recommendations for the categories; it merely provides information on the concentration of purchase spend.

The introduction of the Kraljic portfolio approach has been described as 'a major break-through' in the development of professional purchasing, representing the most important single diagnostic and prescriptive tool available to purchasing and supply management (Syson, 1992). Kraljic (1983) made a reasonable case for the usefulness of the portfolio approach by describing the experiences of four large industrial companies. Studies have shown that a purchasing portfolio model is a powerful tool for:

1. coordinating the sourcing patterns of fairly autonomous strategic business units within companies, resulting in leverage and synergy (Carter, 1997; Gelderman and Van Weele, 2002);
2. differentiating the overall purchasing strategy, with different strategies for different supplier groups (Lilliecreutz and Ydreskog, 1999; Gelderman and Van Weele, 2003);
3. discussing, visualizing and illustrating the possibilities of the development of differentiated purchasing strategies (Gelderman and Van Weele, 2002, 2003);
4. configuring and managing supplier relationships, considering various interdependencies and trade-offs among relationships (Wagner and Johnson, 2004).

Portfolio approaches can be used to improve the allocation of scarce resources (Olsen and Ellram, 1997). A portfolio model provides a framework to understand and to focus a company's supply strategy (Hadeler and Evans, 1994). Portfolio usage has been associated with the level of purchasing sophistication of companies. A portfolio approach can make the difference between an unfocused, ineffective purchasing organization and a focused, effective one (Hadeler and Evans, 1994), especially for those companies that have never thought systematically about their procurement expenditure (Cox, 1997). The utilization of this purchasing methodology may lift the purchasing activity out of the tactical, fire-fighting mode into a strategic role (Elliott-Shircore and Steele, 1985), Moreover, it may convince top management of the effective role that purchasing can play in contributing to a company's profit and success (Carter, 1997).

However, purchasing portfolio models have been severely criticized too. There are doubts and questions with respect to the following measurement issues:

1. The selection of variables. How could one know whether the most appropriate variables are being used (Nellore and Söderquist, 2000)? And how could we deal with the impact of the high sensitivity to the choice of dimensions and weights (Aloini et al., 2019)?
2. The supplier's side. Why is the supplier's side disregarded in most portfolio models (Homburg, 1995; Kamann, 2000)?
3. The operationalization of dimensions. What exactly is meant by profit impact and supply risk (Ramsay, 1996)?
4. The measurement of variables. How should the weighting of factors take place (Olsen and Ellram, 1997)? And does the measurement not merely reflect the purchaser's subjective mindset (Luzzini et al., 2012)?
5. The lines of demarcation. What is the exact difference between a 'high' and a 'low' supply risk (Homburg, 1995)?
6. The simplicity of recommendations. How could one deduce strategies from an analysis that is based on just two dimensions (Dubois and Pedersen, 2002)?

Other criticisms relate to more fundamental issues and objections. Portfolio models have a tendency to result in strategies that are independent of each other (Coate, 1983). They do not depict the interdependencies between two or more items in a matrix (Olsen and Ellram, 1997); instead, they concentrate on separate products (Ritter, 2000), focusing on supply, not on suppliers (Rezaei and Lajimi, 2019). Portfolio models fail to capture context-related dimensions and other important constraints, such as overall business strategy of the company, corporate purchasing policies and the network context (Kang et al., 2012; Aloini et al., 2019). Because portfolio models are limited to analysing products in a dyadic context, they fail to capture all the aspects that are considered vital for buyer–supplier relationships from a network perspective (Dubois and Pedersen, 2002). In line with the foregoing, some are averse to recommendations either to exploit power (Olsen and Ellram, 1997), or to reduce risk associated with the interdependence of companies within an industrial network (Dubois and Pedersen, 2002). From a different perspective, Cox (1997) condemned the portfolio methodology because it does not provide any proactive thinking about what can be done to change the existing reality of power in the various supply chains in which companies are involved.

The arguments supporting portfolio models have been reported in empirical studies, while the counterarguments can be found in conceptual studies (Gelderman and Van Weele, 2005). The critique of portfolio models does not include the experience of practitioners. Experienced users have found a reply to the critique of portfolio models, stressing that that there is no simple, standardized blueprint for the application of portfolio models (Gelderman and Van Weele, 2003). It requires critical thinking and sophistication of the purchasing function. Portfolio usage can be driven by purchasing sophistication (professionalism and position). However, it can also be argued that the introduction of the purchasing portfolio in companies drives purchasing sophistication. Adopting a portfolio approach could work as a catalyst for change within companies (Gelderman and Van Weele, 2005).

ASSUMPTIONS AND THEORETICAL FOUNDATION

Although purchasing portfolio models in general and the Kraljix matrix specifically have been criticized for a lack of adequate theoretical foundations (Luzzini et al., 2012), we posit that all of these models have their roots in portfolio theory. In addition, we will argue that the well-known Kraljic approach is essentially and implicitly based on resource dependence theory (see Gelderman, 2003).

Purchasing portfolio models are all based on general portfolio theory, which is developed for investment purposes. Portfolio theory is essentially concerned with the collective returns from the use of assets, together with their possible redistribution over various options at the discretion of management. All portfolio models are aimed at balancing objectives of high yield and low risk, and the efficient allocation of limited resources.

Resource dependence theory (RDT) provides a theoretical framework for understanding the dependence of one organization on another (Pfeffer and Salancik, 1978). The main principle of resource dependency theory is that it considers the ability to acquire and maintain resources as the key to organizational survival. Organizations require personnel, money, social legitimacy, customers, and a variety of technological and material inputs. In a very broad sense every organization must transact with elements in the environment to acquire the many resources that it depends on. In RDT the importance of a resource is a crucial factor, determining organizational dependence. Subsequently, there are two factors to the importance of any resource exchange: the relative magnitude of the exchange, and the criticality of the resource (Pfeffer and Salancik, 1978, pp. 45–51). It can be argued that the dimensions in the Kraljic matrix correspond with these variables: profit impact can be seen as an elaboration of magnitude, and supply risk as a translation of criticality. In other words, the combination of profit impact and supply risk determines the importance of a particular product category.

More insight in buyer–seller relationships is gained by distinguishing between levels of dependence with respect to both the buyer's dependence and the seller's dependence (Blenkhorn and MacKenzie, 1994; Kumar, 1996; Frazier and Antia, 1995). A distinction can be made between three levels of interdependence: low interdependence (balanced), unbalanced exchange, and high interdependence (balanced). In the case of a mutual dependence, power is in balance. In conclusion, there are four possible combinations of dependence:

1. High mutual dependence (balanced power).
2. Low mutual dependence (balanced power).
3. High supplier's dependence, low buyer's dependence (buyer dominated).
4. Low supplier's dependence, high buyer's dependence (supplier dominated).

Table 30.1   *Kraljic's strategic recommendations and their impact on dependence*

Item category	Strategic recommendations	Objectives	Impact on dependence
Bottleneck	Volume assurance	Prevent shortage of critical supplies	Reduces the negative effects of resource criticality and dependence; Does not remove the sources for the high level of buyer's dependence
Non-critical	Efficient processing	Reduce cost of ordering and materials handling	Does not affect the low level of buyer's dependence
Leverage	Exploit purchasing power	Reduce direct purchasing cost	Increases the supplier's dependence
Strategic (1): buyer's dominance	Exploit power	Increase overall supplier performance, incl. favourable pricing and reduced inventories	Increases the supplier's dependence
Strategic (2): supplier's dominance	Diversify	(a) find material substitutes/new suppliers; or (b) prevent shortage of critical supplies, for example accept higher prices or longer-term obligations	In case of (a) reduces the high level of buyer's dependence; or in case of (b) does not change the high level of buyer's dependence
Strategic (3): balanced relationship	Balance	Develop long-term supply relationships	Increases the high levels of buyer's and supplier's dependence

Sources: Kraljic (1983) and Gelderman (2003, p. 137).

If we take a close look at these four categories, we conclude that this classification is totally in accordance with Kraljic's matrix. The categories refer to very fundamental types of buyer–supplier relationships. That is probably why 'leverage', 'strategic', 'non-critical' and 'bottleneck' are four labels that have found their way into the common language:

1. 'Strategic' refers to high mutual dependence relationships.
2. 'Non-critical' refers to low mutual dependence relationships.
3. 'Leverage' refers to buyer-dominated relationships.
4. 'Bottleneck' refers to supplier-dominated relationships.

Now, we will analyse Kraljic's strategic recommendations from a power and dependence perspective. Table 30.1 summarizes the generic recommendations that are provided for the quadrants of the matrix. In addition, columns are added for the main objectives to be pursued by the strategic recommendations and for their intended and expected impact on the power-dependence relationships with suppliers. 'Volume assurance' and 'efficient processing' are adaptive methods, aimed at other objectives than changing the prevailing power-dependence relationships with suppliers. The recommendations handle problems that are a consequence of the matrix position: the negative effects of a shortage of supplies and the negative effects on the operational purchasing costs.

Quite a different picture is found in the leverage and strategic quadrant, where either the buyer's dependence or the supplier's dependence is increased, or both. In other words, the provided recommendations are aimed at changing the relative power position towards suppliers. Buyers are advised to proactively use possibilities, especially in light of the existing relationships with suppliers, attributed in terms of relative dominance. The exploitation of purchasing power will expand the buyer's dominance in the relationship even more. In cases of supplier's dominance more restraint actions are recommended, such as 'find material substitutes' and 'accept higher prices or long-term obligations to prevent shortages of supply'. Finally, in the case of power balance, an adaptive strategy is recommended to match and to develop the existing (long-term) relationship with the supplier in the strategic quadrant.

Kraljic's seminal article does not provide any reference to a theoretical foundation or comprehensive perspective. The general idea of the portfolio approach is 'to minimize supply vulnerability and make the most of potential buying power' (Kraljic, 1983, p. 112). In an interview, Kraljic acknowledged that the selection of dimensions was based on discussions with purchasing professionals, in search of 'things that really matter in purchasing'. Basically, a matter of common sense. He also confirmed that his portfolio approach was basically concerned with using and changing the balance of power with suppliers. Power and dependence are indeed at the heart of the Kraljic purchasing approach (Gelderman and Van Haaster, 2002). The in-depth analysis of the Kraljic approach, the dimensions and the recommendations, has made a reasonable case for the conclusion that the resource dependence theory should be considered as the (implicitly applied) theoretical foundation for the Kraljic portfolio approach (Gelderman, 2003).

HOW HAS PORTFOLIO THEORY BEEN USED?

Investment and Financial Management

Portfolio theory was foremost and primarily developed as a theory for investment decisions. Markowitz (1952) derived the expected rate of return for a portfolio of assets and an expected risk measure. He showed that the variance of the rate of return was a useful measure of portfolio risk and he derived a formula for computing the variance of a portfolio. Nowadays Markowitz's formula is still being used as the basis for modern investment theory and investment practice. The consequences are far-reaching and provide much guidance for investment decisions. The most important implication is that diversification reduces variability and risk.

Within the financial world, research has developed and widened its scope significantly. Building on the work of Markowitz, Sharpe (1963, 1964) introduced the well-known capital asset pricing model (CAPM). The CAPM is widely used by investors to estimate the return or the moving behaviour of the stock, whereas the Markowitz model is aimed at portfolio diversification (Lee et al., 2016). After the development of CAPM, research and portfolio theory have progressed in various directions, such as behavioural portfolio theory, non-utility portfolio theory, style portfolio theory, portfolio theory with liquidity, portfolio theory with continuous long-term, and value at risk (VaR) portfolio theory (Zhang, 2019). Portfolio theory is a well-known method in economic research, in asset allocations and the potential benefits of diversification for risk-averse agents. Particularly interesting is the application of the principles of portfolio theory in environmental research. Portfolio theory provides flexible tools to support natural resource decision-making (Alvarez et al., 2017). Research addresses land-use management, diversification and trade-off dynamics, since portfolio theory has proved to be useful for its application in environmental research questions (Matthies et al., 2019).

Purchasing and Supply Management and Supply Chain Management

Portfolio theory provides the common foundation for the development of purchasing portfolio models, although the application in the purchasing and supply domain requires that models are tailor-made to include domain-specific content (Luzzini et al., 2012). By using portfolio models, purchasing managers are forced to be aware of the balance between risks and returns. Portfolio theory is based on the principle of efficient allocation of limited resources. The implication is that investors have to select options and strategies, optimizing returns and reducing risks, which is very similar to the work of purchasing managers who have to select (a set of differentiated) purchasing and supplier strategies.

Strategic Management

In seeking answers to questions of strategic planning for the diversified organization, management has a strong need for tools that assist in allocating resources among business units and/ or products. A number of portfolio models have been proposed for this purpose. The first and best known is the Boston Consulting Group's growth share matrix (Henderson, 1970, 1972, 1973). The initial intent of the growth share matrix was to evaluate business units, but the same evaluation can be made for product lines or any other cash-generating entities. In addition to the BCG framework, other scholars and practitioners have developed multifactor portfolio models that use composite dimensions to designate the matrix axes. Well-known examples are the General Electric Business Screen, the Shell directional policy matrix, and the strategic condition matrix. Just as the purchasing portfolio models, the portfolio models in the domain of strategic management have their roots in portfolio theory.

Companies usually have to manage simultaneously and continuously a range of multiple concurrent projects (portfolios). Although each project might be independent, collectively they are interdependent. In this context, project portfolio risk management emerged (Hofman et al., 2017; Teller and Kock, 2013), which resulted in a body of literature 'providing knowledge and understanding about objectives, features, and the impacts of project portfolio risk management' (Micán et al., 2020, p. 68).

Portfolio models in strategic management provide recommendations concerning strategic business units: which to invest in, which to sell off, and which to shut down. In other words, they help companies in how to distribute their limited available resources (Kader and Hossain, 2020). For a long time, companies in the private sector have used portfolio management as a tool for strategic management of multi-business portfolios. Only recently have research and application expanded to organizations in the public sector (Baškarada and Hanlon, 2018). Commonly used criteria (for example, growth potential and market share) are generally not applicable in public sector organizations. Another development is the use of the grey portfolio analysis method. This method is complementary to the well-known BCG matrix, enabling managers to make a dynamic portfolio analysis for data with a high level of uncertainty (Nowak et al., 2020).

Marketing Management

The most common portfolio models in marketing management can be classified into three groups: models for new products or research and development projects, product (line) portfolio models, and customer portfolio models (Gelderman, 2003). The innovation portfolio consists of potential future products, while the product portfolio both informs innovation strategy and provides inputs to future innovation efforts (Brasil and Eggers, 2019). Product portfolio models tend to focus on resource allocation: which projects should be invested in, and which products are expected to produce economic value? Portfolio models in the marketing domain show much resemblance to those for selecting a financial portfolio of investments.

The literature shows a large number of comparable customer portfolio models (Fiocca, 1982; Shapiro et al., 1987; Homburg and Daum, 1997; Netzer et al., 2008; Homburg et al., 2009). These models are preoccupied with customer profitability, balancing costs and financial benefits. Customer portfolio models most commonly calculate expected returns from customers' purchasing history (Holm et al., 2012). They consider only current customers and focus on returns in the short term. Notable exceptions are the models as developed by Johnson and Selnes (2004) and McAlister and Sinha (2021). Companies will only survive if they succeed not merely in keeping customers, but also in attracting new entry-level customers who are turned into loyal customers.

Recently, with the development of big data analytics, companies need and use advanced software tools and platforms. Advanced methods of data analytics have been introduced in the world of customer portfolio analysis. An example is provided by Monalisa et al. (2019) who clustered customers on their customer's life value (CLV), using sophisticated quantitative techniques; for example, a Fuzzy C-means algorithm, the analytical hierarchy process (AHP) and the partition coefficient index (PCI).

HOW HAVE PURCHASING PORTFOLIO MODELS BEEN USED?

Purchasing and Supply Management and Supply Chain Management

In the purchasing and supply chain management literature, purchasing portfolio models have been used for three different purposes. First, purchasing portfolio models have been used in many studies that investigated the development and application of purchasing and supplier strategies. These studies most commonly focused on a specific context: company, industry or topic; for instance, case studies at an oil company (Gelderman and MacDonald, 2008), a chemical company (Gelderman and Van Weele, 2002) and a hospital (Medeiros and Ferreira, 2018). Examples of specific industries are the defence sector (Ekström et al., 2021), the construction industry (Ghanbarizadeh et al., 2019), the boiler industry (Gangurde and Chavan, 2016) and the manufacturing industry (Caniëls and Gelderman, 2007). Examples of specific topics are managing a global supply base (Gelderman and Semeijn, 2006), managing a portfolio of relationships (Olsen and Ellram, 1997; Bensaou, 1999), supplier involvement in product development (Wynstra and Ten Pierick, 2000), lean and agile purchasing (Drake et al., 2013), component purchasing (Lee and Drake, 2010) and commodity buying (Padhi et al., 2012).

Second, purchasing portfolio models have inspired many scholars to adjust and refine the traditional Kraljic matrix. More specifically, scholars have addressed what is believed to be one of the greatest weaknesses of purchasing portfolio models: the limits in operationalizing and measuring variables (Gelderman and Van Weele, 2005; Luzzini et al., 2012). Purchasing portfolio models have been criticized for the rather subjective methods for weighting and positioning objects in a matrix (Montgomery et al., 2018). Examples of quantitative approaches are the analytic hierarchy process (AHP) (Drake et al., 2013; Bianchini et al., 2019), the multi-objective decision analysis (Montgomery et al., 2018), the decision making trial and evaluation laboratory (DEMATEL) (Ghanbarizadeh et al., 2019); fuzzy set theory (FST) (Aloini et al., 2019) and the best worst method (BWM) (Rezaei and Lajimi, 2019). However, other scholars have alternatively embraced the qualitative character of portfolio use (Steele and Court, 1996). They appreciate the flexibility of the tool, allowing for customization and adaption to the needs and requirements of users. Ekström et al. (2021) proposed to use a Delphi method in the context of defence procurement. Some companies use a consensus-based method which is predominantly based on a process of reasoning and discussion by involved stakeholders (Gelderman and Van Weele, 2002). Gelderman (2003) found in his case studies that the positioning of items in the quadrants (the measurement) had to be followed by a process of reviewing the positions in the matrix, and a process of reflection on the consequences. Whatever method was selected, there are always subjective choices, limitations and elements that influence the actual positioning in the matrix.

Third, portfolio models have proved to be particularly useful in research that takes into consideration differences across purchasing categories and purchasing situations. The Kraljic matrix is often used to serve this purpose (Dabhilkar et al., 2016). An example is the study of Knight et al. (2014) that investigated how knowledge and skills vary across a portfolio of purchases. Obviously, effective purchasing requires a differentiated approach, tailored to the required skills for the procurement of specific products. In a related study, Dabhilkar et al. (2016) investigated the effectiveness of purchasing capabilities within the context of sustainability. Tailored approaches were recommended for different purchasing strategies. Another promising stream of research is studies that align purchasing portfolio management with negotiation styles. Depending on the specific buyer–supplier relationship at hand, different technical, commercial, legal and price/cost issues will be put on the agenda (Geiger, 2017). The negotiation context in terms of positions in the Kraljic matrix is likely to impact upon negotiation topics, tactics and outcomes (Lambrechts et al., 2019). Purchasing professionals adapt their negotiation style across the different quadrants of the portfolio matrix (Kang et al., 2018).

OUTLOOK ON FUTURE RESEARCH OPPORTUNITIES

Purchasing portfolio models have been criticized for their limitations and weaknesses. These open issues can be considered invitations for future research opportunities (Aloini et al., 2019). The most pressing issues appear to be:

1. The selection and measurement of variables, since all purchasing portfolio models are sensitive to these design choices (Gelderman and Van Weele, 2005).
2. The impact of the context in which companies work, since deep contextualization and ad hoc analysis are needed for the development of effective purchasing strategies (Aloini et al., 2019).
3. The simplicity and arbitrariness of the recommendations (Dubois and Pedersen, 2002; Knight et al., 2014), since subjective interpretations have a strong impact on the outcomes of portfolio analyses.

More research is also needed to understand the effectiveness of purchasing portfolio models. Future research could include an empirical study on the actual, direct impact of the application of a portfolio approach. The required research methodology should begin with the development of performance measures. A distinction should be made between the impact of the introduction of the tool in companies (first-time use) and the impact of a long-standing application (repeated use). Adopting a portfolio approach could work as a catalyst for change, leading the way to a more professional, mature and sophisticated purchasing function. Immediate success is warranted, considering the new insights that are to be attributed to portfolio use. To gain a deeper understanding of the adoption of the portfolio tool, we recommend a series of action research studies aimed at identifying normative guidelines for the implementation and for the assessment of the full impact of the portfolio approach. These action research studies should include 'before' and 'after' measurement of key variables in order to determine accountable changes. Another possibility would be the use of critical incident techniques to shed more light on complex managerial problems relating to the development and implementation of portfolio-based purchasing strategies.

Even more challenging would be some research focused on the impact of repeated use, in terms of performance measures that count to top management. Only longitudinal studies in companies could provide information about the long-term impact and usefulness of the portfolio approach. Such research requires a complex design. The researcher should overcome the difficulties of attributing results of portfolio use and of comparing the use of the tool in different companies, because several company-specific factors are likely to influence the impact and implementation of portfolio use. In addition, the personality of individual purchasers could be included, describing and explaining the use and effectiveness of the portfolio approach.

REFERENCES

Åhman, S. (2002), 'Strategic sourcing of suppliers in a supply network', paper presented at the 11th International IPSERA Conference, Enschede, The Netherlands, 26 March.

Aloini, D., Dulmin, R., Mininno, V., and P. Zerbino (2019), 'Leveraging procurement-related knowledge through a fuzzy-based DSS: a refinement of purchasing portfolio models', *Journal of Knowledge Management*, 23(6), 1077–1104.

Alvarez, S., Larkin, S.L., and A. Ropicki (2017), 'Optimizing provision of ecosystem services using modern portfolio theory', *Ecosystem Services*, 27, 25–37.

Baškarada, S., and B. Hanlon (2018), 'Corporate portfolio management in the public sector', *Journal of Management Development*, 37(4), 333–340.

Bensaou, M. (1999), 'Portfolios of buyer–supplier relationships', *Sloan Management Review*, 40(4), 35–44.

Bianchini, A., Benci, A., Pellegrini, M., and J. Rossi (2019), 'Supply chain redesign for lead-time reduction through Kraljic purchasing portfolio and AHP integration', *Benchmarking: An International Journal*, 26(4), 1194–1209.

Bildsten, L. (2014), 'Buyer–supplier relationships in industrialized building', *Construction Management and Economics*, 32(1–2), 146–159.

Blenkhorn, D.L., and H.F. Mackenzie (1994), 'The importance of buyer–seller dependence in relationship marketing', paper presented at the Second Research Conference on Relationship Marketing, Emory University, Atlanta, USA, 11 June.

Brasil, V.C., and J.P. Eggers (2019), 'Product and innovation portfolio management', in Aldag, R.J. (ed.), *Oxford Research Encyclopaedia of Business and Management*. Oxford University Press, 1–31. doi:10.1093/acrefore/9780190224851.013.28.

Brealy, R.A., and S.C. Myers (2012), *Principles of Corporate Finance* (international edition). New York: McGraw-Hill.

Caniëls, M.C.J., and C.J. Gelderman (2007), 'Power and interdependence in buyer supplier relationships: a purchasing portfolio approach', *Industrial Marketing Management*, 36(2), 219–229.

Carter, J.R. (1997), 'Supply positioning at SGX Corporation', *Best Practices in Purchasing and Supply Chain Management*, 1, 5–8.

Castro, L.M., Calvas, B.T., and T. Knoke (2015), 'Ecuadorian banana farms should consider organic banana with low price risks in their land-use portfolios', *PloS one*, 10(3), e0120384.

Coate, M.B. (1983), 'Pitfalls in portfolio planning', *Long Range Planning*, 16(3), 47–56.

Cox, A. (1997), *Business Success – A Way of Thinking about Strategic, Critical Supply Chain Assets and Operational Best Practice*, Boston, UK: Earlsgate Press.

Dabhilkar, M., Bengtsson, L., and N. Lakemond (2016), 'Sustainable supply management as a purchasing capability', *International Journal of Operations and Production Management*, 36(1), 2–22.

Drake, P.R.D., Lee, M., and M. Hussain (2013), 'The lean and agile purchasing portfolio model', *Supply Chain Management: An International Journal*, 18(1), 3–20.

Dubois, A., and A.-C. Pedersen (2002), 'Why relationships do not fit into purchasing portfolio models – a comparison between portfolio and industrial network approaches', *European Journal of Purchasing and Supply Management*, 8(1), 35–42.

Ekström, T., Hilletofth, P., and P. Skoglund (2021), 'Towards a purchasing portfolio model for defence procurement – a Delphi study of Swedish defence authorities', *International Journal of Production Economics*, 233, 107996.

Elliott-Shircore, T.I., and P.T. Steele (1985), 'Procurement positioning overview', *Purchasing and Supply Management*, 23, 26.

Fiocca, R. (1982), 'Account portfolio analysis for strategy development', *Industrial Marketing Management*, 11(1), 53–62.

Frazier, G.L., and K.D. Antia (1995), 'Exchange relationships and interfirm power in channels of distribution', *Journal of the Academy of Marketing Science*, 23(4), 321–326.

Gadde, L.E., and I. Snehota (2000), 'Making the most of supplier relationships', *Industrial Marketing Management*, 29(4), 305–316.

Gangurde, S.R., and A.A. Chavan (2016), 'Benchmarking of purchasing practices using Kraljic approach', *Benchmarking: An International Journal*, 23(7), 1751–1779.

Geiger, I. (2017), 'A model of negotiation issue-based tactics in business-to-business sales negotiations', *Industrial Marketing Management*, 64, 1–16.

Gelderman, C.J. (2003), 'A portfolio approach to the development of differentiated purchasing strategies', Doctoral thesis, Eindhoven University of Technology, the Netherlands.

Gelderman, C.J., and D.R. MacDonald (2008), 'Application of Kraljic's purchasing portfolio matrix in an undeveloped logistics infrastructure – the Staatsolie Suriname case', *Journal of Transnational Management*, 13(1), 77–92.

Gelderman, C.J., and J. Semeijn (2006), 'Managing the global supply base through purchasing portfolio management', *Journal of Purchasing and Supply Management*, 12(4), 209–217.

Gelderman, C.J., and P. Van Haaster (2002), 'De portfolio is veel werk en gezond verstand. Interview with Peter Kraljic', *Tijdschrift voor Inkoop & Logistiek*, 18(9), 28–30 ('The portfolio is a matter of hard work and common sense').

Gelderman, C.J., and A.J. Van Weele (2002), 'Strategic direction through purchasing portfolio management: a case study', *Journal of Supply Chain Management*, 38(2), 30–37.

Gelderman, C.J., and A.J. Van Weele (2003), 'Handling measurement issues and strategic directions in Kraljic's purchasing portfolio model', *Journal of Purchasing and Supply Management*, 9(5–6), 207–216.

Gelderman, C.J. and A.J. Van Weele (2005), 'Purchasing portfolio models: a critique and update', *Journal of Supply Chain Management*, 41(3), 19–28.

Ghanbarizadeh, A., Heydari, J., Razmi, J., and A. Bozorgi-Amiri (2019), 'A purchasing portfolio model for the commercial construction industry: a case study in a mega mall', *Production Planning and Control*, 30(15), 1283–1304.

Hadeler, B.J., and J.R. Evans (1994), 'Supply strategy: capturing the value', *Industrial Management*, 36(4), 3–4.

Hartmann, E., Ritter, T., and H. Gemuenden (2001), 'Determining the purchase situation: cornerstone of supplier relationship management', paper presented at the 17th IMP International Conference, Oslo.

Henderson, B.D. (1970), 'The product portfolio', (Perspectives). Boston, MA: Boston Consulting Group.

Henderson, B.D. (1972), 'Cash traps', (Perspectives). Boston, MA: Boston Consulting Group.

Henderson, B.D. (1973), 'The experience curve reviewed: IV. The Growth Share Matrix of the product portfolio', (Perspectives, No. 135). Boston, MA: Boston Consulting Group.

Hofman, M., Spalek, S., and G. Grela (2017), 'Shedding new light on project portfolio risk management', *Sustainability*, 9(10), 1798–1816.

Holm, M., Kumar, V., and C. Rohde (2012), 'Measuring customer profitability in complex environments: an interdisciplinary contingency framework', *Journal of the Academy of Marketing Science*, 40(3), 387–401.

Homburg, C. (1995), 'Single sourcing, double sourcing, multiple sourcing …? Ein ökonomischer Erklärungsansatz. *Zeitschrift für Betriebswirtschaft*, 65(8), 813–834 ('Single sourcing, double sourcing, multiple sourcing …? An economic explanation').

Homburg, C. and D. Daum (1997), 'Die Kundenstruktur als Controlling Herausforderung', *Controlling, Heft 6*, November/Dezember, 394–404 ('The customer structure as a controlling challenge').

Homburg, C., Steiner, V.V., and D. Totzek (2009), 'Managing dynamics in a customer portfolio', *Journal of Marketing*, 73(5), 70–89.

Johnson, M.D., and F. Selnes (2004), 'Customer portfolio management: toward a dynamic theory of exchange relationships', *Journal of Marketing*, 68(2), 1–17.

Kader, M.A., and H. Hossain (2020), 'An analysis on BCG growth sharing matrix', *International Journal of Economics, Business and Accounting Research*, 4(1), 245–252.

Kamann, D.J.F. (2000), 'Kraljic krijgt extra dimensie', *Tijdschrift voor Inkoop & Logistiek*, 16(4), 8–12 ('Kraljic gets an extra dimension').

Kang, M., Hong, P., Bartnik, R. Park, Y. and C. Ko (2018), 'Aligning purchasing portfolio management with sourcing negotiation styles', *Management Decision*, 56(11), 2341–2356.

Kang, M., Wu, X., Hong, P., and Y. Park (2012), 'Aligning organizational control practices with competitive outsourcing performance', *Journal of Business Research*, 65(8), 1195–1201.

Knight, L., Tu, Y.H., and J. Preston (2014), 'Integrating purchasing skills profiling and purchasing portfolio management: an opportunity for building purchasing capability', *International Journal of Production Economics*, 147, 271–283.

Kraljic, P. (1977), 'Neue Wege im Beschaffungsmarketing', *Beschaffung Aktuell*, December, 20–26 ('New ways in procurement marketing').

Kraljic, P. (1983), 'Purchasing must become supply management', *Harvard Business Review*, 61(5), 109–117.

Kumar, N. (1996), 'The power of trust in manufacturer relationships', *Harvard Business Review*, 74(6), 93–106.

Lambrechts, W., Gelderman, C.J., Weelink, R., and J. Semeijn (2019), 'How do buyers actually negotiate with their leverage and strategic suppliers? Analysis of negotiation topics, tactics and outcomes', paper presented at the 28th International IPSERA conference, Milan.

Lee, D.M., and P.R. Drake (2010), 'A portfolio model for component purchasing strategy and the case study of two South Korean Elevator Manufacturers', *International Journal of Production Research*, 48(22), 6651–6682.

Lee, H.S., Sheng, F.F., and C.S. Chuan (2016), 'Markowitz portfolio theory and capital asset pricing model for Kuala Lumpur stock exchange: a case revisited', *International Journal of Economics and Financial Issues*, 6(3), 59–65.

Lilliecreutz, J., and L. Ydreskog (1999), 'Supplier classification as an enabler for a differentiated purchasing strategy', *Global Purchasing and Supply Chain Management*, 11, 66–74.

Luzzini, D., Caniato, F., Ronchi, S., and G. Spina (2012), 'A transaction costs approach to purchasing portfolio management', *International Journal of Operations and Production Management*, 32(9), 1015–1042.

Markowitz, H. (1952), 'Portfolio selection', *Journal of Finance*, 7(March), 77–91.

Matthies, B.D., Jacobsen, J.B., Knoke, T., Paul, C., and L. Valsta (2019), 'Utilising portfolio theory in environmental research – new perspectives and considerations', *Journal of Environmental Management*, 231, 926–939.

McAlister, L., and S. Sinha (2021), 'A customer portfolio management model that relates company's marketing to its long-term survival', *Journal of the Academy of Marketing Science*, 49, 584–600.

Medeiros, M. and L. Ferreira (2018), 'Development of a purchasing portfolio model: an empirical study in a Brazilian hospital', *Production Planning and Control*, 29(7), 571–585.

Micán, C., Fernandes, G. and M. Araújo (2020), 'Project portfolio risk management: a structured literature review with future directions for research', *International Journal of Information Systems and Project Management*, 8(3), 67–84.

Monalisa, S., P. Nadya and R. Novita (2019), 'Analysis for customer lifetime value categorization with RFM model', *Procedia Computer Science*, 161, 834–840.

Montgomery, R.T., J.A. Ogden and B.C. Boehmke (2018), 'A quantified Kraljic portfolio matrix: using decision analysis for strategic purchasing', *Journal of Purchasing and Supply Management*, 24(3), 192–203.

Nellore, R. and K. Söderquist (2000), 'Portfolio approaches to procurement – Analysing the missing link to specifications', *Long Range Planning*, 33(2), 245–267.

Netzer, O., J.M. Lattin and S. Srinivasan (2008), 'A hidden Markov model of customer relationship dynamics', *Marketing Science*, 27(2), 185–204.

Nicholson, A. (1993), 'Strategic management for the purchasing professional', *Purchasing and Supply Management*, 27, 32–32.

Nowak, M., Mierzwiak, R., Wojciechowski, H., and C. Delcea (2020), 'Grey portfolio analysis method', *Grey Systems: Theory and Applications*, 10(4), 439–454.

Olsen, R.F. and L.M. Ellram (1997), 'A portfolio approach to supplier relationships', *Industrial Marketing Management*, 26(2), 101–113.

Padhi, S.S., Wagner, S., and V. Aggarwal (2012), 'Positioning of commodities using the Kraljic portfolio matrix', *Journal of Purchasing and Supply Management*, 18(1), 1–8.

Pagell, M., Wu, Z., and M.E. Wasserman (2010), 'Thinking differently about purchasing portfolios: an assessment of sustainable sourcing', *Journal of Supply Chain Management*, 46(1), 57–73.

Pfeffer, J. and G.R. Salancik (1978), *The External Control of Organizations – A Resource Dependence Perspective*. New York: Harper & Row Publishers.

Ramsay, J. (1996). 'The case against purchasing partnerships', *International Journal of Purchasing and Materials Management*, 32(4), 13–19.

Reilly, F.K and E.A. Norton (2017), *Outlines and Highlights for Investments*, 7th edn. Orlando, FL: Dryden Press.

Rezaei, J., and H. Fallah Lajimi (2019), 'Segmenting supplies and suppliers: bringing together the purchasing portfolio matrix and the supplier potential matrix', *International Journal of Logistics Research and Applications*, 22(4), 419–436.

Ritter, T. (2000), 'A framework for analyzing interconnectedness of relationships', *Industrial Marketing Management*, 29(4), 317–26.

Shapiro, B.P., Rangan, K.V., Moriarty, R.T., and Ross, E.B. (1987), 'Manage customers for profits (not just sales)', *Harvard Business Review*, 65(5), 101–108.

Sharpe, W.F. (1963), 'A simplified model for portfolio analysis', *Management Science*, 9(2), 277–293.

Sharpe, W.F. (1964), 'Capital asset prices: a theory of market equilibrium under conditions of risk', *Journal of Finance*, 19(3), 425–442.

Smeltzer, L.R. and S.P. Siferd (1998), 'Proactive supply management: the management of risk', *International Journal of Purchasing and Materials Management*, 34(4), 38–45.

Steele, P.T. and B.H. Court (1996), *Profitable Purchasing Strategies: A Manager's Guide for Improving Organizational Competitiveness through the Skills of Purchasing*. London: McGraw-Hill.

Syson, R. (1992), *Improve Purchase Performance*. London: Pitman Publishing.

Teller, J., and A. Kock (2013), 'An empirical investigation on how portfolio risk management influences project portfolio success', *International Journal of Project Management*, 31(6), 817–829.

Turnbull, P.W. (1990), 'A review of portfolio planning models for industrial marketing and purchasing management', *European Journal of Marketing*, 24, 7–22.

Wagner, S.M., and Johnson, J.L. (2004), 'Configuring and managing strategic supplier portfolios', *Industrial Marketing Management*, 33(8), 717–730.

Wynstra, F., and E. Ten Pierick (2000), 'Managing supplier involvement in new product development: a portfolio approach', *European Journal of Purchasing and Supply Management*, 6(1), 49–57.

Yorke, D.A. (1984), 'An interaction approach to the management of a portfolio of customer opportunities', *Market Intelligence and Planning*, 2(3), 5–22.

Yorke, D.A., and G. Droussiotis (1994), 'The use of customer portfolio theory: an empirical survey', *Journal of Business and Industrial Marketing*, 9(3), 6–18.

Young, L.C., and I.F. Wilkinson (1997), 'The space between: towards a typology of interfirm relations', *Journal of Business-to-Business Marketing*, 4(2), 53–97.

Zhang, L. (2019), 'Research status and progress of portfolio theory', paper presented at the First International Symposium on Economics, Management, and Sustainable Development, Hangzhou, China.

31. Supply chains as dynamic socio-technical systems

John Gattorna and William Pasmore

INTRODUCTION

Supply chains are dynamic socio-technical systems. They are socio-technical systems because they employ people (social) all along the chain who use technology (technical) as part of a work system in which decisions made about how work is designed can greatly affect motivation and results. They are dynamic because they must adapt constantly to the changing contexts within which they operate. Consequently, human and technical configurations must be designed in an optimal fashion and be flexible so that they can evolve at a pace commensurate with these changes.

This truth defines what supply chains are, but tells us little about what makes a given supply chain efficient or inefficient, static or dynamic, resilient or fragile. In this chapter, we combine the perspectives provided by socio-technical systems theory and the ideas incorporated in dynamic supply chain alignment to offer guidance about the design of supply chains in a disrupted world. We offer specific insights into the actions required to transform a supply chain from its current static state to one of more resilient and dynamic high performance.

KEY VARIABLES AND DEFINITIONS

The focus of dynamic socio-technical system supply design is to create supply chains that perform at the highest possible level over time in the face of turbulence brought about by changes in the business environment. The outcome variables of interest are threefold: (1) efficiency and effectiveness; (2) employee motivation; and (3) adaptability. Key contributions to the development of dynamic socio-technical system supply chain design include Trist and Bamforth (1951), Emery (1959, 1963), Miller (1959), Trist et al. (1963), Emery and Trist (1965), Hill (1971), Cherns (1976), Pasmore (1988) and Gattorna (2010). The key variables involved in the design of dynamic socio-technical system supply chains are: (1) technical arrangements; (2) social arrangements; (3) work system design; and (4) dynamic alignment. These four elements, when combined with a view toward their interdependence in influencing how the supply chain functions and reacts to change, determine the overall goodness of supply chain design. We define each in the following subsections.

Technical System

Supply chains utilize a variety of technologies to accomplish the tasks involved in importing, storing and distributing goods and information. These technologies include both equipment of various kinds and software or platforms that coordinate, track and manage inventory. As noted by Miller (1959) and Emery (1959, 1963), organizations have a wide array of choices when it comes to technologies. Supply chain technologies are evolving rapidly, driven by such concerns as efficiency, cost, control, speed, reliability, and the ability to gain greater insights into the location and flow of goods.

Since the earliest examinations of the effects of technology on the design of work systems, researchers have called attention to the fact that leaders of organizations have choices regarding both the technology they choose to employ and the ways in which they design the jobs of employees to operate whatever technologies are utilized (Trist et al., 1963). The co-equal importance of choices around technology and the design of work systems is emphasized in various studies (Emery and Thorsrud, 1969; Hill, 1971; Rice, 1958; Walton, 1972). The allure of technologies that promise greater efficiency, higher output or increased control can cause leaders to make investments in technology that limit both the motivational aspects of jobs and the ability of employees to intervene when the technology malfunctions. Issues caused by choosing technological arrangements that make it difficult to correct unanticipated deviations and alienate workers are well documented (Perrow, 2011; Trist and Bamforth, 1951).

Social System

Supply chains depend on people to play important roles in supply chain activities, from handling inventory, to planning demands for goods, to determining how the supply chain should operate. As in the case of technical systems, leaders can choose who works in their organization as well as the jobs they are asked to do. Leaders also have choices about how they reward people, whether labour is supplied internally or externally, whether people work alone or in teams, training and development, the determination of policies, the employee value proposition and organization culture. Quite often, those in charge of selecting technologies and setting up workflows are not the same people in charge of thinking about the many choices influencing social system dynamics. In effective socio-technical systems, the capabilities of employees are well suited to the tasks they are asked to perform, and the work employees are asked to do is motivating and fulfilling (Hackman and Oldham, 1980). When careful attention is paid to the impact that technical system design choices have on social system functioning, the overall work system is said to have achieved joint optimization (Cherns, 1976).

The Work System

The work system is the result of choices made about both the technical system and the social system. The design of work systems can vary from lacking consideration of the need for joint optimization to embracing that need. When work systems are designed poorly, they can underperform even with the latest, most efficient technologies. Signs of poor social system design include the inability of people to perform the tasks they are assigned properly, the inability of people to keep up with the demands of the technical system, accidents, systems out of control, quality issues, high absenteeism and turnover, low motivation, sabotage, unionization, and resistance to change. Only when joint optimization takes place can the system reach its peak output and sustain that level of performance over time. As a result of decades of experimentation and research, cited previously, we now know, for example, that people must have control over the work they do so that they can identify and respond to problems as they arise, rather than awaiting help that may never come. We have learned that joint optimization requires

Table 31.1   *Definitions of dynamic socio-technical systems variables*

Key variables/terms	Explanation	Supporting references
Technical system	The technologies used in supply chain work, including both equipment and software.	Miller, 1959; Emery, 1959, 1963; Burns and Stalker, 1961; Hirschhorn, 1986
Social system	Human beings and their influence on the outcomes of work. Key concepts include motivation, commitment, loyalty, interpersonal relationships, teamwork, collaboration, problem solving, creativity, innovation, learning, knowledge work, adult development, capabilities, staffing, adaptability, resistance to change.	Bucklow, 1966; Katz and Kahn, 1966; Thompson, 1967; Hackman and Oldham, 1980; Walton, 1985; Crestani, 2018
Work system	The design of the organization, work and culture that brings technology and people together in search of joint optimization. Key concepts include job design, work design, layout, variances, variance control, efficiency, effectiveness, costs, flexibility, control, risk, safety, speed, degree of interdependence among technical operations and units; timing, length, and physical location of operations; in-house or contracted; software platforms.	Trist and Bamforth, 1951; Rice, 1958; Trist et al., 1963; Emery and Thorsrud, 1969; Engelstad, 1970; Hill, 1971; Cherns, 1976; Pasmore and Sherwood, 1978; Davis and Taylor, 1979; Pava, 1983; Pasmore, 1988; Purser et al., 1992; Perrow, 2011; Zarka et al., 2019
Dynamic alignment	The process of identifying changes that affect desired operational characteristics of the supply chain and builds in the capacity of the supply chain to adapt to these changes; based on open systems theory.	Von Bertalanffy, 1950; Emery and Trist, 1965; Lawrence and Lorsch, 1967; Jayaram, 1976; Gattorna, 1978, 2010, 2015; Chorn, 1987; Gattorna and Ellis, 2020

that human needs are met, demands upon workers are humane, people have the knowledge they need to control technology and are empowered to do so, whole tasks are managed by multiskilled teams or interdependent units, and people are compensated for the value they bring, not just the time they spend. As new technologies are introduced, people should be involved in choices about which technologies are adopted and how the work of supporting those technologies is designed. Overall, the organization should be designed to maximize commitment and adaptability to change.

Dynamic Alignment

We first presented the Dynamic Alignment™ model in 1990 to link the increasing volatility of the external market context to specific decisions that need to be made regarding the internal culture, leadership and operational strategies (Chorn et al., 1990). Additional information on the model is available in Gattorna (2015) and Gattorna and Ellis (2020). Essentially, the model sought to connect the business with the marketplace, including customers, using operational strategy as the bridge between the two entities, all tied together with processes, systems and infrastructure. Up until this time, and unfortunately still this is true today, businesses have tended to take an 'inside-out' view of the world, where they make assumptions about their target market, and then proceed to build marketing, sales and supply chain strategies to support those assumptions. This goes to the heart of the problem, and one that the new model sought to correct: that is, to find a direct link between customers' expectations, and use the insights gained to reverse engineer the business, including the necessary processes, technology, infrastructure and organization structure. We call this 'outside-in' thinking, which is very consistent with the design thinking concepts espoused by Roger Martin (2009) some two decades later.

In the years since the early explorations into the socio-technical design of work systems, there has been a recognition that 'one size fits all' solutions do not exist. Instead, we now know that as the business context changes, resulting in new customer demands, and as technology continues to evolve, offering new opportunities to increase efficiency and effectiveness, 'one size fits all' thinking must give way to developing work systems that constantly adapt to these changes. We call supply chains that are designed in this fashion dynamic socio-technical systems. Table 31.1 and Figure 31.1 help to define the variables and their relationships to outcomes of interest.

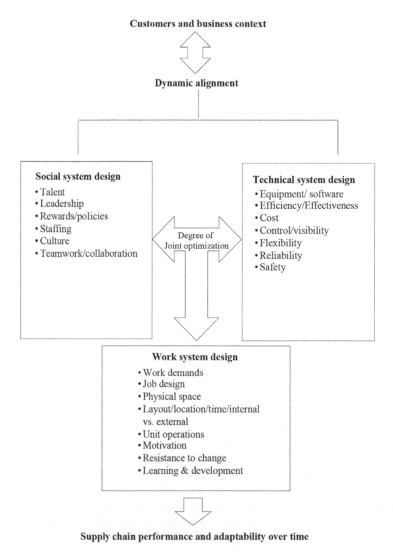

Figure 31.1   Overview of dynamic socio-technical systems elements

DOMAIN WHERE THE THEORY APPLIES

The primary domain where the theory applies is in the design of supply chains for an organizational entity. Of course, some organizations contain multiple supply chains for different products, services or geographies, and the theory can be applied to multiple supply chains as well as to single supply chains. Other organizations serve as distributors; the scope of the supply chain for those organizations should include suppliers/vendors as well. In the modern era, customers and their suppliers are increasingly likely to share linked supply chain platforms, making interoperability easier; in these cases, the theory should be applied to the design of the entire supply chain. As witnessed during the Covid-19 pandemic, unless raw material suppliers are taken into consideration, designing the rest of the supply chain for optimal performance may not help.

RELATIONSHIPS BETWEEN THE VARIABLES

Twenty-first-century supply chains depend heavily on advanced technologies, including information technology platforms, universal product codes, robotics, automated material handling systems, material requirements planning systems, sensor networks, block chain applications, flexible manufacturing systems, three-dimensional (3D) printing and artificial intelligence. However, no matter how advanced the technologies, a supply chain remains first and foremost a socio-technical system.

Supply chains should be designed to take maximum advantage of both technological and human contributions. Because humans are essential to the immediate adaptation and ongoing evolution of the system to meet changing demands, the supply chain should be designed to allow operators to understand and take part in improving technological choices and work methods. Allowing humans to play a meaningful role also enhances their commitment to the well-being of the overall system.

The joint optimization of social and technical systems takes place in a business context that produces ever-changing customer demands. As the complexity and interconnectedness of our world continues to increase, many supply chain designers will feel the need to increase the flexibility and resilience of supply chain arrangements. While the Covid-19 virus pandemic exposed the vulnerability of the existing supply chains in a number of critical industries, the kind of extreme unexpected shock we experienced as a result will surely not be our last. The sources of future shocks may be different: climate change, technological disruption, acts of terrorism, global conflicts or massive population migrations could alter the world in an irrevocable fashion. It is not an overstatement to say that the lives of millions depend on the thought we put into the design of our future supply chains. We need to design supply chains capable of sustained performance, albeit in volatile operating environments.

The ability of an organization to survive over time depends on its built-in capacity to adapt to change. The greater the rate of change in the environment, the more capability and flexibility the organization must possess. Because technology cannot adapt without human assistance, and because environments have become increasingly complex and turbulent, a higher level of human intervention is required to adjust the way the organization goes about what it does to meet external demands. Moreover, because adaptation depends on the alignment and commitment of human actors across the system, it is imperative that the social system be engaged, supportive and capable of helping the system to adapt. This requires an engaging style of leadership rather than the hierarchical approach or command-and-control style. It also requires a social system that has sufficient capability to adapt to the level and complexity of change that is occurring, which in turns requires the hiring and continued development of knowledgeable, skilled workers and leaders. These workers and leaders must possess the authority needed to act to change the system as required and not be constrained unnecessarily by bureaucratic control.

To address the need for adaptability, we first presented the Dynamic Alignment™ model in 1990 to link the increasing volatility of the external market context to specific decisions that need to be made regarding the internal culture, leadership, and operational strategies (Chorn et al., 1990). Additional information on the model is available in Gattorna (2015) and Gattorna and Ellis (2020). This starting position drew on the doctoral research of both Gattorna (1978), and Chorn (1987). The result was a conceptual framework that we initially called the strategic alignment model, but subsequently changed to Dynamic Alignment™ model some years later, when it became obvious from our field research that the model had to withstand changing conditions in the marketplace, as depicted in Figure 31.2.

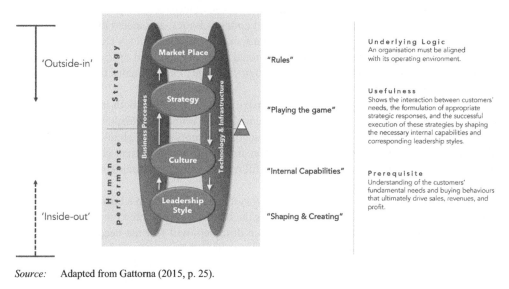

Source: Adapted from Gattorna (2015, p. 25).

Figure 31.2   The Dynamic Alignment™ business model

Essentially, the model seeks to connect the business, made up of levels 3 (cultural capability) and 4 (leadership style), with level 1 (the marketplace, including customers), using operational strategy (level 2) as the bridge between the two entities, all tied together with processes, systems and infrastructure. So even at this early stage in our thinking we recognized that there were social and technical components involved. The way the model works is as follows. Research is conducted in the target market to reveal the range of expectations customers have for the way they prefer to buy specific product/service categories. Once this is known, it is relatively easy to develop a matching range of value propositions and corresponding operational strategies. Then comes the hard part.

Armed with a set of intended strategies, we have to look deeply into the organization (Level 3) to shape the subcultures in such a way that they support and actively underpin and propel these strategies towards the target market segments already identified. As Chorn had previously shown, it is this interface between the organizational culture and strategy where there is serious slippage, to the extent that 40–60 per cent of intended strategies are never delivered, primarily because of internal cultural resistance to change. And sadly, this is still largely true today, irrespective of the newer technologies available to us now. So, the earlier point about systems and people working together is still very valid, and a necessary condition for success.

The final level (level 4), leadership, comes into play as the top team, with one eye on the marketplace, takes action to shape the subcultures inside the business in such a way as to align with the operational strategies that have been devised. The better the alignment between what is happening in the marketplace, in terms of customer expectations, with the corresponding strategies, internal subcultures and leadership styles, the better the enterprise will perform as it delivers value propositions to customers that are most appropriate, avoiding costly over- and underservicing. The key here is precision alignment.

THEORETICAL PREDICTIONS

Over the course of the last 25 years, we have relentlessly continued our field research in an effort to make the original 'alignment' concept more granular, and therefore more practical. By conducting numerous pieces of market research, in many different industries, across multiple geographies, we came to recognize patterns in the customer buying behaviours observed. Consistent with the work of Adizes (1979 [1985]) and Faust (1979), we found a total of 16 archetypes of behaviour, which theoretically pointed to the need for up to 16 matching supply chain configurations. Clearly this is impracticable in a day-to-day operational sense. However, further work convinced us that this number could be resolved down to four or five in order to achieve a very credible 80 per cent coverage of a given target market, and at the same time be workable in terms of how the business organized itself internally to support such a portfolio of supply chain configurations.

Indeed, we will go further and say that a portfolio of four supply chain configurations (collaborative, lean, campaign and agile) is sufficient to cover the business-as-usual (BAU) demands in most product/market combinations. In other words, these four configurations, hard-wired into the business, are designed to service demand which can range from stable (representing say 0–40 per cent CoV[1]), through to a significantly volatile demand (50–100 per cent CoV). Operations within these limits we consider to be business-as-usual.

Beyond that, in times of extreme and unexpected disruption, such as during the Covid-19 crisis, we are likely to witness much higher fluctuations in demand, with CoVs correspondingly much higher, for example over 200 per cent. This is the world of the fully flexible supply chain. Indeed, the difference between BAU and extreme disruption is like managing in a parallel universe, and we have to prepare for both, accordingly.

The focus, technology/information technology (IT) systems and socio-cultural characteristics embedded in these different supply chain worlds are described in Figure 31.3. As customers demand more agility, moving from the relatively stable collaborative pattern, through

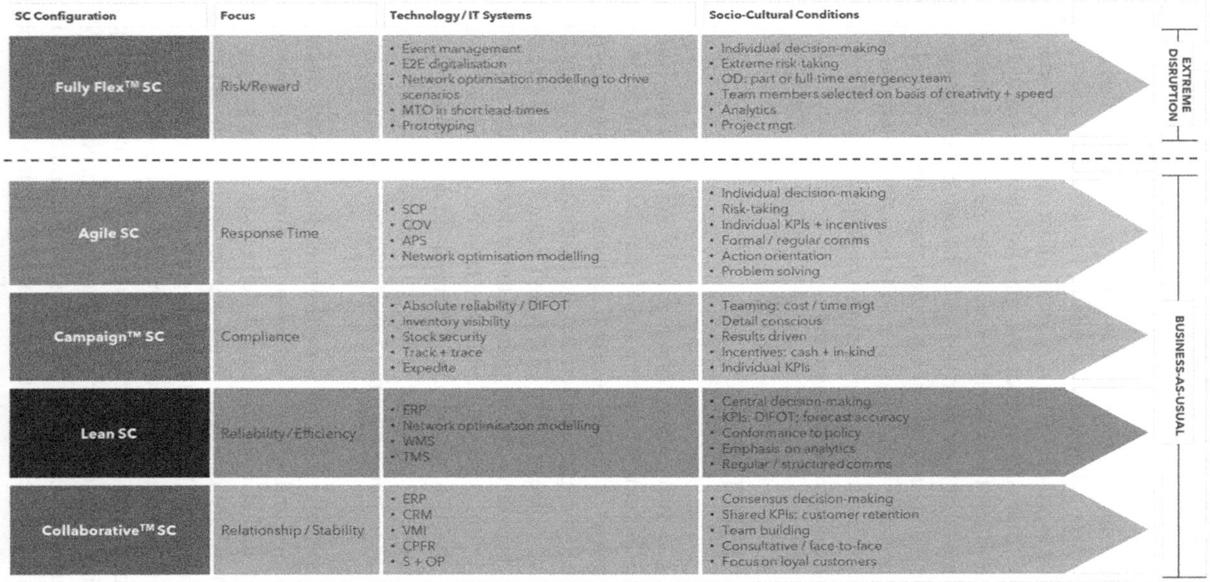

Source: Gattorna Alignment Research.

Figure 31.3   Socio-technical characteristics by supply chain type

to a more volatile pattern in dynamic buying behaviour, and ultimately to extreme disruption as seen in the innovative solutions segment, the need to incorporate socio-technical design principles into the operation of supply chains increases. Whereas collaborative and lean supply chains can be designed for technical optimization because they operate in an environment of certainty in a repetitive fashion, the opposite is true of fully flexible supply chains.

HOW HAS THE THEORY BEEN USED?

Companies such as Zara, Li & Fung, Semco, VF Corporation, The Decathlon Group, Aera Energy and Adidas have been in the vanguard, using different configurations of the self-adaptive team. See Gattorna (2015, Ch. 6) for a full review of the different organization structures experimented with to date. In our view, the best and most practical organization configuration to service fast-moving contemporary markets is to retain the vertical functional specialisms, but complement these with multidisciplinary teams to drive the horizontal cross-functional flows through to specific customer segments. This dual structure would be serviced by a shared services platform of human resources (HR), IT and finance. Examples of this configuration are set out in Gattorna (2015, Chs 7–11).

OUTLOOK ON FUTURE RESEARCH POSSIBILITIES

The goals of introducing dynamic socio-technical systems theory into supply chain research are twofold: (1) to learn how to minimize design features that produce less-than-optimal supply chain operations; and (2) to investigate design features that allow more ready adaptation to turbulent business conditions.

Additional research on the design of supply chains that operate under conditions of extreme volatility would add to our understanding of the factors that are most important to consider as we witness the ever-increasing turbulence and connectedness of global business conditions. As new technologies have emerged, and in particular those based on artificial intelligence (AI), there have been serious debates on whether AI will be a boon or a threat to humanity. As technology plays a greater role in supply chain control, the question is whether employees will see the added assistance as supplementing or diminishing the meaningfulness of work. Investigation into the effects of new supply chain technologies on performance and motivation would be most welcome.

As supply chains become more complex, tying together a greater number of actors who once made decisions independently, there is a greater need for parties to adopt the same platforms and operational arrangements. In doing so, the sheer scope of connected operations could defeat the goal of maintaining flexibility to allow for adaptation. Research into methods to both connect and rapidly change supply chain design will be needed to guide designers who want the best of both.

As new generations of workers enter organizations, it is not clear that the same needs that produced joint optimization in the past will do so in the future. Understanding how needs are evolving at work is necessary to design appropriate work systems for tomorrow's workforce.

Finally, witnessing the disruption to supply chains brought about by Covid-19, it is clear that supply chain design needs to examine how to prepare for extreme disruption, the source and nature of which cannot be predicted.

NOTE

1.   CoV, or coefficient of variation, is a ratio of standard deviation over the mean. The relative size of the CoV is what is important in assessing demand patterns.

REFERENCES

Adizes, I. (1979 [1985]), *How to Solve the Mismanagement Crisis*, 1st printing, Dow-Jones-Irwin; (1985) 5th printing, Santa Monica, CA: Adizes Institute.

Bucklow, M. (1966), 'A new role for the work group', *Administrative Science Quarterly*, 59–78.

Burns, T., and Stalker, G. (1961), *The Management of Innovation*. London: Tavistock Institute.

Cherns, A. (1976), 'The principles of socio-technical design', *Human Relations*, 29(8), 783–792.

Chorn, N.H. (1987), 'The relationship between business-level strategy and organizational culture', unpublished PhD thesis, Witwatersrand University, Johannesburg.

Chorn, N., Myres, K., and Gattorna, J. (1990), 'Bridging strategy formulation and implementation', paper presented to the 10th Annual International Conference of the Strategic Management Society, Stockholm.

Crestani, I. (2018), 'Feeling valued: The role of communication in preparing employees for change', *unpublished PhD Thesis*, Australia: Charles Sturt University.

Davis, L., and Taylor, J. (1979). *Design of Jobs*, Santa Monica, CA: Goodyear.

Emery, F. (1959). Characteristics of socio-technical systems. Document # 527, London: Tavistock Institute for Human Relations.

Emery, F. (1963), Some hypotheses about the way in which tasks may be more effectively put together to design jobs. Document # T176, London: Tavistock Institute for Human Relations.

Emery, F., and Thorsrud, E. (1969), *Form and Content in Industrial Democracy*, London: Tavistock Institute.

Emery, F., and Trist, E. (1965), 'The causal texture of organizational environments', *Human Relations*, 18(1), 21–32.

Engelstad, P. (1970), 'Socio-technical approach to the problems of process control', in F. Bolan (ed.) *Papermaking systems and their control*. British Paper and Board Makers Association.

Faust, G.W. (1979), President, Faust Management Corp., Poway, CA (previously President of the Adizes Institute).

Gattorna, J.L. (1978), 'The effects of innovation on channels of distribution', unpublished PhD thesis, Cranfield University.

Gattorna, John (2010), 2nd edn., *Dynamic Supply Chains*: Delivering Value through People, Harlow, UK: FT Publishing.

Gattorna, J. (2015), 3rd edn., *Dynamic Supply Chains: How to Design, Build and Manage People-centric Value Networks*, Harlow, UK: FT Publishing.

Gattorna, J., and Ellis, D. (2020), *Transforming Supply Chains: Realign Your Business to Better Serve Customers in a Disruptive World*. Harlow, UK: FT Publishing.

Hackman, R., and Oldham, G. (1980), *Work Redesign*, Reading, MA: Addison-Wesley.

Hill, P. (1971), *Towards a New Philosophy of Management*, New York: Barnes and Noble.

Hirschhorn, L. (1986), *Beyond Mechanization*, New York: Barnes and Noble.

Jayaram, J. (1976), Open systems planning, in W. Bennis, K. Benne, R. Chin and K. Corey (Eds.), *The Planning of Change*, New York: Holt, Rinehart & Winston.

Katz, D., and Kahn, R. (1966), *The Social Psychology of Organizations*, New York: Wiley & Sons.

Lawrence, P., and Lorsch, J. (1967), *Organization and Environment*, Cambridge, MA: Harvard University Press.

Martin, R. (2009), *The Design of Business: Why Design Thinking is the Next Competitive Advantage*, Boston, MA: Harvard Business Press.

Miller, E. (1959), 'Technology, territory and time: The internal differentiation of complex production systems', *Human Relations*, 17 (12), 245–272.

Pasmore, W. (1988), *Designing Effective Organizations: The Socio-technical Systems Perspective*, New York: Wiley & Sons.

Pasmore, W., and Sherwood, J. (1978), *Socio-technical Systems: A Sourcebook*, LaJolla, CA: University Associates.

Pava, C. (1983), *Managing New Office Technology: An Organizational Strategy,* New York: Free Press.

Perrow, C. (2011), *Normal Accidents: Living with High Risk Technologies–Updated Edition*, Princeton University Press.

Purser, R., Pasmore, W., and Tenkasi, R. (1992), 'The influence of deliberations on learning in new product development teams', *Journal of Engineering and Technology Management*, 9 (1), 1–28.

Rice, A. (1958), *Productivity and Social Organization: The Ahmedabad Experiment*, London Tavistock Institute.

Thompson, J. (1967), *Organizations in Action*, New York: McGraw Hill.

Trist, E.L., and Bamforth, K.W. (1951), 'Some social and psychological consequences of the longwall method of coal-getting: An examination of the psychological situation and defences of a work group in relation to the social structure and technological content of the work system', *Human Relations*, 4 (1), 3–38.

Trist, E., Higgin, C. Murray, H., and Pollock, A. (1963). *Organizational Choice*. London: Tavistock Institute.

Von Bertalanffy, L. (1950), 'The theory of open systems in physics and biology', *Science*, 111, 23–29.

Walton, R. (1972), 'From control to commitment: How to counter alienation in the plant', *Harvard Business Review*, 50 (6), 70-81.

Walton, R. (1985), 'From control to commitment in the workplace', *Harvard Business Review*, March–April, 77–84.

Zarka, M., Kochanovskaya, E., and Pasmore, W. (2019), *Braided Organizations: Designing Augmented Human-Centric Processes to Enhance Performance and Innovation*, Charlotte, NC: Information Age Publishing.

32. Panarchy theory

Amanda Bille and Andreas Wieland

INTRODUCTION

Supply chain management (SCM) has developed rapidly over the last decades. A multitude of theories have been used to illuminate supply chain phenomena, and it is clear to see how our view on SCM is undergoing constant transformation. Back in 2001, Mentzer et al. presented a famous conceptualization of the supply chain. They demonstrated how the supply chain was more than a simple buyer–supplier relationship. With their 'ultimate supply chain', these authors widened our view of the supply chain and included actors that had previously been left out of supply chain matters (Mentzer et al. 2001). However, the supply chain was still conceptualized as a closed system. Years after, the view on SCM has changed remarkably. Authors introduced the notion of a 'visibility horizon' around focal firms as well as a distinction between the physical and the support supply chain. This highlighted that it is not possible to fully understand the entire supply chain – we can only manage a limited part thereof (Carter et al. 2015). These authors now conceptualized the supply chain as an open system.

In this chapter, panarchy theory will be introduced as a novel approach to SCM. It will show how panarchy theory can be used as yet another conceptualization of the supply chain, where the world is interpreted as a complex system of which the supply chain is a part.

For many years, ecologists have demonstrated the strengths of seeing the complex nature of ecological systems through the lens of panarchy theory. Building on this theory to interpret the changes of processes and structures in ecological systems (for example, rainforests) has proven to be particularly useful to understand how such systems develop and potentially collapse (Holling and Gunderson 2002). With panarchy theory, ecologists have developed a tool that allows analysis of how large and complex systems behave at smaller levels without isolating them from the larger context (Holling 2001). At each level, the development of the system can be described as an adaptive cycle (Holling 2001). Thus, panarchy theory can be especially useful when it comes to addressing issues at the crossroads of economic success, sustainability and innovation, as it can provide an analytical tool for understanding why some systems fail at coping with such issues (Holling et al. 2002). Engineering scholars view resilience as a constant striving to return to a normal and stable state of being (Sheffi 2005), whereas panarchy theory interprets resilience as a flexible, dynamic concept of constant becoming that requires adaption and transformation; not management by control (Davoudi 2012). In Wieland (2021) this logic has been transferred to the context of SCM.

The reasons why panarchy theory is attractive to social scientists, such as SCM scholars, are many. Panarchy theory allows for a manageable analysis of complex matters in a way that is rarely seen in other prevailing theoretical approaches. Such an approach that embraces complexity has been argued to be what is necessary to bring SCM into the twenty-first century (see Nilsson 2019). This is possible because panarchy theory simplifies the analysis without reducing the unit of analysis. Instead of viewing the supply chain as a stable, 'engineerable' entity, interpreting the supply chain as being a part of a social-ecological system, represented by a panarchy, will require SCM scholars to acknowledge that supply chains are subject to constant change (Wieland 2021). Thus, a panarchy is a suitable tool for acknowledging the world's phenomenological complexity while at the same time depicting this in a structured way. It is not novel per se to apply panarchy theory to systems outside ecology. Researchers within fields such as urban planning have shown that it is in fact possible to translate panarchy theory to a social setting, where they have analysed cities as social-ecological systems that are partly unplannable and unpredictable in their nature, making it impossible to stay in complete control of their development (Evans 2011).

On the basis of this theoretical development, this chapter looks into the possibilities of using a panarchical lens on SCM (see Wieland 2021). First, a thorough definition of key elements and definitions related to panarchy theory are provided with the purpose of developing a solid understanding of how panarchy theory are constructed. Next, the assumptions about human nature lying behind panarchy theory are outlined. The chapter then looks into how panarchy theory has previously been used within ecology. The possibilities and previous attempts of applying panarchy theory to a management setting are then investigated and discussed. The chapter concludes with a discussion of how to further develop panarchy theory as an analytical tool in SCM.

KEY ELEMENTS AND DEFINITIONS

The main driver behind developing panarchy theory was to create a model that would provide a structured understanding of complex phenomena without oversimplifying them. Panarchy theory enables us to make sense of ecological systems in a dynamic and prescriptive way, where we can gain a better understanding of the uncertain and unpredictable nature of the systems in question (Holling 2001). Table 32.1 summarizes key definitions in panarchy theory.

The Adaptive Cycle

Panarchy theory takes its point of departure in the adaptive cycle, which is used to explain the evolving nature of social-ecological systems (Allen et al. 2014). Social-ecological systems are special cases of complex adaptive systems that focus on social actors and elements of nature. The adaptive cycle is driven by three different variables: potential, connectedness and resilience. The potential of a system, its 'wealth', describes how much a system can change and provides insight into the different ways in which the system might end up looking in the future. The connectedness denotes how much the system is able to control what it will look like in the future. These controls can either be flexible or rigid, and can be more or less sensitive to deviations. Finally, resilience measures the vulnerability of the system to unexpected shocks (Holling 2001).

It is important to note that the ecological definition of resilience differs from the traditional definition of resilience used in most SCM literature. In an SCM context, resilience often follows the roots of a mechanical-engineering perspective, where the goal is to re-establish the original structure after a disruption, returning to the stable and well-known dynamics from before the change (see Sheffi 2005). Ecological resilience, on the other hand, acknowledges that disruptions and collapses happen, and that the system will not necessarily be able to return to its original shape (Holling 1996). Thus, ecological resilience reflects the unpredictable

Table 32.1   Key definitions in panarchy theory

Element	Explanation	Supporting references
Unit of analysis	A complex adaptive system of nature and people, that is, a social-ecological system.	Holling (2001); Holling and Gunderson (2002); Wieland (2021)
Level of analysis	Often on a macro/global/ecological system level, but with the possibility of zooming in on and out of various elements.	Cash et al. (2006); Drever et al. (2006); Holling (2001)
Key definitions		
Adaptive cycle	A panarchy consists of various adaptive cycles defined by three factors: potential, connectedness and resilience.	Allen et al. (2014); Holling (2001)
Phases of adaptive cycles	All adaptive cycles move through four different phases – exploitation, conservation, release and reorganization – at different paces.	Allen et al. (2014); Biggs et al. (2010); Holling (2001); Holling and Gunderson (2002)
Scales	Scales such as spatial, temporal, quantitative or analytical are used to describe the granularity of a given level within a panarchy.	Cash et al. (2006); Gibson et al. (2000); Westley et al. (2002)
Levels	The unit of analysis located at a certain position on a scale. On some levels, changes are slower; on others they are faster.	Cash et al. (2006); Gibson et al. (2000)
Cross-scale and cross-level linkages	Adaptive cycles are interconnected across scales and levels, for example through 'revolt' and 'remember' linkages.	Berkes and Ross (2016); Cash et al. (2006); Holling et al. (2002)
Assumptions about human nature		
Meaning	Social systems are characterized by trust, interpersonal relations and symbols.	Westley et al. (2002)
Foresight and intention	Human beings are able to predict developments of the panarchy better than animals and plants.	Holling et al. (2002); Westley et al. (2002)
Transfer and storage of experience	Using communication, experience can be stored and transferred.	Holling et al. (2002)
Technology	Human beings can use technology to trigger transformations.	Holling et al. (2002)

and unplannable nature of ecological systems (Evans 2011) and the necessity for adaptation; a view that can be transferred to social-ecological systems (for instance, supply chains) by adding humans' ability to foresee changes (Westley et al. 2002; Wieland 2021). Resilience is then considered to be a dynamic, ever-changing process, requiring adaptation and transformation and not management by control (Davoudi 2012; Holling and Gunderson 2002). Taking all three interpretations into account, supply chain resilience can then be defined as 'the capacity of a supply chain to persist, adapt or transform in the face of change' (Wieland and Durach 2021).

Phases of Adaptive Cycles

The potential, connectedness and resilience of a system allow for defining the four phases of an adaptive cycle: exploitation (r), conservation (K), release (Ω) and reorganization (α) (Holling 1986). The way in which the adaptive cycle moves from one function to another is defined by the degree of potential, connectedness and resilience. As depicted in Figure 32.1, the cycle consists of a front loop and a back loop, each of which represents the development and survival of the system (Allen et al. 2014; Holling 2001; Holling and Gunderson 2002).

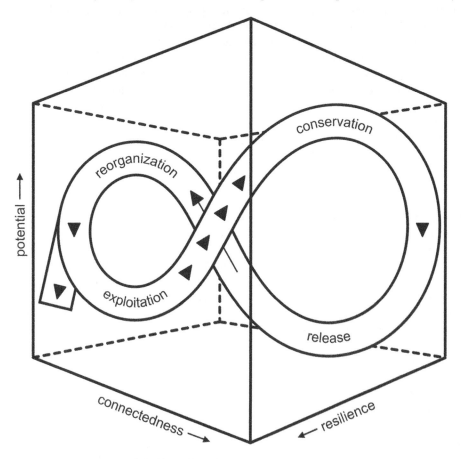

Source: Wieland (2021), based on Holling (1986, 2001).

Figure 32.1   *The four phases of the adaptive cycle*

Systems often move slowly. When moving from r to K, the system goes through a slow process of accumulation of resources; a process that becomes more and more predictable as the system develops over time (Holling 2001). In this front loop, connectedness becomes increasingly high, and the system becomes increasingly rigid and exposed to surprises and disruptions (Holling and Gunderson 2002). In a supply chain context, this rigidity may mean that the cultural and contractual control of the supply chain managers becomes overwhelming (Wieland 2021).

Sometimes, systems suddenly move fast, for example when a system collapses. This leads into the release phase, as a result from moving from K to Ω. The release phase refers to a process of creative destruction, where a rapid release of resources destroys the overwhelming rigidity in K, meaning that the old system can no longer be maintained under the given conditions (Allen et al. 2014; Holling 2001). It may be that a novel business model or a new technology is developed, forcing change upon the supply chain (Wieland 2021). This creative destruction in Ω allows for the system to enter the back loop, as it moves from Ω to α. Unlike the front loop, the back loop is highly unpredictable, as the system is quickly reorganizing the components left after the massive release of resources in Ω. The supply chain may now either reorganize its processes and structure in a way that resembles the old structure from the previous front loop, or it may develop entirely new processes and structures that change the way in which the supply chain operates. Some innovations will fail, and others will survive and carry on in the new front loop from r to K, where yet again resources are slowly accumulated, leading to new rigidity (Holling 2001; Holling and Gunderson 2002).

The adaptive cycle does not necessarily move as smoothly, as described above. Two traps have been proposed to occur in an adaptive cycle: a rigidity trap and a poverty trap. The rigidity trap occurs when the cycle gets stuck in K, the conservation phase. As resources are accumulated and connectedness increases, the system – in this case, the supply chain – can sometimes become so rigid that it is impossible to break out of the front loop and enter the process of creative destruction (Biggs et al. 2010). Moving further along in the cycle, the system may also get stuck in α, the reorganization phase, leading to a poverty trap. This may be because the system is missing innovative force and lacks the ability to develop new structures that will move the system from the chaotic and unpredictable back loop to the safe and stable front loop (ibid.). Thus, these traps counter a key feature of an adaptive cycle to constantly balance between creativity (back loop) and conservation (front loop), leading to ongoing development and transformation of the system (Holling 2001).

The Scales of a Panarchy

A panarchy can be understood through the use of different scales as a means to study the system in question. Such a scale can be spatial, temporal, quantitative or analytical, depending on the purpose of the study and the type of system in question (Gibson et al. 2000). When studying systems of nature – that is, ecological systems – it may, for instance, be useful to be guided by spatial and temporal scales allowing the researcher to investigate both small adaptive cycles (for instance, describing the development and transformation of a leaf) and large cycles (for instance, describing an entire rainforest or even the planet). In a social-ecological system (for instance, a supply chain), a symbolic scale must be included in order to reflect humans' ability to foresee changes in terms of new meanings, visions and narratives (Westley et al. 2002; Wieland 2021).

The Levels of a Panarchy

Systems rarely operate on their own without any impact from other systems that operate at other levels. This is why researchers such as Holling et al. (2002) argue that a nested set of complex systems can be best described by a panarchy. Unlike in a traditional hierarchy, where the system is often influenced by rigid, top-down management, a panarchy consists of various interconnected adaptive cycles that represent the movements of systems. These interconnected adaptive cycles operate at different levels on scales of time, space and symbolic meaning; that is, the adaptive cycles operate at different paces and with different dynamics. Some cycles are small, fast, and are based on a simple narrative – others are large, slow, and are bold in meaning (see Figure 32.2) (Gunderson and Holling 2002).

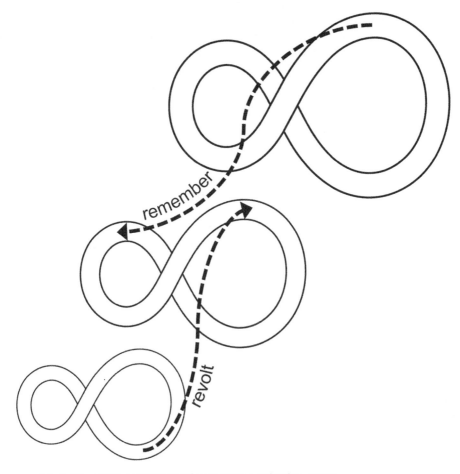

Source: Adapted from Wieland (2021), based on Gunderson and Holling (2002).

Figure 32.2   A panarchy with two cross-level linkages

In theory, it can be imagined that the supply chain panarchy includes a wide variety of levels. In Wieland (2021), a panarchy is presented that includes three levels: the supply chain, political-economic and planetary levels. More generally, the group, functional, organizational, supply chain, political-economic, socio-cultural and planetary levels can serve as starting points to identify a suitable set of levels (Wieland, 2021). Thus, panarchy theory provides a flexible approach to supply chain management, where the structure of a panarchy has to be adapted to the context in which the supply chain operates. One could, for instance, imagine levels of worker communities, consumer communities and, perhaps, a level that represents the media landscape.

Cross-Scale and Cross-Level Linkages

Where Figure 32.2 shows a neatly ordered panarchy that represents a supply chain level, a political-economic level and a planetary level, panarchies usually need to integrate more granularity in terms of additional levels. Actors may be both horizontally and vertically linked across the panarchy (Berkes and Ross 2016). The slower and larger adaptive cycles determine the conditions under which the smaller cycles operate; and the smaller ones can influence the larger ones through overwhelming creative destruction (Holling 2001).

This is only possible because of the cross-level linkages that connect the adaptive cycles nested in a panarchy. Two types of such linkages have received a particularly large amount of attention in the panarchy literature: revolt and remember (see Figure 32.2). The revolt linkage describes how innovations and events at small and fast levels impact or even overwhelm those occurring at larger levels (Holling 2001). This can be observed when the smaller cycle moves into Ω, triggering creative destruction. In some cases, it may be that the creative destruction in Ω becomes so massive that it triggers a crisis at larger and slower levels operating above it (Holling et al. 2002). Such a revolt connection would result in the adaptive cycle at a larger level being forced to enter Ω, even if no resources have been accumulated in K yet (Allen et al. 2014; Holling 2001). Taking an SCM perspective on this, it may be, for instance, that a company develops a new product or technology which completely disrupts the market. This has an effect on the political-economic level, as such a novel invention may require different legislation than was previously the case.

Another cross-level linkage is the 'remember' linkage, which can be observed when cycles on larger and slower levels impact cycles that operate at smaller and faster levels through memory and experiences of previous processes of creative destruction (Allen et al. 2014). The 'remember' linkage is triggered when an adaptive cycle at a larger level is at the peak of K. The knowledge of this cycle then trickles down to the smaller cycles' α, where new and innovative processes will be developed. The smaller cycles will be able to make use of the wisdom from the larger cycles when it comes to delimiting the potential options for developing new processes, rather than entering into a completely new regime to be tested in r (Allen et al. 2014; Holling 2001). An example of such a linkage can be found when legislators at the political-economic level become aware of the larger crises of the planetary system, leading them to pass eco-friendly supply chain laws.

ASSUMPTIONS ABOUT HUMAN ACTORS

Since panarchy theory was originally developed with the intention of better understanding systems of nature, it is important to acknowledge that systems of people and nature behave differently. Therefore, following both ecologists and social scientists using panarchy, certain assumptions can be made about human actors. Holling et al. (2002) identify three key points where human systems differ from ecological systems. First, foresight and intention distinguish humans from trees, algae and even other animals, as human beings are capable of predicting developments of the panarchy far better than animals ever could. Supply chain managers may be able to foresee trends and disruptions, and guide transformations of the supply chains in the face of future challenges. Second, humans are capable of transferring and storing experience using communication. This is valuable when it comes to reorganizing and stabilizing the system after a crisis has occurred. Following a crisis such as COVID-19, managers are able to reflect on the changes in norms and adjust their way of working to fit a new normal. Finally, humans are able to use technology to transform the system, and often advancement in technology is exactly what triggers the movement from K to Ω (Holling et al. 2002). Most of these social factors tend to be context- or even culture-specific, making it important to be aware of norms and values when it comes to applying panarchy to social systems (Berkes and Ross 2016).

Adding to this, Westley et al. (2002) call for an even stronger distinction between applying panarchy to systems of nature, and to systems of nature and people. Since human beings are what the authors define as 'sense-making' animals, the application of panarchy to social settings should reflect this. They argue that where systems of nature are guided by time and space only, social systems are also characterized by meaning, since, for instance, supply chains are characterized by trust, interpersonal relations and symbols. Ultimately, social systems are more resilient to disturbances locally, but at the same time it becomes more difficult for humans to respond to disruptions. At a global level, however, human beings become capable of anticipating long-term changes (for example, environmental changes) much faster, giving social systems the possibility to reorganize before a crisis occurs. This is due to social laws being what the authors call 'mutable', unlike often unchangeable natural laws (Westley et al. 2002).

On the basis of these assumptions about human nature, it is argued that when viewing supply chains in the light of panarchy theory, humans acknowledge that they are a part of a complex reality; a reality that cannot be framed as simple cause–effect relationships. They might not be rational decision makers, since their actions will be characterized by meaning as defined by Westley et al. (2002). Thereby, using panarchy theory calls for a somewhat interpretive reading of supply chain management (see Darby et al. 2019), as managers, for instance, are taking part in an ongoing sense-making process.

THE USE OF PANARCHY THEORY IN ECOLOGY RESEARCH

The notion of panarchy has in itself been revolutionary for the field of ecology. Before its introduction to the field, ecological systems were interpreted as closed systems that are measurable and fully understandable. This had substantial consequences for how ecologists addressed managing ecological systems. Previously, ecologists argued that, once understood, it would be possible to control and maintain ecological systems in an optimal state (Biggs et al. 2010). Standing in clear opposition to this, panarchy theory views ecological systems as complex, evolving and open systems (ibid.) that can never truly be understood and predicted; but a better understanding can be gained of when and where the system is vulnerable (Holling 2001).

Since panarchy theory originates from the field of ecology, the panarchical approach has found numerous applications within ecological contexts. Instead of interpreting ecological systems as something stable, panarchy theory has helped ecologists in gaining immense knowledge about the various levels and scales in order to understand the adaptive cycles and their dynamics (Drever et al. 2006). Drever et al. (2006) further argue that understanding the panarchy will allow forest managers to notice the signs of potential disruptions before they occur, and to understand the long-term impact their actions may have not just on the cycle being managed, but on the entire panarchy.

APPLICATIONS OF PANARCHY THEORY TO MANAGEMENT ISSUES

When applying panarchy theory to social systems, it is important to remember the characteristics of human nature, as they will impact upon the way in which the system develops (Holling et al. 2002). In order to reflect this, Westley (2002) argues that as a supplement to making system-level analyses, as argued by Holling and Gunderson (2002) and several others, it may be relevant to focus on providing rich and deep analyses of a single actor when understanding complex social systems, which is in line with recent calls in SCM for more interpretative research (Darby et al. 2019). Specifically, Westley et al. (2002) used the case of one manager to investigate how to manage adaptively over time. By investigating the adaptive nature of a single actor, these authors argue that it becomes possible to truly understand the complex dynamics within the panarchy. Such research becomes highly contextualized, making it possible to reflect the web of values and norms that influences the panarchy (Westley 2002).

Staying close to ecological phenomena, Brunckhorst (2002) shows how it is necessary for a society and its institutions to understand their roles when it comes to enhancing resilience related to, for instance, the climate crisis. On the basis of panarchy theory, the author argues that there has to be a much stronger integration between social functions and natural functions if we want to ensure sustainability; namely, institutions have to learn how to adapt better to changes (Brunckhorst 2002). Similarly, Linnenluecke and Griffiths (2010) investigate organizational adaptation associated with weather extremes. In order to adapt to the complex issues, it will be necessary for organizations and social-ecological systems in general not just to create strategies to avoid disasters; managers will have to impose structures that will allow them to build up long-term resilience that may make it easier to cope with future events (Linnenluecke and Griffiths 2010). In addition to this, research also suggests that using a panarchical approach to management does not just mean adapting to ecological changes; organizations can play an important role in preventing such changes (King 1995) and can steer substantial changes, shifting adaptive to transformative management (see Wieland and Durach 2021).

Where the research on adaptive management related to ecological issues is quite extensive, the amount of research conducted on other types of management issues remains scarce. In addition to the account of panarchy theory in SCM investigated in Wieland (2021), which is used throughout this chapter, Williams et al. (2019) present their own view on how panarchy theory can serve to investigate SCM phenomena. Taking a point of departure in Unilever's supply chain, these authors investigate how changes in the Borneo rainforest affect Unilever, and vice versa. Their panarchy comprises two adaptive cycles: one that is ecological in nature (representing the changes in the rainforest) and one that is social-ecological in nature (representing those in the supply chain). Where traditional resilience approaches would have tackled El Niño events in isolation and focused on how Unilever might deal with specific supplier risks related to the disruption, these authors move one step further in analysing the cross-level impact that changes in Borneo have on Unilever's supply chain; they argue that the disruption in Borneo will lead to a disruption in Unilever's activities even in other geographical regions.

This approach stands in sharp contrast to the traditional organizational resilience approaches that managers have been guided by (Williams et al. 2019).

Williams et al. (2019) argue that a too narrow focus on optimizing organizational resilience internally may in fact undercut management initiatives with increasing resilience. Instead, managers ought to take a holistic and dynamic perspective on resilience, meaning that in the case of Unilever's supply chain, managers should focus not just on mitigating risk within this supply chain but also on strengthening the stability and agility of the Borneo rainforest. In line with these arguments, Cash et al. (2006) argue for the use of a multitude of scales, such as jurisdictional, institutional, management and network scales, when it comes to addressing complex issues. Following panarchy theory, those who are able to manage their organization with great attention to cross-scale and cross-level linkages will be better at identifying potential disruptions across the system and identifying political and ecologically sustainable solutions to such issues (Cash et al. 2006).

OUTLOOK ON FUTURE RESEARCH OPPORTUNITIES

Previous research has demonstrated that panarchy theory is particularly well equipped for tackling complexities, and there is great potential in developing panarchy theory as a tool to study managerial phenomena. Those complexities can, for instance, be related to ecological issues such as the biodiversity and climate crises as well as forest fires (see, for instance, Holling and Gunderson 2002; Linnenluecke and Griffiths 2010), but as demonstrated by Williams et al. (2019) and Wieland (2021), a wider range of issues may in fact benefit from panarchical approaches. This becomes apparent for SCM, where global supply chain issues are routinely very complex in nature, requiring holistic explanations that go beyond the level of the focal firm (Nilsson 2019). Events in one part of the world may lead to massive shocks in other parts of the world, activating both cross-scale and cross-level linkages, making it difficult for individual managers to employ their conventional supply chain risk management strategies (see Bapuji et al. 2020).

Managers may particularly benefit from the holistic and dynamic view of panarchy theory when managing with an awareness of sustainability-related issues: issues that have previously been difficult to grasp or that have even been overlooked due to their complex nature (Ashby et al. 2012; Quarshie et al. 2016). Applying panarchy theory to sustainability-related issues, where cross-scale and cross-level linkages are indubitably present, will allow SCM researchers to investigate possible global developments and track how the panarchy behaves in the event of a disruption. As argued by Holling et al. (2002) and Westley et al. (2002), this is exactly what characterizes human systems: that one is able to use historic knowledge and experience to predict future changes, and be prepared for how to prevent crises from happening. That is also why 'dancing' is used in Wieland (2021) as a metaphor of a panarchical interpretation of management: humans are able to plan the next steps, but they are not dancing alone. By using a panarchical approach to SCM, scholars in our discipline will be able to better equip managers for future disruptions in a dynamic and holistic way, which is what many have argued is necessary in order to strengthen contemporary SCM (see, for instance, Pagell and Shevchenko 2014).

The holistic and dynamic nature of panarchies requires an extension of the methodological toolset, and even to question the paradigmatic assumptions of SCM research. Particularly, it is necessary to change – or as a minimum, reflect on – the unit of analysis of most SCM research, as this will impact upon the outcome of the research (Allen et al. 2014). Since panarchy theory does not have a predefined set of scales or levels (Cash et al. 2006; Westley et al. 2002), it will be up to the individual researcher to determine: (1) the number of scales to be included; and (2) the number of levels to be included. On the one hand, this gives the researcher a high level of creative freedom, allowing for a multitude of interpretations of the scenario in which the firm operates, which will potentially make it possible to reflect on the complexities of our world (Nilsson 2019). On the other hand, it will be the responsibility of the researcher to thoroughly argue for why those specific scales and levels have been included and, even more importantly, why others have been left out (Wieland 2021).

It seems reasonable to argue that within management studies panarchy theory calls for either qualitative approaches (for example, non-positivist case studies) or those quantitative approaches that explicitly embrace complexity (for example, system dynamics, machine learning). It is in itself not possible to delimit the methodological scope of panarchical research to only a small set of approaches, since many different approaches may be able to inform the application of panarchy theory to SCM. To name a few examples, Williams et al. (2019) use qualitative document data to construct the two adaptive cycles, and within a social science setting, Westley (2002) conducts an in-depth qualitative study of a single manager to reflect on the panarchical nature of the manager's work. However, panarchy theory points towards non-positivist research that allows the researcher to reflect on previous, current and possible developments of the system. Following the arguments of Westley (2002), employing an interpretive perspective on panarchy theory, the SCM scholar will then be able to take a point of departure in one manager or one team, investigating the subjective view on the panarchy, that is, the dominating narratives operating at the levels under study. This would provide practitioners with knowledge on how to adjust their management efforts to take cross-scale and cross-level linkages into account. Similarly, following a critical realist point of view, panarchy theory could be used to investigate the arena in which corporations operate today. A contextualized explanatory case study (see Welch et al. 2011) will make it possible to theorize the changing role of corporations as well as how managers should interact with actors directly or indirectly associated with their supply chain.

To summarize, there are multiple areas where SCM scholars can work with panarchy theory in the future:

- First, panarchy theory may provide us with new knowledge on how to manage supply chains in the twenty-first century, where complex issues are putting managers under pressure.
- Second, SCM researchers are called to investigate the possibilities of using panarchy theory as a means to address sustainability issues.
- Third, it ought to be researched how to determine the number of scales and levels necessary when using panarchy theory in SCM.
- Fourth, researchers should be creative in their application of different methodological approaches and their use of panarchy theory in SCM.

REFERENCES

Allen, C.R., D.G. Angeler, A.S. Garmestani, L.H. Gunderson and C.S. Holling (2014), 'Panarchy: theory and application', *Ecosystems*, **17** (4), 578–589.

Ashby, A., M. Leat and M. Hudson-Smith (2012), 'Making connections: a review of supply chain management and sustainability literature', *Supply Chain Management: An International Journal*, **17** (5), 497–516.

Bapuji, H., F.G.A. de Bakker, J.A. Brown, C. Higgins, K. Rehbein and A. Spicer (2020), 'Business and society research in times of the Corona crisis', *Business and Society*, **59** (6), 1067–1078.

Berkes, F. and H. Ross (2016), 'Panarchy and community resilience: sustainability science and policy implications', *Environmental Science and Policy*, **61**, 185–193.

Biggs, R., F.R. Westley and S.R. Carpenter (2010), 'Navigating the back loop: fostering social innovation and transformation in ecosystem management', *Ecology and Society*, **15** (2). https://doi.org/10.5751/ES-03411-150209.

Brunckhorst, D.J. (2002), 'Institutions to sustain ecological and social systems', *Ecological Management and Restoration*, **3** (2), 108–116.

Carter, C.R., D.S. Rogers and T.Y. Choi (2015), 'Toward the theory of the supply chain', *Journal of Supply Chain Management*, **51** (2), 89–97.

Cash, D.W., W.N. Adger, F. Berkes, P. Garden, L. Lebel, et al. (2006), 'Scale and cross-scale dynamics: governance and information in a multilevel world', *Ecology and Society*, **11** (2). https://doi.org/10.5751/es-01759-110208.

Darby, J.L., B.S. Fugate and J.B. Murray (2019), 'Interpretive research: a complementary approach to seeking knowledge in supply chain management', *International Journal of Logistics Management*, **30** (2), 395–413.

Davoudi, S. (2012), 'Resilience: a bridging concept or a dead end?', *Planning Theory and Practice*, **13** (2), 299–333.

Drever, C.R., G. Peterson, C. Messier, Y. Bergeron and M. Flannigan (2006), 'Can forest management based on natural disturbances maintain ecological resilience?', *Canadian Journal of Forest Research*, **36**, 2285–2299.

Evans, J.P. (2011), 'Resilience, ecology and adaptation in the experimental city', *Transactions of the Institute of British Geographers*, **36**, 223–237.

Gibson, C.C., E. Ostrom and T.K. Ahn (2000), 'The concept of scale and the human dimensions of global change: a survey', *Ecological Economics*, **32**, 217–239.

Gunderson, L.H. and C.S. Holling (2002), *Panarchy: Understanding Transformations in Systems of Humans and Nature*, Washington, DC: Island Press.

Holling, C.S. (1986), 'The resilience of terrestrial ecosystems: local surprise and global change', in W.C. Clark and R.E. Munn (eds), *Sustainable Development of the Biosphere*, Cambridge: Cambridge University Press, pp. 292–317.

Holling, C.S. (1996), 'Engineering resilience versus ecological resilience', in National Academy of Engineering and P. Schulze (eds), *Engineering within Ecological Constraints*, Washington, DC: National Academies Press, pp. 31–43.

Holling, C.S. (2001), 'Understanding the complexity of economic, ecological, and social systems', *Ecosystems*, **4**, 390–405.

Holling, C.S. and L.H. Gunderson (2002), 'Resilience and adaptive cycles', in L. Gunderson and C. Holling (eds), *Panarchy: Understanding Transformations in Human and Natural Systems*, Washington, DC: Island Press, pp. 25–62.

Holling, C.S., L.H. Gunderson and G.D. Peterson (2002), 'Sustainability and panarchies', in L. Gunderson and C. Holling (eds), *Panarchy: Understanding Transformations in Human and Natural Systems*, Washington, DC: Island Press, pp. 63–102.

King, A. (1995), 'Avoiding ecological surprise: lessons from long-standing communities', *Academy of Management Review*, **20** (4), 961–985.

Linnenluecke, M. and A. Griffiths (2010), 'Beyond adaptation: resilience for business in light of climate change and weather extremes', *Business and Society*, **49** (3), 477–511.

Mentzer, J.T., W. DeWitt, J.S. Keebler, S. Min, N.W. Nix, et al. (2001), 'Defining supply chain management', *Journal of Business Logistics*, **22** (2), 1–25.

Nilsson, F.R. (2019), 'A complexity perspective on logistics management: rethinking assumptions for the sustainability era', *International Journal of Logistics Management*, **30** (3), 681–698.

Pagell, M. and A. Shevchenko (2014), 'Why research in sustainable supply chain management should have no future', *Journal of Supply Chain Management*, **50** (1), 44–55.

Quarshie, A.M., A. Salmi and R. Leuschner (2016), 'Sustainability and corporate social responsibility in supply chains: the state of research in supply chain management and business ethics journals', *Journal of Purchasing and Supply Management*, **22**, 82–97.

Sheffi, Y. (2005), 'Preparing for the big one (supply chain management)', *Manufacturing Engineer*, **84** (5), 12–15.

Welch, C., R. Piekkari, E. Plakoyiannaki and E. Paavilainen-Mäntymäki (2011), 'Theorising from case studies: towards a pluralist future for international business research', *Journal of International Business Studies*, **42** (5), 740–762.

Westley, F. (2002), 'The devil in the dynamics', in L.H. Gunderson and C. Holling (eds), *Panarchy: Understanding Transformations in Human and Natural Systems*, Washington, DC: Island Press, pp. 333–360.

Westley, F., S.R. Carpenter, W.A. Brock, C.S. Holling and L.H. Gunderson (2002), 'Why systems of people and nature and not just social and ecological systems', in L.H. Gunderson and C. Holling (eds), *Panarchy: Understanding Transformations in Human and Natural Systems*, Washington, DC: Island Press, pp. 103–119.

Wieland, A. (2021), 'Dancing the supply chain: toward transformative supply chain management', *Journal of Supply Chain Management*, **75** (1), 58–73.

Wieland, A. and C.F. Durach (2021), 'Two perspectives on supply chain resilience', *Journal of Business Logistics*, **42** (3), 1–8.

Williams, A., G. Whiteman and S. Kennedy (2019), 'Cross-scale systemic resilience: implications for organization studies', *Business and Society*, **60** (1), 1–30.

SUGGESTED FURTHER READING

The dynamics of panarchy theory:

Allen, C.R., D.G. Angeler, A.S. Garmestani, L.H. Gunderson and C.S. Holling (2014), 'Panarchy: theory and application', *Ecosystems*, **17** (4), 578–89.

Holling, C.S. (2001), 'Understanding the complexity of economic, ecological, and social systems', *Ecosystems*, **4** (5), 390–405.

How to apply panarchy theory to social systems:

Westley, F., S.R. Carpenter, W.A. Brock, C.S. Holling and L.H. Gunderson (2002), 'Why systems of people and nature and not just social and ecological systems', in L.H. Gunderson and C. Holling (eds), *Panarchy: Understanding Transformations in Human and Natural Systems*, Washington, DC: Island Press, pp. 103–119.

Applying panarchy theory to management issues:

Westley, F. (2002), 'The devil in the dynamics', in L.H. Gunderson and C. Holling (eds), *Panarchy: Understanding Transformations in Human and Natural Systems*, Washington, DC: Island Press, pp. 333–360.

Wieland, A. (2021), 'Dancing the Supply Chain: Toward Transformative Supply Chain Management', *Journal of Supply Chain Management*, **75** (1), 58–73.

33. Preferred customer theory: benefiting from preferential treatment from suppliers through measures on buyer attractiveness and supplier satisfaction

Holger Schiele

HISTORY: REVERSE MARKETING BEGINNINGS COMPLEMENTED BY A THEORY

The fundamental question that preferred customer theory addresses is: How can buying firms gain competitive advantage by getting better access to suppliers than their competitors? For a long time, this question might have been less relevant, and did not get much attention. Also, terms and concepts to describe the situation of getting access to supplier resources and provide solutions were not abundant. The preferred customer theory fills this gap, suggesting solutions for organizations facing factor market rivalry, that is, which compete with rival buying organizations for the attention of the same suppliers.

The basic concept of preferred customer theory is the need of the buying firm to be attractive to its suppliers, in order to ensure privileged access to their resources and hence achieve competitive advantage over rival organizations which rely on the same suppliers. Such ideas of 'reverse marketing' (inverting the traditional view by asking buyers to be attractive to sellers, rather than the other way around) have sporadically appeared in science, but did not develop into a research stream until about a decade ago.

The sporadic occurrences of preferred customer thinking include the simulation study by Hottenstein (1970), which marginally touches upon the idea of firms using preferred customer lists to make decisions on prioritising customers. Also the work of Brokaw and Davisson (1978) suggests that purchasers should apply marketing tools to sell their firm to the supplier. Ten years later the idea of 'reverse marketing' was again picked up by Leenders and Blenkhorn (1988), though they use a different frame; while Williamson (1991) and Moody (1992), based on their case study experience, emphasize the importance of a firm being a 'good' customer. What is noticeable is that these sporadic publications do not seem to refer to each other, nor have they been noticed by many other researchers. In 2002, Christiansen and Maltz presented a model on how firms without leverage could become 'interesting' customers. A few years later, Steinle and Schiele extensively discussed the preferred customer idea, reporting on a case study (Steinle and Schiele, 2008). A year later, Hald et al. (2009) developed an 'attraction theory', which for the first time tried to link this line of thought to social exchange theory. However they did not focus directly on preferred customership, but on a general idea of how to become an interesting or attractive customer. The main body of preferred customer theory – about 50 papers now published – however, emerged around and following a special issue on the topic, edited in 2012 (Schiele et al., 2012). Again rooted in social exchange theory and strategic management theory, the 'cycle theory of preferred customership' was established, arguing that becoming a customer of choice requires satisfied suppliers, which have in the first instance decided to work with this buyer because they perceive it to be sufficiently attractive. Hence, preferred customership requires a multi-stage approach.

PREFERRED CUSTOMER THEORY: THE CYCLE OF ATTRACTIVENESS, SUPPLIER SATISFACTION AND PREFERRED CUSTOMERSHIP

Before discussing the theoretical model as such, its underlying assumptions have to be exposed. In its attempt to explain and provide guidelines to the buying company on how to get privileged resource access to its suppliers – that is, generating a competitive advantage through purchasing – preferred customer theory builds upon several assumptions. Assumptions two to four, shared with social exchange theory, are summarized as 'conditions for equal exchange' (Zeitz, 1980), the last two conditions, linked to resource-based theory, would be the 'strategic conditions' (Ramsay, 2001):

1. Image of man. The underlying assumption is that human nature follows what McGregor (1966) called 'Theory Y': human beings are active, responsible, benevolent and able to follow organizational objectives. Based on such a view, collaborative relationships for mutual benefit are conceivable.
2. Legal equality/voluntary exchange. Parties need to have equal legal rights and, as such, enter the exchange on a voluntary basis. The question of privileged resource access is only relevant if the supplier would not be obliged to deliver; or, respectively, the buyer would not be obliged to accept the supplier and its conditions, for instance because of government regulations.
3. Awareness of cost–benefit. In order to assess benefits and to decide on entering, continuing or discontinuing a voluntary exchange relationship, the parties need to be able to understand their cost–benefit position (Di Domenico et al., 2009). In the case of business-to-business relations, with professionals on both sides, it is assumed that they are able to estimate the value of the relationship, that is, 'the rewards received versus direct and opportunity costs' (Ellis et al., 2012, p. 1260); which, again, is needed to make a non-arbitrary decision upon the relationship. If a supplier is unable to estimate the value of a business relationship, or if it is not possible to differentiate between customers because all deliver exactly the same benefit, preferred customer theory is not applicable.
4. Mutual benefit. Free parties enter into an exchange if (and only if), based on a cost–benefit analysis, both parties perceive that the exchange will benefit them; that is, each ends up better off with than without the deal. Note that the size and the equality of distribution of the benefit is not part of the assumption; only that for each it must have a positive value.
5. Resource heterogeneity. Where input factors – that is, supply goods – are perfectly equal (or at least the differences among them are irrelevant), in terms of both product and conditions of exchange such as price, delivery, and so on, preferred customer theory does not apply. In such factor markets no strategic advantage can be derived from supplier access (Dierickx and Cool, 1989). A condition, then, is that there must be differences among the suppliers and their products, some of them being superior to others.

6. Resource scarcity. Finally, but most importantly, there must be a finite number of suppliers for preferred customer theory to be relevant; that is, no perfect factor mobility. If each customer could have full access to all suppliers on equal terms, no factor market rivalry would emerge, and no attempts need to be made to gain privileged access to any of these abundant suppliers. Scarcity occurs in non-atomistic markets, where the decision of suppliers to serve one customer has a direct influence on its capacity to serve another customer (Pulles et al., 2019). A limited number of products, difficulties in substituting them, and a finite amount of players on the market, thus describe a situation where achieving preferred customer status is crucial.

The conditions of voluntary equal exchange and of strategic resource scarcity can be considered as necessary conditions to apply preferred customer theory. Preferred customer theory, then, is not a universal theory of exchange or a universal supply theory, because its domain is limited to the conditions listed above. There are sourcing situations in which a (quasi-)unlimited amount of homogenous suppliers is available, or situations in which buyer and suppliers are regulated in their choices. In such cases, preferred customer theory does not contribute; or, more precisely, its contribution is not relevant. However, in the case of a voluntary exchange with factor scarcity, preferred customer theory is applicable, and offers explanation and guidelines for action.

Preferred customer theory has two theoretical roots (Schiele et al., 2012): in strategic management theory, the resource-based view of the firm, more precisely: the relational view, in its elaboration on competitive advantage through superior resource command (Barney, 1991; Dyer and Singh, 1998; Sanchez and Heene, 1997; Steinle et al., 1998); and in social exchange theory (Lambe et al., 2001; Pulles et al., 2019; Reichenbachs et al., 2017), though it is not identical to the latter. Social exchange theory originally dealt with interpersonal relationships, but has been found to be very suitable to explain interorganizational relationships as well, and as such contributes to the formation of preferred customer theory (Anderson and Narus, 1984; Harris et al., 2003; Kelly and Hageman, 1999; Lambe et al., 2001).

Social exchange theory scholars introduced the idea of expectations leading to exchanges. Before an actor explores the option to enter into an exchange, the potential partner might need to present a basic level of attractiveness. Once the exchange has started, that exchange is then evaluated against a standard (leading to supplier satisfaction, in the case of the buyer's performance matching the standard applied by the supplier). Then, social exchange theory introduces the 'comparison level of alternatives', arguing that the continuation of a relationship not only depends on general satisfaction, but is also contingent on the availability of alternatives (leading to a classification of a buying organization being a preferred customer, if outperforming the other customers of a supplier) (Schiele et al., 2012; Thibaut and Kelley, 1959).

It is important to highlight that preferred customer theory, while relying on social exchange theory as an explanatory mechanism, has a broader scope. In classical social exchange theory, 'Value creation, viewed as social exchange, is always non-contractual, emphasizing reciprocity and relying on trust' (Tanskanen, 2015, p. 578). From a Blauian social exchange theory perspective (Blau, 1964), the scope of exchange is, thus, a voluntary, non-contractual reciprocal exchange, which would, for instance, explain privileged collaboration in innovation processes, but would not extend to contractually settled delivery or price conditions. Preferred customer theory, however, does not only intend to explain preferential treatment in a social exchange, but – even more from a purchaser's perspective – also encompasses the preferential treatment expressed in contractual relations. In fact, getting better contracts is one target. Preferred customer theory expects the process of achieving such deals to follow the same steps as those which might lead to a more informal preferential treatment. The following conceptual core elements can be grouped to form the 'cycle of preferred customership', offering an explanation for privileged treatment.

Before an organization decides to enter a business relationship with another (or to intensify an existing relationship), it assesses the partner at hand and develops expectations on the cost–benefit relation the exchange may incur. This determines customer attractiveness. To start a (business) relationship, the exchange partner needs to be sufficiently attractive; otherwise, no interest in exchange is expressed. In the worst case for a purchaser, no offer is made; specifically, no bid is submitted by the supplier in response to a request for a quotation. Based on the initial expectations of the supplier towards the exchange relationship, the buyer–supplier relationship is established, and the exchange is executed (a similar argument may apply to the buyer, of course, although the supplier's perspective is highlighted in the subsequent discussion).

In the next step, after an exchange takes place (delivery of products, co-development of innovations, and so on), the outcome of that exchange is judged against basic satisfaction factors and the 'comparison level', reflecting the expectations towards this relationship. In the case of a buyer–supplier relationship, the supplier considers whether this particular exchange is satisfactory.

Please note that in social exchange theory sometimes it is differentiated between general normative elements of satisfaction ('social norms') and individual aspects (called 'cognitive') (McDonald, 1981; Sabatelli, 1988). In a buyer–supplier relationship, for instance, a general normative criterion of satisfaction might be proper payment. On top of this, a supplier might have individual targets with a particular customer; for example, market access to a particular country. As such, satisfaction can be composed of general satisfaction factors and relation-specific expectations, jointly composing the comparison level.

This evaluation results in satisfaction with the relationship once the minimum criteria are surpassed. Supplier satisfaction is important on an operative level, in order to receive good service from the supplier. Following social exchange models, preferred customer theory, however, considers supplier satisfaction only as a necessary, but not a sufficient condition explaining business continuity.

The third building block is based on the so-called 'comparison level of alternatives' (Cl_{alt}), that is, the assumption that actors will use not only absolute (satisfaction) but also relative criteria (namely, comparing this relation to other potential relations), in order to evaluate the outcome of an exchange relationship to eventually opt for continuation or termination (Thibaut and Kelley, 1959). As a next step, the availability of alternatives has a moderating effect on a customer's final classification by the supplier as preferred or regular, or in the extreme case as an 'exit customer': a buyer that the supplier will no longer serve (Helm et al., 2006). Depending on the presence and the quality of alternatives, suppliers classify their customers. Hence, while satisfaction compares to an absolute standard, 'status' is a relative concept, reflecting the position in a ranking (Piazza and Castellucci, 2014). A preferred customer scores higher than other customers in the preference ranking of a supplier. As such, preferred customer status also is different from a buying organization's reputation. Many organizations might have a good reputation (an absolute value), but facing other competitive actors, this does not translate into a high rank order.

Eventually, a customer enjoying preferred status will receive preferential treatment by the supplier – that is, get better services than other customers of that supplier – and, as such, achieves competitive advantages.

In sum: buying firms need to be attractive for a supplier to start engaging in a relationship. Once established, the supplier needs to be satisfied. If the vendor is more satisfied with this relationship than with others, it may award preferred customer status and, eventually, offer privileged services, which provide competitive advantages to the buying firm.

Why is the relationship between the three core concepts of attractiveness, supplier satisfaction and preferred customer status seen as cyclical (Nollet et al., 2012; Schiele et al., 2012)? In business-to-business (B2B) markets, recurrent business relationships are common. The evaluation of one transaction influences the expectation towards future exchanges (Anderson, 1989): 'If good outcomes are experienced in initial contacts or if these contacts lead the persons to anticipate good outcomes in the future, the interaction is likely to be repeated' (Thibaut and Kelley, 1959, p. 20). Provision of a service by one actor precedes reciprocation by the other, which can lead to a mutually enforcing circle (Ellis et al., 2012; Hald, 2012; La Rocca and Snehota, 2021). Tóth et al. even talk about 'relational attractiveness' to stress the multi-period, interactive character of attractiveness development (Tóth et al., 2015). The status a customer is awarded by the supplier influences its expectations, and affects the attractiveness of that customer in the view of the supplier. Even more, it is positioned that the commitment to an existing relationship will lower the expectations towards others, because of the positive experiences created (Cook and Emerson, 1978; Dwyer et al., 1987; Leik and Leik, 1977; Scanzoni, 1979). Therefore, preferred customer theory assumes a vicious circle, instead of a linear relation.

Interpreting the cycle from a reciprocity rule perspective, one party's actions are contingent on the other's behaviour. In this way, interdependence reduces risk and increases collaboration. The process begins when at least one actor takes a step, and the other party recognizes this and reciprocates. Once the process is in motion, each action can create a constantly stronger self-reinforcing cycle (Cropanzano and Mitchell, 2005). However, this circle is not completely endogenous, as it is subject to external influences, namely the availability and characteristics of the alternative partners. The relative nature of preferred customers status can lead to situations of frustration for firms which might have invested a lot and achieved high levels of supplier satisfaction, but still do not benefit from preferential treatment, because their rivals on the supply market scored even better. On the other hand, a supplier might not leave a relation, because of being dependent on this single or largest customer, even though not achieving full relational satisfaction.

Importantly, the three stages – attractiveness, supplier satisfaction and preferred customer status – have been empirically demonstrated (Pulles et al., 2016). Hence, as a precondition to achieving preferred customer status and the associated benefits, a buying organization needs to care about having satisfied suppliers and must make itself known to (potential) vendors, rather than waiting to be found. In other words, the buying organization benefits from practicing reverse (or 'upstream') marketing, understood as the active promotion of the buying company to its (potential) suppliers, which encompasses both positioning the company in the supply market as a marketing activity, and directly contacting potential suppliers.

The preferred customer theory can be enriched by some compatible models, including Hald et al.'s (2009) attractiveness theory and Pulles et al.'s (2019) resource mobilization framework. Hald et al. focus on the first step of the model, attractiveness, and as such can be connected to the cycle of preferred customership in order to better explain customer attractiveness in the first instance. They summarize their model as follows: 'We discuss attraction as the force drawing social exchange actors together and propose an expression derived from social exchange theory describing attraction as composed of three components: Expected value, trust, and dependence' (Hald et al., 2009, p. 961) Following a long tradition seeing dependence as a negative attribute, because it can put the less dependent party in the position of extracting additional rents from the more dependent exchange actor, Hald's attraction theory positions the expectation of dependence as an attraction-reducing mechanism. On the other hand, suppliers may have an expectation of trusting the customer not to abuse its position, which would increase this customer's attractiveness. Interdependence may arise. Finally, the expected value (sales volume, growth, innovation, and so on; in short, what is seen as important) has a positive influence on attractiveness. Hald et al. emphasize a comprehensive value definition, involving the buyer perception, the supplier perception and dyad perceptions on value creation.

While Hald et al. focus on the first phase of the cycle, Pulles et al. (2019) complement mainly in the 'last' part of the cycle. They suggest to expand the cycle of preferred customership by three further elements. First, is supplier segmentation, as a task for the buyer to differentiate vendors, so as to be able to concentrate on improving supplier satisfaction. Further, they introduce, between achieving preferred customer status and restart of the cycle with attractiveness considerations, the explicit steps 'engage in supplier oriented actions', such as supplier development, and 'integrate supplier resources', including establishing the necessary absorptive capacity in the buying organization. The supplier-oriented actions – as a form of reciprocal action by the buyer, once perceiving being awarded preferred customer status by the supplier – can further increase the vendor's perception of that customer as being attractive and, as such, close the cycle.

EMPIRICAL FINDINGS INCLUDING BENEFITS OF PREFERRED CUSTOMER STATUS

In recent years, initial empirical findings testing (at least part of) the cycle of preferred customership have been published. While some studies on preferred customer status have been carried out in such diverse countries as Ghana (Glavee-Geo, 2019) and the United States (Ellis et al., 2012), the bulk of empirical findings come from two lines of research conducted in India and in Europe. Some of the recent studies reported from the 'Indian school' analyse structural relationships between the preferred customer enablers (Kumar and Routroy, 2016a), determine a manufacturer's preferred customer status with suppliers (Kumar and Routroy, 2016), and measure preferred supplier status within manufacturing (Hudnurkar and Ambekar, 2019; Kumar and Routroy, 2016) and service industries (Prakash, 2011). European studies have focused on supplier satisfaction – evolving around the importance of growth, profitability, relational behaviour and operative excellence (Essig and Amann, 2009; Vos et al., 2016) – and its consequence, preferred customer status, both in private (Hüttinger et al., 2012; Pulles et al., 2016) as well as in public environments (Glas, 2018; Schiele, 2020). The importance of distinguishing between preferred customer status and its antecedent, supplier satisfaction, has been empirically evidenced. Supplier satisfaction is a necessary but not sufficient condition for achieving preferred customer status (Piechota et al., 2021; Pulles et al., 2016). Pulles et al.

(2019) advance a comprehensive summary on the current state of the empirical literature on customer attractiveness, supplier satisfaction and preferred customer status.

Complementary empirical findings highlight the benefits firms gain from having achieved preferred customer status; that is, findings that stress the relevance of research on this theory. Here, research has provided insights from very different fields. For instance, in finance, preferred customers received earlier earnings forecast revisions by analysts than the standard customers (Ekholm and von Nandelstadh, 2009). In information techology, preferred customers are served first and enjoy special server capacity to satisfy them (Goes et al., 2010). An energy plant accepted different failure rates for different customers: for standard customers, a maximum of eight hours or three interruptions; whereas for preferred customers, the target was lower than one hour or two interruptions (Holm et al., 2009). This list could continue, but the message is clear: depending on what is important to the particular business, preferred customers received privileged service from their suppliers.

To generalize, preferred customers can receive:

1. particular benefits related to the product at hand;
2. contractual cost and pricing benefits (Hald et al., 2009; Hennig-Thurau et al., 2002; Moody, 1992; Patrucco et al., 2019; Schiele et al., 2011) that have been estimated at 2–4 per cent (Bew, 2007) but may be as high as 5–30 per cent (Blenkhorn and Banting, 1991);
3. innovation access benefits (Ellis et al., 2012; Patrucco et al., 2019; Schiele et al., 2011); and
4. delivery priorities (Bemelmans et al., 2015); that is, operative benefits, including risk reductions (Reichenbachs et al., 2017).

It is worth remarking that these benefits are always relative to the services or products received by other customers of the same supplier. The unit of analysis is a single supplier that serves several customers. Hence, achieving preferred customer status has a strategic component, because it is about obtaining better supplier resource access than competing companies (Pulles et al., 2016).

EVALUATING PREFERRED CUSTOMER THEORY IN LIGHT OF WACKER'S THEORY CRITERIA

Providing a theoretical explanation for a testable phenomenon, the preferred customer theory sums up as a valid theory according to Wacker's (2008, p. 13) model of theory building, which requires valid theory to define its domain, depict assumed relationships and derive predictions.

To clarify, Table 33.1 lists constructs and their definitions and contributes to a model of relationships (Figure 33.1), which make testable predictions, arguing that higher preferred customer status predicts the supplier's contribution to innovation, benevolent pricing, privileged delivery and special benefits.

Considering the circular nature of the model a test not of parts, but the entire cycle, may require a longitudinal study, while its building blocks (such as predicting supplier satisfaction) can be more easily tested. In terms of definitions, Wacker cautions against renaming existing concepts. Preferred customer theory tries not to rename all definitions, but whenever possible tries to keep the original. This is the case with the comparison-level concept, known from social exchange theory. Hence, the question could arise if preferred customer theory is not just

Table 33.1   *Definition of terms*

Concept	Definition	Source
Customer attractiveness	'A customer is perceived as attractive by a supplier if the supplier in question has a positive expectation towards the relationship with this customer. The conditions for this perception of the supplier include an awareness of the existence of the customer and knowledge of the customer's needs.'	(Schiele et al., 2012, p. 1180)
Customer attractiveness factors	The factors that determine the evaluation of the attractiveness of the customer by the supplier.	
Comparison level	'The comparison level is the standard against which the member evaluates … the relationship or how satisfactory it is.'	(Thibaut and Kelley, 1959, p. 21)
Supplier satisfaction	'Supplier satisfaction is a condition that is achieved if the quality of outcomes from a buyer–supplier relationship meets or exceeds the supplier's expectations.'	(Schiele et al., 2012, p. 1181)
Comparison level of alternative	The comparison level of alternatives reflects the evaluation of the relationship in light of potential alternatives and determines the future status of the relationship.	(Thibaut and Kelley, 1959; Schiele et al., 2012)
Preferred customer	'A firm has preferred customer status with a supplier, if the supplier offers the buyer preferential resource allocation.'	(Steinle and Schiele, 2008, p. 11)

a supply chain application of social exchange theory. On the one hand, the scope of preferred customer theory extends beyond pure social exchange, but also includes contractually framed exchanges. Two of the assumptions come from strategic management, the second root of preferred customer theory. And therefore the definition of 'comparison level of alternative' cannot directly be taken over from Thibaut and Kelley's original, because they explicitly are interested only in continuation or discontinuation of a relationship. Importantly, here preferred customer theory differentiates between discontinuation on the one hand, and con-

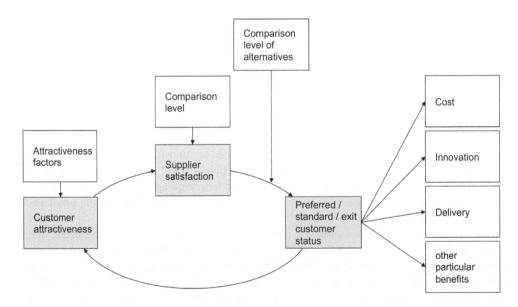

Figure 33.1   *The cycle of preferred customership*

tinuation as standard customer or preferred customer, and as such goes beyond the classical social exchange theory question (Schiele et al., 2012). It is the contribution from strategic management which analyses how firms can gain sustainable competitive advantage; that is, be better than their competitors, not just keep operations running (Barney, 1991). Social exchange theory itself has two roots, and uses the concepts of rewards and costs (which was borrowed from psychology) and resources (which was adopted from economics) to develop propositions on the exchange relationship between two parties. Likewise, preferred customer theory uses concepts from social exchange theory and from strategic management in order to explain buyer–supplier relationships and factor market rivalry. Findings from social exchange theory-based work tend to be compatible with preferred customer theory; those from other theories with different underlying assumptions – for example, Theory X-based principal–agent theory – would be less so.

A further theoretical criterion proposed by Wacker is that a theory should define its domain very specifically: that is, when and where it applies. This is the case with preferred customer theory, which clearly delineates the domain, based on the conditions for equal exchange and the strategic conditions, which specify its scope to voluntary, market-based interactions with finite numbers of heterogenous players.

Finally, Wacker suggests that theory should motivate new areas to explore; that is, its fecundity. Preferred customer theory is a strategic management theory, as it provides an explanation on how firms can gain sustainable competitive advantages through sourcing; more precisely, it offers a theory of how to solve the problem of factor market rivalry and outperform competitors within factor markets (Ellram et al., 2013; Markman et al., 2009). As such, it addresses a new field which has previously been neglected. It has often been argued that purchasing is a strategic function simply because of the monetary volume it is responsible for. But large and important does not equal to strategically relevant. The latter is only so if a sustainable competitive advantage can be achieved (Barney, 1991). While classical resource-based theory would search for resources internal to the firm, extensions of this theory likewise consider external resources, such as suppliers, as sources of competitive advantage, provided they can be tied to the company at hand (Dyer and Singh, 1998; Sanchez and Heene, 1997; Steinle et al., 1998). Becoming a preferred customer of leading suppliers is a way to establish sustainable bonds with external resources, and in this way achieve competitive advantage.

CONCLUSION, PURCHASING IMPLICATIONS AND FUTURE RESEARCH

Preferred customer theory explains how firms can gain sustainable competitive advantage by becoming a preferred customers of suppliers, which is accomplished by ensuring these suppliers' satisfaction with the relationship and initially being an attractive customer. The bonding mechanism is understood as a reinforcing cycle, the cycle of preferred customership.

Preferred customer logic has several implications for supply management. First of all, it is clear that it is not sufficient to conceive a buyer–supplier relationship as a one-to-one affair; rather, according to preferred customer theory, alternative business partners must also be taken into consideration. Further, supplier satisfaction is an absolute standard, but it is only a necessary, not a sufficient condition to achieve preferred customer status. The latter depends on the comparison level of alternatives; a relative comparison. The same absolute level of supplier satisfaction may or may not lead to the supplier awarding preferred status; this depends on the set of available alternatives. For purchasing managers this implies, in practice, that they benefit from having a good understanding of the other customers which their suppliers serve, and how the vendor regards them. Buying companies benefit from actively positioning their organization positively in the factor markets, in a reverse marketing approach (Blenkhorn and Banting, 1991).

Preferred customer theory predicts, within the respective legal situation of each country and industry, a buyer will get preferential prices with a supplier awarding preferred customer status, as the supplier wants to stay in the relationship, and also relational uncertainty is reduced. Such a supplier will also accept dependencies that it would otherwise try to avoid; for example, by assuming bilateral dependencies that emerge in the relationship. As such, a condition for joint innovation is established which requires close collaboration and inevitably creates dependencies. Following this logic, preferred customer theory argues that for a buying firm making sourcing choices, it is not always the 'best' – for example, the technically most advanced – supplier in the market that is the best supplier for a particular firm, if it does not award it with preferred customer status. From the buying firm's perspective, it is not helpful if a supplier could provide a particular service or product, but in this particular situation does not actually do so. Hence, one of the key take-aways from preferred customer theory is to care about understanding how the buying company is regarded by the supplier, and to focus only on those relationships where preference is reciprocal. What is more, firms pursuing a differentiation strategy need to be preferred customers of the leading suppliers for their strategic purchases, otherwise they are predicted to fail to compete in innovation, in cases where they are increasingly dependent upon supplier contributions. Here, we have the case of a purchasing-induced strategy determination: if a firm tries to pursue a differentiation strategy, and for that relies on its supplier's contribution to innovation, it cannot successfully implement such a strategy without ensuring privileged access to these crucial suppliers.

But also in supply chain operations and delivery, preferred customer theory predicts a significant difference, with the preferred customer gaining preferential delivery conditions. Most pronounced, in allocation situations, is that the preferred customer is expected to get supplies, while standard customers are not served. Not being a preferred customer with important suppliers represents a strategic risk. Depending on the supply structure of a firm, it might also be seen as more creditworthy by a bank. A company that can rely on a supplier structure characterized by the fact that the main suppliers offer preferred customer status, compared to one which has a weak supply base which shifts loyalties at the first instance and overcharges the buyer, is evidently less volatile.

To summarize, preferred customer theory focuses on the three cycle stages of attractiveness, satisfaction and preferred customer status, and their interaction. In order to structure the field and classify research, the cycle stages can be depicted as one dimension on how to map preferred customer research (the top dimension in Figure 33.2, Z-axis). At the same time, the diverse benefit classes are relevant: gaining preferential resource allocation from suppliers for cost reduction, innovation enhancement, delivery stabilization, or further industry- or company-specific particular benefits (depicted as the front dimension in Figure 33.2, X-axis). A final dimension which could be added to summarize and sort preferred customer research, and likewise to identify opportunities for future research, is the level of analysis (Schiele et al., 2012): micro (individual; Ellegaard, 2012), meso (buyer–supplier) and macro (country) (levels depicted as Y-axis in Figure 33.2).

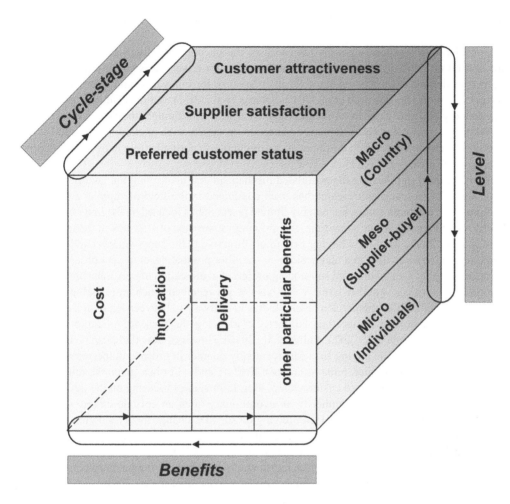

Figure 33.2   The attractiveness cube

For describing the maturing of a theory and exposing the gaps in empirical verification, five steps can be differentiated (Schiele, 2020): (1) the phenomenon that the theory addresses has to be empirically evidenced (here, the existence of customer differentiation and differences in treatment); (2) its relevance depicted (the benefits/threats); (3) antecedents (the mechanism understood; here, the cycle stages); (4) actionable implications (here, the design of preferred customer management tools); and (5) the identification of contingencies needs to be accomplished (for instance, environmental, such as countries; here, the levels of analysis).

First, a recent review of current preferred customer research (Pulles et al., 2019) revealed that the phenomenon of differentiated treatment of customers by their suppliers has been described very often. It was found to be a recognizable business reality. Less research has been conducted into customer segmentation in B2B marketing which, however, could provide a better understanding on objectives, tools and mechanisms of differentiated treatment. There is also the question of purposeful customer segmentation versus intuitive differences in treatment.

Considering the second step, the relevance of the phenomenon, such as shown above in the section on the benefits of preferred customership for buyers, it is striking that there has been considerable empirical evidence for the relevance for innovation and also evidence for the price hypothesis (Patrucco et al., 2019; Schiele et al., 2011), but only limited research on the delivery and risk side. In an increasingly volatile world, though, the aspect of seamless delivery becomes more challenging. For instance, in crises, such as the one induced by the Covid-19 pandemic, preferred customer status might play a particular role to overcome supply shortages (Schiele et al., 2021).

With the third step, testing the postulated mechanism and identifying the factor's antecedents, some initial empirical research has been conducted in the field of supplier satisfaction and preferred customer status, but notably limited research has focused on the first phase of the cycle, attractiveness. At the same time, the growing importance of start-ups in the innovation process stresses the need for a buying firm to be attractive in the supply market and signal its demands, much more than in a classical buyer–supplier product development process, where issues of supplier satisfaction and subsequent preferential allocation of personnel and capacity resources are critical. Another issue which has not yet received much empirical attention is the measurement of the comparison level. Studies identify a gap between supplier satisfaction and preferred customer status, thus indirectly evidencing the presence of more attractive relationships (Piechota et al., 2021; Pulles et al., 2016). However, how these can be identified, categorized, and how the buying firm can eventually counter in order to outperform the rival customers of a good supplier, remains an open field of study. Further, given the multi-period nature of the cycle of preferred customership, long-term studies focusing on the development of such business relationships either in an evolutionary or in an episode-driven way could greatly expand our understanding. Here, relying on social exchange theory's notion that there is a mutual adaptation in a relationship in order to achieve an actor's goals, which may develop into mutually obliged bonds, comes into play (Ellis et al., 2012).

From a management perspective (the fourth step on actionable implications), a few tools have been proposed to help firms implement preferred customer theory. Early on Cordón and Vollmann (2008) proposed 'ten golden rules for becoming an attractive customer', which include internal organizational changes and changes in the conduct towards suppliers. More systematically, and based on the above theory, Nollet et al. (2012) introduce a model on how to become a preferred customer, one step at a time. They collect a series of tactics that purchasers can systematically apply at each phase of the cycle. Schiele (2012) introduces the 'preferred customer matrix', which on one axis depicts the competitiveness of a supplier, and on the other axis differentiates between standard and preferred customer. Such a supplier classification might be the input for the second step ('segment suppliers') in Pulles et al.'s (2019) stage model of supplier resource mobilization. However, it can be said that despite such attempts, literature is still scarce on management applications designed following preferred customer logic. A broad avenue for future research also emerges around upstream or reverse marketing; that is, the purposeful positioning of the buying firm in the supply market. Here, some time ago Biemans and Brand (1995) presented a first draft on how firms could implement a systematic reverse marketing approach, essentially focusing on the identification of preferred suppliers and then the proactive approach towards them.

Contingencies of the theory, fifth and finally, have only started to be researched. For instance, while preferred customer research has been conducted in diverse countries, a comparison between them has yet to be published. Given the underlying understanding of buyer-supplier as a social exchange process, the importance of culture as an influencing factor is almost to be expected. In particular, the country or nation a firm is hosted in might have an influence, for instance, on the perceived attractiveness of this buyer by international suppliers. Most research, so far, has focused on the meso level, analysing the relationship between firms. Interpersonal elements may also influence the decision or the habit of a supplier to award a customer with preferred status (Ellegaard, 2012).

Preferred customer theory enables purchasing to orchestrate competitive advantages for its firm by ensuring better access to supplier resources than competing organizations have. As such, this theory if fully developed could become the driver of a next round in competition.

ACKNOWLEDGEMENT

This chapter has profited from extensive comments by Scott Ellis. The remaining positions and issues are, of course, mine.

REFERENCES

Anderson, E. (1989). Determinants of continuity in conventional industrial channel dyads. *Marketing Science*, *8*(4), 310–323.

Anderson, J.C., and Narus, J.A. (1984). A model of the distributor's perspective of distributor–manufacturer working relationships. *Journal of Marketing*, *48*(Fall), 62–74.

Barney, J.B. (1991). Firm resources and sustained competitive advantage. *Journal of Management*, *17*(1), 99–120.

Bemelmans, J., Voordijk, H., Vos, B., and Dewulf, G. (2015). Antecedents and benefits of obtaining preferred customer status: Experiences from the Dutch construction industry. *International Journal of Operations and Production Management*, *35*(2), 178–200. doi:10.1108/IJOPM-07-2012-0263.

Bew, R. (2007). The new customer of choice imperative: ensuring supply availability, productivity gains, and supplier innovation. Paper presented at the 92nd Annual International Supply Management Conference, Las Vegas.

Biemans, W.G., and Brand, M.J. (1995). Reverse marketing: A synergy of purchasing and relationship marketing. *International Journal of Purchasing and Materials Management*, *31*(2), 28–37. doi:10.1111/j.1745-493X.1995.tb00206.x.

Blau, P.M. (1964). *Exchange and Power in Social Life*. New York: Wiley.

Blenkhorn, D.L., and Banting, P.M. (1991). How reverse marketing changes buyer–seller roles. *Industrial Marketing Management*, *20*(3), 185–191. doi:10.1016/0019-8501(91)90016-9

Brokaw, A.J., and Davisson, C.N. (1978). Positioning a company as a preferred customer. *Journal of Purchasing and Materials Management*, *14*(1), 9–11.

Christiansen, P.E., and Maltz, A. (2002). Becoming an 'interesting' customer: Procurement strategies for buyers without leverage. *International Journal of Logistics: Research and Applications*, *5*(2), 177–195.

Cook, K.S., and Emerson, R.M. (1978). Power, equity and commitment in exchange networks. *American Sociological Review*, *43*(5), 721–739.

Cordón, C., and Vollmann, T. (2008). *The Power of Two: How Smart Companies Create Win–Win Customer–Supplier Partnerships that Outperform the Competition*. Houndmills: Palgrave Macmillan.

Cropanzano, R., and Mitchell, M.S. (2005). Social exchange theory: An interdisciplinary review. *Journal of Management*, *31*(6), 874–900. doi:10.1177/0149206305279602.

Di Domenico, M., Tracey, P., and Haugh, H. (2009). The dialectic of social exchange: Theorizing corporate–social enterprise collaboration. *Organization Studies*, *30*(8), 887–907.

Dierickx, I., and Cool, K. (1989). Asset stock accumulation and sustainability of competitive advantage. *Management Science*, *35*(12), 1504–1511.

Dwyer, F.R., Schurr, P.H., and Oh, S. (1987). Developing buyer–seller relationships. *Journal of Marketing*, *51*(2), 11–27.

Dyer, J.H., and Singh, H. (1998). The relational view: Cooperative strategy and sources of interorganizational competitive advantage. *Academy of Management Review*, *23*(4), 660–679.

Ekholm, A., and von Nandelstadh, A. (2009). Do analysts leak information to preferred customers? *Corporate Ownership and Control*, *6*(4 D Cont. 3), 357–369.

Ellegaard, C. (2012). Interpersonal attraction in buyer–supplier relationships: A cyclical model rooted in social psychology. *Industrial Marketing Management*, *41*(8), 1219–1227. doi:10.1016/j.indmarman.2012.10.006.

Ellis, S.C., Henke Jr, J.W., and Kull, T.J. (2012). The effect of buyer behaviors on preferred customer status and access to supplier technological innovation: An empirical study of supplier perceptions. *Industrial Marketing Management*, *41*(8), 1259–1269.

Ellram, L.M., Tate, W.L., and Feitzinger, E.G. (2013). Factor-market rivalry and competition for supply chain resources. *Journal of Supply Chain Management*, *49*(1), 29–46. doi:10.1111/jscm.12001.

Essig, M., and Amann, M. (2009). Supplier satisfaction: Conceptual basics and explorative findings. *Journal of Purchasing and Supply Management*, *15*(2), 103–113.

Glas, A. H. (2018). The impact of procurement on supplier satisfaction: service, communication, and speed. *International Journal of Integrated Supply Management*, *12*(1–2), 90–117.

Glavee-Geo, R. (2019). Does supplier development lead to supplier satisfaction and relationship continuation? *Journal of Purchasing and Supply Management*, *25*(3). doi:10.1016/j.pursup.2019.05.002.

Goes, P., Ilk, N., Yue, W.T., and Zhao, J.L. (2010). Live-chat agent assignments in two-class e-customer queues under imperfect profiling. Paper presented at the Proceedings of 20th Annual Workshop on Information Technologies and Systems.

Hald, K.S. (2012). The role of boundary spanners in the formation of customer attractiveness. *Industrial Marketing Management*, *41*(8), 1228–1240.

Hald, K.S., Cordón, C., and Vollmann, T.E. (2009). Towards an understanding of attraction in buyer–supplier relationships. *Industrial Marketing Management*, *38*(8), 960–970.

Harris, L.C., O'Malley, L., and Patterson, M. (2003). Professional interaction: Exploring the concept of attraction. *Marketing Theory*, *3*(1), 9.

Helm, S., Rolfes, L., and Günter, B. (2006). Suppliers' willingness to end unprofitable customer relationships: An exploratory investigation in the German mechanical engineering sector. *European Journal of Marketing*, *40*(3–4), 366–383.

Hennig-Thurau, T., Gwinner, K.P., and Gremler, D.D. (2002). Understanding relationship marketing outcomes: An integration of relational benefits and relationship quality. *Journal of Service Research*, *4*(3), 230–247. doi:10.1177/1094670502004003006.

Holm, A., Pylvänäinen, J., Owe, P., Paananen, H., and Bollen, M.H.J. (2009). Customer dissatisfaction index (CDI): Pilot use in network planning. Paper presented at the IET Conference.

Hottenstein, M. (1970). Expediting in job-order-control systems: a simulation study. *IIE Transactions*, *2*(1), 46–54.

Hudnurkar, M., and Ambekar, S. S. (2019). Framework for measurement of supplier satisfaction. *International Journal of Productivity and Performance Management*, *68*(8), 1475.

Hüttinger, L., Schiele, H., and Veldman, J. (2012). The drivers of customer attractiveness, supplier satisfaction and preferred customer status: A literature review. *Industrial Marketing Management*, *41*(8), 1194–1205.

Kelly, M., and Hageman, A. (1999). Marshallian externalities in innovation. *Journal of Economic Growth*, *4*(March), 39–54.

Kumar, C. V. S., and Routroy, S. (2016). An approach for measuring a manufacturer's preferred supplier status. *Asia Pacific Journal of Marketing and Logistics*, *28*(5), 939–963.

Kumar, C. V. S., and Routroy, S. (2016a). Case application of a methodology for determining a manufacturer's preferred customer status with suppliers. *EMJ – Engineering Management Journal*, *28*(1), 25–38. doi:10.1080/10429247.2016.1139911.

La Rocca, A., and Snehota, I. (2021). Mobilizing suppliers when starting up a new business venture. *Industrial Marketing Management, 93*, 401–412. doi:https://doi.org/10.1016/j.indmarman.2020.08.002.

Lambe, C.J., Wittmann, C.M., and Spekman, R.E. (2001). Social exchange theory and research on business-to-business relational exchange. *Journal of Business-to-Business Marketing, 8*(3), 1–36.

Leenders, M.R., and Blenkhorn, D.L. (1988). *Reverse Marketing: The New Buyer–Supplier Relationship.* New York: Free Press.

Leik, R.K., and Leik, S.A. (eds) (1977). *Transition to Interpersonal Commitment.* New Brunswick, NJ: Transaction.

Markman, G.D., Gianiodis, P.T., and Buchholtz, A.K. (2009). Factor-market rivalry. *Academy of Management Review, 34*(3), 423–441. doi:10.5465/AMR.2009.40632072.

McDonald, G.W. (1981). Structural exchange and marital interaction. *Journal of Marriage and the Family, 43*(4), 825–839.

McGregor, D. (1966). *Leadership and Motivation.* Boston, MA: MIT Press.

Moody, P.E. (1992). Customer supplier integration: Why being an excellent customer counts. *Business Horizons, 35*(4), 52–57.

Nollet, J., Rebolledo, C., and Popel, V. (2012). Becoming a preferred customer one step at a time. *Industrial Marketing Management, 41*(8), 1186–1193.

Patrucco, A.S., Luzzini, D., Moretto, A., and Ronchi, S. (2019). Attraction in buyer–supplier relationships: Improving supply network performance through purchasing recognition and proficient collaboration initiatives. *Business Process Management Journal, 25*(2), 347–367.

Piazza, A., and Castellucci, F. (2014). Status in organization and management theory. *Journal of Management, 40*(1), 287–315.

Piechota, S., Glas, A.H., and Essig, M. (2021). Questioning the relevance of supplier satisfaction for preferred customer treatment: Antecedent effects of comparative alternatives and multi-dimensionality. *Journal of Purchasing and Supply Management, 27*(1), 100672.

Prakash, G. (2011). Service quality in supply chain: empirical evidence from Indian automotive industry. *Supply Chain Management: An International Journal, 16*(5), 362–378.

Pulles, N.J., Ellegaard, C., Schiele, H., and Kragh, H. (2019). Mobilising supplier resources by being an attractive customer: Relevance, status and future research directions. *Journal of Purchasing and Supply Management, 25*(3). doi:10.1016/j.pursup.2019.100539.

Pulles, N.J., Schiele, H., Veldman, J., and Hüttinger, L. (2016). The impact of customer attractiveness and supplier satisfaction on becoming a preferred customer. *Industrial Marketing Management, 54*, 129–140. doi:https://doi.org/10.1016/j.indmarman.2015.06.004.

Ramsay, J. (2001). The resource based perspective, rents, and purchasing's contribution to sustainable competitive advantage. *Journal of Supply Chain Management, 37*(3), 38–47.

Reichenbachs, M., Schiele, H., and Hoffmann, P. (2017). Strategic supply risk: exploring the risks deriving from a buying firm being of low importance for its suppliers. *International Journal of Risk Assessment and Management, 20*(4), 350–373.

Sabatelli, R.M. (1988). Exploring relationship satisfaction: A social exchange perspective on the interdependence between theory, research, and practice. *Family Relations, (37)*2, 217–222.

Sanchez, R., and Heene, A. (1997). Reinventing strategic management: New theory and practice for competence-based competition. *European Management Journal, 15*(3), 303–317.

Scanzoni, J. (1979). Social exchange and behavioral interdependence. In R.L. Burgess and T.L. Huston (eds), *Social Exchange in Developing Relationships* (pp. 61–98). New York: Academic Press.

Schiele, H. (2012). Accessing supplier innovation by being their preferred customer. *Research-Technology Management, 55*(1), 44–50.

Schiele, H. (2020). Comparing public and private organisations in their quest to become a preferred customer of suppliers. *Journal of Public Procurement, 20*(2), 119–144.

Schiele, H., Calvi, R., and Gibbert, M. (2012). Customer attractiveness, supplier satisfaction and preferred customer status: Introduction, definitions and an overarching framework. *Industrial Marketing Management, 41*(8), 1178–1185.

Schiele, H., Hoffmann, P., and Körber, T. (2021). Synchronicity management: Mitigating supply chain risks by systematically taking demand changes as starting point – A lesson from the Covid 19 crisis. *IEEE Engineering Management Review, 49*(1), 55–62. doi:10.1109/EMR.2020.3040016.

Schiele, H., Veldman, J., and Hüttinger, L. (2011). Supplier innovativeness and supplier pricing: The role of preferred customer status. *International Journal of Innovation Management, 15*(1), 1–27.

Steinle, C., Eickhoff, M., and Schiele, H. (1998). Zur Perspektivenerweiterung des Strategischen Management: Der ‚innovative Cluster' als Wertschöpfungssystem und die Entwicklung von Kernkompetenzen. *Zeitschrift für Planung, 9*(4), 367–390.

Steinle, C., and Schiele, H. (2008). Limits to global sourcing? Strategic consequences of dependency on international suppliers: cluster theory, resource-based view and case studies. *Journal of Purchasing and Supply Management, 14*(1), 3–14.

Tanskanen, K. (2015). Who wins in a complex buyer–supplier relationship? A social exchange theory based dyadic study. *International Journal of Operations and Production Management, 35*(4), 577–603. doi:10.1108/IJOPM-10-2012-0432.

Thibaut, J.W., and Kelley, H.H. (1959). *The Social Psychology of Groups*. Oxford: John Wiley.

Tóth, Z., Thiesbrummel, C., Henneberg, S.C., and Naudé, P. (2015). Understanding configurations of relational attractiveness of the customer firm using fuzzy set QCA. *Journal of Business Research, 68*(3), 723–734.

Vos, F. G., Schiele, H., and Hüttinger, L. (2016). Supplier satisfaction: Explanation and out-of-sample prediction. *Journal of Business Research, 69*(10), 4613–4623.

Wacker, J.G. (2008). A conceptual understanding of requirements for theory-building research: Guidelines for scientific theory building. *Journal of Supply Chain Management, 44*(3), 5–15.

Williamson, P.J. (1991). Supplier strategy and customer responsiveness: Managing the links. *Business Strategy Review, 2*(2), 75–90.

Zeitz, G. (1980). Interorganizational dialectics. *Administrative Science Quarterly, 25*(1), 72–88.

34. On theories for researching sustainability

Thomas E. Johnsen and Federico Caniato

INTRODUCTION

Recent systematic literature reviews have mapped the use of theoretical perspectives in purchasing and supply chain management (PSCM) research (Chicksand et al., 2012; Spina et al., 2016). These show that transaction cost economics (TCE) and the resource-based view (RBV) are the dominant theories in PSCM research, although a wide array of theoretical perspectives can also be identified. However, TCE and the RBV are old theories that were not developed to guide research in PSCM, and we would question their suitability for researching sustainable PSCM phenomena. In fact, literature reviews that focus on sustainable PSCM (Gimenez and Tachizawa, 2012; Johnsen et al., 2017; Quarshie et al., 2016) show that when researchers carry out studies related to sustainable PSCM they are driven by a different set of theories.

In this chapter we discuss why researchers in sustainable PSCM tend to opt for different theoretical perspectives to guide their research, and why TCE and the RBV are relatively rare. We unpack the reasons why theories that are applicable to PSCM in general may not be easily transferrable or appropriate to research that focuses on sustainability. In brief, we argue that the reasons are twofold. Firstly, the inherent long-term nature of sustainability, as opposed to, for example, the short-term nature of buyer–supplier exchanges or transactions, requires theory that focuses on long-term developmental processes. Secondly, the traditional theories used in PSCM research are limited when researchers seek to understand sustainability from an interorganizational systems (or ecosystems) perspective, focused on networks of actors or stakeholders.

TCE is limited as a theoretical perspective because it is predominantly applied to analyse transactions between buyers and suppliers as the unit of analysis, rather than long-term development processes within complex, multi-tiered networks. Furthermore, TCE is ill-suited as a theoretical perspective because the boundary conditions (Busse et al., 2017) become problematic: the assumptions of TCE theory of short-term optimization and firms being driven by profit maximization and cost reduction – that is, purely economic goals – cannot explain very well the long-term vision of sustainable PSCM.

The RBV is increasingly applied as a theoretical lens in sustainable PSCM research (Johnsen et al., 2017) but also suffers from limitations. In particular, the assumption in traditional RBV theory (for example Barney, 1991; Wernerfelt, 1984) is that strategic resources, including core competencies, must be internally controlled rather than distributed across multiple firms (Granstrand et al., 1997). Later developments of the RBV, including the extended RBV (Lavie, 2006) and the natural RBV (NRBV) dating back to the seminal article by Hart (1995), place more emphasis on the importance of external relationships, and that these can in fact be a source of competitive advantage.

In this chapter we begin by presenting four theoretical perspectives that, with the exception of our fourth suggestion, are widely applied in sustainable PSCM research. Our first proposed theory for researching sustainability is therefore the NRBV. Hart's (1995) NRBV is particularly suitable to studying sustainable PSCM because it assumes that competitive advantage can be achieved through the firm's relationship with the natural environment; in turn achieved by means of pollution prevention, product stewardship and sustainable development. In addition to the NRBV, we propose three theories that are characterized by their focus on the development and management of interorganizational relationships.

We propose stakeholder theory (Freeman, 1984) as the second alternative. Stakeholders include 'any group or individual who can affect, or is affected by, the achievement of a corporation's purpose' (Freeman, 1984, p. vi). Stakeholder theory is particularly useful in research on sustainable PSCM to identify how varying stakeholders exert pressure on companies to implement a sustainable supply chain (for example Darnall et al., 2008; Ehrgott et al., 2011; Hall and Matos, 2010; Walker and Brammer, 2009). Such stakeholders might include, for example, regulators, media, non-governmental organizations (NGOs) or customers. Stakeholder theory is therefore well suited to analyse the question of why companies want to implement sustainable supply chains, as companies are often driven in their decisions by these stakeholders. Mitchell et al.'s (1997) work is frequently used to provide insights into stakeholder salience, focusing on the constructs of power, legitimacy and urgency.

As the third alternative, we propose institutional theory (for example DiMaggio and Powell, 1983), which is also often used to identify drivers of sustainability implementation, but with an emphasis on why companies often adopt similar responses and practices. Borrowing from Weber's (1930) use of the 'iron cage' metaphor, DiMaggio and Powell (1983) emphasize a negative view of the importance of isomorphic institutional pressures; key constructs within institutional theory include the coercive, normative or mimetic nature of external pressures and influences.

Our fourth suggestion is the Industrial Marketing and Purchasing (IMP) Group interaction approach ('IMP') (Håkansson, 1982). Compared with the other three theories we put forward, IMP has been applied far more rarely in studies of sustainable PSCM. However, as argued by Johnsen et al. (2017), IMP is ideally suited to researching sustainable PSCM given its focus on interaction processes within dyadic relationships and the complex industrial networks in which dyads are embedded. Similarly to other network theories, IMP emphasizes the bonds and ties between network actors and the resources they control, as well as links between the activities they perform (Håkansson and Snehota, 1995). Unlike social network theory, IMP examines industrial networks that in many ways resemble supply chains (with important differences).

This *Handbook* contains chapters that are fully dedicated to the four theories. We do not intend to repeat what readers can learn from these other chapters. In this chapter we examine why these four theoretical perspectives are suitable for researching sustainable PSCM.

Having presented the four theoretical perspectives, we put forth some more recent promising theories that introduce some new perspectives that would help researchers to break new ground. The potential problem with relying on the same 'old theories' is that it is very difficult to make new theoretical contributions. Using established theories tends to result in marginal contributions, where the shift from traditional to sustainable purchasing and supply chain models really requires discontinuous or even paradigmatic change (see Wieland, 2021). We would therefore urge ambitious PSCM researchers to consider the use of such new theories; or new at least in the context of PSCM research. In this chapter we briefly present the following: the social resource-based view (SRBV), complex adaptive systems (CASs), the ecologically dominant logic, and panarchy theory.

We begin by comparing the four main theories that we focus on, discussing their strengths and limitations from the perspective of sustainable PSCM research. We then offer some guidance on the types of sustainability themes and research questions that are suitable to study through these perspectives. At the end of the chapter we briefly present the more recent theories.

APPLYING THE NRBV TO RESEARCH ON SUSTAINABILITY

Background

The RBV was originally proposed by Wernerfelt (1984) as a reaction against the prevailing theories in the 1980s that focused on identifying attractive niches in the marketplace with little regard to the necessary resource endowment required to compete in these niches (Wernerfelt, 1984). The RBV focused on the heterogeneity of resource bundles and capabilities and the factors that make these difficult to imitate and are not simply available on 'strategic factor markets' (Barney, 1986, 1991; Dierickx and Cool, 1989). The idea was that the development over time of difficult-to-copy and superior resources could be a source of sustained competitive advantage. Barney's (1991) framework showed that resources need to be valuable, rare, inimitable and non-substitutable.

The fundamental logic of the RBV found its way to the minds of the business world when Prahalad and Hamel (1990) published their famous article in the *Harvard Business Review* on core competences. They described how core competencies, rather than products or markets, could be leveraged, and that core competencies tend to be knowledge-based and involve collective learning (Peteraf, 1993). Of fundamental importance is that core competencies in turn must be protected through what Rumelt (1987) called isolating mechanisms, that will create barriers to imitation. Resources are thus the basis unit of analysis.

Within PSCM the RBV logic has found its way into practice, notably in informing the make-or-buy decision on the basic principle that companies must never outsource resources that are core (Arnold, 2000), as they must be internally nurtured and protected. More recent contributions show how even strategic activities, such as manufacturing, design and logistics, can be outsourced, but RBV analysis can inform such strategic decisions (McIvor, 2009).

One theme within the RBV concerns the risk that core competencies can become core rigidities as companies focus too much on past strengths instead of the future: they become competency traps (Leonard-Barton, 1992). In a rapidly changing world characterized by disruptive technological change (Christensen, 1997), too much focus on past strengths could mean that incumbent firms fall victim to competence-destroying innovations (Henderson and Clark, 1990). The concept of dynamic capabilities has been developed with this limitation in mind, defined as the ability to integrate, build and reconfigure internal and external processes to address rapidly changing environments, where the ability to maintain and adapt these capabilities is the basis of competitive advantage (Teece et al., 1997). Thus, where traditional RBV can be interpreted as a 'stick to your knitting' philosophy, dynamic capability theory emphasizes the need for firms to change and innovate. Prahalad and Hamel's (1994) book *Competing for the Future* captured the spirit of this focus on innovation and long-term competitive advantage, and it has remained at the core of RBV theory development.

From the RBV to the NRBV

One spin-off from the traditional RBV is the NRBV, which links RBV theory to the sustainability agenda. Where the traditional RBV theory places little emphasis on physical resources per se, the NRBV goes in the opposite direction by specifically focusing on natural (or biophysical) resources, and therefore directly ties in the resource debate with an environmental agenda (Hart, 1995). Moreover, as Hart (1995) argues, management theory historically uses 'a narrow and parochial concept of environment that emphasizes political, economic, social, and technological aspects to the virtual exclusion of the natural environment' (pp. 986–987).

Changing from the RBV to the NRBV analysis requires both a dynamic and an interconnected view of resources that emphasizes resource connectivity, to include relationships with external stakeholders. Not only does the NRBV theory not see it as a disadvantage to access resources through interorganizational relationships, but it also suggests that resources gain social legitimacy through stakeholder collaboration. Being able to access strategic resources through external relationships is key to the NRBV. Hart's (1995) conceptual framework consists of three interconnected strategies: sustainable development, product stewardship and pollution prevention; Hart (1995) argues that these constitute potential sources of sustainable competitive advantage. All three of these strategies require close collaboration with a range of external stakeholders.

Although traditional RBV theorized around long-term strategic advantages by referring to sustained competitive advantage, this was essentially in the sense of economic sustainability, and not taking into account environmental and social sustainability. Whether or not these terms themselves indicate a real difference in perspective, traditional RBV certainly did not consider the triple bottom line (TBL) in their concern with how to achieve economic rents (see for example Barney et al., 2011). Even Hart's (1995) original theory did not focus on TBL performance; the ecologically dominant paradigm proposed by Montabon et al. (2016) and the social RBV proposed by Tate and Bals (2018) are recent theoretical developments proposing how to widen the scope from economic to TBL performance, and we discuss these latest developments in our section on the latest theories for researching sustainable PSCM.

Research Themes and Avenues for the NRBV

Building on the use of the NRBV in supply chain management (SCM), researchers have highlighted the interplay between internal and external capabilities for green SCM (Lee and Klassen, 2008), a focus on interorganizational resources to stimulate supplier engagement (for example Foerstl et al., 2010), and the reinforcing effects of collaboration (Vachon and Klassen, 2008) and organizational learning (Carter, 2005). The review by Sarkis et al. (2011) highlights the need for further development of the NRBV by focusing on the interorganizational learning elements and definition of what is meant by competitive valuable resources in this context.

The NRBV has been successfully applied to underpin studies into sustainable PSCM. For example, Paulraj (2011) showed how sustainable supply management can be a socially complex relational capability with significant influence not only on economic but also on environmental and social firm performance. His research therefore ties into the debate about how sustainability management can constitute a source of sustained competitive advantage, and he calls for more research on sustainability competency to understand its broader importance in promoting sustainable PSCM. In a similar vein, Vachon and Klassen (2006) showed how knowledge sharing routines and capability to integrate external resources constitute resources that are difficult to replicate and thus may generate a competitive advantage. This remains an important avenue for future research.

Researchers have also applied the NRBV to study the interplay between internal and external capabilities for green SCM (Lee and Klassen, 2008), and this focus on interorganizational resources and collaboration remains a key topic for NRBV research in SCM research (for example Foerstl et al., 2010). More recently, the NRBV has been used to research circular (or closed-loop) supply chains, and this is a very promising research opportunity as there are still very few studies that have attempted this. Howard et al. (2016) used NRBV theory as a lens to explore the dynamic capabilities that lead to successful product stewardship in developing closed-loop supply chains. Closed-loop supply chain development involves radical supply chain redesign and therefore requires dynamic capabilities and development of new stakeholder relationships. Sarkis et al. (2011) highlights the need for further development of the NRBV in green SCM by focusing on interorganizational learning elements and the meaning of valuable resources and this remains a viable research avenue.

APPLYING STAKEHOLDER THEORY TO RESEARCH ON SUSTAINABILITY

Background

The original work on stakeholder theory by Freeman (1984) can be seen as an attempt to widen the understanding of the range of diverse stakeholders that affect corporate decisions. Where traditional strategy thinking focuses primarily on shareholders, employees, customers and suppliers as the main stakeholders of corporations, stakeholder theory argues that there are many more stakeholders to consider in corporate decision making, such as communities, governmental bodies, trade associations, unions, and so on. Stakeholder theory categorizes these stakeholders on the basis of the 'principle of who or what really counts' (Mitchell et al., 1997). Primary stakeholders are those with a direct interest in the organization, including customers, shareholders, employees, suppliers and regulators; whereas secondary stakeholders are not engaged in transactions with the organization but can nevertheless affect, and be affected by, the organization, including academic institutions, NGOs, neighbouring communities and social activists.

A fundamental premise of stakeholder theory is that relationships do not occur in a vacuum of dyadic ties, but as a network of influences involving multiple stakeholders (Rowley, 1997), that include 'any group or individual who can affect, or is affected by, the achievement of a corporation's purpose' (Freeman, 1984, p. vi). Mitchell et al. (1997) proposed three attributes to characterize the dynamics of interaction amongst stakeholders:

1. Power: the ability of an advocate to influence, produce or affect behaviours, outcomes, processes, objectives or direction.
2. Legitimacy: in keeping with expected behaviours, structures, values, beliefs, norms and rules.
3. Urgency: the stake is critical to the stakeholder and time-sensitive.

Where Freeman's (1984) work originally focused on strategic management, researchers in sustainable PSCM have increasingly used stakeholder theory as a theoretical lens because it helps to understand the pressures not only from traditional supply chain actors, such as customers and suppliers, but also from actors, or stakeholders, that are not traditionally included in supply chain analysis, but with potentially critical influence when the focus shifts to sustainable supply chains.

Research Themes and Avenues for Stakeholder Theory

Stakeholder theory is the dominant underpinning theoretical perspective in sustainable purchasing and supply management research, and its popularity continues to increase (Johnsen et al., 2017). The diversity of stakeholder theory and its facility for identifying and prioritizing conflicting stakeholder pressures is part of the appeal of stakeholder theory in sustainable purchasing and supply management (Johnsen et al., 2017). Many studies (for example Hall and Matos, 2010; Walker and Brammer, 2009) focus on how pressures of primary stakeholders and secondary stakeholders induce companies to embrace sustainable PSCM practices.

Mitchell et al.'s (1997) seminal work on stakeholder salience theory is frequently adopted as part of research into sustainability (for example Parmagiani et al., 2011) where relationship attributes combine the influence of power, legitimacy and urgency. For example, Parmagiani et al. (2011, p. 221) use this framework to argue that firms must learn how to engage with stakeholders: 'adding stakeholder salience with respect to social and environmental issues means that firms may benefit from focusing on a smaller number of rich relationships with both suppliers and activists, as it will take more effort to manage these relationships cooperatively'. Schneider and Wallenburg (2012) focus on the role of purchasing in implementing sustainable sourcing and collaboration with internal and external stakeholders. Building on stakeholder theory, they investigate stakeholder salience to drive the implementation of sustainable sourcing, analysing stakeholder power, legitimacy and urgency.

The appeal of stakeholder theory for research on sustainable PSCM is therefore closely related to the analysis of the influences or pressures that different types of stakeholders exert, and how these form a powerful force in putting pressure on companies to implement sustainable practices within their supply chains. Stakeholder theory has thus often been used to understand why companies want to implement sustainability, but stakeholders can also be instrumental in analysing how companies can implement sustainable supply chains. Gualandris et al. (2015) propose a model for supplier sustainability evaluation and verification. Illustrating how stakeholders can perform roles such as counsellors or advisors, they show how companies can engage with diverse stakeholders to address the problem of accountability, affecting the levels of inclusivity, scope and disclosure. We align with their suggestions that more empirical research is needed to assess how different stakeholders can be involved in supplier evaluation and verification and the effects on inclusivity, scope and disclosure.

Stakeholder theory is limited in its focus on stakeholder power, legitimacy and urgency. For this reason, it is not surprising that the theory is often applied in combination with another theoretical perspective, and one of the frequent combinations is with institutional theory, which we discuss in the following section.

APPLYING INSTITUTIONAL THEORY TO RESEARCH ON SUSTAINABILITY

Background

A fundamental premise of institutional theory is that it explains why companies often adopt similar responses and practices: the study of isomorphism. Where stakeholder theory focuses on stakeholder pressure as a driver of organizational decision making, institutional theory examines three mechanisms, or forms of pressure, that can cause institutional isomorphism: coercive, mimetic and normative pressures (DiMaggio and Powell, 1983).

Coercive isomorphism relates to the formal and informal pressures exerted on organizations by other organizations upon which they are dependent, and by expectations from society (DiMaggio and Powell, 1983). For example, a powerful firm may seek to coerce its suppliers to adopt lean production practices or to comply with its sustainability requirements. This may not lead to efficiencies (Miemczyk, 2008) but can still increase legitimacy. Mimetic isomorphism occurs as a result of uncertainty that encourages imitation (Zsidisin et al., 2005). Consider how the automotive industry in Europe and North America from the late 1980s began to adopt lean production practices based on observations of superior Japanese manufacturers (especially Toyota), thereby mimicking Japanese production and supply chain structures and processes; see for example Oliver and Wilkinson's (1988) *The Japanization of British Industry*. Normative isomorphism stems from employee professionalization, defining the conditions and methods of their work to establish greater legitimacy for their occupation (Gopal and Gao, 2009). DiMaggio and Powell (1983) recognize two aspects of professionalization as sources of isomorphism: formal education and legitimation in a cognitive base produced by university specialists and the growth of professional networks across which new models diffuse.

Institutional theory stipulates that conformance to institutional rules, or organizational isomorphism, increases organizational legitimacy, so organizations will adopt those practices perceived as most legitimate. Where institutional theory differs from other organizational theories is the logic that organizations adopt structures and practices not due to the effectiveness or efficiency of these in producing performance outcomes, but due to the legitimacy that their adoption grants to the organization (Alvesson and Spicer, 2019).

Research Themes and Avenues for Institutional Theory

Institutional theory has been applied across a range of SCM research, such as quality management and adoption of electronic tools (Kauppi, 2013), but in recent times institutional theory has been used widely in sustainable PSCM research (Johnsen et al., 2017). Examples of the application of institutional theory to investigate sustainable PSCM phenomena include Zhu and Sarkis's (2007) research on the role of institutional pressures on emerging green SCM and purchasing practices in Chinese manufacturers, where they use institutional theory to identify the importance of market (normative), regulatory (coercive) and competitive (mimetic) pressure. Zhu's later work (for example Zhu, 2016) has similarly relied on institutional theory to analyse pressures that motivate Chinese firms to adopt sustainability practices. Similarly, Hoejmose et al. (2014) draw from institutional theory to argue that the choice between coercive and cooperative approaches to implement green SCM depends on institutional pressures as well as downstream customer requirements; they find that institutional pressures significantly determine cooperative approaches, but customer pressure more often results in a coercive approach involving, for example, supplier monitoring.

Elsewhere in this book, Kauppi (see Chapter 21) sets out future research opportunities for institutional theory. This includes a suggestion to examine how social sustainability assessment initiatives instigate and use institutional pressures to drive third-party accreditation in supply chains. We would suggest that this might be broadened to include other ways to monitor and foster sustainability in supply networks, and the range of accreditation (or certification) and verification that can be performed by third parties (Gualandris et al., 2015). Kauppi's suggestion to use institutional theory to understand the extent to which technology applications actually get adopted and impact upon daily operations in a supply chain also presents opportunities for sustainable PSCM research. For example, there is much hype about the implementation of blockchain technology to solve transparency and even corruption issues in supply chains, but to date there is little research to evidence the successful adoption of blockchain in supply chains, and what drives such efforts.

APPLYING THE IMP INTERACTION APPROACH TO RESEARCH ON SUSTAINABILITY[1]

Background

The Industrial Marketing and Purchasing (IMP) Group interaction approach dates back to a major international research project, which focused on industrial buyer–seller relationships (Håkansson, 1982; Turnbull and Cunningham, 1981). This research resulted in the interaction model that changed the way in which buyer–seller relationships were understood. Rather than purely focusing on discrete one-off exchange episodes or transactions, the model incorporated long-term aspects of buyer–seller relationships, mutual adaptations and institutionalization processes. The model also depicts the interaction process as taking place within an atmosphere which is described in terms of power/dependence, conflict/cooperation, closeness/distance, and mutual expectations (Håkansson, 1982, p. 20). The model also includes an environmental level surrounding the interaction process and the atmosphere, although this part of the model is less detailed. The fundamental assumption of the interaction model is the active nature of both buyer and seller: the process of interaction. In the context of the 1970s and 1980s, this broke with the tacit assumption of earlier studies, such as organizational buying behaviour theories (Sheth, 1973; Webster and Wind, 1972), where one actor is active whereas the other is merely passive.

The IMP interaction approach later expanded in the direction of industrial networks to emphasize that 'no business is an island' (Håkansson and Snehota, 1990), thereby changing the unit of analysis from the level of the dyadic relationship to the network in which the dyads are embedded. The later model known as the actors–resources–activities (ARA) model provided a conceptual framework to analyse the development of relationships over time as two actors build up activity links, resource ties and actor bonds (Håkansson and Snehota, 1995). This shifted the focus of analysis to the positive or negative effects that network connections can have on interactions within dyads (Blankenburg and Johanson, 1990).

IMP scholars have developed a host of models since the creation of the interaction and ARA models, and the basic assumptions of these models still apply. However, despite the great number of studies that have followed in the wake of these early developments (with the annual IMP conference usually counting hundreds of participants), the IMP interaction approach is not a theory in the sense of offering predictive powers: it is an 'approach'. In fact, the focus appears to have been on providing conceptual frameworks and language to better understand buyer–supplier relationships and networks (Harland et al., 2004), but researchers seeking to apply IMP as a theoretical lens will most likely be looking in vain for proposed or proven causal relationships on which they can build their arguments and hypotheses. We recommend that IMP be used for its specific conceptual frameworks, notably the interaction or ARA models, and as a way of thinking about buyer–supplier interactions, relationships and networks. This can usefully be combined with formal theories that offer predictive powers based on similar assumptions and theoretical constructs; these could be stakeholder and institutional theories.

Research Themes and Avenues for IMP

From the perspective of sustainability research, the appeal of the IMP interaction approach (Håkansson, 1982) lies within its focus on interaction processes and buyer–supplier relationship management: relatively speaking, institutional and stakeholder theories have little to say about relationship management, especially within buyer–supplier, or supply chain, relationships. While both stakeholder and institutional theories provide frameworks to classify actors (or stakeholders) through levels of salience (legitimacy, urgency and power) or institutional logics (routines, rules, laws, conventions, paradigms, and so on), the mechanisms of interaction amongst actors are largely ignored (Johnsen et al., 2017).

In comparison with stakeholder and institutional theories, the IMP interaction approach does not have a focal firm-centric view but, in fact, points to the limitations of a focal firm perspective as it is inconsistent with an interaction perspective where it is not a question of the focal firm being the (sole) active actor, but where all connected actors are equally active and may be acting with or against the focal firm (Ford and Håkansson, 2002). At the network level of analysis, IMP has a distinct focus on understanding the interconnectedness and interdependency of relationships, which is instrumental in analysing sustainability at the multi-tier supply chain or network level, for example to study the diffusion of sustainability across supply networks (Meqdadi et al., 2019; Tate et al., 2013).

Considering the upsurge in multi-tier sustainable supply network research, this is an opportunity for IMP-based research. Here we might highlight the exemplary research by Villena (2019), who investigated how companies build sustainable supply networks by putting pressure on first-tier suppliers to cascade their sustainability requirements to lower-tier suppliers; other researchers could extend or elaborate this research through the IMP perspective to really understand the interactive roles of supply network actors. It follows from this idea that future studies could analyse how supply network actors cope with sustainability initiatives launched by other distant network actors.

Table 34.1   *Comparing the four theoretical perspectives*

Characteristics	NRBV	Stakeholder theory	Institutional theory	IMP
Unit of analysis	The firm: the traditional RBV emphasizes internal resources and the need to protect these; the NRBV values interorganizational relationships and external resources.	Typically a focal firm in relationship with primary and secondary stakeholders. Also, network, whole-system or sector analysis.	The firm (as institutions), but also the institutional environment comprising multiple external and internal institutions.	Dyadic buyer–supplier relationships and business networks processes.
Key variables	Natural or biophysical resources. Resource connectivity. Sustained competitive advantage through strategies of pollution prevention, product stewardship and sustainable development.	Identification of key actors. The motivation of firms: that is, power, legitimacy, urgency. Importance or salience of each actor in relation to the phenomena under investigation.	Legitimacy is gained by responding to institutional pressures. Argues that the institutional environment creates isomorphism (structures and practices) through coercive, normative and mimetic pressures.	Interaction processes in business-to-business (BTB) customer–supplier relationships. Adaptation and institutionalization. Actors' bonds, resource ties, activity links. Network effects and network embeddedness. Interdependency.
Sustainable PSCM relevance	Competitive advantage, through differentiation, can be gained by sustainability actions if based on unique, socially complex resources and capabilities such as collaborative supplier relationships and development.	Concepts such as legitimacy and urgency, as represented in sustainability and stakeholder theory, may take precedence in future over more traditional notions such as power in the supply hierarchy.	Pressures arise from non-economic institutions such as government and NGOs, but also economic actors such as industry associations promoting social standards. These are key drivers for sustainable supply practices. Partnerships with actors seen as important for legitimacy.	Understanding how sustainability diffuses/spreads within networks. Role of interaction with network actors (direct and indirect relationships), interdependency or connectedness, embeddedness and network effects.

COMPARING FOUR THEORETICAL PERSPECTIVES

Table 34.1 compares the four theories we have briefly discussed in this chapter, identifying the differences in units of analysis, key variables and the relevance of the theories for studying sustainable PSCM. These are all characterized by a focus on interorganizational issues and share a common view of the importance of interorganizational relationships as a source of sustainable competitive advantage. However, only IMP considers relationships and exchange processes as the unit of analysis, while the others mainly focus on individual (focal) firms and their interactions with external actors. Therefore, the theories are often combined to benefit from the complementary perspectives that they can bring to the analysis. This is most often the case with stakeholder theory and institutional theory, since each comes with limitations but can usefully be combined to give more comprehensive understanding of the range of pressures or motivations that lead organizations to develop sustainability.

Other theory combinations are less common, but examples are provided by, for example, Shi et al. (2012), who study 'natural resource based green supply chain management' using institutional theory and the NRBV. Blome et al. (2014) rely on the same two theories to study green procurement and green supplier development. They point out that the differences between the NRBV and institutional theory are subtle: where institutional theory interprets legitimization as 'a process of institutionalization, whereby external norms and beliefs are adopted without much thought (DiMaggio and Powell, 1983), the NRBV envisions legitimacy as instrumental, proactive and, more importantly, a deliberate pursuit that can ultimately enhance external beliefs, thereby creating newer and enhanced levels of legitimacy' (Blome et al., 2014, p. 35).

In comparison, IMP researchers tend to be more reluctant to combine the IMP perspective with any other theoretical perspective. The somewhat idiosyncratic nature of the IMP perspective, including the lack of focus on predicting outcomes, could be an opportunity for future research. As explained earlier, we therefore recommend that IMP be used for its specific conceptual frameworks and as a way of thinking about buyer–supplier interactions, relationships and networks, but combined with formal theories that offer predictive powers based on similar assumptions and theoretical constructs, including stakeholder and institutional theories.

NEW POTENTIAL THEORIES TO RESEARCH SUSTAINABILITY

Social Resource-Based View (SRBV)

The NRBV is as an evolution of the RBV focused on natural resources and therefore suitable to investigate environmental sustainability, but neglects the social dimension. More recently, Tate and Bals (2018) proposed a further development to also include the social dimension of sustainability, that is, the social resource-based view (SRBV). They maintained the elements of the RBV and NRBV and added some more, to cover the three dimensions of the triple bottom line (TBL). The SRBV extends the NRBV by adding social capabilities, which are classified into commitments (values), connections (in the value network) and consistency (of behaviour). These social capabilities allow two strategic capabilities to be achieved – that is, the mission-driven approach and stakeholder management – which in turn allow social performance to be achieved. The SRBV also extends the network of relevant stakeholders to be considered and managed, including economic, social and environmental stakeholders. Indeed, a critical capability is value chain partner network design, considering not only suppliers, but also financial providers, institutions, NGOs, and so on. The SRBV is surely a relevant and promising development, extending the RBV to cover the entire spectrum of TBL performance. However, it still assumes the perspective of a single organization which is embedded in a network and needs to design, develop and manage relationships with multiple and heterogeneous stakeholders, but still assuming the point of view of one 'focal' actor.

Complex Adaptive Systems (CASs)

Where supply chains were originally seen as linear systems that were controlled by a central focal firm, more recent developments theorize supply chains as complex networks that are difficult to predict and self-organize (Carter et al., 2015). The complex adaptive system (CAS) perspective focuses on understanding supply networks as complex adaptive systems that emerge and self-organize.

With roots in different disciplinary backgrounds, the CAS and IMP perspectives share a common understanding of networks as self-organizing structures that emerge rather than being deliberately designed and controlled by singular network actors (for example Ford and Håkansson, 2002; Håkansson and Snehota, 1995). A central theme in both is therefore the ability of – and need for – companies to attempt to control the network in which they are embedded, and whether or not such attempts are futile. Choi et al. (2001) propose that supply network control may be detrimental to flexibility and innovation, although they argue that both emergence and control are necessary.

CASs have been used as a theoretical lens to guide a wide range of supply chain and network studies. These include modelling of complexity from a technical or operational research (OR) perspective, such as Hearnshaw and Wilson (2013) and Surana et al. (2005). Pathak et al. (2009) use CASs to investigate the evolution of supply network population and topology to explore network evolution. CASs have also been used in empirical studies, including qualitative case study research, to study issues of control and emergence in complex supply networks, and how companies can use different strategies to reduce complexity and actor interdependencies, such as modularization (Matos and Hall, 2010) and delegation of tasks through tiering (Johnsen et al., 2019).

The question of supply network self-organizing versus control is critically important in sustainable PSCM research, because it is virtually impossible even for large and powerful companies to control the sustainability behaviour of all suppliers across multiple tiers (Villena and Gioia, 2018). Using CASs to study environmental innovations across supply networks, Nair et al. (2016) suggests that deliberate planning be applied when environmental innovation is within the boundary of the dominant firm, but combined with indirect engagement when the innovation process unfolds in the wider network. Managing sustainability across multi-tier supply networks highlights uncontrollable challenges that cannot be managed through traditional SCM approaches. There is clearly scope for more research on the questions of supply network control versus self-organizing, especially in the context of highly complex supply networks as can be found in, for example, the oil and gas, wind power, and aerospace industries.

Ecologically Dominant Logic

Much research on sustainable PSCM focuses on how sustainable supply chain developments are driven by a risk reduction or legislative and regulatory compliance approach (Walker et al., 2008), such as the use of supplier monitoring approaches (Meqdadi et al., 2020; Vachon and Klassen, 2006). However, instead of creating truly sustainable supply chains, a compliance approach is about reducing the damage that companies do. Put differently, compliance approaches are focused on companies not being caught acting illegally or being exposed in the media for unsustainable behaviour. This is about doing less bad, but not about having a positive influence on PSCM practices (Pagell and Shevchenko, 2014).

Markman and Krause (2016) argue that companies need to move from 'do no harm' thinking to 'do good' thinking. Ecologically dominant logic (Montabon et al., 2016) takes point of departure from the three dimensions or pillars of sustainability – that is, people, planet and profit – arguing that instead of simply balancing the three dimensions of sustainability, companies should prioritize ecology first, society second, and commerce third. In other words, the environment comes before social concerns, leaving economic sustainability as a last priority.

Montabon et al. (2016) contrast ecologically dominant logic with the traditional instrumental logic, which treats social and environmental aspects discretely and sequentially, as if such issues are emerging distractions (Gao and Bansal, 2013, p. 241). Where institutional logic is ultimately an inside-out view concerned with focal firm profits, the ecologically dominant logic is an outside-in view, which begins by assessment of economics impact on the environment and society. Akin to the non-focal network actor view of the IMP perspective, ecologically dominant logic takes a wider view of the ecosystem within the stakeholder network.

Finding companies that pursue an ecologically dominant logic rather than a traditional instrumental logic may be hard. Yet there are prominent examples of traditional industries, such as automotive, that have been disrupted by innovative new entrants with radically different business models that centre on transforming the automotive industry towards zero emissions, where incumbent firms are mostly concerned with reducing vehicle emissions, that is, reducing the harmful impact of their products. Implementing as well as researching sustainable PSCM from the perspective of ecologically dominant logic is therefore about (sustainable) innovation and the creation of new business models; in our view this is a highly promising avenue of future research.

Panarchy Theory

As the final new theory, we propose panarchy theory (Wieland, 2021). A full treatment of this new theoretical development is beyond this chapter, but this latest development still deserves a brief introduction.

The panarchy theory of supply chain management reinterprets the supply chain as a social-ecological system, pushing the traditional assumptions of supply chain management even more than the theories we have previously discussed. Rooted in ecology, panarchy theory provides a structure for understanding how a system follows the movement of adaptive cycles on scales of time, space and meaning (Wieland, 2021, p. 59). Like, for example, the IMP and CAS perspectives, the panarchy theory of supply chain management extends the unit of analysis not only from simple linear supply chains to complex adaptive supply networks (Carter et al., 2015), but even further to take in other levels of structure, including political-economic and planetary levels. For example, one such level could be the consideration of local communities if studying social sustainability in supply chains.

A panarchical approach to supply chain management also does away with the traditional notion of managing supply chains. Wieland (2021, p. 59) argues that it is 'time to replace the modernist tropes of designing, planning, and optimizing the supply chain with a new metaphor that accounts for the transformative power of management: that of *dancing the supply chain*'. Thus, echoing several of the long-held arguments of the IMP perspective (Ford and Håkansson, 2002) and CAS (Choi et al., 2001), panarchy theory challenges the fundamental assumptions of the supply chain as a closed system that can be controlled by focal supply chain firms, and which can be modelled and optimized by supply chain researchers rooted in industrial engineering or operations research. These widely differing views of supply chains tie in with current debate about the disciplinary underpinnings and identity of purchasing and supply chain management (Ellram et al, 2020).

CONCLUSION

In this chapter we have discussed and proposed four theories as relevant for researching sustainable PSCM. These include the NRBV, stakeholder and institutional theories, and the IMP interaction approach.

We can conclude that there are important differences between stakeholder and institutional theories on one side, and IMP and the NRBV on the other. The former two theories assume external actors to provide pressures to the firm and therefore require a response to gain legitimacy; such a response can be more 'passive' (as assumed by institutional theory) or 'active' (as assumed by stakeholder theory). In comparison, the latter two theories focus more on the interdependent role of firms: in the case of the NRBV, the firm can access and leverage on external (natural) resources to gain sustainable competitive advantage; whereas in the case of IMP firms interact within networks so can affect and be affected by other network actors. Where the NRBV is a development of traditional RBV theory that focuses specifically on natural resources and therefore sustainability, the domain of IMP is general business-to-business marketing and purchasing, and IMP has not traditionally been used to analyse sustainability phenomena. As we have noted, IMP is also different from the others in that its focus has not been on developing predictive outcomes, but rather on providing conceptual frameworks to aid analysis of interorganizational phenomena.

Therefore, future research on sustainability in PSCM could leverage on the strengths of these theories and their combination in the following ways:

1. Extend the scope of analysis to the multiple tiers of the supply chain and the relationships with relevant stakeholders, thus broadening the perspective of stakeholder and institutional theories by combining them with the IMP approach.
2. Identify and compare reactive and proactive strategies to respond and manage the multiple pressures by actors and stakeholders to achieve sustainable competitive advantage at network level.
3. Extend the NRBV approach to also include social and ethical perspectives, to understand how they can become sources of competitive advantage, while broadening the scope from

focal firms to the supply chain/network. The SRBV is a first and very promising attempt in this direction.

These four theories therefore not only have provided useful and rich insights on sustainability in PSCM so far, but also provide high potential for further research development in the future, in particular by broadening their scope and leveraging on a combination of multiple theories to complement their strengths and overcome their limitations.

Recent theoretical developments highlight the need to question the traditional assumptions of supply chain management, which are becoming untenable especially when the focus is on sustainable PSCM. CASs, ecologically dominant logic and panarchy theory propose radically different perspectives, either by proposing a systemic, decentralized, emergent and dynamic view of networks (CASs and panarchy), or by advocating a radical revision of the priorities to be pursued, defining a clear hierarchy with planet first, people second, and profit third and last (ecologically dominant logic). As often happens, radical ideas may be more difficult to transform into practice, and may (and should) be questioned, but are surely a very important stimulus for innovation and development; and therefore they are not only welcome, but necessary and urgent in these times of unprecedented global challenges.

NOTE

1. What we refer to here as the 'IMP interaction approach' is also called the 'industrial network approach' (see Chapter 21).

REFERENCES

Alvesson, M., and Spicer, A. (2019). Neo-institutional theory and organization studies: a mid-life crisis? *Organization Studies*, 40 (2), 199–218.

Arnold, U. (2000). New dimensions of outsourcing: a combination of transaction cost economics and the core competence concept. *European Journal of Purchasing and Supply Management*, 6 (1), 23–29.

Barney, J. (1986). Strategic factor markets: expectations, luck, and business strategy. *Management Science*, 4 (10), 1231–1241.

Barney, J.B. (1991). Firm resources and sustained competitive advantage. *Journal of Management*, 17 (1), 99–120.

Barney, J., Ketchen, D.J., Jr, and Wright, M. (2011). The future of resource-based theory: revitalization or decline? *Journal of Management*, 37 (5), 1299–1315.

Blankenburg, D., and Johanson, J. (1990). Managing network connections in international business. *Scandinavian International Business Review*, 1, 5–19.

Blome, C., Hollos, D., and Paulraj, A. (2014). Green procurement and green supplier development: antecedents and effects on supplier performance. *International Journal of Production Research*, 52 (1), 32–49.

Busse, C., Kach, A.P., and Wagner, S.M. (2017). Boundary conditions: what they are, how to explore them, why we need them, and when to consider them. *Organizational Research Methods*, 20 (4), 574–609.

Carter, C.R. (2005). Purchasing social responsibility and firm performance: the key mediating roles of organizational learning and supplier performance. *International Journal of Physical Distribution and Logistics Management*, 35 (3), 177–194.

Carter, C.R., Rogers, D.S., and Choi, T.Y. (2015). Toward the theory of the supply chain. *Journal of Supply Chain Management*, 51 (2), 89–97.

Chicksand, D., Watson, G., Walker, H., Radnor, Z., and Johnston, R. (2012). Theoretical perspectives in purchasing and supply chain management: an analysis of the literature. *Supply Chain Management: An International Journal*, 17 (4), 454–472.

Choi, T.Y., Dooley, K., and Rungtusanatham, M. (2001). Supply networks and complex adaptive systems: control versus emergence. *Journal of Operations Management*, 19 (3), 351–366.

Christensen, C.M. (1997). *The Innovator's Dilemma: The Revolutionary Book that Will Change the Way You Do Business.* Collins Business Essentials. New York: HarperCollins.

Darnall, N., Jolley, G.J., and Handfield, R. (2008). Environmental management systems and green supply chain management: complements for sustainability? *Business Strategy and the Environment*, 17 (1), 30–45.

Dierickx, I., and Cool, K. (1989). Asset stock accumulation and sustainability of competitive advantage. *Management Science*, 35 (12), 1504–1511.

DiMaggio, P.J., and Powell, W.W. (1983). The iron cage revisited: institutional isomorphism and collective rationality in organizational fields. *American Sociological Review*, 147–160.

Ehrgott, M., Reimann, F., Kaufmann, L., and Carter, C.R. (2011). Social sustainability in selecting emerging economy suppliers. *Journal of Business Ethics*, 98 (1), 99–119.

Ellram, L., Harland, C., van Weele, A., Essig, M., Johnsen, T., et al. (2020). Purchasing and supply management's identity: Crisis? What crisis? *Journal of Purchasing and Supply Management*, 26 (1), 1–9.

Foerstl, K., Reuter, C., Hartmann, E., and Blome, C. (2010). Managing supplier sustainability risks in a dynamically changing environment – sustainable supplier management in the chemical industry. *Journal of Purchasing and Supply Management*, 16 (2), 118–130.

Ford, D., and Håkansson, H. (2002). How should companies interact in business networks? *Journal of Business Research*, 55, 133–139.

Freeman, R. (1984). *Strategic Management – A Stakeholder Approach*. London: Pitman.

Gao, J., and Bansal, P. (2013). Instrumental and integrative logics in business sustainability. *Journal of Business Ethics*, 112 (2), 241–255.

Gimenez, C., and Tachizawa, E.M. (2012). Extending sustainability to suppliers: a systematic literature review. *Supply Chain Management: An International Journal*, 17 (5), 531–543.

Gopal, A., and Gao, G. (2009). Certification in the Indian offshore IT services industry. *Manufacturing and Service Operations Management*, 11 (3), 471–492.

Granstrand, O., Patel, P., and Pavitt, K. (1997). Multi-technology corporations: why they have 'distributed' rather than 'distinctive core' competencies. *California Management Review*, 39 (4), 1–19.

Gualandris, J., Klassen, R.D., Vachon, S., and Kalchschmidt, M. (2015). Sustainable evaluation and verification in supply chains: aligning and leveraging accountability to stakeholders. *Journal of Operations Management*, 38, 1–13.

Håkansson, H. (1982). *International Marketing and Purchasing of Industrial Goods. An Interaction Approach*. Chichester: John Wiley & Sons.

Håkansson, H., and Snehota, I. (1990). No business is an island: the network concept of business strategy. *Scandinavian Journal of Management*, 4 (3), 187–200.

Håkansson, H., and Snehota I. (1995). *Developing Relationships in Business Networks*. London: International Thomson Business Press.

Hall, J., and Matos, S. (2010). Incorporating impoverished communities in sustainable supply chains. *International Journal of Physical Distribution and Logistics Management*, 40 (1–2), 124–147.

Harland, C.M., Zheng, J., Johnsen, T.E., and Lamming, R.C. (2004). A conceptual model for researching the creation and operation of supply networks. *British Journal of Management*, 15 (1), 1–21.

Hart, S.L. (1995). A natural-resource-based view of the firm. *Academy of Management Review*, 20 (4), 986–1014.

Hearnshaw, E.J.S., and Wilson, M.M.J. (2013). A complex network approach to supply chain network theory. *International Journal of Operations and Production Management*, 33 (4), 442–469.

Henderson, R.M., and Clark, K.B. (1990). Architectural innovation: the reconfiguration of existing product technologies and the failure of established firms. *Administrative Science Quarterly*, 35 (1), 9–30.

Hoejmose, S.U., Grosvold, J., and Millington, A. (2014). The effect of institutional pressure on cooperative and coercive 'green' supply chain practices. *Journal of Purchasing and Supply Management*, 20 (4), 215–224.

Howard, M.B., Miemczyk, J., and Johnsen, T.E. (2016). Dynamic development and execution of closed-loop supply chains: a natural resource-based view. *Supply Chain Management: an International Journal*, 21 (4), 453–469.

Johnsen, T.E., Miemczyk, J., and Howard, M. (2017). A systematic literature review of sustainable purchasing and supply research: theoretical perspectives and opportunities for IMP-based research. *Industrial Marketing Management*, 61, 130–143.

Johnsen, T.E., Mikkelsen, O.S., and Chee, Y.W. (2019). Strategies for complex supply networks: findings from the offshore wind power industry. *Supply Chain Management: an International Journal*, 24 (6), 872–886.

Kauppi, K. (2013). Extending the use of institutional theory in operations and supply chain management research: review and research suggestions. *International Journal of Operations and Production Management*, 33 (10), 1318–1345.

Lavie, D. (2006). The competitive advantage of interconnected firms: an extension of the resource-based view. *Academy of Management Review*, 31 (3), 638–658.

Lee, S.Y., and Klassen, R.D. (2008). Drivers and enablers that foster environmental management capabilities in small- and medium-sized suppliers in supply chains. *Production and Operations Management*, 17 (6), 573–586.

Leonard-Barton, D. (1992). Core capabilities and core rigidities: a paradox in managing new product development. *Strategic Management Journal*, 13 (S1), 111–125.

Markman, G.D., and Krause, D. (2016). Theory building surrounding sustainable supply chain management: assessing what we know, exploring where to go. *Journal of Supply Chain Management*, 52 (2), 3–10.

Matos, S., and Hall, J. (2010). Integrating sustainable development in the supply chain: the case of life cycle assessment in oil and gas and agricultural biotechnology. *Journal of Operations Management*, 25, 1083–1102.

McIvor, R. (2009). How the transaction cost and resource-based theories of the firm inform outsourcing evaluation. *Journal of Operations Management*, 27, 45–63.

Meqdadi, O., Johnsen, T.E., and Johnsen, R.E. (2019). Power and diffusion of sustainability in supply networks: findings from four case studies. *Journal of Business Ethics*, 159 (4), 1089–1110.

Meqdadi, O., Johnsen, T.E., Johnsen, R.E., and Salmi, A. (2020). Strategies for diffusing sustainability in supply networks: case study findings. *Supply Chain Management: An International Journal*, 25 (6), 729–746.

Miemczyk, J. (2008). An exploration of institutional constraints on developing end-of-life product recovery capabilities. *International Journal of Production Economics*, 115 (2), 272–282.

Mitchell, R., Agle, B., and Wood, D. (1997). Toward a theory of stakeholder identification and salience: defining the principle of who and what really counts. *Academy of Management Review*, 22 (4), 853–887.

Montabon, F.L., Pagell, M., and Wu, Z. (2016). Making sustainability sustainable. *Journal of Supply Chain Management*, 52 (2), 1–34.

Nair, A., Yan, T., Ro, Y.K., Oke, A., Chiles, T.H., and Lee, S. (2016). How environmental innovations emerge and proliferate in supply networks: a complex adaptive systems perspective. *Journal of Supply Chain Management*, 52, 66–86.

Oliver, N., and Wilkinson, B. (1988). *The Japanization of British Industry*, 2nd edn. Oxford: Blackwell.

Pagell, M., and Shevchenko, A. (2014). Why research in sustainable supply chain management should have no future. *Journal of Supply Chain Management*, 50 (1), 44–55.

Parmigiani, A., Klassen, R.D., and Russo, M.V. (2011). Efficiency meets accountability: Performance implications of supply chain configuration, control, and capabilities. *Journal of Operations Management*, 29 (3), 212–223.

Pathak, S.D., Dilts, D.M., and Mahadevan, S. (2009). Investigating population and topological evolution in a complex adaptive supply network. *Journal of Supply Chain Management*, 45 (3), 54–57.

Paulraj, A. (2011). Understanding the relationships between internal resources and capabilities, sustainable supply management and organizational sustainability. *Journal of Supply Chain Management*, 47 (1), 19–37.

Peteraf, M.A. (1993). The cornerstones of competitive advantage: a resource-based view. *Strategic Management Journal*, 14 (3), 179–191.

Prahalad, C.K., and Hamel, G. (1990). Core competence of the corporation. *Harvard Business Review*, 68 (3), 79–91.

Prahalad, C.K., and Hamel, G. (1994). *Competing for the Future*. Boston, MA: Harvard Business School Press.

Quarshie, A.M., Salmi, A., and Leuschner, R. (2016). Sustainability and corporate social responsibility in supply chains: the state of research in supply chain management and business ethics journals. *Journal of Purchasing and Supply Management*, 22 (2), 82–97.

Rowley, T. (1997). Moving beyond dyadic ties: a network theory of stakeholder influences. *Academy of Management Review*, 22, 887–911.

Rumelt, R.P. (1987). Strategy, economic theory and entrepreneurship. In D. Teece (ed.), *The Competitive Challenge*. Cambridge, MA: Ballinger Books, pp. 137–158.

Sarkis, J., Zhu, Q., and Lai, K.H. (2011). An organizational theoretic review of green supply chain management literature. *International Journal of Production Economics*, 130 (1), 1–15.

Schneider, L., and Wallenburg, C.M. (2012). Implementing sustainable sourcing – does purchasing need to change? *Journal of Purchasing and Supply Management*, 18 (4), 243–257.

Sheth, J.N. (1973). A model of industrial buying behaviour. *Journal of Marketing*, 37 (4), 50–56.

Shi, V.G., Koh, S.C.L., Baldwin, J., and Cucchiella, F. (2012). Natural resource based green supply chain management. *Supply Chain Management: an International Journal*, 17 (1), 54–67.

Spina, G., Caniato, F., Luzzini, D., and Ronchi, S. (2016). Assessing the use of external grand theories in purchasing and supply management research. *Journal of Purchasing and Supply Management*, 22 (1), 18–30.

Surana, A., Kumara, S., Greaves, M., and Raghavan, U.N. (2005). Supply chain networks: a complex adaptive systems perspective. *International Journal of Production Research*, 43 (20), 4235–4265.

Tate, W.L., and Bals, L. (2018). Achieving shared triple bottom line (TBL) value creation: toward a social resource-based view (SRBV) of the firm. *Journal of Business Ethics*, 152 (3), 803–826.

Tate, W.L., Ellram, L.M., and Gölgeci, I. (2013). Diffusion of environmental business practices: a network approach. *Journal of Purchasing and Supply Management*, 19 (4), 264–275.

Teece, D.J., Pisano, G., and Shuen, A. (1997). Dynamic capabilities and strategic management. *Strategic Management Journal*, 18 (7), 509–533.

Turnbull, P.W., and Cunningham, M. (eds) (1981). *International Marketing and Purchasing: A Survey among Marketing and Purchasing Executives in Five European Countries*. New York: Macmillan.

Vachon, S., and Klassen, R. (2006). Extending green practices across the supply chain – the impact of upstream and downstream integration. *International Journal of Operations and Production Management*, 26 (7), 795–821.

Vachon, S., and Klassen, R. (2008). Environmental management and manufacturing performance: the role of collaboration in the supply chain, *International Journal of Production Economics*, 111 (2), 299–315.

Villena, V.H. (2019). The missing link? The strategic role of procurement in building sustainable supply networks. *Production and Operations Management*, 28 (5), 1149–1172.

Villena, V.H., and Gioia, D.A. (2018). On the riskiness of lower-tier suppliers: managing sustainability in supply networks. *Journal of Operations Management*, 64, 65–87.

Walker, H., and Brammer, S. (2009). Sustainable procurement in the United Kingdom public sector. *Supply Chain Management: An International Journal*, 14 (2), 128–137.

Walker, H., Di Sisto, L., and McBain, D. (2008). Drivers and barriers to environmental supply chain management practices: lessons from the public and private sectors. *Journal of Purchasing and Supply Management*, 14 (1), 69–85.

Weber, M. (1930). *The Protestant Ethic and the Spirit of Capitalism*. T. Parsons, trans. London: Routledge.

Webster, F.E., and Wind, Y. (1972). A general model of organisational buying behaviour. *Journal of Marketing*, 36 (2), 12–19.

Wernerfelt, B. (1984). The resource-based view of the firm. *Strategic Management Journal*, 5 (2), 171–180.

Wieland, A. (2021). Dancing the supply chain: toward transformative supply chain management. *Journal of Supply Chain Management*, 57 (1), 58–73.

Zhu, Q. (2016). Institutional pressures and support from industrial zones for motivating sustainable production among Chinese manufacturers. *International Journal of Production Economics*, 181, 402–409.

Zhu, Q., and Sarkis, J. (2007). The moderating effects of institutional pressures on emergent green supply chain practices and performance. *International Journal of Production Research*, 45 (18), 4333–4356.

Zsidisin, G., Melnyk, S., and Ragatz, G. (2005). An institutional theory perspective of business continuity planning for purchasing and supply management. *International Journal of Production Research*, 43 (16), 3401–3420.

Index

Printed and bound by CPI Group (UK) Ltd, Croydon, CR0 4YY

16/04/2025

14658390-0004